Women Public Speakers
in the United States,
1800-1925

Women Public Speakers in the United States, 1800-1925

A BIO-CRITICAL SOURCEBOOK

EDITED BY
Karlyn Kohrs Campbell

GREENWOOD PRESS
WESTPORT, CONNECTICUT • LONDON

Library of Congress Cataloging-in-Publication Data

Women public speakers in the United States, 1800-1925 : a bio-critical
    sourcebook / edited by Karlyn Kohrs Campbell.
        p.   cm.
    Includes bibliographical references and index.
    ISBN 0-313-27533-5 (alk. paper)
    1. Women social reformers—United States—Biography—Dictionaries.
2. Feminists—United States—Biography—Dictionaries.   3. Women
orators—United States—Biography—Dictionaries.   I. Campbell,
Karlyn Kohrs.
HQ1412.W67   1993
305.42'092'2—dc20   92-14615
[B]

British Library Cataloguing in Publication Data is available.

Library of Congress Catalog Card Number: 92–14615
ISBN: 0-313-27533-5

First published in 1993

Greenwood Press, 88 Post Road West, Westport, CT 06881
An imprint of Greenwood Publishing Group, Inc.

Printed in the United States of America

∞™

The paper used in this book complies with the
Permanent Paper Standard issued by the National
Information Standards Organization (Z39.48–1984).

10 9 8 7 6 5 4 3 2 1

To Lillian O'Connor
who pioneered the study of women in public discourse.

"The woman writer [and speaker] searches for a female
model... because she must legitimize her own rebellious
endeavors."
                         —Sandra M. Gilbert and Susan Gubar,
                                      Madwoman in the Attic, 50

CONTENTS

INTRODUCTION _____

Karlyn Kohrs Campbell

From the nation's beginnings, strenuous efforts have been made to silence U.S. women. Barred from politics by a denial of their citizenship rights; barred from the courts by a lack of standing to sue, bear witness, or make contracts; barred from advanced education and the professions, their voices inevitably were constrained. Yet they spoke. This volume covering the years from 1800 to 1925, and its companion covering the years after 1925, are offered to gain those voices new recognition. They are dedicated to the woman who began the contemporary study of women's rhetoric, Lillian O'Connor.

Women ventured into the public dialogue far earlier than is generally recognized. In 1787, at the initial commencement of the Philadelphia Female Academy, probably the first secondary school for young women in the nation (Woody, 1929, 1:333, 337), the salutatorian, a Miss Mason, welcomed parents and guests with a speech defending a woman's right to use her talents and to contribute to the public dialogue (Mason, 1887; Woody, 1929, 1:338–339). In 1802 DEBORAH SAMPSON GANNETT (names of women for whom there are entries are in all capitals), who had fought bravely in the Revolutionary War, lectured in Massachusetts to attest to her military record as well as to explain her unwomanly behavior. In 1819 EMMA HART WILLARD pleaded with the New York State Legislature to endow Troy Female Seminary. In 1828 Frances Wright, an American by choice and belief, lectured throughout the nation explaining the meaning and implications of the country's basic principles. In a memorable Fourth of July address, she urged its citizens to a higher patriotism that would encompass the world, not just the nation (1972:117–125). In 1831 MARIA W. MILLER STEWART spoke in Boston urging fellow African-Americans to help themselves, castigating colonization proposals, and affirming the citizenship rights of those who in slavery and in freedom had contributed so much to creating the nation's wealth. She called on whites, especially her white sisters, to assist African-American women in overcoming the special barriers they faced.

Beginning in the 1830s, these solo voices became a chorus as women banded together in fledgling organizations to struggle to abolish slavery, aid prostitutes, fight the debilitating effects of the unregulated sale of alcoholic beverages, and claim their rights as persons and citizens. Female anti-slavery societies, moral reform and benevolent societies, and temperance societies sprang up and, along with woman's rights advocates, held conventions, issued proceedings, and aired their views in publications they founded. The movement that is the precursor of modern feminism had begun.

Given their ethical dimensions, these issues heightened the internal conflict in the conception of True Womanhood, which dominated thinking in the early years of the Republic and well into the nineteenth century. Pure, pious, domestic, and submissive were the key terms (Welter, 1976). According to this conception, as naturally domestic creatures, women were to remain entirely in the private sphere of the home, submissive to their fathers, husbands, or sons. At the same time, however, they were deemed naturally to be of greater moral purity and of greater religious piety than their fellows. Consequently, what women saw as moral questions—slavery, prostitution, the devastation wrought by alcohol abuse on families, and the inability of women to protect their maternal obligations through the courts and the ballot box—was at odds with woman's submissiveness and her confinement to the home. In the face of that conflict, women asserted their moral right, indeed, their moral imperative, to breach domestic boundaries in order to protect the home and to apply their greater moral sensitivity and religious piety to issues of great ethical moment.

The result of organization and agitation was collective discourse issued forth in proceedings, pamphlets, and journals, which, in turn, induced acknowledgment, usually hostile, of women's public life in the mainstream press, illustrated by reactions to the 1848 Seneca Falls, New York, convention (*HWS* 1:802–805).

Put simply, although women in this country were largely ignored by scholars until very recently, since the 1830s, they have participated actively and widely in public dialogue on fundamental questions underlying the polity: What is it to be a citizen in a democracy? What kinds of education do democratic citizens require? How shall the well-being of citizens be protected in the workplace, in the home? How shall we ensure the health and well-being of future generations? How should political decisions be made? How shall the economic powers of various interest groups be balanced and protected? Women have answered these questions differently, depending on their political beliefs, their class, their ethnicity, their education, and their religious commitments. However, since those who spoke were, almost inevitably, reformers, they argued for change. If they were conservative, like EMMA HART WILLARD and JULIA WARD HOWE, they argued for change in the name of the most traditional values. If they were freethinkers (anti-clerical individuals who sometimes took agnostic, even atheistic stands), like ERNESTINE POTOWSKI ROSE or VOLTAIRINE DE

CLEYRE, they attacked traditional religious beliefs; many more, such as MA-TILDA JOSLYN GAGE and ELIZABETH CADY STANTON attacked the organized church. If they were deeply religious, even recognized clergy, such as LUCRETIA COFFIN MOTT and ANTOINETTE BROWN BLACKWELL, they found the bases for reforms in scripture and religious principles. If they were anarchists, like VOLTAIRINE DE CLEYRE and EMMA GOLDMAN, they called for radical elimination of the state and criticized their more conservative sister suffragists. If they were socialists, like FLORENCE KELLEY and KATE RICHARDS O'HARE, they called for the application of socialist theory and practice in U.S. society. Many spoke for the poor and the downtrodden; some, like former slave SOJOURNER TRUTH, were poor and uneducated; others, like JANE ADDAMS and MARGARET DREIER ROBINS, were well educated and affluent. Some, like ERNESTINE POTOWSKI ROSE and ANNA HOWARD SHAW, were foreign-born; others, like ABIGAIL SCOTT DUNI-WAY, were of pioneer stock. Some, like CLARA BEWICK COLBY, spent all they had on the movement for woman's rights. Others, like ANNA E. DICK-INSON, used reform lecturing as a path to wealth. Some, like MARY HARRIS "MOTHER" JONES and IDA B. WELLS BARNETT led lives so unusual that they defy belief—no one ever showed greater courage than "Mother" Jones organizing workers in the coal fields or Wells Barnett fighting to discover and expose the facts about the lynching of her people. Although these pages do not encompass all of them, the voices of women of diverse ethnic, religious, and social backgrounds entered the public dialogue; those represented here are merely evidence of the pervasiveness of their claim on the *res publica*.

Despite their many contributions to public dialogue, the history of women's rhetoric is the story of an unending struggle to be heard and to be heeded in the face of the hostility of the church, the courts, the professions, and the press, supported by state and federal courts and legislatures. As Aileen S. Kraditor recognized, hostility was usually justified in terms of three fundamental rationales for keeping women in a separate, inferior place (*IWSM*).

The most fundamental rationale was religious, a theological interpretation of scripture that denied a woman's right to teach, advise, or preach even on those moral and spiritual matters on which she was deemed particularly sensitive and able. Hence, the history of women's public discourse includes a long struggle with theology and clergy over the interpretation of biblical passages. Those who broke the public sound barrier in the earliest years were disproportionately Quakers precisely because that religious group was the first to recognize a woman's equal capacity to feel the promptings of an "inward light" and to express those promptings in terms that other Friends, male and female, should heed (Bacon, 1986). The earliest defenses of a woman's right to speak emerged from the pens of Margaret Askew Fell (1666) and George Fox, the British founders of Quakerism. As a group, Quakers predominated among female reformers; SARAH M. GRIMKÉ, a convert to Quakerism, was the first American to author a woman's rights treatise, and she and her sister ANGELINA GRIMKÉ WELD were among

the earliest white women to raise their voices against slavery; LUCRETIA COF-
FIN MOTT was an early woman's rights and anti-slavery advocate. Similarly,
African-American MARIA W. MILLER STEWART spoke against slavery and
for woman's rights out of a deep religious conviction. But conflicts with religious
authorities over woman's public role persisted. These conflicts were reflected
equally in the attempts at synthesis made by FRANCES E. WILLARD, who
defended woman's right to the pulpit, and in the attacks on religious authority
collected in *The Woman's Bible* edited by ELIZABETH CADY STANTON,
also its primary author, and in MATILDA JOSLYN GAGE's *Woman, Church,
and State*. Those conflicts were revived in the modern period in the works of
feminist theologians and in the struggle over the ordination of women as clergy.

Of almost equal power were barriers created out of biology and physiology
or ignorance of them. Woman's allegedly natural submissiveness and domesticity
were buttressed by her ability to bear children, by her generally smaller anatomy
and physiology, and by fashions that adversely affected her health. It was claimed
that woman's health was incompatible with education, for demands on her brain
would prevent appropriate ovarian and uterine development. According to Harvard medical school professor Edward Clarke, most diseases of the female were
caused by displacement of blood from genital growth to the brain, making
advanced education for women a threat to the nation. Women's smaller, frailer
nerves made her incapable of sustaining the rough and tumble of business or
politics; her smaller brain made her incapable of the deliberations required for
rational decision making; that she *could* bear children meant that, to be a full
and complete adult, she *had to* bear children, and the resulting obligations barred
her from activities in the public sphere. Finally, trailing, heavy skirts and whale-
bone corsets limited her motion and her ability to breathe. The fight against
biological ignorance motivated PAULINA KELLOGG WRIGHT DAVIS, an
early lecturer on anatomy and physiology, and JULIA WARD HOWE, who
satirically refuted the medical profession's strictures against women's education.
In more recent times, psychology has contributed to this rationale, as illustrated
by Naomi Weisstein's classic essay (1971).

Another related rationale for woman's special and limited place grew out of
views of the family as a unit represented publicly by the husband/father in
business, in the courts, and in government, views that denied the personhood
and individuality of a married woman. The effect was to render a wife a legal
nonperson without judicial standing or political rights, including the right to sue
or bear witness, to hold or convey property, or to share in the guardianship of
children. The most conservative early advocates argued that women required
legal and political rights in order to fulfill their maternal and domestic responsibilities. This idea was especially illustrated by the speeches and writings of
CLARINA HOWARD NICHOLS.

Traditional conceptions of womanhood affected all women, even those who
were least able financially to live the kind of lives that these conceptions envisioned and those most burdened by the barriers of racism, nativism, and poverty.

Slave women, free African-American women, most immigrant women, and poor women generally were compelled to leave the private sphere of the home in order to survive. They lacked husbands and fathers capable of earning wages adequate to support a family and were driven into work with low pay and long hours—domestic labor, textile mills, sweat shops, and, often, prostitution. For them, the right to earn was vital, the right to their earnings was of nearly equal importance, education and training were desperately needed, and joining together in unions was vital to improving their working conditions. In the 1830s, African-American and white women struggled to free their sisters from slavery, the most desperate and degrading condition of all. In the 1840s, women in the Lowell textile mills defended their right to seek better working conditions (Mattina, 1986); in the 1870s, woman's rights advocates joined with working women to seek improved conditions; in the 1890s, upper and middle-class women such as JANE ADDAMS gave meaning to their lives by creating settlement houses to aid the poor and founding organizations designed to aid working women in unionizing to improve their working conditions.

Ultimately, for many women, the vote became the focus of their efforts, the central, crucial means through which they believed women would be empowered to effect the changes they so desperately needed. Although woman suffrage was only a part, albeit an important part, of women's public advocacy, it often is viewed mistakenly as the sole issue in relation to which women entered the public dialogue. Suffrage arguments, however, reveal a fundamental disagreement among reformers that persists to this day.

On the one hand, as Kraditor noted, suffragists demanded justice based on natural rights philosophy, encapsulated in the Declaration of Independence. This argument treated women as persons like all others and, indistinguishable from men, entitled to certain fundamental rights—the right to choose those who would represent them in making laws, especially tax laws, and the protection of full legal standing in courts of law. On the other hand, suffragists argued on the basis of difference, affirming the distinctions between the sexes enunciated in the cult of True Womanhood. Given those differences, they claimed, it would be beneficial or expedient to give women the vote so that their distinctive influence could be felt in government and the courts. Women, it was argued, would protect the home and be especially sensitive to the needs of children, and their moral purity and superior spiritual sensitivity would be reflected in their decisions and, hence, would purify government and improve society.

Suffragists not only argued from these conflicting positions, but they also combined these arguments, occasionally in the same discourse. What appears contradictory on its face, however, was not beyond synthesis; combining these arguments was a recognition that, in some sense, both were true. Females were human beings quite apart from their sex, and, simultaneously, women were different from men, acculturated as a gender in ways that made their interests and their perspectives distinctive. In some cases, as illustrated by the discourse of ERNESTINE POTOWSKI ROSE, ABIGAIL SCOTT DUNIWAY, and CAR-

RIE LANE CHAPMAN CATT, these arguments were integrated in highly creative ways. In others, the expediency argument was refined into a highly sophisticated analysis of the impact of women's singular experiences and, hence, particular views and values, an argument echoed in some studies of contemporary U.S. women (Gilligan, 1982).

The women represented in this volume reflect that diversity; as a result, although many of their names are familiar, still others are known only to those in specialized areas of research. They were groundbreakers in many areas in addition to entering the public dialogue. They include the first lawyers, ministers, physicians, labor organizers, newspaper editors and publishers, historians, educators, even soldiers, and many were leaders of large and powerful organizations. They include the first women who ran for the presidency, as well as those who first ran for the U.S. Senate and House of Representatives, in some cases, even before women had the right to vote. They come from different areas of the country, and in some cases, their voices speak with distinctly regional accents. LAURA CLAY was a Southerner to the core; ABIGAIL SCOTT DUNIWAY spoke for her beloved Pacific Northwest; MARY CLYENS LEASE spoke for midwestern populists. Others, exemplified by SUSAN B. ANTHONY, traveled widely for the causes they espoused and, until late in life, had no real home of their own. Still others, such as ROSA FASSEL SONNESCHEIN, spoke to and for a particular ethnic group, in her case, for American women of Jewish-German descent.

Although woman's rights and woman suffrage were important for nearly all the women represented here, those issues were only two areas among the concerns that these women felt and voiced. They fought slavery, they espoused the rights of the poor and of the working class and organized them into unions; they fought to save wounded soldiers and those injured in catastrophes; they struggled to find a means to keep the world at peace. They studied science, including anatomy and physiology; they revolutionized education; they defended the oppressed in courtrooms; they helped to found what became known as sociology and social work; they organized to speak for consumers; and their pioneering studies changed the course of the nation's social policy. Many were nationally, some internationally, known during their lives; perhaps only one, JULIA WARD HOWE, has remained perpetually in the nation's consciousness through the words of her patriotic poem, "Battle Hymn of the Republic." The women represented in this volume are indeed very diverse.

Given their accomplishments and their diversity, one cannot avoid the question, why have they been forgotten and ignored? Two reasons have to do with the history of the field most directly related to their rhetorical endeavors. What is announced under varied titles as Communication Studies, Speech Communication, and Communication Arts and Sciences (see list of contributors) is a field that in its contemporary form is relatively recent, although the study of rhetoric began sometime in the sixth century B.C.E. in ancient Greece. Originally, those who created this field were housed in English departments, although the separation occurred before that field shifted from a historical and biographical emphasis to a focus on practical criticism. Accordingly, the original speech communication scholars focused on public address, which was oral rather than written literature, and on discourse on public policy issues, in contrast to the imaginative character of most fiction, and they studied the impact of speeches on immediate audiences (Black, 1965). Because the works with the most apparent impact were those of men in positions of power, usually political positions of power, the study of public address became the study of the oral discourse of white male political leaders, chiefly presidents and candidates for that office, members of Congress, and, on occasion, the speeches of leading religious figures, lyceum lecturers, lawyers, or leading literary figures whose pronouncements were clearly hortatory, such as Ralph Waldo Emerson's Phi Beta Kappa lecture at Harvard, "The American Scholar." Because women were excluded by law and conventions from the pulpit, the courtroom, and from positions of political power, and were denied access to advanced education and professional training, their discourse, however significant, was usually ignored. The great white male study of public address imitated the great white male study of history on which it rested. Increasing interest in the rhetoric of women and others who have been oppressed and/or excluded from positions of institutional power in part reflects the impact of social history on the study of public discourse and a recognition of more subtle forms of impact and of the long-term effects of social protest that seem to fail in the short term.

Despite the diversity of those included in this volume, critics may find it a female version of the study of great white male rhetoric. On the simplest level, one must begin somewhere, and the first women to whom attention is drawn are those who, as a result of unusual advantages or lucky accidents, were able to overcome the obstacles that defeated their female contemporaries. On a more complex level, such criticism ignores the barriers all women faced and demeans the efforts of these women who literally created the organizations that gave them opportunities for leadership and expression. Many were poor, even destitute; most were compelled to support themselves, to finance whatever education they received, to confront hostility so severe that they were castigated as harlots and heretics. A few came from wealthy families, but even those faced extraordinary obstacles—no institution of higher education would admit them, organizations espousing the causes dear to their hearts would not permit them membership, much less allow them to speak or vote. They were compelled to make their cases and defend their causes to mostly hostile males who held virtually all the political, social, and economic power. That they were extraordinary women, women of unusual talents, intelligence, and perseverance should not be held against them. Moreover, it is their voices that articulated the conditions and the despair of their sisters and pleaded for the changes that enabled other, less extraordinary and less advantaged women, to enter the marketplace of ideas. In other words, when compared to white males, these women, even those rich and educated, were disadvantaged and oppressed.

Another characteristic of the field that studies public discourse has been the dominance of forms of critical analysis that inflicted the worst forms of sexual stereotyping on women. What Edwin Black (1965) labeled neo-Aristotelianism was a system that privileged only certain forms of discourse, those to which women had least access. It also privileged logic and argument and denigrated the emotional appeals, figurative language, and stylistic creativity most likely to appear in the discourse of protestors and reformers. In fact, this critical method tended to see only arguments, and because women were thought naturally deficient in that area, little was done to examine even the argumentation of women speakers.

Finally, the key to this method was its emphasis on effects on immediate audiences. Although immediate effects are rare in any case (even U.S. presidents cannot wave magic wands of argument and obtain enactment of their proposals), that standard privileges the discourse of the powerful who are more apt to achieve their ends than are those who seek fundamental changes in attitude and social policy. Accordingly, one could dismiss the efforts of woman suffrage advocates, whose goals were achieved after more than seventy years of efforts; those who tried to organize women workers and succeeded in achieving only a small part of their goal; those who fought for anarchism, which was never adopted; those who fought for socialism, which was largely rejected; those who fought against lynching, which abated but persisted; and those who fought for prohibition, which was repealed. In addition, issues were divided so that the concerns of women were seen as lying outside the *res publica*, as private, as "women's issues" that did not merit public attention. Hence, women who spoke about child labor, consumer protection, divorce, and prostitution could be dismissed as dealing with unimportant topics, and those who concerned themselves with the civil rights of women—the legal existence of married women, suffrage, education, access to the professions—could be ignored as partial, biased, and self-seeking rather than as reformers perfecting the principles underlying the nation.

But the dominance of such perspectives has come to an end, and increasingly rhetorical scholars are asking questions to which the discourse of women can contribute answers. How does social change occur and what is the contribution of public discourse to those processes? What is excellence and creativity in the human use of symbols? How have the oppressed and disadvantaged strategized to overcome the social barriers that confront them in their efforts to seek change? Perhaps we shall discover that the works of women and other disadvantaged groups, precisely because of the obstacles they face, will be more significant in answering such questions and illuminating the breadth and variety of human symbolic action (Campbell, 1991).

The work that follows is intended to introduce these women as contributors to the public dialogue of their time. Instead of providing detailed biographies, they focus on women's public lives in discourse. References are provided for those readers who seek more information about the subjects' lives. This volume and its forthcoming companion (1925–present) are designed for those readers who seek to understand women's history in the public discourse of the United States and who wish to begin to assess their contributions to the nation's thinking and policy. Following a brief section of biographical background information, each entry includes a short analysis of each woman's rhetoric, outlining areas of particular significance and emphasis. Entries conclude with a listing of primary sources, critical works, and key rhetorical documents, in addition to selected sources of historical and biographical information. Entries vary in length partly because of past attention and partly because of the varied length and complexity of women's public careers. For example, ERNESTINE POTOWSKI ROSE often has been overlooked; here she commands greater attention. Similarly, CARRIE LANE CHAPMAN CATT has received little treatment as a speaker despite a long career in suffrage and antiwar efforts. By contrast, women who have been the subjects of many biographies and whose rhetoric has received more attention have been allotted less space.

In attempting a project such as this, regrettable omissions are inevitable. For example, although she is the subject of a recent biography by Celia Morris Eckhardt (1984), Frances Wright's rhetoric has not received the attention it merits; nonetheless, she is not included. Others who merit inclusion but who are absent include such important African-Americans as Frances Harper and Fannie Barrier Williams. Although some regional figures such as HELEN JACK-SON GOUGAR and CATHARINE WAUGH MCCULLOCH have been in-cluded, others of importance, such as Jane Grey Cannon Swisshelm, are not. No volume could encompass all the contributions of women to the nation's public discourse up to 1925; many volumes will be required before such a history is complete. The omissions noted above and others reflect the difficulty of finding scholars to do what is often copious and difficult primary research to produce entries. That difficulty has resulted in the omission of such figures as Lucy Stone, Dorothy Dix, and Mary Rice Livermore, among others. In two instances, figures I have been forced to omit, Abigail (Abby) Kelley Foster and Lucy Stone, have been the subjects of fine recent biographies that demonstrate their significance as historical figures and as early woman speakers (Kerr, 1992; Sterling, 1991). A few are omitted from this volume because their careers extend beyond the arbitrary end point of 1925. These include Anna Julia Cooper, Leonora O'Reilly, and Mary Church Terrell, who will be the subject of entries in the companion volume. Happily, scholarship is never finished; these volumes will have achieved their end if they stimulate the study of other women rhetors and encourage further study of the women described in the pages that follow.

Any reference work in a relatively new research area raises unexpected questions. That naming should be an issue will come as no surprise to rhetorical scholars who are well aware of the significance of terms of reference. After careful consideration of the options, I decided that the figures discussed would always be referred to by their birth names in addition to whatever names they acquired through marriage. Hence, although she never referred to herself that way, LUCRETIA COFFIN MOTT is always Coffin Mott in second references. (Mott is her husband James.) Originally, I planned to follow that policy only with women who began their public careers prior to marriage, such as IDA B. WELLS or ANGELINA GRIMKÉ, but the longer I worked on the volume, the less satisfactory that became, as the Coffin Mott example illustrates. Hence, throughout this work, whatever their own usage, I have incorporated the subject's birth name into all references to her, and although the practice seemed odd at first, familiarity bred satisfaction. Perhaps it may set a precedent.

Space constraints drew attention to organizational names and sources that recurred very frequently; accordingly, certain abbreviations used throughout are identified in a list of such abbreviations. Abbreviations in references in individual chapters are explained in the section on sources at the end of each chapter.

I owe a debt of gratitude to my editorial board, Professor Janice Schuetz of the University of New Mexico and Emeritus Professor Mary Margaret Roberts, Kansas State University at Pittsburg, who have done so much to improve the entries in this volume. I owe an incalculable debt to the authors, many of whom are former students, who have devoted precious research time to this project. I am hopeful that work for this project will be a springboard for subsequent publications. I also thank the College of Liberal Arts and the Graduate School of the University of Minnesota for the kinds of support that make such a project possible, and members of the Department of Speech–Communication for the support that makes such a project enjoyable, including their wonderful collegiality and penetrating criticisms. My research assistant Nathan Dick was invaluable; I particularly appreciate his careful attention to detail. Finally, I thank Professor Paul Newell Campbell, an unofficial member of the editorial board, who stepped into the breach and brought to bear his fierce feminism, his dedication to elegance and clarity in writing, and his extraordinary organizational skills, and who asked the simple questions that helped to identify the blinders, what Kenneth Burke has called the "occupational psychosis," that overtake all specialists. To the degree that these volumes are intelligible to those without extensive background in women's history, he deserves much of the credit.

SOURCES

Bacon, Margaret Hope. *Mothers of Feminism: The Story of Quaker Women in America*. New York: Harper & Row, 1986.

Black, Edwin. *Rhetorical Criticism: A Study in Method*. New York: Macmillan, 1965.

Campbell, Karlyn Kohrs. "Hearing Women's Voices." *Communication Education* 40 (January 1991):34–48.

Clarke, Edward H. *Sex in Education: A Fair Chance for the Girls*. Boston: James R. Osgood, 1873.

Eckhardt, Celia Morris. *Fanny Wright: Rebel in America*. Cambridge, Mass.: Harvard University Press, 1984.

Fell, Margaret Askew. *Womens Speaking Justified*. 1666; 1667. Intro. David J. Latt.

Publication no. 194. Augustan Reprint Society, William Andrew Clark Memorial Library, University of California, Los Angeles, 1979, pp. 1–19.

Gilbert, Sandra M., and Susan Gubar. *Madwoman in the Attic: The Woman Writer and the Nineteenth-Century Imagination*. New Haven, Conn.: Yale University Press, 1979.

Gilligan, Carol. *In a Different Voice: Psychological Theory and Women's Development*. Cambridge, Mass.: Harvard University Press, 1982.

Kerr, Andrea Moore. *Lucy Stone: Speaking Out for Equality*. Princeton, N.J.: Rutgers University Press, 1992.

Kraditor, Aileen S. *Ideas of the Woman Suffrage Movement, 1890–1920*. 1965. New York: W. W. Norton, 1981.

Mason, Miss. The First Woman's Salutatory. *The Woman's Journal* 17 no. 40 (October 1, 1887):1.3–4.

Mattina, Anne F. "Shattered Silence: The Rhetoric of An American Female Labor Reform Association." Ph.D. diss., Ohio State University, 1986.

O'Connor, Lillian. *Pioneer Women Orators*. New York: Columbia University Press, 1954.

Sterling, Dorothy. *Ahead of Her Time: Abby Kelley and the Politics of Antislavery*. New York: W. W. Norton, 1991.

Vonnegut, Kristin. "Listening for Women's Voices: Revisioning Courses in American Public Address." *Communication Education* 41 (January 1992):26–39.

Weisstein, Naomi. "Psychology Constructs the Female, or the Fantasy Life of the Male Psychologist." *Roles Women Play: Readings Toward Women's Liberation*. Ed. Michele Hoffnung Garskof. Belmont, Calif.: Brooks/Cole, 1971, pp. 68–83.

Welter, Barbara. *Dimity Convictions: The American Woman in the Nineteenth Century*. Athens: Ohio University Press, 1976.

Willard, Frances E. *Woman in the Pulpit*. Chicago: Woman's Temperance Publishing Association, 1890.

Woody, Thomas. *A History of Women's Education in the United States*, 2 vols. New York: Science Press, 1929.

Wright [D'Arusmont], Frances. *Life, Letters and Lectures 1824/1844*. 1834; 1844. New York: Arno Press, 1972.

ABBREVIATIONS _____

ORGANIZATIONS

AERA   American Equal Rights Association

AWSA   American Woman Suffrage Association

NAWSA   National American Woman Suffrage Association

NWSA   National Woman Suffrage Association

WCTU   Woman's Christian Temperance Union

WRC   Woman's Rights Convention

SOURCES

HOW   History of Women Collection, Schlesinger Library, Radcliffe.

HWS   *History of Woman Suffrage*. Vols. 1–3. Eds. Elizabeth Cady Stanton, Susan B. Anthony, and Matilda Joslyn Gage. 1881, 1882, 1886. Vol 4. Eds. Susan B. Anthony and Ida Husted Harper. 1902. Vols. 5 and 6. Ed. Ida Husted Harper. 1922. Salem, N.H.: Ayer, 1985.

IWSM   Aileen S. Kraditor. *Ideas of the Woman Suffrage Movement, 1890–1920*. 1965. New York: W. W. Norton, 1981.

MCSFH *Man Cannot Speak for Her*. 2 vols. Westport, Conn.: Greenwood Press, 1989.

NAW   *Notable American Women: A Biographical Dictionary*. 3 vols. Ed. Edward T. James. Cambridge, Mass.: Belknap Press of Harvard University Press, 1971.

OW   *Outspoken Women: Speeches by American Women Reformers, 1635–1935*. Ed. Judith Anderson. Dubuque, Iowa: Kendall Hunt, 1984.

TWJ   *The Woman's Journal*

WSBH   *We Shall Be Heard: Women Speakers in America*. Eds. Patricia Scileppi
             Kennedy and Gloria Hartmann O'Shields. Dubuque, Iowa: Kendall Hunt,
             1983.

WT   *Women Together: A History in Documents of the Women's Movement in
             the United States*. Ed. Judith Papachristou. New York: Alfred A. Knopf,
             1976.

PROCEEDINGS

AERA 1867   *Proceedings of the First Anniversary of the American Equal Rights As-
             sociation*. New York City, May 9–10, 1867. New York: Robert J. John-
             ston, Printer, 1867.

WRC 1850   *Proceedings of the Woman's Rights Convention*. Worcester, Mass., Oc-
             tober 23 and 24, 1850. Boston: Prentiss and Sawyer, 1851.

WRC 1851   *Proceedings of the National Woman's Rights Convention*. Worcester,
             Mass., October 15, 16, 1851. New York: Fowler and Wells, 1852.

WRC 1852   *Proceedings of the Woman's Rights Convention*. September 8–9, 1852,
             Syracuse, N. Y.: J.E. Masters, 1852.

WRC 1853   *Proceedings of the National Woman's Rights Convention*. Broadway
             Tabernacle, New York, September 6–7, 1853. New York: Fowler &
             Wells, 1853.

WRC 1854   *Proceedings of the National Woman's Rights Convention*. Cleveland,
             October 5–7, 1854. Cleveland: Gray Beardsley, Spear & Co., 1854.

WRC 1856   *Proceedings of the National Woman's Rights Convention*. New York,
             November 25–26, 1856. New York: Edward O. Jenkins, 1856.

WRC 1859   *Proceedings of the National Woman's Rights Convention*. Rochester,
             N.Y.: Steam Press, 1859.

WRC 1860   *Proceedings of the National Woman's Rights Convention*. New York,
             May 10, 1860. New York: Robert J. Johnston, 1866.

Women Public Speakers in the United States, 1800-1925

JANE ADDAMS

(1860–1935), champion of the poor, advocate for peace, suffragist

FRAN HASSENCAHL

Jane Addams was internationally known as the founder of Hull House and as a sociologist, educator, and spokesperson for and supporter of woman's rights, international peace, the labor movement, child welfare, and social reform generally. She wrote and spoke to legislators, heads of state, and the public about the problems of youth, uprooted immigrants, factory conditions for women and children, and the horrors of war. Prior to World War I, the U.S. public viewed her as a saint as well as the social worker of the century. In 1908, the *Ladies' Home Journal* named her "First American Woman"; other surveys ranked her ahead of Theodore Roosevelt, Thomas Edison, and Helen Keller (see entry in volume 2). But her opposition to the war and her proposal to feed all the hungry without asking whether the parents of a hungry child were Italians, our allies, or Dalmatians, our enemies, made her suspect; she was under surveillance by the Department of Justice; and in 1920, she was included in the four-volume Lusk Report that linked peace and women's organizations and other reform efforts with communism, socialism, and bolshevism. Her popularity declined; only a few peace groups continued to invite her to speak.

However, admirers and supporters, especially from outside the country, remained faithful, and almost every year from 1920 until 1930, campaigns were launched to secure the Nobel Peace Prize for her. When the award finally came in 1930, she had to share it with conservative internationalist Nicholas Murray Butler, who had supported U.S. participation in the war. She gave her share of the prize money to the Women's International League for Peace and Freedom (WILPF) and to aid the unemployed in the Hull House neighborhood. Other honors followed. She was again in demand as a speaker and reappeared on lists of the greatest women of the century and, with Thomas Edison and Henry Ford, was seen as one of the seven greatest Americans of all time in popular polls.

As a rhetorician, the sheer volume of her work can but dismay any critic. Addams authored or edited twelve books and produced nearly 500 articles and speeches. There are many studies of her life and work, but she has received only limited attention as a rhetorician. As a result, following brief sections on her family and education and her work at Hull House, the major emphasis of this chapter will be on her suffragist and antiwar rhetoric.

FAMILY AND EDUCATIONAL BACKGROUND

Laura Jane Addams was born on September 6, 1860, at Cedarville, Illinois. She was the eighth of nine children, but only she, two sisters, and an older brother survived infancy. Her mother Sarah Weber died when Addams was two, following the premature birth and death of her ninth child. Like many women who have emerged to play major leadership roles, Jane Addams benefited from a close relationship with her father, John Huy Addams. The death of her mother and her position as the youngest child made her the recipient of much of his attention. He encouraged her to develop intellectually and sent her to Rockford Seminary, where she studied rhetoric, Greek, and Latin, took lessons and participated in debate and oratory, and wrote for and edited the *Rockford Seminary Magazine*. When she was seven, her father married widow Anna H. Haldeman who helped Addams to develop a sense of assurance around those with wealth and culture. Of much importance in her career is that her father was a large landholder and founder and president of a bank in nearby Freeport who had the means to give her a comfortable life and education with opportunities to travel extensively.

Two additional family issues should be noted. First, for some time, her stepmother urged Addams to marry her son George Haldeman. Second, there was strong pressure for her to stay at home and act as the "maiden aunt" who would care for the family's business and emotional needs. Rejecting both proposals, she entered the Women's Medical College in Philadelphia in the fall of 1881. However, she discovered that she was not particularly interested in medicine, and so she left after a semester. With no economic need to work and no marriage plans or interest in teaching, Addams found that her career options were limited.

Here Addams's European travels, made possible by her father's affluence, became significant. Her early trips to the Continent may not have been as important as she later thought them, but it appears that a stay in London in the spring of 1888 was a turning point in her life. There she visited Toynbee Hall and the People's Palace, which housed meeting rooms, a gymnasium, and space for clubs and crafts for working people. She wrote in an essay that she was impressed that the university men who ran them lived in the neighborhood rather than visiting it (SCPC 7–11). They were much like college students on a campus, and the classes, library, and lectures provided a way for the residents to disseminate their knowledge of history, literature, and art to the worker audience. Sharing one's knowledge and culture seemed much more acceptable to her than donating money to the poor or creating a charitable institution. It was probably at this juncture that she decided to live in a working-class neighborhood.

Her interest in neighborhood work and living may also have resulted from her interest in Leo Tolstoy. Addams read his works and visited him in Russia in 1886. But whereas Tolstoy saw rural life as a restorer of community and an answer to the disruptive isolation of the city, she found cities vital and full of potential. However, she shared Tolstoy's ideas on war and nonresistance and his philosophy of art, namely, that art should express the life and labor of the people and draw them together. In 1902, at Chautauqua, New York, she offered a series of lectures revealing the impact of Tolstoy's ideas on her thought. These lectures, "Newer Ideals of Peace," "Arts and Crafts and the Settlement,"

"Count Tolstoy," and "Count Tolstoy's Theory of Life," were published in the *Chautauqua Assembly Herald*.

HULL HOUSE

In January 1889, Addams and Ellen Gates Starr, her best friend and companion on the London trip, took rooms at a Chicago boarding house and began their plans to found a settlement house. After inspecting several neighborhoods, the two women decided to sublet the second floor of the former Charles J. Hull mansion. On September 18, 1889, they moved their books, art, and pieces of family furniture into what Addams would call "home" for the next forty-six years of her life.

Settlement houses, in both England and the United States, drew from the ideas of Christian Socialists and the Social Gospel movement and from optimism that the social sciences could resolve the problems of urban industrial society. Addams quickly decided that the settlement house at Halstead and Polk streets would be a base for understanding and ameliorating social problems.

Hull House activities were widely publicized by the press, which helped raise funds and direct public opinion toward reform efforts. The press simplified Addams's motives by emphasizing a religious rationale for her work and creating an image of her as an angel of mercy. In fact, although she was baptized a Presbyterian in 1888, in later years she became an agnostic.

But Hull House was no place for ministering angels. Rather, it became an internationally important intellectual center where leaders of many disciplines gathered to teach, study, and do research. It grew to become twelve buildings comprising what is now the campus of the University of Illinois, Chicago. Faculty from the University of Chicago Sociology Department lectured there and worked with the emerging labor unions that often met there. Sociologists Albion Small, George H. Mead, Edith Abbot, Charles Henderson, Charles Zueblin, George E. Vincent, Sophonsiba Breckinridge, and W. I. Thomas saw Hull House as a logical extension of their research and humanitarian interests. Addams was a charter member of the American Sociological Association, founded in 1905. She also taught sociology in the University of Chicago Extension and at the Chicago School of Civics and Philanthropy and published in sociological journals, including five articles that appeared in the prestigious *American Journal of Sociology*. Five of her books were reviewed by the journal. *Democracy and Social Ethics* (1902) was well received; in a letter to Addams, William James called it "one of the great books of our time" (September 17, 1902, SCPC).

But Addams's major contribution to the field of sociology was editing *Hull House Maps and Papers* (1895). FLORENCE KELLEY, a Hull House resident and special agent for the State Bureau of Labor Statistics, had conducted a study of Chicago sweat shops and had corresponded with Robert T. Ely, a University of Wisconsin professor and founder of the American Economic Association.

Kelley and Ely were the moving forces behind the research leading to publication of the book, which contained ten essays written by Hull House residents and researchers and two large pull-out maps. One depicted the distribution of eighteen national groups within a third of a square mile area near Hull House. The other showed their wages, occupations, and housing conditions. The essays treated low wages, unhealthy work conditions, specific studies of the Jewish, Bohemian, and Italian immigrants, critiques of social service agencies, and examined the sociology of art.

The book was notable for its impact on the University of Chicago Sociology Department, which continued to focus research on the city and its immigrants and laborers. The development of mapping as a statistical technique to reveal social group patterns became a major contribution of the Chicago School.

But in the postwar period, sociology was to become more scientific and objective, which made it more acceptable to business and to university administrators. As the field left behind its commitment to the critique and reform of societal institutions, male sociologists were hired to teach and do research at the academy, and the writings of women sociologists were characterized as "undisciplined" (Deegan, 1988:145). The period of happy collaboration between Hull House and Chicago sociologists was over. By 1920, women were moved out of the Sociology Department into what was seen as their sex-appropriate sphere, the School of Social Services. Settlement houses were no longer seen as sociological laboratories where research and social experiments could be conducted; instead, they became linked with social work, which was women's work. Rather than the search for solutions to the problems of immigrants, labor, women, and children, the field of sociology shifted its focus to the construction of abstract theories and models that served to legitimize an increasingly male-dominated discipline.

In the postwar period, Addams became more active in social work but continued to identify herself as a sociologist. She was also seen as a sociologist by such leaders in the field as E. A. Ross and Charles Cooley, who quoted her books and assigned them to students to read. As before, she was a role model for and facilitated a network of women sociologists.

BACKGROUND OF ADDAMS'S SUFFRAGIST AND PACIFIST RHETORIC

Addams and her progressive colleagues opposed the Equal Rights Amendment because they feared it would undo the protective legislation for women workers that they had worked so hard to secure. For this reason, some of her more radical contemporaries, such as Alice Paul, did not consider her a feminist. Indeed, Addams wished to reform, not overthrow, the patriarchy and envisioned the expansion of women's roles within it. She believed in the superiority of women's values and world views, but she also believed in marriage, children, and the patriarchal family. She had favored woman suffrage as a college student but was not active in the movement until 1906, when she joined NAWSA, becoming its vice-president in 1911. She worked for municipal suffrage in Chicago and in 1911, joined with 300 women who mounted a major campaign for woman suffrage in Illinois.

Addams believed that when they received the vote, women would make a special contribution to the community. Women who had studied economics would use the ballot to outlaw sweat shops, to secure laws setting minimum wages for all and maximum hours for women, and so forth. Women who were trained in the sciences would be concerned with sanitation, pure water and milk, the control of infectious diseases, infant mortality, and the like. Women needed the vote to secure appropriate educational and recreational programs and facilities for their children; woman suffrage, she claimed, would bring about reforms needed by both men and women.

Addams argued from expediency, but her version of expediency merits attention because it differed from that of many other suffragists. The vote, she believed, was a means to a better society rather than a natural right. In this respect, she differed from earlier suffragists who had argued on the basis of justice and equality of the sexes. Most suffragists were white, native-born, middle-class women, and many had difficulty with the franchise being extended to Blacks and immigrants. Political expediency made it necessary to seek linkages with these groups, but most agreed with ELIZABETH CADY STANTON that there ought to be an educational qualification for voters. Alone among the women on the executive committee of NAWSA, Addams argued for the extension of the franchise to immigrant women on humanitarian grounds. She contended that the problems to be solved were so basic that formal education was not needed. With a series of examples about the experiences of Scandinavian women who had voted in Europe and Russian-Jewish housewives who could not grasp why the United States did not have clean, covered food markets, she emphasized that these women would vote intelligently and that they needed the franchise to feed and clothe their families properly and to insure proper sanitation and police protection.

The statement is sometimes made that the franchise for women would be valuable only so far as the educated women exercised it. This statement totally disregards the fact that these matters in which women's judgement is most needed are far too primitive and basic to be largely influenced by what we call education. (*Newer Ideals of Peace*, 188)

Her observations were borne out by passage in 1917 of a New York suffrage law, made possible by immigrant voters in New York City.

Addam's work in the suffrage movement drew her into party politics. When the Republican National Convention met in Chicago in 1912, she requested a hearing from the platform committee. She was given one hour's notice and seven minutes to make a case for a suffrage plank. Unsuccessful, she turned to the newly formed Progressive party, which adopted a suffrage plank. Its platform also incorporated the recommendations of a special report from a committee on industrial standards of the National Conference of Charities and Corrections. Addams was the first woman president of the conference when the committee was appointed in 1909.

Addams made a campaign tour through fifteen states in support of Theodore Roosevelt's election, delivering a basic speech that focused on the social and industrial reforms in the Progressive party platform. The platform called for legislation to establish a six-day week and an eight-hour day, to protect workers from industrial accidents, to prohibit child labor, and to protect workers against illness and old age with a system of social insurance. Sometimes accompanied by the "Jane Addams Chorus," women vocalists in white dresses, she spoke at rallies. She told audiences that politics would be "infinitely benefited if women were taking a natural and legitimate share in the development and in the administration of governmental activities" (Farrell, 1967:133).

Addams frequently used a municipal housekeeping argument. Women should extend the private sphere into the public realm by tending to municipal tasks as they did household chores. This concept was rooted in her belief in the superiority of women's values and world views, which is to say that she, like most women sociologists trained before 1915, was a cultural, if not an ideological, feminist.

Her arguments for peace reflected her belief in cultural feminism. Her keynote address on January 10, 1915, to the Woman's Peace party in Washington, D.C., is the most concise statement of her opposition to World War I. In this speech, she reminded her audience that she had not maintained that women were better than men, but that they were different, particularly in nurturing life. She asked: "And at last, shall we not say that the sensitiveness to human life, so highly developed in women, has been seriously injured by this war?" (Davis, 1973:63). She reported that children and the aged were dying in some countries in a ratio of five to one to soldiers killed in battle. She noted that war destroys "not only the work of the mother, the nurse and teacher, but at the same time ruthlessly destroys the very conception of the careful nurture of life." In her closing plea, she urged women again to be the conscience of the future and called for an end to warfare. It was up to women to clean up the horror of war, to put the human house in order.

Much of Addams's war and postwar activity was channeled into efforts to feed the hungry and to restore her credibility. Using ideas from Fraser's *Golden Bough*, she wrote and spoke about the history and relevance of the female deities, the corn mother and her daughter. She imagined a scenario in which mothers had planted primitive gardens in an attempt to prevent the loss of their children. She graphically attributed these losses to "the alternation of gorging when the hunt was good and of starving when it was poor" (*Peace and Bread*, 79). She pictured these women insisting that they could not leave an area until the crops were harvested. The exchange of foodstuffs was a basis for the first cooperation between tribes and offered the hope of international cooperation. In a 1917 speech to the Chicago City Club, she asked if it would not be possible for the

United States, now engaged in the war, to tell its allies that it would not enlist in the war for the purpose of starving women and children. Once women reacquainted themselves with the corn mother and her daughter, Demeter and Persephone, they would rediscover their ancient obligation to nurture the world and provide a basis for a new international organization. Hence, women must extend their housekeeping role from the city and state to include the world.

ADDAMS AS A SPEAKER

Whether it was presenting testimony before congressional committees or delivering sermons and eulogies, lecturing to university students and sociologists, or addressing international conferences, Addams was greatly in demand as a speaker. Much of what she said in lectures was incorporated into her magazine articles and books. She prepared her speeches carefully from notes and revised drafts until she had a final manuscript. Ordinarily, she spoke from notes or from memory, rarely extemporaneously or from a manuscript.

Christopher Lasch observes that her argumentation was autobiographical. He comments that both the virtues and defects of her works came from speaking and writing directly about her experiences. Addams's often-used graphic examples added a personal touch and an urgency to her arguments that would not have accrued from a more scholarly approach.

A speech at Carnegie Hall on July 9, 1915, after her return from the First International Conference of Women at The Hague, illustrates her awareness of the power of examples to clarify and intensify an argument. In her introduction, she warned that the war had intensified emotions and created a need for "some careful understanding. You become very afraid of generalizing. The situation is so confused, so many wild and weird things are said about it, that you are afraid to add one word that is not founded upon absolutely first-hand impressions and careful experience" (Davis, 1973:72). The post-conference trip that she and five other women took to nine European countries seeking support for a conference of neutral nations gave her the opportunity to gather first-hand data to support her thesis that there was "the possibility of substituting negotiations for military processes" (Davis, 1973:76).

After arguing inductively that she and her colleagues had found the nine heads of state with whom they had spoken to be supportive of her thesis, she took up the question of whether the war was supported by those who fought. In order not to "get in trouble" and "to back it up, so to speak," she presented examples from both sides. She told of a young, wounded German soldier who "Never during that three months and a half had . . . once shot his gun in a way that could possibly hit another man" (Davis, 1973:79). Other examples included French soldiers who "will not do any fatal shooting" and an angry Cambridge University student/soldier who accused the older generation of "doing their very utmost . . . to perpetuate . . . hate, intolerance, and revenge." She balanced her findings with examples of soldiers, nurses, and mothers who wholeheartedly supported the war, including a patriotic mother who had given five sons and a son-in-law to the war effort and lamented that she had no more sons to give.

Addams employed a clipping service and was aware that she was under attack by the press and fellow reformers for her work with the Woman's Peace party. To counter their arguments that she, a social worker, was out of her realm, she compared the belligerents in Europe to two squabbling boys:

Let us say that there are two groups of boys in a boys' club, and I have much experience of that sort in boys' clubs to draw upon. If one says, "We did this because the other fellows did that," you will simply have to say, "I won't go into the rights and wrongs of this, but this thing must stop because it leads nowhere and gets nowhere." And so with larger groups. (Davis, 1973:86)

Addams chose examples that were consistent with audience beliefs that many on both sides hoped for a mediated end to the war. In her conclusion, she challenged core values when she suggested that soldiers were not motivated by and would not kill for love of country or out of a sense of duty. Rather, they had to be worked up through the use of alcohol:

We heard in all countries similar statements in regard to the necessity for the use of stimulants before men would engage in bayonet charges—that they have a regular formula in Germany, that they give them rum in England and absinthe in France; that they all have to give them the "dope" before the bayonet charge is possible. (Davis, 1973:89)

The response of the press was virulent. Her call for a conference of neutrals was lost in the barrage of attacks on her political expertise and credibility. Earlier, she had been quite successful by virtue of her message and because of who she was and what she represented. For many years, the press had described hers as a life of sacrifice among the poor, and her persuasiveness had been related to her reputation as a reformer, skilled fundraiser, and leader. Biographer Allen Davis suggests that her activities and her calm, gentle demeanor satisfied a longing for an American heroine: "She fulfilled the need for a female religious figure—a saint, a madonna, even a Protestant virgin" (1973:105). Americans refused to permit one they saw as a gentle philanthropist to step out of the mainstream. "By challenging the part of the American dream that saw war as glorious and patriotic, she had fallen from grace" (1973:229).

Much of Addams's rhetoric during the postwar years was an effort to restore her public image. In order to explain her position and to answer charges made against pacifists, in "Patriotism and Pacifists in Wartime," delivered in the spring of 1917 at the Chicago City Club, the University of Chicago, and the First Congregational Church of Evanston, she attempted to differentiate herself and her supporters from those who might properly be labeled passive, unpatriotic, or cowardly. She argued that the peace movement had remained alive through many wars and was tolerated now in war-torn Europe in a variety of forms, including the Women's International Committee for Permanent Peace, which she chaired. She then responded to the character attacks. Pacifists, she explained, were descendants of the founders who had created the Declaration of Independence and the Constitution and had formed a federal government out of thirteen sovereign states. Pacifists advocated that the United States take a leadership role in recreating this model on a worldwide basis. Moreover, she took special care to distinguish this movement toward international government from the "mid-Victorian idea that good men from every country meet at The Hague" where they would pass resolutions mandating the end of wars. A more analogous situation, which boded well for an international federation of states, was the success already achieved by international banks and scientific associations (Davis, 1973:141).

The efforts of the U.S. Department of Food Administration to feed the hungry of Europe, specifically in occupied countries, offered Addams an opportunity to be useful and to link her to causes that were more acceptable to Americans. When Herbert Hoover asked her to lecture to women's clubs on behalf of the department, which he headed, she agreed. Reaction to her opposition to the war could be muted by her intense concern about its effects and the need to feed the hungry. To explain her concern for hungry Germans, the enemy, was more difficult. Nonetheless, she soon was receiving more invitations to speak than she could honor.

Addams wrote and spoke in a descriptive, narrative style enlivened by examples. She used few figures of speech, but bread frequently appeared as a metaphor. In his introduction to the 1945 edition of Addams's *Peace and Bread in Time of War*, John Dewey observed that the need for food was important to her, not only as signified by the juxtaposition of bread and peace in the title, but also in the extensive discussion of food therein. He commented that bread was a symbol for her belief in the natural goodness and primitive affection of people one for another (xix). The metaphor was linked to her past. Her father, grandfather, and great-grandfather had been millers, and she remembered being held up by dusty hands to see the foaming water wheel turning to power the mill stones that ground the "masses of hard yellow wheat."

The association of women with bread was a theme that originated in Addams's first presentation in 1881 at Rockford Seminary. In that speech, she pointed out that, while she and her classmates asserted their independence, they also retained "the old ideal of womanhood" in the sense that "we have planned to be 'Bread-givers' throughout our lives" (*Jane Addams: A Centennial Reader*, 103). In a presidential address to the Pan-Pacific Woman's Conference in 1928, she repeated her theme of women as foodgivers and praised New Zealand women for using suffrage to insure that all children had their "quota of good milk" (Davis, 1973:203–204).

CONCLUSION

Addams was both praised and vilified. The era of settlement houses is now over, but establishment of Hull House alone would have guaranteed her a place

in history. In addition, the WILPF, of which she was the first president, continues
to seek world peace. As a rhetor she was a tireless advocate in support of the
needy, children, immigrants, woman suffrage, labor, civil rights, social reform,
and, of course, peace.

SOURCES

Addams's Papers (JAP), Hull House Association Records (1889–1970), and the Halde-
man-Julius Family Papers (1833–1961) are held in the Manuscript Collection, University
of Illinois, Chicago, Library. The Haldeman Papers (1839–1953), Lilly Library, Indiana
University, contain correspondence with her sister, Alice Haldeman. Rockford College
Archives include information about her as a student and alumna. The Sophia Smith
Collection, Smith College, has two boxes of her papers and the papers of Ellen Gates
Starr, co-founder of Hull House and longtime friend. Chicago Peace Society records and
the Louise Hadduck Bowen [deKoven] Papers are in the Chicago Historical Society.

Other sources are Sophonsiba P. Breckinridge Papers, Library of Congress Manuscript
Division; Florence Kelley Papers, Rare Book and Manuscript Library, Columbia University, and Nicholas Kelley Papers, Manuscript and Archives Division, New York Public
Library; the Angela Morgan Papers, Brantley Historical Library, University of Michigan;
the Emily Greene Balch (see entry in volume 2) Papers, the WILPF records, and the
Woman's Peace Party Papers, Swarthmore College Peace Collection (SCPC); and WILPF
records, Western Historical Collection, University of Colorado.

The Jane Addams' Papers, ed. Mary Lynn McCree Bryan (University Microfilms,
1985), *A Preliminary Checklist for a Bibliography on Jane Addams* (Rockford, Ill.,
1960), comp. M. Helen Perkins, and "Check List of the Jane Addams' Papers" (n.d.)
in the Swarthmore Peace Collection are helpful resources. Farrell has the most complete
bibliography of her works.

Books Written or Edited by Jane Addams

Jane Addams. "The Settlement as a Factor in the Labor Movement." *Hull House Maps
          and Papers*. Ed. Jane Addams. 1895. New York: Arno, 1970, pp. 183–204.
Democracy and Social Ethics. 1902. Ed. and intro. Anne Firor Scott. Cambridge, Mass.
          Belknap Press of Harvard University Press, 1964.
Newer Ideals of Peace. New York: Macmillan, 1907.
The Spirit of Youth and the City Streets. 1909. Intro. Allen F. Davis. Urbana: University
          of Illinois Press, 1972.
Twenty Years at Hull-House, with Autobiographical Notes. New York: Macmillan, 1910.
A New Conscience and an Ancient Evil. 1912. New York: Arno, 1972.
Women at The Hague; the International Congress of Women and Its Results. 1915. New
          York: Garland, 1972. With Emily Greene Balch and Alice Hamilton.
The Long Road of Woman's Memory. New York: Macmillan, 1917.
Peace and Bread in Time of War. Intro. John Dewey. 1922. New York: Garland, 1972.
          Rpts. "Patriotism and Pacifists in War Time."
*The Second Twenty Years at Hull-House, September 1909 to September 1929, with a
          Record of a Growing World Consciousness*. New York: Macmillan, 1930.

The Excellent Becomes the Permanent. 1932. Freeport, N.Y.: Books for Libraries, 1970.
My Friend, Julia Lathrop. 1935. New York: Arno, 1974.

Collections of Writings and Speeches

Addams, Jane. *Philanthropy and Social Progress; Seven Essays Delivered Before the School of Applied Ethics at Plymouth, Massachusetts*. Intro. Henry C. Adams. New York: Crowell, 1893.
"Woman's Conscience and Social Amelioration." *The Social Application of Religion*. Ed. Charles Stelzle. Merrick Lectures, 1907–1908. Cincinnati: Jennings & Graham, 1908, pp. 41–60.
Jane Addams: A Centennial Reader. Ed. Emily Cooper Johnson. New York: Macmillan, 1960. Excerpts writings and speeches. (*CR*)
Jane Addams on Peace, War, and International Understanding 1899–1932. Ed. Allen F. Davis. New York: Garland, 1976. Speech texts and speeches reprinted as magazine articles. (*JAPW*)
McCree, Mary Lynn. "The First Year of Hull House, 1889–1890, in Letters by Jane Addams and Ellen Gates Starr." *Chicago History* 1, no. 2 (1970):101–114.

Dissertations

Culjak, Toni Ann. "Versions of a 'Feminist' Self: The Origins and Representation of Personal Identity in Nineteenth-Century American Feminist Autobiography." Ph.D. diss., University of Wisconsin-Madison, 1988. Ann Arbor: UMI, 1989. AAC 8826039
Joslin-Jeske, Katherine Harriet. "The Social Thought and Literary Expression of Jane Addams and Edith Wharton." Ph.D. diss., Northwestern University, 1984. Ann Arbor: UMI, 1985. AAC 8423252
MacFarland, Susan. "Anti-War Women: The Role of the Feminist-Pacifist-Internationalist Movement in American Foreign Policy and International Relations, 1898–1930." Ph.D. diss., University of Oklahoma, 1990. AAC 9110021
Oglio, Donna Marianne. "The American Reformer: Psychological and Sociological Origins. A Comparative Study of Jane Addams, Louis Dembitz Brandeis, and William Jennings Bryan." Ph.D. diss. City University of New York, 1979. Ann Arbor: UMI, 1980. AAC 8006458
Schmider, Mary Ellen Heian. "Jane Addams' Aesthetic of Social Reform." Ph.D. diss., University of Minnesota, 1983. Ann Arbor: UMI, 1983. AAC 8318127
Shadwell, Delvenia Gail. "Rhetorical Analysis of Selected Speeches by Jane Addams." Ph.D. diss., University of Illinois, 1967. Ann Arbor: UMI. AAC 6801854
Sherrick, Rebecca Louise. "Private Visions, Public Lives: The Hull House Women in The Progressive Era." Ph.D. diss., Northwestern University, 1980. Ann Arbor: UMI, 1980. AAC 8026921

Selected Biographies

Carson, Mina. *Settlement Folk: Social Thought and the American Settlement Movement, 1885–1930*. University of Chicago Press, 1990.

Conway, Jill. "Jane Addams: An American Heroine." *The Woman in America*. Ed. Robert Jay Lifton. Boston: Beacon, 1967, pp. 247–266.

Davis, Allen F. *American Heroine: The Life and Legend of Jane Addams*. New York: Oxford University Press, 1973.

Davis, Allen F. *Spearheads for Reform: The Social Settlements and the Progressive Movement, 1890–1914*. New York: Oxford University Press, 1967.

Deegan, Mary Jo. *Jane Addams and the Men of the Chicago School, 1892–1918*. New Brunswick, N.J.: Transaction, 1988.

Farrell, John C. *Beloved Lady: A History of Jane Addams' Ideas on Reform and Peace*. Baltimore: Johns Hopkins University Press, 1967.

Hofstadter, Richard. *The Age of Reform: From Bryan to F.D.R.* New York: Alfred A. Knopf, 1955.

Lageman, Ellen Condliffe. *Jane Addams on Education*. New York: Teachers College Press, 1985.

Levine, Daniel. *Jane Addams and the Liberal Tradition*. Madison, Wis.: State Historical Society, 1971.

———. *Varieties of Reform Thought*. Madison, Wis.: State Historical Society, 1964.

Linn, James Weber. *Jane Addams: A Biography*. New York: D. Appleton-Century, 1935.

Lynd, Staughton. "Jane Addams and the Radical Impulse." *Commentary* 32 (July 1961):54–59.

The Social Thought of Jane Addams. Ed. Christopher Lasch. Indianapolis: Bobbs-Merrill, 1965.

Chronology of Major Speeches

"Social Settlements." National Conference of Charities and Correction. *Proceedings* (1897):338–346.

"Arts and Crafts and the Settlement; The Newer Ideals of Peace; Tolstoy's Theory of Life." *Chautauqua Assembly Herald* 27 (July 9, 1902):2; (July 10, 1902):6–8; (July 14, 1902):2–3.

"Child Labor and Pauperism." National Conference of Charities and Correction. *Proceedings* (1903):114–121.

"Immigrants and American Charities." Illinois Conference of Charities and Correction. *Proceedings* (1905):11–18.

The Modern City and the Municipal Franchise for Women. Address NAWSA Convention, Baltimore, February 1906. 7 pp. JAP, SCPC.

"The Public School and the Immigrant Child." National Education Association. *Journal of Proceedings and Address* 46 (1908):99–102.

"Woman's Conscience and Social Amelioration." Eds. Charles Stelzle et al. *Social Application of Religion*. [Merrick Lectures, Ohio Wesleyan University, 1907–1908]. Cincinnati: Jennings & Graham, 1908, pp. 41–60.

"Standards of Education for Industrial Life." National Conference of Charities and Correction. *Proceedings* (1911):162–164.

Seconding speech, Theodore Roosevelt's presidential nomination, Progressive party convention. U.S. *Congressional Record* 48, Appendix, 62nd Cong., 2nd Sess., 1912, pp. 564–565.

"The Civic Value of Higher Education for Women." *Bryn Mawr Alumnae Quarterly* 6 (June 1912):59–67.

"A Modern Lear." *Survey* 29 (November 2, 1912):131–137.
"Why Women Should Vote." *Woman Suffrage, History, Arguments, and Results; A Collection of Seven Popular Booklets, Covering Together Practically the Entire Field of Suffrage Claims and Evidence. Designed Especially for the Convenience of Suffrage Speakers and Writers and for the Use of Debates and Libraries.* Ed. Frances Maule. New York, 1913, pp. 139–158.
Testimony, [Dec. 3] U.S. House of Representatives, [Sub-] Committee on Woman Suffrage of the Committee on Rules, *Hearing on Resolutions Establishing a Committee on Woman Suffrage*, December 3, 4, 5. 63rd Cong., 2nd Sess., 1914, pp. 13–18.
Presidential Address, International Congress of Women, The Hague, April 28–May 1, 1915. *Report* (1915):18–22; "What War Is Destroying." *Advocate of Peace* 77 (March 1915):64–65.
Testimony, U.S. House of Representatives, Committee on Military Affairs, To Increase Efficiency of the Military Establishment of the United States, January 6–February 11, 1916 (January 13, 1916), 64th Cong., 1st Sess., 1916, pp. 201–213.
Testimony, U.S. House of Representatives, Committee on Foreign Affairs, Commission for Enduring Peace, *Hearings on H.R. 6921 and H.J. Resolution 32* (January 11, 1916), 64th Cong., 1st Sess., 1916, pp. 3–17.
Testimony, U.S. House of Representatives, Committee on the Judiciary, Espionage and Interference with Neutrality, *Hearings on H.R. 291*, April 9 and 12, 1917, Serial 53, Part 2, 65th Cong., 1st Sess., 1917, pp. 50–52.
"Patriotism and Pacifists in Wartime." *City Club* [Chicago] *Bulletin* 10 (June 16, 1917):184–190.
"World's Food and World's Politics." National Conference of Social Work. *Proceedings* (1918):650–656.
"World's Food Supply and Woman's Obligation." National Education Association. *Journal of Addresses and Proceedings* 56 (1918):108–113.
"Revolt Against War" (July 9, 1919). *JAPW*:72–90.
Opening Address as President of the Women's International League for Peace and Freedom, at the Fourth Biennial Congress, Washington, May 1–8, [1924]. (Geneva, n.d. [1924]).
"The World Court." Jane Addams Collection, SCPC, Box 35, Folder 1926. Typewritten ms.
"Social Consequences of the Immigration Law." National Conference of Social Work. *Proceedings* (1927):102–106.
Presidential Address. *Women of the Pacific, Being a Record of the Proceedings of the First Pan-Pacific Women's Conference, Honolulu, August 9–19.* 1 (1928):13–14.
"World Peace and Disarmament." Jane Addams Collection, SCPC, Box 36, Folder 1931. Typewritten ms.

SUSAN B. ANTHONY
(1820–1906), radical egalitarian of woman's rights

KATHLEEN L. BARRY

Susan B. Anthony's public career as a spokeswoman for and leader of the woman's rights movement spanned fifty-six years—the entire second half of the nineteenth century into the early years of the twentieth. During that time, she witnessed small gains for women, such as slowly evolving access to higher education, and large losses, such as repeated defeats of constitutional amendments granting women suffrage. In the 1840s, her early career as a school teacher eventually led her into public speaking on temperance issues. In the early 1850s, she discovered her talent for arousing women to action in their own behalf as she built organizational structures from local societies to state and national associations. She increased opportunities for women to speak in public by organizing national woman's rights conventions and petition campaigns throughout the 1850s, even after many women activists had returned to their family responsibilities.

By the time of her arrest in 1872 for voting, Anthony had gained recognition as the charismatic leader of efforts for woman's rights. By the 1880s, she had taken her campaigns to Europe and laid the foundation for an international movement. From then until her death in 1906, in both her organizing efforts and her lectures, her focus was on women's political power through suffrage. Recognized for giving her life to the cause of women's emancipation, by the turn of the century she had become the international spokesperson of woman's rights.

BACKGROUND

Nothing in Anthony's early life presaged her extraordinary and, for many of the early years, notorious public career as the leader of woman's rights. Her name would become synonymous with the cause. She retained a charismatic appeal because she came to be viewed as embodying the very liberation she fought for in behalf of women. And yet she was an ordinary woman who was born in 1820 to a rural Massachusetts Quaker family, the third of six children. Her father was a strong temperance man who turned from farming to become one of the early developers of the northeastern cotton mills that ushered the Industrial Revolution into the United States. Quakerism made family life austere even when the family economy improved. When Anthony was seventeen, her father lost his business and even the family household possessions in an economic crash. To remove herself as an economic burden to her family, Anthony went out to teach, bringing her own rudimentary education to a halt. After ten years in the classroom, she delivered her first speech in 1849 in the small village of

Canajoharie, New York, on behalf of the local Daughters of Temperance (EOF 3:Appendix 10–16). She soon bored of the classroom and became so caught up by the spirit of reform that she resigned from teaching and began to search for a public career.

ANTHONY, ADVOCATE OF WOMAN'S RIGHTS

Anthony's work placed her before the public more than any other woman at that time. She conducted conventions, made appeals to legislatures, and traveled the lecture circuits for months at a time each year. Without particular connection to the reform aristocracy and without the class privilege that brings with it entitlement, she rose to become a national and then an international leader of woman's rights. Her persuasiveness on the lecture circuit was due in significant part to her similarities to the women in remote villages whose interests she championed. Her early life had typified the ordinariness and economic meager- ness of the lives of the girls and women of her time. Women saw in her the common woman of their own lives.

In her formative years, Anthony had been inculcated with the traditional ideology of True Womanhood of her time, which she adopted with special fervor in early adulthood. As a young woman, still years away from the public platform, she was selectively fervent about the moralistic piety that defined True Wom- anhood, choosing to ignore its intention to keep women in their assigned private sphere. Her early temperance lectures reveal some of the moralistic piety and righteousness that she eventually transformed into political consciousness and a civil, publicly responsible morality. From the beginning, hers was a search to find and challenge the root cause of women's suffering and their inferior status. She began with the woman abuse that came from men's intemperance:

We would that some means were devised, by which our Brothers and sons shall no longer be allured from the *right* by the corrupting influences of the fashionable sippings of wine and brandy, those sure destroyers of Mental and Moral Worth, and by which our Sisters and daughters shall no longer be exposed to the vile arts of the gentlemanly appearing gallant, but really half-inebriated seducers. (Harper, 1898, 1:53)

In this speech, Anthony was searching for ''plans which may produce a radical change in our Moral Atmosphere,'' but her words had not yet matched the actual roots of women's subordination. Lecturing fed her developing political con- sciousness because it connected her to women's daily lives. In turn, she converted her new knowledge into political consciousness. On the lecture circuit, speaking in villages throughout New York State in the early 1850s, she discovered the limitations of her temperance campaigns. She talked with women in their kitchens and saw the actual conditions of their lives. She left behind the old morality of True Womanhood and turned her intense energy toward initiating lecture cam- paigns and petition drives to secure married women property rights in an age when marriage suspended women's legal existence and, thus, their rights to inherit, own property, conduct their own businesses, or even share custody of their own children. Petitioning was a means to tie the woman's rights messages of her lectures to political action that involved her audiences.

However great Anthony's ties were to common women, by the mid-1850s she herself was rising to national prominence. Few women sustained full careers as public orators at this time. Furthermore, she was neither a wife nor an "old maid," neither comfortably middle-class nor poor; she supported herself solely on the little money she earned from lecturing. At this time she and ELIZABETH CADY STANTON met. Their lifelong friendship and deep, loving commitment to each other provided Anthony with a peer—a true equal—in friendship and politics. This friendship would sustain her through her long tours of duty on the lecture circuit.

Historical research abounds with studies determined to elevate the one leader over the other, depending on whether Cady Stanton's philosophical speeches or Anthony's pragmatic organizing are in vogue. But the hierarchies constructed by scholars were unknown to the two women. For Anthony, theirs was "a most natural union of head and heart" in which she was loved and where her deep convictions often found direction. More than once, she helped Cady Stanton get back on the right track after Cady Stanton was diverted by one political crisis or another. They needed and complemented each other in more profound ways than can be revealed by scholars who, in favoring theory over action, tend to elevate Cady Stanton over Anthony. Nor do the reformers represent the reality and political impact of this powerful couple when they take Anthony as the symbol of woman's rights and ignore Cady Stanton's incisive political analysis.

Anthony elevated Cady Stanton over herself in one area: with each new organization she founded, from the Woman's State Temperance Society in 1853, to the Woman's National Loyal League in 1862, to NWSA in 1866, to the International Council of Women in 1888, to NAWSA in 1890, she always nominated Cady Stanton for president. In this way she both honored the woman who opened the way for woman's rights when she issued the called to the Seneca Falls Convention and insured that her coworker's persuasive presence would always open their meetings. For five decades, Anthony accepted positions in her organizations as vice-president or secretary when Cady Stanton's continued presidency was secured. She herself accepted the presidency of NAWSA only after Cady Stanton's full, permanent retirement from public work.

The 1850s was the woman's rights decade of radicalism and political consciousness in which speeches produced by Anthony and Cady Stanton together, along with their separate statements, became the foundation of the politics and philosophy of their movement. Together they penned "On Educating the Sexes Together," a speech that Anthony delivered in New York and Massachusetts in 1856. It bore the strong influence of Cady Stanton's analysis of natural rights. In demanding coeducation, they reasoned that if it would be ridiculous to talk of male and female atmospheres, male & female rains, male & female sunshine, or male & female elements in any part of nature, how much more ridiculous is it in relation to mind, to soul, to thought, where there is as undeniably no such thing as sex, to talk of male & female education & male and female schools. (SBAP, LC)

Anthony's own politics were less shaped by studied philosophies and movement ideologies than were Cady Stanton's, nor did her own rhetoric reflect them. In expounding her views, Anthony drew from pieces and patches at hand, the way she had in making quilts when she was growing up at home. Natural rights became mixed with some Quaker egalitarianism, fired by some of her father's temperance convictions—all of which took on a new, different meaning when she developed them into her own woman's rights rhetoric.

As Anthony cultivated her own ideas and direction for her woman's rights work, her rhetoric became focused on her belief in the unlimited human potential for progress, development, and growth, a key theme of liberalism and its ideas of progress. She fitted these ideas into a conception of woman's enlightenment that was neither natural rights philosophy nor the ideology of liberalism. It was a new, vital woman-oriented consciousness that shaped philosophy as it emerged in political action. The foundation of Anthony's politics, her speeches, and her organizing was her belief in human immortality. "There is indwelling in every human being irrespective of color, or sex, or condition, the indestructible, though perchance from unfortunate circumstances of birth and surroundings, scarcely recognizable germ of immutable life, susceptible of unlimited culture, growth and development." This belief in something spiritual that could not be destroyed even by all the oppression she saw around her motivated her to work, campaign, and struggle through defeats and sometimes seemingly insurmountable odds. What the idea of progress had given to the theme of the common man, which encouraged men to move upward and outward in society, Anthony articulated to create a utopian vision for women. She formulated this dream in her 1857 speech "The True Woman," which gives much of the basis of her politics and thinking. To incorporate women into the idea of progress, she developed an egalitarian image of a new true woman:

The true woman will not be exponent of another, or allow another to be such for her. She will be her own individual self,—do her own individual work,—stand or fall by her own individual wisdom and strength. . . . She will proclaim the "glad tidings of good news" to all women, that woman equally with man was made for her own individual happiness, to develop every power of her three-fold nature, to use, worthily, every talent given her by God, in the great work of life, to the best advantage of herself and the race. (SBAP, HOW)

Anthony was not the originator of this radical vision of the new woman. It was an emerging consciousness that developed as women challenged the limits imposed on them in activism, in their personal lives, and in literature. Charlotte Brontë's *Jane Eyre*, published in 1848, contained an early image of the new true woman. Elizabeth Barrett Browning's *Aurora Leigh*, Anthony's favorite book, published in the same year that she wrote and delivered "The True Woman," presaged the independent, self-sufficient woman who would endure economic and emotional hardship rather than concede to dependency on a man. Equality was the first basis for love and enduring relationships as well as the foundation of society.

Here in the utopianism of Anthony's woman's rights rhetoric is one of the subtle differences between her rhetoric and that of Cady Stanton. Their differences were reflected in the literature that fed their revolutionary spirits. While for both the oppressive conditions of women's lives represented the starting point for their political theories and speeches, it was Anthony's work in the early years that was visionary and went beyond present conditions of women's oppression to future possibilities and responsibilities. She found reinforcement for her own thinking in the works of Barrett Browning and Brontë; she emphatically disliked the novels of George Eliot, which she found depressing because they did not offer hope and vision. By contrast, Eliot's novels, like *Mill on the Floss*, fed Cady Stanton's anger against injustice. They revealed the hopelessness of woman's situation and her inability to change it as well as how strong and unjust were the conditions of her subjugation. She told Anthony that she would "long to pour forth from my own experience the whole long story of woman's wrongs." Their different outlooks were framed in part by the difference in their marital status. In the 1850s, Cady Stanton was struggling in a marriage in which she sometimes felt like a "caged lioness," while Anthony was trying to find a way to live her singleness in a public, political life without being drawn into the dependency of the traditional "old maid's" role. Because of their different life situations, when these two women combined, they gave force to their convictions beyond what either could have exerted alone.

From temperance to property rights for married women to woman suffrage, Anthony's strategy of petitioning and using the lecture circuit to raise consciousness on the issues kept her on the road several months a year. In those early years of woman's rights, the gains women won were temporary. In 1860, the New York State Legislature, after years of Anthony's petitioning, granted limited property rights to married women, most of which they retracted the following year.

Anthony's and Cady Stanton's campaigns for legal equality in marriage culminated with a demand for the right to divorce. Cady Stanton appealed to the logic of contract theory and formulated marriage as a contract like any other that, when broken, was dissolved. Anthony strongly defended the proposal during the controversy it caused at the 1860 Woman's Rights Convention: "Marriage has ever been a one-sided matter, resting most unequally upon the sexes. By it, man gains all—woman loses all; tyrant law and lust reign supreme with him— meek submission and ready obedience alone befit her" (HWS 1:735). The *His-*

tory of Woman Suffrage and the Harper biography (1898) record many of the
important, spontaneous statements Anthony made during convention debates.

By the mid-1850s, Anthony was in as much demand on the anti-slavery circuit
as she was on woman's rights. While she grew up in a family that was not
directly involved in the abolitionist movement, she was surrounded with the
values of anti-slavery, which were strong among some Quakers of that time.
Her speeches were optimistic and visionary. More important, they were solidly
lodged in her belief in the inviolability and immortality of the human being.
That belief was the foundation for her lifetime commitment to the universality
of rights and equality. Her rhetoric centered on the integrity and potential of the
human being, which made her egalitarianism universal whether she was discussing marriage, slavery, working women, or suffrage. Her universal rights
approach and her moral suasion made her sought after by other reformers. She
became an advocate for the emancipation of African-Americans when, in 1857,
the Anti-Slavery Society invited her to join them and to take New York State
as her territory as an abolitionist. By 1862, on behalf of the Woman's National
Loyal League that she had founded, she challenged Lincoln's hesitation to grant
immediate, unconditional emancipation to all slaves. As the public and the
president worried about what the slaves would do with their emancipation,
Anthony had found the needed clarity:

What will the black man do with himself, is a question for him to answer. I am yet to
learn that the Saxon man is the great reservoir of human rights to be doled out at his
discretion to the nations of the earth. . . . What arrogance in us to put the question what
shall we do with a race of men and women who have fed, clothed and supported both
themselves and their oppressors for centuries. (''Civil War and Slaves,'' SBAP, HOW)

The same tough-minded, unswerving egalitarianism that attracted abolitionists
to her in the 1850s turned them away in the 1860s when it was clear that her
standards were universal: she would not subordinate woman's rights to any other
cause. The radicalism of Anthony and Cady Stanton, reaching as it did to the
roots of women's subordination in marriage, caused reformers, especially the
abolitionists, to turn against them. Anthony was undaunted. When William Lloyd
Garrison told her she should not offer refuge to an abused wife of a prominent
politician, she relied on analogy to convey the universality of her politics:

That I should stop to ask if my act would injure the reputation of any movement never
crossed my mind, nor will I now allow such a fear to stifle my sympathies or tempt me
to expose her to the cruel, inhuman treatment of her own household. Trust me that as I
ignore all law to help the slave, so will I ignore it all to protect the enslaved woman.
(Harper, 1898, 1:203)

This letter to Garrison reveals the conformity of Anthony's public rhetoric
and action to her private correspondence. For her there was no difference in the
two worlds. Her universal approach to rights became the basis of her singular

commitment to championing woman's rights when the abolitionists rejected universal suffrage. After the Civil War, the abolitionists proposed amendments to the U.S. Constitution to extend suffrage to African-American men that would still exclude all women. She protested against the amendments, and when she continued to champion woman suffrage, she was called a racist. This name-calling intensified when she accepted support from some racist Democrats. What followed split the women's movement, which broke along the lines of earlier divisions on marriage and divorce. The radicals including Anthony and Cady Stanton separated from the reformers, who accepted the abolitionist position on granting national suffrage only to men and agreed to work around it.

Opposition to Anthony was the strongest in this period. Abolitionists attempted to discredit her as a public advocate with accusations that she misused funds. She feared that even though she was exonerated, she would lose her effectiveness as a woman's rights leader. But however much she alienated reformers by her undivided commitment to woman's rights, she attracted women. Radicalism was no longer ascendant in these times, but it continued to speak to the realities of women's lives. The more she was subjected to ridicule from her enemies as "the shrewish maiden" or the "hobgoblin of the public mind," the more women who followed her came to revere her as their "Napoleon" and "America's Joan of Arc."

Anthony made working women the focus of her campaigns and organized Working Women's Associations that she used to break the sex and race barriers of the National Labor Union Congress in 1868. Her economic arguments in behalf of working women were based on her vision of the true woman, which required women's economic independence. As Anthony articulated it, the problem was in the structure of economic oppression: women supported themselves in the face of discrimination that marginalized their labor bargaining, and as long as women were not a recognized labor force, strikes held no power for them. She saw that, as long as women did not have equal *political* power with men, that is, suffrage, they would remain marginalized economically.

By 1870, Susan B. Anthony had become a charismatic leader. By this time, it was known that her life was the cause of women; that she withstood the rigors of demanding daily lectures for months at a time staying in the field long after others left to recuperate; that she lived frugally allowing herself one new dress a year, always a black one so the gaiety of colors and prints that she loved would not detract from her message.

By 1870, when she realized that without political power women would not be able to achieve and secure equal status, Anthony focused on suffrage in her speeches but always connected it to the wide range of women's issues. She had come to see denial of suffrage as the root cause of women's secondary status because it denied women the political power to shape their destinies. In her speeches Anthony enumerated the arguments raised by opponents of woman's rights—that men supported women so they did not need to support themselves, that work degraded women. Then she marshalled facts to answer these arguments, bringing all the issues to bear on woman's political disfranchisement. She always fitted her examples to her particular audience (working women, married women, teachers). In each speech she made a specific appeal to the men who, as she knew, held the family purse and the right to vote for woman suffrage. Her strategy was to ask them to take the higher road and not debase themselves to the condition of slave master as other men were doing in examples she gave.

Anthony's speeches were unadorned with the evangelical flourishes typical of that period. "I come tonight neither as an orator nor a philosopher, but as a representative of the working women," began one of her many logical, pragmatic lectures (*San Francisco Evening Bulletin*, July 13, 1871). She never considered herself a good speaker, and many of her long, handwritten speeches are laborious to read. But their oral delivery, fortified with her passion, gave them added power.

In some cases she was just too far ahead of her time, as in her speech "The Homes of Single Women," which was written when she was hosted by single women during her long campaigns on the road. Although she used the same approach in this as in other speeches and began by answering the objections to single women having homes of their own, the speech fell flat. In this case, her visionary politics seemed to outstrip her audience's sense of possibility. She called for an "epoch of single women," a transition period in society, during which women would live in "self-sustained, self-supported homes, where her [*sic*] freedom and equality shall be unquestioned," that would create the conditions needed to realize her ideal of the new, true woman. But in the later stages of the women's movement, when reform ideology had supplanted the revolutionary rhetoric of earlier stages, this speech was out of time and place.

Anthony's persuasive powers were strongest when she spoke extemporaneously. In her public appearances, she always dressed in loosely fitting clothes to prevent any confinement when she was on the public platform. At her 1873 trial for voting, these elements combined with her charismatic appeal to produce one of her finest and most enduring rhetorical works (MCSFH 1:105–119). After she sat through the mockery of a trial and heard the federal judge direct the jury to bring in a verdict that she was guilty of having voted in the national elections of 1872, the judge asked, "Has the prisoner anything to say why sentence shall not be pronounced?" In court she had been caught by surprise when the judge refused to turn the case over to the jury, but now she spoke her mind without notes or written statements:

In your ordered verdict of guilty you have trampled under foot every vital principle of our government. My natural rights, my civil rights, my political rights, my judicial rights, are all alike ignored. Robbed of the fundamental privilege of citizenship, I am degraded from the status of a citizen to that of a subject; and not only myself individually but all of my sex are, by your honor's verdict, doomed to political subjection under this so-called Republican government. (HWS 2:687)

The essence of Anthony's charismatic message was her indignation and her refusal to recognize a court, laws, or a country that violated her (and all women's) rights. She would not acknowledge or concede to being a subject to unjust rule. She ignored rebukes from the judge that he would not tolerate her speech, and she also ignored his orders to sit down and be silent. Her speech in this trial established her reality outside the law she refused to recognize. Finally, when the court ordered her to pay a fine of $100 and costs of prosecution, she placed herself squarely outside of his authority:

May it please your honor, I will never pay a dollar of your unjust penalty. All the stock in trade I possess is a debt of ten thousand dollars incurred by publishing my paper *The Revolution*—the sole object of which was to educate all women to do precisely as I have done, rebel against your man-made, unjust, unconstitutional forms of law, which tax, fine, imprison and hang women, while denying them the right of representation in the government; and I will work on with might and main to pay every dollar of that honest debt, but not a penny shall go to this unjust claim. And I shall earnestly and persistently continue to urge all women to the practical recognition of the old Revolutionary maxim, "Resistance to tyranny is obedience to God." (Harper, 1898, 1:441)

When the judge refused to enforce these penalties by jailing Anthony, she was denied an opportunity to take her case to a higher court.

Anthony had been the publisher of the *Revolution* from 1868 to 1870, and when it failed, she was forced to work the lecture circuit for six years to pay off the $10,000 debt. When that was paid, she began work on financing the *History of Woman Suffrage*, as well as financing one suffrage campaign after another, which kept her full time on the lecture circuit to support the movement and herself.

By the 1880s, Anthony had become conscious that in championing woman's rights, she and her movement were not only making history but were also creating a historical legacy for future generations. She was determined that women would write their own history. With Cady Stanton and MATILDA JOSLYN GAGE, she produced and published three volumes of the *History of Woman Suffrage*. She produced a fourth volume with Ida Harper, who also wrote the three-volume *Life and Work of Susan B. Anthony* that she insisted be written as she came to realize that her own life had also become a history of the movement.

Through her travels to Europe in the 1880s, Anthony generated an international woman's movement. Although she organized its first meeting in 1888, it was not until 1902, four years before her death at age eighty-six, that she saw the International Council of Women unite in the struggle for suffrage. She considered this accomplishment the climax of her career. To the end of her life universal rights and a pragmatic approach to political action marked her approach to her public work, which had become synonymous with her private life. In the 1890s, she refused to support racist and class-based proposals for educated suffrage, which would exclude the poor, most immigrants, and African-Americans. When considering who was qualified to vote, she argued for an economic analysis to expose how misuse of power, and not necessarily poverty, corrupts: "[T]he greatest wrongs in our government are perpetuated by rich men, the wire pulling agents of corporations and monopolies, in which the poor and the ignorant have no part" (Harper, 1898, 2:922).

A debate over the last major work of Cady Stanton's life, *The Woman's Bible*, reveals the difference between Anthony's and Cady Stanton's political orientation, which can be understood as the difference between a materialistic and an idealistic analysis. Cady Stanton firmly believed that the ideas in the Bible were wrong. Anthony did not necessarily disagree, but she insisted that it was not ideas but material reality in the form of economic and political subordination that hurt people. Admitting that she had no interest in religious issues, she argued to Cady Stanton that "men who hold me in durance vile—won't care a dime what the Bible says—all they care is what the saloon says" (Letter, July 24, 1845, Huntington Library). When liquor dealers were paying drunks to go to the polls to defeat woman suffrage as they did in the California campaigns of the 1890s, Anthony persisted in political action that would give women control of the ballot with which she assumed they could change the material conditions of domination. She was more interested in changing behaviors that produced human injustice than in correcting the ideas behind them. As change requires action in both material and ideal realms, the difference between them was really one of emphasis and priority, but these factors loom large for activists and leaders.

Although she felt strongly about Cady Stanton's *Woman's Bible* project, Anthony defended her lifelong friend before the NAWSA convention that proposed to censure it. She acknowledged that Cady Stanton might well be ahead of her time with this work, as she was with the Seneca Falls Convention. In addition, Anthony firmly defended freedom of ideas and speech asking, "Who is to draw the line? " and threatening that "When our platform becomes too narrow for people of all creeds and of no creeds, I myself shall not stand upon it" (HWS 4:264).

CONCLUSION

The last two decades of Anthony's life were as filled with rigorous lecture schedules and state-by-state campaigns as were the first two of her public career. In 1891, suffragist women throughout the United States came together to restore the Anthony home for her and to present her with a lifetime annuity. From then on, her unrelenting traveling and lectures were matters of will, not economic necessity. In her utopian vision she continued to be future-oriented for the movement. She tried to prepare women leaders to take over after she was gone, and she raised a fund to continue the work for woman suffrage after her death. In her work she created a legacy for women. When in 1900 at the age of eighty, she turned over the presidency of NAWSA to CARRIE LANE CHAPMAN CATT, Lane Catt acknowledged, "Miss Anthony will never have a successor" (HWS 4:388). As her speeches grew shorter in the last few years of her life, Anthony's presence now conveyed her message. One month before her death at 86, she mustered enough strength to attend the annual suffrage convention. She left the movement and her cause with the optimism of her last words in public, "Failure is impossible!"

SOURCES

The speeches of Susan B. Anthony are found in the Library of Congress, Susan B. Anthony Papers (SBAP) on microfilm; the Schlesinger Library on the History of Women (HOW) in America at Radcliffe, Susan B. Anthony Papers; and the Appendix to Volume 2 of *The Life and Work of Susan B. Anthony (LW)* by Ida Husted Harper, 1898. Fragments of lectures and spontaneous statements recorded at the time are found in the Harper biography, the *History of Woman Suffrage*, vols. 1–4, and the Susan B. Anthony scrapbooks on microfilm at the Library of Congress. Appendices to Harriett Grim's dissertation (EOF) include copies of some texts and reconstructions of others from newspaper reports.

Biographies

Anthony, Katharine. *Susan B. Anthony: Her Personal History and Her Era*. Garden City, N.Y.: Doubleday, 1954.
Barry, Kathleen L. *Susan B. Anthony: A Biography of a Singular Feminist*. New York: Ballantine, 1988, 1990.
Dorr, Rheta Childe. *Susan B. Anthony: The Woman Who Changed the Mind of a Nation*. New York: Frederick A. Stokes, 1928.
Harper, Ida Husted. *The Life and Work of Susan B. Anthony*. 3 vols. Indianapolis: Bobbs-Merrill, 1898, 1908.
Lutz, Alma. *Susan B. Anthony, Rebel, Crusader, Humanitarian*. Boston: Beacon, 1959.

Critical Sources

Berman, Ruth Florence. "A Critical Evaluation of the Speeches of Susan B. Anthony." M.A. thesis, University of Wisconsin, 1947.
Campbell, Karlyn Kohrs. "Contemporary Rhetorical Criticism: Genres, Analogs, and Susan B. Anthony." *The Jensen Lectures: Contemporary Communication Studies*. Ed. John I. Sisco. Tampa: University of South Florida, 1983, pp. 117–132.
———. "Seeking a Judicial Route to Suffrage: Anthony in Behalf of Herself." *MCSFH* 1:105–119.
Grim, Harriett Elizabeth. "Susan B. Anthony, Exponent of Freedom." 3 vols. Ph.D. diss., University of Wisconsin, 1937. EOF
McDavitt, Elaine E. "Susan B. Anthony, Reformer and Speaker." *Quarterly Journal of Speech* 30 (1944):173–180.
Merriam, Allen H. "Susan B. Anthony." *American Orators Before 1900: Critical Studies and Sources*. Eds. Bernard K. Duffy and Halford R. Ryan. Westport, Conn.: Greenwood, 1987, pp. 28–34.
Twichell, Doris Yoakam. "Susan B. Anthony." *A History and Criticism of American Public Address*. Ed. Marie Kathryn Hochmuth. New York: Longmans, Green, 1955, pp. 97–132.

Chronology of Selected Speeches

Address first delivered at Batavia, New York, in company with Emily Clark (Temperance), (May 1852). HOW, Fol. 21.

"On Educating the Sexes Together." With Cady Stanton (1856).

"The True Woman" (1857). HOW, Fol. 24.

"No Government" (c. 1858). HOW, Fol. 25.

"The Civil War and Slaves" (1862).

"Fourth of July Address" [Framingham, Mass.] (1862). HOW, Fol. 27; EOF 3:App., 46–65.

"Reconstruction" (1865). Harper 2:960–967

"Suffrage and the Working Woman." *San Francisco Daily Evening Bulletin* (July 13, 1871).

"Constitutional Argument" (1873). *HWS* 2:630–647.

Address of Susan B. Anthony, Delivered in twenty-nine of the post office districts of Monroe, and twenty-one of Ontario, in her canvass of those counties, prior to her trial in June 1873. *An Account of the Proceedings on the Trial of Susan B. Anthony on the Charge of Illegal Voting, at the Presidential Election in Nov., 1872.* 1874. New York: Arno Press, 1974, pp. 151–178. *MCFSH* 2:279–316.

"Social Purity" (1875). *LW* 2:1004–1012; EOF 3:App. 124–146.

"Homes of Single Women" (1877). SBAP; Harper 2:1004–1012.

"Woman Wants Bread Not the Ballot" (1870–1880). *LW* 2:996–1003; EOF (reconstructed) 3:App., 67–85.

"Demand for Party Recognition" (1894). *LW* 2:1015–1021; *OW*:11–16

"The Status of Woman: Past, Present, and Future." *The Arena* (May 1897):901–908. HOW, Fol. 26.*

"Susan B. Anthony to National Negro Race Conference" (1900).

"Woman's Half Century of Evolution." *North American Review* 175 (December 1902):800–810.*

*These articles represent the content of Anthony's speeches in the 1890s.

CLARA BARTON
(1821–1912), advocate for the American Red Cross

MARY M. ROBERTS

After reading Jean Henri Dunant's vivid descriptions of war-wounded soldiers' sufferings in 1859 in *Un Souvenir de Solferino*, Dr. Theodore Maunoir declared, "We must get up an agitation" to prevent such misery in the future (Dulles, 1950:7). With three others, Maunoir and Dunant formed a Committee of Five that met in Geneva in September 1863, which became the International Committee of the Red Cross, and thus founded the international organization.

Within six years, twenty-four countries had signed the Treaty of Geneva and established Red Cross societies to insure the neutrality of the wartime wounded and their caretakers. The United States did not sign; in 1864 and in 1865, Secretary of State William Seward advised "holding aloof" from the agreement. In 1869, Dr. Henry W. Bellows, president of the American Association for Relief of the Misery of the Battlefields and former president of the Civil War Sanitary Commission, campaigned unsuccessfully for approval. His Battlefields organization dissolved in 1872.

After doing civilian relief work in Strasbourg and elsewhere during the Franco-Prussian War, in the summer of 1877 Clara Barton received approval from the International Red Cross to begin a concerted agitation for U.S. approval of the Geneva treaty, which resulted in Senate passage in 1882. In 1959, Charles Hurd called the Red Cross "one of the great moral movements in the history of mankind" and credited U.S. participation to the "practical maneuvering of a diminutive, dedicated woman already internationally famous for her battlefield work in the Civil War" (Hurd, 1959:13). Barton, he declared, "had the imagination to develop a long-range public relations program that . . . modern practitioners of that art might well copy" (49).

Clara Barton is well known as a heroic Civil War nurse and founder of the American Red Cross. She was not considered seriously as a feminist, however, until the 1970s, and especially after Elizabeth Brown Pryor's revisionist biography appeared (1987). Pryor asserted that Barton's achievements as a feminist are "of equal importance" to her war nursing and Red Cross accomplishments, and include functioning as "the first female American diplomat . . . who participated in an astonishing number of the nineteenth century's major events . . . a personal friend of figures as varied as Susan B. Anthony, Frederick Douglass, Benjamin Butler, and Kaiser Wilhelm" (ix). On February 21, 1866, she may have become the first woman to testify before Congress when she appeared before the Joint Committee on Reconstruction (Pryor, 1987:147). This chapter argues that she deliberately kept her feminism implicit, a decision that was a canny adaptation to the circumstances of her time.

In his introduction to Mary Massey's *Bonnet Brigades* (1966), Alan Nevins wrote, "Clara Barton exaggerated very little when she said that the war had left women at least fifty years in advance of the position they would have held if peace had endured" (xv). Barton contributed significantly to those advances, and after the war, she continued to do so in her role as noble woman leader of the Red Cross.

Barton's atypical family background prepared her to succeed as a Civil War nurse. Lecturing about her experiences as a nurse and tracer of missing and dead soldiers won her a national reputation. That fame as well as assiduous persuasive efforts enabled her to gain approval for the American Red Cross and to guide it as president for some twenty years. Always persuasive, she mingled internationally with Red Cross and government leaders, made hundreds of speeches, penned countless letters, and wrote the story of her childhood, histories, and other treatises on the International and the American Red Cross. She epitomized Kenneth Burke's ideal of "using all there is to use" to promote her cause. Until late in her declining years, her rhetorical judgment was shrewd and sound.

BACKGROUND

Clarissa Harlowe (named for an aunt who had been named for the romantic heroine of Samuel Richardson's novel) Barton was born at Christmastime, 1821, the youngest child of Captain Stephen and Sarah Stone Barton, in North Oxford, a small Massachusetts town a few miles south of Worcester. Pryor writes that the birth of this daughter, eleven years following the birth of the last child, was marked by the purchase of a set of Blue Willow china and a tea service, major investments for a middle-class household of the period.

Barton identified with the men of the family—her father and two elder brothers, Stephen and David—more than with her mother and sisters, Dorothea and Sally. Mrs. Barton gave her daughter little nurturing, being preoccupied with doing twice as much housework as the ordinary housewife and in half the time. Full of nervous energy and early conviction that women were entitled to some rights, she entertained visiting lecturers with enthusiasm but was unpredictable and difficult to please, argued and fought openly with her husband before the children, and sometimes behaved somewhat irrationally. The young Barton internalized her mother's nervous energy, compulsive work habits, intellectual curiosity, and openness to woman's rights.

The sisters, each of whom taught school for a time, encouraged Clara's literary and scholarly interests. Dorothea, however, experienced a nervous breakdown when Clara was six years old and thereafter was confined in a locked upstairs room. Subject to depression herself in periods of inactivity, Barton always feared that she might suffer her sister's fate.

Her father, a community leader, treated his youngest daughter with affection and respect, sharing his values and experiences. He told her of family members who had fought bravely in the English Wars of the Roses and the American Revolution and of his own satisfying military career with General Anthony

Wayne in the Indian wars. He instilled values of patriotism, courage, duty, and philanthropy in his children. Stephen, David, and other male cousins taught Barton to enjoy riding bareback on fast horses and playing ball, running, and similar active pursuits that gave her greater strength and endurance than most of her female peers and a greater willingness to take risks.

As the youngest child, Barton naturally endured some teasing, but she gained respect during a three-year stint, beginning in 1832, of devotedly nursing her brother David after his fall at a barnraising. A shorter period of nursing smallpox-infected neighbors produced similar rewards, reinforcing her conviction that service to others was the path to recognition. She tried working the looms in her father's cotton mill, which she enjoyed, but the project ended when the factory burned. Nevertheless, she acquired a taste for productive activity and achievement, although, as a female, she felt limited in her options. Moreover, she was somewhat fearful of leaving home. But wishing to avoid financial dependency, sometime between the ages of sixteen and eighteen, she took her first real job teaching in an ungraded summer school in North Oxford.

As a woman teacher, Barton drew lower wages than her male colleagues. However, at one school where she taught she won a man's salary by insisting on it. Pryor recorded that in 1845 she prepared a "major speech" favoring school redistricting in Oxford, but had to hear it presented by a male mill-owner because women could not speak at the meeting (p. 29).

After ten years of highly successful teaching in a number of schools, Barton studied for a year at Clinton Liberal Institute in Clinton, New York. She then taught again for a time, ending her career in education in 1853 by establishing a "free school" in Bordentown, New Jersey, which did so well that it was determined a man should be its head rather than a woman. Severely disappointed, she fell into ill health and depression for a time. She rallied and with a friend went to Washington, D.C., to do therapeutic cultural reading at the Library of Congress. There she began cultivating friends and friends of friends, until in July 1854 she was able to obtain a Patent Office copyist-clerk's job at the impressive salary of $1,400 a year. As one of the first women to be employed in government, she endured the usual harassment of the woman pioneer but managed to hold the position for three years before retreating to North Oxford. After Lincoln's election, she was able to return to Washington as a temporary copyist.

Pryor notes that Barton quickly became a shrewd observer and an analyst of the Washington scene. Next, she decided to court Massachusetts Senator Henry Wilson (for some years chair of the Military Affairs Committee) for aid in her personal and charitable projects. When conventional social approaches through a mutual friend failed to produce a meeting, she visited him in his office to call attention to unfavorable working conditions in the Patent Office. When they met, they felt an immediate rapport that inspired Senator Wilson to use his influence in behalf of her various projects.

By this time Barton had developed considerable self-confidence as a result of her paid work as a teacher and clerk. In addition to feelings of professional competence, she was also experiencing the elation of social success. Her high-energy vivacity and ability to converse insightfully about politics and other subjects that interested men made her welcome at Washington gatherings. By the time the Civil War began, she had acquired an extensive circle of friends in high places. Thus, she could participate in significant social events where policy attitudes were influenced; she was laying the groundwork for becoming an effective lobbyist for the Red Cross. Her diaries are full of references to calls she made—and those she tried repeatedly to make until successful—on government officials. After the war, however, she did not need to rely on the force of her male friends. Now she could also invoke her own reputation as the noble battlefield angel who had saved the lives of many soldier sons of those whose support she was seeking. She became a person whose personal entreaties could not long be refused.

Since the favorable public image that she had crafted so effectively was largely the product of her postwar lectures, it is rhetorically rewarding to examine the content and method through which she presented herself to her listeners.

BARTON'S RHETORICAL CAREER

Barton was both an unproclaimed natural rights feminist and a realistic pragmatist. As a feminist, she believed in "the full right of woman to all the privileges and positions which nature and justice owed to her in common with other human beings. Perfectly equal rights—human rights" (Address to the New England Woman's Suffrage Association, quoted in Smith, 1981:158). Ellen Henle explains that Barton linked a woman's status as a second-class citizen to "her exclusion from war . . . men denied women a role in the *decision* to go to war because women lacked the suffrage and . . . men *justified* denying the vote to women because women had no military responsibility to the state" (Henle, 1978:154, italics added). Barton correctly regarded such reasoning as "circular." In the concluding appeal of her post–Civil War "Lecture #1" for help for the "lonely widowed mother" and "the fatherless children she is raising in toil and penury" because "their father fill[s] a martyr's grave," she declared: "Her country tells her she is weak—and its laws make her powerless—she can only raise sons to fill its armies." She then pictured orphan children as appealing to listeners to "preserve their rights and liberties, that they may not only live,— but *live like citizens*" (italics added). Barton may have intended those words to mean that the slain soldiers' daughters should gain the right to vote, along with their brothers. However, she seems to have been dubious that suffrage per se would improve women's position significantly. Somewhat similarly, she accepted the existence of war as a fact of life and preferred to invest her energy in ameliorating its terrible effects rather than in crusading for an elusive peace.

As a realistic pragmatist, Barton was too prudent to campaign for woman's rights as such. Instead, insofar as it was possible without overtly challenging the status quo, she enacted her ability to participate in public life. When the war offered her the opportunity to work as a nurse and her father did not object, she took it. Her first task was to help re-outfit the Massachusetts Sixth whose luggage had been lost on April 19, 1861, in the Baltimore fracas. Thus, she began to enlist the help of neighboring women and of friends in ever-expanding circles to give her items needed by the troops: clothing, bandages, food treats, medicines, and so on. For the sake of propriety, she took two women with her on her first expedition into battle but later traveled only with men because women lacked the stamina to be useful helpers.

Nina Smith explains that in general the nurses, most of whom were supervised by Dorothea Dix of the Sanitary Commission, were quite safe "because those soldiers were American: bred to respect ladies under all circumstances." Moreover, a sort of "chivalrous comradeship . . . grew up between the soldier and nurse, who saw themselves as standing together against the doctor and the officer . . . and both fighting for the same thing: what Barton called 'the life of every institution which had protected and educated me!' " (Smith, 1981:85, 86).

Barton viewed with some pessimism the nursing qualifications of the majority of women brought up in the cult of True Womanhood, but she was generous in praise and support of those who served well. For years after the war, she used her persuasive powers to obtain pensions for these women, most of whom had served in hospitals. Barton was the first and one of only a few nurses who went onto battlefields while the conflict raged.

In March 1865, with Lincoln's authorization, Barton began another major task: compiling lists of war dead and finding and marking their graves. Advertisements in newspapers announced that any family member who wished information about the fate of a loved one could contact Barton. She succeeded in supplying definite information about some 22,000 casualties. She shared the saddest news from Andersonville, Georgia, where hundreds of federal prisoners of war had died of starvation or other hardships.

All this correspondence, in addition to the letters she wrote home for individual soldiers and to women's groups to request and acknowledge supplies, made Barton's name widely known. Thus, after the war's end, when she asked her supportive aunt Frances D. Gage what she should do next to finance her work on the death lists and to supply a new challenge, Gage suggested that she travel, lecturing on her war experiences. The idea seemed practical, although not personally appealing. Nonetheless, Barton undertook several demanding tours from 1866 to 1869. At first she spoke in her own New England, and later she went west to Ohio and as far as Iowa and Minnesota. Her lectures were billed under such titles as "Incidents of Army Life" and "More Incidents of Army Life." Even when she presented two or three lectures in a city or returned for a later tour, she did not repeat her stories.

Since childhood, Barton had heard, enjoyed, and discussed many public lectures. She was perceptive enough to know what the public wanted and that she was in a position to supply it. Victorious Northerners were eager for "bloody shirt'' rhetoric that would permit them to hiss the defeated Southerners as treasonous villains. They wanted entertainment: vivid stories of their soldiers' heroism, the excitement of battle, and the exhilaration of victory without danger to themselves. As a woman speaking on the war, Barton had little, if any, competition, and, of course, no one else could recount her particular experiences. Nevertheless, as a woman, she still had to justify her appearance on the public platform before mixed audiences of men and women and her departure from woman's sphere to participate in war, the most masculine of activities.

Barton's choice of patriotism to describe her motivation was truthful. In addition, Smith notes, "The argument for patriotism offered protection, glorious self-fulfillment, and identification with the national future; no more impregnable and satisfying defense could have been devised'' (1981:155). The lecture's theme was patriotism, and it was an entertaining ceremonial speech of praise to believing audiences that glorified victory over the South. Barton extolled the nation, the common soldiers, the gallant officers and noble surgeons, the contributions of the homefront women, and—by implication—the speaker, as the heroine of "events in which I was either a witness or an actor.''

The materials were exciting narratives with descriptions of cannons roaring and musketballs whizzing overhead. There was an abundance of violence but no sex. Now more than forty-five years old and having earned her living as a school teacher for ten years, Barton stressed her sisterly relationship to the soldiers, her collegial relationship to the officers and surgeons, and an implicitly pedagogical relationship to the teamsters and other civilian male employees. Implicitly, her message was that a woman could work with strange men without a sexual relationship. In addition, she showed that the women who had worked with the Sanitary Commission and who had sent supplies from home had made major contributions. Despite these implications, Barton succeeded rhetorically because, Smith notes, "Opponents could not attack women's work in the Civil War without attacking the Union cause and the elements that had made it triumphant'' (1987:155).

Her metaphors were homely. She often personified elements of nature which she usually represented as sorrowing at the carnage. She included few literary quotations. There was an occasional biblical reference, along with brief quotations from a Scottish military poem and a martial poem by Robert Browning as well as a phrase from JULIA WARD HOWE's "Battle Hymn of the Republic'' about living "among the dews and damps.'' Most suggestive was a quotation from John Greenleaf Whittier's "Barbara Fritchie'' celebrating her as the "bravest of all in Fredericktown'' because it might have stimulated listeners to regard the speaker as "the bravest'' in the exploits described.

In addition to demonstrating that her motivation was praiseworthy, Barton indicated throughout that she had been competent for her tasks physically, attitudinally, and in respect to skills and judgment. In addition, through all hardships, she had preserved her image as a modest, womanly "lady.''

Recognizing that gentlemen were the decision makers, Barton addressed them first in her lecture: "Gentlemen and ladies." Once done, however, she also recognized the women as she moved to explain her motivation as a nurse and a lecturer: "If I have been permitted to stand by your loved ones, when the trial came and their brave lives went . . . and there [sic] last look was turned upon my face instead of yours . . . the knowledge is not mine,—it belongs to you, to all my countrymen." Eloquently, she asserted, "I dropped a tear for her, who could not go, blessed the grave in the south she could not see and come to tell you." Barton dutifully had gone to battle to become a volunteer nurse to *represent* all the women who could not go because of home responsibilities, to care for their wounded and ill sons, brothers, and husbands. Modestly, she asked her listeners, "Be patient with my story, cast aside all which pertains to myself, remembering only the brave men of whom I speak." Similarly self-deprecating utterances were sprinkled throughout the speech to reassure listeners that she did not think her unusual deeds had elevated her above the status of an ordinary woman who did her duty and demanded no thanks.

The most emotional story of the lecture depicted her vividly in this womanly stance. Early in the war during her first night in the field after a terrible battle near Fairfax Station, Virginia, she and a few helpers "worked and wept, . . . put socks and slippers on their cold damp feet,—wrapped blankets and quilts about them, and when we had no longer these to give . . . covered them in the hay." At about three o'clock in the morning, a surgeon appeared to ask her to go with him to a dying lad who was calling for his sister Mary. She went, hearing his cries of "Mary—Mary Sister Mary—Come—Oh, come. . . . Don't let me die here alone, Oh, Mary, Mary come." Barton dismissed her companions and approached him alone: "Oh, Mary, Mary have you come? I knew you would come if I called you." She kissed him on the forehead and lifted him on her lap, without calling him "brother," and he soon fell asleep. When he awoke, he saw she was not his sister and asked who she was: "I said it was simply a lady who, hearing he was wounded, had come to care for him." He carried a letter from his mother, saying he was her only son, and he begged to be put on a train to Washington so she could get news of his death and perhaps even claim his body. This prospect was unlikely in the Virginia field.

Barton then pleaded in his behalf, and his evacuation was arranged. Back in Washington a few days later, she went to the hospital where he would have been taken and inquired about him—she learned that his name was Hugh Johnson. His parents and sister Mary had reached him in time, but at that moment they were accompanying his body from the ward to the depot. Barton did not reveal herself to them: "There was no need of me,—he had given his own messages,— I could add nothing to their knowledge of him, and would fain be spared the scene and the thanks. Poor Hugh! thy piteous prayers reached and were answered."

This lengthy story, embellished with many details, came early in the speech and helped to establish Barton's character and competency. It illustrated her truthfulness in refusing to lie about her identity, and it reinforced her determination not to usurp other women's relationships with the soldiers. It also showed her winning an argument through logic with the surgeon in charge of the train to Washington in order to have Hugh Johnson put aboard. When the surgeon said it was impossible to take the lad, implying that Johnson would not survive the trip, she asked whether he could guarantee the lives of all the other wounded men on the train. When he admitted that half of them would die of their wounds and hardships, she pleaded, "Then give this lad his chance with them,—he can only die—and he has given good and sufficient reasons why he should go." In her pragmatic view, logic superseded gender and hierarchy. Aware of the sensibilities of her audience, however, she was careful to minimize her role and assert that the surgeon "yielded nobly and kindly."

Another incident with implicit gender overtones occurred when an officer asked Barton's advice as the officer in charge of a herd of cattle destined to be food for the troops. He told her that a nearby house was being used as a hospital for Confederate troops. Its commander had informed him that meat was needed to keep the patients alive; however, he was "a bonded officer, and responsible for the property under . . . [his] charge." She suggested that he discover some reason to ride on ahead, since she was "neither bonded, nor responsible." As he did so, she chose a large white ox at the edge of the herd to be encouraged to linger on the grass near the hospital. This incident, which revealed both male respect for her judgment and her skill in artful rationalization, probably elicited a chuckle from the audience—no doubt welcome as an instance of humor in an intensely dramatic recital. But she quickly grew serious again, contrasting the gift of the ox to the Confederates with their policy of starving Union soldiers at Andersonville prison.

Barton implied her sagacity, tact, and persuasive problem-solving ability as she described her own response to her early observation that the order of vehicles in army wagon trains was contrary to the interests of the wounded. Ammunition came first and then food, with medical supplies and personnel at the rear. The result was that wounded soldiers usually lay for days without help before the medical wagons arrived. Barton told her listeners that, without arguing with anyone that the order of march should be changed, she instead "resorted to strategy."

At one o'clock in the morning, she and her small crew of men "rose, breakfasted, fed—harnessed, and moved on past the whole train." Thus, they gained ten miles and "were up with the artillery," in advance even of the ammunition. When the battle came to the waiting men of the Army of the Potomac, Barton presented herself and her supplies to "one of the kindest and noblest surgeons" she had ever seen, who asked, "How did you get from Virginia so soon . . . to supply our necessities, and they are terrible." He explained that men were bleeding to death because he had no bandages, and surgeons had only the chloroform they carried in their pockets. In the lecture, she profusely thanked the women of her audience who had sent her their "sacred old household linen . . . for you arose [sic] the tender blessings of those grateful men."

Twice more, the speaker specifically acknowledged the women for their contributions, stressing their importance to the war effort. She had been dismayed in her first battlefield experience at the lack of utensils with which to serve the food she had prepared for the hungry wounded. Then, upon opening boxes sent by generous women, she had discovered not only jellies and jams and other treats, but also jars and glasses and small boxes in which these items had been sent; these she used to serve the men. On another occasion, when she had been desperate for food, she opened nine barrels of wine packed in sawdust; then she found three barrels that had been packed in meal, which she transformed into lifesaving gruel. These details reinforced her point that female contributions had been significant to the war effort: volunteer women had furnished food and utensils, while she herself had resourcefully cooked and served it to the men in addition to helping dress their wounds. When speaking in the West, she also included a special tribute to Western women for their creation of hospitals and their other "Christian deeds at Cairo, Port Hudson, Shilo[h], and Chattanooga," in which she felt "womanly pride."

Descriptions of her own hardships, which demonstrated her physical qualifications for army service, were frequent and vivid. Barton left Washington on her first assignment on a steam freight train that had no seats, no windows, no conveniences. She subsequently covered so many miles as part of an army mule train that she declared she "came to understand mules"—another item that might have roused a chuckle. Her patients' needs kept her from "tasting food" from Saturday afternoon until Monday evening during the battle of Chantilly, a detail reported in the *Chicago Times* (March 2, 1867). Sleeping provisions in a tent or wagon were primitive, and her tent floor was once so full of water that she feared it would flow into her ears. Extreme weariness was normal. She asserted that, on one occasion, "You have the full record of my sleep from Friday night—till Wednesday morning—two hours." Pryor treats this report as an example of Barton's tendency to frequent exaggeration; with her largely uncritical lecture audiences, it appears to have been highly effective.

The dangers she endured that demonstrated her mental and emotional fitness for army nursing were even more impressive. One dramatic recital concerned her ability to ride horses bareback. Because she had that skill, Barton was able to stay and minister to the wounded for several hours longer than she could have, before a retreat, if she had needed to depart in a wagon. Her closest brush with death occurred when she was supporting a soldier with her arm to give him a drink, and a "ball" (reported variously in newspapers as coming from a cannon and a musket, though the musket seems more likely) went between her body and her arm and passed through the man's chest "from shoulder to shoulder." He "fell back, quivering in the agonies of death." She did not spare her listeners the grim details that had been a part of the nation's glorious victory against "treason."

Through all hardships and dangers, Barton preserved her ladylike image, even in dress. More than once she declared that she had to stop to wring blood or water or both from her long skirts. She referred to herself as learning to be an outdoor "housekeeper, if that may be said of one who had no house to keep, but lived in fields, and woods, and tents, and wagons with all out of doors for a cooking-range—mother earth for a kitchen-hearth—and the winds of heaven for a chimney.''

Audiences and newspapers received her lectures favorably. Democratic newspapers understandably showed less enthusiasm than Republican publications, but practically all credited her with noble motives and skill as an entertaining speaker. For example, the *Chicago Times* (March 2, 1867) reported that her battlefield experiences were "well told, and elicited the frequent and emphatic applause of the audience. . . . Miss Barton has not the voice of Miss [Anna] Dickinson, but she has a sweeter and more attractive face. She has not the assurance of the former lecturess [*sic*], but is rather a *true woman*, telling tales of touching pathos, especially to all who have lost sons or brothers on the battlefield" (italics added). The *New York Tribune* (March 18, 1868) announced that she soon would return from a Western tour for a reception in her honor at Steinway Hall where she would speak and cited her "acknowledged talent as a lecturer . . . *blending her own personal history with that of the war* in many stirring episodes" (italics added). It declared that her "love for her work . . . as well as her devoted effort to preserve the name and record of our fallen heroes on every field, must secure for her a place in every soldier's heart and a warm greeting from an appreciative public." The *New Bedford Mercury* (December 1867) commented with approval: "Miss Barton is what we call a strong hearted woman; *not 'strong minded'* in the invidious sense of the term" (italics added).

These lectures made Barton famous, and her eventual founding of the American Red Cross, which they helped to make possible, was her crowning achievement. However, she led the Red Cross in the same way as she had conducted her battlefield nursing and the search for missing soldiers. Each was essentially a one-person operation involving a small group of anonymous assistants in stressful tasks; no one had time to spend in careful financial recordkeeping. Both in her searches for missing men and in her Red Cross leadership, Barton was accused of carelessness in handling funds, although she was extremely frugal and there was no evidence of dishonesty. Other women leaders had led their organizations for life. Not surprisingly, Barton also expected to do so, but eventually she was persuaded to resign when criticism of her leadership became too great. She founded the National First Aid Association of America and served as its honorary president instead.

Barton had vision in addition to persuasive and practical skills. It was her idea to involve the American Red Cross in relief activities during natural disasters as well as in wartime. The international organization adopted the concept with enthusiasm as "the American idea." She was a superb agitator-promoter for the Red Cross; she did not campaign for woman suffrage because she felt such activity would impair her reputation and that of her organization, which were closely entwined. Nevertheless, she and SUSAN B. ANTHONY—another strong-willed single Massachusetts woman whose life was identified with her cause and who also was accused unjustly of fund mismanagement (Barry, 1988:325)—were good friends, and she had strong woman's rights sympathies. On one occasion, misguided promoters had billed Barton as a speaker on patriotic themes, not on woman's rights, "after the style of Susan B. Anthony and her clique." At the end of her lecture, she read the advertisement to the audience, defended Anthony, endorsed her cause, and led her loyal Grand Army of the Republic supporters in three cheers for Anthony (Pryor, 1987:151, 152).

CONCLUSION

Barton demonstrated that a capable woman who was willing to avoid the appearance of threatening the patriarchal status quo could participate in U.S. public life—even in two fields, medicine and the military, that were most strongly identified with masculine values. Enacting rather than advocating her woman's rights sentiments was a highly appropriate strategy for her time.

Evidence of Barton's continuing influence appeared in a recent article concerning current Red Cross President Elizabeth Hanford Dole's visit to Kuwait to "bring the attention to the American Red Cross's Gulf Crisis Fund Campaign." After recounting the activities of the indefatigable Hanford Dole in Kuwait, inspecting hospitals, encouraging U.S. soldiers and Red Cross workers, conferring with General Norman Schwarzkopf, and so on, the article concluded that "the new leader of the American Red Cross has a lot in common with the famed Barton. A genteel background, attractive, and fiercely determined—and of course, 'sensitive by nature, refined by culture' " (Wallo, 1991:30).

SOURCES

Primary sources are the Clara Barton Papers, Manuscript Division, Library of Congress (CBPLC), and the collection at the Clara Barton National Historic Site, Glen Echo, Maryland. Other sources include the Clara Barton Papers, Sophia Smith Collection, and William Barton Papers, Smith College Archives, Northampton, Massachusetts; the Clara Barton Papers, American Antiquarian Society, Worcester, Massachusetts; the Clarissa Harlowe Barton Papers, Manuscript Department, Duke University Library, Durham, North Carolina; the Clara Barton Papers, Henry E. Huntington Library, San Marino, California, and the Elwell Papers, Western Reserve Historical Society, Cleveland, Ohio. Letters exist in many collections throughout the country, for example, the Mugar Library Manuscript Division, Boston University.

Dissertations

Henle, Ellen Langenheim. "Against the Fearful Odds: Clara Barton and American Philanthropy." Ph.D. diss., Case Western Reserve University, 1977.
Smith, Nina Bennett. "The Women Who Went to the War: The Union Army Nurse in the Civil War." Ph.D. diss., Northwestern University, 1981.

Selected Secondary Sources—Articles

Gangwer, Constance W. "Civil War Nurses and Society's View of Women." *Kansas Nurse* (December 1988):11–12.

Henle, Ellen Langenheim. "Clara Barton, Soldier or Pacifist?" *Civil War History* 24 (June 1978):152–160.

Matejski, Myrtle P. "Ladies' Aid Societies and the Nurses of Lincoln's Army." *Journal of Nursing History* 1 (April 1986):35–51.

Parramore, Thomas C. "The Bartons of Bartonsville." *The North Carolina Historical Review* 51, no. 1 (1974):22–40.

Wood, Ann Douglas. "The War Within a War: Women Nurses in the Union Army." *Civil War History* 18, no. 3 (1972):197–212.

Selected Secondary Sources—Books

Barry, Kathleen. *Susan B. Anthony: A Biography of a Singular Feminist*. New York: New York University Press, 1988.

Boardman, Mabel T. *Under the Red Cross Flag at Home and Abroad*. Philadelphia: J. B. Lippincott, 1915.

Dulles, Foster Rhea. *The American Red Cross: A History*. New York: Harper & Brothers, 1950.

Hurd, Charles. *The Compact History of the American Red Cross*. New York: Hawthorn Books, 1959.

Massey, Mary Elizabeth. *Bonnet Brigades*. New York: Alfred A. Knopf, 1966.

The Tribune Association, publishers. *A List of the Union Soldiers Buried at Andersonville*. Copied from the Official Record in the Surgeon's Office at Andersonville. New York, 1866.

Wallo, Terri J. "Elizabeth Dole Provides Impetus for Gulf Crisis Fund." *COMPASS Reading* (May 1991):30.

Whitman, Alden, ed. *American Reformers*. New York: H. W. Wilson, 1985.

Biographical Sources

Significant biographies are listed in *American Reformers* with the exception of Pryor, Elizabeth Brown. *Clara Barton: Professional Angel*. Philadelphia: University of Pennsylvania Press, 1987.

Rhetorical Works

Books by Barton are listed in *American Reformers*.

CBPLC has a number of speeches, including a handwritten copy of "Lecture #1" and a file called "Lecture Notes" that contains additional stories and descriptions used in other lectures. Both are undated but appear to be 1866. It also contains an address to the International Council of Women, Washington, D.C., March 27, 1888. The Clara Barton Papers, Sophia Smith Collection, include a manuscript of "Work and Incidents of Army Life," probably 1866, and her Memorial Day Address of May 30, 1888.

The 1881 address advocating approval of the Geneva Convention is included in her

The Red Cross: A History, as is her address to a congress of women in 1895 or 1896 on
"What Is the Significance of the Red Cross in Its Relation to Philanthropy?"

The writer would like to thank Mari Tonn for her contribution, as a Title III research
grant assistant, to the preparation of this chapter.

BELVA BENNETT MCNALL LOCKWOOD
(1830–1917), lawyer, equal rights advocate, presidential candidate

Looking back on her five-year struggle for admission to practice before the U.S. Supreme Court, Belva Bennett Lockwood said, "I never stopped fighting" (*New York World*, November 3, 1912). These words aptly sum up her career as teacher, suffragist, lawyer, presidential candidate, and promoter of universal peace through international arbitration. Among her many achievements, she was the first woman to be admitted to practice before the U.S. Supreme Court and the U.S. Court of Claims (1879) and to the bar of Virginia (1894) and to receive a doctor of laws degree (1909). She was also instrumental in securing equal pay for female federal employees and in obtaining for women of the District of Columbia equal property rights and equal guardianship of their children (1896). She ran for the U.S. presidency on the Equal Rights party ticket in 1884 and 1888, and is considered the first legitimate woman candidate for that office. Her name was presented to President William Howard Taft as a possible Supreme Court justice when John Harlan died in 1911 (unidentified newsclipping SCPC).

BACKGROUND

Born October 24, 1830, Belva Ann Bennett was the second of five children born to Hannah Green and Lewis J. Bennett, farmers who lived near Royalton in western New York. She attended local one-room schools, studied for a year at Royalton Academy, a preparatory school, and at age fifteen began teaching in the district schools. She immediately encountered discrimination—her salary was approximately half that of males doing the same work. Her protests were in vain. When told that that was the way of the world, she resolved to change it, if ever an opportunity presented itself ("My Efforts," 216; Winner, 1958:325).

Hopes of a career based on higher education were set aside because colleges generally would not admit women. In 1848, she was married to farmer and sawmill operator Uriah H. McNall; a daughter, Lura, was born on July 31, 1849. However, Bennett McNall continued to study and contributed pieces to the local press. In 1853, McNall died as a result of a sawmill accident. Faced with the necessity of supporting herself and her daughter, she sought additional education with a view to teaching or other suitable employment. General sentiment during the 1850s was that pursuing higher education was unladylike. Nonetheless, she studied at Gasport Academy, attended first Genesee Wesleyan Seminary, and than Genesee College, from which she earned a B.S. degree with honors in 1857. Some thirteen years later, she was granted a master's degree from Genesee College, now Syracuse University ("My Efforts," 217–218).

After completing a bachelor's degree, she became principal of the Lockport Union Academy. Among other changes, she instituted a required course in public speaking for girls, a program endorsed by SUSAN B. ANTHONY, whom she met at state teachers' meetings ("My Efforts," 218–219).

Bennett McNall accepted a similar post at Gainesville Female Seminary in 1861. After it was destroyed by fire, she taught at Hornellsville for the rest of the year. There she distressed the principal by teaching the girls calisthenics and recommending ice skating as a useful form of exercise (Winner, 1958:331–332). Thereafter, she operated a young ladies' seminary in Oswego, but after three years, she moved to Washington, D.C., where she taught at a local seminary while familiarizing herself with the nation's capital and its possibilities ("My Efforts," 221; Winner, 1958:332). She acquired Union League Hall, turning it into living quarters, classrooms, and a hall that could be rented for meetings. McNall's Ladies Seminary opened in 1866, but the next year the school became coeducational, one of the first such institutions in the city (Winner, 1958:332).

While operating her school, Bennett McNall found time to study the Constitution, politics, and law. She also began to participate in the organizations that met in Union League Hall. Most significant were equal rights groups advocating woman suffrage. Ultimately, the Universal Franchise Association of Washington, D.C., was formed, which affiliated with NWSA. On March 11, 1868, Bennett McNall was married to Ezekiel Lockwood, a dentist and former Baptist minister, who was to support and encourage her until his death in 1877 ("My Efforts," 221–222, 227).

In the fall of 1869, Bennett Lockwood applied for admission to the law department of Columbian College (now George Washington University) and was rejected on the grounds that her presence would distract the male students ("My Efforts," 222). Undaunted, in 1870, she applied to the newly opened National University Law School and was one of fifteen women admitted and one of two who completed the two-year course of study, which included segregated lectures and recitations. Although she finished the course in 1872, prejudices against women were sufficient to deny her inclusion in the graduation ceremonies and a diploma. Only after writing to President Ulysses S. Grant, *ex officio* president of the school, did she receive her law degree—more than a year after finishing the course ("My Efforts," 222–224).

In the meantime, Bennett Lockwood had espoused the cause of female government employees who faced inequities similar to those she had encountered as a teacher. Working with Representative Samuel M. Arnell, she wrote legislation that he introduced as H.R. 1571 on March 21, 1870 (*Cong. Globe*, 2094). Two years later the Arnell Bill passed to provide equal pay for equal work for federal employees.

Shortly afterward, on September 24, 1873, Bennett Lockwood was admitted to the bar of the District of Columbia, judicial rules having been changed two years earlier to permit women to practice law in the District. In April 1874, she applied for admission to practice before the U.S. Court of Claims. The justices, noting that she was "a woman" and "a married woman," delayed for seven weeks, finally concluding that a federal court could not admit a woman ("My Efforts," 224–226).

Dissatisfied with a practice limited to paperwork for claims cases and with hiring male lawyers to present her cases in court, Bennett Lockwood sought admission to practice before the U.S. Supreme Court. She reasoned that if she were admitted there, admission to practice before all other federal courts would follow. The rule governing admission was: "Any attorney in good standing before the highest court of any State or Territory for the space of three years shall be admitted to this court when presented by a member of this bar" ("My Efforts," 226). In 1876, she appealed the decision of the Court of Claims to the Supreme Court. The justices rejected her appeal on the grounds that the Court knew of no English precedent for the admission of women. Thus, her application would be denied unless public opinion demanded it or special legislation allowed it ("My Efforts," 227).

Bennett Lockwood immediately turned to Congress, and in 1876 and 1877, bills were introduced, only to fail passage. Then, on November 5, 1877, H.R. 1077, "An Act to relieve certain legal disabilities," was introduced, reported favorably by the Judiciary Committee, and passed on February 21, 1878 (*Cong. Rec.*, 1235); it was passed by the Senate on February 7, 1879 (*Cong. Rec.*, 1082–1084), and the "Lockwood Bill" was signed by President Rutherford B. Hayes on February 15, 1879. On March 3, 1879, she was admitted to practice before the Supreme Court and three days later to the U.S. Court of Claims. After years of intense personal lobbying for its passage, this act, in her words, "virtually opened the doors of all the Federal courts in the country to the women of the land, whenever qualified for such admission" ("My Efforts," 229).

A committed reformer, unceasingly active on matters related to equal rights, Bennett Lockwood maintained a full law practice from which she contributed significantly to the betterment of the human condition. She commented, "I have never lacked plenty of . . . work. . . . There is no class of case that comes before the court that I have not ventured to try. . . . I have been patient, painstaking, and indefatigable" ("My Efforts," 225). As Madeleine Stern observes, "she was a joiner of joiners—committee woman, chairman [*sic*], president of any and all associations that carried her standard" (1963:227). In 1884, she was to carry the standard of equality for all women as a candidate for the nation's presidency.

Perhaps it was VICTORIA CLAFLIN WOODHULL's abortive candidacy in 1872, which she briefly supported, that suggested such a move. Perhaps it was the example of ELIZABETH CADY STANTON who ran for Congress in 1866. Perhaps it arose out of frustration with the major parties, neither of which would support woman suffrage. In any case, Bennett Lockwood refused to endorse the Republican candidate, James G. Blaine, as she was urged to do by Cady Stanton and Anthony.

Instead, on August 10, she wrote a letter to Marietta L.B. Stow of San

Francisco, editor of the *Woman's Herald of Industry*, in which she said: "If women in the states are not permitted to vote, there is no law against their being voted for, and if elected, filling the highest office in the gift of the people. . . . It is quite time that we had our own party, our own platform, and our own nominees." The letter inspired a group of San Francisco women convening as the Equal Rights party to nominate her ("How I Ran," 729). She accepted, and her fourteen-point platform stressed equal rights for all (including African-Americans, Native Americans, and immigrants), temperance, peace, education, and a moderate tariff. Her campaign was opposed by suffragists Cady Stanton and Anthony, but she felt that it might be "the entering wedge—the first practical movement in the history of Woman Suffrage" (Stern, 1963:224). She undertook a campaign tour that included Pennsylvania, Kentucky, Ohio, Michigan, and New York. Rather than delivering purely political speeches, she lectured, using the proceeds to pay her expenses. As one might expect, the novelty of a woman candidate aroused much interest and considerable ridicule. After a bitter campaign between the major parties, Grover Cleveland emerged the victor, but to the surprise of many, Bennett Lockwood received 4,149 of the tabulated votes from six states. She also claimed Indiana's electoral votes, one half of Oregon's electoral votes, and noted that her Pennsylvania votes were discarded ("How I Ran," 733).

Bennett Lockwood's presidential candidacy energized her career as a lecturer traveling under the auspices of the Slayton and White Lecture Bureau of Chicago (Letter to Darwin C. Pavey, March 8, 1885). She was nominated for the presidency again in 1888 by the Equal Rights party, which convened in Des Moines, on May 15 (Stevens 1988:44). Once again, lecturing was the basis for her campaign, but this time her candidacy stirred little interest. However, in addition to campaigning, she had begun to work for world peace.

As early as 1868, she had been impressed by the principles of the Universal Peace Union, which urged an international agreement for the settlement of disputes through arbitration, and she became an active supporter. A delegate to international peace congresses in Paris in 1889, London in 1890, and Rome in 1891, she ultimately crossed the Atlantic at least eight times. The last such congress she attended was held in Budapest in the summer of 1913. Selected to be the dean of the delegates, she commented: "I expect this to be the crowning glory of my old age" (Letter to Lella C. Gardner, April 30, 1913).

Yet the practice of law, especially claims cases, was the foundation for all her other activities. Gradually, Bennett Lockwood won the respect of colleagues and judges before whom she practiced until, by the end of her active career in 1915 at age eighty-five, she was the acknowledged "elder stateswoman" of Washington, D.C. As early as 1879, a petition signed by 160 attorneys of the District of Columbia supported Senate passage of the "Lockwood Bill" (*Cong. Rec.*, 1083–1084). After his retirement, Judge Charles C. Nott, who had denied her admission to practice before the U.S. Court of Claims in 1874, said to her, "Mrs. Lockwood, I turned you down once, can you forgive me?" In 1910,

Justice Stanton M. Peele of the Court of Claims responded this way when a question of improper intervention on her part was posed: "Mrs. Belva A. Lockwood has been a member of this bar for over 25 years, and during that time she has always deported herself like a lady, has never neglected her cases, or her duty to her clients. This motion will be dismissed" (Biographical materials, SCPC).

Of the thousands of cases with which Bennett Lockwood was associated during her forty-three years before the bar, the most noted was a claims case against the United States by the Eastern and Immigrant Cherokees, which ultimately came before the Supreme Court. Its decision, delivered April 30, 1906, found in favor of her clients in the amount of some $5 million. It was reported that "her argument before that body was one of the most noted ever heard before that tribunal and stands out as one of the ablest pleas ever presented, drawing the highest praise from the chief justice" (*Bartlesville [OK] Enterprise*, August 15, 1910). Assistant Attorney General Louis A. Pradt, who presented the government's case, called her "decidedly the most noted attorney in this country, if not in the world" (O-W Misc.).

At age eighty-five in 1915, Bennett Lockwood addressed the Court of Claims for the last time in a case involving settlement of the estate of John Sevier, first governor of Tennessee (Biographical materials, SCPC; Clark, 1935:215–216). In the fall, she supported Woodrow Wilson's candidacy for a second term (Washington, D.C., *Evening Star*, October 24, 1916). Ironically, only shortly after he began his second term, on April 2, 1917, Wilson called on Congress to pass a declaration of war. Six weeks later, at age eighty-six, this ardent advocate of peace through arbitration died.

BENNETT LOCKWOOD'S RHETORICAL CAREER

From the beginning of her professional career, Bennett Lockwood relied on the power of persuasion. Whether she was pursuing educational goals as a teacher, addressing suffragist conventions or peace congresses, lobbying or testifying before congressional committees, arguing before the courts, or appearing before popular audiences as a lecturer, she was advancing her cause through the use of rhetoric. Like many other women reformers, popular audiences often greeted her with derision. However, she actively organized the like-minded into suffrage and peace associations. Although a committed reformer, she was a pragmatist. She said, "I am intensely practical," and criticized fellow reformers, saying, "Professional suffragists talk too much and are not always practical" (*New York World*, November 3, 1912).

The foundation of her rhetoric was the principle of equal rights for all. Although she articulated that principle in many ways, one expression was particularly apt: "Integrity and intelligence, virtue and morality, should constitute the civil service examination for statesmanship; and not wealth, sex, or brawn and on these alone can be securely built the pillars of a republic" (O-W Misc., 142).

In the same work, referring to the Fourteenth and Fifteenth amendments, she wrote: "He is a bold man today who dares deny that a woman is a *person*; if a person then a citizen; if a citizen then entitled to the ballot" (147). Despite what appears today to be irrefutable logic, Bennett Lockwood went on to note that nothing in the Constitution or its amendments prevented women from being appointed or elected to any position, and that only "that most potent and subtle of all powers, *public opinion*," was keeping the vote from women (147–149). It was against the power of public opinion that she was to contend.

Her efforts for woman's rights and for world peace were linked by her view of war as a violation of human rights. On February 28, 1895, in Washington, D.C., she said:

We are one people. . . . Why should we destroy each other, taking away lives that we cannot give . . . and for what? . . . War is civilized murder that brings no blessing . . . and leaves the cause of the difficulty to be settled later by arbitration, by compromise. (*Growth of Peace Principles*, 9)

On August 23, 1897, to another Washington audience, she said that "war is a relic of the barbarism of the past, that settles nothing but the superiority of low cunning or brute force" and that "arbitration contains a panacea for all neighborhood difficulties, contentions between States and nations" ("Arbitration and the Treaties," 3). To a third Washington audience, she acknowledged that, in 1902, the war in the Philippines was unreal for the general public, like "a legend or a myth, . . . something beyond them in which they have no responsibility. . . . [T]he public conscience," she noted, "is not aroused" ("Peace Versus Militarism," 1–2).

It was this lethargic public conscience or public opinion that she sought to arouse, and although she did not live to see passage of the Nineteenth Amendment, Bennett Lockwood anticipated its coming. As early as 1915, she said, "Suffrage is no longer an issue. . . . It is an accomplished fact" (Stern, 1963: 233). Public opinion regarding universal peace through an international arbitration court, however, had not become so acceptable. As she wrote to Alfred Love, president of the Universal Peace Union: "I addressed the Secular League of this City on Peace, May 11, and the Woman's Press Association on May 16, . . . but peace meetings are still against the grain in Wash. [*sic*] and are not popular" (Letter, May 19, 1902).

In speaking outside the courtroom, she typically structured her materials inductively, citing examples of women's achievements, which, she argued, would ultimately lead to equal rights, including the franchise. Bennett Lockwood frequently cited her own experiences to illustrate what might be accomplished. For example, during her second campaign for the presidency, she told of her struggles for admission to the bar, a story that constituted a major part of her lecture, "Women in the Professions," delivered at the Grand Opera House, New York, August 5, 1888 (*New York Times*, August 6, 1888:5). In "The New Woman," she not only used her own experiences and those of other successful women, but she also attacked those who denigrated woman's abilities and made her timid to test her potential:

Has God given to one half of his creatures talents and gifts that are but as a mockery,— wings but not to fly? reasoning ability but not to think; the power of poesy but not to write; the ability to conceive grand ideals but not to paint; the power to give life to the marble but not to use the chisel; the power to sway the multitude with her eloquence but not to voice the thought? The power of control but not to rule? We tell you nay!

Were I a voice—a still small voice—an eloquent voice—a persuasive voice, I would whisper into the ear of every young woman, improve and exercise every talent that has been given to you; improve every opportunity, obey your inspirations,—give no heed to the croakings of those narrow minds who take old hide bound and musty customs for religion and law, with which they have no affiliation, and who tell you with remarkable ease that these professions were never intended for women; as though they were the keepers of the conscience of the great I Am, and knew exactly what he intended women for when he created her, and made them his confidant. (O–W Section 1:20–21)

Both her arguments and her style were aimed at empowering female listeners.

Her most popular lecture was "Social and Political Life in Washington," which was based on her own observations. In this lecture she discussed the presidential family, lobbyists, newspaper reporters, society mothers, consular service personnel, and department clerks (*Lafayette [Ind.] Daily Courier*, December 15, 1886) and satisfied the desire of audiences for inside information about the government and political celebrities. The lecture "Across the Continent and What I Saw" was also popular, exploiting curiosity about other regions of the country. As reported in the Denver *Tribune-Republican* (November 13, 1885), "the subject-matter . . . was excellent, setting forth many facts which were relieved by frequent bursts of eloquence and poetical descriptions."

"The Growth of Peace Principles" was a lecture closer to her reformist concerns. In it, Bennett Lockwood argued that "the history of mankind has been one of war" and reviewed that history, era by successive era, concluding with the possibility of interrupting that historical flow by instituting arbitration. Similarly, "Arbitration and the Treaties" surveyed international peace conferences and their accomplishments. Thus, like many other successful lecturers, she combined entertainment with instruction and reform.

Bennett Lockwood's style generally was educated and elevated. She had a knack for graphic description, and she used rhymes and puns. For example, in discussing the clashes between religious groups, she cleverly punned: "Orthodoxy is my doxy; heterodoxy is your doxy" ("Growth of Peace Principles," 2). She also used poetry to make a point and to inject humor. For example, in an extant manuscript fragment, she wrote:

Taxation without representation
Is tyranny; just this is meant,

One person shall not rule another
Except by that person's consent.

It was this in the logic of Lincoln
That served the proud Douglas to vex;
With them it related to color,
With us it's a question of sex. (O-W 6:143–145)

In addition to her argumentative skills, ably illustrated in her brief to the
Senate refuting the Court's assertion that admission of a woman to practice
before it was contrary to English precedent (*HWS* 3:106–107), Bennett Lockwood's primary rhetorical resource was her own character. Gradually, with time,
her ability, conduct, and growing reputation won for her a grudging respect and,
ultimately, admiration and the "acclaim of millions of people" (*Washington
Herald*, November 10, 1912). She was forceful, yet feminine (Clark, 1935:219),
and she avoided offense by dressing immaculately and conservatively. Perfect
posture and the "compact intensity of dedication to a cause" blunted inclinations
to jeer (Stern, 1903:227).

CONCLUSION

Bennett Lockwood's impact on her audiences over a span of fifty years is
apparent in newspaper reports. For example, the Mt. Pleasant, Iowa, *Free Press*,
November 26, 1885, commented:

We have in previous years had most of the queens of the platform in Mt. Pleasant—
Mrs. Stanton, Susan B. Anthony, Anna Dickinson, Mrs. Livermore, and others. Some
of them may excel Mrs. Lockwood in richness of voice or some other single feature, but
as a whole, in real strength, in clear, comprehensive grasp, in brilliancy, in the rare
blending of wit and earnestness, we have not heard her superior.

The *Dubuque [IA] Daily Telegraph*, May 6, 1887, said:

Mrs. Lockwood's candidacy was, west of the Alleghenies, considered by many a huge
joke. Three years roll by, . . . and she is everywhere greeted with the most intelligent
audiences and learned men, and but a few years since radical opposers, now recognize
the ability of this woman.

The *Brooklyn [N.Y.] Daily Eagle*, July 27, 1888, reported:

The candidate of the Equal Rights party for the Presidency unfolded a manuscript and
read from it an exceedingly able and interesting address. . . . Her hearers expressed their
gratification audibly and frequently. They paid tribute to her talents even if they could
not endorse her candidacy. A Brooklyn audience never fails to recognize brains, and
brains are what Belva is troubled with.

On the basis of her lifelong dedication to the cause of equal rights, whether for equal pay for government employees, the right of a woman to study law and practice as an attorney, or the right of women to vote, Bennett Lockwood contributed as much as any other individual to the attainment of that goal. Thus, the power of her rhetoric lay not only in the arguments she advanced, but also in who she was and what she achieved. Many held her up as an example worthy of emulation. Late in life, she noted that she had some forty or fifty namesakes (*Washington Herald*, October 25, 1912). However powerful her arguments were before courts of law, attested by the many in which she was successful, and however eloquent her speeches to reformers, on the hustings, or in lecture halls, the most significant single element of her rhetoric was her image, her example. She had opened doors and pointed the way for those who would follow. As she said, "I never stopped fighting. My cause was the cause of thousands of women" (*New York World*, November 3, 1912).

SOURCES

There is no major collection of the Bennett Lockwood Papers. The Belva A. Lockwood Papers in the Swarthmore College Peace Collection (SCPC) include biographical materials, correspondence, some articles and newspaper clippings, and several pamphlets based on speeches concerning peace through arbitration. The Belva Lockwood Papers in the Ormes-Winner Collection (O-W), New York State Historical Association, include approximately 500 pages of handwritten manuscripts divided into (1) The New Woman; (2) Women in the Professions; (3) On Marriage; (4) On Prosperity and Existing Conditions; (5) On Equal Rights for Women; (6) Across the Continent—Suffrage—Memorial Day; (7) On Temperance; (8) Miscellaneous. Although some are lengthy, none is complete.

Biographical Sources

Scholarly works include:

Clark, Allen C. "Belva Ann Lockwood." *Records of the Columbia Historical Society* (Washington, D.C., 1935) 35–36:206ff, 209f, 212.
Filler, Louis. "Lockwood, Belva Ann Bennett McNall." *NAW* 2:413–416.
Stern, Madeleine B. "The First Woman Admitted to Practice Before the United States Supreme Court, Belva Ann Lockwood." *We the Women*. New York: Schulte, 1963, pp. 205–234.
Stevens, Peter F. "When the Women Came to Des Moines." *The Iowan* (Spring 1988):44–47.
Winner, Julia Hull. "Belva A. Lockwood—That Extraordinary Woman." *New York History* 39 (October 1958):321–340.

Two articles by Bennett Lockwood are also informative: "My Efforts to Become a Lawyer," *Lippincott's Monthly Magazine* 41 (February 1888):215–229; and "How I Ran for the Presidency," *National Magazine* (March 1903):728–733.

Partial biographies include:

Dunnahoo, Terry. *Before the Supreme Court, the Story of Belva Lockwood*. Boston: Houghton, 1974.

Fox, Mary Virginia. *Lady for the Defense, A Biography of Belva Lockwood*. New York: Harcourt, 1975.

Rhetorical works

"Arbitration and the Treaties." SCPC, Box 1, Doc. grp. 98.

"The Growth of Peace Principles and Methods of Propagating Them" (pamphlet). Washington, D.C.: J. S. Tomlinson & Son, 1895.

"Peace Versus Militarism." May 18, 1902. SCPC

"Across the Continent and What I Saw (partial ms.). O-W 6

"The New Woman" (partial ms.) O-W 1

"The Present Phase of the Woman Question." *Cosmopolitan* 5 (October 1888):467–470.

"Women in Politics; A Woman's View [of the Presidential Contest]." *American Journal of Politics* 2 (January and April 1893):36–41, 385–387.

CLARA BEWICK COLBY
(1846–1916), a "free lance" leader and spokesperson

E. CLAIRE JERRY

Clara Bewick Colby was one of the most active and versatile participants in the nineteenth-century woman's movement, both in the United States and abroad. She was an editor and publisher, an orator, a writer, an administrator, an organizer, a philosopher, and an international activist. However, she was first and foremost, in the words of her biographer Olympia Brown, a "free lance" (Brown, 1917:xi). She was a close friend and coworker of many leaders who recognized her influential role in the woman suffrage movement, and she held a number of appointed and symbolic positions. Nonetheless, official positions of prominence eluded her. She was never elected to office in a national suffrage organization, she published without organizational and financial backing, and she held to unpopular positions even when they divided her from her friends. Nonetheless, for almost forty years, she was a persistent and effective spokesperson for the causes she embraced.

BACKGROUND

Clara Bewick was born in England in 1846; her family immigrated to Wisconsin eight years later. Her father, himself a well-educated man, supported some education for girls, believing it to be good preparation for a teaching position in rural schools. As a result, Bewick regularly attended the local public school, but at an early age she ended her own education to become a teacher. After two or three years in the district schools, she desired additional formal education. At the age of nineteen, she enrolled in the normal department at the State University of Wisconsin at Madison. She graduated with honors in 1869 and was the valedictorian among that university's first class of women. She remained at the university teaching Latin and history and taking graduate courses in chemistry until her marriage to Leonard W. Colby caused her to move to Beatrice, Nebraska, in 1872.

Bewick Colby quickly became involved in community activities. For example, in 1873, she was instrumental in establishing the first library in Beatrice. She was an officer in the Ladies Library Association, and, by 1878, she was serving as the librarian. She began the first community theater in Beatrice and edited a column called "Woman's Work" in the local newspaper. This column was recognized as a forum for discussing and publicizing woman's rights activities. It is the earliest indication of her interest in Nebraska suffrage work. The Nebraska Woman Suffrage Association (WSA) was founded in 1881, and Bewick Colby was elected vice-president-at-large, a position she held until she advanced to the presidency in 1883. In 1883, she also began what was to be the focus of her professional life, the publication of a suffrage newspaper, the *Woman's Tribune*. She served as president of the Nebraska WSA until 1899.

Over the years, Bewick Colby participated in a number of suffrage and reform organizations, such as the National Woman's Press Association and the Women's Freedom League, and she was an appointed officer in groups such as the International Women's Union, the Association for the Advancement of Women, the Federal Suffrage Association, and the International New Thought Alliance. She was an active member of NWSA (and later the NAWSA), chairing the Federal Suffrage Committee and the Committee on Industrial Problems Relating to Women and Children. She also appeared on the convention platform regularly between 1886 and 1914. Throughout these years she lectured extensively to popular audiences as well as to legislative and congressional committees. She personally participated in suffrage work throughout the country, and she expanded her involvement beyond domestic venues. Accordingly, she served as a delegate to the International Congress of Women (1899), the first International Moral Education Congress (1908), the first International Races Congress (1911), the International Woman Suffrage Alliance (1913), and the International Peace Congress (1913). She spent most of her time from 1909 to 1912 touring and speaking in England, but she also toured Ireland, Scotland, Hungary, Holland, and Germany, occasionally speaking in German.

Although she identified herself primarily as a suffragist, Bewick Colby had a general instinct for reform. She was interested in temperance, social purity, labor reform, peace, and New Thought, but she saw all issues as related to the central fight for suffrage. In defense of her wide-ranging interests, she argued: "It has been said that such matters are outside the scope of a woman suffrage paper, but the Tribune in its search after truth and liberty has ever held to the motto of Terence: 'There is nothing human that is no concern of mine' " (*Woman's Tribune*, [October 6, 1905]:69). Moreover, she felt that suffrage was the broadest of all possible issues: "This is why it is the greatest mistake possible to call the woman suffrage question a question of Woman's rights. It is a question of human rights. . . . There is no woman question. He who speaks one word for woman speaks two for man and three for the race" ("Spiritual Significance").

BEWICK COLBY'S COMMUNICATIVE CHANNELS

Throughout her long career as a suffrage advocate, Bewick Colby used three main outlets for her reform rhetoric. First and foremost, from 1883 to 1909 she was the editor and publisher of the *Woman's Tribune*. Second, from 1890 to 1896, she published an offshoot circular, the *National Bulletin*, a "missionary" paper designed "to supply Woman Suffrage Societies with information and argument at a low price" (*National Bulletin*, Prospectus). Third, she was a reform speaker, appearing on national platforms from 1880 until her death in 1916. Through all three avenues, she demonstrated remarkable consistency in her philosophy and rhetorical strategies, yet in each she exhibited adaptations to different audiences and goals. In fact, it was her willingness to adapt in order to reach a wide range of potential audiences that enabled her to overcome the inherent limitations of her lack of an official leadership position in a national suffrage organization.

In all her rhetorical media, Bewick Colby argued primarily from a natural rights philosophy. Echoing the founders of the movement at Seneca Falls, she recognized that "Suffrage is a fundamental right, underlying all other rights and essential to their possession and preservation" (*WT*, [January 13, 1900]: 1). She even went so far as to argue that "equality of the sexes" is "divinely intended" ("Woman in Marriage"). She was always aware of the alternative basis for suffrage arguments, expediency, but she held to the primacy of natural rights: "If we deny natural rights we are lost in the quagmire of expediency and government becomes a shifty evasion of problems instead of a fearless meeting them on the broadest terms of principle and statesmanship" ("Human Rights"). In fact, she worried that expediency arguments would cloud women's judgment about the need for continued effort:

We must not rest upon past achievements. The danger threatens that having accomplished so many practical ends so fully and successfully that they no longer need the woman suffragist's help, and already scarcely own their origin, we will be left without the connecting link between the abstract right on which we stand and the common heart and sympathy which must be enlisted for our cause ere it can succeed. ("Labor Question")

Even though her personal philosophy remained remarkably consistent, Bewick Colby was more than willing to encourage others to adapt to reach potential supporters. She always assumed that, once gained, the ballot would be used for good: "The giving of the ballot will be laying home upon each woman's soul her responsibility to use her new powers & possibilities for the good of all" ("Human Rights"). She recognized that, to win support for the general public, it was this "good of all" that would have to be addressed and made to appear most important. Her speech "The Relation of the Woman Suffrage Movement to the Labor Question" was a defense of both natural rights and expediency as grounds for enfranchisement, as well as a primer for those seeking argumentative strategies. She introduced her subject with the statement that "All revolutions of thought must be allied to practical ends." She continued:

The idealist must harness his Pegasus to the market cart of the realist, then they shall both ride in the chariot of the gods. Only as the woman suffrage movement is seen to be a practical endeavor to benefit humanity, can it secure the co-operation of even enough persons to arrest the attention of the age. It is the practical bearings of the movement that have led the marshalled hosts of the White Ribbon army to give it their hand. Women who draw back cold and scornful when spoken to of their abstract right to the ballot and and [*sic*] the fundamental necessity for the equality of the sexes, pledge themselves to effort, when Frances Willard points out the value of the ballot as a temperance weapon.

For the good of the movement as a whole, she was willing to adapt to the requirements of audiences it needed to enlist. For example, this speech concluded with a proposal to capture the attention of the "wage-earning classes" by offering suffrage as an answer to the question, "how shall the economic resources of the country be so utilized as to make life worth living for each man and woman?" She saw no inconsistency in arguing for expedient gains from what belonged to women by natural right.

All three of these avenues (*Woman's Tribune*, *National Bulletin*, speeches) were based on this natural rights philosophy as tempered by however much expediency seemed likely to gain adherents. In spite of similarities in arguments and themes, the very adaptation that enabled Bewick Colby to gain her influence in the movement often resulted in different emphases and different styles. Seen as related parts of her overall career, these three avenues of rhetorical activity account for her influence.

The *Woman's Tribune*

Although begun as the organ of the Nebraska Woman Suffrage Association, full responsibilities for publication of the *Woman's Tribune* fell to Bewick Colby in 1884. The paper was not initially intended to be a competitor with established national papers, but it quickly grew into a publication with national focus and impact. From the beginning, Bewick Colby, who did all the editorial writing herself, had three purposes for the paper, each designed to reach and draw in a different potential audience. Her first purpose was to be a suffrage organ, that is, to reach women already interested in suffrage but who, perhaps because of geographic or financial isolation, were unable to participate actively. In other words, the paper provided knowledge, information, and experiences of the suffrage movement for women who could not take part directly, and the *Tribune* reported suffrage action on both the state and national levels. The most significant way she accomplished this was to report on suffrage conventions in detail, recounting resolutions, debates, songs, and prayers, and transcribing in full as many speeches as possible. Because of her preference for and ties to the NWSA, the *Tribune* featured the work of SUSAN B. ANTHONY and ELIZABETH CADY STANTON. In fact, the *Tribune* was the initial publication point for both Cady Stanton's autobiography and for her more controversial work, *The Woman's Bible*. For a time, the *Tribune* was considered the unofficial organ of the NWSA, but it lost any organizational standing when the reunited NAWSA favored the *Woman's Journal* (*TWJ*).

In addition to reporting suffrage meetings, Bewick Colby wrote about suffrage successes and failures. She included columns from states where various suffrage measures were pending and recounted the results. When there was good news, as with the adoption of suffrage by Wyoming, she praised the workers and looked hopefully to the future. When, as was more frequently the case, the outcome was negative, she made an optimistic interpretation, as if to inspire the faithful. For example, when much hard work failed to bring the desired result in South Dakota, her conclusion found the little good that could be salvaged:

[E]very vote cast for it is that much of a victory over ancient customs, prejudice and conservatism gained by education and agitation. Doubtless many men in South Dakota are berating themselves to-day for having neglected to vote for the amendment which they really wished to have carried. (*WT*, [December 31, 1898]:97)

Bewick Colby took very seriously the *Tribune*'s second purpose, education for her readers. She saw the paper as "devoted not only to woman's political interests but to her interests in all fields of labor and thought" (November 1, 1883:1). This educational element made the paper appealing to women who did not yet identify themselves as suffragists but who could be brought into the movement through columns focusing on their particular interests. For example, information for the home was covered in long-running columns such as "Home Hints," "Hygiene and Medical Progress," and "Health, Beauty, and Dress." New opportunities for women were presented through the reports of women who had succeeded in fields such as education, music, city government, religion, art, science, medicine, the theater, and journalism. Colleges and medical schools that admitted women ran advertisements in the *Tribune*. As women made inroads into unusual occupations such as gold mining, exploration, dry cleaning, river piloting, and agriculture, Bewick Colby encouraged others to follow.

For those women who were not yet committed to a suffrage organization, a wide range of women's associations was featured in the *Tribune*. For example, Bewick Colby reprinted speeches given before the Association for the Advancement of Women, Chautauquas, the WCTU, and national and international Woman's Congresses. Speeches from national fairs and expositions were another popular feature. To make her accounts of the Lewis and Clark Exposition in 1904 even more accessible and more educational, she added pen and ink drawings of the major buildings. Finally, she discussed a range of topics designed to broaden women's experience of the world. She wrote about music study, current literature, lyric poetry, and sports. But by far the most common way in which she attempted to expand her readers' horizons was through travelogues. Traveling herself on suffrage business or for personal reasons, she wrote about what she saw. In the early years of the paper she provided information about both suffrage and scenery in Oregon, Wyoming, Louisiana, and Kansas. Later she wrote about Iowa, the Black Hills of the Dakotas, and "Dixie." In the last decade of the *Tribune*, she added an international flavor, writing of her travels in England and Holland. She never forgot that she had access to people, places, and information that, while edifying and entertaining for her readers, would never be available to them except through the pages of her paper. Moreover, once a woman was attracted to the paper for its educational features, she might also find herself educated by the suffrage columns running alongside.

The third purpose for which Bewick Colby envisioned the *Tribune* was as a general circulation newspaper, thus appealing to men as well as to women generally interested in current events: "The main feature of current history and national politics will be given in as brief space as possible, that busy men as well as women may learn to look here for a mention of such things about which no intelligent person should be ignorant" (January 1, 1884:1). With a nonpartisan attitude atypical of nineteenth-century publishers, she averred that she would present "not so much argument and theory, but facts and information" (January 1, 1884:1). She desired readers to build their convictions based on "the logic of events" that a paper can report (November 1886:2).

Bewick Colby achieved this goal by reporting on general, newsworthy events of the day. For example, the "Notes" of March 22, 1890, a typical column, reported the proposal for direct election of senators, the use of Bedloe's Island as an immigration landing, the establishment of a post office in Yellowstone, and laws about real estate loans (89). Other examples that demonstrated her determination to cover the news included reports on the use of Colorado public lands, the return of 1847 war trophies to Mexico, the building of a Nicaraguan Canal to promote the sale of U.S. grain, an eight-hour day for streetcar employees, phosphate mining, income tax law, and the regulation of milk sales.

Another emphasis in Bewick Colby's news reporting can be classified as a concern with rights and liberty. For example, she was opposed to the U.S. annexation of Hawaii, and she expressed her disfavor in front-page columns: "From henceforth the Sandwich Islander is doomed to subordination and destruction. Hawaii as an American state . . . may furnish a fine field for the commercial greed and political ambition of Americans, but ethnologically it will cease to be interesting if the gentle and intelligent Hawaiian is not to be allowed to work out his own destiny" (February 4, 1893:29). This concern was also prominent in her coverage critical of U.S. involvement in the Philippines: "Thus, the policy of the administration is for the first time plainly announced. It is not to use our purchased vantage ground to keep all hands off this people and let them work out their own self government; it is to establish sovereignty over these islands to the ruin of everybody that stands in the way" (April 8, 1899:25). Of course, once she reached an audience that was generally sympathetic to the plight of persons denied their rights by the U.S. government, she could hope they would make the connection to women who were equally downtrodden.

Diversity, which was the watchword of the *Woman's Tribune*, made it unique among reform newspapers. Because she recognized that women did not and could not live by political rights alone, Bewick Colby strove to give her paper variety and practical utility. As her readership changed to a more cosmopolitan and leisure class, the need for this type of reporting diminished. This was undoubtedly frustrating for her because, as Olympia Brown observed: "She wanted to help everybody and instruct everybody. Unfortunately many people do not wish to be instructed and some cannot be helped" (57). Moreover, as she expanded news and educational reporting in the *Tribune*, she was chastised by her friends and allies. Nonetheless, she maintained her commitment to the varied audiences and purposes the *Tribune* represented, and the paper remained the primary focus of her rhetorical energies for twenty-six years.

The *National Bulletin*

Bewick Colby published the *National Bulletin* as an offshoot of the *Woman's Tribune* from 1890 to 1896 (The initial issue, the Prospectus, appeared somewhat earlier in October 1887.) The *Tribune* typically ran full-size issues of eight to sixteen pages, but the *Bulletin* was substantially shorter and smaller. However, the circulation of the *Bulletin* occasionally quadrupled that of the *Tribune*. The difference in circulation numbers may be accounted for by their differences in purpose. Whereas the *Tribune* was designed for individual subscriptions to be read and digested at home, the *Bulletin* was designed "to supply Woman Suffrage Societies with information and argument at nominal prices for free distribution" (*NB* Prospectus). She envisioned the *Bulletin* as "a neat little document" to give to visitors to one's home, enclose in letters, and distribute at fairs and gatherings (*WT* [May 14, 1891]:84). The *Bulletin* was unabashedly a form of "missionary work" (*WT* [February 27, 1892]:61), openly claiming to be "propaganda" (*WT* [March 14, 1896]:30). Although she published much of her own work in the *Bulletin*, it was frequently a forum for the publication of speeches, essays, and articles from other suffrage supporters. The *Bulletin* was apparently quite successful for a while. Some issues sold as many as 50,000 copies at a time, while others were lauded as "the very best literature yet prepared for the Suffragist use in the South" and "the best document that has ever been published" (*WT* [March 14, 1896]:6; [September 4, 1987]:70).

The *National Bulletin* was filled with arguments supported by historical example and statistical proof. The example typically illustrated that suffrage existed throughout the United States and the world, and that no terrible disadvantages had resulted. This argument was the very first used by the *National Bulletin*; the Prospectus of October 1887 was entirely devoted to woman's municipal vote in Kansas. Kansas was the first state in which women obtained the municipal ballot, and in 1887, a larger percentage of registered women voted than registered men. This example also refuted the commonly held idea that only "bad" women would respond to the suffrage opportunity:

Practical refutation of the oft-repeated argument that only disreputable women would vote is abundant. Out of seventy-five in Dodge City only *two* registered. A physician of Wichita states that, in that city, but five or six appeared at the polls, among the three or four hundred ladies who voted.

Moreover, "the ballots of the good women outnumbered and destroyed what would have been the evil effects of the ballots of bad men" (Prospectus). Other historical examples came from Washington and Colorado. For example, she included testimony from Representative John F. Shafroth of Colorado that the success in Colorado was "complete refutation" of any objections to woman suffrage (*NB*, May 1896). International examples such as the British Empire, the Isle of Man, and New Zealand also supported this line of argument. From the Isle of Man came the report that "the quiet manner in which they have exercised their rights is perhaps the best answer to those who credit women with extreme revolutionary tendencies" (*NB*, May 1896).

The three *Bulletin* issues based on the historical example of Wyoming also provided Bewick Colby's most dramatic statistical demonstration of the positive outcomes of woman suffrage. The statistic-laden November 1895 *National Bulletin* is the best representation of this strategy. For instance, according to the editor, during the decade in which Wyoming gave women the ballot, the U.S. population increased 24.6 percent; Wyoming's population increased 127.9 percent. She claimed this was because immigrants were drawn to a suffrage state. She credited suffrage with lowering the crime rate in Wyoming and specifically argued that suffrage improved "the morals of the female part of the population" because there were no women criminals in Wyoming in 1890. She also posited that suffrage was conducive "to a tranquil state of mind and a high degree of intelligence," proven by the fact that there were no idiots in Wyoming and only three insane people (all men).

Marriage also benefited from suffrage. The number of what she labeled "undivorced marriages" in the United States declined 138 percent between 1870 and 1880. In the western states, excluding Wyoming, the decrease was 216 percent. In Wyoming, however, undivorced marriages increased 140 percent in the same decade, giving a couple a 50 percent better chance of staying married if they lived in Wyoming.

Furthermore, Bewick Colby documented that there had been no loss of virtue in Wyoming, there was better justice, school attendance was mandatory, and men were more respectful there. Sexual crimes were more clearly defined in Wyoming law, and the suffrage legislation included a literacy requirement. The only people opposed to woman suffrage in Wyoming were convicts who had been convicted by juries that included women. Overall, the state had concluded that suffrage had done "great good." Her interpretation of these statistics was rather extreme, but her extensive use of them added credibility, as much for the demonstration of her logical skill as for their own status as proof. Although these Wyoming reports were later republished in the *Woman's Tribune*, they demonstrate the different types of evidence and emphasis that Bewick Colby initially used in the *Bulletin*.

Although the *Bulletin* was relatively short-lived, it illustrates Bewick Colby's concern for different kinds of audiences. The *Bulletin* was designed to provide compact arguments and persuasive appeals for the individual not yet committed to the suffrage cause. Through mass distribution techniques and a very low cost, she was able to target persons who would not otherwise seek out the suffrage message. This was consistent with her general belief that publishing was superior to lecturing. Even though she was herself an orator, she always maintained, at least in the pages of the *Tribune*, that "The spoken word has its power for the day, but for building up a new line of thought in the popular heart there must be the written word, which shall be quietly digested and made part of the reader's own thought. Then the change in belief comes irresistibly" (*WT* [March 1885]:2). She repeatedly argued that newspapers were more enduring than speeches and that they could be used passively to engage nonbelievers in the movement:

But while the lecture amuses and interests for an hour or two, often the many cares and interests of our complex life sweep away the impression immediately, while the paper read in quiet moments gradually makes conviction, and the reader instead of being transitorily influenced by the opinion of another, builds up opinions of his own from the logic of events, a faith that cannot be shaken. (*WT* [November 1886]:2)

Her subscription pitches for the *Tribune* demonstrated how a full-fledged paper and a small, missionary circular might be able to work together:

SUPPORT of the suffrage papers should be the first pledge of loyalty to the cause of woman suffrage. The first personal need of those who want to have an intelligent interest in this movement is to take a paper as surely as a man needs the organ of his party: and the first duty in suffrage work is to get our literature into the hands of others. (*WT* [June 21, 1890] 172:2)

The *Tribune* was designed to serve the role of movement organ, while the *Bulletin* was a sample of "our literature."

Bewick Colby's emphasis on publishing was especially interesting because of the constant struggle it represented for her. Denied the support and financial backing of a national organization, she assumed total responsibility for her papers. She often did all the work herself, from the writing and typesetting of articles to the folding and mailing of the finished products. Divorced late in life, she had few other sources of income at a time when the *Tribune* was a major financial drain. She was so impoverished in the final years of her life that she had to move repeatedly to find cheaper housing, and she counted every $1 ticket she sold to one of her speeches as a significant step toward the next day's meals. But she never considered abandoning her editorial work; to the end of her life she believed in the contribution of her paper and regarded it as her leadership offering to the cause.

Public Speaking

Bewick Colby was an orator of note. Her convention addresses were described as "excellent," "convincing," "effective," "eloquent," and "replete with beauty and pathos," although Olympia Brown observed that she lacked "spontaneity and magnetism" (1917:43). Her speeches are somewhat more difficult to assess than are her publications because she spoke almost exclusively from notes in an extemporaneous style, and many of her speeches are only partially

extant. However, the thirteen speeches that are available reveal her keen awareness of audience expectations and needs. In speeches to suffrage associations
she addressed the audience as peers and experts, encouraging them and providing
examples of how they might speak to the unconverted. She saw her speeches
as opportunities to provide arguments and evidence that her listeners could take
away with them and use in their own attempts to persuade.

What one finds in the speeches that is less clearly apparent in her prepared
editorials and essays are the rhetorical devices she favored. For example, her
imagery was more elaborate than in her written rhetoric, as in this passage from
"Human Rights":

What woman's sphere may be who shall dare to say? It is as varied as the form that
water takes which is always according to the vessel that holds it or the channel in which
it flows. With one it is as a spring bubbling up in a silent place from a deep underground
fountain; with another a brook dancing merrily in the sunshine; and again it may be the
majestic river which bears the destiny of nations in its bosom. All are natural and all
reach the ocean at last. It is only the stagnant water that is pestiferous.

She occasionally used the imagery of others, making dramatic allusions to significant speeches of the day. For example, in an address she sent to be read at
the National Convention of the National Populist party, she echoed the eloquent
plea of fellow populist William Jennings Bryan's "Cross of Gold" speech delivered only two weeks before: "Do not longer press upon the brows of your
mothers, wives and daughters the crown of thorns of the degradation of disfranchisement, or continue to crucify them on the same political cross with
lunatics, criminals and idiots" (*WT* [July 25, 1896]:69).

Bewick Colby's speeches also reveal, more than any other source, the two
most salient features of her rhetoric in the last years of her life, her commitment
to federal suffrage (woman suffrage as granted in preexisting constitutional provisions rather than through state routes or an amendment) and her belief in and
her reliance on the images of religion. The first commitment is most apparent
in a series of speeches she made before congressional committees on behalf of
federal suffrage as derived from Article I of the U.S. Constitution. Again indicating her sensitivity to specific audiences, she built her arguments on government precedent, citing James Madison, the Articles of Confederation, the
Declaration of Independence, the Constitution, and several Supreme Court cases.
She also turned to her audience's own experiences when she observed that
"Twenty-two Senators and forty-one Members of the House of Representatives
sit in Congress by the votes of women." In her final federal suffrage circular,
she demonstrated the intensity with which she was prepared to defend this
position: "What a farce it is to construe the Constitution which women had
helped to establish for the Nation, which they had helped to build, in such a
way as to prevent [that which it] was framed to secure!" (Brown, 1917:113).

The second feature of Bewick Colby's oral discourse, her reliance on religious imagery, had been prominent from the beginning of her public speaking career. She concluded her first national address, "Concerning Farmers' Wives," delivered in 1880, with an unusual analogy to Eastern religion:

As, according to Hindoo [sic] mythology, Maya is followed by Vishnu through all her transformations from the lower orders of animal life to the higher, he always being the male of her species, until she becomes the woman goddess and he the god man,—so woman, in her ascent, will take man and the race with her, until together, they shall stand on the sublime heights of divine unity.

In her speech "The Spiritual Significance of Woman Suffrage," she said: "Woman's uprising is obedience to God. It is her soul answering to the command 'Him only shalt thou serve.' " This speech, given many times to many audiences, connected her vision of reform to her understanding of spirituality:

All great world movements have a spiritual basis. . . . The Woman Movement is the Feminine principle in the Universal seeking to manifest [itself] on the external plane. . . . Jacob Boehme has said[,] "The mission of woman to save man ends only when he has found the Celestial Virgin within himself." This man is slowly doing. Man & woman are one . . . it is necessary for a human being to blend the essential permanent elements of both to make that full-statured man referred to by Paul when he said "Till we all come to the fullness of the stature of a perfect man in Christ Jesus."

Nowhere is Bewick Colby's belief in the power of religious thought and imagery more eloquently expressed than in the conclusion of a New Thought[1] speech, "The Strength of Non-Resistance":

They who can enter into the freedom and power of this glorious conception [of non-resistance] will meet all situations without fear and without failure. In the presence of pain, of loss, of injury, of injustice, of misunderstandings, and aggressive wrong, they will stand unmoved, instantly allying themselves with that infinite strength which under the name of Faith operated of old so that, as the Bible says, those who practiced it stopped the mouths of lions; quenched the violence of fire; escaped the edge of the sword; out of weakness were made strong.

This belief in the Great Divine as manifested in New Thought became a more prominent theme in her rhetoric in the last decade of her life. Her increasing attempts to link suffrage with this philosophy further distanced her from the mainstream of the movement. In "The Radiant Center," one of her last major speeches, she defined New Thought as "the philosophy which recognizes man's inherent divinity" and indicated its relevance to reform work:

By the Radiant Center I mean that from which all physical manifestation, all sense of beauty, all intellectual activity, and all spiritual aspirations have come forth. . . . You cannot take anything away from the Infinite. You cannot separate anything from Omnipresence. You cannot know anything apart from Omniscience. . . . [W]hile the rest of creation appropriates unconsciously and negatively the heat and light of the Spiritual Center, man has to supply the moral conditions which make him the recipient of it consciously and positively.

In the last years of her life, to support herself she offered courses, series of lectures for which a fee was charged, with such "philosophical" titles as "The Philosophy of Henri Louis Bergson," "The Inspiration of Margaret Fuller," and "The Cosmic Significance of Sacred Structures." What had once been a rhetorical strategy gradually became the central focus of her speeches as a whole.

CONCLUSION

In spite of her significant contributions to the rhetoric of woman's rights, Clara Bewick Colby has not been seen by her contemporaries or by history as a leading figure in the woman suffrage movement. The shift of the entire movement away from the broader arena of woman's rights caused her and her rhetoric to be seen as fringe, radical, and even detrimental to the cause. The mainstream body of the movement and its leadership narrowed the focus to suffrage alone and to suffrage via a constitutional amendment. With her emphasis on a range of issues and her insistence on suffrage as inherent in the Constitution from its beginning, she was left out, passed by in the final push toward the goal.

Nonetheless, Bewick Colby contributed substantially to the movement. The *Woman's Tribune* lasted twenty-six years, marking the second longest span for all movement papers and the longest one for papers without official organizational backing. Unlike most other suffrage publications, it had a national circulation and a national perspective; at its peak as a daily it reached more readers than any other paper representing its cause. Through the pages of her publications, she took suffrage issues, arguments, and activities to women who were too isolated to participate in the movement directly. By combining suffrage with other issues, she enabled her cause to reach individuals who were not interested in a specific reform. This targeted audience included not only uncommitted women but also, and perhaps more important, men. She also never lost sight of the larger context of suffrage for U.S. women. Throughout her rhetorical career, she wrote and spoke on a wide range of woman's rights topics, and she saw rights in the United States as part of rights for women worldwide. Her speeches were well received, and her writing universally praised. Working through three interrelated avenues, Bewick Colby addressed many audiences who might otherwise have ignored woman's issues and, thus, successfully fulfilled her self-proclaimed role as an influential movement leader.

SOURCES

Those who wish to study her rhetoric must rely heavily on the Clara Bewick Colby Collection held in the State Historical Society of Wisconsin Library (MSS 379). Many extant speech texts not recorded elsewhere are available there. Many of her speeches are reprinted in full only in the *Woman's Tribune* (*WT*). The University of Wisconsin Library holds a complete set of the *Tribune* and most available issues of the *National Bulletin* (*NB*). The *Tribune* is available on microfilm from the Library of Congress, the History of Women Collection (HOW), and the Gerritsen Collection. The *Bulletin* is also available on microfiche in the Gerritsen Collection. Volume 4 of the *History of Woman Suffrage*, 1883–1900, contains excerpts of a number of her speeches. The Henry E. Huntington Memorial Library, San Marino, California, has a substantial collection of Bewick Colby materials, primarily correspondence.

Critical Studies

Jerry, E. Claire. "Clara Bewick Colby and the *Woman's Tribune*: The Free Lance Editor as Movement Leader." *A Voice of Their Own: The Woman Suffrage Press, 1840–1910*. Ed. Martha Solomon. Tuscaloosa: University of Alabama Press, 1991, pp. 110–128.
Jerry, E. Claire. "Clara Bewick Colby and the *Woman's Tribune*: Strategies of a Free Lance Movement Leader." Ph.D. diss. University of Kansas, 1986.

Selected Biographies

Brown, Olympia, ed. *Democratic Ideals: A Memorial Sketch of Clara B. Colby*. Federal Suffrage Association, 1917. (*OB*)
Green, Norma Kidd. "Colby, Clara Bewick." *NAW* 1:355–357.
Leonard, John William, ed. *Woman's Who's Who of America, 1914–1915*. New York: American Commonwealth, 1914, p. 191.
Who Was Who in America, 1897–1942. Vol. 1. Chicago: Marquis Who's Who, 1943, p. 240.

Chronology of Major Speeches and Documents

"Concerning Farmers' Wives." Association for the Advancement of Women, Boston, October 1880. MSS 379; HOW
"The Relation of the Woman Suffrage Movement to the Labor Question." NWSA Convention, Washington, D.C., February 17, 1886. *WT* (March 1886):1; excerpted in *HWS* 4:70–71.
"Woman in Marriage." NWSA Convention, Washington, D.C., January 23, 1889. *WT* [March 2, 1889]:90; excerpted in *HWS* 4:151–152.
"Address, National Populist Party" [written]. National Convention, St. Louis, July 23, 1896. *WT* (July 25, 1896):69.
"Our Great Leaders." NAWSA Convention, Washington, D.C., February 9, 1900. MSS 379.
"Remarks of Mrs. Clara Bewick Colby." Senate Committee on Woman Suffrage, Washington, D.C., December 17, 1904. GPO Senate Hearings 3–9. *WT* (April 15, 1905):25–27; MSS 379.
"Remarks of Mrs. Clara Bewick Colby." Senate Committee on Woman Suffrage, Washington, D.C., as published in *WT* (February 3, 1906):9–10; MSS 379.

"The Strength of Non-Resistance." Fellowship Circle of Portland, Oregon, as published
      in *WT* (January 25, 1908):5.
"The Radiant Center." San Francisco, August 30, 1915. OB:87–102.
"Federal Suffrage Circular," prepared 1916. OB:109–116.

Speeches Delivered on Multiple Occasions

"Human Rights the Foundation of Government." MSS 379.
"The Spiritual Significance of Woman Suffrage." MSS 379.
"Women in the Building of America." MSS 379.

NOTE

1. New Thought was related to nineteenth-century spiritualist movements such as
Theosophy and Freethinking, which were largely non-Christian, if not anti-Christian.
Many of their principles were influenced by the Hindu-based teachings of Madame Helena
Petrovna Blavatsky and the spiritual leadership of Annie Besant. Bewick Colby appears
to have considered herself a New Thought follower, although she never defined that
approach more clearly than she does in these few speeches. Her family felt she had left
Christianity, although she herself seemed to believe that she accepted all religious principles. Brown summed up her eclectic religiosity: "She was essentially a devoted reli-
gionist. Adhering to the Congregational church, she yet had an open mind to all the
various forms of new thought and wondrous spiritual suggestion of our times. . . . Her
cry, like that of Goethe when he died, was ever 'more light' " (1917:57).

ANTOINETTE BROWN BLACKWELL
(1825–1921), speaker, writer, and first ordained woman minister

BARBARA S. SPIES

In 1853, Antoinette Brown became the first woman to be ordained into the ministry of a Protestant denomination in the United States. This is reason enough to record her name in the annals of history, but she did much more. In addition to preaching, she spoke regularly on the northeastern circuit in support of temperance, abolition of slavery, social purity, and woman's rights, including suffrage, and through her speaking and writing, she gained a national reputation. In a 1916 address, NAWSA president CARRIE LANE CHAPMAN CATT included her in a list of women who had "builded with others the foundation of the political liberty for American woman" (*MCSFH* 2:494).

Brown attended Oberlin College, one of the first institutions of higher education to admit women and Blacks. She first completed the undergraduate women's literary course and then the postgraduate theological course. For many years, ordination as a minister had been her goal, but despite fulfilling all requirements, she was denied ordination by the college. Instead, she had to search out a church that would call and ordain her. Eventually, a small New York Congregational church in South Butler asked her to be their pastor and ordained her in 1853. A year later she became a Unitarian, and in 1856, she married Samuel Blackwell.

Tracing Antoinette Brown Blackwell's career as a speaker during the second half of the nineteenth century reflects the development of early woman's rights rhetoric. Like many others, hers was a voice in transition that moved from a more conservative position grounded in religion to a more radical statement of woman's rights. The shifts in her argumentation reflect a growing understanding of the roots of women's problems. The evolution in her thought is especially interesting given the views of some historians that the radical voice left the movement as the turn of the century approached (e.g., IWSM).

Brown Blackwell is also important because of her work for the elimination of prostitution. She joined the New York Committee for the Prevention of State Regulation of Vice, later the American Purity Alliance, speaking regularly at its conventions and becoming a vice president in March 1895. She argued forcefully against the legalization of prostitution. Unlike others who saw a lack of moral purity as the cause of vice, she stressed that only an elimination of the double standard of morality would restore social purity.

Brown Blackwell was also a well-published author. Her articles appeared in the *New York Tribune*, the *Oberlin Quarterly Review*, the *Atlantic Monthly*, and the *Woman's Journal*, and she wrote nine books. These works, which span the period 1855–1915, reflect the evolution of her thought.

EARLY VOICE

From the outset, Antoinette Brown struggled to be heard. As an Oberlin student, she early experienced the constraints placed on women. Biographer Elizabeth Cazden notes: "Training in rhetoric was an essential part of the preparation of Oberlin men, most of whom expected to become lawyers, ministers, or teachers. Such training was considered unnecessary for female students, who were not expected to enter the professions for which it was needed" (1983:26). In response, Brown, with others including her close friend Lucy Stone, formed a secret women's debating society (Cazden, 1983:28). Later, in the theological course, she had to fight "Oberlin's general prohibition against women's oral recitation" (38). Her frustrations as a student and a minister must have fueled her ambition to work to advance woman's rights. However, many of her earlier speeches reflect a cautious, even conservative approach, and many early arguments were grounded in biblical authority.

In a speech to the 1852 woman's rights convention in Syracuse, she argued for women's equality, asserting: "God created the first pair equal in rights, possessions, and authority. He bequeathed the earth to them as a joint inheritance; gave them joint dominion over the irrational creation; but none over each other" (BFP, 242). She claimed that the equality that existed in the beginning continued after the fall from God's grace. That man would rule over woman was properly translated as a prediction, not as God's command.

After being denied the rostrum at the World's Temperance Convention in New York in 1853, Brown addressed the Whole World's Temperance Convention and again used biblical argument to make her points. Referring to male criticism of woman's rights, she said: "They try to show us our errors, but if we attempt to justify by argument the ground we have taken, they cry aloud that we are obstinate and unreasonable, especialy [sic] when we quote text for text, as Christ did when talking with a certain person of old" (BFP, 263). Matthew 4:1–11 and Luke 4:1–12 tell of Satan tempting Jesus in the wilderness; in each instance, Satan used scripture in his attempts to ensnare Jesus, who quoted "text for text" in response. Brown's allusion suggested that woman's rights was the genuinely religious position and that opponents who condemned them were misinterpreting the scriptures.

Given her theological training, it is not surprising that Brown often used biblical arguments. For example, as a student and a pastor, men regularly questioned her ability, but she reacted to such doubts optimistically in the same 1855 address.

The day is dawning when the intellect of woman shall be recognized as well as that of man, and when her rights shall meet an equal and cordial acknowlegment [sic]. The greatest wrong and injustice ever done to woman is that done to her intellectual nature. That, like Goliath among the Philistines, overtops all the rest. (BFP, 264)

Goliath, whom David fought in 1 Samuel 17, was noted among the Philistines for his height and strength, and as their champion, he taunted the Israelites. Just as Goliath represented the worst of the Philistines, so attacks on women's intelligence represented the worst of the injustices done to them, but just as David slew the giant, so women would triumph over men's attacks.

Brown's focus on biblical argument early in her speaking career reflected her more conservative stance. She took Galatians 3:28 as her basic text, a verse asserting that there is "neither male nor female in Christ Jesus." Thus, at the 1852 National WRC in Syracuse, she "Resolved: That the Bible recognizes the rights, duties and privileges of woman as a public teacher, as every way equal to those of men; that it enjoins upon her no subjection that is not enjoined upon him; and that it truly and practically recognizes neither male nor female in Christ Jesus" (BFP, 349). Her caution was even more evident in an *Oberlin Quarterly Review* (July 1849) article, where she wrote:

It is not proposed at the present time to discuss the question of the propriety or the expediency of woman's becoming a public teacher, nor to enquire whether it would be at all consistent with her nature and her relations to be engaged to any extent in public life; but simply to examine what has supposed to be the Bible prohibition against this, and to ascertain if possible the real meaning of an inspired teacher. (BFP, 87)

The article made a powerful argument concerning the biblical bases for woman's right to teach in public, but did not pursue its implications to consider whether women should be public speakers.

Brown did not rely solely on biblical arguments. She also argued for woman suffrage based on basic democratic ideals. In a speech at the 1852 Syracuse WRC, she said:

Man cannot represent woman. They differ in their nature and relations. The law is wholly masculine; it is created and executed by man. The framers of all legal compacts are restricted to the masculine standpoint of oberservation [*sic*], to the thought, feelings, and biases of man. The law, then, could give us no representation as woman, and therefore no impartial justice, even if the present law-makers were honestly intent upon this; for we can be represented only by our peers. (BFP, 246)

Brown attacked the paternalism of current laws. The assumption that women could not make political decisions for themselves was ridiculous to her. For years she focused on the franchise as the answer to women's problems, but in later years she realized that the vote alone was not sufficient. Basic inequality was the root cause, but for the time being, she stressed the paternalistic nature of the male franchise. At the Seventh National WRC, New York City, in 1856, she stated:

The central claim for Woman is her right to be, and to do, as well as to suffer. Allow her everywhere to represent herself and her own interests. Custom and law both deny her this right. If she is too cowardly to contend with custom, let her remain its slave. But the law has bound her hand and foot. Here she cannot act. The law-makers have forged her chains and riveted them upon her. They alone can take them off. Shall we not, then, at once demand of them—demand of every sovereign State in the Union—the elective franchise for women? With this franchise she will make for her a civil and political equality with man. Without it she is utterly without power to protect herself. She does not need to be protected like a child. She does need freedom to use the powers of self-protection with which her own nature is endowed. (BFP, 368)

She saw denying women political equality as enslavement.

Brown continued to speak in public and struggled against hostility to women speakers. In her biography, she described the response of some audience members when she spoke: "On July 4, 1853, of the next year I delivered the Independence Day address at South Butler, the first year the giving of patriotic addresses by women is a matter of record. . . . All the ministers of the town disapproved and the Baptist minister left the grove while I talked" (BFP, 163). Such reactions were not uncommon.

Brown participated in the northeastern lecture circuit in the 1850s. Before her ordination, as she wrote in her biography, she spoke in many locations: "I went to Pennsylvania, Ohio, and New England, lecturing in various towns generally taking up a collection, sometimes having a small admission fee. My subjects were Woman's Rights, Anti-Slavery, Temperance, and whenever I could get permission and admission to a church, I preached a sermon on Sunday" (BFP, 138).

She was a popular speaker, though perhaps more notorious than famous. A positive review in the *National Anti-Slavery Standard* (December 17, 1853) described a lecture delivered in Providence as

sprinkled all over with rich metaphors, with graphic figures, and that rare quality of modern productions "originality." The ideas expressed were clothed in beautiful language, such as none but the finest intellectual gifts could produce, sentences superbly framed, periods rounded with a grace not surpassed by the numberless gems of the great English essayist. (BFP, 351)

These comments suggest that Brown was able to fulfill nineteenth-century oratorical expectations.

Although Brown Blackwell supported woman's rights, she did not agree with some woman's rights leaders on the question of divorce. ELIZABETH CADY STANTON and ERNESTINE POTOWSKI ROSE, for example, stressed the importance of women's ability to leave marriages that were not in their best interests; Brown Blackwell did not see any circumstance under which divorce was appropriate. At the 1860 National WRC in New York, she spoke in support of the following:

Resolved, That as a parent can never annul his obligations towards even a profligate child, because of the inseparable relationship of the parties, so the married partner cannot annul his obligations towards the other, while both live, no matter how profligate that other's conduct may be, because of their still closer and alike permanent relationship; and, therefore, that all divorce is naturally and morally impossible, even though we should succeed in annulling all legalities. (*MCSFH* 2:203)

This resolution and her speech in support of it reflected her more conservative views. Circumstances did not affect the nature of the marriage covenant; it was a permanent agreement. Once again, she fell back on religious argument to make her point: "I believe that all the laws which God has established are sacred and inviolable; that his laws are the best which exist; that they are all founded on the natures or relation of things, and that he has no laws which are not as eternal as the natures and relations to which he has given existence" (*MCSFH* 2:205).

Although she rejected divorce, she believed that, while women lacked equal rights, marriage would be an imperfect institution. She explained that "as long as you make women helpless, inefficient beings, who never expect to earn a farthing in their lives, who never expect to do any thing outside of the family, but to be cared for and protected by others throughout life, you cannot have true marriages; and if you try to break up the old ones, you will do it against the woman and in favor of the man" (*MCSFH* 2:213). She believed that if divorce were made easier, men would abandon their wives at the slightest whim. Instead, she proposed: "The cure for the evils that now exist is not in dissolving marriage, but it is in giving to the married woman her own natural independence and self-sovereignty, by which she can maintain herself," adding: "So long as society is constituted in such a way that woman is expected to do nothing if she have a father, brother, or husband, able to support her, there is no salvation for her, in or out of marriage" (*MCSFH* 2:213–214).

RADICAL VOICE

As time passed, Brown Blackwell became convinced that the franchise alone could not solve women's problems. She sought the root of the problem and found it in the inequalities inherent in relations between men and women. While there were traces of radicalism in her earlier speeches, her concern with the roots of the problem became more pronounced in her later rhetoric.

In 1875, Brown Blackwell published *The Sexes Throughout Nature*, in which she offered an argument countering Herbert Spencer's extension of Darwin's views to the evolution of the sexes. In the preface, she noted, "Many women have grievously felt the burden of laws or customs interfering unwarrantably with their property, their children, or their political and personal rights" (6). She believed that laws rendering the sexes unequal were buttressed by current opinions about evolution and nature. Thus, she offered her ideas, "believing that they contain the germs of a new scientific estimate of feminine nature, from its earliest dawning in the planet up to developed womanhood in all its present complexity" (7).

Brown Blackwell accepted the nineteenth-century view of women as primarily mothers, but she saw this as a reason for a more equal division of work. She explained: "Other things equal—during the whole child-bearing age, at least— if family necessity compels to extra hours of toil or care, these must belong to the husband, never to the wife. The interests of their children *must not be sacrificed* by her over-exhaustion, even though she were willing and eager for the sacrifice of herself" (*The Sexes*, 115). She also argued that evolution had blessed the females of many species with more gifts than the males; their role in procreation was more significant: "Among the beings of a lower type, plant and animal, all the more recent observations indicate that Nature herself systematically favors the females—the mothers of the destined races" (*The Sexes*, 144).

In this book, Brown Blackwell called attention to an assumption that is still prevalent—that men are normal and women are a deviation. This assumption is reflected in the second account of creation in Genesis in which woman was made from the rib of man and was, therefore, a subset of man. She noted:

There is a convenient hypothesis that the intellect of the female, among all the higher orders of being, has acquired a development intermediate between the young of the species and the males, as their bodies and brains are intermediate in size. It is a theory closely akin to the time-honored assumption that the male is the normal type of his species; the female the modification to a special end. Also, it is nearly allied to any scheme of Evolution which believes that progress is effected chiefly through the acquirement and transmission of masculine characters. (*The Sexes*, 122)

This view of male superiority was especially powerful because it grounded women's inferiority in scientific theories of evolution.

Brown Blackwell also noted that females were not judged as individuals, but rather on the basis of how well they represented their sex. She must have felt this judgment herself, both as a student and as a minister. She pointed to this double standard of evaluation:

In schools, the abilities of the girls are tested by those of the boys. . . . The failure of any one is felt, perhaps unconsciously, by all the others, almost as a personal grievance, as a failure which involves the whole sex. Comparatively, a boy may succeed or fail for himself alone. For his confreres, all the ages past are illuminated by examples which cover his deficiencies with their vail [*sic*] of light. (*The Sexes*, 198–199)

Brown Blackwell's purpose was to prove scientifically that evolution had not favored males over females in any species and to identify the evil effects of that inaccurate assumption. Her writing was another means to attack the causes of women's problems.

In addition to writing, Brown Blackwell continued to speak publicly in the 1880s and 1890s. An 1880 circular of the Woman's National Lyceum Bureau announced: "Rev. Antoinette Brown Blackwell, A. M. Subjects—'What the Yankees are Whittling.' 'The A.B.C. of Nature.' 'School Suffrage for

Women.' '' (BFP). Although few texts of her lyceum speeches are available, many of her speeches on social purity still exist.

Brown Blackwell's speeches on social purity called forth her most radical statements on woman's rights. The only evident restraint was her reference to prostitution only with euphemisms such as "vice" and "fallen women." Most of these speeches were printed in the *Philanthropist*, the organ of the American Purity Alliance (APA), which in 1895 grew out of the New York Committee for the Prevention of State Regulation of Vice. The APA fought against proposed laws similar to the Contagious Diseases Acts in England, which regulated prostitution by making women register as prostitutes and submit to physical exams to prevent the spread of social diseases. The APA opposed these acts because they supported the continuation of prostitution and because they treated men and women unequally. Brown Blackwell argued that, in addition to basic inequalities between the sexes, prostitution was caused by the double standard of morality.

She explained the problems caused by the double moral standard in remarks at an 1887 meeting: "Popular sentiment does not expect, does not strenuously demand chastity from young men. It is currently assumed that crimes in that direction may be lightly regarded. Even members of churches are tolerant of this vice in others, and sometimes in themselves also" (*Philanthropist*, March 1887:6). She amplified the implications of the double standard:

The prevalent code of morals has never fairly considered the woman at all, for her own sake and in the light of her interests. Men, even as teachers, have made almost no attempts to put themselves in the woman's place and to realize the appalling effect of this moral code upon her. Women have suffered great wrongs from society in many things, both through customs and legislation, but there is no other wrong which is so utterly heartless, so cruelly heathenish as this one. No other crime is so little removed from brutality, so absolutely indifferent to the interests of another. (*Philanthropist*, March 1887:7)

As Brown Blackwell saw it, society condoned prostitution. If vice were truly deemed wrong, society would fight against it vehemently. In remarks at an 1889 purity meeting, she argued: "This class of wrongdoing is not held up in the sunlight as more intensely inhuman than any other class of crime; if it was firmly believed to be crime, as murder is crime, it would be sternly suppressed" (*Philanthropist*, March 1889:5). She held that using a prostitute was a crime as evil as murder.

The sometimes timid arguments of Brown Blackwell's earlier speeches no longer appear in her purity speeches. She blatantly attacked the male system that perpetuated prostitution. Her language was harsh, and she made her points emphatically. In "Woman and the Regulation System," delivered at an 1892 purity meeting, she stressed that "The instinctive feeling of women, of the good and the bad alike, is a shuddering repugnance to the regulation system. It would never have originated with them. Its patent insincerities are detestable, and every detail which it prescribes is intensely repellent" (*Philanthropist*, January 1892:2).

She described the regulation system as one that only men could have designed: "The entire scheme is a man's invention, a pure masculine scheme for protecting male humanity at the pitiful expense of the tenderer and younger, the less self-helpful, the more ignorant, poorer, and more friendless and already outcast by social ban, of the weakest, least self-assertive elements of feminine humanity" (*Philanthropist*, January 1892:2).

The issues were confronted directly: regulation of prostitution was itself criminal, she contended. With such phrases as "shuddering repugnance," "detestable," and "repellent," her evaluation was clear. At the same time, she created sympathy for and identified with the women victimized by prostitution through adjectives describing them as "tenderer," "younger," "outcast," and "weakest."

Those who supported regulation of prostitution argued that it would protect women from disease. Brown Blackwell identified what she saw as the true concerns of proponents in the 1892 address:

A provision to save unhappy women from shameful suffering! if this has ever been proposed, intended, considered in any practical light and haltingly adopted, we have abundant evidence to prove that not for their sake was this done; but as a more indirect measure established in the interest of the idle soldier who might one day fight for his country, of the sailor in port who adorns the navy or who is the right hand of commerce, of the voting citizen numbered in a political constituency. (*Philanthropist*, January 1892:2)

In her 1892 address, Brown Blackwell compared prostitution and its regulation to slavery. Proponents of regulation contended that women desired it, but she doubted the veracity of that claim:

And they, that pitiable class of the other women, we are told that many of them even petitioned for a continuance of regulative supervision! Yes; we were told once that the slaves were deeply in love with slavery, were humbly grateful for its protecting shield, almost ready to kneel in the dust and beg that they might always have a master to rule over them and might never be permitted to enjoy the perilous gift of freedom. If the masters had been enterprising enough, doubtless they might have rolled up a long list of just such petitioners. Intimidation will accept stones for bread, and even while it feels the sting of the serpent may affirm that it is only a fish. (*Philanthropist*, January 1892:3)

Any woman who said she favored regulation probably had been coerced into taking that position.

The true source of the problem was inequality. Brown Blackwell stressed that men had made all the rules and even tried to divide women in order to achieve their goals. In her 1892 address, she said: "Makers of provisions like those realized no need of advice or endorsement from 'females,' good or bad. Both sets of women were very well in their respective places, and these men were confident of being able to draw the lines in just about the right way between them" (*Philanthropist*, January 1892:3). If women were divided into two classes, men more easily could maintain their superiority to both. Without a sense of connection, women could not unite to throw off their bonds. Yet she held out the possibility of equality when she added, "But women are learning that from the same heavens comes the flooding sunlight which enfolds the daughters as warmly as the sons of equally dependent humanity" (*Philanthropist*, January 1892:3).

The need for woman suffrage was linked to arguments against the regulation system. Regulation would ensure that a woman, once registered, would be labeled a prostitute forever. Brown Blackwell saw this proposal as additional evidence of women's need for the franchise as a means of protection against the control of men. In remarks at an 1895 purity meeting, she said: "A helpless forlorn army of women legally to be forced to take their lives into the absolute control of the infamous commission—to be made over to their care, their literal bond women. If anything could make us all believe in the largest and fullest suffrage for all womanhood, it would be proposals of this character" (*Philanthropist*, March 1895:7). At an 1895 National Purity Congress, Brown Blackwell made one of her most powerful addresses opposing regulation. She relied on religious commonplaces and strong language to demonstrate its wrongs. She criticized the double moral standard that perpetuated prostitution and made clear her belief that the unequal position of men and women was the root of the problem.

As in the 1853 speech in which she compared men who argued against woman's rights with Satan and women who responded with Christ, Brown Blackwell again stressed the Christ-like qualities of women in contrast to proponents of regulation. She presented those who support the system as traitors to humanity:

So obvious have such facts become, that regulation has been abolished where once established, as worse than useless; and wherever it is still maintained it is upheld both by immoral men and by the shameful greed of moneyed interests ready either to urge on the guilty or to betray the innocent for the thirty pieces of silver. (Powell, 1896:21)

Just as Judas received silver for betraying Christ, men would benefit financially from betraying innocent women into prostitution and its regulation.

Women became Christ-like in still another comparison she made:

The woman's point of view is so totally outside of all existing regulative systems, legal or illegal, that if the best women remained silent, and the stones did not cry out, the leaves on the trees would bleed with compassion over the dumb helplessness of fallen womanhood. Every silent green thing would droop and blacken because of unuttered sympathy. (Powell, 1896:27)

In Luke 19:40, Jesus answered the Pharisees, who said that he should order his disciples to stop praising him as he made his triumphal entry into Jerusalem on Palm Sunday, by saying: "I tell you, if these were silent, the stones would shout out." Similarly, she argued, "Fallen womanhood" should be supported by the voices of "the best women," but even if they could not speak, nature herself would cry out in their behalf.

Over and over, Brown Blackwell pointed out the despicable nature of the double moral standard. Without legal rights, women were subject to the whims of men. Prostitution was just one of the many examples of masculine power gone awry. She attacked the entire unequal relationship when she said:

This is a paternalism to which heathendom never attained. Barbarism had no double standard either of morals or of remedies. Sheer savagery never laid one brutal hand heavily upon the woman, beating her into the dust while the other arm uplifted and upheld the man, seeking, despite his fall, to clothe him in honor and dignity. (Powell, 1896:25)

Because of the sexual hierarchy, men had the power to create two classes of women: the pure for their wives and daughters, and the tainted for their own gratification. Brown Blackwell described this process and showed how the regulation system fitted in: "It was only after it was decided to divide womankind into the sheep and the goats, and give men the privilege of associating with both, that the double standard of morals was erected and the device of seeking to protect fallen men at the sole expense of fallen women was invented" (Powell, 1896:25). The only people who benefited from regulation were men; women were harmed more and more by the legal perpetuation of prostitution, she argued: "The regulation scheme is a shield manufactured and uplifted exclusively for men. It recognizes only their perils, needs, and wishes to be protected along a line of admitted debasement" (Powell, 1896:26).

The proponents of regulating prostitution consistently countered this claim by arguing that the health of women and children would be protected if prostitutes were required to have regular medical examinations, which assumed that prostitutes are the only source of sexually transmitted diseases. Brown Blackwell responded, noting: "If it were in earnest in its claim to furnish safeguards for innocent wives and children, it would deal directly with the men rather than with the women; it would require both men and women to take out licenses for prostitution and be able to show a clean bill of health or be placed in an hospital" (Powell, 1896:26).

Her radical statements opposing regulation continually pointed to inequality as the source of the problem. She summed up her views at an 1895 National Purity Congress: "In the face of the actual facts, one-sided sanitary regulations become inexpressibly ignoble. They are grounded in the assumption that for a common sin, the woman shall forfeit everything: but, so far as law or manufactured opinion can help him, the man shall forfeit nothing" (Powell, 1896:27).

Because she had pointed to the inequality between the sexes as the cause of prostitution, her obvious solution was to make women and men equal partners. Brown Blackwell recognized the obstacles that she faced because, even though the regulation system was not in effect, a kind of code among men had already put the system into effect. As she commented: "Authorized legalization has scarcely dared yet to lift its head in our own country; yet the police service has often pandered to vice and its claims, unrebuked,—if not liberally rewarded. Often they virtually execute an unwritten law which favors social depravity'' (Powell, 1896:24).

She criticized the effectiveness of rescue work as a method of eliminating prostitution. Many claimed that, if only a pure moral attitude were maintained and those who had been enslaved by prostitution were rescued, then prostitution could be eliminated. Brown Blackwell rejected this claim in her response to addresses of welcome at an 1896 purity meeting:

Rescue work to most people means the rescue of poor girls led astray; but did you ever think that, while the double standard of morals prevails everywhere, the rescue of one girl means merely the drawing down of another? It is all but hopeless to rescue women, while public opinion remains what it is. (*Philanthropist*, January 1896:12).

In order to root out the problem, inequality between the sexes had to be eliminated. When women cannot work to support themselves, prostitution may seem the only alternative. In the same 1896 response, she argued strongly for a system in which women would not find it necessary to turn to prostitution. She said: ''We shall never have social purity so long as work is regarded as disgraceful, or so long as the sex of the worker is paid rather than the work'' (*Philanthropist*, January 1896:12).

CONCLUSION

Antoinette Brown Blackwell was a dedicated woman's rights advocate. She faced obstacles in education and in her profession because of her sex. She did not give up on her quest for woman's rights because of these difficulties. Like so many women of her time she struggled that others might not face the barriers that she had encountered.

As a minister, she preached regularly, despite male attacks on her modesty for doing so, but she did not confine herself to the pulpit. She spoke regularly at woman's rights conventions, social purity meetings, and on the lyceum circuit, and her understanding of the barriers to women's equality evolved over the half century of her speaking career.

At the beginning, she spoke with a more conservative voice. Her arguments were often restrained and sometimes, as in the 1860 divorce debate, she opposed the views of leaders of the woman's rights movement. In her early speeches, she usually relied on biblical arguments.

Over time, Brown Blackwell developed a more radical voice. She sought to discover the underlying causes of women's problems. In later speeches, she identified the source as women's inequality in relation to men. Prostitution, she argued, did not result from immorality, but rather from an unequal relationship between women and men that resulted in a double moral standard. Although the vote would improve women's position, legal and economic inequalities were the root problem that she identified in her rhetoric.

SOURCES

The Blackwell Family Papers (BFP), Schlesinger Library, Radcliffe College, are cataloged as A–77, A–145, and A/B632/a3. They contain her autobiography, including her *Oberlin Quarterly Review* article; "New Departure in Education," *Oberlin Alumni Magazine* 5, no.6 (March 1909); "Consciousness and Its Helpers," delivered to the Medico-Legal Society in 1898; and "Sex Injustice," delivered to the APA, in an 1897 pamphlet printed by the *Philanthropist*. Other primary sources include:

"Shadows of Our Social System." *New York Tribune*. Published serially, 1855.
"Sex and Work." *Woman's Journal*. Published serially, 1874.
The Philanthropist. APA organ. Previous title: *Vigilance*. Volumes 1–27, January 1886–January 1914. HOW
Powell, Aaron. *The National Purity Congress: Its Papers, Addresses, Portraits*. 1896. New York: Arno, 1976.

Biographical Sources

Cazden, Elizabeth. *Antoinette Brown Blackwell: A Biography*. Old Westbury, N.Y.: Feminist Press, 1983.
Deen, Edith. *Great Women of the Christian Faith*. New York: Harper & Brothers, 1959.
Hardesty, Nancy A. *Great Women of Faith: The Strength and Influence of Christian Women*. Grand Rapids, Mich.: Baker Book House, 1980.

Critical Sources

Campbell, Karlyn Kohrs. "A Movement in Transition: The Debate of 1860." *MCSFH* 1:71–86.

Chronology of Major Works

"Exegesis of Certain Texts of St. Paul." *Oberlin Quarterly Review* (July 1849). WRC, Syracuse, 1852. Excerpts, BFP
Whole World's Temperance Convention, New York, 1853. Excerpts, BFP
Seventh National WRC, New York City, 1856. Excerpts, BFP
Resolutions and speech, debate on divorce, National WRC, New York City, 1860. *MCSFH* 2:188–228.
The Sexes Throughout Nature. 1875. Westport, Conn.: Hyperion, 1976.
APA, New York, 1887. *Philanthropist* 2, no. 3 (March 1887):6–7.
APA, New York, 1889. *Philanthropist* 4, no. 3 (March 1889):5–6.
"Woman and the Regulation System." APA, New York, 1892. *Philanthropist* 7, no. 1 (January 1892):2–3, 8.
APA, New York, 1895. *Philanthropist* 10, no. 3 (March 1895):7–8.

"Immorality of the Regulation System." National Purity Congress, Baltimore, Md., October 1895. Powell:21–29.

APA, New York, 1896. *Philanthropist* 11, no. 1 (January 1896):12.

"Sex Injustice." APA, New York, 1897. *Philanthropist* 12, no. 7 (July 1897):7–9.

ELIZABETH CADY STANTON
(1815–1902), woman's rights philosopher, speaker, and writer

KARLYN KOHRS CAMPBELL

Elizabeth Cady Stanton was one of the great public advocates of the nineteenth century, but she remains a controversial figure for several reasons. First, she espoused positions that were radical for her time, some of which, such as anticlericalism, have remained controversial. Moreover, she distanced herself from woman's rights organizations for much of her life, first because she was burdened with many young children and later because she preferred to take the case for woman's rights to the public in lectures. However, throughout her life she remained the movement's preeminent public spokeswoman. Finally, she is sometimes damned by contemporary feminist scholars because, despite strong support for the abolition of slavery, in the aftermath of struggles over the wording of the Fourteenth and Fifteenth amendments, which excluded women, she espoused ethnocentric and elitist positions. Yet she identified with the plight of slave women in advocating abolition, launched what became the social movement for woman's rights including woman suffrage, and was the early movement's preeminent philosopher and rhetorician.

Because her parents were landed gentry and her father a judge, Elizabeth Cady had opportunities available to few women of her time. She was the only girl to graduate from the Johnstown, New York, high school, and, although barred from higher education by her sex, for two years she attended Troy Female Seminary, a finishing school with a somewhat enlarged curriculum. (See EMMA HART WILLARD.) A clergyman neighbor tutored her in Greek, and by her own report, she read some law in her father's office. However, she was largely self-educated, and she was a voracious reader throughout her life.

Because she fulfilled traditional expectations for women of her time, she was a more credible woman's rights advocate. In 1840, she married Henry Brewster Stanton and traveled with him to London where she met LUCRETIA COFFIN MOTT and observed the refusal of the World's Anti-Slavery Society to seat women delegates (Tilton, 1868:344). The Stantons were the parents of seven children. Despite family responsibilities, which were unusually onerous for her because her husband was often absent on business for months at a time, she became an active reformer. In addition to being the moving force behind the first woman's rights convention in 1848 at Seneca Falls, New York, she was a founder and president of the New York Woman's Temperance Society, 1851–1853, a founder and president of the AERA, 1867–1869, a founder and president of NWSA, 1869–1890, and president of the merged NAWSA, 1890–1892. In 1866, she became the first woman to run for the U.S. Congress (from the Eighth District of New York), exploiting the inconsistency that prohibited women from voting but not from running for office (''To the Electors of the Eight Congressional District," quoted in Tilton, 1868:352– 354). For eight months of the year between 1869 and 1882 she lectured, usually twice a day, on the lyceum circuit; her most popular offering was "Our Young Girls" (holograph ECSP; Waggenspack, 1989:141–158).

A variety of women had offered rationales for woman's rights. In England, in 1666, Quaker founder Margaret Askew Fell had asserted woman's right to preach, and in 1792, Mary Wollstonecraft had made a case for her right to be educated. In the United States, Scotswoman Frances Wright and Americans MARIA W. MILLER STEWART, Margaret Fuller, Judith Sargent Murray, and ANGELINA and SARAH GRIMKÉ had recognized and articulated women's legal and civil disadvantages. But Cady Stanton launched what became a social movement for woman's rights. She was one of five women who in 1848 issued the call for the first woman's rights convention and who refashioned the Declaration of Independence into a Declaration of Sentiments proclaiming women's grievances. The resolutions adopted at the Seneca Falls Convention, including a controversial demand for woman suffrage, were reaffirmed at later conventions and led to organized agitation to change state laws regarding woman's legal rights and to pass a federal woman suffrage amendment (*MCSFH* 1:49–70).

Many others made important contributions to the cause of woman's rights and woman suffrage, but Cady Stanton merits special recognition for several reasons. During her life, she was the movement's chief public advocate. From 1848 until her death in 1902, her voice and pen were dedicated to woman's rights. Her output was prodigious. In addition to countless newspaper articles and letters to the editor, she made numerous speeches, frequently to legislative bodies, many of which were published in newspapers and as tracts. With SUSAN B. ANTHONY as publisher, she and Parker Pillsbury edited the *Revolution* (1868–1870); with SUSAN B. ANTHONY and MATILDA JOSLYN GAGE, she compiled and edited the first three volumes of the *History of Woman Suffrage* (1881, 1886). In addition, she published an autobiography (1898), and was the editor and chief author of the two volumes of *The Woman's Bible* (1895, 1898).

In addition to launching what became a social movement and acting as its chief public advocate, in her speeches and writings Cady Stanton articulated the philosophy or ideology underlying the early movement. Certain principles echoed in contemporary feminism are evident. First, even as she worked for temperance and the abolition of slavery, she argued that woman's rights were fundamental. For example, in her opening address to the New York Woman's Temperance Society in 1853, she explained:

We have been obliged to preach woman's rights, because men, instead of listening to what we had to say on temperance, have questioned the right of a woman to speak on any subject. . . . Let it be clearly understood, then, that we are a woman's rights Society; that we believe it is a woman's duty to speak whenever she feels the impression to do so. (*HWS* 1:495)

Second, she saw all reforms as inevitably tied to civil rights for women. For example, in the speech just cited, she made an impassioned plea for consistency between emotional appeals based on women's plight and political action for their rights:

[S]hall these classes of sufferers [drunkards' wives, children, widows, and orphans] be introduced but as themes for rhetorical flourish, as pathetic touches of the speaker's eloquence; shall we passively shed tears over their condition, or by giving them rights bravely open to them the doors of escape from a wretched and degraded life? . . . If in showing her wrongs, we prove the right of all womankind to the elective franchise; to a fair representation in the government; to the right in criminal cases to be tried by peers of her own choosing, shall it be said that we transcend the bounds of our subject? (*HWS* 1:496)

Third, despite the severe economic, social, and political disabilities under which they labored, Cady Stanton sought to convince women of their power to effect social change. At Seneca Falls, she asserted that "woman herself must do this work," calling attention to the rhetorical power of women speaking for their rights and to women's deeper understanding of women's problems (*MCSFH* 2:42). In 1860, speaking to the American Anti-Slavery Society, she said: "[A] privileged class can never conceive the feelings of those who are born to contempt, to inferiority, to degradation. Herein is woman more fully identified with the slave than man can possibly be, for she can take the subjective view." She then illustrated her claim with a uniquely woman-centered appeal for the abolition of slavery:

Are not nearly two millions of native-born American women at this very hour, doomed to the foulest slavery that angels ever wept to witness? Are they not doubly damned as immortal beasts of burden in the field, and sad mothers of a most accursed race? Are not they raised for the express purpose of lust? . . . And this is the condition of woman in republican, Christian America, and you dare not look me in the face and tell me that, for blessings such as these, my heart should go out in thankfulness. (*Liberator*, 78)

Cady Stanton can be called a feminist in the contemporary meaning of the term because, unlike most early woman's rights advocates, she believed men and women had identical natures, that differences between them reflected socialization. Accordingly, her arguments were grounded in natural rights philosophy, a perspective that inevitably led to an enlarged conception of woman's sphere. Her philosophical position was apparent when, in speaking to the New York Legislature in 1860, she said: "If, then, the nature of a being decides its rights, every individual comes into the world with rights that are not transferable" (*MCSFH* 1:168). In 1867, addressing the American Equal Rights Association, she made the link between natural rights and civil rights:

To discuss this question of suffrage for woman and negroes, as women and negroes, and not as citizens of a republic, implies that there are some reasons for demanding this right for these classes that do not apply to "white males".... as if they were anomalous beings, outside all human laws and necessities. (*HWS* 2:185)

Sometimes she used the linkage sarcastically to raise the consciousness of the audience, as in 1860 when she said to white male New York legislators: "We may safely trust the shrewd selfishness of the white man, and consent to life under the same broad code where he has so comfortably ensconced himself" (*MCSFH* 2:176).

Cady Stanton's role as movement philosopher was enhanced because, from the outset, she recognized the fundamental arguments that had to be discredited if women were to attain full citizenship. Her speech at Seneca Falls was a detailed refutation of the major justifications used by opponents to limit woman's sphere, that is, the biological argument that anatomy is destiny; the theological argument that God ordained woman's limited and subservient place; and the sociological view that, as a member of the family unit, woman is publicly represented by her husband or some other male. Her early insistence on the goal of female enfranchisement reflected her inclusive, holistic view of the struggle. She shocked the New York Woman's Temperance Society in 1852 by advocating liberalized laws to permit women to divorce husbands who were perpetual drunkards. As early as 1853, she was writing to Susan B. Anthony that "this whole question of woman's rights turns on the pivot of the marriage relation" (*LDR* 2:49). She took the position that marriage was a contract like any other, not a religious sacrament; she expressed this view in speeches advocating liberalized divorce laws. She recognized that the church, the clergy, and theology were major obstacles to woman's rights, and she spoke and wrote in support of that view throughout her life. Such views were highly controversial, and her final major work, *The Woman's Bible*, was repudiated by NAWSA, despite the impassioned pleas of her revered friend and co-worker, SUSAN B. ANTHONY (*HWS* 4:263–264). Cady Stanton is often described as speaking for the less conservative wing of the movement, and she described herself as a radical in public as early as 1852. Late in life she wrote in her diary what other suffragists would not have disputed: "I tell her [Anthony] that I get more radical as I grow older, while she seems to grow more conservative" (*LDR* 2:254).

Cady Stanton was such an effective public advocate for woman's rights because she grounded her appeals in traditional cultural values—natural rights philosophy and the principles underlying the American Revolution and the Protestant Reformation. This highly consistent philosophical position made her less vulnerable to attack and strengthened the refutation she made of opponents' arguments. Despite the unchanging character of her basic premises, she was skilled in adapting to diverse audiences. For instance, in addressing the joint Judiciary Committees of the New York Legislature in 1854, she organized her speech to consider woman as citizen, wife, widow, and mother. This topical structure allowed her to combine appeals for the natural rights that women claimed as citizens with appeals to the chivalry of her male audience to protect women in their traditional roles. As she was addressing lawyers on legal matters, she drew her evidence from the state and federal constitutions, statutes, and legal authorities. As she was appealing to male chivalry, she told moving stories of the plight of widows and mothers under current laws. To these were added religious appeals based on the Golden Rule and an invidious comparison of the attitudes of southern planters toward their slaves and of males toward females. Although her proposals were rejected in 1854, in 1860 the legislature passed laws alleviating most of the conditions she had deplored in 1854.

Like others who spoke and wrote frequently to many different audiences, Cady Stanton repeated arguments and themes. For example, there were echoes of speeches given earlier that year in her first speech of the 1867 Kansas referendum campaign, delivered at Lawrence. However, her speech was crafted for this time and place. Her introduction reflected her adaptive skills and hinted at the meaning of "Kansas" for reformers of her time, particularly those who had labored in the anti-slavery movement:

How shall I find fitting words to express all I would say as I stand for the first time before an audience in Kansas? As the pious Catholic on entering his cathedral kneels and with holy water makes the sign of the cross upon his brow before lifting his eyes to the Holy of Holies, so would I reverently treat this soil as the vestabule [sic] to our Temple of Liberty, the opening vista to the future grandeur of the new republic. (MCSFH 2:260–261)

She invited Kansas voters to play a historic role:

Fresh from the corrupting influences of Kings and Courts, it was a great thing for our Fathers to get the idea of equality on paper, . . . but it is a greater thing for you today to make it a fact in the government of a mighty state. . . . [I]f you realize what you propose, to you will belong the honor of solving the national problem that has so long perplexed our political leaders, for as in war freedom was the key note in victory, so now is universal suffrage the key note of reconstruction. (MCSFH 2:264)

She was a particularly effective advocate because she understood the persuasive barriers that the movement faced. For example, speaking to the national NWSA convention in 1870, she said:

Knowing that we hold the Gibraltar rock of reason on this question, they resort to ridicule and petty objections. Compelled to follow our assailants, wherever they go, and fight them with their own weapons; when cornered with wit and sarcasm, some cry out, you have no logic on your platform, forgetting that we have no use for logic until they give us logicians at whom to hurl it, and if, for the pure love of it, we now and then rehearse the logic that is like a,b,c, to all of us, others cry out—the same old speeches we have heard these twenty years. (HWS 2:349)

As her statement implies, Cady Stanton understood that woman's rights advocates had to vary their rhetorical strategies. The chief resources in her rhetorical arsenal were tightly reasoned deductive arguments based on legal evidence and authority, and skillful use of analogy, example, metaphor, vivid depiction, and humor.

No brief excerpt can adequately illustrate Cady Stanton's argumentative prowess. Her speeches to the New York Legislature in 1854 and 1860 and to U.S. congressional committees in 1890 are masterworks of discursive proof. Some examples from her speeches give a flavor of her skill in argument. For instance, she frequently used natural rights principles to pose a dilemma for her male audiences:

If the sexes are alike in their mental structure, then there is no reason why women should not have a voice in making the laws which govern her. But if they are not alike, most certainly woman must make laws for herself; for who else can understand her wants and needs? (*MCSFH* 2:171)

She could make her refutation clear and vivid. For example, in April 1894, in an essay entitled "Women Do Not Wish to Vote," she wrote:

We do not fence the cornfields because we think the cattle will not eat the corn, but because we know they will. And the word "male" in the Constitution [Fourteenth Amendment], is a standing admission that men know women would vote if the barriers were down, no matter what they say to the contrary. (*National Bulletin*, 1–4)

As this quotation illustrates, her discourse was replete with metaphors, analogies, and descriptive language by which she made ideas vivid and enabled audience members to associate the new ideas and proposals with the homey and familiar. In 1867, a St. Louis newspaper described her language as "choice and her metaphor abundant" (ECSP Reel 5, Cont. 9). Her 1854 speech to the Judiciary Committees of the New York Legislature concluded by transforming a familiar feminine image into rebuttal of the argument that woman's rights advocates did not speak for all women:

[W]ho are they that we do not now represent? But a small class of fashionable butterflies who, through the short summer days, seek the sunshine and the flowers; but the cool breezes of autumn and the hoary frosts of winter will soon chase all these away; then, they too will need and seek protection, and through other lips demand, in their turn, justice and equity at your hands. (*MCSFH* 2:166)

Exploiting abolitionist sentiment, Cady Stanton made detailed comparisons between the *legal* positions of slaves and women, as in her 1860 speech to the New York Legislature:

How many of you have ever read the laws concerning them [women] that now disgrace your statute books? In cruelty and tyranny, they are not surpassed by any slaveholding code in the Southern States. . . . The negro has no name. He is Cuffy Douglas or Cuffy Brooks, just whose Cuffy he may chance to be. The woman has no name. She is Mrs.

Richard Roe or Mrs. John Doe, just whose Mrs. she may chance to be. Cuffy has no right to his earnings; he cannot buy or sell, or lay up anything he can call his own. Mrs. Roe has no right to her earnings. (*MCSFH* 2:172–173)

She went on to recount other legal similarities in regard to child custody, legal recognition, and physical restraint and chastisement, effectively exploiting audience revulsion regarding the treatment of slaves.

Humor, frequently satirical, regularly appeared in her speeches. In an 1867 speech to the New York Legislature urging that women be allowed to vote for delegates to the state constitutional convention, she recalled that women had voted in New Jersey between 1776 and 1807, and then asked:

Did the children, fully armed and equipped for the battle of life, spring Minerva-like, from the brains of their fathers? Were the laws of nature suspended? Did the sexes change places? Was everything turned upside down? No, life went on as smoothly in New Jersey as in any other State in the Union. (*HWS* 2:277)

Later, in the same speech, she drew an ironic contrast:

Does the North consider its women a part of the family to be represented by the "white male citizen," so views the South her negroes. And thus viewing them, the South has never taxed her slaves; but our chivalry never fails to send its tax gatherers to the poorest widow that holds a homestead. (*HWS* 2:279)

Finally, she told a story to support her view that suffrage should be universal and without qualification: "In the old days of the Colonies when the property qualification was £5 that being just the price of a jackass—Benjamin Franklin facetiously asked, 'If a man must own a donkey in order to vote, who does the voting, the man or the donkey?' " (*HWS* 2:279).

Her most controversial rhetoric appeared in the period immediately following the Civil War. Republicans who dominated Congress excluded women from the provisions of the Fourteenth and Fifteenth amendments to the Constitution in order to ensure ratification and Republican political domination of the South, and abolitionists viewed suffrage for freedmen as a matter of survival that would be threatened if linked to woman suffrage. The creation of the American Equal Rights Association out of the National WRC of 1866 was an explicit assertion of support for universal suffrage. In the words of Cady Stanton, "Has not the time come . . . to bury the black man and the woman in the citizen? . . . Any work short of this is narrow and partial and fails to meet the requirements of the hour" (*HWS* 2:174). However, in arguing that this was the "Negro's hour," Republicans and abolitionists pitted freed Black men against women, and the frustration of woman's rights advocates erupted in ethnocentric and elitist statements. In 1865, as this conflict emerged, Cady Stanton fulminated:

The representative women of the nation have done their uttermost for the last 30 years to secure freedom for the negro, and so long as he was lowest in the scale of being we were willing to press *his* claims; but now, as the celestial gate to civil rights is slowly moving on its hinges, it becomes a serious question whether we had better stand aside and see "Sambo" walk into the kingdom first. (*HWS* 2:94)

Originally, women's efforts in the 1867 Kansas referendum campaign espoused universal suffrage, attempting to build support for proposed amendments to the state constitution that would remove both "white" and "male" as barriers to enfranchisement. However, Kansas and national Republican leaders refused to publicize their speeches or to support their efforts for woman suffrage. In the face of this betrayal, Susan B. Anthony and Cady Stanton accepted the support of George Frances Train, a pro-slavery Democrat, in order to publish the *Revolution*. By 1869 they had formed a pro-woman, anti-Negro suffrage organization. In her speech to the first NWSA convention, she asked why women, "the daughters of Adams, Jefferson, and Patrick Henry," were denied the vote while "iron-heeled peasants, serfs, and slaves, exalted by your [the government of males] hands, tread our inalienable rights into dust?" (*HWS* 2:351). Moreover, she said:

If American women find it hard to bear the oppressions of their own Saxon fathers, the best orders of manhood, what may they not be called to endure when all the lower orders of foreigners now crowding our shores legislate for them and their daughters. Think of Patrick and Sambo and Hans and Yung Tung, who do not know the differences between a monarchy and a republic, who cannot read the Declaration of Independence or Webster's spelling-book, making laws for Lucretia Mott, Ernestine L. Rose, and Anna E. Dickinson. (*HWS* 2:353)

Subsequently, her invective rose to new heights: "[S]hall American statesmen, claiming to be liberal, . . . make their wives and mothers the political inferiors of unlettered and unwashed ditch-diggers, boot-blacks, butchers, and barbers, fresh from the slave plantations of the South, and the effete civilizations of the Old World?" (*HWS* 2:354) Her words reflected the sense of betrayal of those who had been abandoned despite their support of abolitionist and Republican goals, but her indignation revealed the deeply entrenched ethnocentrism and classism of middle-class, white, woman's rights advocates. If a choice was to be made, advantaged white women were to be preferred to lower class immigrants and freedmen: "if you will not give the whole loaf of suffrage to the entire people, give it to the most intelligent first" (*HWS* 2:383), in the words of Anthony at the 1869 AERA convention. Cady Stanton viewed continued disfranchisement as the loss of dignity and respect as women:

On the blackest pages of history there is no record of an act like this, in any nation, where native-born citizens, having the same religion, speaking the same language, equal to their rulers in wealth, family, and education, have been politically ostracized by their own countrymen, outlawed with savages, and subjected to the government of outside barbarians. (*HWS* 2:355)

To her credit, even her acrimonious utterances retained her commitment to the principle of universal suffrage; to her discredit, in the face of betrayal, she abandoned the less fortunate to proclaim the rights of advantaged, white, middle–class women.

For the lyceum, Cady Stanton developed a variety of lectures that dealt with the issues of greatest concern to her. The most popular was "Our Young Girls," a lecture that vividly illustrated her ability to adapt controversial views for a popular audience. She wrote to her daughter Margaret from Austin, Minnesota: "You would laugh to see how everywhere the girls flock round me for a kiss, a curl, an autograph. They all like so much my lecture, 'The Coming Girl' '' (December 1, 1872, ECSP, Reel 1, Cont. 1). In it she described "the coming girl" as "healthy, wealthy, and wise. . . . an independent, self-supporting being, not as today, a helpless victim of fashion, superstition, and absurd convention-alisms" (holograph ECSP; Waggenspack, 1989:144). She appealed to cherished national values as well as young women's desires to be attractive and productive, entertained with humor, and made arguments based on common sense and but-tressed with examples. Cautioning parents, she said: "Remember, vice recruits her palsied ranks not from the children of lust but from the gay, the fashionable, the helpless, those who know not how to work, but yet must eat" (holograph ECSP; Waggenspack, 1989:153). To their daughters, she spoke with humor and common sense:

I will give you a recipe, dear girls, for nothing, that will prove far more serviceable in preserving your beauty than Hagan's Magnolia Balm at 75 cents a bottle. . . . For the hair, complexion, and clear, bright expression of the eye, there is nothing you can do like preserving your health by exercising regularly, breathing pure air in all your sleeping and waking hours, eating nutritious food, and bathing every day in cold water. Not three times a day, . . . that would wash all the constitution out of you. Don't imitate our financiers, the Vanderbilts and the Fisks, who water their stocks so freely as to take all the value out of them. Eat pure roast beef and vegetables, good bread and fruits; do not munch chalk, clay, cloves, india rubber, peanuts, gum or slate pencils—always chewing, chewing, chewing like a cow with her cud. (ECSP; Waggenspack, 1989:151)

More liberated views were integrated with these more conventional ideas:

In the second place, the coming girl is to be wealthy, that is, she is to be a creator of wealth herself. . . . There cannot be too much said on the helpless condition in which a girl is left when thrown alone on the world without money, without friends, without skill or place in the world of work. . . . marriage as a profession nine cases in ten time proves a sad failure because the wife is pecuniarily dependent. . . . Beside in the most fortunate marriages, women are not secure against want, for good husbands sometimes die bankrupt, leaving a young wife with half a dozen little children to provide for. (ECSP; Waggenspack 1989:152)

She also urged women to be married by Methodists because their clergy had dropped the word "obey" from marriage ceremonies. Moreover, she celebrated unusual women of achievement: "All honor to the Mary Carpenters, Florence Nightingales, Maria Mitchells, Harriet Hosmers, Louisa Alcotts, Rosa Bonheurs, Anna Dickinsons, Susan B. Anthonys, and the long line of geniuses, saints, and philanthropists, who have directed themselves to art, religion, and reform" (ECSP; Waggenspack, 1989:156). She took to the lyceum to earn money and to spread her message to a wider audience; seeing her in person may also have eroded some common stereotypes. For example, the *Greenfield* [Ohio] *Transcript*, January 24, 1880, wrote:

It has become so common however to look upon these reformers, and especially lady speakers, as being a set of semi-masculine viragoes with gaunt [?] figures, brazen faces, sharp visages, fiery eyes, shrill, cracked voices, and impudent over-bearing manner, that we were wont to expect something of the kind in Mrs. Stanton. It may be that those who found themselves unable to cope with them in argument may have resorted to the ready stratagem of deriding their personal appearance as a substitute. (ECSP Reel 5, Cont. 9)

However reassuring her demeanor, her speeches combined appeals for self-help with calls for institutional change. Her rhetorical skills enabled her successfully to mix her unconventional views of woman's rights and roles with the sorts of material that drew audiences to her lectures and gained her regular bookings.

CONCLUSION

Many of the causes Cady Stanton espoused were successful in her lifetime as a broad array of state statutes were enacted enlarging woman's rights. Full woman suffrage came only after her death; other goals she fought for have yet to be achieved. A statement she made before the U.S. Senate Committee on Woman Suffrage, April 2, 1888, provides a context for viewing her achievements and those of the early woman's rights/woman suffrage movement: "[William Edward Hartpole] Lecky, the historian, has well said the success of a movement depends much less on the force of its arguments, or upon the ability of its advocates, than the predisposition of society to receive it" (13). Despite what she described as "the merciless storm of ridicule and persecution, . . . [being] ostracized in social life, scandalized by enemies, denounced by the pulpit, scarified and caricatured by the press" (13), she spoke where few or no women had spoken before, and she was honored in her lifetime as one of the greatest women the United States had produced.

Such an estimate is confirmed rhetorically. She produced one of the masterpieces of rhetorical literature, "The Solitude of Self," a speech she made to committees of the U.S. House and Senate and to the national NAWSA convention in 1892 (*MCSFH* 2:371–384). The address is a manifesto for humanistic feminism and a lyric expression of the experience of human life. It remains an enduring rationale for individual rights based on our republican tradition, the Protestant concept of the priesthood of believers, and the American credo of individualism and self-reliance (Campbell, 1980; *MCSFH* 1:133–144).

Not only was Cady Stanton an advocate who influenced the U.S. public for over half a century, but she was also a leader in a great social movement. Her works still speak to us because they address issues of continuing concern, her arguments are grounded in cherished cultural values, and her skills with metaphor, analogy, and humor bring her ideas vividly before our eyes.

SOURCES

Elizabeth Cady Stanton's rhetoric is found in these major sources: the Elizabeth Cady Stanton Papers, Library of Congress, available on microfilm (ECSP, Reels 1–5); the History of Women microfilm collection (HOW), incorporating materials from many special collections; the journals that were the major outlets for woman's rights advocates such as the *Lily, Una, Revolution, Woman's Journal, Woman's Tribune,* and *National Bulletin*; and the *Papers of Elizabeth Cady Stanton and Susan B. Anthony*, eds. Patricia G. Holland and Ann D. Gordon. Amherst: University of Massachusetts, 1990, microfilm and guide. Other primary sources are:

Elizabeth Cady Stanton As Revealed in Her Letters, Diary, and Reminiscences. 2 vols. Eds. Theodore Stanton and Harriot Stanton Blatch. New York: Harper & Brothers, 1922. *(LDR)*
Stanton, Elizabeth Cady. *Eighty Years and More: Reminiscences 1815–1897.* 1898. Intro. Gail Parker. New York: Schocken, 1971.
Stanton, Elizabeth Cady, and the Revising Committee. *The Woman's Bible.* 2 vols. 1895, 1898. Seattle: Coalition Task Force on Women and Religion, 1974.

Critical sources

Campbell, Karlyn Kohrs. "Stanton's 'The Solitude of Self': A Rationale for Feminism." *Quarterly Journal of Speech* 66 (October 1980):304–312.
———. *MCSFH* 1:49–103, 133–144.
Goodman, James E. "The Origins of the 'Civil War' in the Reform Community: Elizabeth Cady Stanton on Woman's Rights and Reconstruction." *Critical Matrix: Princeton Working Papers in Women's Studies* 1, no. 2 (1985):1–29.
Kern, Kathi L. "Rereading Eve: Elizabeth Cady Stanton and *The Woman's Bible*, 1885–1896." *Women's Studies* 19 (1991):371–383.
McCurdy, Frances. "Women Speak Out in Protest." *The Rhetoric of Protest and Reform, 1878–1898.* Ed. Paul Boase. Athens, Ohio: Ohio University Press, 1980, pp. 185–211.
Waggenspack, Beth M. *The Search for Self-Sovereignty: The Oratory of Elizabeth Cady Stanton.* Westport, Conn.: Greenwood, 1989, pp. 1–93. Texts in this source are replete with errors.

Biographical Sources

Banner, Lois. *Elizabeth Cady Stanton: A Radical for Women's Rights.* Boston: Little, Brown, 1980.

Bullard, Laura Curtis. "Elizabeth Cady Stanton." *Our Famous Women.* Ed. Elizabeth Stuart Phelps et al. Hartford, Conn.: Hartford Publishing, 1888.
Griffith, Elisabeth. *In Her Own Right: The Life of Elizabeth Cady Stanton.* New York: Oxford University Press, 1984.
Lutz, Alma. *Created Equal: A Biography of Elizabeth Cady Stanton.* New York: John Day, 1940.
———. "Stanton, Elizabeth Cady." *NAW* 3:342–347.
Tilton, Theodore. "Mrs. Elizabeth Cady Stanton." *Eminent Women of the Age.* Hartford, Conn.: S. M. Betts, 1868, pp. 332–361.

Chronology of Major Speeches

Address delivered at Seneca Falls and Rochester, New York, WRCs, July 19 and August 2, 1848. *Proceedings.* New York: Robert J. Johnston. ECSP Reel 5, Cont. 9; HOW; *MCSFH* 2:41–70; holograph ECSP, Reel 2, Cont. 3.

Address, New York State Temperance Convention, Rochester, New York, April 20 and 21, 1852. ECSP, Reel 5, Cont. 8; *HWS* 1:481–483; *Lily* 4 (May 1852):1.

Address, First Annual Meeting, Woman's State (NY) Temperance Society, Rochester, June 1 and 2, 1853. ECSP, Reel 5, Cont. 10; *HWS* 1:494–497.

Address to the Legislature of New York, adopted by the State WRC, Albany, February 14 and 15, 1854. Albany, N.Y.: Weed, Parsons, 1854; ECSP, Reel 5, Cont. 8; HOW; *HWS* 1:595–605; *MCSFH* 2:145–166.

Address, New York Legislature [A Slave's Appeal], February 18, 1860, as published May 11, 1860, ECSP, Reel 5, Cont. 8; from convention proceedings, *MCSFH* 2:167–186.

Speech on Marriage and Divorce, Tenth National Woman's Rights Convention, New York City, May 12, 1860. *Proceedings of the Woman's Rights Convention, 12 May 1860.* New York: Robert J. Johnston, 1860, pp. 66–73; *MCSFH* 2:187–202.

Speech, Anniversary of the American Anti-Slavery Society, New York City, May 18, 1860. *Liberator,* May 25, 1860:78.

Address on the Divorce Bill before the Judiciary Committee of the New York Senate, February 8, 1861. Albany, N.Y.: Weed, Parsons, 1861; ECSP, Reel 4, Cont. 6, Reel 5, Cont. 9; *MCSFH* 2:235–250.

Address to the New York Legislature on universal suffrage, January 23, 1867. Albany, N.Y.: Weed, Parsons, 1867. HOW; ECSP, Reel 3, Cont. 4, Reel 5, Cont. 9.

Speech, AERA convention, New York City, May 9, 1867. *Proceedings of the American Equal Rights Association,* May 9 and 10, 1867. New York: Robert J. Johnston, 1867.

First speech, 1867 Kansas referendum campaign, Lawrence, n.d. Holograph, mss. collection, Kansas State Historical Society, Topeka, 62 pp.; *MCSFH* 2:259–278.

President's Address, NWSA Convention, May 10, 1870. *Revolution* (May 19, 1870):305–307.

Address, House Judiciary Committee, January 10, 1872; Senate Judiciary Committee, January 12, 1872, ECSP, Reel 3, Cont. 5.

Our Young Girls [1872]. ECSP, Reel 3, Cont. 5; *Revolution* June 25, 1868:394; *Revolution,* January 29, 1868:51. Also "Our Girls, 1872." Waggenspack, 1989, 141–158.

Address of Welcome, International Council of Women, March 25, 1888. *Report of the*

International Council of Women. Washington, D.C.: Rufus H. Darby, 1888, pp. 31–39; holograph, ECSP, Reel 4, Cont. 6; *Woman's Tribune* (March 27, 1888):5; *TWJ* (March 31, 1888):103, 106.

"Statement of Mrs. Elizabeth Cady Stanton," Hearing before the Committee on Woman Suffrage, United States Senate, April 2, 1888, 50th Cong., 2d sess. Report #2543, pp. 9–16.

Speech, U.S. Senate Special Committee on Woman Suffrage, February 8; House Judiciary Committee, February 12, 1890. ECSP, Reel 4, Cont. 6, Reel 5, Cont. 10; HOW; *Woman's Tribune* (February 15, 1890):50–53.

"Change Is the Law of Progress." President's Address, NAWSA Convention, February 18, 1890. *Woman's Tribune* (February 22, 1890):58–61; holograph, ECSP, Reel 4, Cont. 7.

"The Solitude of Self." House Judiciary Committee and NAWSA Convention, January 18; Senate Committee on Woman Suffrage, January 20, 1892. ECSP, Reel·4, Cont. 7; HOW; *HWS* 4:189–191; *MCSFH* 2:371–384; *TWJ* (January 23, 1893):1, 32.

VICTORIA CLAFLIN WOODHULL
(1838–1927), a radical for woman's rights

SUZANNE E. CONDRAY

Distinguished in 1872 as the first woman to promote herself as a candidate for the nation's presidency, Victoria Claflin Woodhull used oral and written rhetoric to challenge social and political norms with her views on woman's rights, social freedom, and economic and political reform. Assailed by the press, the church, and the state for her radical views, she was ridiculed by supporters of the institutions she sought to transform.

BACKGROUND

Born in rural Homer, Ohio, Claflin acquired the principles of Methodism and spiritualism from her mother Roxanna Hummel. With only two years of formal education, she pursued self-education throughout her life and amassed an extensive personal library. Accompanied by her father Reuben Buckman Claflin, she and her sister Tennessee learned the skills of self-promotion as clairvoyants traveling the region. At age fifteen, she married Cincinnati physician Channing Woodhull, whose alcoholism and extramarital affairs ignited his wife's interest in woman's rights and social freedom. After an unhappy eleven-year marriage, she divorced Woodhull, retaining his name for the sake of their children, Zula Maud and Byron.

During these years, Claflin Woodhull embraced spiritualism, traveling as a clairvoyant and later marrying Colonel James Blood who introduced her to the American Association of Spiritualists, a national organization that she afterward served as president and chief spokesperson. In the 1860s, the Claflins and Bloods moved to New York where the sisters presented themselves as spiritualist physicians.

Intrigued by their beauty and their ability to predict the movements of the stock market, the wealthy Cornelius Vanderbilt helped the sisters establish themselves as the first women stockbrokers. In February 1870, Woodhull, Claflin and Company opened at 44 Broad Street. Vanderbilt introduced the sisters to an influential New York clientele and provided the financial means for their success. They enjoyed being touted by the New York press as "queens of finance" and "bewitching brokers." The sisters sparked press publicity for daring to breach societal constraints and for challenging other women to act on their own initiative.

CLAFLIN WOODHULL'S RHETORICAL CAREER

Claflin Woodhull began her rhetorical career late in 1870, after her first public declarations on political and social matters appeared in *Woodhull & Claflin's*

Weekly, which the sisters published. Between May 1870 and June 1876, the radical *Weekly* endorsed woman suffrage, sexual freedom, marriage reform, spiritualism, international justice, and economic and labor reform. The paper, whose masthead proclaimed "Progress, Free Thought, Untrammeled Lives," gave her a forum from which to discuss the tenets of natural philosophy and socialism. These ideas eventually found their way into her public speeches.

During her speaking career, Claflin Woodhull's rhetoric evolved from reformist advocacy to more radical stances and eventually took a somewhat philosophical bent. Predictably, her views were more readily embraced during her reformist period and were attacked more and more vehemently as she espoused increasingly radical stands. She regained some public acceptance in the last phase of her career but never recaptured the attention and support that she had attracted at the outset.

As a reformist, Claflin Woodhull relied on traditional forms of argument, including syllogistic reasoning, and petitioning. She based her arguments on what she saw as the premises underlying constitutional rights. She claimed that she was acting on her own initiative in deciding to take her case for woman suffrage directly to the Judiciary Committees of Congress (*VWR* IIA1:4). As the first woman to speak before these bodies, she put forward a legal argument for woman suffrage (see also *HWS* 2:407–416) in her "Memorial to Congress" of December 19, 1870. In this speech she petitioned the Senate and House of Representatives to recognize the constitutional rights of citizenship that she and other aggrieved women claimed under provisions of the Fourteenth Amendment. She outlined the constitutional grounds for woman's rights, called attention to the absence of constitutional distinctions between citizens based on sex, and charged the legislature to make laws necessary to remedy the political plight of women (*VWR* IIA1:1) A month later, she appeared before the Judiciary Committees to speak in support of her petition.

In this and similar speeches on woman's rights, Claflin Woodhull began with a quasi-logical argument comparing the sovereignty of the state to that of the individual. Whereas American colonists asserted themselves against the monarchy to establish national sovereignty, by analogy, she claimed that the citizen must assert her or his citizenship rights as an act of self-sovereignty. Furthermore, she cited evidence demonstating the legal grounds for suffrage, including women's ability to meet the criteria of citizenship and naturalization, to own and control property, and to pay taxes. She indicated contradictions in the arguments of those who opposed woman's right of suffrage, saying, "The male citizen has no more right to deprive the female citizen of the free, public, political expression of opinion than the female citizen has to deprive the male citizen thereof" (*VWR* IIA1:2).

According to her interpretation of the Fourteenth and Fifteenth amendments, race and color by their nature comprehend both genders. Therefore, she rebuked the Congress for its willingness to allow some states to abridge the rights of female citizens. In January 1872, in "Carpenter and Cartter Reviewed," she argued: "Either the states have the right to deny the right to vote to all citizens, or they have no right to deny it to any citizen" (*VWR* IIA3:6). She appealed to the legislative authority of Congress to prevent such acts of injustice against women.

Based on their familiarity with and support for woman suffrage, Claflin Woodhull relied on enthymematic constructions in her speeches before national suffrage conventions more than she did before the Judiciary Committees. However, in her May 1871 speech, "A New Political Party and a New Party Platform," presented to suffragists in New York's Apollo Hall, she argued syllogistically that:

> All persons [as specified in the Fourteenth Amendment]—men and women—are citizens.
> Citizens have the right to vote.
> Therefore, women have the right to vote. (*VWR* IIB6:1)

Moreover, she contended that the right to vote remained an inherent right of citizenship in a participatory democracy; to ignore the rights of some individuals, she reasoned, suggested the constitution of another form of government.

Despite opposition from Congress and the courts, Claflin Woodhull found suffragists sympathetic to her arguments, recognizing the "vitality of spirit and fresh ideas" of their new champion. ELIZABETH CADY STANTON and Isabella Beecher Hooker welcomed her to share the platform with them at several suffrage meetings. LUCRETIA COFFIN MOTT and Martha Coffin Wright wrote that audiences were charmed with her beauty, grace, knowledge, and enthusiasm (SSC, March 15, 1871). On February 11, 1871, *TWJ* editors even chastised those who ignored her petition, heralding it as "the spirit of the age" and agreeing that it "must finally prevail" (45). By 1871, as many as 30,000 women supported her declaration on behalf of women.

Riding a wave of popularity in 1871, Claflin Woodhull proposed other political initiatives, including a new party with a platform more humanitarian than that of either the Republicans or Democrats. In her May 1871 Apollo Hall speech, she endorsed election and civil service reform, domestic improvements in commerce and transportation, public benefits and national education, employment and tax reform, an international legal tribunal, and a program by which criminals would reimburse victims' families (*VWR* IIB6:1). In her peroration, she championed a political agenda that would expose "the most complete equality which humanity can attain" (*VWR* IIB6:7).

As Claflin Woodhull began to recognize the institutional forces poised against woman suffragists, she adopted a more radical tone. Her rhetoric became more confrontational, castigating social, political, and economic evils represented by those institutional forces. To lead this political revolution, she offered herself as a candidate in the 1872 presidential election campaign, in her words, "chiefly for the purpose of bringing home to the mind of the community woman's right to fill any office in America, from the Presidency down'' (*VWR* IIA4:4). Her intentions were first publicly recorded in the *New York Herald* (April 2, 1870). In June 1872, the Equal Rights party she had created, convening in New York, nominated her by acclamation. Recognizing the boldness of this gesture, later that month, she admitted:

I am not much given to the habit of conforming to conventionalities. In fact, if there be one thing that I hold more lightly in esteem than any other, it is the doing, or the refrain from doing, anything, simply because it is in accordance with an established custom to do so. (*VWR* IIB9:1)

Claflin Woodhull relied on ridicule in a number of her speeches, particularly when she perceived herself among allies. In ''Carpenter and Cartter Reviewed,'' she scornfully referred to the ''logic'' and ''wisdom'' of the court and government (*VWR* IIA3:9). When one senator claimed that an argument supporting woman suffrage was ''the slimmest he ever heard,'' she urged him to revise his claim in favor of a more recent pronouncement she had heard from the opposition. In the same speech, she ridiculed a justice who argued that allowing women to vote would destroy civil government. She countered mockingly with a series of analogies, that since some men showed bad judgment in voting, women probably ought not vote; that since some people abuse their stomachs, perhaps one ought not have a right to eat or drink as one pleased; and that since some people steal, the right of possession might best be nullified. She ended her litany by ridiculing her opposition saying, ''I stand abashed before the awful majesty of such wisdom'' (*VWR* IIA3:25).

Shortly after *Woodhull & Claflin's Weekly* published the first U.S. edition of the *Communist Manifesto*, Claflin Woodhull embraced Marxist philosophy and the idea that production ought to fulfill human needs, not line the pockets of the rich as profit. By this time, she not only sought to enlist the support of suffragists, but she also appealed to the laboring classes. Her experience as a stockbroker and her earlier support of the International Workingman's Association enhanced her credibility with male and female workers. In her speeches, she endorsed the eight-hour working day, full employment, and redistribution of wealth. Her deeds and words in behalf of labor established her credibility with those supporting economic reforms.

As Claflin Woodhull began to identify and align herself with those divorced from institutional power, her rhetoric evolved in a more agitational direction. Equating wealth with monarchy, in her speech to the Equal Rights party in June 1872, she urged listeners to summon the spirit of ''the men and women who barefooted trod the wintry roads of Valley Forge, blood marking their way'' (*VWR* IIB9:2). Appealing to laborers, she insisted that workers' toil generates all wealth for the employer. Thus, ''You should know that instead of this power being your master, it should be your servant since all it is it owes you'' (*VWR* IIB9:1).

Claflin Woodhull's speeches on the economic system proposed radical reforms and claimed that any indictment of the system was a "just" indictment. Speaking on "The Impending Revolution," in February 1872, in Boston and New York, she defiantly held: "I would rather be the unwilling subject of an absolute monarch than the willing slave of my own ignorance" (*VWR* IIIA2:11). She attacked the system using rhetorical questions that challenged workers to consider their role in the production of the country's wealth. She unabashedly identified those who, as landowners, stock manipulators, and industrial barons, robbed nineteenth-century America of its public wealth. In the same manner that she earlier positioned women against those institutions governed by physical and military power, she cast laborers as enslaved protagonists seeking to escape their own bondage. In structuring her arguments for economic reform, she presented examples and illustrations that evoked the frustration of working men as struggling against governmentally sanctioned monopolies, subsidies, land grants, and dividends.

Although Claflin Woodhull audaciously attacked the inequities of the economic system, she drew the greatest criticism for her speeches and writings on social freedom. Attacking the clergy for preaching the crucifixion rather than social justice in "The Impending Revolution," she identified Jesus as "a communist of the strictest sort" and herself as one of "the most extreme kind" (*VWR* IIIA2:28). In the *Weekly* of March 1871, she endorsed the licensing of prostitutes (2). Later that year in "The Principles of Social Freedom," she argued that in some cases marriage was a form of legalized prostitution whereby partners sold themselves for economic or social reasons without mutual respect and love. In this infamous speech, she reasoned that marriage must be based on *either* love *or* law. In her eyes, government had no right to interfere in a contractual relationship between parties who united or withdrew from one another. Instead, government should foster each party's freedom and pursuit of happiness; she insisted: "Marriage consists of a union resulting from love, without any regard whatever to the sanction of law, . . . and marriages of convenience . . . characterized by mutual or partial repugnance are adulterous" (*VWR* IA1:17).

Of all her pronouncements, the passage in that speech that most shocked Victorian audiences was her acceptance of the doctrine of "free love":

Yes, I am a free lover . . . I have an *inalienable*, *constitutional*, and natural right to love whom I may, to love as *long* or as *short* a period as I can, to *change* that love *everyday* if I *please*, and with *that* right neither *you* nor any *law* you can frame have *any* right to interfere. (*VWR* IA1:23–24)

Despite her explanation that she chose the concept "free love" because of its literal meaning and not to advocate promiscuity, she was attacked vehemently by the press and public. More conservative suffragists castigated her as "universally odious" for raising this "social evil question." In *Harper's Weekly*

(February 12, 1872), cartoonist Thomas Nast caricatured her as "Mrs. Satan" who was leading women astray (Sachs, 1928:150).

Despite these attacks, curious audiences flocked to hear her controversial views. An estimated 3,000 people reportedly attended the infamous Steinway Hall speech, and hundreds more tried unsucessfully to obtain admission. ELIZABETH CADY STANTON and LUCRETIA COFFIN MOTT rallied to her support, noting the hypocrisy of those who attacked her. In Claflin Woodhull's defense, Cady Stanton heralded her as "one of the ablest speakers and writers of the century, sound and radical, alike in religious and social principles. Her face, form, manners, and conversation all indicate the triumph of the moral, intellectual, spiritual, over the sensuous in her nature" (SSC, April 1, 1871).

The hypocrisy of her attackers became more apparent when the *Weekly* (November 2, 1872) disclosed that the renowned Henry Ward Beecher, minister of Plymouth Church, New York City, was having an affair with parishioner Elizabeth Tilton. Upon her return from a speaking engagement in Chicago, Claflin Woodhull and her sister Tennessee were arrested and jailed on obscenity and libel charges for publishing these accusations. Her presidential bid was abandoned during the seven months she spent in and out of jail and fighting the Reverend Anthony Comstock in the courtroom. Nonetheless, the article was a symbolic gesture of defiance at clergyman Beecher's hypocrisy in preaching purity while practicing promiscuity.

In January 1873, disguised as a Quaker, Claflin Woodhull, appeared at Cooper Institute to deliver "The Naked Truth," which refuted press and judicial charges and denounced the "ten thousand forms of domestic damnation visited upon women" (*VWR* IA3:26). Sachs wrote, "All the furies stirred with her arraignment of the courts, the press and public opinion" (1928:196) as she spoke before the transfixed crowd. At the conclusion of the hour-and-one-half speech, marshals led her to Ludlow Street Jail where she was indicted on additional obscenity charges.

By 1874, the radicalism of Claflin Woodhull's rhetoric escalated. In the *Weekly* of October 1874, she outraged opponents by endorsing woman's right to birth control. Then, in "Tried as by Fire," she addressed the ills of legally contracted marriages and the need for sex education, a speech she delivered in 1874 and 1875 to audiences estimated at 250,000 (*VWR* IA5:1). With the zeal of a religious revivalist, she boldly pointed out the inconsistencies between society's reverence for marriage and the abusive conditions of women enslaved by wedlock. With deep emotion, she spoke of "the living corpse in my breast," a metaphorical reference to an imbecile son she had borne out of her own ignorance, "because I knew no better than to surrender my maternal functions to a drunken man" (*VWR* IA5:27). She linked her own plight to that of other women existing in circumstances of legal servitude.

Eventually, the curious crowds that had thronged to hear this "demonic, Mrs. Satan" (Sachs, 1928:150) lost interest in her radical ideas. The furor surrounding the Beecher-Tilton scandal and continuing lawsuits left her wearied and destitute, the *Weekly* fell into financial distress, and Colonel Blood separated from her. Broken in spirit and exhausted by a grueling schedule of appearances and continued assaults on her character, she was persuaded to leave the United States for England in 1877.

In the third phase of her rhetorical career in England, Claflin Woodhull abandoned the radicalism of earlier periods to embrace a philosophical posture closely related to scientific positivism and spiritualist beliefs in the power of the body. She allied herself with those who accepted the scientific method as the key to knowledge and who believed in the magnetic powers of the human psyche.

After a brief respite in London, Claflin Woodhull returned to the podium to deliver a ten-part series, "The Human Body, The Temple of God," before receptive crowds in St. James Hall. Tempering her language for Victorian audiences, she spoke of the body as a spiritual instrument "for the virtuous production of healthful humanity" and implored mothers to educate their children on sexual matters (Sachs, 1928:290). She presented "The Garden of Eden" as an allegory, equating the four rivers of Eden with the incubation, birth, growth of intelligence, and millennium of civilization. In an 1880 article in the *London Court Journal*, she repudiated the doctrine of free love and those identified with it. Several years later in a libel suit against the British Museum, she clarified her opposition to "anything that binds woman against her will" (*Martin v. British Museum Trustees*, 338). Accused of contradicting previous positions, she maintained her support of marriage based on love and her opposition to the hypocrisy of those who remained together after love ceased.

In 1883, Claflin Woodhull was married to John Biddulph Martin, a wealthy London banker and member of the Royal Statistical Society. As a result, she became more involved in the British reform movement. In the late 1880s, she used pamphlets to express her support for the unpopular eugenics movement. In February 1888, she published "Stirpiculture, or The Scientific Propagation of the Human Race," in which she examined the tenets of the pseudoscientific Malthusian theory. Interspersing passages from the writings of St. Paul with Hindu teachings on the spiritual nature of the human body, she argued against the perpetuation of hereditary disease and suffering. Reasoning by analogy, she indicted society for its attention to animal breeding and its inattention to the same principles among humans. Claiming the significance of maternal influence on prenatal development and the government's responsibility for human welfare, she proposed a program of procreative education that would serve women in particular and humankind in general. In "The Rapid Multiplication of the Unfit," she used inductive reasoning and the testimony of physiologists and Darwinians to conclude that "The best minds of to-day have accepted the fact that if superior people are desired, they must be bred; and if imbeciles, criminals, paupers, and otherwise unfit are undesirable citizens they must not be bred" (*VWR* IB7:38).

Still concerned with economic inequities and somewhat knowledgeable about the principles of finance, Claflin Martin endorsed a fixed currency in pamphlets, "Humanitarian Money" and "The Financial Crisis in America." Between 1892 and 1901, with the editorial assistance of her daughter Zula Maud, she wrote regularly on these and other reforms in her newly established monthly, the *Humanitarian*. She devoted the monthly to examination of the social and scientific questions confronting humanity, proposing that the magazine offer a dialectical forum independent of any sect or party and void of distinctions of race and creed. Tempered by age and perhaps by social position but steadfastly dedicated to woman's rights, she adopted a tone more typical of an idealized quest for knowledge than of an act of defiance. In the foreword to the August 1893 issue she wrote:

The regeneration of humanity will not be complete until the light of knowledge shall have dawned on the darkness of ignorance and superstition. . . . The pioneer of the dawn must be the idealized woman, who through her perfected offspring will guide man in his aspirations to higher aims of life. She will henceforth hold aloft the crown of science, and will lead the nations of the world in their march towards the goal. (ii)

She reprinted many of her earlier speeches, including "A Lecture on Constitutional Equality," "The Principles of Social Freedom," and "The Human Body," in an attempt to circulate her ideas more widely. Between 1895 and 1896, in a series on "The Pharmacy of the Soul," she returned to some of her earlier spiritualist beliefs about the body's magnetism and untapped natural power.

At the turn of the century, after the death of her husband, she retired to the Martins' Cotswold estate where she died in June 1927. Ever the ardent reformer, she spent her last years engaged in bettering the educational and economic conditions of women in the surrounding countryside. She founded a coeducational village school, established the International Agricultural Club to train young women in horticulture and animal husbandry, and opened a lyceum for the discussion of English-American relations.

CONCLUSION

Throughout her life, Victoria Claflin Woodhull advocated political, social, and economic reforms with revolutionary zeal. Ostracized by a society more Victorian than farsighted, she persevered amid public persecution. Her words, radical by every nineteenth-century measure, urged the creation of a society based on political equality and social justice and economically beneficial to all. Because of her stridency and perceived impropriety, she was victimized and shunned by a society almost entirely unwilling to condone her advocacy of radical change.

SOURCES

The Victoria C. Woodhull Papers, Southern Illinois University, Morris Library Archives, and the Schlesinger Library, Radcliffe, hold speeches and writings. Pamphlets, correspondence, and speech announcements are found in the Isabella Beecher Hooker Papers, Stowe-Day Library, Hartford, Connecticut; Olympia Brown Papers, Schlesinger Library; Martha Coffin Wright and Lucretia Mott Papers, Sophia Smith Collection, Smith College (SSC); and Ohio Historical Society Library Archives, the New York Historical Society, the New York Public Library, the Fawcett Library, London, and the British Museum. Other primary sources are:

"Martin and Wife v. British Museum Trustees." 10 *Times Law Report* 215. London: Queens' Bench Division. 1894.

Martin, Victoria Woodhull. *The Human Body: the Temple of God, or The Philosophy of Sociology.* London, 1890.

The Victoria Woodhull Reader. Ed. Madeleine B. Stern. Weston, Mass.: M & S Press, 1974. (This work is paginated only by item. It is divided into Parts, designated by Roman numerals, which are divided into sections, designated by capital letters. In each section, items are designated by Arabic numerals; page numbers are those of the original publication. Hence, a quotation identified as IIA2:5 refers to Part II, Section A, item 2, page 5.)

Selected Critical Studies

Condray, Suzanne. "Church State and Press: Institutional Attacks on the Rationality of Victoria Woodhull's 1872 Presidential Bid"; "Victoria C. Woodhull and the Suffragists." Unpublished papers, Denison University, 1990.

Ek, Richard A. "Victoria Woodhull and the Pharisees." *Journalism Quarterly* 49 (Autumn 1972):453–459.

Madson, Lynda Phillips. "The Rhetoric, Strategy, and Style of a Liberationist: Victoria C. Woodhull 1838–1927." Ph.D. diss., Ohio University, 1974. AAC 0294397

Stapen, Candyce Homnick. "The Novel Form and *Woodhull & Claflin's Weekly*, 1870–1876, A Little Magazine Edited by Women and Published for Suffragists, Socialists, Free Lovers, and Other Radicals." Ph.D. diss., University of Maryland, 1979. AAC 8001656

Selected Biographies

Brough, James. *The Vixens: A Biography of Victoria and Tennessee Claflin.* New York: Simon & Schuster, 1980.

Johnston, Johanna. *Mrs. Satan: The Incredible Saga of Victoria C. Woodhull.* New York: G. P. Putnam's Sons, 1967.

Kisner, Arlene, ed. *Woodhull & Claflin's Weekly, The Lives and Writings of Notorious Victoria Woodhull and Her Sister Tennessee Claflin.* Washington, N. J.: Times Change, 1972.

Legge, Madeleine. *"Two Noble Women, Nobly Planned."* Victoria C. Woodhull Martin. *Tennessee Claflin, Lady Cook.* London: Phelp Bros., 1893.

Marberry, M. Marion. *Vicky; a Biography of Victoria C. Woodhull.* New York: Funk & Wagnalls, 1967.

Martin, Victoria Woodhull. *A Fragmentary Record of Public Work Done in America, 1871–1877.* London; G. Norman & Son, 1887.

Meade, Marion. *Free Woman: The Life and Times of Victoria W. Woodhull*. New York: Alfred A. Knopf, 1976.

Sachs, Emanie. *The Terrible Siren: Victoria Woodhull*. New York: Harper & Brothers, 1928.

Stern, Madeleine Bettina. *We the Women: Career Firsts of Nineteenth-Century America*. New York: Burt Franklin Reprints, 1974.

Tilton, Theodore. *Victoria C. Woodhull: A Biographical Sketch*. New York: Golden Age Tract No. 3, 1871.

Chronology of Major Speeches

"Memorial of Victoria C. Woodhull." December 19, 1870. *HWS* 2:443; *VWR* IIA1:1.

"Speech Before Judiciary Committee." U.S. House of Representatives, January 2, 1871. *HWS* 2:444–445; *VWR* IIA1:1–6.

"A Lecture on Constitutional Equality." Lincoln Hall, Washington, D.C., February 16, 1871. *VWR* IIA2:1–33; *WSBH*:108–129.

"Great Social Problem of Labor and Capital." Reform Labor League, Cooper Institute, New York City, May 8, 1871. *VWR* IIIA1:1–29.

"A New Political Party and a New Party Platform." NWSA convention, Apollo Hall, May 11, 12, 1871. *VWR* IIB6:1–8.

"Principles of Finance." Cooper Institute, New York City, August 3, 1871. *VWR* IIIB4:1–29.

"The Principles of Social Freedom." Steinway Hall, New York City, November 20, 1871. *VWR* IA1:1–44; *OW*:227–251.

"Carpenter and Cartter Reviewed." NWSA Convention, January 10, 1872, Lincoln Hall, Washington, D.C. *VWR* IIA3:1–36.

"Impending Revolution." Music Hall, Boston, February 1, 1872; New York Academy of Music, February 20, 1872. *VWR* IIIA2:1–39.

"Speech [nomination acceptance], Ratification Meeting of the Equal Rights Party." June 22, 1872. *VWR* IIB9:1–2.

"Naked Truth; or, the Situation Reviewed!" Cooper Institute, New York City, January 9, 1873. *VWR* IA3:1–26.

"Reformation or Revolution, Which?" Cooper Institute, New York City, October 17, 1873. *VWR* IIIA3:1–39.

"Tried As by Fire: or, the True and the False, Socially." Various audiences, 1874. *VWR* IA5:1–44.

"The Human Body, the Temple of God." St. James Hall, London, December 1877. *Humanitarian* 2 (March 24, 1893):49–55.

"Stirpiculture; or, The Scientific Propagation of the Human Race." London, February 1888. *VWR* IB6:1–31.

"The Garden of Eden," London, 1890. Excerpts, Sachs, 1928:292–293.

"The Rapid Multiplication of the Unfit." London, 1891. *VWR* IB7:1–39.

"Humanitarian Money: The Unsolved Riddle." London, 1892. *VWR* IIIB5:1–26.

"Pharmacy of the Soul." *Humanitarian* 6 (September 1895):172–6; 6 (October 1895):249–255; 6 (November 1895):328–336; 7 (January 1896):7–13.

"The Financial Crisis in America." *Humanitarian* 7 (November 1896):330–339. *VWR* IIIB6:1–10.

LAURA CLAY
(1849–1941), a southern voice for woman's rights

JOHN M. MURPHY

For forty years, Laura Clay was an active woman's rights advocate, Democratic party politician, and social reformer in the state of Kentucky and throughout the South. She has seldom been recognized for her accomplishments, however, because of her philosophical commitment to a strict construction of the Constitution. Like many southern Democrats, Clay's political positions flowed directly from her view that the powers of government should be strictly limited. She supported woman suffrage as a necessary check on the power of patriarchal government to oppress women. Her adherence to the doctrine of states' rights, however, led her to oppose the Susan B. Anthony (later the nineteenth) Amendment to the Constitution enfranchising women because, while granting women the vote, it gave the federal government unchecked powers to supervise state elections. This position resulted in her estrangement from the movement's mainstream. Nonetheless, she deserves critical attention because she articulated an alternative rationale for woman's rights, a justification grounded primarily in a profound distrust of unchecked power of any sort.

BACKGROUND

Clay was born on February 9, 1849, to a prominent and affluent Kentucky family. Her father Cassius M. Clay was a cousin of Henry Clay and an outspoken abolitionist who later served Presidents Andrew Johnson and Ulysses S. Grant as ambassador to Russia. Her mother Mary Jane Warfield was from a prominent family in Lexington and was an active supporter of woman's rights. After Ambassador Clay deserted his family, which resulted in a messy, public divorce in 1878, Mary Warfield Clay rejuvenated the family farms and provided for the education of her daughters. Clay's older sisters married late in life and served the cause of woman suffrage with distinction; Mary B. Clay, for instance, was AWSA president in 1883–1884 (*HWS* 4:407).

Laura Clay followed the family tradition of independent thought and devotion to the public good. She remained single, dividing her time between suffrage work and shrewd management of a 245-acre farm. She graduated from the Sayre Female Institute in Lexington, Kentucky, a school for girls with an unusually broad curriculum; she studied mathematics, history, English literature, and philosophy in addition to the standard women's classes. She attended a finishing school in New York, and she later attended the University of Michigan for a year and the State College of Kentucky (now Transylvania University) for a semester. Because of her growing commitment to the woman suffrage movement, she never finished her college degree (Fuller, 1975).

Her parents' divorce clearly influenced Clay. Under Kentucky law, despite his open adultery and violent disposition, Cassius Clay could have won control of his children and all of the couple's financial assets, including the Warfield properties inherited by his wife. He chose not to do so, but his unlimited power under Kentucky law must have shocked his youngest daughter. Clay dated her involvement in the woman's rights movement to her decision to help found the Kentucky Equal Rights Association (ERA) in 1888. From then on, she worked to change these laws, win the vote for women, and bring about a number of other reforms. She was president of the Kentucky ERA from 1888 to 1912, a member of the WCTU, a speaker for the Woman's Peace party from 1915 to 1917, auditor of NAWSA from 1896 to 1911, a delegate to the Democratic National Convention in 1920, a state Senate nominee for the Democratic party in 1923, and a speaker for Al Smith in 1928. A devout Episcopalian, she campaigned for a larger role for women in the church. She also spearheaded successful efforts to make the University of the South coeducational. She died at age ninety-two on June 29, 1941 (Fuller, 1975).

Although Kate Gordon, a Louisiana suffragist, and others were active suffrage campaigners in the South, Clay was the preeminent spokeswoman for the southern wing of the woman's rights movement (IWSM, 185). While she participated in the national movement and was devoted to SUSAN B. ANTHONY, her political philosophy led her to break with the second generation of suffrage leaders, such as NAWSA presidents CARRIE LANE CHAPMAN CATT and ANNA HOWARD SHAW. Her stance as a traditional southern Democrat provided the foundation for her rhetorical action.

CLAY AND THE AMERICAN SOUTH

Clay not only spoke for her region but also reflected its culture. Despite (or because of) her Republican father, she was a classic southern Democrat. She envisioned the role of the federal government as limited and spoke constantly of the need for checks and balances on all power (a position that may have evolved from her recognition of her father's unlimited power over her mother). In fact, much of her justification for woman suffrage came from this philosophical foundation. In 1913, she told a reporter for the *Knoxville Sentinel*:

I hold that human nature is dual in all its elements and requires the influence of both sexes for the best development. It is this dual element, this mixture of the man and woman, this establishment of checks and balances that we need in politics at present, and woman suffrage offers it.

She saw a woman's ability to vote as a check on the power of men to abuse women. As she argued in 1919:

For 364 days of the year, not only in homes and in churches, but in the factories, the shops, the offices, in all the busy marts of labor, women are found side by side with men. Is it right, is it wise, that on the 365th day, election day, men only go to the ballot box, and by their votes alone make the laws which control all the conditions of women's work, its hours of toil, its protection from dangerous machinery, the sanitation of its surroundings, in short, all the things which go to make up their industrial weal or woe? ("Women and the Ballot")

Clay saw the ideal government as one limited in power by a variety of checks and balances, that allowed states and localities to make as many of their own decisions as possible, and that acted primarily to create a level playing field between appropriate contending interests. She supported progressive reforms, such as pure food and drug laws, because she felt industrial interests had abused their power and needed to be checked. She opposed the Anthony Amendment because it would expand federal power without any corresponding check. In other words, as a southern Democrat, she was an advocate of limited government, and her outlook was similar to that of predecessors such as Patrick Henry and successors such as William Fulbright and Ernest Hollings.

CLAY'S RHETORIC

As might be expected of an active rhetor, Clay developed a "stock" speech in support of woman suffrage that reflected her political philosophy. Her speeches were characterized primarily by their chronological structure and deductive argument. She began with the founding of the country, detailed its political and economic evolution, and concluded with a vision of the future. Naturally, she explained the place of women at each stage of this history. Accounts of the past revealed the principles of natural rights that animated the founders, values that she used in the second section of the speech to construct deductive arguments that supported woman suffrage. She generally concluded with the advantages that it would bring to the country in the future.

Almost invariably, Clay began her speeches with a discussion of the nation's founding. This strategy established a woman's natural right to vote. In her 1895 speech to the South Carolina Constitutional Convention, she praised the state's "long record of brilliant statesmanship" and argued that the principles for political action were to be found "in the old bill of rights." Similarly, at Kentucky's 1890 Constitutional Convention, she spoke movingly of her trip to "our Mother State, Virginia." She detailed her visits to the "old church in which Patrick Henry spoke those immortal words, 'Give me liberty or give me death.' " What "thrilled most through my heart," however, were the words of the "Burgesses of Virginia" guaranteeing " 'a firm adherence to justice, and a frequent adherence to fundamental principles' " ("Elections"). Those principles, she felt, demanded woman suffrage. As she noted in 1919, women "have never advanced any new theory of government in defense of their claims." Instead, "they stand loyally and firmly on the fundamental principles of government accepted by our people for more than a century and a quarter of glorious national life" ("Women and the Ballot").

Clay then drew on the traditional principles of the Republic to make deductive arguments in support of woman suffrage in the second section of the speech. She noted that "men had come into their heritage of political liberty prior to women," but that those rights must now be applied to women. She argued:

"Taxation without representation is tyranny." Women are taxed. "Governments derive their just powers from the consent of the governed." Women are governed. The demand for suffrage for women is not a revolution; it is only an evolution in the application of these principles. ("Women and the Ballot")

Consistent with her political philosophy, she reasoned that the Declaration of Independence and the Constitution had guaranteed women certain "inalienable rights." Men had denied those rights in an unreasonable exercise of power. In fact, she claimed that "the burden of proof lies upon those who deny their [natural rights] application to women" ("Women and the Ballot").

In her discussion of the current condition of women, Clay also used economic premises to support her political claims for equality. The new economic status of women demanded that they have the vote to protect themselves from exploitation. She noted that, in the past, women had worked primarily in the home, but that economic changes had thrust women "into the world of law and politics." The Industrial Revolution had taken women's work out of the home and into the factory or, in modern terms, out of the private sphere and into the public one. She emphasized the new economic situation through a vivid use of synecdoche: "Could a woman of a century ago dream that her spinning wheel, the companion of her daily toil, would first be relegated to the garret, and then brought forth as an antique and become an idle ornament in the home of her great-granddaughter?" ("Women and the Ballot").

This economic revolution had brought "seven millions of women" into the marketplace, "most of them young, many of them receiving very small wages, all of them withdrawn from the protection of the home, which had been the safeguard for all the preceding generations of women" ("Women and the Ballot"). Clay then claimed that, with "no commensurate extension of the protection of the law to replace that which has been lost to them," these women were helpless. Again, she denounced unchecked power, of employers in this case, and argued that suffrage would be the remedy. She used the changes wrought by the Industrial Revolution to support her political arguments for equality.

In the third section of the speech, she refuted opposition views of the horror woman suffrage would bring and offered her own vision of the future. She made frequent use of humor to demonstrate the absurdity of opponents' claims. Critics argued, for instance, that babies would suffer as women voted. According to the *Knoxville Sentinel* report of February 1, 1911, Clay, like ANNA HOWARD SHAW in 1915 (*MCSH* 2:451), dealt humorously with this issue. She related the story of an election in Colorado where a "quiet-looking young man" stood outside of the polling place and held the babies of several women voters. Bemused, an observer finally asked his identity: "And the answer came back, 'Why that's one of the candidates.' " In the same report, in response to the claim that women had no time to vote, she stated: "Nothing is so labor-saving as a vote, properly applied." In a more serious vein, she maintained that woman suffrage would ensure a brighter future for the country. In "Women and the Ballot," she argued from analogy by comparing the doubts of many that the American Revolution could succeed to the doubts about woman suffrage. The United States had written a glorious page of history in 1776, she claimed, and it could do the same again. She also compared voting to education, arguing that many had tried to stop women from going to college and that those fears had proven groundless. Finally, she portrayed a future in which the "sharp eyes of housekeepers" would force public officials to keep the streets clean, to enforce public health ordinances, and to pass pure food legislation.

Clay's rhetoric in support of woman suffrage was ideally adapted to her southern, conservative audience. Her robust humor and refutation were familiar to a generation of audiences used to the political rhetoric of Populist and racist "Pitchfork" Ben Tillman, South Carolina governor (1890–1894) and U.S. senator (1895–1918), and others. Moreover, her proud heritage (she was often introduced as Henry Clay's cousin) protected her from the disdain that otherwise might have resulted from these "unwomanly" tactics. Constant repetition of the political heritage of the South and the nation made her arguments attractive to conservatives. Her economic arguments made sense to a "new," industrial South. Most important, she consistently articulated her arguments in the language of states' rights. While that theme undergirded her "stock" speeches, it was most apparent in the three major crises of her political career.

The first challenge was the question of race. As a Southerner of her time, Clay believed in the superiority of whites. She had some sympathy with the successful campaign by southern states to disfranchise their African-American populations in the 1880s through the early 1900s, but she doubted the constitutionality of such efforts. Thus, she supported the enfranchisement of educated women, regardless of race. She faced the task of persuading white men, engaged in the work of denying the ballot to nonwhites, to grant educated women the vote. Second, she felt that state-by-state suffrage campaigns were the best way to proceed. In the early 1900s, she sought to persuade the movement and the national leadership to continue with the state campaigns and deemphasize the national amendment drive. Finally, after women's enfranchisement, she actively campaigned for the Democratic party during the 1920s, one of the most difficult periods in its history. As she crafted her rhetorical responses to each one of these issues, she was guided by her distrust of unlimited power.

It is easy to classify Clay as a typical racist and to characterize her discourse in those terms. In truth, she was a white supremacist although her views were more complex than those of most of her fellow Southerners. She did not regard nonwhites as equals; she was maternalistic, regarding African-Americans as rebellious children who, through education and Christian charity, could be "brought up" to be responsible citizens. For example, throughout her life, she contributed money and time to the self-help programs of an African-American Episcopal church in Lexington. This racism can in no way be excused; at the same time, these attitudes created different policies and an alternative rhetoric to that of firebrands such as Kate Gordon of Louisiana (IWSM:185–196).

She perceived the problem of race in the South as having two dimensions. First, she felt that the vast majority of southern African-Americans were not up to the responsibility of voting and government. As she wrote in a newspaper column in 1890:

What the South has a right to complain of is not that negroes have a representation at the ballot box, but that they have a representation all out of proportion to the intelligence and virtue they bring to the support of Republican government, and the true problem set before the South is how she may restore a due supremacy of the more highly developed race without corrupting the ballot box, or repudiating the principles of true Democracy, which defends the right of every class to representation. ("The Race Question Again")

Clay's racial attitudes were evident here; whites were superior but not inherently better, simply "more highly developed." Her logic dictated that representation should be based not only on class, but also on "the intelligence and virtue" that various groups brought to governance. Currently, she argued, the sizable electoral power of African-Americans outweighed the "intelligence and virtue" of white Southerners. Thus, although Blacks "were being developed," as it were, she felt that whites should dominate the electoral process.

The practical question of a means to this end was the second question that troubled Clay. She reasoned that schemes for the disfranchisement of the non-white population would be found unconstitutional or, in accordance with Section 2 of the Fourteenth Amendment, southern representation in Congress would be reduced. In addition, her elitism was partly colorblind. She concluded that there were a large number of illiterate whites who did not deserve the vote; thus, she proposed an educational test. She argued, however, that the Supreme Court would not accept any restrictions on current voters. Qualified woman suffrage, then, would fit the needs of the time. The "best" women would receive the vote; in this way, she sought to tie woman suffrage to white supremacy. She acknowledged that educated African-American women would receive the vote, but in "The Race Question Again" she argued:

The white men, reinforced by the educated white women could "snow under" the negro vote in every State, and the white race would maintain its supremacy without corrupting or intimidating the negroes, a present method that is fraught with reactionary danger to the integrity of our institutions.

The implication was clear. Failure of the South to act on woman suffrage would lead to federal action, which would result in the end of white supremacy.

Unfortunately for Clay, she miscalculated the political situation during the

1890s in two important ways. First, white Northerners were more than willing to reduce African-Americans to second-class citizenship, regardless of the dubious nature of various schemes for doing so. In 1896, the *Plessy v. Ferguson* decision created the separate but equal doctrine. In 1898, the *Williams v. Mississippi* decision validated the most egregious southern plan to deny African-Americans the vote, the 1890 Mississippi Constitution. Woman suffrage was not required to ensure white supremacy (Fuller, 1975).

Second, her elitist attitudes contrasted sharply with the growing power of populists in the South. These leaders wanted no part of qualified suffrage, which threatened their often illiterate political base, and they came to power in many southern states during the 1890s. Her efforts to bring about woman suffrage by linking it to white supremacy failed.

Despite the defeat of woman suffrage by a variety of southern constitutional conventions throughout the 1890s, Clay remained convinced that a federal amendment granting woman suffrage would be wrong. At various times, she proposed alternatives, arguing, for instance, that Congress already possessed the authority to pass a law enfranchising women. As the federal amendment gained momentum, however, she faced a personal and political crisis. Although she wavered somewhat in the early twentieth century, she generally remained opposed to a federal amendment. She decided to campaign against ratification of the Nineteenth Amendment, despite a lifetime of work for woman suffrage. Her views alienated the vast majority of her former colleagues and damaged her historical standing in the movement. Given her perspective (and other conflicts with ANNA HOWARD SHAW), she was defeated for reelection as auditor for NAWSA in 1911 and, thereafter, gradually withdrew from the national movement.

Clay built her case against the Nineteenth Amendment with arguments based on principle and expediency. In a letter to the people's forum of the *Lexington Herald* (February 25, 1919), she detailed her objections. First, she claimed that the doctrine of states' rights was an inviolable principle of U.S. governance. She argued that woman suffrage "in the Anthony Amendment is its minor proposition." She contended that the second, major proposition of the amendment violated states' rights because "it plainly adds to the enumerated powers of the Federal Government one of the rights originally reserved to the states" by giving Congress the power to supervise state elections. Admittedly, the Fifteenth Amendment did the same, but, she argued, it was passed only as a result of military coercion; ten southern states were occupied by federal forces and compelled to ratify it. The Fifteenth Amendment lacked legitimacy; it put in only a "thin wedge" to transfer one of the reserved powers. The "Anthony Amendment drives in the wedge still further." The second section of the amendment, she argued, "grants to Congress a new power never contemplated by the framers of the Constitution and one for which no Constitutional check is provided" ("People's Forum").

In her view, the consequences were potentially catastrophic. Congress could manipulate state election laws until they received whatever state legislation they wanted. Clay specifically cited the Force Bill of 1870, which was drawn to enforce the Fifteenth Amendment, as an example of the problems that could occur. She argued that that bill did not help "the negro man in his constitutional right to vote." Instead, it "quickly became an instrument to exploit the States subjected to it for the advantage of the party holding the majority in Congress and not the will and interests of the majority of the people of the states." In other words, the amendment made Congress "the most autocratic legislative body in any constitutional government" ("People's Forum").

Clay also claimed that the Anthony Amendment was not the most expedient way to gain woman suffrage. She argued that, when

fifteen states have full suffrage already and twenty-five have partial suffrage by state action; when women can vote for 336 out of 531 presidential electors and every political party of 1916 declared for woman suffrage, a federal amendment is too late to be [of] prime importance for woman suffrage, whatever it may have been in 1878 when it was first proposed. ("People's Forum")

Moreover, in a speech delivered to the 1916 NAWSA Convention, she maintained that ratification of the Anthony Amendment was unlikely. Arguing that the Nineteenth was a repetition of the Fifteenth, she did some arithmetic: "It is hardly to be supposed that the ten coerced States now will subscribe voluntarily to a principle which they rejected formerly; and if even three of the eight others which refused to ratify the Fifteenth Amendment remain of the same mind, the Anthony Amendment cannot be ratified."

On the grounds of principle and expediency, then, Clay urged the movement to deemphasize the Anthony Amendment. Unfortunately, the issue of states' rights *had* been decided by force from 1861 to 1865, and her views had lost. Argument was unlikely to reverse the outcome. When her effort to persuade the movement failed, she argued against ratification. That effort also failed.

As is evident by now, Clay was always a committed partisan of the Democratic party, even when she could not vote. Her party identification was so strong that she even foreswore her opposition to the Anthony Amendment briefly when Woodrow Wilson endorsed it. She was elected as an at-large delegate to the 1920 Democratic Convention, and in the midst of the long deadlock between James A. Cox and William G. McAdoo, she was nominated for the presidency and received one vote. She was the first woman so honored by a major party convention (*New York Times*, June 30, 1941).

Clay was concerned less with honors than with concrete progress. She felt that many women, particularly young women, were not using their right to vote, and she cast about for a means to inspire them. She decided to run for the Kentucky Senate in 1923, although she faced formidable odds because her district was heavily Republican.

She won the Democratic primary without opposition, but her position in favor of parimutuel betting machines doomed her in the general election. She argued in favor of these machines for reasons based, as usual, in principle and practicality. She argued on principle that the decision to make a bet was a moral choice that "must be left between a man's [sic] conscience and his God. Any attempt to do so by civil government is a usurpation of the authority of conscience abhorrent to our governmental principles." In addition, as a practical farmer and former financial officer of the NAWSA, Clay saw the revenue possibilities in such machines. She argued that, under the current system, gambling was "uniformly united with cheating" and outside of "police guardianship." The machines would control the cheating and allow legislators to place taxes on the machines. She claimed: "It is the aim of legislators to place taxation upon the unnecessary expenses or the luxuries of the people; and betting in parimutuel machines certainly comes under that head." Unfortunately, her Republican opponent painted her as an opponent of family values. She lost the election, but gained public acclamation for her stirring run for office at the age of seventy-four.

Her last hurrah as a politician began in 1928 when she campaigned in support of Al Smith's presidential candidacy. Clay's devotion to the Democratic party was in evidence here. She had been a member of the WCTU for many years, although it seems clear that she spoke about temperance primarily in order to argue for suffrage ("A New Tool"). Nonetheless, it came as a surprise to many Kentuckians when she announced her support for the "wet" Al Smith. She simply argued that prohibition had been a mistake and should be repealed (Fuller, 1975).

Clay's extant speech from that campaign, however, avoided the issue. Instead, she argued for Smith based on the philosophy and performance of each party, and then refuted the major attacks on him. She reminded her southern audiences of the traditional Democratic party support for states' rights and argued that Smith hewed to that line. She scored the Republican party in the strongest terms for the Teapot Dome scandal and their betrayal of the "ages old law 'Thou shalt not steal.' "

In a most impressive move, Clay concluded the speech with an eloquent plea for religious toleration. Evidently, her reading of the constitutional imperative for separation of church and state led her to develop a strong argument in support of Smith. She opened the section with a touch of humor:

And then, Gov. Smith is a Catholic. Now as I am an old dyed-in-the-wool Protestant Episcopalian, I would greatly prefer that he should be an Episcopalian, or even a member of another Protestant denomination. But he is a Catholic; that is the faith in which he tries to walk humbly with his God.

She then returned to her political philosophy, noting that "I am a Jeffersonian Democrat," and, using Jefferson's familiar stance in support of toleration, established the right of religious freedom. Citing sources ranging from Jefferson's

Virginia statute of religious freedom to the U.S. Constitution, she argued that to reject Smith for religious reasons was to be un-American. She angrily refuted charges that the Pope would run the country or that children would have to go to Catholic schools. She said that "we are not going to elect a dictator in November, but a President." In sharp words, she charged that only "snakes" would spread such whispers. She concluded that

religious intolerance just now is abroad in the land. It is an evil passion of the heart which dies hard. In this campaign, it is hiding itself behind many disguises, diverting attention from the main issues of the campaign so that even people who would be ashamed of it if they recognized it seem liable to be led astray by it. When it is seen without any disguise, it is a hateful thing, despised by all. This campaign is a call to every true American of whatever party to stand firmly for the principle of religious freedom.

At seventy-nine, she had lost little of her fire.

Although Smith lost, Clay continued to campaign against prohibition. Five years after the election, she was elected to the state convention that met to consider the Twenty-first amendment. In her last major public appearance, she was honored with the convention's temporary chair and, predictably, denounced the Eighteenth Amendment as a violation of states' rights.

CONCLUSION

While Laura Clay has generally been dismissed as a regional figure, her rhetoric is significant for its philosophical grounding, its success within her native region, and its relationship to the mainstream movement. She articulated an alternative rationale for woman suffrage based on an essentially Madisonian view of the necessary checks and balances on governmental power. Men held unlimited political and economic sway, power that needed to be checked by woman suffrage. Unlike many suffragists (and other reformers), she held to that philosophy even when the temptation existed to use the power of the federal government for the good of her cause. Perhaps as a result of her southern heritage and the experience of Reconstruction, she never forgot that the power wielded by the government was a double-edged sword. It could be used to help women today, but also to hurt them tomorrow. Thus, she fought consistently to limit the writ of government as much as was humanly possible. More so than other suffrage advocates, she saw the vote not so much as the means to achieve power, but as a protection from power.

Clay's articulation of this philosophy led to success within her native region, particularly in Kentucky. She was undeniably effective in achieving many changes in the status of women. The Married Women's Property Act (1894) and a co-guardianship act (1910) ensured that no woman would ever again be placed in the horrendous position of Mary Warfield Clay. Her efforts played a major role in creating a coeducational state university system and in obtaining better treatment for women in prisons, hospitals, and other state institutions. Finally, her run for office and her influential political career blazed the trail for many women to follow (Fuller, 1975).

Clay's limited effectiveness on the national level, however, was also due to her political philosophy. Woman suffrage in the South was inextricably entwined with states' rights. The people of the South held strong views on states' rights, and she ably represented those views to the unreceptive national leadership of the movement. Unfortunately for her and her constituency, major movement leaders rejected her fears of federal power in favor of using that power to gain the ultimate goal of suffrage.

Finally, Clay's rhetoric reveals, more clearly than most, the racism of the woman suffrage movement. She adapted her arguments to her native South, but found that her views were welcome in most of the country. Her rhetoric of the 1890s anticipates the movement's gradual abandonment of any pretense of sympathy toward African-Americans in the early 1900s (IWSM:199–205). Her racism cannot be excused, but it was not especially rare among suffragists. However, she should not be remembered solely for these views. She was one of the "foot soldiers" that every movement needs; she spoke in virtually every state suffrage campaign whose leaders asked her to appear. She was an inexhaustible rhetor, even in her late seventies during the campaign for Al Smith. While she was not an Elizabeth Cady Stanton or a Susan B. Anthony, Laura Clay spoke simply, often, and well for her gender, for her party, and for her state.

SOURCES

Scholars of rhetoric must rely almost entirely on the Laura Clay Papers (LCP), University of Kentucky, Lexington. Her work occasionally appeared in the women's journals of the day, copies of which are found in her voluminous scrapbooks. The collection also contains a large number of letters between Clay and most of the major figures in the woman suffrage movement.

Selected Biographical Materials

Boyer, Paul S. "Clay, Laura." *NAW* 1:346–348.
Fuller, Paul E. "Laura Clay." *Encyclopedia of Southern History*. Eds. David C. Roller and Robert Tyman. Baton Rouge: Louisiana State University Press, 1979, p. 238.
Fuller, Paul E. *Laura Clay and the Woman's Rights Movement*. Lexington: University Press of Kentucky, 1975.
"Miss Laura Clay, Noted Suffragist." *New York Times* (June 30, 1941):17.

Chronology of Major Works

"Miss Clay on Kentucky Law." [1890s]. LCP, Box 17.
"The Race Question Again." *Kentucky Gazette*, April 1890. LCP, Box 17, Scrapbook.
"Elections." December 12, 1890. *Proceedings and Debates in the Convention Assembled*

at Frankfort, on the eighth day of September, 1890, to adopt, amend or change
the Constitution of the State of Kentucky. 2:2090–2093. Frankfort, Ky.: E. Polk
Johnson, 1890.

"Argument from Bible Teachings." Address, 1894 NAWSA Convention. *Woman's*
Tribune (February 20, 1894). LCP, Box 17, Scrapbook.

"Miss Clara M. [Laura] Clay's Speech." 1895 South Carolina Constitutional Convention,
Columbia, South Carolina. *Weekly News and Courier* [Greenville, S.C.]. September 25, 1895. LCP, Box 17, Scrapbook.

"All Women Have Vote in Next Ten Years." Speech excerpt and interview with Laura
Clay. *Knoxville Sentinel* (February 1, 1913). LCP, Box 16, Scrapbook 1.

"A New Tool." Address, WCTU banquet in Lexington, Kentucky, February 11, 1913.
LCP, Box 16.

"NAWSA Speech." Atlantic City, N.J., September 1916. LCP, Box 10.

"War Savings Bonds." Delivered throughout June 1917. LCP, Box 12.

"Women and the Ballot." February 1919 address [appears to be "stock" speech for
woman suffrage]. LCP, Box 11.

"Sees Link Between Two Measures." *Lexington Herald*, February 16, 1919. LCP, Box
11.

"People's Forum." *Lexington Herald*, February 25, 1919. LCP, Box 11.

"The Citizens Committee for a State Suffrage Amendment: Open Letter to the Public."
June 12, 1919. LCP, Box 11.

"Need of Self-Expression." Address, Hamilton College, December 1919. LCP, Box 11.

"Parimutuel Machines." October 1923. LCP, Box 12.

"Why I Am Going to Vote for Al Smith." October 1928. LCP, Box 12.

"Why I Am a Democrat." *Democratic Woman's Journal.* December 1929, LCP, Box
12.

MARY CLYENS LEASE

(1850–1933), "raising hell": for Populism and woman's rights

THOMAS R. BURKHOLDER

"What you farmers need to do is raise less corn and more hell!" Thus, we are told, Mary Clyens Lease admonished Kansas farmers in 1890. According to Katherine Clinton, "every account of Populist history mentions this female orator. Yet her fame rests largely on [that] single piece of advice. . . . Ironically, Lease twice denied ever having made the famous statement" (1969:52). None-theless, through ignorance or perhaps a simple desire to tell a good story, his-torians and rhetoricians alike seized on the line and created a legend only slightly larger than the life of this remarkable woman. The advice she "allegedly gave to Kansas farmers," said O. Gene Clanton, "has come down to the present time undiminished, and is remembered by even the most casual student of American history" (1968, 190).

Despite Clyens Lease's notoriety as an orator, primarily as a leading voice of Populism in Kansas and throughout the nation, but also as an advocate of wom-an's rights and woman suffrage, until 1988 (Burkholder, 1988) no detailed analysis of her discourse existed, nor was there a comprehensive collection of her speeches and essays. Populist rhetors as a group, however, have been studied (Ecroyd, 1973, 1980; Gunderson, 1940). Her speeches and essays are scattered through unindexed copies of old newspapers, and, when located, they are often fragments rather than complete texts. Nevertheless, analysis of those texts reveals that Clyens Lease was a rhetor of considerable sophistication and wit and a formidable debater and campaigner with the ability to adapt her message to a variety of situations.

BACKGROUND

Mary Elizabeth Clyens was born in Ridgeway, Pennsylvania, on September 11, 1850, the sixth of eight children of Joseph P. and Mary Elizabeth Murray Clyens, Irish Catholics who immigrated sometime after 1842 (Paulson, *NAW* 2:380; Clanton, 1968, gives 1853 as her birth date). In 1871, she moved to Osage Mission, Kansas, where she taught briefly at St. Ann's Academy for girls (Blumberg, 1978:3). In 1873, she married Charles L. Lease, a local pharmacist. In 1874, the couple moved to Denison, Texas. There, she accepted the invitation of Sarah Acheson, wife of her husband's employer, to join the WCTU. "She was asked to speak at one of their meetings," Dorothy Rose Blumberg reported. "Her eloquence was the surprise of the evening and marked the first step toward her future career as orator and advocate" (1978:4). By 1884, the Lease family had moved again, first to a farm in Kingman County, Kansas, and eventually to Wichita, where she began her career as a professional lecturer. Clyens Lease lectured in behalf of the Irish National League, claiming Irish birth to enhance her ethos. She advocated prohibition and woman suffrage, helped to organize the Wichita Equal Suffrage Association, and founded the Hypatia Society where women met to discuss current issues (Blumberg, 1978:4; Clanton, 1968:191; Paulson, *NAW* 2:381). She studied law at home and under the direction of Charles Ebey, a Wichita attorney, and became one of the first women admitted to the Kansas bar (Blumberg, 1978:5).

As Clyens Lease's lecturing reputation grew, her political interests shifted from the Irish cause to domestic reform issues, including woman's rights and suffrage. Her involvement with the agrarian reform movement began in June 1886, when she was invited to address two meetings of the Farmers' Alliance, forerunner of the People's party, in Harper County, Kansas. The invitation, Blumberg reported, was "probably" due to "her reputation as an inspiring speaker." But the Alliance also shared at least some of her concern for woman's rights. "For the first time," said Blumberg, "[she] found herself in an organization in which women took their place, at least nominally, on an equal basis with men" (1978:5).

The Farmers' Alliance and the People's party or, more simply, the Populist movement grew from the formidable economic and social problems that confronted farmers throughout the West and South in the 1880s and 1890s. Burdened with heavy mortgages, unable to pay their debts because produce prices were deeply depressed, and at the mercy of Eastern bankers for capital and Eastern railroad companies that charged extremely high freight rates for transportation of their goods, farmers faced destruction of their way of life. Convinced that their plight resulted from a gigantic conspiracy among land speculators, bankers, railroaders, and corrupt politicians, they sought to replace the existing political leadership with their own representatives. They sought more radical solutions as well, advocating nationalization of transportation systems, currency reform, the free coinage of silver, and the establishment of a national banking system (Clanton, 1969:; Hicks, 1931; Miller, 1925).

The spectacular Populist political successes in Kansas in 1890 and 1892 are well documented (Argersinger, 1967, 1972). Her oratorical skill made Clyens Lease a major figure in that effort. In August 1890, she delivered the opening address and served on the nominations committee at the party's state convention in Topeka. According to Blumberg, throughout the 1890 campaign, she "traveled hundreds of miles, crisscrossing the entire eastern half of Kansas, spoke in 16 counties, in perhaps 50 cities, towns, and picnic groves, sometimes two speeches in one day, an estimated total of 160 appearances" (1978:6). Ross Paulson added that

in 1891 she carried her campaign into Missouri, the Far West, and the South. At the St. Louis Populist convention of February, 1892, she was appointed to the committee that launched the party onto the national political scene. At its nominating convention in July she seconded the name of Gen. James B. Weaver for president and that fall campaigned with Weaver in the West and South. (*NAW* 2:381)

She was instrumental in Populist victories and was recognized throughout the nation as a party leader. As Clanton argued: "Unquestionably, Mrs. Lease had played a mighty role in that first whirligig campaign of 1890. . . . And her name is closely and justly associated with the victories the new party won, inside and outside Kansas, between 1890 and 1892" (1968:190).

A VOICE FOR "THE PEOPLE"

Philosophically and ideologically, Clyens Lease's discourse, like that of other Populists, was grounded in the agrarian myth (Burkholder, 1988, 1989). "Like any complex of ideas," Richard Hofstadter explained, "the agrarian myth cannot be defined in a phrase, but its component themes form a clear pattern." Those themes, he continued, cast the "yeoman farmer" as hero. The central conception of the myth was "the notion that [the yeoman farmer] is the ideal man and the ideal citizen." According to Hofstadter: "The yeoman . . . was the incarnation of the simple, honest, independent, healthy, happy human being. Because he lived in close communion with beneficent nature, his life was believed to have a wholesomeness and integrity impossible for the depraved populations of cities." Consequently, he concluded, "agriculture, as a calling uniquely productive and uniquely important to society, had a special right to the concern and protection of government" (1955:24–25).

That special right was threatened when industry emerged as the dominant economic force in society, mechanization of agriculture significantly increased productivity, and railroads opened vast new markets for agricultural products. Those factors, combined with growing financial dependence on Eastern lending institutions, destroyed the simple, self-sufficient life of the mythic yeoman. At the mercy of these forces, and faced with deepening economic depression and perceived political oppression that seemed to threaten their very way of life, agrarian reformers naturally sought to reassert their primacy in society. To do so, they drew on ideals implicit in the myth to justify the agrarian past out of which their culture grew and to explain why the simple yeoman had been, and should continue to be, the foundation of U.S. society. By what seemed to Populists a natural extension, those mythic ideals characterized all members of the "productive classes." Thus, all labor was dignified. As Hofstadter remarked, Populists saw

a natural harmony of interests among the productive classes. To the Populist mind there was no fundamental conflict between the farmer and the worker. . . . The underlying interests of the productive majority were the same; predatory behavior existed only because it was initiated and underwritten by a small parasitic minority in the highest places of power. (1955:64)

In her Populist rhetoric, Clyens Lease frequently developed two interrelated rhetorical strategies from this ideological foundation. Those strategies appealed directly to her target audience of disgruntled farmers and laborers, but also risked enraging her political opponents.

First, the myth provided criteria for delineating good and evil. Bankers, land speculators, railroaders, corrupt politicians, or simply "the money powers" were evil. In opposition were the forces of good: farmers, laborers, the productive classes, or simply "the people." Second, the myth provided appeals to induce "the people" to transcend sectional and occupational differences, unite within the People's party, and oppose the money powers. In campaign speeches, Clyens Lease typically arranged those strategies in problem/solution order: evil and corrupt money powers had conspired to oppress and deprive the people; the people must unite to confront evil, regain their rightful place in society, and solve the nation's problems.

In March 1891, Clyens Lease addressed a Populist rally in Kansas City. "Wall Street owns this country," she began. Then, through a series of antithetical pairs, she delineated the sides of good and evil, placing blame for the people's plight on the Eastern money powers:

It is no longer a government of the people, by the people and for the people, but a government of Wall Street, by Wall Street and for Wall Street. The great common people of this country are slaves, and monopoly is the master. The West and South are bound and prostrated before the manufacturing East. . . . Our laws are the output of a system which clothes rascals in robes and honesty in rags. (*OW*, 106–107)

Her words echoed Lincoln, the common railsplitter, the archetypal yeoman hero who, like a latter-day Cincinnatus, left the western prairies to lead the nation in its time of greatest peril. For her listeners, no other national hero could have been more closely identified with the ideals of the agrarian myth.

To bridge sectional differences, she reminded her Kansas City audience: "In this People's Party we find not only the boys who wore the blue but the boys who wore the grey." Lingering sectional discord, she argued, was the product of the same evil forces that oppressed the people: "The North and South have been kept separated because of the unscrupulous scheming of the leaders of both political parties." She then urged all people to transcend sectional differences and unite in their common oppression. "The mortgage indebtedness and the opposition by the money power rests just as heavily on the Southern states as on the Federal states just as heavily on the Democratic brother as on the Republican brother." And she exhorted the people to confront their oppressors: "We will stand by our homes and stay by our firesides by force if necessary, and we will not pay our debts to the loan shark companies until the government pays its debts to us. The people are at bay; let the bloodhounds of money who dog us beware!"

In September 1893, she addressed the Labor Congress in Chicago (*Monitor*,

September 7, 1893). Her speech demonstrated the affinity Populists saw between farmers and other laborers. She first deplored the vast wealth accumulated by "your Vanderbilts, and Goulds and Wanamakers and Stanfords" and the inability of the country to "distribute this wealth so that no one may want, and each may have accordingly as he has produced." Failure to solve this problem, Clyens Lease argued, resulted in oppression of the productive classes:

Because we have failed to solve this problem you men of Chicago are today on the verge of a slumbering volcano that may break forth at any time; because you have ignored the word "justice" a great army of unemployed men in the city of Chicago are crying out today for bread and work. Because hungry men have asserted their right to peaceably assemble and discuss their wrongs they are clubbed down in the street like dogs. Because of political mismanagement our country has become practically an annex to England with its imperial gold basis.

Blame was again placed on the money powers or "plutocrats" who conspired with corrupt politicians of the major parties. In the last election (1892), Clyens Lease said, "you voted for [Benjamin] Harrison or for [Grover] Cleveland, and what difference did it make for which you voted? Everybody knows that there is no difference between a plutocratic Republican party and a plutocratic Democrat party. . . . My God," she exclaimed, "how any patriotic man today can be a Republican or a Democrat is past my comprehension." Consistent with Populist ideology, she saw action by the yeomanry as the solution. "The farmers in every conflict that has swept this country from the battle of Lexington to the great rebellion have always come to the front and have solved the great questions involved successfully," she said. "Today they are called on to solve the labor question. You may club down the laborers in cities and make them the slaves of plutocracy, but you cannot, thank God!, starve and club down the farmers of this country, who stand ready to save it." The labor audience was invited to unite with western farmers in that effort.

Before an eastern labor audience, at Cooper Union in New York City in April 1894, Clyens Lease echoed her Chicago speech (*New York Tribune*, March 1, 1894). "We see pale mothers and starving children in the midst of us," she said. "Three-quarters of the people of this city are crowded into one twenty-fifth of the city's area . . . [in] densely-packed layers of human beings in the New York tenement houses." The suffering, she contended, was not confined to eastern cities: "We learn that 24,000 people are in possession of more than one half of the wealth of the land, and that 4,000,000 people are denied the privilege of that divine injunction, 'Earn bread in the sweat of your brow.' There are 4,000,000 men out of work whose families are starving." The allusion to Genesis 3:19 placed those who oppressed and starved the people in violation of God's command. Those evil forces were "political leaders" who failed to hear "the cry of the poor for bread," like Grover Cleveland, whom she called a "great smoke extinguisher," "a menace to the republic," and "a blight to prosperity and liberty.'' And in a passage certain to startle her listeners, she accused the church itself of complicity:

We live a gigantic lie. We profess christianity [sic] and fail to practice it. You build monumental piles of stone and brick and dedicate them to God, and still you allow your children to starve. Your ministers are afraid to preach a doctrine antagonistic to plutocracy. You ask why your laboring men are leaving the church, and I answer, because the churches hold the hay too high for the sheep. Our social conditions have no part with the teaching of Christ. If you are afraid to attack the plutocrats, then you need a new Christ—one who will hobnob with the rich, and who will preach Heaven for the rich and Hell for the tramps.

She again assured eastern laborers that western farmers stood ready to combat evil. ''We have heard out on the prairies of the West, the cry of your starving thousands,'' she said. ''But your monopolies and corporations cannot starve down the farmers of this broad, free land. The farmers are the hope of the nation.'' Farmers and laborers would unite under the banner of the People's party and supplant the forces of evil. Assuming the persona of prophet, she warned: ''Punishment will come to your leaders. . . . The giant of labor in this country is aroused. The light of justice is in his eyes. Men will not starve in the sight of plenty. Aristocracy may well start from its slumber as it dreams of the French revolution. It is a struggle for justice, and those who long ignore it cannot survive.'' And the labor audience was urged to support Populist candidates because, she said, ''if you vote for any other party you vote for a hell on earth.''

Clyens Lease's performance as a debater, clashing directly with her opponents, was equally forceful. Perhaps her most effective debate strategy consisted of a healthy dose of ridicule combined with turning her opponents' own words back on them to expose their inconsistency. In Atlanta, Georgia, in August 1891, she responded to a speech given the night before by her favorite target, John J. Ingalls, the eighteen-year Republican U.S. senator from Kansas, defeated by the Populists earlier that year (Industrial Advocate, August 20, 1891). ''It has been announced . . . that I was to answer here tonight the able argument—or rather able speech of John J. Ingalls,'' she said. With acid wit, she continued:

I falter with my woman's heart before dissecting such a cadaverous and ungainly specimen of humanity as the ''so-called statesman out of a job.'' It is a pity to waste ammunition on a dead duck, and I know of no man who is deader politically than Ingalls. He is dead beyond all resurrection.

For her southern audience, she ridiculed Ingalls, saying that he ''had done more to stir up partisan bitterness and strife between the sections'' than anyone else. During the Civil War, however, ''when their country needed defenders and they were bravely at the front, Ingalls was skulking at home, seeking office and his only war record consists of the fact that he courtmartialed a chicken thief.'' As for the ''arguments'' Ingalls had made, ''I know of no more effective way to answer John J. Ingalls than to place Ingalls versus Ingalls," she said. "He is the most inconsistent and illogical speaker in the United States." To illustrate, she explained:

He said to you, "I know of no valid reason why woman has not as much right to the ballot as man." On February 26, 1888, in the city of Salina, Kan., Ingalls said: "Woman has been placed under the ban of her Creator since the days of Eve. My objection to woman's voting is because she is a woman." I mention this to show you how he has been converted since that Salina speech, and by the way, that was the speech that caused his defeat.

In a debate with Republican Judge Keenan before the Wichita Literary League on February 5, 1892, Clyens Lease responded to her opponent's claims that the People's party taught a "doctrine of hate" (*Kansas Commoner*, February 11, 1892). "I propose to show," she said, " . . . that the Republican leaders and their partisan Republican press, in their efforts to misrepresent the demands of the people have injured the state by their falsehoods." To do so, she employed a variation of her favorite strategy, this time using Republican sources as reluctant authorities to refute her Republican opponent. Keenan claimed that a Wichita Populist had called the Republican party "the meanest organization in existence, because it had become so corrupt," a statement Keenan found "unpardonable." In response, she encouraged Keenan to

Look over the back files of the leading Republican paper of the state,—the *Wichita Eagle*,—[where] he will find Mr. M. Murdock in the editorial column using the following language: "Corporations, monstrous enough to induce revolution, have been enthroned in big places under Republican rule, and they, the leaders, have become the whipped whelps of corporate greed." . . . Bravo Murdock! But, if an Alliance man said that, you would call him an anarchist. But listen to his brother, Sen. T. B. Murdock . . . :"The Republican party has become so vile, so rotten, that angels are compelled to hold their noses as they fly over Kansas."

Thus did she turn Republican sources back on Keenan, revealing the double standard employed by her opponents.

These excerpts demonstrate that style also served an important strategic function for Clyens Lease. Present are examples of high style commonly associated with nineteenth-century oratory: antithesis, repetition, parallelism, and allusions to national heroes and to the Bible. But her style was also consistently fierce, combative, profane, or "masculine," what Ernest G. Bormann called "ungenteel" (1969, 1985:99–119). Use of such language by a woman might have shocked listeners with refined sensibilities, but it was well adapted to ingratiate her with her audience of disgruntled, angry farmers and laborers.

Nevertheless, her artistry was perhaps better illustrated by her ability to adapt her Populist message to those occasions that demanded high style. Her Kansas Day address at the 1893 Columbian Exposition in Chicago was a striking stylistic contrast to her campaign speaking; it was an encomium to Kansas that demonstrated her skill as an orator in the grand tradition of the nineteenth century, yet still echoed Populist ideology (*Kansas Sunflower*, December 1893). She began:

He that can paint a picture in marvelous beauty, that can pencil a landscape tinted with the glory of the dawn, that can strike a harp and make its responsive chords burst into a glad melody of song, that can tint a rainbow, give glory to the flowers, sublimity to the sea, majesty to the landscape and with the hand of Liszt bring melody from pattering rain and whispering breeze, evolve the music of the spheres from rustling corn and billowy wheat, may hope to picture Kansas, that old land which men call new.

The people of Kansas received equal praise. "The principles of patriotism and valor and integrity permeates [*sic*] every Kansas heart," she said, "and they are as staunch, as tried and true as our Kansas soil that the sunshine and rain have kissed into teeming life and power." Faith in the people and in the beneficence of nature, characteristic of the agrarian myth, echoed in her words and helped adapt her Populist message to this ceremonial occasion. "Patrick Henry plead [*sic*] for liberty," she said; "Washington fought for it; the philosophy of Jefferson perpetuated it; but Kansans live it." For her, the spirit of the nation's heroes continued to dwell within Kansas Populists who opposed the new tyranny, the money power. In high style, and again with the voice of a prophet, she concluded:

From Kansas shall come the fulfillment of scripture. Up from her plains, baptized with the blood of martyrs, shall come the prophet of Ezekiel's vision, that breathing upon the dry bones of the world's oppressed will clothe them with new life, resurrecting the wisdom of the seers, the justice of Christ, and all humanity will enjoy that liberty which the winds of Kansas forever play on aeolian harps, and all the world shall come up the path which we have blazed and bask in the light which we have kindled and kings shall be no more, and the world will not tolerate hungry poor or idle rich; neither shall be found tyrants, small or great, but they who obey the divine injunction to earn their bread in the sweat of their face; honest toilers shall constitute a state.

As a voice of Populism, Clyens Lease was a sophisticated, forceful campaigner and debater with the ability to adapt her message to a variety of situations. Her discourse contrasted sharply with that of many women advocates, distinctive in its aggressive, angry tone and ungenteel, "masculine" style, which delighted allies and dismayed opponents. Her advocacy of woman's rights was no less skillful.

A VOICE FOR WOMAN'S RIGHTS

Like other woman's rights advocates, Clyens Lease confronted opposition based on three interrelated rationales: theological—that God had ordained a subservient role for women; biological—that women were the "weaker sex" not only physically, but also mentally and emotionally; and sociological—that for the good of society, women must be limited to a domestic role (IWSM:14–42). Her response was typically twofold: she linked woman's oppression to those rationales; and she sought to refute the premises on which they were based, frequently by turning her opponents' own arguments back on them.

In an essay published in 1884, she recognized that the three rationales were interrelated: "Nine tenths of the men actually believe that by a wise dispensation of providence the quality and quantity of female brains is far below the average in the male and consequently no amount of care or culture will bring woman to a level of equality with themselves. Many of them do not hesitate to say," she continued, "that she fulfills her whole mission . . . when she makes herself as pretty and agreeable as possible and devotes the proper time and attention to the discharge of her domestic duties" (*Kingman County [Kans.] Citizen*, January 21, 1894). Such reasoning, she argued, kept women in "the background . . . vibrating between the condition of slave and superintendent of the kitchen; taught nothing but those flimsy accomplishments which would catch . . . [a] husband or master; ridiculed or rebuked whenever she attempted to escape from silken serfdom."

In response, Clyens Lease argued that "such disparaging ideas of woman are based upon ignorance and error." Proof was found in numerous women who lived the antithesis of the stereotype: "Mary Somerville, and Caroline Herschel, in science, Queen Elizabeth, and Madam [*sic*] Roland, in politics; Charlotte Bronte, George Elliott [*sic*], Browning, Hemings [*sic*], Stowe, Eliza Cook and a host of others in literature; Joan of Arc, in War; Baroness Brudette Conts, in finance; . . . thousands and hundreds of women who might be named to prove there is no inevitable, and inexorable war of inferiority waging against them." A week later in the same newspaper, she listed eleven women who had made significant accomplishments in journalism (*Kingman County [Kans.] Citizen*, February 7, 1894). Together, the two essays provided compelling evidence that destiny was not determined by sex.

The "theological" rationale was the foundation of opposition to woman's rights. Clyens Lease attacked that foundation in an essay published in 1891, arguing that the male-dominated church, not the Bible itself, was responsible for woman's plight (*Farmer's Wife*, October 1891). As in her Populist speeches, she began her refutation by ridiculing her opponents: "It has been my lot more than once to have the Bible thrown at my head both on the rostrum and through the press, by some valiant Pharisee who prefixed 'Rev.' to his name." Then, she employed the Bible as a reluctant authority, turning its words back on the "valiant Pharisees":

There is an abundance of material in the Bible to make it an effective weapon . . . against those who profess to be guided by its teachings. The women of the Bible are the grandest conceptions of history. . . . How Godlike Miriam stands outlined against the centuries. What an illustration we have in Deborah that the good mother of a household can also be the good mother of a nation. . . . when God wished to perfect some mighty plan . . . a woman was selected as the instrument of communication, whether a Judith delivering her besieged kinsmen in the beleaguered city, or the daughter of a Pharaoh rescuing from the Nile the leader of God's chosen people.

Strategically, the passage functioned as a subtle enthymeme, inviting readers to conclude that the Bible itself provided ample evidence of woman's ability and accomplishment, thus eroding the foundation of the opposition's argument.

Much of the essay took the form of a *prosopopoeia*, the classical stragegy in which a rhetor engages in mock debate with opponents, refuting examples of their arguments. For instance, she reminded readers: " 'But the very fact that God created the male first gives him precedence and superiority,' we are told." In response, she asked: "Well, then we find that God created the fowls of the air, the fishes of the sea, and every creeping thing upon the earth; does precedence in creating give them superiority over man?" Finally, she suggested: "Rather let us reason that . . . the lower animals were God's experiment, man the culmination of His practice, and woman, because LAST, the crowning masterpiece of His workmanship."

She then demonstrated woman's role as preacher and prophet in the early church, drawing evidence from sources usually considered woman's worst theological enemies, St. Paul and St. Peter. She accused St. Augustine, who claimed that women had "dealings with the devil," of perpetuating "witch-craft laws" by which "nine million women were burned at the stake, victims of the insatiable church." And she concluded that "enough has been said to show that the church and not the Bible is responsible for the slavery and degradation of woman."

Clyens Lease was as forceful from the podium as in the press. Speaking in Topeka in February 1894, she employed irony to illustrate woman's position in society (*[Garnett] Kansas Sunflower*, February 1894). "Women, of right and necessity, must enter the field of competition and join in the . . . struggle for existence," she said. And yet:

We have fettered her with man-made laws, enslaved her and her children to debts she had no part in incurring, made her amenable to laws she had no voice in making, denied her representation, while imposing upon her taxation and penal legislation, denied to her that right, guaranteed by the constitution to the citizens of the United States, "the right to trial by a jury of her peers," obeying in dumb silence, laws of man.

Despite her aggressive style and her reputation as a radical Populist, much of her speech in Topeka was fundamentally conservative, designed to enhance her appeal with male voters. For example, once again employing irony, she said:

We cannot teach reverence for laws that will prevent my girl or yours from holding or selling property, or attaining her majority until she is 18 years of age, then enact, by legislation, that when that little, innocent child is 10 or 12, or 14 years of age (and in some states, the law fixes the age of consent at 7 years), she may barter her soul, sell her virtue and be lost in the hell of man's baser passions.

Although her tone remained combative, the appeal was conservative in that it placed her in woman's traditional role as family protector, and played upon fathers' emotions for their daughters.

Clyens Lease employed much the same strategy as she seemed to accept the sociological rationale that cast woman in a domestic role, but argued that suffrage was essential for woman to perform that function. "It has been said that woman has a higher and holier sphere within the home," she said, "but the government, whose laws we must obey, whose laws we have no hand in making, comes unbidden into every home and broods at every fireside." Those laws, she continued, prevented women from fulfilling their ordained duty:

Masculine politics have invaded and degraded the home. We carefully and tenderly guard our boys in infancy and childhood; we baptize them with tears and sanctify them with a mother's prayers. They go forth at the dawn of manhood, from the shelter of the home roof. We may not follow them. The wild beasts of lust and drunkenness beset their paths. Man-made laws interfere, and they say to the mother: "Go back to your home. . . . You are women."

Ultimately, the argument turned the sociological rationale back upon opponents, justifying suffrage as a means of fulfilling woman's traditional role in society. "The ballot is power, and power makes respect," she said, "and when placed in the hands of the home-keepers of this nation, it will be a power for the uplifting of humanity, and woman's wants will not be treated with contempt, as they are to-day."

CONCLUSION

Along with other Populist rhetors, Clyens Lease was initially successful in building an effective political coalition of farmers, industrial laborers, and other workers. But the coalition was short-lived because, ultimately, their strategy of separating the forces of good and evil along lines suggested by the agrarian myth became divisive. The strengths and weaknesses of those Populist rhetorical strategies have been examined previously (Burkholder, 1988, 1989).

Nevertheless, Clyens Lease's career as a public advocate was distinctive because she not only championed woman's rights, but also was a major force in the People's party. As a voice of Populism, she achieved more short-term political success than almost any other woman advocate of her time. For that success, and for her distinctive rhetorical style, she was deified by supporters and vilified by opponents. As Clinton observed, "even more than is the case with most political figures, one's view of Mrs. Lease was likely determined by one's political affiliation" (1969:55). Thus, it was ironic that, ultimately, she raised hell with almost everyone. In 1895, she published a book entitled *The Problem of Civilization Solved*, which, according to Clanton, "was filled with nativistic and racist nonsense, and in which she called for a Napoleon to liberate the industrial world" (1968:200). By 1896, she denounced her former Populist allies, primarily for their cooperation with Democrats (Clanton, 1968:195–196). Before the end of the decade, she moved to New York City to be a professional lecturer. In 1900, however, she returned to Kansas and Nebraska to campaign against William Jennings Bryan, once the Populist nominee for president, and for Republican candidates, once her enemies (Clinton, 1969:58; Clanton, 1968:200).

The ambivalence with which many contemporaries came to regard Clyens Lease was clearly expressed by William Allen White, the Republican newspaper editor, once her bitter foe, whose view of her eventually mellowed. When the Populist revolt ended, White said, she "left Kansas and made an honest and honorable living in New York City and died a respected citizen. But she flashed across Kansas in that day of turmoil, a harridan in the eyes of her enemies, a goddess to her friends. Looking back across a generation, I think she was a litle of both" (1946:219).

SOURCES

Biographical information on Clyens Lease, like the texts of her speeches, is scattered through various sources. Most histories of the Populist movement, especially those focusing on Kansas, include some material, but no full-length biography exists. Especially useful in completing this study were:

Blumberg, Dorothy Rose. "Mary Elizabeth Lease, Populist Orator: A Profile." *Kansas History* 1 (Spring 1978):3–15.
Clanton, O. Gene. "Intolerant Populist? The Disaffection of Mary Elizabeth Lease." *Kansas Historical Quarterly* 34 (Summer 1968):189–200.
Clinton, Katherine B., "What Did You Say, Mrs. Lease?" *Kansas Quarterly* 1 (Fall 1969):52–59.
Paulson, Ross E. "Lease, Mary Elizabeth Clyens." *NAW* 2:380–381.

Other sources on the development of Populism in Kansas and the nation contain scattered references to Clyens Lease. Most useful were:

Argersinger, Peter H. "Road to a Republican Waterloo: The Farmers' Alliance and the Election of 1890 in Kansas." *Kansas Historical Quarterly* 33 (Winter 1967):443–469.
———. "The Most Picturesque Drama: The Kansas Senatorial Election of 1891." *Kansas Historical Quarterly* 38 (Spring 1972):43–64.
Clanton, O. Gene. *Kansas Populism: Ideas and Men.* Lawrence: University Press of Kansas, 1969.
Hicks, John D. *The Populist Revolt: A History of the Farmer's Alliance and the People's Party.* Minneapolis: University of Minnesota Press, 1931.
Miller, Raymond Curtis. "The Background of Populism in Kansas." *The Mississippi Valley Historical Review* 11 (March 1925):469–489.

White, William Allen. *The Autobiography of William Allen White*. New York: Macmillan, 1946.

Critical Sources

Portions of this analysis on the influence of the agrarian myth on Populist rhetoric appeared earlier in two sources:

Burkholder, Thomas R. "Mythic Conflict: A Critical Analysis of Kansas Populist Speech-making, 1890–1894." 2 vols. Ph.D. diss., University of Kansas, 1988. AAC 8903985
———."Kansas Populism, Woman Suffrage, and the Agrarian Myth: A Case Study in the Limits of Mythic Transcendence." *Communication Studies* 40 (Winter 1989):293–307.

Other useful sources were:

Bormann, Ernest G. "The Rhetorical Theory of William Henry Milburn." *Speech Monographs* 36 (1969):28–37.
———.*The Force of Fantasy: Restoring the American Dream*. Carbondale: Southern Illinois University Press, 1985, pp. 99–119.
Ecroyd, Donald H. "The Agrarian Protest." *America in Controversy: History of American Public Address*. Ed. Dewitt Holland. Dubuque, Iowa: Wm. C. Brown, 1973, pp. 171–184.
———."The Populist Spellbinders." *The Rhetoric of Protest and Reform, 1878–1898*. Ed. Paul H. Boase. Athens: Ohio University Press, 1980, pp. 132–152.
Gunderson, Robert G. "The Calamity Howlers." *Quarterly Journal of Speech* 26 (October 1940):401–411.
Hofstadter, Richard. *The Age of Reform: From Bryan to F.D.R.* New York: Alfred A. Knopf, 1955.
Kraditor, Aileen. "The Rationale of Antisuffragism." *The Ideas of the Woman Suffrage Movement, 1890–1920*. New York: Columbia University Press, 1965, pp. 14–42.

Textual Sources

No comprehensive collection of speeches and essays exists; however, six of the ten texts used in this study—her 1891 speech in Atlanta, her 1892 speech to the Literary League in Wichita, her 1893 speech to the Labor Congress in Chicago, her 1893 Kansas Day address at the Chicago World's Fair, her 1894 address at Cooper Union, New York City, and "The Legal Disabilities of Women," Topeka, 1894—are in Burkholder, "Mythic Conflict," vol. 2.

In order of citation, the ten texts used in this study are:

"The Red Dragon of Wall Street Vs. the Farmer." [Kansas City] *Star*. April 1, 1891. *OW*:106–7.
Speech before the Labor Congress, Chicago Art Palace, September 1893. [Abilene, Kans.] *Monitor*, September 7, 1893.

Address at Cooper Union, New York City, April 30, 1894. *New York Tribune*, March
    1, 1894. Rpt. [Garnett, Kans.] *Agitator*, March 8, 1894.
Address in Atlanta, Georgia, August 1891. [El Dorado, Kans.] *Industrial Advocate*,
    August 20, 1891.
Speech to the Literary League, Wichita, Kansas, February 5, 1892. [Wichita] *Kansas
    Commoner*, February 11, 1892. That the debate occurred in Wichita is conjecture;
    because it was her home and because the text first appeared in the *Kansas Com-
    moner*, that is likely. Rpt. [Lawrence, Kans.] *Jeffersonian*, February 25, 1892.
Kansas Day Address, Columbian Exposition, Chicago. [Garnett] *Kansas Sunflower*, De-
    cember 1893 and January 1894.
"Are Women Inferior?" *Kingman County [Kans.] Citizen*, January 21, 1884.
"Are Women Inferior?" *Kingman County [Kans.] Citizen*, February 7, 1884.
"The Church and not the Bible." [Topeka, Kans.] *Farmer's Wife*, October 1891.
"The Legal Disabilities of Women, Representative Hall, Topeka, February 7, 1894."
    [Garnett] *Kansas Sunflower*, February 1894.

LUCRETIA COFFIN MOTT

(1793–1880), religious reformer and advocate of the oppressed

LESTER C. OLSON AND TRUDY BAYER

"Let me urge such faithfulness to the light which you have, as shall prepare you to become able advocates for the oppressed."

—Lucretia Coffin Mott

Lucretia Coffin Mott ranks among the most significant reformers influencing nineteenth-century U.S. culture. As a Quaker minister and public speaker, she advocated a broad range of reforms on issues such as peace, poor relief, penal servitude, temperance, public education, anti-slavery, women's equality, humane treatment of the mentally ill, economic issues of the working class, and rights of Native Americans. Although generally represented as a woman's rights advocate and abolitionist, religious reform was central in her public speaking. Other issues—even her deep and abiding concerns over anti-slavery and woman suffrage—were secondary to it. Above all, she was committed to equality for each and every person.

Coffin Mott spoke often about the need for peace and nonviolence (e.g., "The Subject of Peace," *Voice of Peace*, October 1869; "A Faithful Testimony Against Bearing Arms," *Voice of Peace*, November 1875; "A Warlike Spirit," *Voice of Peace*, July 1876, quoted in *CSAS*:343–348, 375–379, 379–383). This commitment shaped her analysis of appropriate methods of handling all other issues. For example, even though she was opposed to slavery, she deplored the use of violent or military means to end the peculiar institution ("To Carry Out Convictions for Peace," May 6, 1877, *Voice of Peace*, June 1877, quoted in *CSAS*:385–386). Her comments on John Brown's raid on Harper's Ferry reflected ambivalence resulting from agreement with Brown's goals but disagreement with his choice of means ("I Am No Advocate of Passivity," *National Anti-Slavery Standard*, November 3, 1860, quoted in *CSAS*:261–262). Toward the end of her life, she averred: "Even the woman question, as far as voting goes, does not take hold of my every feeling as does war" (Letter to Richard Webb, January 22, 1872, quoted in Bacon, 1980:212).

In addition to her lifelong commitment to the Society of Friends, Coffin Mott was a founder of the Philadelphia Female Anti-Slavery Society (1833); a primary organizer of the Anti-Slavery Convention of American Women (1837); an active member of the American Anti-Slavery Society and an officer in its branch, the Pennsylvania Anti-Slavery Society (1839); a delegate to the 1840 World's Anti-Slavery Convention in London where she was denied her seat because of her sex (*Diary*); founder of the Association for the Relief of Poor Women (1844); a primary organizer of the Seneca Falls WRC (1848); president of the WRC, Syracuse (1852); a founder of the Friends' College at Swarthmore (1864); first president of the American Equal Rights Association (AERA; 1866–1867); president for a decade of the Pennsylvania Peace Society (1870–1880); and vice-president of NWSA (1876).

In this chapter we examine Coffin Mott's public address by first describing the principal source of her rhetorical invention as grounded in her experience as a Quaker, especially the inward light, and then characterizing features of her invention that cannot be ascribed specifically to her Quakerism. Next, we identify the salient topics of her speeches, employing them as both a category and a source of propositions to explore her style and argumentation. Finally, we analyze her rhetorical strategies with special emphasis on her use of evidence.

INWARD LIGHT AS A SOURCE
OF RHETORICAL INVENTION

Lucretia Coffin Mott was a Hicksite Quaker, a branch of the Society of Friends that separated itself from orthodox Quakers based, in part, on commitment to social reform, especially anti-slavery. Those religious views constituted the principal source of her rhetorical invention on the political, moral, and social issues of her lifetime. Specifically, her experience of the "inward light," which was fundamental to all Friends, shaped and unified her world view. The inward light was that of God, the divine spirit in each person. She said: "I am sometimes asked if I do not believe in the divinity of Christ. I say, yes, not only in the divinity of Christ, but of all men" ("A Faithful Testimony Against Bearing Arms," September 19, 1875, *Voice of Peace*, November 1875, quoted in *CSAS*:377–378). The inward light demystified the "kingdom of God" in that each individual, as an exponent of the divine, contained this kingdom. The leading of the inward light was the ultimate source of truth for each individual; because of direct participation in and with the divine, one needed no outward authority. Her slogan, "truth for authority; rather than authority for truth," summarized her belief in each individual's ability and obligation to discern the truth and to judge what was right ("Religious Aspects of the Age," January 3, 1869, FHL, quoted in *CSAS*:315, 322).

In the Quaker tradition, one spoke only when moved by the inward light ("Quarterly Meetings," November 6, 1849, FHL, quoted in *CSAS*:139). Accordingly, Coffin Mott spoke extemporaneously, commenting in the introductions of her speeches that she had not prepared any remarks (*Discourse*, 3). The extant texts of her public address were recorded by stenographers and have been collected in an anthology.

Faithfulness to the light led to a life of righteousness, which was the willing and doing of good as displayed in everyday actions. Like Jesus of Nazareth, who best exemplified the divine nature of humanity, all people were called on "to promote the benign and holy principles of peace, justice, and love" ("Likeness to Christ," September 30, 1849, FHL, quoted in *CSAS*:108). Righteousness transcended specific forms of worship in that one ministered to the common well-being of humankind through the practice of these divine principles ("Progress of the Religious World," Anti-Sabbath Convention, Boston, March 23–24 1848, *Proceedings*; quoted in *CSAS*:67). Because the world had not yet actualized these principles, those who were faithful to the light had to participate as nonconformists in reform. Coffin Mott glorified the work of reform and characterized the reformer as "prophet," "messiah," and "blessed of the age," waging a "moral warfare" in the cause of progress and Christian democracy. She reminded audiences of each individual's personal responsibility for remediating injustice by promoting the divine principles to create the millennium now.

The dialectical tension between light and dark—good and evil—was thematic in her rhetoric. Paraphrasing the words of Jesus in John 3:19, she remarked: " 'Those only who are in the wrong dread discussion. The light alarms those only who feel the need of darkness.' It was sound philosophy, uttered by Jesus, 'He that doeth truth cometh to the light, that his deeds may be made manifest, that they are wrought in God' " (*Discourse*, 4).

As a prophetic ministry, the Quaker tradition exemplified the difference between the roles of prophet and priest. Quakers rejected hiring or training priests to minister to their needs; instead, they chose to depend on the divine inspiration of each and every person acting as prophet. Like other Friends, Coffin Mott distinguished between Christianity and its various types of formal institutions, often disparaging "sectarian theology" and the merely formal, ritualistic, or ceremonial features of worship (e.g., "The Truth of God," September 23, 1841, *Liberator*, October 15, 1841, quoted in *CSAS*:33; *Righteousness*, quoted in *CSAS*:35, 39, 43; "Progress of the Religious World," Anti-Sabbath Convention, Boston, March 23–24 1848. *Proceedings*, quoted in *CSAS*:59–60; Sermon at Bristol, June 6, 1860, *JLMLL*:523, 525, quoted in *CSAS*:254, 256). Instead, she believed that emphasis should be placed on integrating a practical Christianity in one's everyday life characterized by service to others (e.g., "Progress of the Religious World," Anti-Sabbath Convention, Boston, March 23–24 1848, quoted in CSAS:64, 67; "Worship in Spirit and in Truth," November 11, 1866, *The Friend*, December 1866, quoted in *CSAS*:272). Like other Quakers, she believed that the best human society could take place only within the divine plan. Accordingly, she subscribed to a civil religion that integrated Christianity and the state, though not necessarily church and state ("When the Heart Is Attuned to Prayer," Pennsylvania Peace Society, November 19–20, 1868, *The Friend*, January 1868, quoted in *CSAS*:305–306, 309; *Sermon*, 18–19).

Quaker experience of the inward light also shaped Coffin Mott's views of original sin and atonement, the coequality of women and men, personal accountability, and appreciation of diversity (Bacon, 1969:5). She rejected the theory of the inherent evil of humankind (*Righteousness*, quoted in *CSAS*:36–37; "Religious Instinct in the Constitution of Man," September 26, 1858, *Liberator*, October 29, 1858, quoted in *CSAS*:241; "Religious Aspects of the Age," January 3, 1869, FHL, quoted in CSAS:318), toward the end of her life characterizing it as a major cause of violence and war. She also objected to the concept of vicarious atonement ("Unity of Spirit in the Bond of Peace," September 2, 1849, FHL, quoted in *CSAS*:98–98). She often called on her audiences to assume personal accountability for doing right and to respect and tolerate diversity (e.g., "Religious Instinct in the Constitution of Man," September 26, 1858, *Liberator*, October 29, 1858; quoted in *CSAS*: 235–251). Her sermon at Bristol, June 6, 1860 (*JLMLL*:522–528), details basic features of her commitment to practical Christianity, duty, reform, and the divine principles.

Because respect and tolerance of others were fundamental tenets of Coffin Mott's religious convictions about the inward light, she continued to grow in her capacity to honor "that of God" in others. For example, in her earlier sermons she preferred the term *true Christianity* to describe the divine and central principles of peace, love, justice, and mercy, while encouraging her audiences to honor these principles in the Jewish tradition. Toward the end of her career, she extended respect and tolerance to other religious approaches by describing "true religion" so that it explicitly included faiths other than Judeo-Christianity: "Let it be called the Great Spirit of the Indian, the Quaker 'inward light' of George Fox, the 'Blessed Mary, mother of Jesus,' of the Catholics, or Brahma, the Hindoo's God—they will all be one, and there will come to be such faith and such liberty as shall redeem the world" (Address, Free Religious Association, May 30, 1873, *JLMLL*:555; quoted in *CSAS*:364).

Coffin Mott's experience as a Quaker enabled her to hold a theory of knowing that valued reasoning, intuition, and personal experience equally. Although she reminded her audiences of the divine gift of reason and asked them to use their intellect to think issues through for themselves, she also relied on intuition, instinct, and experiential knowledge (e.g., Sermon at Bristol, June 6, 1860, *JLMLL*:522–528, quoted in *CSAS*:253–260; "When the Heart Is Attuned to Prayer," November 24, 1867, *The Friend*, January 1868, quoted in *CSAS*:299–310). These qualities of her epistemology distinguished her from enlightenment rationalists because, to her, personal revelation was an adequate foundation for knowledge (Greene, *CSAS*:12; for an opposing view, see Sillars, 1991). Accordingly, her rhetoric depended extensively on divine inspiration.

Although Coffin Mott's experience as a Hicksite Quaker profoundly shaped these features of her rhetoric, other important features cannot be attributed to Quaker experience specifically. Most important, she conceived of problems such as war, poverty, slavery, and sexual inequality as systemic in that they were deeply rooted in cultural practices and embedded in society's institutions. In her moral philosophy, both the system and those participating in it in any measure were equally immoral. For example, she believed that northern manufacturers who profited from cheap cotton products and consumers who purchased items made by slave labor were as guilty as the southern slaveowners (e.g., *Righteousness*, quoted in *CSAS*:35–51; "Law of Progress," May 9, 1848, *National Anti-Slavery Standard*, May 18, 1848, quoted in *CSAS*:71–79). This conviction explains the Motts' decision to market woolen products instead of cotton ones (Bacon, 1980:38–42). Illustrating her concern about the systemic roots of injustice, "We Have Food While Others Starve" (May 31, 1850, FHL, quoted in *CSAS*:181–189) exemplifies recurring characteristics of her discourse: it was introspective; it took an everyday action as its starting point; and it refuted errors in sectarian religion and affirmed her view of "true Christianity." The speech asked the audience to consider how the individual's own actions contributed to injustice and called for personal responsibility for reform, using poverty as an instance.

Coffin Mott's invention displayed a sophisticated awareness of the complex interplay of individual and systemic change, systemic barriers, and further change, as a sustained example of women's inequality illustrates. She described inequity in women's education in a public school in London; then she mentioned that the conditions in Pennsylvania were even worse: "We have as yet no high school for girls" (*Discourse*, 18). She identified inequities in the legal system related to suffrage, lawmaking, and officeholding as barriers to women (*Discourse*, 15–17; National WRC, New York, May 10, 1866, *Proceedings*, 1866, quoted in *CSAS*:267). She emphasized how religious ceremonies and civil laws limited women, observing, "In marriage, there is assumed superiority, on the part of the husband, and admitted inferiority, with a promise of obedience, on the part of the wife" (*Discourse*, 13). In her extant speeches there is no reference to divorce reform, a reform that Bacon, her primary biographer, argues that she supported (1980:175–177). The clergy of the various denominations constituted one of the most serious, systemic barriers to women, in her view ("Abuses and Uses of the Bible," November 4, 1849, FHL, quoted in *CSAS*:132; National WRC, New York, November 25–26, 1856, *Proceedings*, 1856, quoted in *CSAS*:232). She commented, "we deny that the present position of woman is her true sphere of usefulness; nor will she attain to this sphere, until the disabilities and disadvantages, religious, civil, and social, which impede her progress, are removed out of her way" (*Discourse*, 7).

The combined force of cultural practices in various institutions supported a conception of woman that defined her as inferior to man, not as a result of arbitrary convention but of nature. In *Discourse on Woman*, one of her most widely reproduced and discussed speeches, Coffin Mott called this conception of woman into question by quoting and refuting Richard Henry Dana, Sr.'s claims: "While man assumes that the present is the original state designed for woman, that the *existing* 'differences are not arbitrary nor the result of accident,' but grounded in nature; she will not make the necessary effort to obtain her just rights" (7). She conceptualized the reluctance of many women to work toward equality as a consequence of their internalized oppression.

Coffin Mott's convictions about the systemic root of inequality influenced her rhetorical invention, for example, in that she saw a need to make women aware of the underlying cultural practices contributing to their oppression: "I would that woman would wake up to a sense of the long-continued degradation and wrong that has been heaped upon her!" (National WRC, *Proceedings*, 1856, quoted in *CSAS*:232; also National WRC, *Proceedings* 1866, quoted in *CSAS*:269). She argued that the reason some women did not want the vote or claimed to have adequate rights was because of the oppression they had internalized through cultural influences. She contended, however, that "The unwillingness of some to vote (assuming such to exist), does not destroy the right of a class" (WRC, New York, September 6–7 1853, *Proceedings* 1853, 19, quoted in *CSAS*:205). She argued that women must have equal rights to choose to exercise, even though none would be required to exercise them (*Discourse*, 14–15).

Coffin Mott also strategically defined the removal of systemic barriers as a right: "Let woman then go on—not asking as favor, but claiming as right, the removal of all the hindrances to her elevation in the scale of being" (*Discourse*, 19; similarly 12–13). She identified specific institutional sites where women and men could seek change: she proposed equal education (*Discourse*, 18–19), changes in civil law (*Discourse*, 16; National WRC, *Proceedings*, 1866, quoted in *CSAS*:267; AERA Convention, *Proceedings*, 1867, quoted in CSAS:287), access to the pulpit (*Discourse*, 5–6; Whole World's Temperance Convention, September 1–2, 1853, *Proceedings*, 1853, quoted in *CSAS*:208; National WRC, Cleveland, October 5–7, 1853, *Proceedings*, 1854, quoted in *CSAS*:217: "When the Heart Is Attuned to Prayer," November 24, 1867, *The Friend*, January 1868, quoted in *CSAS*:303), and to business opportunities (*Discourse*, 18). She advocated expanding the range of roles that women could fulfill, while assuring those who wished to do so that they could continue within a domestic sphere.

In Coffin Mott's analysis, the institutions that oppressed women could be countered by developing institutions to uplift them. At the 1853 National WRC in Cleveland, she underscored the value of meeting in such conventions: "These Conventions ought to give encouragement to the steps of advancement" (*Proceedings*, 1854, quoted in *CSAS*:218). Generally, she urged, "Young women of America, I want you to make yourselves acquainted with the history of the Woman's Rights movement, from the days of Mary Wollstonecraft. . . . I want to note the progress of this cause, and know now that Woman's redemption is at hand, yea, even at the doors" (National WRC, New York, May 10, 1866, *Proceedings*, 1866, quoted in *CSAS*:270).

Along with *Discourse on Woman*, her speeches at the WRC, New York, September 6–7, 1853 (*Proceedings*, 4–5, 19–20, 54–57, 85–86, quoted in *CSAS*:203–210), best illustrate her awareness of the barriers facing women and her faith in women's ability to overcome them. They used a wide range of rhetorical techniques: enumeration of model women, reinterpretation of Paul's comments about women, rebuttal of claims that women do not wish to vote, refutation by reversal, and, above all, a brilliant reframing of mob conduct to prove that women have enacted their capability to handle political responsibility. The final lines of her last speech paraphrased SOJOURNER TRUTH's speech at the 1851 Akron, Ohio, WRC.

RHETORICAL TOPICS

The "leading of the inward light" shaped Coffin Mott's lines of argument about recurring themes in her discourse—righteousness, personal responsibility, nonconformity, the divine work of reform, progress, Christian democracy, and the millennium. These were rhetorical topics in two senses: they were headings or categories that typified the content of her speeches, and they were the locations or places for propositions serving as underlying premises in her argumentation, in a classical sense of *topoi*. These topics merit scrutiny because they are vital to understanding aspects of her rhetorical style and argument such as her diction and major premises. These topics, informed by the leading of the inward light, were intricately interrelated and internally consistent.

Of the recurring topics in Coffin Mott's speeches, the inward light was most fundamental, followed closely by righteousness. Here we focus on how other noteworthy topics emerged out of them. If one accepted her assumptions about the inward light and righteousness, then the other propositions associated with the remaining topics followed logically: if righteousness, then personal responsibility, nonconformity, and reform; if reform, then progress, Christian democracy, and the millennium now.

According to Coffin Mott, if individuals heeded the leading of the inward light and led lives of righteousness, then each would contribute to correcting injustice by assuming personal responsibility for it. For example, she asked audiences to consider what actions of their daily lives contributed to the system of slavery and could be changed:

Whether you should act in organized societies, or as individuals, it is not for me to decide for any; but we all have a part of the work to perform, for we are all implicated in the transgression. Let us examine our own clothing—the furniture of our houses—the conducting of trade—the affairs of commerce—and then ask ourselves, whether we have not each, as individuals, a duty which, in some way or other, we are bound to perform ("The Truth of God," September 23, 1841, *Liberator*, October 15, 1841, quoted in *CSAS*:31–32).

In other words, a life devoted to righteousness led to scrutiny and transformation of daily conduct ("Quarterly Meetings," November 6, 1849, FHL, quoted in *CSAS*:140).

Coffin Mott criticized individuals and institutions that failed to assume responsibility by distancing themselves from the causes and cures of injustice. She condemned portrayals of injustice as the result of acts of providence, implicitly objecting to the teachings of organized religion and the gospel of wealth, which held that one's material conditions corresponded to one's spiritual state. She denounced detached approaches to correcting evil, such as prayer alone, as ways of denying one's own culpability: "Who is so unenlightened as to regard the sufferings as the direct visitation of Providence? As though God did not design that all his children should be happy. Let us . . . be concerned to discover how far we are implicated, individually and nationally, in war, slavery and other oppressions'' ("Unity of Spirit in the Bond of Peace," September 2, 1849, FHL, quoted in *CSAS*:99–100).

Faithfulness to the light and a life of righteousness would lead individuals into conflict with the systems that obfuscated truth and obstructed justice: "Let us then, be faithful to the light; be obedient even though it may lead us into greater non-conformity" ("The Duty of Prayer and Its Effects," October 14, 1849, FHL, quoted in *CSAS*:120). To think for oneself and to do what was right required confronting oppressive systems of belief. The righteous were noncon- formists who dialectically enjoined apologists of the status quo. Accordingly, Coffin Mott encouraged hearers to assume the roles of "nonconformist," "in- fidel," and "heretic," reflecting her belief in skepticism and critical thinking as prerequisite to the revelation of truth.

As a result of her nonconformity, Coffin Mott acknowledged her own vul- nerability to the charge of heresy, as in her widely reproduced *Sermon to the Medical Students*, February 11, 1849, in which she said: "I confess to you, my friends, that I am a worshipper after the way called heresy—a believer after the manner which many deem infidel" (6). Yet she distinguished between types of heresy: Praiseworthy heresy confronted the status quo, whereas blameworthy heresy colluded with it; praiseworthy heresy resulted from the leading of the inward light, whereas blameworthy heresy resulted from the leading of such darkness as superstition, ignorance, and evil. She warned: "Beware of the heresy that will lead us into the belief, that we should do nothing to remove the great evils that are in the earth" ("Quarterly Meetings," November 6, 1849, FHL, quoted in *CSAS*:141, also 136).

Coffin Mott alerted her audiences that if they, too, heeded the inward light, they would have to prepare themselves for charges of heresy. By pointing to Jesus of Nazareth as an exemplar, she reframed its meaning: "I want to say to those who have much to say about following Jesus, that they should remember to follow him in his non-conformity, in his obedience to the right, however much it might conflict with the popular beliefs and ceremonies of the day" (Address, Free Religious Association, May 31, 1872, *JLMLL*:552–553; quoted in *CSAS*:361). She noted that Jesus's nonconformity also resulted in charges of heresy: "Jesus taught the heresy of that age, and it was his opposition to the cherished forms and creeds of that day that constituted his greatest offense" (*Righteousness*, quoted in CSAS:38, also 41).

For Coffin Mott, reform activity necessarily resulted from the leading of the inward light: "The apostolic in every age, the sent-of-the-Father, are ever calling for a higher righteousness, a better development of the human race, a more earnest seeking to equalize the condition of men" ("Worship in Spirit and in Truth," November 11, 1866, *The Friend*, December 1866, quoted in *CSAS*:276). She saw reform as divine and blessed, affirming, "The more we are disposed to enter this reforming theatre of the world, the greater will be the promise of improvement of the social system, and the nearer the approach to the true end of human existence" (Sermon at Bristol, June 6, 1860, *JLMLL*:527, quoted in *CSAS*:258). Though often few in number, reformers were living testimony to the power of truth and righteousness ("The Spirit of Peace Must Be Cultivated in Our Hearts," Third Annual Women's Peace Festival, June 2, 1875, *Voice of Peace*, July 1875, quoted in *CSAS*:371). The accomplishments of reformers were evidence of progress and "the possibility of removing mountains on the side of right" ("A Warlike Spirit," Women's Peace Festival, Philadelphia, June 2, 1876, *Voice of Peace*, July 1876, quoted in *CSAS*:380). She stated that "nothing so enlarged my spirit . . . as the wonderful success attendant on the comparatively small labors of those who have been engaged in the reformatory movements in the several generations past. It is wonderfully designed that 'one shall chase a thousand, and two put ten thousand to flight' " ("There Is a Principle in the Human Mind," March 14, 1869, FHL; quoted in *CSAS*:336).

Coffin Mott believed that the inward light led to reform and, thus, to social progress—the continuing advancement of truth. For example, she claimed that prophets of old preached "moderation in alcohol consumption," but the nineteenth-century temperance prophet called for " 'total abstinence' from all intoxicating liquors" ("Law of Progress," Fourteenth Annual Meeting, American Anti-Slavery Society, New York, May 9, 1848, *National Anti-Slavery Standard*, May 18, 1848, quoted in *CSAS*:72). Similarly, the Protestant Reformation chipped away at the hierarchy of priestcraft, but nineteenth-century religious reformers called for complete rejection of all priestcraft and ceremony. She saw further evidence of progress in many reform movements: "The prisons are visited; insane hospitals are erected for meliorating the condition of suffering humanity; efforts are made to remove the gallows and other barbarous inflictions from our midst" (*Sermon*, 18). Despite her belief in progress, Coffin Mott was by no means naive about the remaining barriers, yet declared them "not insurmountable" (WRC, New York, September 6–7 1853, *Proceedings*, 5, quoted in *CSAS*:204).

Implementing Christian democracy was a principal method for promoting reform and progress. Her conviction that each individual embodied the inward light was the foundation for her belief in Christian democracy, which she defined ostensively through examples of its objective and practice. The aim of Christian democracy was to foster a society in which each individual's divinity justified equal status, rights, and opportunities. Humanity could achieve this end if each individual recognized the divinity of every person and thus felt compelled to eradicate injustice by actualizing the divine principles.

Christian democracy encompassed all aspects of one's life, including politics. Coffin Mott's emphasis on Christian democracy distinguished her from most other contemporary leaders in the woman suffrage movement such as ELIZABETH CADY STANTON in that Coffin Mott founded her claims on the divinity of each person, rather than on the natural rights philosophy (Greene, *CSAS*:19–20). If religious principles and civil government came into conflict, religion took priority: "you will bring your religion right into your politics" ("When the Heart Is Attuned to Prayer," November 24, 1867, *The Friend*, January 1868, quoted in *CSAS*:309). When elected representatives failed to practice divine principles, individuals had a moral right to disobey their enactments, as in the instance of the Fugitive Slave Law.

If individuals followed the leading of the inward light, acting in accord with the dignity of their respective natures, then the true end of existence—a world of peace, love, justice, and mercy—could be realized. According to Coffin Mott, each person's mission, like that of Jesus of Nazareth, was to bring the Kingdom of God to the earth. She encouraged her audiences to bring about the millennium now: "There has been a disposition to look for the millenium [*sic*] in the future, but we are learning better, and realizing that the Kingdom of God is now at hand, if we will only work for it in the right way" (Remarks, Pennsylvania Peace Society, September 19, 1875, *Voice of Peace*, November 1875, quoted in *CSAS*:377).

RHETORICAL STRATEGIES

Coffin Mott used several types of evidence to promote her reasoning about reform in the United States and abroad. Her view of argument from authority was noteworthy in that she regarded personal authority, the inward light of each individual, as more reliable than the authority of others, claiming that individuals should rely on their own judgments to scrutinize scripture, the teachings of the church, and all other outward authority ("Progress of the Religious World," Anti-Sabbath Convention, Boston, March 23–24, 1848, *Proceedings*, quoted in *CSAS*:59; "Abuses and Uses of the Bible," November 4, 1848, FHL, quoted in *CSAS*:123–125; National WRC, Cleveland, October 5–7, 1853, *Proceedings* 1854, quoted in *CSAS*:217; "This Internal Light of the Soul," January 23, 1870, FHL, quoted in *CSAS*:353). In her public address, she described the inward light as the source of instruction: "I would not weary you with words, fully believing that each has a Teacher within himself; and obeying this, we need not that any man should teach us" (*Sermon*, 19).

Despite her conviction that men and women had equal personal authority, she realized that the larger society did not value women's knowledge and experience as highly as that of men. Coffin Mott commented on this prejudice as a barrier to her credibility as a reformer and speaker: "I have seen that there is an objection, which seems reasonable to many minds, against woman's stepping forth to advocate what is right. Let me endeavor to remove these prejudices and these objections" ("The Truth of God," September 23, 1841, FHL, quoted in *CSAS*:26). Her Quaker affiliation posed an additional barrier to her credibility in mainstream forums ("Religious Instinct in the Constitution of Man," *Liberator*, October 29, 1858, quoted in *CSAS*:237–238). She used numerous rhetorical strategies to overcome these limitations on her personal authority, refuting and reinterpreting scripture, and identifying these forms of prejudice to minimize their force (*Righteousness*, quoted in *CSAS*:43). At times, she would also describe herself as prepared to incur "ridicule" in her endeavor to promote transcendent concerns ("The Truth of God," September 23, 1841, *Liberator*, October 15, 1841, quoted in *CSAS*:26–27, 29; WRC, New York, September 6–7, 1853, *Proceedings*, 4, quoted in *CSAS*:203).

She believed that the testimony or authority of others could be held in the "inward light" so that its truth could be ascertained. She valued such truth wherever it could be found—in the writings of recent thinkers and classical authors as well as in biblical figures in both the Old and New Testaments, and, above all, in personal experience: "Truth speaks the same language in every age of the world and is equally valuable" ("Likeness to Christ," September 30, 1849, FHL, quoted in *CSAS*:109, 111). Her use of testimony from such authorities as the Unitarian minister William Channing and her willingness to criticize passages in scripture resulted, at times, in charges that she was a heretic ("To Speak Out the Truth," October 20, 1846, *Christian Register*, October 31, 1846, quoted in *CSAS*:53–54; "When the Heart Is Attuned to Prayer," November 24, 1867, *The Friend*, January 1868, quoted in *CSAS*:307; see Bacon, 1980:94). For Coffin Mott, true authority ultimately was personal. Thus, she used argument from authority only in the technical sense that she quoted the ideas of others to support her claims and make them convincing to audiences ("This Internal Light of the Soul," January 23, 1870, FHL, quoted in *CSAS*:353).

When Coffin Mott used evidence from the Bible, she displayed her subtle and fluent understanding of scripture and her love of it. She frequently invoked the beatitudes or the Sermon on the Mount ("Religious Instinct in the Constitution of Man," September 26, 1858, *Liberator*, October 29, 1858, quoted in *CSAS*:248; Sermon at Bristol, June 6, 1860, *JLMLL*:523, quoted in *CSAS*:254), which summarized the divine principles succinctly. However, her sermons distinguished between the source that inspired the Bible and the text itself: "My education has been such, that I look to the Source whence all the inspiration of the Bible comes. I love the truths of the Bible . . . but I never was educated to love the errors of the Bible" (National WRC, Cleveland, October 5–7, 1853, *Proceedings*, 1854, quoted in *CSAS*:224; "There Is a Principle in the Human Mind," March 14, 1869, FHL, quoted in *CSAS*:338).

Beginning with her earliest public speeches, she refuted interpretations of scriptural authority, especially those resting on the apostle Paul's comments in 1 Cor. 14:34–35 to prove a divine sanction for women's subordination (e.g., "The Truth of God," September 23, 1841, *Liberator*, October 15, 1841, quoted in *CSAS*:26; *Discourse*, 5–6; WRC, New York, September 6–7, 1853, *Proceedings*, 56–57, quoted in *CSAS*:208; National WRC, Cleveland, October 5–7, 1853, *Proceedings*, 1854, quoted in *CSAS*:216; AERA Convention, New York, May 9–10, 1867, *Proceedings*, 1867, quoted in *CSAS*:287). She reframed and reinterpreted biblical passages to argue that Paul's instructions were merely local or circumstantial, not universal, because Paul himself had provided instructions to women on how to preach and prophesy ("The Truth of God," September 21, 1841, *Liberator*, October 15, 1841, quoted in *CSAS*:26; *Discourse*, 5–6).

Coffin Mott distinguished between "true Christianity" and sectarian religion. She granted little authority to sectarian religion, for she believed that the trappings of organized religion shrouded the light in ignorance and often justified inequity ("To Improve the Condition of Our Fellow Beings," December 23, 1849, FHL, quoted in *CSAS*:168). She often expressed anguish over the Bible's misuse as in "Abuses and Uses of the Bible" (November 4, 1849, FHL, quoted in *CSAS*:123–134). In other instances, she objected that leaders of religious sects employed the Bible to sanction "war, and slavery, wine drinking, and other cruel, oppressive and degrading evils" ("Likeness to Christ," September 30, 1849, FHL, quoted in *CSAS*:111; also "Abuses and Uses," "We Have Food While Others Starve," March 31, 1850, FHL, quoted in *CSAS*:176; National WRC, Cleveland, October 5–7, 1853, *Proceedings*, 1854, quoted in *CSAS*:215; "Religious Instinct in the Constitution of Man," September 26, 1858, *Liberator*, October 29, 1858, quoted in *CSAS*:246). She condemned the "usurpations of the church and clergy, by which woman has been so debased, so crushed, her powers of mind, her very being brought low" ("Abuses and Uses of the Bible," November 4, 1849, FHL, quoted in *CSAS*:132; similarly, *Discourse*, 5–7).

Coffin Mott criticized the church and clergy for endorsing biblical translations that excluded women from the pulpit and silenced them in general. For example, the term that was translated as "*servant*" for women became "*minister*" for men (*Discourse*, 6). Later, she made a similar argument about mistranslation: "wives of deacons" should have been "*the female* deacons" (WRC, New York, September 6–7, 1853, *Proceedings*, 56, quoted in *CSAS*:208; National WRC, Cleveland, October 5–7, 1853, *Proceedings*, 1854, quoted in *CSAS*:217). Near the end of her life, she said: "I know the veneration there is for the scriptures. Taken as a whole it is far too high" ("Religious Aspects of the Age," January 3, 1869, FHL, quoted in *CSAS*:321–322).

Although emphasis on the inward light led her to hold this circumscribed view of the authority of scripture and the church, she made extensive use of biblical images, allusions, and metaphors throughout her speeches, referring to truth with images of light (129 and 144), to society as the "the field white to the harvest," and to reformers as laborers sent forth into this field: "Blessed shall he be who is ready to say here am I, O Lord, send me into the great harvest field of reform where there shall be labor and this labor shall be done" ("Quarterly Meetings," November 6, 1849, FHL, quoted in *CSAS*:142). Use of biblical images, allusions, and metaphors enabled her to emphasize common ground with her predominantly Christian audiences, to establish her interpretations of scripture, and to bring biblical authority to the support of her causes. In contrast, she rarely used literary allusion—except when it promoted true principles as in the case of Harriet Beecher Stowe's *Uncle Tom's Cabin* (National WRC, Cleveland, October 5–7,

1853, *Proceedings*, 1854, quoted in *CSAS*: 220, 222; Bacon, 1980) or William Cowper's long poem, "The Task" (*Discourse*, 14).

Coffin Mott's public address made extensive use of examples; frequently, stories from the life of Jesus were presented as a guide for human behavior. To prove women's capabilities, she listed great women in the Bible such as Deborah, Phebe, and Anna (*Discourse*, 5–6) and in science such as Maria Mitchell, Mary Sommerville, and Caroline Herschel (*Discourse*, 12). She generated lists of women such as Elizabeth Gurney Fry, Dorothea Dix, and Myra Townsend who fulfilled domestic roles, while making significant contributions to public life (*Discourse*, 10; National WRC, Cleveland, October 5–7, 1853, *Proceedings* 1854, quoted in *CSAS*:222). Her own ability to work for reform while fulfilling the duties of housewife contributed to her credibility in the eyes of some contemporaries (Bacon, 1980:68).

Certain comparisons recurred regularly in Coffin Mott's speeches. She compared the condition of U.S. women to that of Hindu women and that of U.S. slaves, although she qualified her arguments to suggest that she saw the condition of slaves as worse (*Discourse*, 17; National WRC, Cleveland, October 5–7, 1853, *Proceedings*, 1854, quoted in *CSAS*:219, 221–222; American Anti-Slavery Society, December 3–4, 1863, *Proceedings . . . Third Decade*, 1860, quoted in *CSAS*:265; National WRC, New York, May 10, 1866, *Proceedings* 1866, quoted in *CSAS*:268). She specifically compared women's internalized oppression to that of the slave in that it accounted for the reluctance of some within each social class to labor for their own liberation:

Like the poor slave at the South, too many of our sex are insensible of their wrongs, and incapable of fully appreciating the blessings of freedom. I therefore submit . . . the following resolution: Resolved, That as the poor slave's alleged contentment with his servile and cruel bondage, only proves the depth of his degradation; so the assertion of woman that she has all the rights she wants, only proves how far the restrictions and disabilities to which she has been subjected have rendered her insensible to the blessings of true liberty. (National WRC, New York, November 23–26, 1856, *Proceedings*, 1856, quoted in *CSAS*:233; also National WRC, New York, May 10, 1866, *Proceedings*, 1866, quoted in *CSAS*:269; AERA Convention, New York, May 9–10, 1867, *Proceedings*, 1867, quoted in *CSAS*:287–288)

As a matter of style, she used antithesis and opposition extensively to make her meaning precise.

Coffin Mott skillfully synthesized argumentative techniques, as when she combined biblical allusion and repetition in her sermon, "This Internal Light of the Soul." She began with a passage from Isaiah 30:20: "Thine eyes shall see thy teachers; and thine ears shall hear a word behind thee, saying, This is the way, walk ye in it" (January 23, 1870, FHL, quoted in *CSAS*:349). She then repeated the exact wording as a refrain connecting a series of related arguments and used the images of teaching and walking in the light as visual motifs unifying the sermon. In another instance, she used the testimony of a male expert on law, who compared the legal status of women and slaves (*Discourse*, 15). She had drawn this comparison herself, but she gave the argument a quality of reluctant testimony by using white male authority.

Coffin Mott's extraordinary ability to marshall evidence and reasoning on behalf of reform cannot be reduced to a standard taxonomy of evidence. She developed arguments based on changes in the visible shape and height of the pulpit and the increasing number of women in it. She referred to both as evidence of a general tendency toward progress in Christianity (Fourteenth Annual Meeting, American Anti-Slavery Society, New York, May 9, 1848, *National Anti-Slavery Standard*, May 18, 1848, quoted in *CSAS*:73). She often reframed and reinterpreted scripture, either by juxtaposing passages or by distinguishing between merely local and universal meanings (e.g., National WRC, New York, November 25–26, 1856, *Proceedings*, 1856, quoted in *CSAS*:229–231). She was skilled in reversal as a refutational strategy, as when she responded to a man who sought to deny women the right to vote: "If he lay stress on his Scripture argument, that the wife must obey the husband, it may in some cases come to cut the other way; as in mine, for example, because *my* husband wishes me to vote, and therefore, according to the Scripture, the gentleman must, even in his own reasoning, allow me the right to vote" (WRC, New York, September 6–7, 1853, *Proceedings*, 85–86, quoted in *CSAS*:209).

A brilliant example of Coffin Mott's rhetorical skill occurred during the 1853 WRC in New York City. The meeting had closed the first day in "uproar and confusion" owing to a disruptive gang of men (Bacon, 1980:1–7). She opened the following day's proceedings by synthesizing several argumentative techniques—reframing, rhetorical question, and enactment:

I suppose, no transactions of a body assembled to deliberate, were ever more outrageously invaded by an attempt to turn them into a mere tumult; yet, though voices were loud and angry . . . not a scream was heard from any woman, nor did any of the "weaker sex" exhibit the slightest terror, or even alarm, at the violent manifestations which invaded the peace of our assemblage.

I felicitate the women on this exhibition of fortitude; of calm moral courage. Should not our opponents, if they have any reason among them, reflect, that these exhibitions are, in reality, some of the strongest arguments that can be offered to support the claims which we stand here to advocate? Do they not show, on the one hand, that men, by whom such an overpowering superiority is arrogated, can betimes demean themselves in such a way as to show that they are wholly unfit for the lofty functions which they demand as their exclusive right? And, on the other hand, do they not conclusively show, that women are possessed of, at least, some of those qualities which assist in calmness of deliberation, during times of excitement and even danger! I think it was really a beautiful sight to see how calm the women remained during last evening's excitement; their self-possession, I consider something truly admirable. . . . Had there been here a company of women who were taught to rely upon others, they would, doubtless, have felt bound to scream for "*their protectors*"; but the self-reliance displayed, which must have its basis in a consciousness of the truth and justice of our cause, and which kept the members of the Convention unmoved, amid all the prevailing confusion, gives us matter of real congratulation. (WRC, New York, September 6–7, 1853, *Proceedings*, 55, quoted in *CSAS*:206–207)

Beyond the presence of mind, courage, and integrity that she enacted as she spoke, this series of rhetorical moves was brilliant, in part, because she appropriated an act calculated to intimidate and silence the women. She also redefined it to provide dramatic evidence of how men oppress women and proof of the very claims about woman's rights that the women had gathered to advance. She and her audience became heroines who survived and prevailed during the experience of overt oppression. As such, they could not be defined as the ''weaker sex,'' expressly enacting a refutation of the myths about women's need for protection. She took this argument even further by alluding in the final line to the women's calm self-reliance as evidence for the truth, justice, and moral righteousness of their cause.

CONCLUSION

Lucretia Coffin Mott's public speeches merit study because she represents a singular voice in nineteenth-century U.S. reform. The most distinctive quality of her rhetoric was the degree to which she relied on a religious foundation for her arguments about all reform, a foundation firmly rooted in her experience as a Quaker. This foundation was the basis for her complex rhetoric about the means to realize a world replete with equality, peace, and justice. Although her way of thinking was characterized by broad, abstract principles, its elements— her epistemology, moral and political philosophy, and rhetoric—were intricately related and internally consistent.

Furthermore, Coffin Mott's discourses merit study in that she addressed virtually every reform movement in nineteenth-century U.S. life. Her rhetoric displayed her ability to draw explicit connections among diverse movements. These connections were evident to her because of her central belief that the inward light ''equalized'' all humanity (Bacon, 1980:73; Greene, *CSAS*:9).

Finally, Coffin Mott's discourses merit study because of the range of her rhetorical techniques and her distinctive style. She was an extemporaneous speaker of remarkable eloquence whose rhetoric was beautifully crafted and is still moving more than a century later. Her style was characterized by connecting broad principles with everyday actions to exemplify them, to make them accessible to people of diverse backgrounds, and to empower them actively to improve society. Her style and highly imagistic language enabled her to connect spiritual insights to contemporaneous contexts. Above all, she held before her audiences a vision of an ideal society and sought to persuade them that their choices and actions had the potential to make that society real.

SOURCES

The Mott Papers and the Sermons Collection, Friends Historical Library (FHL), Swarthmore College, contain speech texts. See also the Miscellaneous Women's Papers Collection, Wilkes College Library, and Sylvina Maria (Dewey) Green Papers, University of Rochester Library.

Other types of primary source material are found in Anne Elizabeth McDowell Papers, Brookline, Massachusetts, Public Library; Anti-Slavery Manuscripts, Elizabeth Stanton Papers, Boston Public Library; Adelaide Johnson Papers, Elizabeth Stanton Papers, NAWSA Records, 1839–1961, Library of Congress, Manuscript Division; Anna Bassett Griscom Papers, Lucretia Mott Papers, Elizabeth Powell Bond Papers, Howland Family Papers, Manuscript Journals Collection, Northern Association of the City and County of Philadelphia For the Relief and Employment of Poor Women Records, Swarthmore College, Friends Historical Library; Anna Lord Strauss, Oral History Collection, and Griffling Papers, Rare Book and manuscript Library, Columbia University; Austin Craig and Craig Family Papers, Minnesota Historical Society, Archives and Manuscripts Division; Ella (Sargent) Montgomery Papers, University of Rochester Library; Florence (Woolsey) Hazard Papers, Cornell University, Department of Manuscripts and University Archives; Florence (Woolsey) Hazard Papers and Garrison Family Papers, Sophia Smith Collection, Smith College; Gardner Family Papers, American Antiquarian Society; Ida A. (Husted) Harper Papers, Huntington Library; Lucretia Mott Papers, Matilda Gage Papers, Schlesinger Library, Radcliffe; Salem Female Anti-Slavery Society Records, 1834–1866, Essex Institute; WRC Records, Seneca Falls, New York, Historical Society; Women's Suffrage Collection, Chicago Historical Society.

Published Primary Materials

James and Lucretia Mott: Life and Letters. Ed. Anna Davis Hallowell. Boston: Houghton, Mifflin, 1884. See Appendix for speech texts. (*JLMLL*)

Mott, Lucretia (Coffin). *Discourse on Woman . . . delivered at the Assembly Building, December 17, 1849*. 1850. Philadelphia: W. P. Kildare, 1869. HOW; *MCSFH* 2:71–97.

———. *Lucretia Mott, Her Complete Speeches and Sermons*. Ed. and intro. Dana Greene. New York: Edwin Mellen Press, 1980. (*CSAS*) A full chronology of her speeches is provided here.

———. *Righteousness Gives Respect to Its Possessor*. Sermon, Unitarian Church, Washington, D.C., January 15, 1843. R. B. Davis, Stenographer. Davis & Pound Printers, Salem, Ohio, 1843.

———. *A Sermon to the Medical Students, delivered by Lucretia Mott, at Cherry Street Meeting House, Philadelphia, on First-day Evening, Second Month; 11th, 1849*. Philadelphia: Merrihew & Thompson, 1849, pp. 3–21. HOW

———. *Slavery and "The Woman Question": Lucretia Mott's Diary of Her Visit to Great Britain to Attend the World's Anti-slavery Convention of 1840*. Ed. Frederick B. Tolles. Haverford, Pa.: Friends' Historical Association, 1952.

Proceedings of the Anti-Sabbath Convention [Boston, March 23–24, 1848]. Port Washington, N.Y.: Kennikat Press, 1971.

The Whole World's Temperance Convention Held at Metropolitan Hall in the City of New York, September 1–2, 1853. New York: Fowler & Wells, 1853.

Selected Biographical Sources

Bacon, Margaret Hope. "Lucretia Mott: Holy Obedience and Human Liberation." *The Influence of Quaker Women on American History: Biographical Studies*. Eds. Carol Stoneburner and John Stoneburner. Symposium papers at Guilford College in 1979. Lewiston, N.Y.: Edwin Mellen Press, 1986.
———. *The Quiet Rebels: The Story of Quakers in America*, New York: Basic Books, 1969.
———. *Valiant Friend: The Life of Lucretia Mott*. New York: Walker, 1980.
Burnett, Constance (Buel). *Five For Freedom; Lucretia Mott, Elizabeth Cady Stanton, Lucy Stone, Susan B. Anthony, Carrie Chapman Catt*. New York: Greenwood, 1968.
Cromwell, Otelia. *Lucretia Mott*. Cambridge, Mass.: Harvard University Press, 1958; New York: Russell & Russell, 1958.
Greene, Dana. "Quaker Feminism: The Case of Lucretia Mott." *Pennsylvania History* 48 (1981):143–154.
Hare, Lloyd Custer Mayhew. *The Greatest American Woman, Lucretia Mott*. 1937. New York: Negro University Press, 1970.
Sterling, Dorothy. *Lucretia Mott, Gentle Warrior*. Garden City, N.Y.: Doubleday, 1964.

Historical Background

Bacon, Margaret Hope. *Mothers of Feminism*. San Francisco: Harper & Row, 1986.
———. "Friends and the 1876 Centennial: Dilemmas, Controversies, and Opportunities." *Quaker History* 66 (Spring 1977):41–50.
———. "Quaker Women and the Charge of Separatism." *Quaker History* 69 (1980):23–26.
Brown, Ira V. "Cradle of Feminism: The Philadelphia Female Anti-Slavery Society, 1833–1840." *Pennsylvania Magazine of History and Biography* 102 (April 1978):143–166.
———. "The Woman's Rights Movement in Pennsylvania, 1848–1873." *Pennsylvania History* 32 (1965):153–165.
Hamm, Thomas D. *The Transformation of American Quakerism: Orthodox Friends, 1800–1907*. Bloomington and Indianapolis: Indiana University Press, 1988.
Hewitt, Nancy A. "Feminist Friends: Agrarian Quakers and the Emergence of Woman's Rights in America." *Feminist Studies* 12 (1986):27–50.
Ingle, H. Larry. *Quakers in Conflict: The Hicksite Reformation*. Knoxville: University of Tennessee Press, 1986.

Critical Studies

Campbell, Karlyn Kohrs. "Responding to Opposition Based on Theology: Proposing a Single Moral Standard." *MCSFH* 1:37–48.
———. "Pluralism in Rhetorical Criticism: The Case of Lucretia Coffin Mott's 'Dis-

course on Woman' ''; A. Cheree Carlson, "Old Teacher in a New School: Lucretia Coffin Mott and the Transformation of Femininity"; Michael C. Leff and Margaret D. Zulick, "Time and the 'True Light' in Lucretia Coffin Mott's 'Discourse on Woman' ''; Malcolm O. Sillars, "From Scripture to Enlightenment: Lucretia Coffin Mott's 'Discourse on Woman' ''; Martha Solomon and Lucy Hogan, "Extending the Conversation; Sharing the Inner Light." Western State Speech Association Convention, Tempe, Ariz., 1991.

Dissertations

Bass, Dorothy Courtenay. "The Best Hopes of the Sexes: The Woman Question in Garrisonian Abolitionism." Ph.D. diss., Brown University, 1980.
Green, John Heyward. "The Rhetoric Antecedent to the Women's Liberation Movement from 1776–1850." Ph.D. diss., Florida State University, 1981.
Halbersleben, Karen Irene. "She Hath Done What She Could: Women's Participation in the British Antislavery Movement, 1825–1870." Ph.D. diss., S.U.N.Y., Buffalo, N.Y., 1987.

VOLTAIRINE DE CLEYRE
(1866–1912), anarchist feminist

CATHERINE HELEN PALCZEWSKI

Voltairine de Cleyre lectured and wrote for and about the anarchist and Free Thought movements from 1887 until her death on June 20, 1912. Originally a freethinker and socialist, she became an anarchist feminist. Although she departed in important ways from anarchist thought, she nevertheless saw anarchism as the solution to social ills, including those faced by women (Marsh, 1981). Despite physical and financial constraints, she was an active lecturer who left a discursive legacy that demonstrates keen understanding of the physical, social, institutional, psychological, and emotional oppression faced by workers and women of all classes. Her speeches and essays on anarchy celebrate a form of individual autonomy that dovetailed with her calls for the emancipation of women and with radical elements of today's feminism. Finally, she delivered many eulogies, notably for the Haymarket martyrs, which transformed their deaths into inspiration for her cause.

De Cleyre's success as a rhetor was astounding, given the obstacles she faced. Because she chose to live a life consistent with her ideals, she took no payment for her anarchist work, supporting herself entirely by teaching English to Jewish immigrants. She rejected all state power, and, in a particularly telling incident when she was the victim of an assassination attempt by a former pupil, she not only refused to press charges but also petitioned for money to help pay for the defense of the man who shot her (*Free Society*, January 11, 1903:5). Long work hours, coupled with chronically bad health, lessened her ability to travel the lecture circuit. Biographer Paul Avrich writes:

Had she been granted the financial means, the physical constitution, and the necessary leisure for sustained writing and speaking, Voltairine de Cleyre might have emerged in the forefront of both the anarchist and feminist movements. As it was, however, she was compelled to work long hours to earn a meager living, with the result that she remained largely in the background and out of the public consciousness, gaining sudden but fleeting prominence on a few dramatic occasions. (1978:6)

Nonetheless, her lectures had an extraordinary impact on her contemporaries. For example, George Brown, the most popular anarchist orator in Philadelphia, wrote of her:

To me, she was the most intellectual woman I ever met; the most patient, brave, and loving comrade I have ever had. She spent her tortured life in the service of an obscure cause. Had she done the same work in some popular cause, she would have been famous and the world would have acclaimed her, as I believe her to have been, the greatest woman America ever produced. (Quoted in Avrich, 1978:101)

As a cause, anarchism also limited the attention paid her. Paul Avrich writes: "Of all the major movements of social reform, anarchism has been subject to the grossest misunderstandings of its nature and objectives. No group has been more abused and misrepresented by the authorities or more feared and detested by the public" (1978:xiii). Anarchism entailed a radical critique of inequality that was understood by few and frightening to many.

Moreover, as the suffrage movement was moving away from appeals to justice and toward celebrations of women's traditional attributes as an expedient rationale for suffrage, de Cleyre was criticizing the pervasive belief in the inequality of the sexes and calling for absolute liberty. Such a rhetorical stance was unlikely to have wide appeal (Marsh, 1981:48, 64). Typical of anarchist feminists of her time, she believed that women needed both economic and emotional independence from men. She also held that marriage as an institution was inherently oppressive of women, and she argued for its rejection. Accordingly, she never married. Her radical views on the Woman Question and marriage fit well with her advocacy of absolute individual liberty, the basis of her anarchism.

BACKGROUND

Voltairine de Cleyre was born on November 17, 1866, in Leslie, Michigan, the daughter of a poor seamstress and an itinerant tailor. She was named for Voltaire by her father, who hoped his third child would be a son (Avrich, 1978:19). She was raised in extreme and unrelieved poverty, and her formal schooling in a Catholic convent, Our Lady of Lake Huron, Sarnia, Ontario, ended when she was seventeen years of age (Avrich, 1978:20). In 1887, she left the family circle and moved to Grand Rapids where she published her first essays and stories in the *Progressive Age* under the pseudonym Fanny Fern, began her association with the Free Thought movement, which eventually led her to anarchism (Avrich, 1978:39), and from which she traveled to lecture on the Free Thought circuit in Michigan.

Although originally driven to Free Thought by her convent experience, she soon turned to anarchism as a way to implement her defense of liberty. Her conversion to anarchism was completed by the injustice of the trial of the Haymarket martyrs, the external event that precipitated internal change; in her words, it was "the specific occasion which ripened tendencies to definition" ("The Making of an Anarchist," *SW*:156).[1]

De Cleyre turned to anarchism rather than to the suffrage movement because the suffrage movement was too conventional, "although she considered herself a feminist and expressed admiration for the suffragists" (Marsh, 1981:128). In the *Freethinkers Magazine* (June 1890), she castigated suffragists for becoming too political: "The original founders of the party, Freethinkers though they are, have become so oneideaed [*sic*] on the suffrage subject as to lose their own moral dignity and truckle to numbers, an incident by no means isolated, which, to my mind, shows the unavoidable corruption of politics itself" (Marsh,

1981:327). However, in February 1892, she formed the Ladies' Liberal League, which may have been modeled after MATILDA JOSLYN GAGE's Women's National Liberal Union (Marsh, 1981:61). The League was designed to be a forum for debating issues related to prohibition, sex, crime, anarchism, and socialism (Avrich, 1978:97). Marsh argues that the League functioned in ways quite similar to those of the consciousness-raising groups that emerged during the second wave of feminism (1981:61).

De Cleyre was a particularly persuasive defender of anarchism for two reasons related to her personal history. First, she willingly admitted that she, too, initially believed the Haymarket anarchists guilty of terrorist activities ("The Eleventh of November 1887"). Accordingly, she was able to speak from her own conversion experience in explaining anarchy to nonanarchists. Second, the indoctrination and regulation that she experienced during schooling in a Catholic convent, to which she was sent for discipline as well as education, left an indelible mark. In "The Making of an Anarchist," her account of why she became an anarchist, she wrote, "there are white scars on my soul yet where ignorance and superstition burnt me with their hell-fire in those stifling days" (SW:156). Her personal knowledge of religious authority fueled her analyses of the perniciousness of the Catholic Church, illustrated by "Secular Education," delivered to Free Thought gatherings, and her memorial lecture "Francisco Ferrer" (SW). Avrich comments: "Being a former pupil in a convent, she was a particularly effective speaker, as she could talk from first hand experience, like the runaway slaves who addressed abolitionist gatherings before the Civil War" (1978:40).

RHETORICAL IMPORTANCE

De Cleyre is an important rhetorical figure for three reasons. First, her anarchist feminism was a precursor of many of the radical critiques of women's status that came out of the second wave of feminism. In *Anarchist Women*, Marsh examines the radical critique of women's position presented by anarchists and argues that the foremothers of today's radical feminism are these turn-of-the-century anarchists. Marsh coined the phrase "anarchist feminist" to describe the philosophical beliefs of those like de Cleyre. Although the prominence of the suffrage movement makes it a more readily available forerunner of contemporary feminism, the ideological link to the work of anarchist feminists is stronger (Marsh, 1981:5). These connections are most evident in contemporary feminist explorations of gender and sexuality. The writings of Jo Freeman and Sheila Cronin and such collections as *The Sexual Liberals and the Attack on Feminism*, *Powers of Desire: The Politics of Sexuality*, and *Pleasure and Danger: Exploring Female Sexuality* present arguments similar to those made by de Cleyre a century ago.

In her study of anarchist women, Marsh identifies de Cleyre's discourse as "the most complete articulation of the anarchist-feminist position to appear in the nineteenth century'' (1981:132). She dates de Cleyre's active exploration of the Woman Question from 1891, the year after her son's birth, explaining: "Prior to that time, although she had demanded the freedom to make her choices as a human being without the hindrance of feminine constraints, she was less aware of the costs of such an assertion; motherhood forced her to confront the consequences of her stance'' (1981:131–132).

De Cleyre rarely combined her views of women and anarchism in the same discourse. The two were always closely linked in her thought, however, as illustrated by her consistent use of workers, women, and slaves as examples of the need for liberty. The one exception to this separate treatment was "Why I Am an Anarchist," delivered in Scotland and England during her 1897 tour (Avrich, 1978:120) and later published in *Mother Earth* (1908).

In that speech, de Cleyre traced her ideological development and isolated the ways in which women, as a class, were denied liberty: by socialization, by the institution of marriage, and by the social pressure to reproduce, which, in turn, were offered as part of the grounding for her turn to anarchism:

Above all, [the reason I am an anarchist is due to] a disgust with the subordinated cramped circle prescribed for women in daily life, whether in the field of material production, or in domestic arrangement, or in educational work; or in the ideals held up to her on all these various screens whereon the ideal reflects itself; a bitter, passionate sense of personal injustice in this respect; an anger at the institutions set up by men, ostensibly to preserve female purity, really working out to make her a baby, an irresponsible doll of a creature not to be trusted outside her "doll's house." A sense of burning disgust that a mere legal form should be considered as the sanction for all manner of bestialities; that a woman should have no right to escape from the coarseness of a husband, or conversely, without calling down the attention, the scandal, the scorn of society. That in spite of all the hardship and torture of existence men and women should go on obeying the old Israelitish command, "Increase and multiply," merely because they have society's permission to do so, without regard to the slaveries to be inflicted upon the unfortunate creatures of their passions. (20–21)

The institutions that bound women to men and children caused de Cleyre to question the role women were allotted in life. She concluded that liberty, not the state, was the solution:

I had meanwhile come to the conclusion that the assumptions as to woman's inferiority were all humbug; that given freedom of opportunity, women were just as responsive as men, just as capable of making their own way, producing as much for the social good as men. I observed that women who were financially independent at present, took very little to the notion that a marriage ceremony was sacred, unless it symbolized the inward reality of psychological and physiological mateship; that most of them who were unfortunate enough to make an original mistake, or to grow apart later, were quite able to take their freedom from a mischievous bond without appealing to the law. Hence, I concluded that the State had nothing left to do here; for it has never attempted to do more

than solve the material difficulties in a miserable, brutal way; and these economic independence would solve for itself. (30)

De Cleyre recognized the role that economic dependence, institutionalized by
marriage, played in women's subordinate status. However, her radicalism did
not stop there. She also called for sexual independence, which extended from
reproductive freedom to sexual choice. Marsh analyzes two speeches that support
this interpretation, "The Gates of Freedom" (1891), and "The Case of Woman
vs. Orthodoxy" (1896), in which the issues of marriage and economic independence are intertwined (132). De Cleyre thought that opposing marriage solely
on the basis of economic dependency was insufficient; women also needed
emotional independence (Marsh, 1981:132). In her analysis of sexuality, the
need for emotional independence is translated into a strategy for social change;
she believed that women should expect nothing from men or from an organized
movement; the struggle for independence was best achieved on an individual
level (Marsh, 1981:133).

In "Sex Slavery" (1890), a defense of Moses Harmon (Avrich, 1978:157–
158), and in "Those who Marry Do Ill" (1907), she defined the boundaries of
sexuality, which included both its pleasures and its dangers. De Cleyre argued
that rape could occur in marriage and that men had no right to force women to
bear children, identifying these as the most serious forms of oppression:

And that is rape, where a man forces himself sexually upon a woman whether he is
licensed by the marriage law to do it or not. And that is the vilest of all tyranny where
a man compels the woman he says he loves, to endure the agony of bearing children that
she does not want, and for whom, as is the rule rather than the exception, they cannot
properly provide. It is worse than any other human oppression; it is fairly *God*-like!
("Sex Slavery," *SW*:345)

The apologists for this slavery were the traditional anarchist demons: church and
state. Responding to these institutional shackles, de Cleyre voiced a battle cry
that seems to presage more contemporary demands: "The questions of souls is
old—we demand our bodies, now" ("Sex Slavery," *SW*:350).

De Cleyre evidenced a deep understanding of the plight of women caught in
marriage. Her solution to sex slavery was not that marriage be improved, but
that, like any permanent sexual and economic relationship, it should be done
away with ("Sex Slavery," *SW*:356). This theme is echoed in "Those Who
Marry Do Ill":

By marriage I mean the real thing, the permanent relation of a man and a woman, sexual
and economical, whereby the present home and family life is maintained. . . . It is the
permanent dependent relationship which, I affirm, is detrimental to the growth of individual character, and to which I am unequivocally opposed. Now my opponents know
where to find me. (502)

To those who said women could leave bad marriages, she responded:

If there is one thing more than another in this whole accursed tissue of false society, which makes me angry, it is the asinine stupidity which with the true phlegm of impenetrable dullness says, "Why don't the women leave!" Will you tell me where they will go and what they will do? ("Sex Slavery," SW:351)

The stupidity of the question rested on the lack of alternatives for women in the late nineteenth century. Accordingly, she recommended a form of guerrilla warfare: "[T]here is no refuge upon earth for the enslaved sex. Right where we are, there we must dig our trenches, and win or die" ("Sex Slavery," SW:352).

De Cleyre not only saw the dangers in sexual relations but also recognized women's sexual needs. In "Sex Slavery," she criticized contemporary fashions because they hid human sexuality (SW:353). In "Those Who Marry Do Ill," she explicitly recognized that sexuality was a normal part of the human condition:

No: I do not believe that the highest human being is the unsexed one, or the one who extirpates his passions by violence, whether religious or scientific violence. I would have people regard all their normal instincts in a normal way, neither gluttonizing nor starving them, neither exalting them beyond their true service nor denouncing them as servitors of evil, both of which mankind are wont to do in considering the sexual passion. (503)

The second reason that de Cleyre is rhetorically noteworthy is that her appeals to and explanation of emotion as a rhetorical device are illuminating. Anarchists prided themselves on their rationality and tended to dismiss emotion. Hence, it is significant that she filled so many of her speeches with vivid imagery that evoked passionate response. She recognized her attachment to her subject; she did not speak as a detached, "objective" observer. Presaging the work of such contemporary feminist philosophers as Gloria Anzaldúa and those anthologized in *Discovering Reality* (1983), *Feminist Perspectives in Philosophy* (1988), and *Feminist Perspectives: Philosophical Essays on Methods and Morals* (1988), she saw emotion as equal to rationality. She contended that feeling was often more authentic than thought because any oppression could be reasoned away.

De Cleyre's most explicit defense of emotion appeared in "Why I Am an Anarchist," in which she argued that emotion and rationality were proportioned with "nine parts feeling to one part thought" and commented that anarchists too often "have prided themselves on the exaggeration of the little tenth, and have chosen to speak rather contemptuously of the 'submerged' nine parts" (17). In explaining her own move to anarchism, she discussed her emotions:

[O]ur feelings are the filtered and tested results of past efforts on the part of the intellect to compass the adaptation of the individual to its surroundings. The unconscious man [*sic*] is the vast reservoir which received the final product of the efforts of the conscious— that brilliant, gleaming, illuminate point at which mental activity centers, but which, after all, is so small a part of the human being. So that if we are to despise feeling we must equally despise logical conviction, since the former is but the preservation of past struggles of the latter. (18)

Accordingly, she refused to expunge references to feelings or emotional appeals in order to adapt to the logical requirements of anarchism. She developed and followed her own notions of piety, as would any true anarchist.

In "Why I Am an Anarchist," de Cleyre guided audience members through a montage of events, feelings, and sights that led her and, if successful, would lead them to embrace anarchism. She justified her approach in her introduction, arguing that personal narratives are more persuasive than pure generalizations (16). She then explained how constant mental activity—"I must do something with my brain" (16)—led her to question the injustices of the present system and to discover their remedy. Thus, unless a person lacks mental activity, she or he, too, will opt for anarchism.

While reflection constituted the first reason for her anarchism, sentiment provided the second. She acknowledged that her approach was a departure from anarchist thought and practice, saying: "I may very likely not be recommending myself to my fellow Anarchists, who would perhaps prefer that I proceeded immediately to reasons" (17). She argued that rehearsing her feelings was appropriate because "my feelings have ever revolted against repression in all forms, even when my intellect, instructed by my conservative teachers, told me repression was right" (18). Feelings were more accurate barometers of social ills than was reason. She equated sentiments and feelings with instincts, explaining that "the instinct of liberty naturally revolted not only at economic servitude, but at the outcome of it, class lines" (18). She catalogued her "instinctive decision" that education should not be constrained by wealth, her "inward protest" against unequal education, her "wild craving" for freedom from conventional dress, speech, and custom, her "eager wish" for less mundane education, her "constant seeking" for better literature, her "unspeakable ennui" at typical literature, her "general disgust" at the ideal woman, her "steady dissatisfaction" with conventional sculpture and art, and "[a]bove all, a disgust with the subordinated cramped circle prescribed for women in daily life" (18–20). She wrote:

All these feelings, these intense sympathies with suffering, these cravings for something earnest, purposeful, these longings to break away from old standards, jumbled about in my ego, produced a shocking war . . . they demanded an answer,—an answer that should coordinate them all, give them direction, be the silver cord running through this mass of disorderly, half-articulate contentions of the soul. (21)

Arguing that emotion had enabled her to comprehend what reason obscured, she claimed that feelings had opened her eyes to the potential of anarchism. To the extent that audiences identified with her feelings, they, too, needed to make sense of them. She provided a way.

De Cleyre used the emotional appeals she justified in "Why I Am an Anarchist'' in many other speeches. She often blended descriptions with emotional language so that listeners were forced to question their rational understanding of the situation. Such a technique was particularly useful in her role as "emissary of anarchism to the non-anarchist world" (Marsh, 1981:135–136). In her 1901 Haymarket memorial speech, she outlined the horrors of the world, in parallel constructions describing what she "saw." This led her to question the system:

[T]heir death drew to my notice, took me up, as it were, upon a mighty hill, wherefrom I saw the roofs of the workshops of the little world. I saw the machines, the things that men had made to ease their burden, the wonderful things, the iron genii, I saw them set their iron teeth in the living flesh of the men who made them; I saw the maimed and crippled stumps of men go limping away into the night that engulfs the poor. . . . I saw the rose fire of the furnace shining on the blanched face of the man who tended it, and knew surely as I knew anything in life, that never would a free man feed his blood to the fire like that. I saw the swarthy bodies, all mangled and crushed. . . . I saw beside the city streets great heaps of horrible colored earth, and down at the bottom of the trench from which it was thrown, so far down that nothing else was visible, bright gleaming eyes, like a wild animal's hunted into its hole. And I knew that free men never chose to labor there. . . . I saw deep down in the hull of the ocean liner the men who shoveled the coal—burned and seared like paper before the grate. . . . I saw the scavenger carts go up and down, drawn by sad brutes driven by sadder ones; for never a man, a man in full possession of his selfhood, would freely choose to spend all his days in the nauseating stench that forces him to swill alcohol to neutralize it. And I saw in the lead works how men were poisoned; and in the sugar refineries how they went insane; and in the factories how they lost their decency; and in the stores how they learned to lie; and I knew it was slavery made them do all this. (*FM*:25–26)

Through enumeration, de Cleyre led the audience through the experiences that had radicalized her, showing them the true face of capitalism. Although it had taken her time to realize the pain in the world, the audience could apprehend it through her speech. The parallel statements of pain seen and the repeated conclusion that this was the work of something other than freedom, constituted a powerful emotional argument. At the end of this graphic description of the results of capitalism, she concluded: "I knew the Anarchists were right—the whole thing must be changed, the whole thing was wrong—the whole system of production and distribution, the whole ideal of life" (*FM*:26).

The third reason for de Cleyre's importance as a rhetorical figure is her consummate skill as a eulogist. She had an ability to reconstitute commemorations rhetorically so that they became a means through which the dead lived on. Her eulogies for the Haymarket martyrs not only present a call to the movement on behalf of those who died, but also attempt to keep their memory alive and, hence, to maintain the memory's radicalizing influence. In her eulogies, she created a secular afterlife for the martyrs. She repeated their words, keeping their memory alive, and incorporated them into the moment. For her, eulogies were not occasions to consign the dead to the past, but to reintegrate them into the present and to link them to the living.

The distinctiveness of de Cleyre's eulogies is clarified by comparison. Kathleen Jamieson and Karlyn Kohrs Campbell describe the typical eulogy as responding

to those human needs created when a community is sundered by the death of one of its members. In Western culture, at least, a eulogy will acknowledge the death, transform the relationship between the living and the dead from present to past tense, ease the mourners' terror at confronting their own mortality, console them by arguing that the deceased lives on, and reknit the community. ("Rhetorical Hybrids," *Quarterly Journal of Speech* 69 [1982]:147)

In this instance, the community of anarchists was sundered by the state-sponsored murder of five of its most powerful voices. Initially, de Cleyre had to justify the willingness of the Haymarket martyrs to die. These men did not recognize the promise of an afterlife; they had to envision their deaths as effecting some material "good." While traditional eulogies seek to transform the relationship to the dead from present to past, the role of martyrdom in a social movement creates incentives for a speaker to take the audience back to the past and to maintain its relationship to the present. By collapsing past and present, the energizing power of martyrdom can be maintained.

De Cleyre attempted this temporal collapse in a number of ways. She referred to the disembodied voices of the martyrs and to their "ghosts" (1895, *FM*:4), "spirit" (1907, *FM*:36), and "Martyr Ghosts" (1910, *FM*:50). The dead were not formless and ethereal; they embodied the present struggles of their followers. In the first Haymarket memorial, she said: "Wherever in the horrible conflict between laborers and soldiers a shattered, shredded striker is borne away by his comrades, who looking on his blood hate deeper, there walks the mangled corpse of Louis Lingg" (*FM*:4). She always repeated the martyrs' words because as long as their words were remembered, they would live on.

De Cleyre's understanding of death is clearest in a eulogy for Katherine Karg Harker, who was an anarchist but not a Haymarket martyr. She said: "To her, to us, it [death] means a melting out of the individual 'I' into the universal All" (5). Transformation into the "all" occurred on two levels: the physical and the spiritual. De Cleyre described this reintegration eloquently:

She [Karg Harker] believed, we believe in the Universal Kinship of all. The blush of a rose leaf or a human cheek, the light of a star or a human eye, the music of a waterfall or a beloved voice, all these are interwoven, interlocked parts of the great panorama of the universe. One law binds all—we are perpetually allied to the infinitelylittle [*sic*], and when all is said we do not know which is great and which is small. But resting sure upon the truth that beyond the all we cannot drift, we know that Death only returns us to our deathless elements. And as of the body, so of that other part of us which religion calls the soul—that part which thinks and feels and loves and hopes and suffers. This, too, returns to its elemental sea, never again to reappear among the living, but ever to reappear in other forms, in other souls, in all the generations yet to come, in all the unborn ones, wherever plain and simple duty is to be done, wherever truth is to be told, wherever liberty is to be served, wherever superstition is to be torn away, wherever the race is to be lifted up—there, I say, will the elements of the soul of her who lies here, the elements of devotion, sincerity, fearlessness, idealism, gleam out purer, stronger, brighter, because she has lived, and been moved by them, and strengthened them in this life. These were the real person, and these deathless. A gift from the past she was, now given to the future. (5)

Insofar as the living embody their beliefs, the dead live on.

De Cleyre also distinguished herself stylistically. Her predilection for writing poetry and short stories shone through in the detailed crafting of her speeches, illustrated by the enumeration in "Why I Am an Anarchist," cited earlier. Quoting from an autobiographical sketch (Wess Papers), Avrich explains:

She considered herself "more of a lecturer than an orator, and more of a writer than either," to quote her own rather modest description. "I am not an orator," she insisted, "and I have a good deal of contempt for extemporaneous speaking, as a rule. It's so disjointed and loaded with repetition. So I usually write my stuff." (41–42)

Consistent with her emphasis on style, she closely guarded her work; editing was not allowed (Avrich, 1978:79).

CONCLUSION

De Cleyre's distinctiveness as a rhetorician came from her deep understanding of the plight of women and the case she made for anarchism as the solution to women's problems, her use of emotional appeals, her ability to create rhetorical afterlives for those who had died for anarchism, and her stylistic skills.

De Cleyre is a largely untapped feminist resource. As feminism attempts to grapple with the dangers and pleasures of sexuality, it should turn to thinkers of earlier times who analyzed the problems and conditions of women. As Marsh writes: "Among the anarchist women of a century ago we find the kind of serious probing of sexual and familial relationships that could serve as a preface to a new feminist analysis" (1978:5).

NOTE

1. A demonstration on May 4, 1886, in support of demands for an eight-hour working day was organized by anarchists and drew a crowd of some 1,500 people to Haymarket Square in Chicago. When police attempted to break up the demonstration, a bomb exploded and rioting ensued. Seven police officers and four others were killed; more than 100 were wounded. Eight anarchist leaders were tried. No evidence was produced that they had made or thrown the bomb; however, they were convicted of inciting violence. Four were hanged, one committed suicide, and the remaining three—after imprisonment for seven years—were pardoned in 1893 by the governor of Illinois on the grounds that the trial was unjust. See *Haymarket Scrapbook*, eds. David Roediger and Franklin Rosemont (Chicago: Charles H. Kerr, 1986).

SOURCES

The Labadie Collection (Lab), University of Michigan, the most complete collection of anarchist material in the United States, holds letters, manuscripts, and other documents by de Cleyre, as well as rare copies of anarchist and Free Thought publications in which she published, for example, *Mother Earth, Free Society, Lucifer, Alarm, Firebrand, Open Court, Twentieth Century, Rights of Labor, Magazine of Poetry, Truth, Chicago Liberal, Boston Investigator, Truth Seeker, Liberty, Independent,* and *Regeneraciòn.*

The Joseph Ishill Collection (Ish), Houghton Library, Harvard University, holds letters and manuscripts collected for a multivolume publication of de Cleyre's writings that was never completed. Other primary sources include:

de Cleyre, Voltairine. *The First Mayday: The Haymarket Speeches, 1895–1910.* Ed. and intro. Paul Avrich. Orkney, N.Y., and Minneapolis: Cienfuegos Press, Libertarian Book Club, & Soil of Liberty, 1980. (*FM*)
Selected Works of Voltairine de Cleyre. Ed. Alexander Berkman. Biographical sketch by Hippolyte Havel. New York: Mother Earth, 1914. Only one speech is identified, but see below. (*SW*)

Biographical Sources

Avrich, Paul. *An American Anarchist: The Life of Voltairine de Cleyre.* Princeton, N.J.: Princeton University Press, 1978.
de Cleyre, Voltairine. "The Past and Future of the Ladies' Liberal League." *Rebel* (October 20, 1895–January 1896). Lab.
Falk, Candace. *Love, Anarchy and Emma Goldman.* New York: Holt, Rinehart & Winston, 1984.
Marsh, Margaret S. *Anarchist Women, 1870–1920.* Philadelphia: Temple University Press, 1981.
Mother Earth 7 (July 1912). Tribute issue; essays by de Cleyre, Harry Kelly, George Brown, Mary Hansen, and Alexander Berkman.
Written in Red: Selected Poems. Ed. and intro. Franklin Rosemont. Chicago: Charles H. Kerr, 1990.

Critical Studies

Greco, Michael Douglas. "The Remembrance of the Haymarket Martyrs: A Marcusean Analysis of the Rhetoric of Voltairine de Cleyre." M.A. thesis, University of North Carolina, 1991.
Rosteck, Thomas, and Michael Leff. "Piety, Propriety, and Perspective: an Interpretation and Application of Key Terms in Kenneth Burke's *Permanence and Change.*" *Western Journal of Speech Communication* 53 (Fall 1989):327–341.

Contemporary Feminist Works

Anzaldúa, Gloria. "Speaking in Tongues: A Letter to Third World Women Writers." *Speaking for Ourselves: Women of the South.* Ed. Maxine Alexander. New York: Pantheon, 1984, pp. 225–231.

Cronin, Sheila. "Marriage." *Radical Feminism*. Eds. Anne Koedt et al. New York: Quadrangle, 1973, pp. 213–221.

Discovering Reality: Feminist Perspectives on Epistemology, Metaphysics, Methodology, and Philosophy of Science. Eds. Sandra Harding and Merrill B. Hintikka. Boston: D. Reidel, 1983.

Feminist Perspectives in Philosophy. Ed. Morwenna Griffiths and Margaret Whitford. Bloomington: Indiana University Press, 1988.

Feminist Perspectives: Philosophical Essays on Methods and Morals. Ed. Lorraine Code et al. Toronto: University of Toronto Press, 1988.

Freeman, Jo. "The Building of the Gilded Cage." *Radical Feminism*. Eds. Anne Koedt et al. New York: Quadrangle, 1973, pp. 127–150.

Pleasure and Danger: Exploring Female Sexuality. Ed. Carole S. Vance. Boston: Routledge & Kegan Paul, 1984.

Powers of Desire: The Politics of Sexuality. Eds. Ann Snitow et al. New York: Monthly Review, 1983.

The Sexual Liberals and the Attack on Feminism. Eds. Dorchen Leidholdt and Janice G. Raymond. New York: Pergamon, 1990.

Chronological List of Major Speeches (Sources identifying texts as speeches are in parentheses.)

"Secular Education." November 1887 Free Thought meetings. *Truth Seeker*, December 3, 1887.

"Thomas Paine." (Probably) Paine Memorial Convention, December 1887, Linesville, Pa. (Avrich, 1978:45), or 1889, Alliance, Ohio (Avrich, 1978:43). The Introduction suggests this was a lecture. *SW*:276–283

"The Drama of the Nineteenth Century." December 16, 1888, Pittsburgh Secular Society (advertisement in Lab). Pittsburgh: R. Staley, Wood Street & Fourth Avenue, 1888?. *SW*:381–406

"The Economic Tendency of Free-thought." Boston, 1890, auspices, American Secular Union. *Liberty*, February 15, 1890.

"Sex Slavery." Probably 1890 (Avrich, 1978:157–158). *SW*:342–358

"The Gates of Freedom." Liberal Convention, March 15, 1891, Topeka, Kans. *Lucifer* April 10, 17, 24; May 1, 8, 15, 22, 29 1891. Lab; Ish

"In Defense of Emma Goldman and the Right of Expropriation." December 16, 1893, New York City. After Goldman's imprisonment for addressing a rally for the unemployed, de Cleyre "delivered a rousing protest against the suppression of free speech" (Avrich, 1978:85). *Free Society* (May 1, 1904):1–3. *Free Society* dates it as 1894, which Avrich contests, *SW*:205–219

"Dyer D. Lum." Probably April 6, 1894, at a memorial; the introduction suggests it was a speech. *SW*:284–296

"The Fruit of the Sacrifice." November 17, 1895. Boston. *FM*

"The Case of Woman vs. Orthodoxy." *Boston Investigator* (September 18, 1896):1–3. (Headnote; also Avrich, 1978:157–158). Lab

"Why I Am an Anarchist." Delivered in Scotland and England during 1897 tour (Avrich, 1978:120). *Mother Earth* 3 (March 1908):16–31, which identifies it as delivered in Hammond, Indiana.

"November 11th." Probably 1897, Philadelphia. *FM*

"November Eleventh." Chicago, November 11, 1899. *Free Society* (November 26, 1899):1+. *FM*

"Our Martyred Comrades." Philadelphia, November 17, 1900. *FM*

"The Eleventh of November 1887." Chicago, November 11, 1901. *Mother Earth* 2 (November 1907). *FM*; *SW*

"Obituary." (Katherine Karg Harker funeral; reread by friend at grave of Kate Austin). *Free Society* (November 30, 1902):5.

"Crime and Punishment." March 15, 1903, Social Science Club, Philadelphia (Avrich, 1978:130); September 17, 1903, London (Avrich, 1978:184). *SW*

"Memorial Address," November 10, 1906, Chicago. *FM*

"Anarchism in Literature." Chicago Social Science League, November 1906 (Avrich, 1978: 192). *Free Society* (March 30, 1902):1–2+. *SW*

"They Who Marry Do Ill." April 28, 1907, Radical Liberal League, Philadelphia; the opposite view was defended by Dr. Henrietta P. Westbrook. *Mother Earth* 2 (January 1908):500–511.

"November Eleventh, Twenty Years Ago." November 11, 1907, New York City. *FM*

"Broad Street Speech." February 20, 1908. *Public Ledger* (February 21, 1908):1. Lab

"Anarchism and American Traditions." March 26, 1909, Harlem Liberal Alliance, New York (Avrich, 1978:205); New York State, for example, Common Council Chamber, Rochester City Hall, October 1910 (Avrich, 1978, 216); mentioned "Tour Impressions II." Pamphlet. New York: International Anarchist Publishing Committee of America, n.d.; Chicago: Free Society Group, 1932. *Mother Earth* 3 (December 1908):344–350; 3 (January 1909):386–393. *SW*

"On Liberty." June 30, 1909, Cooper Union Protest Meeting, National Free Speech Committee (Avrich, 1978:203). *Mother Earth* 4 (July 1909):151–155. Rpt. *Mother Earth* 7 (July 1912):141–145.

"Our Police Censorship." October 8, 1909, Philadelphia. *Mother Earth* 4 (November 1909):297–301.

"Literature the Mirror of Man." October 7, 1910, New York, Workmen's Circle (Avrich, 1978:216). *SW*

"Modern Educational Reform." October 1910, New York State, with "Anarchism and American Traditions" and "The General Strike" (Avrich, 1978:216). *SW*

"Francisco Ferrer." October 13, 1910, Buffalo, N.Y., at a memorial for Ferrer (Avrich, 1978:217–219). *SW*

"The Defiance of August Spies." November 11, 1910, Chicago. *FM*; Lab (handwritten, edited manuscript).

"The Mexican Revolution." October 29, 1911, Chicago. *Mother Earth* 6 (December 1911):301–306; 6 (January 1912):335–341; and 6 (February 1912):374–380. *SW*

"Direct Action." January 21, 1912, Chicago. Pamphlet, *Mother Earth* Publishing Company, 1912. *SW*

ANNA E. DICKINSON

(1842–1932), stump speaker, woman's rights advocate, lyceum star

KARLYN KOHRS CAMPBELL

Intense resistance to women's public speaking continued well into the 1860s, although a number of women had broken the sound barrier in their efforts to abolish slavery and in support of other reforms. Beginning in the 1860s, the speaking career of a singular woman, Anna E. Dickinson, eroded resistance and opened the doors for other women speakers.

Anna Dickinson was the youngest child of a devout Quaker and abolitionist family of Philadelphia. Her father, who died when she was a small child, was an able speaker. Moreover, both of her father's grandmothers had been eloquent Quaker preachers (Chester, 1951:12). Dickinson's formal education in Quaker schools ended when she was fifteen, but she was exposed to literary classics by her mother.

On February 22, 1856, Dickinson first expressed her views publicly when the *Liberator* published her outraged response to reports of the ill treatment of an abolitionist schoolmaster in Kentucky. She first spoke briefly in 1860 at a Friends of Progress meeting at Clarkson Hall, Philadelphia, on "The Rights and Wrongs of Women." Her success at this and subsequent meetings led to invitations to speak in neighboring towns. In the fall, she was invited to the twenty-third anniversary meeting of the Pennsylvania Anti-Slavery Society, which was attended by such leading abolitionists as James and LUCRETIA COFFIN MOTT. According to a *Philadelphia Press* reporter, she "made the speech of the occasion," stoutly defending her view that "If the word 'slave' is not in the Constitution, the *idea* is" (Chester, 1951:19–20).

On February 27, 1861, after being introduced by Lucretia Coffin Mott, Dickinson delivered a two-hour lecture on "The Rights and Wrongs of Women" in Concert Hall, Philadelphia, before some 800 people (Chester, 1951:23; Stanton, 1868:491). Later that year at the annual meeting of the Pennsylvania Anti-Slavery Society, she analyzed the course of the war, and, in an emotional outburst, charged that the battle of Ball's Bluff had been lost "not through ignorance and incompetence, but through the treason of the commanding general, George B. McClellan" (Chester, 1951:29; Stanton, 1868:492). When news of her speech reached the director of the U.S. Mint in Philadelphia, he fired her from her job there, forcing her to seek other means of support. While visiting friends, she spoke on "The National Crisis" in Newport, Rhode Island, a speech repeated in Concert Hall, Philadelphia. At this point she appealed to William Lloyd Garrison, and with his help she was invited to address Theodore Parker's congregation in the immense Music Hall, Boston. Emerson and Wendell Phillips, among others, were also scheduled to speak from this platform (Stanton, 1868:495). With a local anti-slavery committee, Garrison also arranged for her to lecture for a fee in Massachusetts towns three nights a week for four weeks.

As a result of her successful Massachusetts tour, Dickinson received her first lyceum engagement: an invitation to address the Boston Fraternity of the Twenty-eighth Congregational Society for a fee of $100 in a lecture series that included Henry Ward Beecher, George William Curtis, and Wendell Phillips. Her lecture, "Hospital Life," was well received, but no other invitations followed. However, the secretary of the Republican State Central Committee of New Hampshire had heard her lecture (Stanton, 1868:497). Consequently, her career was revived by the 1863 election campaigns, which would determine whether state governments would be headed by supporters of the federal government's war policies.

Dickinson began speaking in small towns in New Hampshire; because of the impact of her speeches, the Republican State Committee put aside its prejudices and hired her as a campaign speaker (Chester, 1951:46). In these speeches, she attacked the Democratic party as being sympathetic to the rebels and disloyal to the Union and called on her audiences to support the administration and the Republican party at the ballot box. They did so by the narrowest of margins, but the governor-elect as well as state Republican papers attributed that result to her speeches.

Dickinson was equally successful speaking in Connecticut, where a bitter election campaign was fought over the recently enacted National Conscription Act. In announcing her arrival, the *Hartford Daily Post* of March 24, 1863, called her "a Joan of Arc that God sent into the field, as many half believed, to maintain the cause of the country at this dreadful and last crisis" (51). The *Hartford Press* reported on her opening speech there on March 25:

In certain powers as a speaker we have never heard her excelled. . . . Her peroration we have never heard equalled. With figure dilating, face impassioned, eye flashing, she poured forth that wonderful illustration and appeal, and the audience, breathless, almost translated, hung upon her words, and, when her voice ceased but slowly regained their self-possession and broke forth into cheering and the most extravagant demonstrations of delight, which continued several minutes. (Quoted in Chester, 1951:52–53)

In the twelve days that remained before the election, she spoke throughout the state, and her repartee with hecklers made these occasions dramatic encounters. When the votes were in, the Republican candidate had won; Connecticut would continue to support the Union cause (Stanton, 1868:499–500).

Her successes culminated in a triumphal address to an audience of 5,000 at Cooper Institute, New York City, on May 7, for which she was paid $100 ("The National Crisis"). She was introduced by Henry Ward Beecher from a platform on which were seated such luminaries as New York Governor Edwin Morgan, Horace Greeley, and other political and literary figures. The *New York Post* report is cited by ELIZABETH CADY STANTON (1868:501–502). Several months later on July 6, 1863, along with Frederick Douglass and Judge W. D. Kelley, she spoke at National Hall, Philadelphia, in an effort to recruit three regiments of African-Americans, whose right to fight had recently been authorized by the secretary of war.

Other important election campaigns remained. In her home state of Pennsylvania, Supreme Court Chief Justice George W. Woodward, an outspoken secessionist, opposed Republican Governor Andrew Curtin, one of Lincoln's strongest supporters. Dickinson was offered the astonishing fee of $1,000 a day for twelve days of speaking, which reflected her unique capacity to campaign for the Republicans in the mining counties where no man dared go (Chester, 1951:70). Despite fears for her safety, she was successful. According to one report, her courage in standing her ground after a curl on her head was shot off gained her a hearing from one group of miners (Chester, 1951:71). The Republicans prevailed in the election, but her fee was never paid, a Republican betrayal she never forgot (Stanton, 1868:504).

Her work for the Republicans led to an invitation to speak in the House of Representatives to members of Congress and their guests (Stanton, 1868:505–507). The invitation was signed by more than one hundred members of Congress, including Vice-President Hannibal Hamlin, and was carried by Judge W. D. Kelley, representing the Congress, and John Nicolay, secretary to President Lincoln. Introduced by Vice-President Hamlin as a Joan of Arc sent by Providence to save the nation (Chester, 1951:5–6), she spoke on Saturday evening, January 16, 1864. She assigned the proceeds (even members of Congress were charged admission) to the Freedmen's Bureau. Response to "Words for the Hour" was positive. The *New York Tribune* briefly noted: "The lecture and the lecturer were enthusiastically received, and the general opinion was of wonderment at the versatility, admiration of the eloquence, and enthusiasm at the patriotism of the lady." The proceeds were estimated at "between $1000 and $1200" (January 18, 1864, 6:5). This unprecedented invitation put her name on the front pages of newspapers throughout the country; she was overwhelmed with invitations to speak (Stanton, 1868:508).

Once the war was over, Dickinson's speaking career shifted from the stump to the lyceum. Lyceum lecturing reached its peak of popularity in the decade following the Civil War. Under the management of such agencies as Redpath and Fall's Boston Lyceum Bureau and the American Literary Bureau in New York, a host of outstanding orators traveled the country from October to May of each year. Although Dickinson was only twenty-three, she immediately became one of the most successful lyceum lecturers. In 1872, at the height of her career, this "Queen of the Lyceum" was grossing more than $20,000 a year, an amount rivaled by only one or two male lecturers and at a time when the president's salary was $25,000 (Chester, 1951:86). Her obituary in the *New York Times* reported: "it was said her earnings as a speaker exceeded a quarter of a million dollars" (October 25, 1932, 19:1).

Dickinson's lecture career ended in the 1870s for a variety of reasons. During the 1871 and 1872 lyceum seasons, she began lecturing on the economic and political implications of postwar industrialization. In "Demagogues and Workingmen" and "Things Hoped For," she opposed monopoly capitalism and criticized the growing trade union movement, positions that lost her important friends and much popular support (Chester, 1951:146). In 1872, she made the fateful decision to denounce President Ulysses S. Grant's renomination. In a speech in Pittsburgh on April 2, she attacked the graft in Grant's administration and criticized the president for abusing the powers of his office. She repeated that speech several times, ending at New York's Cooper Institute. Finally, at the end of October, she spoke again at Cooper Institute to announce her support for the candidacy of Horace Greeley in a speech entitled "Is the War Ended?" Her biographer Giraud Chester found it forceful and persuasive: "As an indictment of an administration in power, it would be difficult to find its superior" (136). But Greeley's cause was hopeless, and her decision was costly; some $14,000 of her lyceum engagements were canceled because of it (Chester, 1951:141).

In the same period, in a dispute over fees, she severed her connection with the Redpath and Fall Lyceum Bureau. In retaliation, some lyceum managers circulated an announcement that she was leaving the platform (Chester, 1951:145). Finally, the panic of 1873 dealt such a severe financial blow to the lyceum that it never fully recovered. With her career in decline, in the spring of 1875, she attempted a special tour into the South where audiences applauded her "Jeanne d'Arc" but were not large enough to make the tour a financial success (Chester, 1951:162–163).

As early as 1868, Dickinson had attempted a career as a writer by publishing a novel called *What Answer?*, but poor reviews and weak sales forced her to focus all her energies on the lyceum as a source of income. On May 8, 1876, she attempted still another career when she appeared in Boston at the New Globe Theatre starring in *Anne Boleyn, or A Crown of Thorns,* a play she had written. As a playwright and an actor, she faced staggering obstacles—the animus of former political opponents and the jealousy of professional theater people, particularly the *New York Tribune*'s drama critic William Winter, who was the most influential of the New York drama critics. Reviews appearing in the Boston papers were favorable, but Winter sarcastically panned both the play and the performance. Although Dickinson toured successfully in New England and in the Midwest, when the play opened in New York in April 1877, the performance was uneven, primarily because the theater manager had failed to rehearse the resident cast. The critics' reviews were scathing. Dickinson made a daring choice—to address the audience following the play and to advertise that she would do so. When she appeared, she responded to her critics, correcting some facts and appealing for a fair hearing. Her attempt failed, not least because the newspapers had too much at stake in the critical reputations of their writers to allow them to be disparaged. Her words were summarized and editorialized by the very men whose judgments she was disputing. The Associated Press, then the only national wire service, so distorted her remarks that at least two of its members published editorials rebuking the agency for its coverage of the speech. Within a week, the play closed.

Dickinson wrote other plays, but only *An American Girl*, a comedy-drama written for actor Fanny Davenport, was a success. However, Dickinson returned to the platform briefly with a lecture, "The Platform and the Stage," in which she asserted that the theater was potentially more influential than lectures, books, the press, and the pulpit (*New York Tribune*, January 18, 1879). She also obtained some lecture bookings for "Jeanne d'Arc."

In 1891, with her career in shambles and her health poor, Dickinson's sister Susan applied to have her committed to the State Hospital for the Insane in Danville, Pennsylvania. Dickinson fought for vindication from these charges in both the courts and the press. The first trial in 1895 resulted in a divided jury; in the second, the jury declared her sane at the time of her incarceration but awarded her damages of only six and one-quarter cents, compelling her to pay court costs of about $3,500. She lived in obscurity in Goshen, New York, until her death on October 22, 1932.

DICKINSON'S RHETORICAL SIGNIFICANCE

Dickinson was preceded by many other women speakers, but she was the first to achieve financial success and national prominence and to win the approval of highly influential male political and literary figures. As a result, she opened doors for other women speakers. Moreover, her ongoing efforts in support of woman's rights and woman suffrage contributed to changes in attitudes that altered state laws and eventually led to full suffrage for women. Her successes resulted from her skills as a political stump speaker and her ability to create lyceum lectures that fused entertainment with education. Her successes were quite remarkable given the controversial topics on which she spoke and the extreme hostility she encountered as a woman speaker. Newspaper headlines spoke of "A Crowing Hen on the Rostrum" (*New York Mercury*, March 3, 1863) and of "Anna E. Dickinson and the Gynaekokracy" (*Geneva, N.Y. Gazette*, March 12, 1866). The latter article includes these comments:

Among the excrescences upon the body politic is one which may be best described by its Greek name Gynaekokracy, which manifests itself in the absurd endeavors of women to usurp the places and execute the functions of the male sex. It is a moral and social monstrosity—an inversion, *bouleversement* of the laws of nature, which have assigned to each sex its appropriate relations and duties; and a subversion, so far as it prevails, of some of the fundamental principles of morality and social order.

Some criticized her style in terms that reflect the limits of what was considered acceptable for a woman speaker. For example:

Miss Dickinson tells stories dramatically, and collocates exceptional instances with an effect that makes them look like general rules. Her pathos is not real. It is artistic. She varies the facts by every resource of color, piles sentence on sentence till Ossa becomes a wart, and then drives all home by a dexterous vocal sinking. The result is rhetorical not spontaneous, and it reaches the audience through their heads and not their hearts.

Her fun is all sarcasm, and not humor. It is spiteful and not good natured. But it smarts the more for it. (Unidentified clipping, AEDP)

In effect, Dickinson had two related rhetorical careers—first as a stump speaker for the Republican party and then as a lyceum lecturer. The textual evidence that remains of her speeches in the 1863 election campaigns demonstrates her command of the strategies needed to be successful on the hustings, a rough-and-tumble form that included heckling from the audience. Her speeches laid out one clearly developed argument. She claimed that only three options were available in responding to the southern rebellion—compromise, division, or a war to subjugate. She detailed the prewar history to demonstrate that compromise was no solution; then she considered division and inquired:

Who will draw the dividing line? How shall we divide the Mississippi, our forts, navy, dock-yards? Some of the Border States already accept the President's plan of emancipation. Are you ready to give them up? Are you ready to yield up the grave of Washington to Jeff. [sic] Davis and his crew? (Hartford Courant, April 6, 1863)

Having eliminated these options, she concluded that war to suppress the rebellion was the only possible course. She therefore urged voters to use their ballots to elect those who supported the Republican administration, which would pursue the war with diligence and end it quickly.

This simple, clear argumentative progression was buttressed by strong efforts to identify the Union with values cherished by her audiences and to associate the Confederacy with people and principles that were abhorrent. For example, in the same speech, she said: "The people of the South claim to be the most aristocratic people in the world. They call you, laboring men, the 'mudsills of society,' 'greasy mechanics,' 'small-fisted farmers,' 'filthy operatives,' and the like." She also claimed: "Across the water the operatives of Lancashire and Manchester are sending their 'God speed the right!' to the North. The autocrats of Europe are on the side of the South." She reminded listeners of the suppression of free speech and free press in the South, freedoms her immigrant audiences had come to the United States to obtain. She used the widely publicized activities of Quantrill's raiders as evidence: "The fact that slavery and free institutions cannot go hand in hand together has been abundantly proved in Kansas. There the homes of free men were burned over their heads, their schools destroyed, and their teachers hung [sic]" (Hartford Courant, April 6, 1863). She refuted charges made against her in the Hartford Times and replied to heckling with clever, sometimes witty repartee. At one point, an audience member, presumably a copperhead, hissed, and she responded: "Loyal men have a good hearty ring of the hand. The men on the other side express themselves according to their nature (Great applause)." Similarly, she engaged listeners directly, asking and answering the questions she assumed were in their minds. For example, she said:

You have nothing to gain, laboring men, by voting for slavery. Give the slaves their liberty in the South, and they will stay there. Refuse it, and they will come to the North, and slave labor will be in competition with your own. Which do you prefer? (Applause.) (*Hartford Courant*, April 6, 1863)

Dickinson's two careers are linked by the topics on which she spoke. She began defending the rights of women, calling for the emancipation of slaves, and supporting policies of Radical Reconstruction. With perhaps the single exception of her most famous lecture, "Jeanne d'Arc," all of her speeches addressed political topics directly, preeminently the legal, economic, and political rights of women, appraisals of the progress of the Civil War and policies that should follow it, and analyses of the postwar rise of monopoly capitalism and trade unionism. As such a catalogue indicates, throughout her public career she spoke on subjects that were deemed completely unsuitable for a woman. Moreover, she took highly controversial stands and seemed to relish struggling to influence hostile audiences.

That she was so successful can be explained by her mastery of dramatic and poetic strategies, elements that made her speeches entertaining as well as highly persuasive. Arguably, she transmuted elements that had made her so successful as a stump speaker into her lyceum lectures. Heckling and repartee became simulated dialogue; political differences over war policy and slavery were transformed into controversial social and political questions; dramatic techniques and emotional language that stirred early audiences to support the Union and Republican candidates became a dramatic style that made her lectures exciting. In other words, by combining discussion of controversial political issues with entertainment, she perfectly amalgamated the educational and recreational functions of the lyceum. In the words of James Redpath: "The lyceum lecture is a failure if it succeeds in imparting instruction only. It should afford pleasure as well" (Horner, 1926:193).

Dickinson's lectures nearly always incorporated simulated dialogue in which she imagined members of the audience asking questions or raising objections that she answered. For example, in "Idiots and Women," a lecture supporting expanded legal rights and full suffrage for women, transitions from one point to another were frequently made through simulated dialogue. She concluded one section by saying, "I would make these women care for the State by a stake in it." Subsequent sections began with questions that might have been posed by audience members:

One cries out in answer to this, she has not time &c. . . . A second exclaims, her proper sphere is home, there is her work. . . . A third declares that women do not know anything about politics, and therefore should not be entrusted with any part of their keeping. . . . Doubted, cries a fourth, denied utterly indeed. . . . (holographic version)

In addition, she enumerated extreme examples, often hypothetical cases, to dramatize the evils she was condemning. In the same lecture, she refuted the claim that women have all the rights they need:

The widows who see the homes they have helped to earn, the lands they have helped to buy, the very house with which they have been served their household work—swept away from them by an unjust decision of a dying husband, and a wicked law. Are these duly represented and have they all the rights they want already? The toiling wives who, struggling hard to save a home, to educate their children properly and clothe them decently see their wages week after week, year after year, paid to their husbands or taken afterwards by them to be squandered in folly and vice, yet living on, staying on, enduring all things rather than part from their children whom the law would give to the degrading control of the husband. Are these duly represented and have they all the rights they want already?

As the quotation illustrates, her lectures were pleasing; argumentative development was punctuated by a refrain, and descriptions incorporated parallel structure and highly emotive terms.

Dickinson's use of vividly descriptive, emotive language is also illustrated by the introduction to "Whited Sepulchres," a lecture on polygamy:

It was at the close of a lovely day in June that I first saw this "City of the Saints." A great stretch of level plain; beyond it, an inland sea of sapphire reflecting a sapphire sky; all about it, range after range of stately mountains, glowing through the marvelously clear air, masses of amber and purple and gold, whilst over all ranged, diamond bright, the eternal walls of snow. In the midst of such surroundings,—the fair things and wonderful things of God's handiwork,—lies this "Whited Sepulchre"; fair indeed to the eye, pleasant to the traveller who knoweth not that the dead are there, and that her inhabitants are in the depths of Hell. (Stenographic holograph)

Later, she used highly emotive terms to paint the moral scene:

I saw hundreds of young girls growing to womanhood, and so growing, approaching a life of sorrow, degradation and shame; I saw on all sides of me coarseness, vulgarity, indecency, and obscenity, dressed in the garb of piety and covered by the cloak of religion, and seeing and hearing and comprehending all this, such an awful sense of degradation and despair took possession of me as a woman, that I covered up my face and cried, "my God, let me die"; and then I bethought me, no! that would be a coward's part; let me live to work; there is need of me.

Although most of the audiences she addressed despised the practice of polygamy, the conclusions she drew were anything but conventional. After asking why these practices were met with "the silence of the press, of the pulpit, of society, of government, and above all, the silence of women elsewhere," she concluded:

In Salt Lake City, they call it religion; in New York, Boston, or Philadelphia, they call it "a young man sowing his wild oats," because things here go uncovered and brazen-faced that elsewhere move masked and vailed [sic] because the underlying theory,—See you I do not say polygamy; I do not say illegal abominations,—but the underlying theory in regard to the proper place and subordination of women, whereon this whole system of polygamy is reared, is precisely the same in Salt Lake that it is in London, Paris, New York, Boston, or Philadelphia, that this woman was sent into the world, not for herself, but for another, and that other, of necessity, a man; that she was put here, not as an individual, not as an entity, not as an entire human being; but as a finishing out and a supplementing and adorning, an after thought, of some other human being, and that other human being, of necessity, a man; that the proper relation between these two is that he should govern and she serve, he rule, she submit, according to that eloquent scholar and divine, Dr. Horace Bushnell, till Heaven shall release her. . . . Stripped of all sentimentality and all glamour; of delicate words and airy sentences, full of idle compliments that signify nothing, the actual theory of these men finds its legitimate consequence in Utah.

Claiming that polygamy was the logical extension of traditional conceptions of womanhood was a shocking challenge to her audiences, yet the lecture was one of her most popular. Surely the drama of her presentation entertained her listeners, and the detailed examples allowed them to savor the delights of an alien, somewhat mysterious sexuality, as the argument challenged them to reconsider the implications of traditional views of women.

A similar willingness to confront the audience is apparent in her lectures on prostitution, a subject deemed unfit for public discussion, particularly by a young, unmarried woman. Dickinson challenged such a view. According to one reporter, she said that "People who would willingly discuss drunkenness, and vice, and poverty, elevated their noses in high disdain at the mention of the degraded of the weaker sex, and their cowardice was not unfrequently [sic] mistaken for delicacy, and their selfishness for refinement of feelings" ("A Woman's View of the Social Evil," New York Times, March 6, 1875). Her success in overcoming the taboo was evident from comments in the Brooklyn Daily News: "The speaker proved that the subject can be publicly treated, even by a woman, without any infraction of feminine propriety or any forfeiture of womanly delicacy or self-respect" (March 6, 1875).

Audiences thronged to Dickinson's lectures to be entertained as well as to be informed about current issues. The controversial topics on which she spoke dramatized issues and heightened the emotional charge of the positions she espoused, as illustrated by her lectures on prostitution, polygamy ("Whited Sepulchres"), women's legal and civil disadvantages ("Women's Work and Wages"; "Idiots and Women"; "Men's Rights"; "Standard Bearers in the Teacher's Battle"), and monopoly capitalism and trade union power ("Demagogues and Working men"; "Things Hoped For"). A Dickinson lecture was politically challenging and emotionally exciting—a dramatic encounter with a controversial issue. Even the nonpolitical "Jeanne d'Arc" treated an ambiguous, troubling woman warrior (Campbell, 1989:94–98).

Despite these highly successful adaptations to audience expectations, Dickinson's views consistently reflected her commitment to natural rights principles, which were the premises from which she argued for woman's rights and full suffrage and for full citizenship for former slaves. She also espoused the principles of universal justice, the premises underlying her arguments for fair treatment of all, including the lowliest workers, especially women. She did not pander to audience beliefs; she frequently championed positions that she knew would be anathema to those she addressed. In all likelihood, part of her appeal to audiences was her courage in demanding a fair hearing for unpopular causes.

CONCLUSION

The contemporary critic might turn to Dickinson's stump speeches as paradigmatic examples of this type of rhetoric at its most effective. Similarly, her lectures are nearly ideal exemplars of lyceum speeches, a form of popular culture that integrated diversion and edification. Finally, all her speeches vividly illustrate the dramatic, somewhat flamboyant style typical of nineteenth-century U.S. oratory.

SOURCES

The Anna E. Dickinson Papers (AEDP), Library of Congress, MS. Collection 17,984, contains holographic texts and newspaper clippings, including published reports of her lectures. Citations are from AEDP unless otherwise indicated. Published texts are:

Addresses of the Hon. W. D. Kelley, Anna E. Dickinson, and Frederick Douglass at a Mass Meeting, Held at National Hall, Philadelphia, July 6, 1863, for the Promotion of Colored Enlistments. Philadelphia, 1863. New York Public Library.

Anna E. Dickinson's "Jeanne D'Arc." *Texts in Context: Critical Dialogues on Significant Episodes in American Political Rhetoric.* Eds. Michael C. Leff and Fred Kauffeld. Davis, Calif.: Hermagoras Press, 1989, pp. 279–310.

Biographical Sources

The most complete is Giraud Chester's *Embattled Maiden: The Life of Anna Dickinson.* New York: G. P. Putnam's Sons, 1951, which lacks annotation but is based on the materials in AEDP. Other sources include:

Anderson, Judith. "Anna E. Dickinson: A Biographical Sketch." M.A. thesis, Lehigh University, 1934.

——. "Anna Dickinson, Antislavery Radical." *Pennsylvania History* 3 (July 1936):147–163.

Horner, Charles F. *Life of James Redpath.* New York: Barse & Hopkins, 1926.

Stanton, Elizabeth Cady. "Anna E. Dickinson." *Eminent Women of the Age; Being Narratives of the Lives and Deeds of the Most Prominent Women of the Present Generation.* Hartford, Conn.: S. M. Betts, 1868, pp. 479–516.

Young, James Harvey. "Anna Elizabeth Dickinson and the Civil War." Ph.D. diss., University of Illinois, 1941. AAC 0144452

————. "Anna Elizabeth Dickinson and the Civil War: For and Against Lincoln."
    Mississippi Valley Historical Review 31 (June 1944):59–80.
————. "Anna Dickinson as Anne Boleyn." *Emory University Quarterly* 5 (October
    1949):163–169.
————. "A Woman Abolitionist Views the South in 1875." *Georgia Historical Quarterly*
    32 (December 1948):241–251.
————. "Dickinson, Anna Elizabeth." *NAW* 1:475–476.

Critical Sources

Campbell, Karlyn Kohrs. "*La Pucelle D'Orleans* Becomes an American Girl: Anna
    Dickinson's Jeanne D'Arc." Eds. Leff and Kauffeld, *Texts in Context*. Davis,
    Calif.: Hermagoras Press, 1989, pp. 91–112.
Caroli, Betty Boyd. "Women Speak Out for Reform." *The Rhetoric of Protest and
    Reform, 1878–1898*. Ed. Paul Boase. Athens OH: Ohio University Press, 1980,
    pp. 212–231.
Linkugel, Wil, and Robert Rowland. "Response to Karlyn Kohrs Campbell's Anna E.
    Dickinson's Jeanne D'Arc: Divergent Views." Eds. Leff and Kauffeld, *Texts in
    Context*. Davis, Calif.: Hermagoras Press, 1989, pp. 113–120.

Chronology of Speeches (Those listed are complete or relatively complete
texts; unless indicated, all are from AEDP.)

"The Three Ways of Peace." *New York Mercury*, March [?] 3, 1863. Connecticut
    Campaign Speech, Allyn Hall, Hartford, Conn., *Hartford Courant*, April 6, 1863.
"The National Crisis." Cooper Institute, May 7 [1863]. Unidentified clipping.
Speech of Anna E. Dickinson at the Southern Loyalists' Convention in Philadelphia,
    September 6, 1866. Unidentified clipping; also "The Pending Canvass," uni-
    dentified clipping.
"Our Political Situation." *Daily Evening Express*. Unidentified clipping, 1866?
"My Policy." *City Bulletin*, 1866?
"We the People." Unidentified clipping, 1866–1867?.
"Women's Work and Wages." New York. Unidentified clipping, April 1867?
"Idiots and Women." Holograph; Parker Fraternity Lectures. *Boston Post*, November
    6, 1867.
"Fair Play." *Boston Post*, January 1, 1869.
"The Struggle for Life." *Daily Gazette* [Ohio?], April 3, 1869.
"To the Rescue." Unidentified clipping, 1870?
"Whited Sepulchres." Holograph by stenographer James A. Slade, as delivered January
    6, 1870, Quincy, Massachusetts.
"Men's Rights." Undated partial holograph, AEDP; *New York Daily Tribune*, January
    11, 1871; "Woman's Work," *Louisville Courier-Journal*, March 13, 1873.
"What's to Hinder?" *Daily Gazette*, Wednesday, March 12, 1871?
"Things Hoped For." *The Press*, October 24, 1872.
"Is the War Ended?" [New York] *Sun* [October 26, 1872].

"Jeanne D'Arc." Undated holograph, 1870?, transcribed in Leff and Kauffeld, 1989;
    also Jeanne D'arc. *New Brunswick Daily Times*, Saturday Evening, 1874?
"Platform and Stage." *New York Daily Tribune*, January 18, 1879.
"Standard Bearers in the Teacher's Battle." Holograph, n.d.

MARGARET DREIER ROBINS

(1868–1945), rhetorical link between two great social movements

PAULA TOMPKINS PRIBBLE

Margaret Dreier Robins was president of the National Women's Trade Union League (NWTUL) from 1907 to 1922, as well as a primary force in its activities during that period. She was a speaker of national prominence whose rhetoric addressed the tension between the woman suffrage movement, with its middle-class orientation, and unionism, with its working-class, masculine orientation. In addressing reform and labor groups, she attempted to expand the masculine definition of work and employment to include the experience of working women. She helped middle-class audiences, particularly women, to understand the problems of working women and inspired sympathetic middle- and working-class women to join together to solve those problems. Her rhetoric was an important link between the woman suffrage and the union movements.

BACKGROUND

Margaret Dreier was one of five children born to middle-class German immigrant parents. The Dreier children were well educated. German was spoken in the home; they were taught by an English governess and in private schools; the equivalent of higher education came through private tutoring and other educational opportunities. In work that would be invaluable later, Margaret Dreier studied public speaking with Lucia Gilbert Runkle, the first woman to write for the editorial page of a major newspaper (*Biographical Cyclopedia*, 113). Moreover, the Dreiers recognized a tradition of female independence and social involvement that encouraged their daughters to pursue careers outside the home. Margaret Dreier's mother was involved in developing industrial education and day-care programs for indigent children and in supporting a vacation and recreation house in Brooklyn for indigent mothers. Dreier's religious upbringing in the German Evangelical Church, which emphasized religious experience, moral earnestness, and social service, was another important basis for her work.

Dreier joined the NWTUL in 1904, believing that it could address the root causes of poverty and prostitution. She served as its treasurer and as president of the New York chapter. In 1905, she met and married Raymond Robins, an ordained minister and a respected member of the Chicago settlement and reform community. She moved to Chicago and became president of the NWTUL and of its Chicago branch in 1907. Her husband's reform activities gave her entrée to labor circles rarely given a female reformer, particularly a suffragist. She was a member of the executive council of the Chicago Federation of Labor (CFL), 1908–1917, and found a sympathetic ear for the problems of working women in its president, John Fitzpatrick. By contrast, her relations with American Federation of Labor (AFL) president Samuel Gompers were rocky, and Gompers and the AFL abandoned their small program for organizing women in 1914.

THE NATIONAL WOMEN'S TRADE UNION LEAGUE

The National Woman's Trade Union League was founded during the AFL convention in 1903 and established its headquarters in Chicago. In the words of Nancy Schrom Dye, the NWTUL "launched organizing campaigns among women throughout the country, attempted to persuade AFL officials to make unionizing women a federation priority, and worked to educate middle-class Americans to the necessity of trade unions for all American workers, male and female (5). The NWTUL, was the only significant woman's rights organization of its time to concentrate on the problems of working women. In this organization, what were labeled middle-class "allies" joined with union women to organize working women into locals that would then join AFL-affiliated unions. Allies were expected to drop out of the organization as more working-class women joined and learned the business of running the NWTUL. Given its makeup, class differences were an important source of tension and conflict within the organization, just as they were with the working women the NWTUL tried to organize and the middle-class women from whom it solicited support (Dye, 1980:40–60).

The financial support of wealthy allies, including Dreier Robins and her sister Mary Dreier, was critical to the NWTUL's survival. In addition to the usual problems of financing small unions, working-class women who committed themselves to union organization were treated as social outcasts by the community and sometimes by their families, thereby increasing their need for outside support (Hyman, 1985:30).

As NWTUL president, Dreier Robins organized support for striking women, sometimes marching in the picket lines herself (Payne, 1988), and the NWTUL provided funds and favorable publicity to women on strike throughout the country (Dye 1980:6). Occasionally, she was involved in the actual negotiation of contracts. Of particular note was her role as a negotiator in the 1910–1911 strike against the Chicago retailer Hart, Schaffner and Marx, which won her the respect of the male Chicago union community and facilitated her election to the executive board of the CFL. Under her leadership, the NWTUL played an important part in organizing women telephone operators, cigar makers, printers, textile workers, and, in particular, the International Ladies' Garment Workers Union (ILGWU). For her, as for many other league members, World War I was a watershed: "The antiradical hysteria the war generated and the social and political repression that followed in its wake killed much of their early enthusiasm and vitality" (Dye, 1980:162). Although she was president of the International Federation of Women Workers from 1919 to 1923, her belief in the efficacy of such work declined. She resigned as NWTUL president in 1922 and moved with her husband to Florida, where she worked in the YWCA, the Red Cross, and the League of Women Voters.

DREIER ROBINS'S RHETORICAL CAREER

In speeches and published writings, Dreier Robins reveals herself as what might be called an idealistic pragmatist. She tried to bring together unionists, working women, and middle-class women in an effort to realize human potential regardless of class or gender: "[R]eally the industrial question is nothing but food and babies and shelter and the love of man for woman and woman for man, and the building of a home in which and through which spring free manhood and womanhood and the gladdest childhood is to find expression" ("Association as Cooperative Agency," 4). She chose not to treat the volatile question of whether women should work, but bluntly stated that they already did:

[T]he great fact which is new in the world's history is not that women have been working or are working, because women have worked from time immemorial, but the fact which is new is that about one hundred years ago the work was taken, by the intervention and through the ingenuity of great minds, from the individual home to the factory. ("Association as Co-operative Agency," 1)

The issue was how to solve the special work-related problems of women. Her discourse presents a dismal picture of the world of the single working woman or working mother. Single women were often sexually harassed or recruited into better paying jobs as prostitutes. In their desperation to feed and clothe their children, mothers endured intolerable conditions for long hours at wages too low to meet their families' needs. Her solution to such problems was the unionization of working women. Thus, her challenge was to convince middle- and working-class women as well as male unionists to organize women into union locals that could strike, negotiate, and administer contracts for themselves.

Union audiences and, to a lesser extent, audiences of working-class women viewed working women through the lens of traditional gender roles, whereas middle-class audiences saw working women through the lens of class. Understanding the rhetorical constraints these audiences placed on Dreier Robins is crucial in assessing her importance as a rhetorician whose efforts linked the labor and woman suffrage movements. In the end, her rhetorical stratagems were more effective in bringing together the interests and concerns of middle- and working-class women than in bridging the interests and concerns of male unionists and working-class women.

Apparently, Dreier Robins had few opportunities formally to address male-dominated unions, although she sometimes published in trade union journals. In Chicago and at the national level, she worked with male unionists and attended national American Federation of Labor (AFL) conventions as a delegate from the NWTUL. AFL-affiliated unions, however, generally were opposed to organizing women, with some union constitutions or bylaws explicitly excluding women from membership. Early in its history, the NWTUL defined its union legitimacy as approval by the AFL, making criticism of AFL policies problematic, if not impossible. AFL policies increased the negotiating power of its unions by requiring them to organize only craft or skilled workers and prevented the establishment of ''dual'' unions that would meet the special needs of disadvantaged groups such as women or minorities. These policies made it almost impossible for the NWTUL to meet the AFL's standards of trade union legitimacy for two reasons. First, most women workers were unskilled or semiskilled industrial workers and, second, some of their experiences and problems in the workplace, for example, sexual harassment and need for childcare, were significantly different from those of men. The AFL did not recognize that women experienced greater tension between their work and family roles than did men and that unions must address that tension successfully to organize women workers.

Support for woman suffrage by Dreier Robins and the NWTUL also strained relations with AFL-affiliated unions. Relations between unions and woman's rights advocates in the nineteenth and early twentieth centuries varied greatly and often were antagonistic. SUSAN B. ANTHONY rejected a basic premise of unionization, that of not crossing picket lines during strikes. This opened woman's rights advocates to charges of scabbing and strikebreaking. Many unionists, including MARY HARRIS (''MOTHER'') JONES, argued that woman's place was in the home or that cheaper women's labor undercut the living wages of husbands and fathers.

In attempting to allay the doubts of unionists about organizing women, Dreier Robins chose to focus on a phenomenon known as underbidding, which struck at the heart of union wage rates. Union wage demands were based on the ideal of a family wage that developed in the nineteenth century. This ''living wage'' would enable working families to attain the cultural standards of an ideal family, which, by the twentieth century, included the idealized gender roles for women in the cult of true womanhood (May, 1985:5, 8–9). Employers who paid women workers less than their male counterparts for the same work created a downward pressure on wages. Women who were anxious to find work would accept lower wages and underbid the wage rate negotiated in union contracts, encouraging employers to pay everyone less.

As noted, Dreier Robins strategically sidestepped the issue of whether women should work to argue that unionization was the solution to the problem of women as underbidders. Through unionization, women workers could be educated to understand the forces that caused them to be underbidders in the workplace; ''to teach girls of fourteen receiving five cents an hour and women working for three dollars a week, the true value of their labor; to show and interpret to them the tragedy of the underbidder and the certainty with which low wages react in injury to women and the ruin of the home'' (*American Federationist*, 717).

By focusing on underbidding, Dreier Robins highlighted similarities in the working experience of men and women and minimized differences. While she was initially successful in convincing the AFL of the need to organize women, she did not succeed in explaining how women's needs in the workplace and the union differed from those of men. AFL-affiliated unions remained uninterested in modifying their traditions so as to conduct successful organizing drives among women workers. This failure, combined with sexism and prejudices against unskilled and semiskilled workers, prompted the AFL's withdrawal of economic support for organizing women workers by 1914.

The majority of Dreier Robins's extant rhetoric appears to be directed to audiences of middle-class reformers or working women generally sympathetic to the goals of the NWTUL. Her personal papers contain texts or notes for speeches addressing the biennial conventions of the NWTUL and what appear to be middle-class reform groups. There are no notes or texts of addresses to audiences of working women not affiliated with the NWTUL. However, some of the themes and arguments she used to address male unionists and middle-class women were probably used in addressing unorganized working women, most likely during organizing campaigns or strikes. Nonetheless, understanding some of the characteristics of working women as an audience is useful in assessing Dreir Robins's rhetorical career.

However inaccurate their perceptions, working women of this era generally envisioned themselves as working at unskilled or semiskilled jobs until marriage and then becoming homemakers supported by their husbands. Working women generally had a strong sense of family responsibility and a desire to be part of a family (Eisenstein, 1983; Montgomery, 1989, 138–148). Because immigrant women often outnumbered the U.S.-born women in particular industries, Dreier Robins and the NWTUL had to adapt to closely held traditional cultural roles for women, particularly in Italian, Russian, East European, and Jewish communities (Hyman, 1985:27–31).

For many of these women, work was a necessity, not a choice. Work and family were parts of an uneasy alliance, necessary for the family's survival. It was also a potential threat to the family's existence, especially when a job required working long hours for low wages in unsanitary work conditions. Single mothers, of course, had to work to support themselves and their children, but married women and young girls sometimes were compelled to work because husbands and fathers could not earn enough to support their families. Although such work initially was more an act of survival than of self-actualization, the experience of working fostered a sense of independence and self-reliance (Eisenstein 1983). To such audiences, Dreier Robins's descriptions of jobs with long hours and low wages, unsanitary conditions, sexual harassment, or discrimination would ring true because these were the jobs women working in industry often were compelled to accept.

Middle-class women, who comprised a substantial part of the audiences to whom she spoke, either as members of reform groups or as NWTUL allies of working women, posed a different rhetorical challenge. With these women, Dreier Robins needed to overcome prejudices against unions rooted in middle-class values of individualism and capitalism. This encouraged viewing employment relationships in economic rather than social terms and workers as free agents who entered into employment contracts at will.

In early speeches before reform groups, Dreier Robins questioned society's acceptance of the economic laws of supply and demand in controlling human relationships for the production of wealth. This acceptance, she argued, allowed members of the middle class to avoid their moral responsibilities to society. Instead, the industrial question should be seen in terms of adequate food, establishing homes, promoting health and mental and spiritual development. "My Friends, it is the moral law which is violated when we deprive men and women of their chance, of their opportunity to grow to the full capacity of their manhood and womanhood, and what lasting basis has any economic law but the basis of the moral law? ("Industrial Conditions and Public Opinion," 5; also "Industrial Conditions in Large Cities" and "Association as a Co-operative Agency"). In two speeches in 1913 advocating the minimum wage, she described society as a " 'wealth producing, poverty-breeding' industrial chaos" in which industries paying low wages were parasites living off of the community "through its reformatories and its prisons, through its alms houses and homes for the aged" ("Minimum Wage," 5; 1913 Convention, 5). People, not wealth, she said, are the most important asset and product of a nation. "Is it not, therefore, time for us to insist that the State cannot afford to put in so great an investment only to reap the continuous loss of the defeated young lives that go under in the industrial world[?]" (1913 Convention, 7). She argued that with industrial democracy the working class could establish the conditions under which this youthful potential would blossom.

To convince middle-class audiences to support the NWTUL, Dreier Robins had to confront their biases against unions: "I know that there is a great prejudice against trade unionism, and I think that prejudice has its root in some of our finest traditions . . . that the individual must work out his own salvation" (1906 Address, 6). When middle-class audiences applied the presumption of individual freedom and initiative to economic relationships, the poor were held responsible for their poverty because they freely chose their contract of employment. She often challenged middle-class audiences with the question of whether it is possible for women or men who work to survive, to exercise the individual freedom cherished by the middle class.

Has the woman who, by virtue of this freedom of contract, works 18 hours a day, has she really as great a chance and opportunity to work out her individual life as the woman who works ten hours or eight hours a day? Does the chance to work out one's individuality live in the number of hours one must work for one's absolute necessities[?] Aren't we perhaps quibbling in words when we speak of the freedom of contract, when on the one side we have a man plus his capital and on the other side we have a man or a woman plus very probably starvation? (1906 Address, 7)

Her view of individualism distinguished her from middle-class woman suffragists such as SUSAN B. ANTHONY and ELIZABETH CADY STANTON who argued from premises of natural or legal rights that emphasized the value of the individual, illustrated by Cady Stanton's eloquent statement of nineteenth-century feminism, "The Solitude of Self." On issues such as protective legislation for working women and the Equal Rights Amendment, Dreier Robins's views and the official views of the NWTUL set them apart from some suffragists, including the National Woman's party. For working-class women, embracing the value of individualism aggravated problems they faced as workers. By contrast, subordinating individual will to the group in order to strike, negotiate, and administer labor contracts created the power necessary to change working conditions, wages, and hours. Only then could working women reach their intellectual and spiritual potential.

Dreier Robins actively supported and worked for suffrage as a stump speaker, as chair of the Chicago Woman Suffrage party (1911), and as a member of the Leslie Woman Suffrage Commission (1917–1920), a national lobbying group for passage of a federal amendment. But she argued that unionization took priority for working women because women could organize themselves and directly affect their working conditions, while they had to wait to convince men to pass woman suffrage (1908 Address). However, suffrage was very important to working women.

Few of Dreier Robins's speeches that support suffrage survive, but her 1910 testimony in congressional hearings on woman suffrage offers a glimpse of her rhetorical strategy. She employed an expediency argument, claiming that the ballot would protect the health and, thus, the motherhood of women who worked in deplorable industrial conditions. Suffrage would augment the power of unionized women to organize locals, negotiate contracts, strike, and lobby for protective legislation, making working women more effective unionists.

When these young women come together to protest and take collective action, they generally form themselves into a union. The women, an unorganized group of women, get together and take collective action, and they find themselves not fighting their industrial battles in the economic field, but they find that they are fighting their industrial battles in the political field, and the weapons that are most certain and most consistently used against them with the greatest success are the political weapons. Now, in these two strikes, and in every other strike, we had our young girls arrested. We had the power of the police used against the girls in many instances. We had the power of the courts used against the girls in many instances. We had injunctions used against the girls in many instances. And whenever we try to meet that political power, or the expression of that political power, we are handicapped, because there is no power in our hand to help change that political power (2–3).

Her testimony reveals the dual burden of class and gender borne by the working woman and further illuminates her rhetorical problem as an advocate for working women before middle-class audiences. Here, she had few common values on which to build an argument for aiding working women. Claims grounded in individual rights could not be used because of the collective values of unionism. Her commitment to unionism clashed with the laissez-faire capitalist values of her audience. Her refusal to question whether women should work clashed with the middle-class cultural roles of woman as wife and mother. With such audiences, her professed concern for the motherhood of working women would ring false; presumably, working women should be encouraged to stay at home and care for their families. Given these class differences, on what basis could middle-class and working women cooperate?

Dreier Robins believed that all women were bound to one another by nurturing qualities that found expression in motherhood, literally or figuratively. The NWTUL ideal of motherhood was represented in its emblem, which showed a woman holding a toddler and shaking the hand of a shield-bearing Athena with the caption, "National Women's Trade Union League. The Eight-Hour Day. A Living Wage. To Guard the Home" (Payne, 1988). While president, she also hung in her office a lithograph representing the reality of motherhood for the working woman. Entitled *Sacred Motherhood*, the lithograph showed an exhausted working woman in a tenement, suckling an infant while operating a sewing machine to support herself and her three children (Payne, 1988: frontispiece). This lithograph was used on stationary in a NWTUL campaign to raise funds to provide milk for the children of striking women (Payne, 1988:134).

Dreier Robins argued that people and societies (of Christian conscience) must judge their actions by whether or not they create an environment for raising children into intellectually, morally, and spiritually capable adults. For a working woman, this produced a cruel irony. By working at a low-paying job to support herself or her family, her wages served to undermine the wage rates necessary for a minimum standard of living for the working-class family, assuring its eventual demise. Neither remaining at home nor working in industry aided unorganized working-class women in fulfilling their ultimate human responsibility, bearing and raising the next generation. In a union, however, the experience of working women would change. "Can we not teach our young women that to lower the wage or increase the hours is to lower the income of their future home, and that to stand together in the demand for a shorter work day, in the demand for social control of wages and hours both through trade organization and legislation is to guard and protect the home of the people, their own and that of the race?" (1909 Convention, 6). Middle-class women would be more likely to aid in unionizing working women if they understood that unions gave women the freedom to raise and educate future generations.

Although she often spoke of motherhood in the physical sense of bearing and raising children, Dreier Robins was childless. But helping children and even adults to realize their full potential as human beings in a democratic society was, for her, the ultimate moral responsibility for both women and men.

Workers in particular were prevented from realizing their human potential or participating in democratic society because of the conditions of an autocratic workplace. Unions brought industrial democracy, nurturing the native intelligence and creativity of workers. The benefits to women were threefold. First, a young working girl, in particular, had an opportunity to "grow into the power of her womanhood" in fellowship with other women (1909 Convention, 4). Second, a union of workers, the equal of management at the negotiating table, could establish the living wages, reasonable hours, and healthy working conditions needed for workers to develop their physical, intellectual, and spiritual potential. This potential was of particular importance for women who bear and raise the next generation. Third, working with one's peers to negotiate and administer a union contract was an exercise in self-government and training for citizenship in a democratic society ("Association as Co-operative Agency," 4–7; see also 1911 Convention, 4–5). Participation in political democracy naturally followed from participation in industrial democracy.

Dreier Robins did not argue that woman is the nurturer and protector of the home while man is not, although she recognized that working women felt the tension between work and family keenly. In addressing male unionists, her depiction of women as unknowing underbidders of union wage rates highlighted similarities and minimized differences between the experiences of working men and women. This approach is significant because of the contrast with expediency arguments by other suffragists, who expanded the cultural images of women as nurturant wives and mothers beyond the home to the public sphere of men. Instead, Dreier Robins presented both working-class men and women as victims of industrial society. Because men were unable to support their families, their wives and daughters had to join them in the workplace. A widow had no recourse but to find a job to support her family because of the nearsightedness and immorality of industrial capitalism. Men and women enter the workplace for the same reason: to support the family.

However, Dreier Robins saw women, not men and women, as ultimately responsible for children. This viewpoint is reflected in the issues the NWTUL addressed as concerns of women that traditional unions ignored (e.g., childcare, health, nutrition, sexual harassment, and prostitution) and in the visual rhetoric of the NWTUL emblem and the lithograph *Sacred Motherhood*, described earlier. This view of the similar nature and experiences of working women and men blunted the impact of her persuasive efforts to help traditional unions understand the distinctive plight of the working woman. Her claims that both working men and women strive to ensure the survival of the family and are victims of industrial capitalism provided traditional unions with little reason to change their organizing strategies and policies to accommodate the needs of women workers. Whatever differences existed would be addressed through traditional union structures and activities. Accordingly, if traditional approaches failed in organizing women workers, the fault lay with women, not unions.

By contrast, audiences of middle-class women who believed that the bonds of womanhood extended to all women and distinguished them from men, and who had been convinced to support suffrage because it would help women protect the home, would find Dreier Robins's vision of the distinctive nature of the working woman's experience more convincing. These audiences would be more likely to focus on her themes of bearing and raising future generations and threats to the health of working women, which pointed to the ways that the experiences of working women were distinctive. Such audiences would see the need for special union efforts directed toward women workers. In sum, Dreier Robins's rhetoric presented two conflicting views of men and women: that their experiences as workers were alike and that their needs as workers were different. Before union audiences, she did not clearly distinguish the experiences of men and women workers or make such distinctions compelling, which enabled male unionists to continue to overlook the specialized needs of women workers. Instead, they could focus on her descriptions and analyses of the shared class experience of men and women workers, which she had to present to earn credibility as an advocate of unionization.

Before audiences of middle-class women, however, Dreier Robins's rhetorical efforts were more successful in pointing out fundamental class differences, while emphasizing the need for unity so that all women could fulfill their natural and moral purpose, to bear and raise future generations. Her rhetorical style, which was both refutational and inspirational, was a key factor in her success.

Dreier Robins's speeches before middle-class audiences were clearly refutational. She rejected the relevance of many middle-class values for the working class and substituted the values of organization and industrial democracy. A common strategy was to use rhetorical questions to ask why middle-class truisms were inadequate to explain the persistence of social ills such as poverty, unemployment, or prostitution:

For instance I presume that each one of us has been taught that if a man be but honest and industrious and thrifty he will thereby win for himself larger opportunities of education and leisure and thought; but if the economic question can be translated into everyday language to mean a demand for shelter and food—the demand that the love of man for woman and woman for man express itself in the building of a home—then the economic question stands as the great denial to thousands of men and women in our country who are honest and industrious and thrifty. What is it we are asking of women when we ask them to work for five or six dollars a week with no chance of promotion? When we know that wage to be independent of the result attained and unrelated to the quality or ability of the work or the worker? (1906 Address, 2–3; also 1908 Address; 1913 Convention)

Dreier Robins used a variety of supporting materials to substantiate and illustrate her claims, refuting conventional wisdom with statistics, U.S. census data, examples, analogies, and expert and personal testimony. Using a more inductive approach, she often presented the new social virtues created by union organization—fellowship and industrial democracy. Living by these values would bring freedom to working-class women:

Unorganized she has to accept conditions as she finds them, low wages, long hours, abusive language, unsanitary conditions, locked doors, fire dangers, work destructive of her physical strength with its promise of the future, work destructive of her moral and spiritual development. Alone she cannot even protest against these conditions, except at the risk of losing her job. She has tried,—she now knows. She loses her job when she asserts her fundamental right to have a voice as to the conditions under which she works. Self-government is essential to the making of a free people, and self-government in the day's work can be had only by the united action of the workers.'' (1913 Convention, 2)

Although her refutation convinced many middle-class women of the need to address the problems of working-class women, it did not convince audiences of the inevitability of success or inspire them to join this cause. Such motive force was needed to convince middle-class audiences to bridge class boundaries and aid their working sisters. Narratives provided an impetus in two ways.

Dreier Robins openly professed a love of pageantry and storytelling. She used narratives to augment her authority as a speaker. Stories of her own experiences established her as someone with first-hand knowledge of the problems of working women. Third-person narratives had a subtly different effect, presenting her as a knowledgeable mother figure. From a position of relative omniscience, she would recount the plight of "every working woman," and then instruct audiences in what had to be done.

The girl who is hungry and tired and lonely is likely to take "a long chance," and when invitations come from foreladies as well as foremen in the department stores or factories, or are brought by leading customers of her employer, her instinctive friendliness naturally responds. That there is commercialized vice, organized for the purpose of betraying the youngest of our sisters, we now all know, and that it sends its representatives into the day's work of factory and story and business we all know. The only protection for the girl under those circumstances is to be found in her trade union organization. . . . To strengthen the hands of the girls so that they are empowered to protect themselves within the four walls of their work is the imperative duty of every man or woman who wishes to combat social wrong. (1913 Convention, 6)

Such narration subtly legitimized Dreier Robins's moral instructions to her audience, presenting them as natural and factual. The "we" linking her to the audience was more an assertion of her authority than of agreement. Especially in her discussions of the social importance of motherhood, such narratives helped shape her persona as that of a mother figure who nurtured and inspired her listeners to a heightened moral awareness.

Characterization and plot were often inspirational, depicting working women and their supporters as engaged in a utopian struggle to protect the home. The romantic plot structure implied the inevitability of NWTUL success. Dreier Robins pictured working women as striving for virtue in difficult or impossible situations, as in the above example of recruiting working women for prostitution. When these innately virtuous women were allowed to follow their natural tendencies in an atmosphere of industrial democracy, the sanctity of the home and the health of future generations was assured. The message of her stories was clear; with unionization, working women would succeed in fulfilling their moral responsibilities.

Middle-class women exhibited a different virtue: that of supporting their working-class sisters in their efforts to establish industrial democracy. Dreier Robins's 1910 address, "The Association as a Co-operative Agency for the Industrial Improvement of the Women of the Community," is an important speech because in it she tells a different story of success, of middle-class and working-class women cooperating to win a dressmakers strike in Philadelphia. In one passage, she states:

I remember when Mrs. Biddle came to me and said, "What can I do for you?" I said, "Just two things; will you go bonds [sic] for us, and then would you mind if your daughter got arrested?" She said, "I will go bond [sic] for you the first chance you give me, and Constance can get arrested." (11–12)

This dialogue portrays a virtuous middle-class woman willing to stand beside working-class women in defense of womanhood. In the romantic logic of this act of solidarity, success is the necessary outcome of virtuous women united in action.

Dreier Robins used refutational and narrative techniques to illuminate fundamental differences and similarities in the experiences of middle- and working-class women and to urge middle-class women to support their working-class sisters. These strategies induced identification with, yet a distancing from, working-class women, which made it possible for middle-class women to recognize that class differences limited their understanding of working women as women and mothers. When these differences were acknowledged, it was logical to employ special, even unusual, efforts to aid working women in fulfilling their maternal responsibilities.

But a strategy of pointing out similarities and differences between working women and men is not equally evident in discourse directed toward union audiences. Because of the AFL's policy against dual unions and prejudices against unskilled workers, the use of such a strategy probably would have caused the AFL to question NWTUL members' legitimacy as unionists. The rhetorical obstacles the AFL and its unions posed were too difficult for Dreier Robins to overcome, especially given limited opportunities to address union audiences. Although they had many successes in organizing women workers, particularly in the needle trades, neither Dreier Robins nor the NWTUL was able cogently to articulate to male unionists the special needs of working women. As one historian points out,

the WTUL was never able to synthesize feminism with unionism or its commitment to sorority with its commitment to class solidarity. Nor was the WTUL able to confront the labor movement on its own ground. The league's difficulties were not unique. Feminists have yet to formulate an analysis that comes to terms with working women's dual status, and feminism has yet to make a significant impact on the American labor movement. (Dye, 1980:4)

CONCLUSION

Dreier Robins's legacy to the labor and the woman's rights/woman suffrage movements is an important one. Although she neither produced a rhetorical masterpiece nor served as a guiding force behind landmark legislation, her efforts to explain and solve the problems of working women were a rhetorical link between these two great social movements. She saw a natural affinity between struggles for civil rights for women and for industrial democracy in addressing the plight of working women, and she sought to speak to both and bring them together.

SOURCES

The Margaret Dreier Robins Papers, University of Florida, Gainesville, and those of other WTUL women, are available on microfilm as *Papers of the Women's Trade Union League and Its Principal Leaders* (PWPL; Dreier Robins Papers, Collection 1, especially reel 12). *Proceedings of the Biennial Convention of the NWTUL* (PBC), Library of Congress, are on microfilm; one essay and the 1913 NWTUL convention address are in HOW, Reel 944.

Selected Biographical Sources

Biographical Cyclopedia of American Women. Vol. 2. Ed. Erma Conklin Lee. New York: n.p., 1925.

Dreier, Mary E. *Margaret Dreier Robins: Her Life, Letters and Work*. New York: Island Press, 1950.

Estes, Barbara Ann. "Margaret Dreier Robins: Social Reformer and Labor Organizer." Ph.D. diss., Ball State University, 1977.

Payne, Elizabeth Anne. *Reform, Labor, and Feminism: Margaret Dreier Robins and the Women's Trade Union League*. Urbana, Ill.: University of Chicago Press, 1988.

Selected Studies of the NWTUL and Working Women

Dye, Nancy Schrom. *As Equals & As Sisters: Feminism, Unionism, and the Women's Trade Union League of New York*. Columbia: University of Missouri Press, 1980.

Eisenstein, Sarah. *Give Us Bread But Give Us Roses: Working Women's Consciousness in the United States, 1890 to the First World War*. Boston: Routledge & Kegan Paul, 1983.

Hyman, Collette A. "Labor Organizing and Female Institution-Building: The Chicago Women's Trade Union League, 1904–1924." *Women, Work & Protest: A Century*

of US Women's Labor History. Ed. Ruth Milkman. Boston: Routledge & Kegan
    Paul, 1985, pp. 22–41.
May, Martha. "Bread Before Roses: American Workingmen, Labor Unions and the
    Family Wage." Women, Work & Protest, pp. 1–21.
Montgomery, David. The Fall of the House of Labor: The Workplace, the State and
    American Labor Activism, 1865–1925. Cambridge, England: Cambridge Univer-
    sity Press, 1987.

Chronology of Major Speeches (Unless indicated, all are in PWPL.)

Address on Industrial Conditions and Public Opinion, 1906.

Address on Industrial Conditions in Large Cities, 1908.

Presidential Address to the 1909 NWTUL Convention, Proceedings, pp. 4–7. PBC

Statement of Mrs. Raymond Robins of Chicago, Women's Suffrage Hearing, Washington,
    D.C., April 19, 1910.

"The Association as a Co-operative Agency for the Industrial Improvement of the Women
    of the Community." Lake Geneva, Wis., August 23, 1910.

Presidential Address to the 1911 NWTUL Convention, Proceedings, pp. 4–6.

"The Minimum Wage." Progressive Conference, Springfield, Ill., April 29, 1913.

"Need of a National Training School for Women Organizers, the Minimum Wage, and
    Industrial Education." Presidential Address, 1913 NWTUL Convention. PWPL;
    PBC; HOW

"Working Women and Organization." American Federationist September 1914:717–
    719.

Presidential Address to the 1915 NWTUL Convention. PBC

Presidential Address to the 1917 NWTUL Convention. PBC

Presidential Address to the 1919 NWTUL Convention.

Address on the Industrial Question. 1922.

Address, First Baptist Church, Philadelphia. March 2, 1922.

"The Human Side of the New Industrial South." 1929 NWTUL Convention.

ROSA FASSEL SONNESCHEIN

(1847–1932), editor and publisher of the *American Jewess*

SANDRA J. BERKOWITZ

Woman's rights, broadly defined, addressed the concerns of all women, whereas woman suffrage was a tool that women of diverse backgrounds saw as a way to achieve their ends. However, as illustrated by the rhetoric of such figures as MARIA W. MILLER STEWART, SOJOURNER TRUTH, and IDA B. WELLS, some issues were of special concern for women of distinctive ethnic backgrounds. In this instance, Jews of German heritage immigrated to the United States prior to the waves of immigrants from Eastern Europe and Russia that aroused intense anti-Semitism in the United States (e.g., Cohen, 1984; Howe, 1976). Given their Western European heritage, German Jews found it easier to fit into the new society. Moreover, Reform Judaism, which had taken hold in Germany earlier, eased this process. By the 1890s, Louise A. Mayo notes that "social mobility had enabled a sizable number of Jews to become wealthy. The children and grandchildren of the German Jewish immigrants of the middle of the century were increasingly educated and genteel" (1988:183). However, despite their education and their ability to adapt and prosper in their new country, German Jews continually dealt with the problem of creating an identity for themselves that would decrease, if not eliminate, anti-Semitism.

In American society, Jews, even German Jews, were still viewed as "others," but in Europe, more systematic, organized, and legally sanctioned forms of anti-Semitism were built into the political and social systems. In the United States, the emphasis on individualism and separation of church and state meant that anti-Semitism was not codified in law. Although very different from European anti-Semitism, Jews in the United States still faced a social, private form of anti-Semitism (Endelman, 1986; Mayo, 1988). One result of anti-Semitism is a questioning of the self:

The Jew who feels rebuffed by gentiles inevitably asks himself [*sic*]: "Was it I who erred by some inappropriate word or act, or was it my Jewishness that gave offense irrespective of what I said or did?" The effect of this uncertainty is a recurrent anxiety that taxes emotional equilibrium. It arouses fear that a false move will provoke prejudiced judgment: "That is indeed what one would expect from a Jew." (Meyer, 1990:36–37)

In answer to such questions, some Jews gave up their Jewish identity to seek complete assimilation into U.S. society. For many this was not acceptable. Naomi Cohen contends, "First and foremost, the psychological and emotional needs of the immigrant Jews kept them within the fold. Nineteenth-century Americans also preferred immigrants to identify with any religion rather than with none at all" (1984:161). The desire to remain Jewish sparked a debate within American Judaism (Braude, 1981). Jonathan Sarna explains the substance of this debate:

Jews' simultaneous desires both to identify and break with their past express a basic tension in American Jewish life: the tension between tradition and change. Ambivalence about the past reflects ambivalence about the past's religious legacy, ambivalence about the Old World heritage, and ambivalence about assimilation. Many nineteenth-century American Jews displayed conflicting attitudes in all these cases. (1986:74)

For Jewish women, the tension between tradition and change was particularly pronounced. Many hoped that Reform Judaism would provide the way to maintain ties to the community and religion, while facilitating assimilation and an end to negative stereotypes (Sarna, 1986:70–71). Jews wanted the "right to be treated equally while remaining in some, even minor, way different from gentiles" (Meyer, 1990:51–52). Unfortunately, Reform Judaism did not provide easy answers. Even with the further development and growth of Reform Judaism in the United States, inconsistencies between traditional and contemporary views remained.

The traditional, Orthodox, view of woman's role was to facilitate man's religious study. For the Jewish woman, the private sphere was of primary importance. Her role was to enact the "Woman of Valor." Historian Jacob Rader Marcus describes the history and reality of this role:

The acrostic Hebrew prose poem which begins with Proverbs 31:10 had for millennia determined the role in life of the Woman of Valor:

The heart of her husband doth safely trust in her,
And he hath no lack of gain.

It is all so simple; she works, he prospers, but he must not fail to praise her on the public square; her children must rise up and call her blessed. The cult of true womanhood was thus outlined by a Jewish gnomic writer centuries before the rise of Christianity. (1989:674)

This particular definition allowed the Jewish woman limited access to the public sphere, but only to make money so that men could pursue the more important work of learning and studying. Whether a woman should remain in the private realm of wife and mother or should and could become an active participant in the public sphere was a pressing issue for Jewish women in the United States in the 1890s. The *American Jewess*, edited and published by Rosa Fassel Sonneschein between 1895 and 1899, was the first English-language Jewish woman's newspaper published in the United States. It focused on issues related to whether or not a Jewish woman in the United States could remain faithful to her traditional role while embracing more liberated conceptions of woman's identity. Fassel Sonneschein was responsible for addressing these issues directly.

BACKGROUND

Rosa Fassel Sonneschein immigrated into this continually evolving Jewish community in the United States. She was born March 12, 1847, in Prossnitz,

Moravia, which was then part of Austria, and she was the youngest of nine children of Oberrabiner Hirsch-Baer Fassel and Fannie Sternfeld. Her father was a well-known orator and Talmudic scholar who was decorated by several emperors. According to her grandson,

She grew up amid the luxury permitted to the rabbi of Nagykanisza [Hungary], the wealthiest congregation in the country. Her mother died when she was very young, but she was the darling of the whole family—father, childless stepmother, older half-brothers and sisters. (Loth, 1985:43)

Favored by her parents, she was privileged to study in her father's library and to be party to intellectual discussions. She was permitted to refuse her first two marriage proposals, but "such unprecedented liberality would not be repeated. She would soon be seventeen and an old maid, so her father's third choice would be final" (Loth, 1985:43). In this religious, yet relatively liberal, atmosphere, she spent her youth.

In 1864, Rosa Fassel was married to her father's third choice, Solomon Hirsch Sonneschein, a twenty-five-year-old rabbi from Warasdin. Rabbi Sonneschein, an intelligent, well-spoken man, had degrees from the universities of Hamburg and Jena. Soon after their marriage, he was called to Prague, where they became the parents of three children. In an attempt to alleviate problems caused by her husband's drinking, she persuaded him to take a position in New York; she believed "that Americans consumed less alcohol than Europeans" (Loth, 1985:44).

The move to the United States did not resolve their conflicts, although she bore another child. She found that her life in the United States was less busy and less stimulating intellectually than her life in Europe. As an outlet for herself and other women in the St. Louis community where the family ultimately settled, on January 25, 1879, Fassel Sonneschein founded the "Pioneers," the first regular Jewish woman's literary club in the United States (Glanz, 1976:128).

Despite her efforts to find expression for her talents and energies, Fassel Sonneschein was still unhappy in her marriage. Divorce was a practical, if not altogether socially acceptable, solution in the Jewish community and in society at large. David Loth quotes his grandmother as saying, "I wished to be rid of him, not ruin him" (1985:44). To save the rabbi the embarrassment of being sued for divorce, she allowed him to sue her; they were divorced in 1893 (Porter, 1980:126). Divorce enabled her to look for creative work but also left her in need of a way to support herself. With these goals in mind, she attended the 1893 Columbian Exposition and indicated her desire to publish a newspaper for Jewish women (Porter, 1981:158). It took her two more years to raise the money she needed to start the paper.

JEWISH WOMEN IN THE NINETEENTH CENTURY

Jewish women in the United States faced barriers to their individual development that stemmed from being women and Jews. Based on the traditional role, Jewish women were stereotyped as "seductress," "princess," or dutiful daughter (Mayo, 1988). In order to combat prejudice in the United States and to resist the limitations of the tradition, Jewish women had an alternative: that of assimilating into the white, Protestant middle class. Jewish women looking to gentile society for a role model found the True Woman, who was pure, pious, domestic, and submissive (Welter, 1966:152). Many German-Jewish women emulated this gentile ideal of womanhood (Baum, Hyman, and Michel, 1976:28–29; Neu, 1976). But the choice of assimilation entailed the abandonment of their Jewish identity (Golumb, 1980:55).

Alternatively, women could insulate themselves within the Jewish community. This choice was made more attractive given the modernization in doctrine brought about by the Reform movement. Reform Judaism was more evolutionary than Orthodox Judaism. As practiced, Reform Judaism acknowledged contact with the secular world and was, therefore, modified by it over the generations. "In a word, Reform Judaism differentiates between *tradition* and *the tradition*; it considers itself, too, a link in the chain of Jewish tradition" (Philipson, 1931:3). The result of changes brought about by Reform was a devaluing of custom and legal precedence. However, by devaluing custom and legal precedence, the Reform movement undercut the religious principles that made Jews, and especially Jewish women, unique. Their legal standing in traditional Judaism gave women their distinctive identity in the home and community. By changing the customary legal standard, Reform Judaism took away the foundation of women's identity. Riv-Ellen Prell explains:

Reformers believed that the non-Jewish vision of women was superior. Yet, by freeing Judaism of the legalism of Jewish Orthodoxy, Reformers ultimately made women at best invisible, at worst failed men. . . . In selecting an emancipation model for addressing the problem of gender, that is, in seeking legal equality, classical Reform eroded the only status Judaism had offered women, legal uniqueness. Hence, they made women invisible as they made women equal. (1982:576)

Jewish women faced a dilemma: if they gave up their traditional role, they were left with the mutually undesirable choices of assimilation, in which they lost their identity as Jews, or Reform Judaism, in which they lost their identities as females.

Jewish women studied the implications of these alternatives and struggled to find some resolution. Those who did not wish either to assimilate or to isolate themselves in the Jewish community sought to create an identity that would allow them to retain those aspects of their culture they considered important. The *American Jewess* was born in response to this desire.

When the first issue of the *American Jewess* appeared in April 1895, it became part of the journalistic traditions of the nineteenth century. One tradition flowed from the woman's press. From the early days of the country, columns, if not entire newspapers, were published to serve the needs of women. These journals helped women to recognize their common problems and empowered them to seek change. Linda Steiner describes another important function of the woman's press: "The nineteenth-century woman's rights publications were also necessary given that 'new women' then had relatively few opportunities to meet in person, to see what these new women actually looked like" (1991:183). Newspapers such as the *Revolution*, the *Woman's Journal*, the *Woman's Tribune*, *Woodhull and Claflin's Weekly*, and the *Woman's Exponent* provided forums for the discussion of issues relevant to diverse groups of women. Although many of these early magazines were thwarted by male prejudice, they still created a new clientele of female readers.

Another journalistic influence came from the Jewish press. During the nineteenth century, many religious periodicals appeared that appealed to those in various denominations, and among them were small but important English and Yiddish papers that appealed to Jews (Aronin, 1966), including a fair number of national and community newspapers (Goren, 1987; Singerman, 1984). These publications dispersed vital information to various parts of the American Jewish community, and they served as bridges between the immigrant and the U.S. cultures.

The *American Jewess* helped reconceptualize an identity for Jewish women in the United States. Although the journal does not present a blueprint for the "New Jewish Woman," one who had clearly navigated these conflicting roles, by articulating a Jewish version of social feminism, Rosa Fassel Sonneschein succeeded in capturing and holding a sizable readership. Put differently, she rationalized changes in the traditional Jewish woman's role effected by Reform Judaism as beneficial to the traditional feminine values of the Jewish community. As a result, the Jewish women she addressed were encouraged to seek advanced education, to work outside the home, and to revise traditional customs as a means to realize more fully their place in American society and their more limited but important role in maintaining Jewish values. Indeed, the unresolved ambivalence found in the pages of *American Jewess* raised more questions than it offered answers. The journal had great appeal to those Jewish woman who were trying to develop an identity that would allow them access to American society while permitting them to maintain some parts of their particular identities as Jews.

Fassel Sonneschein comprehended the significance of the debate over image that was going on within the Reform German Jewish community. Furthermore, she recognized a lack of concern over issues related to women and the absence of women's voices in the debate. The *American Jewess* was in a unique position to help its audience address the issues in the debate and to link that debate to the concerns of women. As Fassel Sonneschein reiterated in several of its issues, the audience it targeted was significant for the Jewish community as well as for advertisers:

The *American Jewess* is the *only* Jewish magazine in the world devoted to the interests of Jewish women. It is the *only* illustrated monthly. It is the *only* Jewish publication sold on news-stands throughout the United States. Advertisers ought to bear this in mind, if they wish to gain as patrons a class of people not reached by any other publication. [emphasis in the original] ("Publishers Notes," September 1895:314)

In discussing issues of importance to Jewish women, the paper developed lines of argument that balanced traditionally feminine and more contemporary feminist interests. Thus, in its unique way, the *American Jewess* espoused a kind of social feminism that emphasizes the values and experiences of women. Naomi Black distinguishes between different types of contemporary feminist thought that shed light on the position adopted by Fassel Sonneschein. She writes:

I accept a division among feminists. . . . I suggest the term "equity feminism" for all those many belief systems which focus on women's similarity to men and demand equality for women on that basis. Equity feminism can exist in relation to any ideology, and it has argued for assimilation into fascist as well as democratic systems, collectivist as well as individualistic societies. By contrast, I focus on the "social feminism" that derives from women's specificity an argument for wider public action on the part of women. (1989:11)

For example, K. Kohrs Campbell argues that social feminist arguments, particularly those espoused by FRANCES E. WILLARD in the late nineteenth century, "succeeded in enlarging woman's conception of her sphere, and . . . enabled 'true women' to perceive the ballot as consistent with femininity" (MCSFH, 1:122). Although the ballot was not their chief concern, the argumentative balance for Jewish women was similar.

The *American Jewess* was a bridge between cultures for a large and relatively diverse segment of American Jewish women who were predominantly middle-class and from German-speaking backgrounds. Its moderate price assured a stable readership, which grew to 29,000 by 1899, when it ceased publication. This readership was a testament to Fassel Sonneschein's ability to identify and respond to the needs of her audience. According to the report of her grandson, "her target was a particular segment of American-Jewish women. . . . She saw a need for a magazine to sustain these middle-class women [recent immigrants of German-speaking backgrounds] in their Jewish traditions" (Loth, 1985:43). Because of her own experiences, she understood and sympathized with the competing demands of traditional Jewish and contemporary American culture. However, the journal did not foreclose interest from others who might benefit from the information it contained.

In order to reach and satisfy its target audience, the *American Jewess* opened its pages to diverse authors to discuss a variety of issues. Writers contributed serialized fiction, news of the National Council of Jewish Women, editorials, and letters to ongoing but anonymous conversations in a column entitled "The Woman Who Talks." In its columns and departments, many issues were discussed, including woman's sphere, marriage, motherhood, religious questions, and woman suffrage. However, no issue dramatizes the problems of developing an identity for American Jewish women more than that of assimilation. Fassel Sonneschein described the Jewish woman's commitment to Judaism, even when faced with the advantages of assimilation:

The pulpit pointed out to the Jewess' mind as religious contradiction almost everything upon which her mother looked with reverence. But in spite of these teachings the American-born Jewess could not entirely free herself from parental religious influence, and she thus became a sort of link between her progenitor and her progeny—the Ghetto Jewess and the subject of our article—the present liberty-loving American Jewess. ("The American Jewess," February 1898:206)

Indeed, in the April 1898 issue, the editor indicated that she believed that the *American Jewess* had done a service for the Jewish woman by bringing her into the public eye. She wrote: "That which we outlined at the start we have to a large extent achieved. We have created a bond of sisterhood, doing our share to weaken existing prejudices against the Jewess by bringing to public notice the Jewess to-day" (22). While the magazine brought the Jewish woman before the public, the Reform movement and life itself brought Jews into close contact with American society. The result was that, as Rabbi Adolph Moses explained in an article entitled "A Glimpse of the Past and Future of Judaism": "We are Americans with every fibre of our being" (*The American Jewess*, September 1896:629). This was an important affirmation. Without a legal foundation for their identity, either within Reform Judaism or society in the United States, the *American Jewess* argued that Jews could maintain both allegiances.

Although such issues as marriage, religious duties, and work outside the home were discussed, there was uncertainty about how these dual allegiances could be maintained in areas of such religious and secular significance. This unresolved ambivalence is best illustrated in a February 1898 article entitled "The American Jewess." Acting as a reporter and as an American Jewish woman, editor Fassel Sonneschein had been asked to write about the American Jewish woman for a European magazine. The article that appeared in the *American Jewess* was a reprint. Yet one audience for the article was Jewish women in the United States. Thus, the article was also exhortative because, in describing an American Jewish woman's identity, she made it an ideal to which all could aspire. By crafting a message that was both descriptive and prescriptive, she tried to redefine the American Jewish woman's role in a nonthreatening way.

When seen as a change from the old ways, assimilation can create "moral conflict." However, Fassel Sonneschein hoped that the radical or threatening dimensions of assimilation would be tempered. As she described the new role, its ultimate goal was not to obliterate traditional values, but to sustain the values of home and family. She described the role of the American Jewish woman this way:

The family life of the American Jewess has shaped itself to the general customs of the country. She enjoys to the full all the liberties granted to her Gentile sisters. In her home she may still occupy the place assigned to her by *"das Hohelied"* ["The Song of Songs"] as the wise, watchful, tireless ruler of the household, but she is by no means a home-body. She is in universal evidence—in the streets, in the shops, at the restaurants, and at the parks. While she guards her daughters with a watchful eye, they are like other American girls—totally independent of her in social matters (208).

After reminding her readers of the ultimate goal, Fassel Sonneschein described some of the changes that had taken place. Those that had occurred should not be threatening because they maintained many traditional values. About marriage and family, for example, she wrote:

Marriage is the foremost aim of the American Jewess, as it was of her grandmother, but in its accomplishment she is not assisted by "shadchan" or parents; and indeed it is not uncommon for a Jewish maiden to surprise her parents with the announcement of her engagement. She may love her father and mother as did Jewesses of bygone ages, but she lacks in reverence. Children regard their parents as dear, good friends, but not as authority. This condition, creditable or not, is simply American. (208)

According to this description, the Jewish woman comfortably lived in and revered many aspects of the traditional sphere. Yet, this description of the beliefs and actions of the Jewish woman was too simple. It did not address ambivalence toward Jewish history or toward assimilation that was prevalent in the community at the time.

Similarly, the Jewish woman's ability to move outside her traditional sphere was wrought with uncertainty. Movement outside of the traditional sphere was acceptable to an extent because she did so to protect important aspects of the traditional sphere. According to the Reverend Ella E. Bartlett, the "new woman" was no different from the women of the past in Israel. Through the repeated use of rhetorical questions, the reader was led to the conclusion that the changes that past and present Jewish women wanted placed the home in the primary position. For example, Bartlett asked, "Does the new woman manifest, with voice and pen, an interest in questions of national importance?" to which she answered, "Did not Miriam, the prophetess, the sister of Moses, do the same as well as other women in the days of Saul and David, and in still later days?" ("The New Woman," July 1895:169). Seen this way, Jewish women had always made contributions outside the home. The analogy to Miriam indicates a desire to adapt to the Jewish audience, but it does little to indicate how the "new" Jewish woman is different from the old stereotype.

On the issue of women and work, another point of potential conflict between

190   Women Public Speakers in the United States

traditional formulations of the public and private spheres, Fassel Sonneschein commented:

In the busy world of American womanhood she is yet a mere cipher. Protected, as she is, by the male members of the family, she does not work unless compelled to do so. She is, however, commencing to show some signs of intellectual activity, as we hear now and then that a Jewess has become a doctor, lawyer, writer, artist or poet. American society has as yet given the Jewess but few opportunities to display her abilities as a leader, if indeed she has any. ("The American Jewess," 208)

Apparently, Jewish women had only begun to explore their opportunities. Indeed, she suggested that opportunities for work were limited only by the prejudices of U.S. society and the Jewish community.

Desire for a new identity for Jewish women was created, in part, by the influence of American society on Reform Judaism. The decreased reliance on culture and tradition changed the community members' understanding of their religious rights and responsibilities. Accordingly, Fassel Sonneschein sought to redefine the religious sphere for women. Jewish women, especially those who were married, were religiously disfranchised. Various articles explored the differences in the religious duties of men and women. The argument was made that, without equal responsibilities, women indeed were powerless. Any notion that religious emancipation would destroy the traditional values held by women was refuted in a December 1897 editorial:

As time passes the Jewish woman will unfold more and more divinity in her mission. The uncontrollable advance of knowledge may rob her of some of her ancient traditions, but will in the long run not antagonize her piety. Ministers of religion who proclaim against her present strides, will soon recognize in her the truest champion of reform— purified religion. (142)

Religious emancipation was not seen as something that would destroy the traditional sphere, but rather as a mechanism that would enable Jewish women and men to carry out their duties more effectively.

In 1893, before the Press Congress of the Columbian Exposition, Fassel Sonneschein had indicated that she wanted to produce a newspaper that would "connect with the cord of mutual interest the sisters dwelling throughout the length and breadth of the country" (quoted in Porter, 1981:158). The imagery of an umbilical cord uniting women is consistent with the idea that feminist discourse works to create a sense of community. Arguably, the *American Jewess* was the only public, printed matter through which these women could address issues that were pertinent to the development of a new Jewish identity.

CONCLUSION

The rhetorical significance of the *American Jewess* is in its focus on issues of assimilation. Through the *American Jewess*, Rosa Fassel Sonneschein provided a forum for discussing the Jewish frustrations with the evolution of the Jewish community and with the process of assimilation. Although she envisioned a community of Jewish women who were educated and religious wives and mothers, women who used their intellect to cultivate their families, a clear articulation of that ideal would take time, more time than the newspaper was in existence.

The *American Jewess* did not offer a radical feminist reinterpretation of an existing vision. There was no acceptable preexisting ideal to reinterpret. Instead, Rosa Fassel Sonneschein and the *American Jewess* used arguments grounded in benefits rather than rights to begin a reconceptualization of Jewish women's identity. This social feminist reconceptualization attempted to maximize the goals both of evolving Jewish views and of modern American views of woman's role. Jonathan Sarna explains:

By becoming involved in shaping their own image, American Jews sought to meet all these challenges at once, demonstrating Judaism's complete compatibility with American life. Not all Jews, of course, took part in this effort. Those who did, however, considered re-conceptualization and elimination the best means of affecting negative Christian views. They presumably reasoned that if Christians would change their negative stereotypes at the same time as Jews showed how little they now resembled those stereotypes, then the so-called Jewish problem would be solved. (1986:70)

The strategy of rethinking their role offered Jewish women a way to begin to envision change in a nonthreatening way. Thus, the importance of social feminism extends beyond FRANCES E. WILLARD's enactment of the female Christian soldier who enters the public sphere in order to protect the home and family (MCSFH 1:121–132). Rosa Fassel Sonneschein and the *American Jewess* addressed the values and experiences of Jewish women in the United States. Readers could envision change in ways that appeared less threatening and, perhaps, as necessary for the maintenance of Jewish ideals.

The *American Jewess* played a significant role in the evolution of an identity for Jewish women in the United States. Although Rosa Fassel Sonneschein did not create a new Jewish woman's identity, she did bring Jewish women to public notice by providing a forum for women's concerns and ideas. Indeed, for the first time, Jewish women began to have a voice in defining themselves. The work that she began would be continued by others. The *American Jewess* appeared before Jews in the United States, particularly Jews of German descent, were prepared to resolve issues of identity more fully in relation to the special conditions in this country in the late nineteenth century. Moreover, as a result of fatigue and hearing loss, a frustrated Fassel Sonneschein gave up control of the business aspects of the paper in 1898, although she retained some editorial influence (Loth, 1985:46). The newspaper ceased publication with the August 1899 issue. When the world became silent for Rosa Sonneschein, she withdrew from public life. She moved back to St. Louis where she died just short of her eighty-fifth birthday on March 5, 1932.

Although nearly a century has passed since it ceased publication, the *American Jewess* continues to have relevance today. Contemporary women are challenged to find a usable past. An important part of finding such a past is to identify and reclaim rhetoric that has been lost. The *American Jewess* provided a forum for women who had previously been silent. In the final analysis, then, with unresolved ambivalence about the identity of the "new" Jewish woman, the *American Jewess* and Rosa Fassel Sonneschein allowed Jewish women to take the first steps in creating their own identity.

SOURCES

A microfilm of many issues of the *American Jewess* is found in the HOW Periodicals collection distributed by Research Publications, New Haven, Connecticut. Complete copies of all issues of the *American Jewess* exist in the microfilm collection at the American Jewish Archives (AJA), Cincinnati Campus, Hebrew Union College/Jewish Institute of Religion.

Selected Critical Studies (None is complete; most contain errors.)

Baum, Charlotte, Paula Hyman, and Sonya Michel. *The Jewish Woman in America*. New York: New American Library, 1976.

Beifield, Martin P. "A Study of the American Jewess." Unpublished essay, May 16, 1972. AJA

Berkowitz [Stafford], Sandra J. "In the Interest of Jewish Women: A Rhetorical Analysis of the *American Jewess*." M.A. thesis, Wake Forest University, 1987.

Berrol, Selma. "Germans Versus Russians: An Update." *American Jewish History* 73 (1983):142–156.

Braude, Ann. "The Jewish Woman's Encounter with American Culture." *Women and Religion in America*. Eds. Rosemary Radford Ruether and Rosemary Skinner Keller. San Francisco: Harper & Row, 1981. vol. 1:150–174.

Glanz, Rudolf. *The Jewish Woman in America: Two Female Immigrant Generations 1820–1929*. Vol. 2. New York: KTAV; New York: National Council of Jewish Women, 1976.

Kuzmack, Linda Gordon. *Woman's Cause: The Jewish Woman's Movement in England and the United States, 1881–1933*. Columbus: Ohio State University Press, 1990.

Lebeson, Anita Libman. *Recall to Life: Jewish Women in American History*. South Brunswick, N.J.: A. S. Barnes, 1970.

Marcus, Jacob Rader. *The American Jewish Woman, 1654–1980*. New York: KTAV; Cincinnati: American Jewish Archives, 1981.

———. *The American Jewish Woman: A Documentary History*. New York: KTAV; Cincinnati: American Jewish Archives, 1981.

Porter, Jack Nusan. *The Jew as Outsider: Historical and Contemporary Perspectives: Collected Essays, 1974–1980*. Washington, D.C.: University Press of America, 1981.

———. "Rosa Sonnenschein [*sic*] and *The American Jewess*: The First Independent English Language Jewish Women's Journal in the United States." *American Jewish History* 68 (1978):57–63.

———. "Rosa Sonneschein and *The American Jewess* Revisited: New Historical Information on an Early American Zionist and Jewish Feminist." *American Jewish Archives* 32 (1980):124–131.

Singerman, Robert. "The American Jewish Press, 1823–1983: A Bibliographic Survey of Research and Studies." *American Jewish History* 73 (1984):422–444.

Sochen, June. *Consecrate Every Day: The Public Lives of Jewish American Women 1880–1980.* Albany, N.Y.: SUNY Press, 1981.

Sokolow, Norman. *History of Zionism, 1600–1918.* 1919. New York: KTAV, 1969.

Selected Biographies

Loth, David. "The American Jewess." *Midstream* (February 1985):43–46.

Sonneschein, Rosa. *American Jewish Year Book.* Eds. Cyrus Adler and Henrietta Szold. Vol. 6. Philadelphia: Jewish Publication Society of America, 1904.

Historical and Critical Background

Aronin, Ben. "The Jewish Press." *"The Sentinel's" History of Chicago Jewry, 1911–1961.* Chicago: Sentinel Publishing, 1966.

Black, Naomi. *Social Feminism.* Ithaca, N.Y.: Cornell University Press, 1989.

Cohen, Naomi. *Encounter With Emancipation: The German Jews in the U. S., 1830–1914.* Philadelphia: Jewish Publication Society, 1984.

Endelman, Todd M. "Comparative Perspectives on Modern Anti-Semitism in the West." *History and Hate: The Dimensions of Anti-Semitism.* Ed. David Berger. Philadelphia: Jewish Publication Society, 1986, pp. 95–114.

Flexner, Eleanor. *Century of Struggle: The Woman's Rights Movement in the United States.* Rev. ed. Cambridge, Mass.: Belknap Press, 1975.

Golumb, Deborah Grand. "The 1893 Congress of Jewish Women: Evolution or Revolution in American Jewish Women's History." *American Jewish History* 70 (1980):52–67.

Goren, Arthur A. "The Jewish Press." *The Ethnic Press in the United States: A Historical Analysis and Handbook.* Ed. Sally M. Miller. Westport, Conn.: Greenwood Press, 1987, pp. 203–228.

Howe, Irving. *World of Our Fathers.* New York: Harcourt, 1976.

Marcus, Jacob Rader. *United States Jewry, 1776–1985: Vol. 1.* Detroit: Wayne State University Press, 1989.

Mayo, Louise A. *The Ambivalent Image: Nineteenth Century America's Perception of the Jew.* Rutherford, N.J.: Fairleigh Dickenson University Press, 1988.

Meyer, Michael A. *Jewish Identity in the Modern World.* Seattle: University of Washington Press, 1990.

Neu, Irene D. "The Jewish Businesswoman in America." *American Jewish Historical Quarterly* 66 (1976):137–154.

Philipson, David. *The Reform Movement in Judaism.* Rev. ed. New York: Macmillan, 1931.

Prell, Riv-Ellen. "The Dilemma of Women's Equality in the History of Reform Judaism." *Judaism* 130 (1981):418–426.

———. "The Vision of Women in Classical Reform Judaism." *Journal of the American Academy of Religion* 50 (1982):575–589.

Sarna, Jonathan D. "The 'Mythical Jew' and the 'Jew Next Door' in Nineteenth Century America." *Anti-Semitism in American History*. Ed. David A. Gerber. Urbana: University of Illinois Press, 1986, pp. 57–78.

Singerman, Robert. "The American Jewish Press, 1823–1983: A Bibliographic Survey of Research and Studies." *American Jewish History* 73 (1984):422–444.

Steiner, Linda. "Evolving Rhetorical Strategies/Evolving Identities." *A Voice of Their Own: The Woman Suffrage Press, 1840–1910*. Ed. Martha M. Solomon. Tuscaloosa: University of Alabama Press, 1991, pp. 183–197.

Welter, Barbara. "The Cult of True Womanhood, 1820–1860." *American Quarterly* 18 (1966):151–174.

EMMA GOLDMAN
(1869–1940), feminist anarchist

MARTHA SOLOMON

When sixteen-year-old Emma Goldman arrived in the United States as an immigrant from Russia in 1885, almost nothing in her background suggested her future fame as a strident advocate for anarchism, a scathing critic of cherished U.S. institutions, and an influential figure in U.S. intellectual and social history. With little formal education and less money, she, like most immigrants, saw the United States as the land of opportunity. Still, her experiences with repressive politics in Russia, her identification with the radical idealism of the Russian Nihilists, and her reading of revolutionary literature had sown the seeds for her commitment to social change (*Living My Life*, 26–29). While the trial and execution of the Haymarket anarchists in 1887 distressed her deeply, the injustice of their fate also provided her with a direction for her enormous energies. Their deaths, she later recalled, "gave me the first impulse towards the vision for which the Chicago men had been done to death by the blind furies of wealth and power" (Johann Most, *American Mercury*, June 1926:158). Inspired by their martyrdom, she began regularly attending socialist meetings and eagerly writing for advertised literature. "I devoured every line on anarchism I could get," she wrote in her autobiography (*Living My Life*, 9–10).

BACKGROUND

With her ideology still evolving, in 1889 Goldman moved to New York City and into the active radical community there. Here a chain of circumstances led her to assume the role of public advocate for anarchism. She immediately met Johann Most, whose radical writings had inspired her growing commitment to anarchism. Himself a renowned and effective orator, Most perceived Goldman's potential as a public speaker. Encouraging and training her, he soon arranged speaking engagements. Those initial lectures, in which she simply parroted Most's ideas, taught her two important lessons as a speaker. Embarrassed by her inability to respond effectively to questions from the audience, she realized "the need for independent thinking"; also emboldened, she "wept with the joy of knowing . . . I could sway people with words" (*Living My Life*, 51–53).

A commitment to women's causes grew out of her work as a practical nurse in impoverished areas of New York City. There the scourge of unwanted pregnancies and unsafe abortions among poor women deepened her commitment to fundamental economic and political change. These experiences also convinced her that women suffered particularly from the pressures of institutionalized religion and conventional morality.

Although she initially confined her work to Yiddish-speaking audiences, as did many immigrant activists, she realized the necessity of agitating in English to native-born Americans, if she was to achieve widespread social change (*Living My Life*, 155). From 1896 to 1901, Goldman toured widely. Her flamboyance and her radicalism earned her the epithet "Red Emma." Public outrage in 1901 over the assassination of President William McKinley by an alleged anarchist forced Goldman to curtail her public agitation for anarchism, but assuming an alias, she continued her work for other radical causes. In March 1906, with financial backing from friends, Goldman published the first issue of *Mother Earth*. From this date until her trial and subsequent deportation in 1917, Goldman employed two media for her advocacy: the lecture platform and her monthly periodical.

From 1906 until her deportation, Goldman was the primary spokesperson for American anarchism and an active participant in many other social and political causes. In her efforts to promote change, she was indefatigable and her output was prodigious. She spent several months of each year on hectic speaking tours, which typically stretched across the upper Midwest, culminating in California, where she toured more extensively. Goldman lectured to audiences on a host of topics from education to the liberation of women to anarchism. Her most popular lectures were those on the modern drama, in which she used the works of Ibsen and others to illustrate the author's awareness of social problems and to alert her audience to the activist political messages conveyed in the plays. Her discussions of these plays sometimes focused on the plight of the worker or on the destructive impact of social conventions, including the problems women faced. In every case, she encouraged audiences to consider literature as a source of social messages.

In addition to her very active speaking schedule, Goldman wrote monthly columns and frequent essays for *Mother Earth* and, except when she was on a lecture tour, was its primary editor. She also wrote for other periodicals, including the popular *American Mercury*, where she could expand her audience. During these years, she also edited two books based on her lectures, *Anarchism and Other Essays* and *The Social Significance of the Modern Drama*. Despite her busy schedule, she was a habitué at more informal gatherings for discussion and debate, including Mabel Dodge's famous salon, where her ideas and personality influenced many young intellectuals.

During these hectic years, the vivacious and rambunctious Goldman reached the acme of her popularity and renown. If crowds came more to be entertained than informed, as she feared, they came in large numbers. According to her own estimates, she spoke to between 50,000 and 75,000 people every year (Letter to Alfred Knopf, August 12, 1929, Amsterdam; quoted in Wexler, 1984:166). Frequent police harassment made it difficult to find a hall to speak in, but her defiance and the publicity she garnered from her flamboyance increased her fame. Such publicity was not without cost, however; police surveillance of her speaking was commonplace. With the outbreak of World War I and her outspoken opposition to it and to conscription, she was increasingly targeted as a threat to national security. She was finally arrested on charges of conspiracy to resist conscription. In many ways, her subsequent trial was confirming evidence for her indictment of the spurious "freedom" of U.S. institutions. Her legal guilt was questionable, but her fate with a jury of antianarchist "peers" was certain. With little hesitation, the jury found her guilty; she was sentenced to two years in prison. Because she was a citizen only through marriage to another immigrant, the judge ordered her deported after internment. Her career on the U.S. platform ended abruptly.

Goldman's later books on her disappointing experiences in Russia after her deportation and her well-publicized autobiography, *Living My Life*, gave her some access to the U.S. public she sought to influence. In 1934, a ninety-day lecture tour, on which she was limited to discussions of the modern drama, proved a failure. Forced to live in exile in France, Goldman maintained her devotion to and work for anarchist causes until her death in 1940. But neither she nor her cause ever regained the prominence in American life they had enjoyed during the turbulent years before 1917. On her death, her body was returned to Chicago to be buried near the graves of the Haymarket anarchists who had inspired her life.

GOLDMAN AS PHILOSOPHER AND PUBLIC ADVOCATE

Goldman's forte was vigorous public advocacy; she was not a theoretical philosopher. For anarchist theory, she drew on the works of others like Pierre Proudhon, Michael Bakunin, and Max Stirner; Nietzsche's call for a "transvaluation of all values" was a continuing inspiration to her on many fronts. From these thinkers, she developed her own version of individualistic anarchism, the kernel of which she expressed succinctly in "Anarchism: What It Really Stands For": "ANARCHISM:—The philosophy of a new social order based on liberty unrestricted by man-made law; the theory that all forms of government rest on violence, and are therefore wrong and harmful, as well as unnecessary" (50). For her, "The individual is the heart of society," and "the individual instinct is the thing of value in the world. It is the true soul that sees and creates the truth alive, out of which is to come a still greater truth, the re-born social soul" (52). The sanctity of the individual soul was the essential tenet of all Goldman's thinking. From that premise, she derived all her critical analyses of existing institutions and her arguments for social transformation.

Because the individual was supremely important, Goldman reasoned, any force that constrained or thwarted his or her full, natural development was anathema. On the contemporary U.S. scene, Goldman perceived three such forces, which she consistently excoriated in her discourse. Capitalism, the nation-state, and institutionalized religion with its conventional ethics all enslave humankind because they dominate thought and behavior, degrading and debasing individuals by making them responsible to forces outside themselves. In her rhetoric, Goldman not only explained her opposition to these tyrannies, but she also traced their impact on an individual's self-image and relation to the social environment. For example, she argued that U.S. democracy encouraged the unenlightened mass to dominate and stifle the inspired individuals of the minority ("Minorities," 69–78); that religion under the aegis of pious morality repressed human sexuality, with disastrous results, especially in women ("Hypocrisy," 167–176); and that capitalism, by depriving individuals of the fruits of their labor, reduced some to automatons and drove others to crime ("Psychology of Political Violence," 79–126).

In attacking established institutions, Goldman assumed the rhetorical role of a physician to society, diagnosing and prescribing cures for social diseases. Her self-described mission in life was "to ascertain the cause of our social evils and of our social difficulties. As a student of social wrongs it is my aim to diagnose a wrong" (Address to the Jury, 363). She saw herself as able to expose the popular misconceptions and superstitions around marriage and to "dissect" the "modern fetish" of suffrage with cool-headed reason and clear vision. By adopting the persona of a scientist studying society's ills, she presented her interpretations and analyses as factual and objective accounts, free from the shackles of conventional superstitions.

Because she saw the majority as lacking reason, judgment, originality, and moral courage, Goldman did little to mollify them. Her target audience was the enlightened few who were capable of moving beyond the common herd. In her essay "Minorities Versus Majorities," she indicates her great faith in the enlightened few:

Always, at every period, the few were the banner bearers of a great idea, of liberating effort. Not so the mass, the leaden weight of which does not let it move. . . . In other words, the living, vital truth of social and economic well-being will become a reality only through the zeal, courage, the non-compromising determination of intelligent minorities, and not through the mass. (75, 78)

Obviously, her chosen rhetorical role, her radical doctrine, and her target audience presented substantial rhetorical challenges. Indirect evidence suggests that Goldman was aware of some of these problems. Although she undoubtedly knew that her approach was too confrontational for most audiences and the changes she advocated were too daunting, she never tried to mollify the "unenlightened mass" in her lectures. From her perspective, attempts to be less combative or to adopt a more conciliatory tone would have been both hypocritical and counterproductive. She sought to stimulate thought and to assault established ways of thinking. Moreover, her individualistic ideology prized assertive iconoclasts. In some senses, then, any standard inventory of rhetorical obstacles and Goldman's management of them is inappropriate to her ideological agenda.

Goldman herself gradually realized that the public platform was not well suited to her goals with her target audience. In the Preface to her first book *Anarchism and Other Essays* (1911), Goldman elucidated two limitations she saw in that forum and acknowledged her frustration with oratory as an instrument of education:

> My great faith in the wonder worker, the spoken word, is no more. I have realized its inadequacy to awaken thought, or even emotion. Gradually, and with no small struggle against this realization, I came to see that oral propaganda is at best but a means of shaking people from their lethargy: it leaves no lasting impression. . . . In meetings the audience is distracted by a thousand non-essentials. The speaker, though ever so eloquent, cannot escape the restlessness of the crowd, with the inevitable result, that he will fail to strike root. In all probability he will not even do justice to himself. The relation between the writer and the reader is more intimate. True, books are only what we want them to be; rather, what we read into them. That we can do so demonstrates the importance of written against oral expression. . . . I am not sanguine enough to hope my readers will be as numerous as those who have heard me. But I prefer to reach the few who really want to learn, rather than the many who come to be amused. (41–43)

This realization led Goldman to rely on essays to reach her target audience and to prompt careful thought.

This rhetorical adaptation is important in two respects. First, Goldman's decision to rely on the written word rather than oral presentations suggests that she recognized and sought to deal with some of the obstacles she confronted in advocating individualistic anarchism. Second, her essays provide us with a better index of her rhetorical skills than other extant materials. Because she enjoyed interacting with her listeners, Goldman spoke extemporaneously from brief notes. Thus, the few extant copies of notes for her speeches are brief and give few clues about her actual rhetorical strategies. Her essays, which she indicates were derived from her speeches, allow us to assess her rhetorical strategies in fuller form. Moreover, because popular press coverage of her speeches was both scant and usually highly biased against her, her initially self-published essays are fairer indications of her rhetorical approaches.

Goldman's essays indicate that her goals and her audience determined her rhetorical approach. In her writings she relies on clearly organized, reasoned analyses supported by varied forms of evidence and stinging rebuttals of anticipated objections to her view. Emphatic, vivid language characterizing her own positions and scathing sarcasm toward her opponents make her presentations lively. Structurally, many of Goldman's texts are social critiques that analyze the causes and consequences of contemporary practices. A few, like her essay on anarchism, are straightforward expositions of her ideas. In either case, the texts are well organized and argumentatively effective, with succinct introductions followed by unambiguous expositions of her thesis. For example, she begins her essay opposing woman suffrage by labeling that cause a "modern fetish" that appeals especially to women who are prone to worship such idols. Then, she presents evidence that woman suffrage has been ineffective in solving social problems where it has been tried and argues that women's "narrow view of human affairs" makes it unlikely that they will use the ballot wisely (205). After identifying such social problems as prostitution or the conditions in prisons, she typically traces their roots to the injustices perpetrated by one or more of the three repressive institutions before picturing anarchism as the solution to the underlying problems.

To reinforce her interpretations, she invokes the authority of those in the intellectual avant garde, including "freethinkers" like Havelock Ellis, Oscar Wilde, and George Bernard Shaw. Her essays and presumably the speeches on which they were based are usually filled with illustrations from history, literature, and contemporary life, substantiating her claims. For example, her book on the modern drama, ostensibly offered as literary criticism, really shows that the best contemporary authors advocate in their works an analysis of social problems identical to her own. Sometimes she uses objective data to illustrate the extent of a problem or to drive an argument home. In discussing the kinds and causes of crimes in the United States, she alleges that "there are four and a half times as many crimes to every million population today as there were twenty years ago." She adds: "The most horrible aspect is that our national crime is murder, not robbery, embezzlement, or rape as in the South. London is five times as large as Chicago, yet there are one hundred and eighteen murders annually in the latter city, while only twenty in London. Nor is Chicago the leading city in crime, since it is only seventh on the list" ("Prisons," 112). In castigating patriotism and how it leads to militarism, Goldman cites the expenditures of various governments on armaments and indicates the rank of the United States among those nations in terms of the proportion of national revenue spent on armies. She moves on to translate these numbers into a per capita tax on the population. Although she cites no sources for her facts, they work effectively to prove her contention that "patriotism is a rather costly institution" ("Patriotism," 130–132).

To anticipate objections to her views or to expose the fallacies of current thinking, Goldman often turns to refutation. For example, her essay "The Traffic in Women" critiques the current solutions to prostitution. She begins by castigating zealous reformers for their belated and simplistic analysis of the issue: "How is it that an institution, known to almost every child, should have been discovered so suddenly? How is it that this evil known to all sociologists, should now be made such an important issue?" She refutes the idea that the problem is new, citing its roots in religious practice. Later, she answers the argument that women involved in prostitution are foreigners by citing their excellent command of English and their "Americanized" habits and appearance (177, 189). By systematically exposing the fallacies in the moral arguments of her opponents, Goldman adds force to her contention that the root cause of prostitution is a capitalism that makes even human sexuality a commodity.

Clearly, one could dispute the starting points of Goldman's arguments or question the evidence, especially the expert testimony, which she offers. But her forceful, clear arguments and the proof she presents for them reveal a keen sense of the necessity of reasoning with her readers. In that respect, her approach suggests that she recognized that her analyses would be controversial, and she sought to fend off objections by arguing her case vigorously and clearly.

As social physician, Goldman's rhetorical bedside manner was far from gentle. While she expresses genuine sympathy for victims of unjust social institutions, including prisoners, her vitriolic tone toward those she opposes is sometimes startling and rhetorically disconcerting. On the one hand, she writes compassionately of the victims of economic exploitation:

America is particularly boastful of her great power, her enormous national wealth. Poor America, of what avail is all her wealth, if the individuals comprising the nation are wretchedly poor? If they live in squalor, in filth, in crime, with hope and joy gone, a homeless, soulless army of human prey. ("Anarchism," 54)

She describes the plight of married women robbed of access to effective birth control:

Thanks to this Puritan tyranny, the majority of women soon find themselves at the ebb of their physical resources. Ill and worn, they are utterly unable to give their children even elementary care. That, added to economic pressure, forces many women to risk utmost danger rather than continue to bring forth life. The custom of procuring abortions has reached such vast proportions in America as to be almost beyond belief. ("The Hypocrisy of Puritanism," 172)

On the other hand, castigating public opinion as the lowest common denominator, she writes contemptuously:

Publishers, theatrical managers, and critics ask not for the quality inherent in creative art, but will it meet with a good sale, will it suit the palate of the people? Alas, this palate is like a dumping ground; it relishes anything that needs no mental mastication. ("Minorities Versus Majorities," 71)

Her critique of the Beatitudes in "The Failure of Christianity" is representatively caustic:

Take the Sermon on the Mount, for instance. What is it but a eulogy on submission to fate, to the inevitability of things? "Blessed are the poor in spirit, for theirs is the Kingdom of Heaven." Heaven must be an awfully dull place if the poor in spirit live there. How can anything creative, anything vital, useful and beautiful come from the poor in spirit? The idea conveyed in the Sermon on the Mount is the greatest indictment against the teachings of Christ, because it sees in poverty of mind and body a virtue, and because it seeks to maintain this virtue by punishment and reward. (236)

"Every intelligent being," she continues, realizes that the "worst curse" in society is this poverty of spirit which tolerates all the evil and misery in the world in anticipation of a reward in the afterlife" (236–237).

Vivid diction, metaphors, and figurative analogies pepper her essays. For example, in explicating anarchism, she animates religion as "a black monster," personifies capitalism in the form of private property as a beast that "recognizes only its own gluttonous appetite for greater wealth, because wealth means power . . . to subdue, to crush, to exploit, . . . to enslave, to outrage, to degrade," and analogizes the state as "the altar of political freedom . . . like the religious altar . . . maintained for the purpose of human sacrifice" ("Anarchism," 53, 54, 57). Another beast, patriotism, is "inexorable and, like all insatiable monsters, demands all or nothing" ("Patriotism," 140). At her 1917 trial, she belittles the actions of the marshal who arrested her with a comparison to a Barnum and Bailey circus performer and ridicules the courtroom proceedings as a "three act comedy" ("Address to the Jury," 359, 360).

In contrast to her caustic belittling of opponents, her depictions of her ideals are often romantically visionary. For example, looking forward to the day when women achieve emancipation from their internalized conventional morality, she idealizes a reborn, authentic relationship between the sexes:

A true conception of the relation of the sexes will not admit of conqueror and conquered; it knows of but one thing: to give one's self boundlessly, in order to find one's self richer, deeper, better. That alone can fill the emptiness, and transform the tragedy of woman's emancipation into joy, limitless joy. ("The Tragedy of Woman's Emancipation," 225)

Goldman's style is not eloquent; at its best, it is direct, forceful, and vivid; sometimes it seems unpolished and inept. Hers is a rhetoric, whether in assigning praise or blame, that eschews moderation. Like the woman herself, her style tends to extremes. Her dogmatic intensity is evident in her frequent use of exclamation points. Reports of her delivery indicate she was an unusually energetic, lively orator, whose rapid rate of speaking effectively conveyed her enthusiasm for her cause. Thus, her essays are more remarkable for the spirit behind and within them than for their stylistic grace.

CONCLUSION

Two factors complicate an assessment of Goldman as a rhetor. First, her ideology led her to critique three central institutions in U.S. life and to advocate a transvaluation of dominant cultural values. With this doctrine, widespread popular success in the early twentieth-century United States was probably impossible. She urged too many painful changes within her audience and in society to make her message palatable.

Second, she was a dynamic, assertive, and flamboyant woman in an age that still severely constrained women's roles. Nonetheless, for her target audience, the avant garde, Goldman became a paradigm of the free spirit. Prominent writers and intellectuals usually rallied to her defense, even when they disagreed fundamentally with her ideology or her approaches to individual issues. Although she did not convert the U.S. public to her doctrine in any significant numbers, she made an indelible impression on the many who heard her and many who knew of "Red Emma" only by reputation. Some select few in her target audience successfully enacted the ideals she advocated. But the very factors that made her attractive to those persons impeded her immediate success as a public advocate. The immoderate stridency and the resistance to "common-sense" compromise that made her an ideal of intellectual and ethical commitment to the avant garde made her seem dangerous and sometimes ridiculous to most Americans.

On an artistic level, however, Goldman's rhetoric is notable. Even her enemies testify to her charisma on the platform. The organization and argumentation in her essays show her mastery of many rhetorical strategies. She was so effective as a platform debater that many of her opponents refused to confront her. At its best, her style alternates effectively from sharp ridicule of present institutions to a romantic vision of future human fulfillment. Her essays are filled with vivid metaphors, effective figurative analogies, and emphatic language. In short, her works reveal her mastery of an impressive array of rhetorical techniques, marshalled to stimulate consideration of her controversial ideas.

Her greatest rhetorical contribution, however, was in her influence on American life. Ironically, although Goldman primarily sought to advance the cause of anarchism, her greatest rhetorical impact was in other areas. Her advocacy of educational reform helped spawn alternative schools in New York; her work in behalf of strikers and of other individuals like Thomas Mooney often turned the tide in their direction (Drinnon, 1970:175–183); and her lectures on the modern drama introduced many Americans to important and socially significant works. Perhaps more important, attempts to abridge her First Amendment right to free speech and her resistance encouraged the formation of Free Speech Societies and the creation of the American Civil Liberties Union (ACLU). Richard Drinnon, labeling her the woman behind Roger Baldwin's founding of the ACLU, writes: "If she had done nothing else than set Baldwin off on his career, her role . . . behind the organization of the American Civil Liberties Union would have made her fights for free speech an outstanding success" (1970:140).

Goldman's greatest continuing impact, however, may be her contribution to the enlightenment and liberation of women. Not only were women's problems a frequent topic in her speeches, but also five of the twelve essays in *Anarchism and Other Essays* treat feminist concerns. An early and open advocate of birth control, she defied legal prohibitions to offer women information about practical methods (Drinnon, 1970:165–174). Speaking against suffrage as ideologically insignificant without concomitant changes in women's self-identity, she urged women to work to free themselves from what modern feminists have called "the enemy who has outposts in your head." The real problems confronting women, in Goldman's view, stemmed from their socialization. Conventional morality made them deny their sexuality and pursue marriage for security, finally reducing them to economic parasitism and narrow conservatism. In other words, Goldman argued forcefully, ''The right to vote, or equal civil rights, may be good demands, but true emancipation begins neither at the polls nor in courts. It begins in woman's soul'' (''The Tragedy of Woman's Emancipation,'' 224). Goldman's potent arguments in behalf of women's liberation and the example she provided— sometimes painfully—in her own refusal to be bound by conventional morality inspired many of her contemporaries and continue to be inspiring today.

SOURCES

The Joseph A. Labadie Collection, University of Michigan, and the Emma Goldman Papers, New York Public Library, are the major sources of correspondence and memorabilia in this country. The Labadie Collection also includes pamphlet copies of some of her essays, the most important of which are reprinted in *Red Emma Speaks*. The most complete archive, which contains most of her major extant manuscripts, is the Goldman-Berkman Archives, International Institute for Social History, Amsterdam. In addition, microfiche of *Mother Earth*, available in many libraries, contains copies of her essays published there. Versions of many of these essays are available in *Red Emma Speaks*. *Mother Earth* (April 1916) contains ''The Social Aspects of Birth Control,'' an essay pertinent to Goldman's feminism that is not available elsewhere.

A comparison of titles suggests that Goldman's essays were derived from her speeches, of which there are no complete manuscript copies in this country. Thus, the two collections of essays that she published and the essays she published in *Mother Earth* (*ME*) are the best sources of texts. *Red Emma Speaks* includes essays from *Mother Earth* and other sources.

Goldman, Emma. *Anarchism and Other Essays*. 1911. New York: Dover, 1969.
————. *The Social Significance of the Modern Drama*. Boston: Richard G. Badger, 1914.
Red Emma Speaks: An Emma Goldman Reader. Comp. and ed. Alix Kates Shulman. 1972. New York: Schocken, 1983.
The Traffic in Women and Other Essays on Feminism. Ed. Alix Kates Shulman. New York: Times Change, 1970.
Vision on Fire: Emma Goldman on the Spanish Revolution. Ed. David Potter. New York: Commonground, 1983.

Selected Biographical Sources

Drinnon, Richard. *Rebel in Paradise: A Biography of Emma Goldman*. Boston: Beacon, 1970.
Falk, Candace. *Love, Anarchy, and Emma Goldman*. New York: Holt, Rinehart & Winston, 1984.
Goldman, Emma. *Living My Life*. 1932. New York: Dover, 1970, and Salt Lake City, Utah: Peregrine Smith, 1982.
————. *My Disillusionment in Russia*. 1923, 1924. New York: Thomas Y. Crowell, 1970.
Harris, Frank. ''Emma Goldman, the Famous Anarchist.'' *Contemporary Portraits*. 4th series. New York: Brentano's, 1923, pp. 222–249.

Shulman, Alix Kates. *To The Barricades: The Anarchist Life of Emma Goldman*. New York: Thomas Y. Crowell, 1971.
Wexler, Alice. *Emma Goldman: An Intimate Life*. New York: Pantheon, 1984.
———. *Emma Goldman in Exile: From the Russian Revolution to the Spanish Civil War*. Boston: Beacon, 1989.

Selected Critical Sources

Berry, Elizabeth. "Rhetoric for the Cause: The Analysis and Criticism of the Persuasive Discourse of Emma Goldman, Anarchist Agitator, 1906–1919." Ph.D. diss., University of California, Los Angeles, 1969. AAC 7008115
Ewing, Christine Combe. "Emma Goldman's Participation in the Labor Free Speech Fight in San Diego 1912–1915." M.A. thesis, University of North Carolina, 1975.
McManus, Mark. "The Rhetorical Failure of Emma Goldman: A Dramatistic and Dialectic Conflict Analysis." M.A. thesis, Auburn University, 1982.
Solomon, Martha. *Emma Goldman*. Boston: Twayne, 1987.
———. "Ideology as Rhetorical Constraint: The Anarchist Agitation of 'Red Emma' Goldman." *Quarterly Journal of Speech* 74 (May 1988):184–200.

Chronology of Major Texts

From *Anarchism and Other Essays*, 1911

"Anarchism: What It Really Stands For." 53–73.
"Minorities vs. Majorities." 75–84.
"Prisons: A Social Crime and Failure." 115–132.
"The Hypocrisy of Puritanism." 173–182.
"The Traffic in Women." 183–200.
"Woman Suffrage." 201–217.
"The Tragedy of Woman's Emancipation." 219–231.
"Marriage and Love." 233–245.

Reprinted in *Red Emma Speaks*

"The Child and Its Enemies." *ME* (April 1906):7–14.
"The Failure of Christianity." *ME* (April 1913):41–48.
"Intellectual Proletarians." *ME* (February 1914):363–380.
"Preparedness: The Road to Universal Slaughter." *ME* (December 1915):331–338; OW:70–75.
"The Philosophy of Atheism." *ME* (February 1916):410–416.
"Address to the Jury, 1917." Printed as a pamphlet by Mother Earth Publishing Association; *WSBH*:219–233.
"Was My Life Worth Living?" *Harper's Magazine*, December 1934.

ANGELINA GRIMKÉ WELD

(1805–1879), pioneer advocate for human rights

PHYLLIS M. JAPP

Angelina Grimké Weld was one of the first women speakers in the United States. Although her public career spanned less than a decade, her status as a woman orator and her contribution to abolitionism and woman's rights are widely acknowledged. She was born in the South, the daughter of John Grimké, a wealthy South Carolina judge and plantation owner. Although she had little formal education, the Grimké family encouraged intellectual pursuits; the children had access to the family library, read widely, and engaged in discussions of law, politics, philosophy, and history. Grimké Weld continued to educate herself throughout her life.

At a young age, she became convinced that slavery was evil, a belief that put her at odds with her family and the southern society in which she lived. She was also unusually religious for a young woman of her time. Born into an Episcopalian family, she was converted in the revivalistic wave of the early nineteenth century and became a Presbyterian. She followed her sister Sarah into the Quaker faith but was excommunicated for marrying outside the church. Later in life, she held no formal church membership but continued to devote much time to reading and interpreting the Bible.

When Judge Grimké fell ill and needed medical treatment, SARAH GRIMKÉ accompanied her father to Philadelphia. She later decided to settle permanently in the North and encouraged her younger sister to join here there. Angelina Grimké left the South in 1829 at the age of twenty-four. Long concerned about slavery, she eagerly absorbed the abolitionist teachings popular in Quaker circles. Her private convictions became public knowledge when a letter she wrote to William Lloyd Garrison was published in his anti-slavery journal, the *Liberator*. The letter attracted the attention of many in the abolitionist movement. Among the readers was Theodore Weld, the abolitionist orator, who invited Grimké to become one of his anti-slavery agents.

Although she was horrified at the publicity generated by the appearance of her letter, Grimké felt she must do whatever she could to aid the abolitionist efforts. Thus, the two Grimké sisters began writing and speaking of their first-hand experiences with the system of slavery and recruiting women to the work of abolition. Together they lectured throughout New England in 1837 and early 1838. During this period, the sisters also wrote prolifically on both abolition and woman's role in social reform. Angelina Grimké authored *Appeal to the Christian Women of the South* (1836), a tract that laid out her challenge to southern women. This was followed by *Appeal to the Women of the Nominally Free States* (1837), Grimké's address to the Anti-Slavery Convention of American Women. Meanwhile, Catharine Ward Beecher published a series of letters opposing the sisters' public performances as an unsuitable activity for women. Angelina Grimké responded to Beecher in *Letters to Catharine E. Beecher* (1838). With her sister, Angelina Grimké began to formulate ideas for a tract on woman's rights, but left Sarah Grimké to complete and publish *Letters on the Equality of the Sexes* (1838).

Angelina Grimké married Theodore Weld in 1838, a few days before her last public lecture. Weld was a major force in the evangelical branch of the abolitionist movement and Grimké's mentor in her public activities. He encouraged the sisters to lecture, tutored them in abolitionist principles, and trained them in the art of public speaking. Weld was not opposed to woman's rights but firmly believed the issue should not be intruded into the abolitionist cause. As their convictions on the subject grew, however, the sisters found it difficult to confine their public remarks to abolitionism. They believed abolition and woman's rights were fundamentally related, being based on the same moral and political principles.

Her disagreement with Weld certainly was one reason for Grimké Weld's retirement from public lecturing following her marriage, although there are no indications that she intended her silence to be permanent. Initially, marriage provided her an excuse to rest and recover from an extremely arduous travel schedule. The sisters (the newlyweds had invited Sarah Grimké to live with them) plunged enthusiastically into a domestic routine. The Welds' first child was born in 1839, soon followed by three others. Grimké Weld's health remained fragile, which was another reason she did not return to public lecturing. In addition, the Welds were deeply disturbed by the factions that had arisen among abolitionists and withdrew rather than take sides on a number of issues. Although she collaborated with her husband on *American Slavery As It Is* shortly after her marriage, Grimké Weld did not lecture or write extensively after 1838. However, her correspondence indicates that she remained committed to both abolition and woman's rights. Grimké Weld died in 1879 at the age of seventy-four.

PUBLIC ADVOCATE FOR ABOLITION AND
WOMAN'S RIGHTS

Grimké Weld's significance as a public advocate lies in her position as one of the first women to speak in public, in her example of a woman enacting her rights as a "moral and political being," to use one of her favorite phrases, and in the philosophy of human rights developed in her writings and speeches.

Although DEBORAH SAMPSON GANNETT, Frances Wright, and MARIA W. MILLER STEWART preceded her to the public platform, Angelina Grimké was a groundbreaker in woman's oratory who inspired others to follow her example. Abby Kelley Foster and Lucy Stone, among others, found in her the impetus for their own public careers. She was a worthy role model. Her character was above reproach by the standards of the time, her appearance and demeanor were "ladylike" enough to deflect the sort of criticism leveled at Wright, while the cause for which she served, abolition, was an issue of national concern, raising her above accusations of selfish publicity-seeking.

Grimké's first public document, the letter published in the *Liberator*, provides a succinct example both of her abolitionist philosophy and of her eloquence of expression. The letter contains themes she later developed in her writings and lectures, for example, the belief that the nation faced a moral crisis, a sense that she was called to participate in the work of abolition, a willingness to suffer and even to die for her convictions. Her moral fervor and the authority of her first-hand experience are formulated in clear and compelling terms that almost demand oral performance. For example:

If persecution is the means which God has ordained for the accomplishment of this great end, EMANCIPATION; then, in dependence *upon him* for strength to bear it, I feel as if I could say, LET IT COME; for it is my deep, solemn, deliberate conviction, that *this is a cause worth dying for.* I say so, from what I have seen, and heard, and known in a land of slavery, where rests the darkness of Egypt, and where is found the sin of Sodom. Yes! LET IT COME—let *us* suffer, rather than insurrections should arise.

Little wonder that both Garrison and Theodore Weld, the man she later married, realized the publicity value of a Southerner who was able so eloquently to declaim the evils of slavery!

Having recruited Grimké, Weld trained her as one of his seventy anti-slavery agents, the only woman among the group. Her first-hand experience with the system of slavery enhanced her credibility with the northern audiences to whom she lectured on abolition. This experience as a southern eyewitness to slavery was her unique contribution to the abolitionist cause, her raison-d'être as an abolitionist speaker.

Grimké and her sister began their public careers in 1837, meeting informally with women in homes but soon lecturing to audiences of women engaged in social reform. In a tour of Massachusetts, supported by the Boston Female Anti-Slavery Society, they found much encouragement from both male and female abolitionists. Their first formal public lecture was delivered before a meeting of that organization. As the sisters' fame grew, men began filtering into their audiences, and they soon found themselves lecturing to mixed groups. Writing to her friend, Jane Smith, Grimké told of her reaction on finding a man in the audience: "so there he sat and somehow I did not feel his presence at all embarrassing and went on just as tho' he was not there" (February 4, 1837). In Lynn, Massachusetts, the sisters addressed their first "promiscuous" audience of about 1,000 men and women and also encountered similarly mixed audiences at Salem and Amesbury. At the latter location, they engaged in a well-attended public debate with two young men who had recently visited the South. The Grimkés reportedly "demolished" their opponents. At Lowell their audience was estimated at 1,500 persons of both sexes, including a large number of mill girls (Melder, 1977:82–83).

Grimké's letters indicate some apprehension about speaking—''the day I have to speak is always a day of suffering,'' she wrote to Smith (January 20, 1837)— but she obviously grew in confidence and for the most part enjoyed performing. Her ''timidity,'' she explains, was not based on her gender but on her lack of experience and education: ''I feel that I am inferior in as much as I have not had the advantages of a liberal education'' (Letter to Amos Phelps, August 17, 1837). She worked diligently on effective delivery techniques. Weld trained his agents in a vibrant, emotional style, reminiscent of the religious revivalists of the time. As a woman, however, Grimké had to work out her own mode of performance within that model. Confiding in Smith, she wrote:

some friends think I make too many gestures, one thinking females ought to be motionless when speaking in public, another fearing that *other* denominations might be offended by them because they were unaccustomed to hear women speak in public. I think the more a speaker can yield himself entirely to the native impulses of feeling, the better, and this is just what I do. (February 4, 1837)

Although aware that public decorum demanded that she appear reluctant to assume a public role, she confessed privately to Smith, ''Dear Jane, I love the work. I count myself greatly favored in being called to it'' (January 20, 1837). Certainly there is every indication that she emerged from the lecture tour a poised, polished, and experienced public speaker. Her sister was less enthusiastic—''I am not very comfortable in the performance of those duties to which I have been called,'' Sarah Grimké confessed in the same letter, and from all accounts, she was not an effective public speaker. In fact, Weld was quite critical of Sarah Grimké's performance and encouraged her to withdraw and leave the platform to her younger sister.

The Grimkés' practice of speaking to mixed audiences not only generated public criticism but also aroused concern within abolitionist circles. Woman speaking to women was something men could ignore. Woman lecturing to men, however, was intolerable to many. Organized religion, with the exception of the Quaker faith, condemned the practice. Even some Quakers felt the sisters were overstepping their bounds when they began addressing mixed audiences. Male abolitionists also had differing opinions. Many were strongly opposed; others, like Weld, believed in woman's rights but did not want the subject to become an issue that might detract from abolition. Still others, Garrison among them, insisted that the abolitionist struggle was for *all* human rights, including those of women.

Abolitionist women were equally divided on the topic. Maria Weston Chapman heartily endorsed the Grimkés' public activities, arguing that woman's ''true sphere'' was to oppose slavery, ''speaking freely against it whenever opportunity arose'' (Melder, 1977:95). Juliana Tappan was torn by the dilemma, observing that

On the one hand, we are in danger of servile submission to the opinions of the other sex & on the other hand in perhaps equal danger of losing that modesty, & instinctive delicacy of feeling, which our Creator has given as a safeguard to protect us from dangers. (Ginzburg, 1990:30)

Certainly, Catharine Ward Beecher was harshly critical of the Grimkés' activity. Her treatise, *An Essay on Slavery and Abolitionism with Reference to the Duty of American Females Addressed to Miss A.E. Grimké*, provoked Grimké's equally forthright response in which she articulated her arguments for women's public role in the movement.

Angelina Grimké Weld was quite conscious of her status as a role model for women. She realized that what she *did*—not what she *said*—would be the most convincing proof of woman's abilities. Her very presence challenged those who denied woman's intellectual capacities and political acumen, as she stood alone on a public platform and lectured in a strong, compelling voice for over two hours at a time, as she advanced biblically and politically sound arguments for the freedom of slaves and the rights of women. For a time she seemed content to demonstrate, rather than articulate, her convictions regarding woman's rights, developing arguments in her writing but not explicitly addressing the topic in her public lectures. Recognizing public resistance to woman speaking, even within abolitionist circles, and sensitive to Weld's request that she not intrude her concern with woman's rights into the abolitionist agenda, she allowed her presence and her competence to serve as her primary oral arguments for woman's capacity to assume a public role.

There is ample evidence, however, that Grimké Weld felt increasingly compelled to voice her well-reasoned arguments for woman speaking. To Gerrit Smith she confided that she felt "quite ready for the discussion about women." The public was ignorant, she believed, of the principles upon which she acted, and she was convinced it might be best to "throw them [her arguments for woman's rights] open for their consideration, just letting them have both sides of the argument to look at, at the same time" (August 26, 1837). Grimké rightly realized that her careful delineation of the moral, political, and spiritual precedents for woman speaking was unique. She felt that arguments from principle might serve to convince the reluctant when arguments from expediency failed. She reported to Smith a conversation with a "Dr. Miller," who was quite prejudiced against women speaking. When she articulated her reasons for "women's preaching," however, she convinced him, for he "had no idea so much could be adduced from the Bible to sustain the ground I had taken." Miller thereupon insisted that she ought "tell the people *why* you believed you had a right to speak" (October 24, 1837). Garrison agreed, but Weld was angry and upset at such a prospect.

Grimké's enactment responsibilities extended beyond her public performance. She viewed Weld's proposal of marriage as a sign to the world that she had not been contaminated by her public activities and was still desirable as a woman.

She was convinced that the world would be watching her performance as a wife and mother, that any failure to live up to expectations would reverberate to the detriment of women. She refused to hire domestic help, for example, and did her own cooking and housework in an attempt to demonstrate that public activities had not ruined her abilities to fulfill her wifely duties. Concurrently, she attempted to continue her self-education, maintained correspondence with a large number of abolitionists, and assumed responsibility for organizing and editing Weld's *American Slavery As It Is*. This nineteenth-century version of the Superwoman syndrome was undoubtedly one reason for her frail health.

Grimké Weld's two surviving speech texts demonstrate her oratorical prowess and illustrate her use of the enactment strategy. No text remains of what was undoubtedly her standard oral presentation, her life narrative and her conversion experience. Thus, the two texts may be somewhat atypical of her oratorical style because both are adapted for particular audiences on specific occasions. The first, delivered on February 21, 1838, was an appearance before the Massachusetts Legislature, presenting petitions containing 20,000 signatures opposing slavery. The other was a speech given in Pennsylvania Hall, Philadelphia, on May 16, 1838. The occasion in Philadelphia was deliberately conceived as a "promiscuous" event in two senses, advertising a slate of speakers that included males and females, Blacks and whites.

Both speeches demonstrate her vision of woman's moral and political responsibilities, albeit in dramatically different ways. In the Massachusetts Legislature speech, Grimké used the biblical example of Queen Esther, who entreated King Ahasuerus to spare the lives of Jewish citizens, lest the judgment of God fall upon the nation. In the Pennsylvania Hall address, she assumed a more assertive role, that of a scolding Old Testament prophet, reminiscent of Isaiah.

Esther, Grimké's persona in the Massachusetts Legislature address, was an especially effective choice for a woman who wanted to focus, not on woman's right to speak, but on the exigency of a situation that virtually compelled her to act for the welfare of her nation. The reluctant prophet—epitomized in the Old Testament by Jonah as well as by Esther—came forth only under duress, with "fear and trembling" in times of crisis, to speak the words that recalled a nation to its moral responsibilities. The assumption, of course, was that when the crisis was resolved, the prophet could retire again into obscurity. This temporary role was not, of course, what Grimké was advocating for women in general, but the strategy was useful in deflecting criticism of woman's public role and highly appropriate to the situation.

The Pennsylvania Hall address called for a different strategy. The occasion was designed to generate publicity and even to provoke controversy. The "trembling woman" stance of the earlier speech is replaced by an assertive, forceful prophetic voice that echoes Old Testament prophets calling Israel into account for sins of omission and commission and warning of divine retribution if the nation refused to repent. Grimké Weld speaks with the voice of moral authority, as one ordained of God to bring a message to the people. Yet even here she did not explicitly lay out her justification for woman's appropriation of that role, but implicitly argued divine sanction by her enactment of the role.

GRIMKÉ WELD AS POLITICAL PHILOSOPHER

Abolitionist historians have acknowledged Grimké Weld's activism but have ignored the political philosophy developed in her writings, whereas feminists have focused almost exclusively on her woman's rights rhetoric. Yet the woman's rights rhetoric is but part of a philosophy of human rights that encompasses the plight of all oppressed and politically disempowered minorities. Her need to locate political, moral, and social support for the rights of women and slaves generated unique insights on the nature of society, race and gender relations, individual rights, moral obligations, and public responsibilities.

In her *Appeal to Women of the Nominally Free States*, Grimké argued that slaves are human beings and women are human beings. Therefore, both should immediately be accorded all the rights and privileges guaranteed by the Creator and the state. She refused to base her appeal for woman's rights on the commonly accepted idea that woman's moral character and moral duty were different than man's. She wrote:

We have hitherto addressed you more as moral and responsible beings, than in the distinctive character of women; we have appealed to you on the broad ground of *human rights* and human responsibilities, rather than on that of your peculiar duties as women. . . . In order to prove that you have any duties to perform, it is necessary first to establish the principle of moral being—for all our rights and all our duties grow out of this principle. *All moral beings have essentially the same rights and the same duties*, whether they be male or female. This is a truth the world has yet to learn. (19)

She wrote to Smith that she considered woman's rights part of the "great doctrine of human rights," and thus a natural and necessary extension of the abolitionist cause (August 26, 1837). She felt that "it must be discussed whether there is such a thing as *male and female virtue and male and female duties* etc. My opinion is that there *are none* and that this false idea has driven the plowshare of ruin over the whole field of morality" (August 10, 1837).

In *Appeal to the Women of the Nominally Free States*, Grimké's vision of woman as a moral being is irresistible:

Woman is now rising in her womanhood, to throw from her, with one hand the paltry privileges with which *man* has invested her, of conquering by fashionable charms and winning by personal attractions, whilst with the other she grasps the right of woman to unite in holy copartnership with man, in the renovation of a fallen world. She tramples these glittering baubles in the dust, and takes from the hand of her *Creator*, the Magna Charta of her high prerogatives as a *moral*, an *intellectual*, an accountable being. (69)

The essence of her human rights doctrine was that all—regardless of race or gender—were political, moral, and spiritual beings, equal before God and the law. Thus, emancipation of both slaves and women should be immediate, an appropriation of rights already foreordained.

The Bible was the principal authority on which Grimké built her human rights argument. This is not surprising, given the nature of the times, Grimké's own deep religious convictions, and the evangelical emphasis of the abolitionists with whom she worked. The Bible was not merely the authoritative source in which she grounded her arguments but the perceptual frame through which her life experiences were defined. For example, commitment to the abolitionist cause was understood as a conversion experience, a move from sin to salvation, from darkness to light. The converted were disciples and evangelists, working to convert others in turn and laboring to purge the nation of the evil of slavery.

When she began to develop the arguments supporting woman's right to speak, Grimké naturally turned to the Bible for guidance. Moreover, since much of the opposition to her activity came from religious authorities, she knew she must ground her argument for her activities in religious principles. Although Quakerism allowed women to *preach* (as did LUCRETIA COFFIN MOTT), Grimké centered her authority on woman's right to *prophesy*, basing her vision of "woman as prophet" on biblical precedent. Citing both Old and New Testaments, she pointed to Esther, to Deborah, and to Huldah prophesying to the nation of Israel, to the prophet Anna in the Gospels, to the women in Acts who were "baptized" with the spirit and sent out to spread news of the ascension of Christ.

Again turning to the Bible, she argued that the prophet, not the priest, served as the moral conscience of a society and as the vehicle for conveying the voice of God to a nation. As the catalyst for moral reform, a prophet must of necessity assume a public role—admonishing, warning, predicting—in leading the populace to repentance and renewal. Thus, when convinced of the consequences that would befall the nation if certain evils (in this case slavery) were not repented, women could, indeed must, speak out in warning. To fail to do so was to abdicate their moral, spiritual, and political responsibilities. Although Grimké Weld refused to appropriate any special moral role for women, her "woman as prophet" argument neatly coopted the opposition of those who did so. If woman *did* have a unique moral responsibility to society, she would be filling the role of prophet and would therefore be free to engage in the activities that role entailed.

CONCLUSION

Although her public career was brief, Grimké Weld deserves her status as a pioneer of woman's oratory and woman's rights rhetoric. Not only was she a source of inspiration to many women of her time, but she also provided future generations of women with a model of oratorical excellence worthy of emulation. By all accounts, her skill as a speaker was exceptional; even her critics admired her abilities. She was highly intelligent, well versed in philosophy, history, and theology, a writer of eloquence, and a person of great moral conviction. When these qualities combined with her attention to delivery and her ability to adapt

214 Women Public Speakers in the United States

to her audiences, the impression she made on all who witnessed her public performances can be envisioned. Her insistence that woman was endowed with the same moral and political rights and responsibilities as man presaged the argument advanced by the suffrage movement in the decades to follow. Her early retirement from public life is unfortunate. How she might have further refined her oratorical skills and developed her philosophy of human rights can only be imagined.

SOURCES

The Grimké-Weld collection, Clements Library, University of Michigan, contains the correspondence of Angelina Grimké, Sarah Grimké, and Theodore Weld, some of which is published in *Letters of Theodore Dwight Weld, Angelina Grimké Weld and Sarah Grimké, 1822–1844*. Eds. Gilbert Barnes and Dwight Dumond. 2 vols. New York and London: D. Appleton-Century, 1934. The Weld collection, Library of Congress, has several of Grimké Weld's letters from a later period that offer insight into her religious development. The American Anti-slavery Collections, Boston Public Library, contain information on Grimké Weld's activities in abolitionist organizations.

The Public Years of Sarah and Angelina Grimké: Selected Writings, 1835–1839. Ed. and annot. Larry Ceplair. New York: Columbia University Press, 1989.

Biographical Sources

Abzug, Robert H. *Passionate Liberator: Theodore Dwight Weld and the Dilemma of Reform*. New York: Oxford University Press, 1980.
Bartlett, Elizabeth. Introduction. *Sarah Grimké: Letters on the Equality of the Sexes and Other Essays*. Ed. Elizabeth Bartlett. New Haven, Conn.: Yale University Press, 1988.
Birney, Catherine H. *The Grimké Sisters, Sarah and Angelina Grimké: The First American Women Advocates of Abolition and Woman's Rights*. 1885. Westport, Conn.: Greenwood Press, 1969.
Friedman, Lawrence J. *Gregarious Saints: Self and Community in American Abolitionism, 1830–1870*. New York: Cambridge University Press, 1982.
Ginzburg, Lori D. *Women and the Work of Benevolence: Morality, Politics, and Class in the Nineteenth-Century United States*. New Haven, Conn.: Yale University Press, 1990, pp. 67–97.
Hersh, Blanche Glassman. *The Slavery of Sex: Feminist-Abolitionists in America*. Urbana: University of Illinois Press, 1978.
Lerner, Gerda. *The Grimké Sisters from South Carolina: Rebels Against Slavery*. Boston: Houghton Mifflin, 1967.
Lumpkin, Katherine Du Pre. *The Emancipation of Angelina Grimké*. Chapel Hill: University of North Carolina Press, 1974.
Lutz, Alma. *Crusade for Freedom: Women of the Anti-Slavery Movement*. Boston: Beacon Press, 1968, pp. 115–144.
Melder, Keith E. *Beginnings of Sisterhood: The American Woman's Rights Movement, 1800–1850*. New York: Schocken, 1977.

Critical Sources

Campbell, Karlyn Kohrs. "The Struggle for the Right to Speak." *MCSFH* 1:22–36.

Daughton, Suzanne. "Enactment as Empowerment: Angelina Grimké at Pennsylvania Hall." Unpublished ms. Southern Illinois University, 1990.

Gold, Ellen Reid. "The Grimké Sisters and the Emergence of the Woman's Rights Movement." *Southern Speech Communication Journal* 46 (Summer 1981):341–360.

Japp, Phyllis M. "Esther or Isaiah?: The Abolitionist-Feminist Rhetoric of Angelina Grimké." *Quarterly Journal of Speech* 71 (August 1985):335–348.

Yellin, Jean Fagan. *Women & Sisters: The Antislavery Feminists in American Culture.* New Haven, Conn.: Yale University Press, 1989.

Chronology of Speeches and Writings

Letter to the *Liberator*, August 30, 1835. Published September 19, 1835.

Appeal to the Christian Women of the South. 1836. New York: Arno, 1969. Excerpt WT:10–12.

Appeal to the Women of the Nominally Free States, Issued by an Anti-Slavery Convention of American Women Held by Adjournment from the 9th to the 12 of May, 1837. New York: W. S. Dorr, 1837. HOW

Letters to Catherine E. Beecher, in Reply to "An Essay on Slavery and Abolitionism Addressed to Angelina E. Grimké." Boston: Isaac Knapp, 1838. HOW

Speech, Massachusetts Legislature, February 21, 1838. *Liberator* (March 2, 1838):35; Lerner, 1967; Ceplair, 1989:310–312; HOW excerpt WT:15–16;

Speech at Pennsylvania Hall, May 16, 1838. *A History of Pennsylvania Hall, Which Was Destroyed by a Mob on the 17th of May, 1838.* [Ed. Samuel May]. Philadelphia: Merrihew & Gunn, 1838; Entry, *American Slavery As It Is: Testimony of a Thousand Witnesses.* New York: American Anti-Slavery Society, 1839. Ceplair, 1989:318–323; Lerner, 1967; *MCSFH* 2:25–32; *WSBH*:23–30; *Forerunners of Black Power: The Rhetoric of Abolition.* Ed. Ernest R. Bormann. Englewood Cliffs, N.J.: Prentice-Hall, 1971, pp. 183–192.

Letter to the Woman's Rights Convention, 1852. HOW

"The North, Go On! Go On!" May 14, 1863, Women's National Loyal League Convention, New York City. *HWS* 2:54–56. *OW*:76–79.

SARAH M. GRIMKÉ

(1792–1873), author of first U.S. woman's rights treatise

KRISTIN S. VONNEGUT

Sarah Moore Grimké played an essential but neglected role in the abolition and woman's rights movements in the United States. Because nearly all her speeches have been lost and only a few essays still exist, some have considered her rhetorically insignificant. Furthermore, the relative brevity of her public career may have caused her to be overlooked. Grimké is best known for her work on slavery and woman's rights in the years 1836 through 1838. Although she was active as a reformer only briefly, she was the first U.S. woman to write an important treatise on woman's rights.

BACKGROUND

Grimké's training as a wealthy southern lady was usual for nineteenth-century females of her class. As the daughter of Judge John Faucheraud and Mary Smith Grimké, South Carolina plantation owners, she studied in the company of her older brother Thomas, but when he began to study Latin and the law, she was excluded. Unlike other upper class southern women, however, she partially overcame the societal norms that limited female education by studying law secretly. Of that period, she wrote:

I was naturally independent, longed for an education that would elevate me above the low pursuits of sense, but I was a girl & altho' well educated as such, yet the powers of my mind were not called into exercise. I looked with longing eyes on my brother's superior advantages & wondered why the simple fact of being a girl should shut me up to the necessity of being a doll. (WGM, Box 10)

Grimké's dissatisfaction with the life of a southern lady led her at age twenty-eight to leave South Carolina and to join a Quaker meeting in Philadelphia. It was unusual for an unmarried young woman to leave her family, but her need for independence was a force stronger than nineteenth-century notions of propriety. For nearly fifteen years, she struggled to become a minister in the Society of Friends, but her path was blocked by self-doubt and obstacles raised by fellow Quakers. In 1836, she chose to leave Philadelphia and move with her younger sister, Angelina, to New York. There, the Grimké sisters began a two-year stint as the first female lecturers for the American Anti-Slavery Society.

The sisters' lectures were well attended by both men and women, which disturbed some religious leaders. Even some members of the American Anti-slavery Society wanted to "protect" them from male intruders during their lectures (Barnes 1957:153–160). Moreover, as the Grimkés became more familiar with the injustices suffered by slaves, they were able to compare the plight of the slave to that of white women. Ultimately, that comparison impelled Grimké to address woman's oppression in a series of letters addressed to Mary Parker, president of the Boston Female Anti-Slavery Society. Originally, the letters appeared in the *New England Spectator*, an organ of the Congregational church, and the *Liberator*, an abolitionist newspaper in 1837. Subsequently, they were published as *Letters on the Equality of the Sexes and the Condition of Woman* (1838). Although many women were stirred by her arguments, some American Anti-Slavery officials believed that one whom they had seen as their advocate was wasting her time and talents on a cause far less important than abolition.

In the spring of 1838, Grimké retired from public speaking at the request of her friend and brother-in-law, Theodore Weld. He was among the abolitionists who disapproved of her woman's rights work, although he maintained that his advice was based on her sister's greater effectiveness as a speaker. Angelina's rhetorical style was dramatic; she incorporated biblical language and appealed to the emotions of the audience. Sarah relied on a more argumentative, legalistic approach to persuade audiences. For instance, in order to defend woman's right to preach, she asserted:

Before I proceed to prove that woman is bound to preach the gospel, I will examine the ministry under the Old Testament dispensation. Those who were called to this office were known under various names. . . . They were denominated men of God, seers, prophets, but they all had the same great work to perform, viz. to turn sinners from the error of their ways. This ministry existed previous to the institution of the Jewish Priesthood, and continued after its abolition. *It has nothing to do with the priesthood.* It was rarely, as far as the Bible informs us, exercised by those of the tribe of Levi, and was common to all the people, women as well as men. It differed essentially from the priesthood, because there was no compensation received for calling the people to repentance. . . . I believe the secret of the exclusion of women from the ministerial office is, that that office has been converted into one of emolument, of honor, and of power. Any attentive observer cannot fail to perceive, that as far as possible, all such offices are reserved by men for themselves. (86)

The elder Grimké's assertive style and sarcastic tone were less likely to please than her younger sister's speeches, which emulated the more flamboyant style traditional in the nineteenth century. Furthermore, because of its biblical, poetic character, Angelina's rhetoric may have been seen as more appropriately feminine than the more austere argumentation of her older sister. Whatever Weld's reasons for censuring Sarah, it is noteworthy that both sisters abandoned their speaking careers in that year.

THE ROOTS OF GRIMKÉ'S WOMAN'S RIGHTS THEORY

Although she retired from public speaking in 1838, Grimké continued to write about woman's rights. She developed her woman's rights theory from two important theoretical bases: Quaker theology and abolitionism. Quaker belief in the "inner light" led members to reject ritualized services and to accept all believers as potential ministers, no matter their sex. Although the orthodox Quaker sect to which she belonged did not give women an equal voice in governance, the right to speak during meetings was an important privilege for nineteenth-century females. In fact, a predecessor and a founder of the Society of Friends, Margaret Askew Fell, had defended woman's right to minister in her 1666 pamphlet *Womens [sic] Speaking Justified*, a work from which Grimké borrowed some arguments (Vonnegut, 1991).

Even more fundamental for Grimké than the right to minister, however, was the right of all followers of the faith to interpret the Bible for themselves. This provision enabled her to question traditional restrictions placed on women consistent with narrow biblical exegesis. In the first of her *Letters* (1838), she affirmed the right of individual interpretation, not just of the scripture as translated but in its original form:

In examining this important subject, I shall depend solely on the Bible to designate the sphere of woman, because I believe almost every thing that has been written on this subject, has been the result of a misconception of the simple truths revealed in the Scriptures, in consequence of the false translation of many passages of Holy Writ. My mind is entirely delivered from the superstitious reverence which is attached to the English version of the Bible. King James's translators certainly were not inspired. I therefore claim the original as my standard, *believing that to have been inspired*, and I also claim to judge for myself what is the meaning of the inspired writers, because I believe it to be the solemn duty of every individual to search the Scriptures for themselves, with the aid of the Holy Spirit, and not be governed by the views of any man, or set of men. (31–32)

Grimké also drew from a second major source, abolitionism. The abolitionists were inspired by a moral imperative to work for the emancipation of slaves. The idea that anti-slavery advocacy was a religious duty appealed to her. For the first time, her desire to speak out on reform issues was countenanced by God. Moreover, it was the abolitionists' broad approach to human rights that allowed her to make the connection between the rights of the slave and the rights of woman. In her *Letters* (1838), she discussed woman's legal disabilities. More than a decade before the Seneca Falls, New York, WRC, she quoted William Blackstone's statement, "*the very being, or legal existence of the woman* is suspended during the marriage." Then she analyzed the implications of these legal norms for women by comparing them to slave laws:

Here now, the very being of a woman, like that of a slave, is absorbed in her master. All contracts made with her, like those made with slaves by their owners, are a mere nullity. Our kind defenders have legislated away almost all our legal rights, and in the true spirit of such injustice and oppression, have kept us in ignorance of those very laws by which we are governed.(72)

Grimké's experiences with Quakerism and abolitionism provided the foundation on which she built a path-breaking theory of woman's rights.

RHETORICAL OBSTACLES: GENDER

Abolitionist agents were not always welcome visitors in northern states. Considered radical troublemakers, agents were often run out of town by angry crowds. The experience of John Alvord was representative. He wrote: "All still until about 8 when in came a broadside of Eggs, Glass, Egg shells, Whites, and yolks flew on every side" (*LTDW* 1:260). If abolitionists in general were perceived as extremist fanatics, women abolitionists were the worst of the lot. According to Barbara Welter (1966), women in the nineteenth century were expected to work within a restricted domestic sphere and be modest, pious, and submissive. When confronted with the evils of slavery, however, women experienced conflict in their traditional role. As pious women, many felt called to do God's work in the abolition movement; as submissive women, they understood that anti-slavery advocacy would compel them to work outside the home and outside their "proper" sphere (Hersh, 1978:3).

Moving into the public arena proved difficult for Grimké; it was a domain in which she felt alien. In every forum, she faced a potentially hostile audience. Although the sisters rarely met with extreme violence during their lecture tours, they were subjected to terms of abuse and missiles of rotten food. In the midst of one lecture by Angelina, rocks and bricks were hurled through the windows. Furthermore, as the Grimkés began to intersperse woman's rights arguments into their abolitionist lectures, they encountered still more opposition. Their friend and fellow abolitionist, John Greenleaf Whittier, wrote to them:

In regard to another subject, "*the rights of woman*," you are now doing much and nobly to vindicate and assert the rights of woman. . . . Why, then, let me ask, is it necessary for you to enter the lists of controversial writers on the question? . . . Is it not forgetting the great and dreadful wrongs of the slave in a selfish crusade against some paltry grievance of our own? (*LTDW* 1:424)

Whittier's letter reveals the depths of the hostility engendered when women stepped out of their sphere. As an abolitionist, he saw the need to recruit women for the public struggle against slavery; but as a man, he resisted the idea that women might have their own grievances. Not only did he subsume women's oppression under the heading of white people's grievances, but he also ignored the African-American females who constituted a large percentage of the slave population he wanted to save.

RHETORICAL OBSTACLES: CULTURE

In addition to constraints of gender, Grimké had to overcome cultural barriers as well. She was not simply a nineteenth-century woman or even a southern woman. She also was a southern *lady*, and as such her duty was to charm and nurture those around her as well as to be pure, pious, submissive, and domestic. Her life was devoted to home and church. In this setting she cultivated a persona that would perpetuate the cultural traditions of home and family. ''Ladies'' who evidenced ''too much'' learning were deemed unpleasant company; those who considered careers endangered their status within the community; those who wrote for an audience were charged with unladylike self-display (Fox-Genovese, 1988:246, 259).

The phenomenon of the southern lady did not appear in a vacuum; it had strong ties to important cultural institutions, including slavery. The institution of slavery strengthened the patriarchal system that stifled women and enabled southern gentlemen to remain in absolute control. Like their children and slaves, women were expected to remain in subjection to their masters. If any one rebelled, the delicate balance would be upset, leaving southern plantation culture in disarray (Scott, 1970:17).

A second institution that socialized southern ladies into the domestic role was the church. Although it supplied women with a legitimate outlet for community action outside the home, the messages from the pulpit replicated those emanating from the head of the dinner table. Moreover, the charity work required of all southern ladies was considered best done from the home. By dispensing charity from the domestic sphere, ladies were protected from unmonitored interaction with the lower classes (Fox-Genovese, 1988:44,234).

That Grimké was pressured to abide by doctrines of proper behavior for a southern lady is indicated in a letter she received from her mother Mary Smith Grimké, who wrote of Sarah's public work:

Before you calculate upon the good you *think* you have done; look to the emense [*sic*] evil that may ensue if your schemes were accomplished. Thus as God permitted you to go this far! but he has now provided for you, a happy home & I trust will there keep you. (WGM, Box 6)

For Smith Grimké, the best thing possible had happened to her unmarried daughter; she had been removed from the public eye and had found a home to call her own.

RHETORICAL STRATEGIES

To overcome the constraints of gender and culture that hindered her rhetorical efforts, Grimké experimented with two powerful strategies. She created a variety of roles or personae, and she assayed a variety of genres in an attempt to become an effective rhetor.

Developing a public persona is never an easy task, but for women rhetors it is almost impossible. Because rhetoric is perceived as part of the public domain, and women's gender roles restrict them to the domestic sphere, their rhetorical efforts are likely to be considered unfeminine. Thus, according to K. Kohrs Campbell and E. Claire Jerry (1988), for a woman to appear credible either she must find a public role that reaffirms her femininity while giving her authority to speak, or she must assume a persona acceptable for both men and women. In an attempt to fortify her credibility, Grimké employed both strategies.

Developing a public persona that empowered both Grimké and her audience proved particularly difficult. Her first effort in 1836, in *An Epistle to the Clergy of the Southern States*, probably left her audience of southern clergymen un-- persuaded. She chose to write an apostolic letter after the manner of St. Paul. In assuming the role of an apostle, one commissioned by Christ, she treated the ministers as parishioners rather than as her spiritual guides, which would have been their traditional relation to her. Malinda Snow explains that "the very composing of an epistle (as a proxy sermon) defines one's audience as people who are to be advised, guided, and convinced" (1985:330).

As an apostle, that is, simultaneously as a religious peer and guide, she wrote: "Let me beseech you then, my dear brethren, to pause, and learn from the tremendous past what must be the inevitable destiny of those who are adding year after year, to the amount of crime which is treasuring up 'wrath against the day of wrath' " (9). Here Grimké's tone was loving but reproachful. She, like Paul whom she quoted, wanted to warn her countrymen that they were not exempt from the punishments of God.

Of course, she violated woman's sphere by lecturing publicly to these men. Nancy F. Cott (1977) has noted that, although the clergy valued women for their support of the church, they did not accept women as teachers or preachers of the word. Moreover, Grimké lacked biblical precedent to justify her choice of roles; no woman had been a disciple or had assumed the role of apostle. This violation was likely to disturb her secondary audience of abolitionists as well. They might have hailed her efforts on behalf of the slave, but adopting what this highly religious group perceived as a male persona was probably as outra- geous to them as to the southern ministers she addressed directly.

Although a poor choice for persuading southerners and more conservative abolitionists, assuming an apostolic persona was apparently an experience con- ducive to Grimké's personal development. This role permitted her to address the ministers and other men as equals and empowered her to speak out against their countenancing and condoning the injustices she had witnessed. That she drew strength from the effort is evidenced in a letter she wrote a few weeks after *An Epistle to the Clergy* was published. In a burst of newly discovered self- confidence, she exclaimed: "The present is a new era in my life and I daily praise God that he condescended to let me enter the ranks of the Abolitionists and mingle with those who are maintaining the holy principles of freedom (*LTDW* 1:357).

The second problematic persona Grimké appropriated was that of a parent or guardian. In her 1837 speech, "An Address to Free Colored Americans," she was able to assume a position of power while adopting a persona deemed suitable for women because it was associated with the private sphere. Speaking as a representative of a group (the committee in charge of preparing the ''Address'') and appropriating a parental role without clear ethnic or gender connotations, she took on a persona that protected her from accusations of behaving in an unfeminine manner. Furthermore, as a representative of the committee, she was only partially responsible for the words she spoke and for their impact (Vonnegut, 1991). If audience members disputed her suggestions, they were challenging the committee she represented, not Grimké herself. The paternalistic views of the committee as well as her assumption of a parental role were clear from the tone in which the African-American audience was addressed. Speaking as the voice of the committee, she said: ''With deep regret we have heard that some of our colored brethren and sisters in our great cities frequent the theatre. This is a sink of vice from which we earnestly beseech you to keep yourselves entirely separate'' (12).

Speaking in the role of parent gave Grimké power, provided the free African-Americans she addressed were willing to assume the role of children, but it did little to empower her primary audience. Indeed, by assuming a superior role, she discouraged identification between herself or the committee and the African-American audience. Rather, the identification she encouraged was between free African-Americans and their enslaved brothers and sisters. She explained:

You are, dear friends, in a peculiar manner fellow sufferers with those who are in bondage; because the whites, having reduced their colored brethren to slavery . . . have labored to impress on the mind of the community, the unfounded calumny that the people of color are unfit for freedom. (5)

Such an identification, when merged with suggestions for passive behavior, may have left free African-Americans feeling even less able to struggle against their lot.

The third major persona that Grimké adopted in her rhetoric was that of a sister, and here she struck rhetorical gold. In *Letters on the Equality of the Sexes and the Condition of Woman* (1838), she feminized her role as public advocate by playing the part of a loving, more experienced sister to the women in her audience. As with the parental role, acting as a sister was compatible with the domain of woman's sphere. Moreover, the role was appealing to the women she addressed. Drawing on the culture of nineteenth-century sisterhood gave her entrée into the hearts and minds of her female audience. In that role, she encouraged her sisters to consider their situation and to take action to change woman's position in society. Using an intimate, conversational approach, for the first time, she empowered her audience by addressing them as capable interpreters of scripture. For instance, she confided in her sisters, airing her doubts about Eve's guilt in the Fall: ''Now, whether the fact that Eve was beguiled and deceived, is a proof that her crime was of deeper dye than Adam's who was not deceived, but was fully aware of the consequence of sharing in her transgression, I shall leave the candid reader to determine'' (96).

In the process of enabling other women to recognize their oppression, Grimké may have limited her own development as a rhetor. By speaking as a sister and adopting the personal letter form (discussed below), she diminished the obstacles to reception of her message, but her choices enlarged her sphere of public action only a little. Both her persona and the genre in which she wrote were anchored in the domestic sphere.

Although her sisters were just beginning to grapple with the implications of their limited role as women, Grimké was ready to take specific action. Yet she needed the support of others to move ahead. In the face of Theodore Weld's disapproval of her public role and her sister's retreat into the domestic sphere after marrying Weld, in addition to earlier discouragements, she chose to join her sister in relative seclusion.

Grimké's use of the apostolic epistle as a rhetorical form was linked to the development of her persona. Initially, she relied on its conventions to provide her with formal guidelines for writing her *Epistle* (1836). For an inexperienced advocate, generic characteristics would have facilitated the creation of a unified, coherent essay. In addition, as the written equivalent of a sermon (Reicke, 1964), the apostolic epistle allowed her to minister to her audience without addressing them face to face. Her recent negative experiences ministering in the Quaker faith had made her reticent about speaking to another congregation. Furthermore, the apostolic epistle was a form familiar to her audiences. Thus, she may have believed the work would receive a fair hearing from fellow Christians, whether southern ministers or abolitionists.

The apostolic epistle, however, did not correspond well to Grimké's situation. The author of an epistle relies on a religious bond that is a link to his or her audience (Mullins, 1968). Furthermore, the audience should consider the writer a credible authority—the equivalent of an apostle. Although southern ministers and northern abolitionists were familiar with the apostolic epistle as a form, neither group had a close relationship with Grimké, and neither was ready to grant her such authority.

Furthermore, Grimké's subject matter, abolition, did not allow her to adopt the genre fully. Apostolic letters followed a basic format from which she was forced to stray. The salutation from author to audience in the New Testament epistles was brief and usually included a wish for peace. The body of most epistles began with a discussion of doctrine followed by an author's admonition to the congregation to act in accord with that teaching. Finally, most apostles closed their epistles with greetings and a blessing on the congregation (Reicke, 1964).

Although Grimké used many of the conventions developed by her apostolic predecessors, of necessity her approach was less friendly. Her introduction included an attempt to identify with her audience. However, her words, ''To my dear native land, to the beloved relatives who are still breathing her tainted air''

(1–2), were not likely to seem welcoming to her southern audience. Her conclusion was unlike the generic model as well. She asked God to ''influence the ministers of his sanctuary, and the people committed to their charge'' to enable the ''year of jubilee'' to come. These words can hardly be called a blessing.

In addition to difficulties with adaptation of the genre, the epistle was a problematic form for Grimké because of its identification with the public sphere. Although other letter forms were acceptable for women's use, the apostolic epistle was a letter addressed to wide and diverse congregations of converts rather than to members of one's family or to friends, for example, the individuals who were deemed appropriate recipients of women's correspondence. Using such a public, male-identified form opened her to attacks from those who believed that there was no place for woman outside the domestic sphere and that they were enjoined by scripture from assuming religious authority.

In contrast to the apostolic epistle, the personal letter is a form associated with the private sphere. Characteristics of the nineteenth-century woman's letter, such as intimate address, description, and moral judgment (Motz, 1983), made Grimké's *Letters* (1838) especially appealing to a female audience. She found her rhetorical metier by using this familiar, intimate form that was part of woman's private sphere. She personalized her *Letters* by addressing their supposed recipient, Mary Parker, as ''My dear sister.'' She used the format of the personal letter to encourage women like Parker to consider woman's rights reform in both her *Letters* and later essays.

An example of Grimké's appeal may be found in letter fifteen, ''Man Equally Guilty with Woman in the Fall.'' She wrote:

The immense usefulness and the vast influence of woman have been eulogized and called into exercise, and many a blessing has been lavished upon us, and many a prayer put up for us, because we have labored by day and by night to clothe and feed and educate young men, whilst our own bodies sometimes suffer for want of comfortable garments, and our minds are left in almost utter destitution of that improvement which we are toiling to bestow upon the brethren. (98)

Here she used description to challenge an image of woman heralded by popular culture. She drew on experiences shared by her sisters and helped them to see their ''sacrifices'' in a harsher light.

Writing in an acceptable female role in a form deemed appropriate for women enabled Grimké to question the social structure and to offer opinions concerning woman's condition without appearing to violate rules of propriety. Letters exchanged between sisters in which one woman considered the problems women faced could not be judged as harshly as authoritative public assertions on the same subject. Finally, her use of the personal letter was a particularly important rhetorical strategy because it spoke in a style suited to the experiences of her female audience, empowering them to question their roles.

Still, speaking in the role of sister through the private letter form might not have been ideal for Grimké's growing sense of woman's rights. The same elements that made the personal letter attractive to women just beginning to consider woman's condition might have made that form confining for her. For a woman who had braved intense hostility on the public platform and had enjoyed success as a lecturer, limiting her expression to the format of a private letter, even if published, and speaking only as a sister might have been an intellectual retreat.

In composing her *Letters*, however, Grimké chose a highly effective rhetorical strategy for her audience: she made the private sphere public; she published these "personal" letters. Now, readers who would not grant her personal letters the same respect they might an essay addressed to a mixed audience were confronted with published letters. An intimate feminine genre had been transformed into a public form. It was a rhetorical coup.

Sarah Grimké's *Letters* inspired many of her nineteenth-century sisters to question their roles. Later advocates for woman's rights testified to their influence. They reinforced Lucy Stone's desire to fight for the freedom of her sisters (Melder, 1977). They served as a model for ELIZABETH CADY STANTON in writing *The Woman's Bible* (Nies, 1977). They may have aided ANTOINETTE BROWN BLACKWELL in formulating *Exegesis of I Corinthians, XIV., 34, 35; And I Timothy, II., 11, 12* (1849) and FRANCES E. WILLARD in setting forth her arguments in *Woman in the Pulpit* (1888) (Vonnegut, 1991). Finally, LUCRETIA COFFIN MOTT considered Grimké's *Letters* second only to Mary Wollstonecraft's *A Vindication of the Rights of Woman* and turned to them in 1849 when formulating her *Discourse on Woman* (Cromwell, 1958).

Others before Grimké had questioned woman's role in society. In 1666, Margaret Askew Fell had argued for woman's right to speak in the church; in 1792, Mary Wollstonecraft had pleaded for equal education for girls and boys; and in 1798 in *Alcuin*, Charles Brockden Brown had considered the middle-class white woman's situation in the United States. Only Grimké, however, was able to provide a broad perspective on woman's situation. She identified the depth of the problem as well as the scope, addressing the needs of women from various classes and races. To that extent, her work surpassed that of her predecessors and was more insightful than many works by later woman's rights advocates.

In her *Letters*, Grimké recognized the restraints placed on women's personal, religious, affiliative, and natural rights—issues raised by woman's rights advocates some ten years later at the first woman's rights convention (*MCSFH* 1:49–69). Like those women, she understood the debilitating effects of poor education and unequal remuneration for working women. In addition, she discussed woman's role in the church and pointed to inconsistencies in biblical exegesis that stifled women, points that were also raised at the Seneca Falls Convention. She was a forerunner in understanding the U.S. legal system and its disregard for the rights of single and married women as well, foreshadowing many of the ideas discussed by her sisters in woman's rights advocacy. Her ability to identify these important constraints placed on women by society established her as a harbinger of the woman's rights movement in the United States.

CONCLUSION

In addition to introducing important theoretical concepts adopted by later advocates and intellectuals, Grimké recognized and fought against the oppression of African-American and all working-class women. Cady Stanton and most other leaders of the woman's rights movement did little to promote the interests of women other than those of the white middle and upper classes. Although Grimké's *Letters* did not discuss woman suffrage or divorce laws or provide as thorough an analysis of woman's subjugation as Cady Stanton did in her address at Seneca Falls, Grimké offered a strong theoretical base on which the next generation of advocates might build.

Rhetoric has long been the domain of those in power. In the United States, the powerful have been and continue to be elite white males. Sarah Grimké and others like her attempted to change that state of affairs by addressing societal problems in the public arena. She faced numerous obstacles throughout her brief rhetorical career. Her rhetorical efforts to overcome these barriers make her an apt representative of the majority of nondominant speakers, especially women who faced similar barriers and creatively invented strategies to overcome them.

SOURCES

Primary materials are in two major sources, the Theodore Dwight Weld, Angelina Grimké Weld, and Sarah Grimké Papers, William L. Clements Library, University of Michigan (WGM), and the Antislavery Manuscripts, Boston Public Library.

Letters of Theodore Dwight Weld, Angelina Grimké and Sarah Grimké, 1822–1844. 2 vols. Eds. Gilbert H. Barnes and Dwight L. Dumond. 1834. Gloucester, Mass.: P. Smith, 1965. (*LTDW*)

Grimké, Sarah. *Letters on the Equality of the Sexes and Other Essays.* Ed. Elizabeth Ann Bartlett. New Haven, Conn.: Yale University Press, 1988.

The Public Years of Sarah and Angelina Grimké: Selected Writings, 1835–1839. Ed. and annot. Larry Ceplair. New York: Columbia University Press, 1989.

Selected Critical Studies

Barnes, Gilbert H. *The Antislavery Impulse, 1830–1844.* Gloucester, Mass.: Peter Smith, 1957.

Bartlett, Elizabeth Ann. "Liberty, Equality, Sorority: Origins and Interpretations of American Feminist Thought: Frances Wright, Margaret Fuller, and Sarah Grimké." Ph.D. diss., University of Minnesota, 1981. AAC 8206325

Campbell, K. Kohrs, and E. Claire Jerry. "Woman and Speaker: A Conflict in Roles."

Seeing Female: Social Reality and Personal Lives. Ed. Sharon S. Brehm. Westport, Conn.: Greenwood Press, 1988, pp. 123–133.

Cott, Nancy F. *The Bonds of Womanhood: "Woman's Sphere" in New England, 1780–1835*. New Haven, Conn.: Yale University Press, 1977.

Cromwell, Otelia. *Lucretia Mott*. Cambridge, Mass.: Harvard University Press, 1958

Fell, Margaret Askew. *Womens Speaking Justified Proved and Allowed by the Scriptures*. 1666. London: Pythia, 1989.

Fox-Genovese, Elizabeth. *Within the Plantation Household: Black and White Women of the Old South*. Chapel Hill: University of North Carolina Press, 1988.

Gold, Ellen Reid. "The Grimké Sisters and the Emergence of the Woman's Rights Movement." *Southern Speech Communication Journal* 46 (Summer 1981):341–360.

Hersh, Blanche Glassman. *The Slavery of Sex: Feminist Abolitionists in America*. Urbana: University of Illinois Press, 1978.

Melder, Keith. *Beginnings of Sisterhood: The American Woman's Rights Movement, 1800–1850*. New York: Schocken, 1977.

Motz, Marilyn Ferris. *True Sisterhood: Michigan Women and Their Kin*. Albany: State University of New York Press, 1983.

Mullins, Terence Y. "Greetings as a New Testament Form." *Journal of Biblical Literature* 87 (1968):418–426.

Nies, Judith. *Seven Women: Portraits from the American Radical Tradition*. New York: Viking, 1977.

Reicke, Bo. "Introduction to the Epistles of James, Peter, and Jude." *The Anchor Bible*, Vol. 37. New York: Doubleday, 1964, pp. xv–xxxviii.

"Sarah M. Grimké's 'Sisters of Charity.' " Ed. and Intro. Gerda Lerner. *Signs* 1 (Autumn 1975):246–256.

Scott, Anne Firor. *The Southern Lady: From Pedestal to Politics, 1830–1930*. Chicago: University of Chicago Press, 1970.

Snow, Malinda. "Martin Luther King's 'Letter from Birmingham Jail' as Pauline Epistle." *Quarterly Journal of Speech* 71 (August 1985):318–334.

Vonnegut, Kristin S. "'If You Would Have Freedom, Strike for It': Sarah Moore Grimké's Struggle for the Rights of Woman." Ph.D. diss. University of Minnesota, 1991.

Welter, Barbara. "The Cult of True Womanhood: 1820–1860." *American Quarterly* 18 (1966):151–174.

Selected Biographies

Birney, Catherine H. *The Grimké Sisters: Sarah and Angelina Grimké: The First American Women Advocates of Abolition and Woman's Rights*. 1885. Westport, Conn.: Greenwood Press, 1969.

Lerner, Gerda. *The Grimké Sisters of South Carolina: Pioneers of Woman's Rights and Abolition*. 1967. New York: Schocken, 1971.

Lumpkin, Katherine Du Pre. *The Emancipation of Angelina Grimké*. Chapel Hill: University of North Carolina Press, 1974.

Chronology of Major Rhetorical Works

An Epistle to the Clergy of the Southern States. New York:1836. HOW, Reel 942, No. 8439; Ceplair, 1989, 90–115.

"An Address to Free Colored Americans." New York: William S. Dorr, 1837; *Proceedings of the Anti-Slavery Convention of American Women, 1837.*

Letters on the Equality of the Sexes and the Condition of Woman Addressed to Mary S. Parker, president of the Boston Female Anti-Slavery Society. Boston: I. Knapp, 1838. Bartlett, *Letters*; HOW, Reel 166, No. 1070.

MARY HARRIS "MOTHER" JONES

(1830?–1930), "Mother" and messiah to industrial labor

MARI BOOR TONN

Mary Harris Jones, known simply as ''Mother'' Jones, was among the industrial labor movement's most colorful and charismatic personalities, its most prolific, charismatic, and inventive rhetors, and its most effective agitators. For nearly half a century, this tiny, immigrant widow spoke extemporaneously, sometimes several times a day and in every imaginable circumstance in behalf of her working-class constituency: child laborers, workers in breweries and mills, streetcar and railroad employees, and even Mexican revolutionaries (*Autobiography*; Fetherling, 1979; Long, 1976; Steel, *Correspondence*).

Her closest and most famous alliance, however, was with the United Mine Workers of America (UMWA), which hired her as a paid organizer sometime in the 1890s (Dix, 1970:7; Fetherling, 1979:28; Foner, 1979:52; Steel, *Correspondence*, xxiv–xxv), when its locals closed their membership and commonly even meetings to females (Schofield, 1980). Nonetheless, her success as an agitator before such daunting male audiences was nothing less than legendary. Her ability to arouse impoverished miners to a frenzy, to persuade them to risk starvation, imprisonment, and even death to join the union helped to make organized labor a political force with which to be reckoned. Eugene Debs claimed that no one—man or woman, living or dead—rivaled Harris Jones as a mine organizer (''To the Rescue''), a view often echoed in labor organs. Elizabeth Gurley Flynn (see entry in volume 2) termed her ''the greatest agitator of our time'' (quoted in Foner, 1983:68). Among her legion of admirers were more than a few establishment figures, including politicians, reporters, and socialites who viewed her as among the nation's greatest women (Fetherling, 1979:152; Mooney, 1967:132). Conversely, coal company owners and operators dubbed her ''The Old Hag'' and called her the ''vulgar old woman'' (quoted in Long, 1976:21), and a West Virginia prosecutor considered her ''the most dangerous woman in America'' (quoted in Michelson, 1913:8). The enemies of labor routinely threatened her and imposed injunctions, deportations, and jail terms in futile attempts to silence the woman whom millions affectionately called ''the miners' angel'' (Fetherling, 1979:85–177).

Harris Jones was extraordinarily effective in overcoming the formidable rhetorical barriers she confronted as a female labor union organizer because she had an intensely intimate appeal to workers. This appeal was based largely on the strategic roles or personae she assumed. In the traditional role of mother, she nurtured males in her audiences by tending to their basic psychological and physiological needs. In the charismatic role of prophet, she offered discouraged workers hope and vision. Both roles also provided this female agitator with authority over male audiences and the freedom to speak publicly for labor.

BACKGROUND

According to the autobiography published in 1925, Mary Harris was born on May 1, 1830, in Cork, Ireland (11). As with certain other aspects of her life, this widely quoted date—both the year and the highly symbolic day for labor— appears to have been chosen to suit her rhetorical purposes, specifically to enhance the roles in which she cast herself—as labor's prophet and matriarch.

More certain than her birth date is her heritage of protest. The eldest child of poor tenant farmers active in the Irish rebellion, she first lost her paternal grand-father to hanging by the British and then her insurgent father to exile in the United States. Some years later, she and her family joined her father in Canada, where she attended high school and excelled in debating. At seventeen, she qualified as a grammar school teacher, a profession she alternated with dress-making and practiced in Canada, New England, and Michigan (Atkinson, 1978:10–11; Fetherling, 1979:2–3).

In 1861, she married a staunch member of the Iron Moulder's Union in Memphis (*Autobiography*, 12; Fetherling, 1979:3). Her husband's name—like those of her mother, some of her siblings, and her children—is debated; all family names except her father's are omitted from her autobiography. Most accounts, including her life story, report that the couple quickly produced four children (12), although their actual number and gender are uncertain (Atkinson, 1978:36; *Autobiography*, 286; Fetherling, 1979:3, 5, 193, 228n.13; Foner, 1979:41; Mikeal, 1965:2; Steel, *Correspondence*, xxiii; Werstein, 1969:17–18, 20–21, 23). In 1867, a yellow fever epidemic seized Memphis (Fetherling, 1979:4–5), and Harris Jones's autobiography includes her husband and children among its victims (12). Less probable is an alternative tale she occasionally told in mining towns of losing her only son to illness or accident and her husband in a mining explosion or in strike violence (Long, 1976:3; Skubitz personal communication August 5, 1986), which was probably told to strengthen iden-tification with all-male coal mining audiences.

Shortly thereafter, the widowed Harris Jones returned to Chicago and opened a dressmaking shop, which burned with her other possessions in the Chicago Fire of 1871 (*Autobiography*, 13; Fetherling, 1979:2). Without home, family, or personal belongings, she found both physical and spiritual refuge at local Knights of Labor meetings. She joined this large labor organization, which was the first to admit women on an equal basis with men (*Autobiography*, 14; Fetherling, 1979:6).

Many details of the first quarter century of Harris Jones's involvement in the labor movement are shadowy, but there are certain clues to some of the forces that shaped her philosophy and distinctive rhetorical style. During the 1870s, she may have traveled to Europe to study labor conditions there ("About Mother Jones"; Nies, 1977:102), reportedly worked in California as a sandlot speaker with the Working Men's party, formed in 1877 to protest the importation of Chinese labor (Long 1976:3; Michelson, 1913:8), and became involved in the Pennsylvania Railroad strike (*Autobiography*, 15–16; Fetherling, 1979:12). She spent much of the 1880s in Chicago where she was influenced by anarchist demands for fairer working conditions such as the eight-hour workday (*Autobiography*, 17–23). At the same time, her alliance with the Knights of Labor was rumored to have unraveled with their failure to use massive worker demonstrations rather than mere words to prevent the executions of the Haymarket martyrs (Werstein, 1969:56), although she maintained a lifelong friendship with Knights leader Terence Powderly. She may also have worked as an organizer of women's auxiliaries to labor unions prior to her involvement with the UMWA ("Mother Jones Dies"), although the dates and places of these alleged activities are unknown. Some claim that the bawdy language that would characterize her rhetoric was acquired in her years as a miner's boarding house proprietor in Colorado sometime in the late 1880s or early 1890s (Coleman, 1943:59; Mikeal, 1965:7; Nies, 1977:106), an establishment the enemies of labor would later call a "brothel." They embellished their account with seamy details and had it inserted in the *Congressional Record* during the pivotal coal strike in Colorado in 1914 in which Harris Jones played a key role (Fetherling, 1979:134–136; Foner, 1983:139; McGovern and Gutteridge, 1972:48, 135–136; Mikeal, 1965:6). In 1894, she joined Coxey's Army in a march of the unemployed to the nation's capitol ("About 'Mother' Jones"). As a participant, she apparently witnessed at first hand the effectiveness of revivalistic rhetoric, drama, and flamboyance in attracting the notice of the press.

Some credit her with directing her first coal strike in 1891 in Norton, West Virginia, from which she would emerge as "Mother" Jones (Fetherling, 1979:16; Mikeal, 1965:7; OW:85). Other dates range from as early as 1882 in Ohio (Michelson, 1913:8) to as late as 1897 in West Virginia and Pennsylvania (Coleman, 1943:59; Nies, 1977:106).

In the two decades on either side of the century, Harris Jones also became entrenched in socialism. In 1895, she assisted J. A. Wayland and three others in launching the *Appeal to Reason* (*Autobiography*, 28–29), an inexpensive socialist newspaper that grew to be the most widely circulated weekly in the country in the decade and a half prior to World War I (Fetherling, 1979:23–24). In 1898, she and socialist comrade Eugene Debs founded the Social Democratic party, a forerunner to the Socialist party of America, which was formed three years later (Fetherling, 1979:76–78; Foner, 1979:283). But her formal alliance with socialism, as with so many other causes in her life, eventually would be strained. In 1911, she reputedly was expelled from the party for accusing the national secretary of dishonesty (Steel, *Correspondence*, xxix). In 1916, she further alarmed socialist stalwarts by campaigning for Debs's Democratic opponent, who had won her allegiance by securing her release from prison in West Virginia (Fetherling, 1979:153).

In the summer of 1903, Harris Jones captured headlines by spearheading a 125-mile, three-week march of impoverished, disfigured mill children to President Theodore Roosevelt's home in New York State. The dramatic spectacle— complete with marching band and bejeweled effigies of capitalists—did not immediately spawn child labor legislation. However, it triggered overdue attention in the press to the exploitation of child labor (*Autobiography*, 73–83; Fetherling, 1979:49–57).

Harris Jones's only experience in forging movement ideology occurred in 1905, when she was the only woman to sign the *Manifesto* of the International Workers of the World ("Wobblies"), an organization designed to embrace all trades, races, and both sexes (Fetherling, 1979:70–72; Foner, 1979:392–393; Ginger, 1949:237–239). But within months, she had severed all ties with the organization whose doctrine she had helped form ("Mother Jones, 81").

By 1909, Harris Jones had begun her lengthy involvement in the insurgency against Mexican President Porfirio Diaz. This cause elevated her to folk heroine status in that country for decades (*Autobiography*, 140–144; Fetherling, 1979:79–81; Mooney, 1967:79–83; Steel, *Correspondence*, xxxv).

The zenith of her career as an agitator came when she was past eighty. Between 1912 and 1914, Harris Jones's inflammatory rhetoric, murder indictment, and repeated imprisonments and deportations earned her star billing in bloody coal strikes in West Virginia and Colorado (*Autobiography*, 51, 164–65; Beshoar, 1942:129–135; Fetherling, 1979:58, 95–102, 114–122; Lee, 1968:17–18; McGovern and Gutteridge, 1972:147, 165–174; Michelson, 1913:8; Mooney, 1967:15).

Other significant strikes involving Harris Jones included those by coal miners in Colorado and West Virginia in 1903 and 1904; iron miners in Minnesota and copper miners in Arizona in 1907; brewery workers in Milwaukee in 1910; steel workers in Pennsylvania in 1919; and coal miners in West Virginia in 1921 (*Autobiography*, 98, 218–227; Fetherling, 1979:58–69, 79–83, 155–162, 186–190; Foner, 1983:55–56, 137–140; Mooney, 1967:68–69, 90–91; Steel, *Correspondence*, xxvii). Several incarcerations also prompted her prison reform efforts in West Virginia in 1919 (Fetherling, 1979:144–148, 179–180; Steel, *Correspondence*, xxxiii–xxxiv).

Six years later, she published her autobiography with the assistance of Mary Field Parton. This was Harris Jones's only published writing other than a few short articles in the *International Socialist Review* and *The Miners' Magazine*. In 1926, Harris Jones delivered her last public speech in Athens, Ohio, as the guest of honor at a Labor Day celebration (Steel, *Correspondence*, xxxviii). Her final public appearance occurred on May 1, 1930, during her one hundredth birthday celebration in Silver Spring, Maryland, where she died on November 30 of that year (Fetherling, 1979:203; MHJP).

PUBLIC ADVOCATE AND PHILOSOPHER

In several respects, Harris Jones was a study in contrasts and contradictions. She preached unalloyed allegiance to the union, for example, but was herself a maverick who answered only to her own instincts, often orchestrating wildcat strikes or campaigns to oust union leaders with whom she personally disagreed.

The policy of ethnic inclusiveness she preached was compromised by her prejudice against Asians ("Mother Jones, 81") and by her doubts about the intelligence of African-Americans, whom she was not above calling "niggers" and "darkeys" (Barnes, 1985:99; UMWA, Cleveland, September 9, 1919:538). Her fervent opposition to temperance did not preclude her from occasionally lecturing miners on the evils of excessive drink, and her views on the use of violence and strikes were always colored by the situation.

The most salient of Harris Jones's inconsistencies was her frequent contention that women should be denied the ballot because they belonged in the home, a prescription she herself flagrantly violated.

To Harris Jones, only one position was not subject to revision: securing economic justice for workers. "The whole philosophy of the labor movement," she told Pittsburg, Kansas, miners on April 30, 1914, "is the battle of right for the [working] class" (202). She remained steadfast in her belief that the one means to empowering workers was through their collective action. The specific issues she championed in that struggle included securing adequate compensation, safe working conditions, and forty-hour work weeks, abolishing child labor, and eliminating such labor practices as special assessments that further diminished already shamefully low wages.

RHETORICAL STRATEGIES

Adding to the enigma of Harris Jones were her mercurial personality and dramatic rhetorical style. She appropriated the trappings of orthodox motherhood conspicuously, yet she infused this traditional role with decidedly radical dimensions: dressed always in black silk and white lace, the woman who answered only to "Mother" also drank, swore incessantly, openly courted danger, occasionally incited violence, and deferred to no one. She liberally pirated the language and culture of the Judeo-Christian faith, yet she excoriated organized religion at every turn. Similarly, her extemporaneous speeches were a mix of compassion and confrontation, eloquence and coarseness, pathos and wit. She spoke often in intimate and tender terms to her "children," her "boys," but in the next breath, she berated them for cowardice and openly baited her enemies with name-calling and threats.

Yet her unorthodox, dramatic style was the key to Harris Jones's remarkable success in overcoming a complex of rhetorical obstacles. The most salient of these obstacles was the tension between the demands of her agitational mission and turn-of-the-century gender expectations. Despite awareness that their own wives, sisters, and daughters had to work outside the home if families were to survive, her lower class, immigrant male audiences nonetheless were hostile to the social and political enfranchisement of women. Harris Jones occasionally acknowledged this obstacle in her speeches and writings. "I have come to the final conclusion that those fellows don't want a woman in the field," she wrote a comrade on November 15, 1901 (Letter to William Bauchrop Wilson, quoted in Steel, *Correspondence*, 16). Besides this obvious constraint, coal miners were a formidable group to mobilize in other respects as well. A mix of nationalities, mining communities festered with ethnic animosity fueled by language barriers. The paternalistic system of company-owned housing, schooling, and medical care also inhibited the miners' capacity to make personal choices. Similarly, the use of scrip or "coupon" wages, which could be redeemed only at company-owned stores, inhibited them from seeking alternative employment. And, most significant, the miners' efforts at organizing engendered costly reprisals: immediate termination, blacklisting, beatings, and, on occasion, murder (See Coleman, 1943; Lantz, 1958; Lee, 1969; McGovern and Gutteridge, 1972; Mooney, 1967). Mother Jones recognized their needs. Speaking to a congressional committee in 1914, she explained: "These men are aggravated to death at times, and it takes someone who understands the psychology of this great movement we are in to take care of them when they are annoyed and starved and plundered and shot" (H. Res. 387:2927).

In response to these rhetorical problems, Harris Jones assumed her own versions of the strategic personae of mother and prophet and adopted an interactive, narrative style.

Clearly, Harris Jones's most inventive and overt strategy was invoking and incarnating symbolic motherhood to create a relationship with male audiences, to imbue herself with authority, and to provide herself with the license to campaign publicly and ferociously for labor. Although she was neither male nor a miner, her role as a nurturing mother enabled male audiences to identify with her and accept her. In her autobiography, she wrote of an early incident that helped to validate her sobriquet: "We took [a boy badly beaten by gunmen] to a local hotel and sent for a doctor. . . . I sat up all night and nursed the poor fellow. He was out of his head and thought I was his mother" (44).

Harris Jones wielded the affective power earned in such mother-child relations in every imaginable setting. She augmented her maternal authority with numerous tales of her courageous exploits and references to her advanced age, which she strategically accelerated to position herself as labor's matriarch. She commonly assumed credit for the accomplishments of respected union officials whom she claimed to have reared, a ploy that afforded her authority over others as well. Illustrative of such moves were comments she made to the Pan American Federation of Labor in January 1921:

There is sitting behind me a young man [Fred Mooney of West Virginia] who was nothing but a child when I first saw him. He spent fourteen hours in the subterranean caverns of earth for twenty-five cents from his master for fourteen hours a day in darkness. He dug the wealth and sent it out. Today he is secretary of nearly 70,000 miners. I schooled them; I used to give them literature long ago. . . . I knew the poor man sitting there before me when he went barefoot in West Virginia many years ago. I have known Mr. Tobin for many long years. I have known this man [James Lord] with the red head, since he was a kid. I have hammered him often. I know them all. (75–76)

As "Mother," Harris Jones justified her notorious defiance of social custom and civil law by invoking the more basic and enduring authority of natural law. To a *New York Times* reporter in June 1913, for example, she explained her disarming fearlessness as the universal maternal instinct: "The brute mother suckles and preserves her young at the cost of her own life, if need be" ("Mother Jones Talks Sociology"). Similarly, in a speech to West Virginia miners on August 4, 1912, she alluded to slave mothers both to emphasize the inhumanity of certain statutes and to illustrate maternal bravery and effectiveness: "In the old chattel slavery days the old black mammy took up the battle and dug through the earth, and said to the young slaves, 'Come and dig with me.' They made a tunnel to get away" (Wallace Papers, n.p.).

Perhaps most important, the nurturing role of mother was an ideal means to address the severe emotional and developmental needs of her oppressed audiences. Because low self-esteem, isolation, and submissive dependency were more crippling than poverty and disease, her rhetoric was designed to cultivate self-worth, build identification among diverse audience members, and generate hope and independent thought and action. Her intimate terms of address, and even her scolding, allowed audiences to feel noticed, perhaps for the first time. As is common with natural mothers, she sometimes merged her voice with those of her listeners both to create a sense of oneness and to move them to action. To Pittsburg, Kansas, miners on April 30, 1914, Harris Jones said, "*I* will give them a fight to the finish and all *we* have to do is to quit being moral cowards, rise up like men and let the world know that *you* are citizens of a great nation and *you* are going to make it great" (219; emphasis added).

Harris Jones's interactive style also encouraged participation, a critical step in union organizing. In fact, her speeches resembled simulated dialogues in which she answered her own rhetorical questions, revealed her own reactions, and invited her listeners to concur and act. Her comments to Missouri miners on September 17, 1915, are illustrative: "Don't blame the mine owners. I would skin you, too, if I was a mine owner—if you'd let me do it. They combine, don't they? Sure. Why? Because they realize that as individuals they could not do anything" ("Mother Jones at Jop[1]in"). Occasionally, she actually engaged in extended exchanges with her audiences, which fostered camaraderie and increased commitment by providing her listeners with "ownership" of union rhetoric. An excerpt from a speech to West Virginia miners on August 15, 1912, is illustrative:

I will knock a few of these Senators down before I die.
    (Cries of: Tell it, Mother, I heard it.)
I will tell you. I want you to be good.
    (A voice: Yes, we will. We are always good.)
They say you are not, but I know you better than the balance do. Be good. Don't drink. Only a glass of beer. The parasite blood-suckers will tell you not to drink beer, because

they want to drink it all, you know. They are afraid to tell you to drink, for fear there will not be enough for their carcass.

(Cries of: The Governor takes champagne.)
He needs it. He gets it from you fellows. He ought to drink it. You pay for it, and as long as he can get it for nothing any fellow would be a fool not to drink it. But I want you to be good. We are going to give the Governor until tomorrow night. He will not do anything. He could if he would, but the fellows who put him in won't let him.

(Cries of: Take him out.) I don't want him out, because I would have to carry him around. (Wallace Papers, n.p.)

Like many natural mothers, Harris Jones was essentially a storyteller who influenced her audiences through examples and metaphorical tales. Contrary to strictly logical form, all of her thirty-one surviving speeches are structurally episodic with each vignette supporting her thesis: the need for concerted action. Her intimate tone, inductive structure, and heavy reliance on testimony, personal experience and examples as evidence resemble what Karlyn Kohrs Campbell has identified as consciousness-raising rhetoric ("Women's Liberation"; "Femininity"). Through numerous examples of industrial injustice everywhere, Harris Jones fostered empathy among diverse individuals and encouraged them to reason inductively in order to develop accurate generalizations about themselves and their situation. In recognizing the commonality of their oppression, workers could conclude that its basis was a political system rather than personal flaws, thereby prompting them to act to effect a political solution. Similarly, she often told stories that resembled fables and parables in which the morals were implied rather than explicit. The rhetorical force of such stories, critics argue, is their capacity to generate self-persuasion by fostering participation, understanding, judgment, and decisive behavior (Bennett, 1978; Kirkwood, 1985). A story she told to miners in Williamson, West Virginia, in June 1920 exemplifies this process; her comments indicate her understanding of the process and its relation to her maternal role:

Now, if you had the brains of a little boy out in Chicago you would be all right. A fellow came along one morning and asked a boy, "How far is it to the B. & O. Station, do you know?" "Oh, yes, I know, sir. Go down to the corner, look up that way, you see a tower with a clock on it. It is the B. & O. Station." "Thank you, my boy. Let me give you a ticket to [my] lecture tomorrow night . . . I will show you the way to heaven." The boy said, "How in the hell can you show me the way to heaven if you don't know the way to the B. & O. Station?" The boy used the gray matter in his head. He knew nobody could show him the way to heaven, and he had sense and wisdom. Nobody can show you the way to freedom, and I wouldn't free you tomorrow if I could. You would go begging. My patriotism is for this country to give the nation in the days to come highly developed citizens, men and women. (Army Intelligence Report, RG 165 10634/11, n.p., quoted in SWMJ:219–220)

Also important was Harris Jones's prophetic persona, which she presented as a natural extension of her role as mother. As was true of her maternal role, her religious characterization afforded her the freedom to speak and authority over any audience. She often linked motherhood to salvation, capitalizing on the prevailing belief that mothers enjoyed a special relationship with God. In a speech to West Virginia miners in Montgomery on August 4, 1912, she told a story of a time when Jesus gave his holy vision to a woman who, like her, understood the misery of poverty:

Away back in Palestine they were robbing and plundering them. There was a humble carpenter that came. It was not the leaders that came to him, it was not a member of the church that came to him, it was not a society woman, she would shame him then as she would now. It was that woman crushed by economic wrongs that came to wash his feet with her tears and wipe them with her hair—then he gave her the hope, the light of the economic age. It was she in gratitude that fell at his feet and paid tribute to him—it was on her sacred head he placed his hands. (Wallace Papers, n.p.)

Typical of many leaders of oppressed groups, Harris Jones made frequent allusions to the emancipation of the Israelites in order to fashion hope from despair. To a group of West Virginia miners in Charleston on August 15, 1912, for example, she redefined the liberation of God's chosen people from Egypt as the labor movement's first victory:

The labor movement was not originated by man. The labor movement, my friends, was a command from God Almighty. He commanded the prophets thousands of years ago to go down and redeem the Israelites that were in bondage, and he organized the men into a union and went to work. And they said, "The masters have made us gather straw, they have been more cruel than they were before. What are we going to do?" The prophet said, "A voice from heaven has come to get you together." And they got together and the prophet led them out of the land of bondage and robbery and plunder into the land of freedom. And when the army of the pirates followed them the Dead Sea [sic] opened and swallowed them up, and for the first time the workers were free. (Wallace Papers, n.p.)

She typically depicted Moses and Jesus as agitators like herself, and she sometimes sandwiched Christ's parables between her own. And Harris Jones frequently suggested that her history of surviving successive tragedies was evidence of her "contract with God Almighty to stay with you until your chains are broken" (Charleston, W. Va., August 1, 1912, n.p.). Perhaps her most eloquent acknowledgment of her holy role was in response to a reporter in 1915 who questioned her about the impetus for her unorthodox career:

That is the question that forty million other fools before you have asked. How does thunder or lightning have its start? How does the world start—it has its birth in the struggle. I was born of the wheel, a brat of the cogs, a woman of the dust. For even iron has its dust, and when a laborer sweats his sweat of blood and weeps his tears of blood a remedy is thrust upon the world. I am remedy. (Barnes, 1985:97–98)

Indeed, for literally millions of oppressed workers, Mary Harris "Mother" Jones was the remedy. Thousands journeyed miles, often in inclement weather and always under threat of severe repercussions, just to hear her tell them that their suffering was shared by others like themselves. With her help, many became convinced of their inherent worth and their collective might. This awareness stirred in them the will to continue a long and painful fight. Eventually, other voices would join the workers' cries for change, and labor would achieve the power to define itself.

CONCLUSION

Few, if any, rhetors have faced more formidable rhetorical problems or have overcome them as effectively as did Mary Harris "Mother" Jones. The obstacles facing turn-of-the-century woman speakers and labor union agitators were compounded because she was both. Her mission was intensely controversial, even life-threatening, and her audiences were divided, defeated, and all-male. Yet through her dramatic style, she successfully addressed the intense needs of her oppressed audiences while resolving the tension between the expectations of "womanhood" and the militant demands of labor agitation. Her most significant strategies, using her roles as "mother" and "prophet," empowered her and her working-class audiences. Tapping the inherent and universal power of the mother-child relationship and the cultural force of Judeo-Christian traditions afforded her the authority to speak publicly and to protest grim human conditions. For oppressed audiences, the nurturing and protective role of mother was ideally suited to their intense physiological and psychological needs. As one who actually lived among them, she cared for them in tangible ways: giving them food, tending to the everyday needs of their wives and children, and dressing their wounds. Rhetorically, her intimate tone, conversational style, storytelling mode, and use of "family" and "motherhood" as cultural ideals cultivated a sense of self-worth and respect, fostered a sense of belonging to the group and social responsibility, and encouraged individual thought and action. And as a prophet, she was able to supplant the workers' despair with hope, the most crucial element of all.

SOURCES

The public papers of Mary Harris "Mother" Jones (MHJP), Department of Archives and Manuscripts, Catholic University of America, Washington, D.C., contain letters and newspaper clippings but few complete speech texts. They contain *Pan American Federation of Labor*, Proceedings of Third Congress, Mexico City, January 10–18, 1921, pp. 72–76, and *United Mine Workers of America*, Proceedings of Special Convention Called to Consider the Strike in the Anthracite Field, Indianapolis, July 17–19, 1902, pp. 81–91.

The public papers of George Wallace, West Virginia Collection, University of West Virginia, Morgantown, contain six important speeches made in West Virginia on August

1, August 4 [two speeches], August 15, September 6 and September 21, 1912, recorded by stenographers hired by the coal operators of Kanawha Valley. All are reprinted in *The Speeches and Writings of Mother Jones* (SWMJ).

The Correspondence of Mother Jones. Ed. Edward M. Steel. Pittsburgh: University of Pittsburgh Press, 1985.

Mother Jones Speaks: Collected Speeches and Writings. Ed. Philip S. Foner. New York: Monad Press, 1983. Contains many significant errors in dates, locations, and transcribing.

The Speeches and Writings of Mother Jones. Ed. Edward M. Steel. Pittsburgh: University of Pittsburgh Press, 1988. (*SWMJ*) The most complete and accurate anthology, including texts recorded by coal company stenographers and military intelligence agents. Does not contain congressional testimony.

United Mine Workers of America, District 14, April 30, 1914. *Proceedings of 15th Consecutive and 1st Biennial Convention, Pittsburg, Ks., 27 April–5 May 1914*, pp. 201–223. (This is the first surviving text containing her discussion of the Ludlow massacre in Colorado, which occurred ten days earlier.) *SWMJ*

United Mine Workers of America. National Office, Washington, D.C. Minutes of many local and national meetings, unindexed. Sample text, Proceedings of 27th and 4th Biennial Convention, Cleveland, September 9, 1919, pp. 537–543.

U.S. Congress. House. Subcommittee of the Committee on Mines and Mining. *Conditions in the Coal Mines of Colorado.* 63rd Cong., 2nd Sess. H. Res. 387. Washington D.C.: Government Printing Office, 1914, 2:2917–2940.

U.S. Congress. Senate. Commission on Industrial Relations. *Report and Testimony on Industrial Relations.* 64th Cong., 1st Sess. S. Rept. 415. Washington D.C.: Government Printing Office, 1916, 11:10618–10646.

Biographical/Historical Works

"About Mother Jones." *Wilkes-Barre Record* (March 30, 1901):n.p. MHJP

Atkinson, Linda. *Mother Jones, The Most Dangerous Woman in America.* New York: Crown, 1978.

Barnes, Djuna. *Interviews.* Ed. Alyce Barry. Washington D.C.: Sun & Moon Press, 1985. Harris Jones's interview, February 7, 1915.

Dillar, Irving, and Mary Sue Dillard Schusky. "Jones, Mary Harris." *NAW* 2:286–288.

Dix, Keith. "Mother Jones." *People's Appalachia* 1, no. 3 (1970):6–13.

Fetherling, Dale. *Mother Jones, The Miners' Angel.* Carbondale and Edwardsville, Ill.: Southern Illinois University Press, 1979.

Green, Archie. "The Death of Mother Jones." *Labor History* 1, no. 1 (1960):68–80.

Jones, Mary Harris. *The Autobiography of Mother Jones.* Ed. Mary Field Parton. 3rd ed. rev. Chicago: Charles H. Kerr, 1980.

Long, Priscilla. *Mother Jones, Woman Organizer.* Cambridge, Mass.: Red Sun Press, 1976.

Michelson, Peter C. " 'Mother' Jones." *The Delineator*, May 1913, p. 8.

Mikeal, Judith E. "Mary Mother Jones: The Labor Movement's Impious Joan of Arc." M.A. thesis, University of North Carolina, 1965.

"Mother Jones at Jop[l]in." [Pittsburg, Kansas.] *Workers' Chronicle* (September 17, 1915):5.

"Mother Jones Dies." *Washington Post* (December 1, 1930):1, 3.
"Mother Jones, 81, Leads Labor War in West Virginia." *Brooklyn Daily Eagle* (June 1, 1913):9.
" 'Mother' Jones, Mild-Mannered, Talks Sociology." *New York Times* (June 1, 1913):sec. V:4.
Nies, Judith. *Seven Women: Portraits from the American Tradition*. New York: Viking, 1977.
Steel, Edward M. "Mother Jones in the Fairmont Field, 1902." *Journal of American History* 57, no. 2 (1970):290–307.
"To the Rescue of Mother Jones." [Girard, Kansas.] *Appeal to Reason* (May 3, 1913):1.
Werstein, Irving. *Labor's Defiant Lady: The Story of Mother Jones*. New York: Thomas Y. Crowell, 1969.

Critical Analyses

Bennett, Lance. "Storytelling in Criminal Trials: A Model of Social Judgment." *Quarterly Journal of Speech* 64, no. 1 (1978):1–12.
Campbell, Karlyn Kohrs. "Femininity and Feminism: To Be or Not to Be a Woman." *Communication Quarterly* 31, no. 2 (1983):101–108.
———. "Hearing Women's Voices." *Communication Education* 40, no. 1 (1991):33–48.
———. "The Rhetoric of Women's Liberation: An Oxymoron." *Quarterly Journal of Speech* 59, no. 1 (1972):73–86.
Goldfarb, Ruth. "A Rhetorical Analysis of Selected Speeches of Mary Harris 'Mother' Jones." M.A. thesis, Ohio University, 1966.
Kirkwood, William G. "Parables as Metaphors and Examples." *Quarterly Journal of Speech* 71, no. 1 (1985):422–440.
Scholten, Pat Creech. "Militant Women for Economic Justice: The Persuasion of Mary Harris Jones, Ella Reeve Bloor, Rose Pastor Stokes, Rose Schneiderman, and Elizabeth Gurley Flynn." Ph.D. diss., Indiana University, 1978.
———. "The Old Mother and Her Army: The Agitative Strategies of Mary Harris Jones." *West Virginia History* No. 40 (1979):365–374.
Tonn, Mari Boor. "The Rhetorical Personae of Mary Harris "Mother" Jones: Industrial Labor's Maternal Prophet." Ph.D. diss., University of Kansas, 1987.

Historical and Critical Background

Beshoar, Barron B. *Out of the Depths: The Story of John R. Lawson, A Labor Leader*. Denver: World Press, 1942.
Coleman, McAlister. *Men and Coal*. New York: Farrar & Rinehart, 1943.
Foner, Philip S. *Women and the American Labor Movement*. New York: Free Press, 1979.
Ginger, Ray. *The Bending Cross: A Biography of Eugene Victor Debs*. New Brunswick, N.J.: Rutgers University Press, 1949.
Lantz, Herman R., with J. S. McCrary. *People of Coal Town*. New York: Columbia University Press, 1958.
Lee, Howard B. *Bloodletting in Appalachia*. Morgantown: West Virginia University Library, 1969.

McGovern, George S., and Leonard F. Gutteridge. *The Great Coalfield War*. Boston: Houghton Mifflin, 1972.

Mooney, Fred. *Struggle in the Coal Fields: The Autobiography of Fred Mooney*. Ed. J. W. Hess. Morgantown W. Va.: West Virginia University Library, 1967.

Schofield, Ann. "The Rise of the Pig-Headed Girl: An Analysis of the American Labor Press for Their Attitudes Toward Woman, 1877–1920." Ph.D. diss., SUNY at Binghamton, 1980.

EMMA HART WILLARD
(1787–1870), pioneer educator and lobbyist

SISTER SHARON DEI

Higher education for women was not a popular cause in the early nineteenth century. Although some clergy and more enlightened male citizens encouraged parents to educate their daughters, few Americans supported advanced learning for girls. Education for women was feared. Some distinguished medical men warned that overtaxing the youthful female brain would drain blood from the reproductive organs and lead to problems in childbearing. Wits joked about who would make the pies and puddings if women became scholars. Doomsayers predicted that college-bred females would never marry or, worse yet, that educated brides would bring their books to bed. Moralists feared that the home and family would suffer from radical ideas of "free love" and political equality. Many more worried that too much education might lure young women from their proper sphere, the home, which protected and thrived on the virtues proper to middle-class American womanhood.

In 1822, while dedicating a female seminary at Saugus, Reverend Joseph Emerson said:

[M]ay we not indulge the enrapturing hope, that the period is not remote, when female institutions, very greatly superior to the present, will not only exist, but be considered as important, as are now our colleges for the education of our sons. The distinguished honor is probably reserved for our rising republic, to exhibit to the world examples of such female seminaries as the world has never witnessed. (Green, 1979:39)

He was prophetic, but few of his contemporaries would have agreed with him. A majority of women tended to side with critics who felt that female higher education harbored dangers for society. Prominent male supporters included Henry Barnard, Matthew Vassar, Edward Hitchcock, Charles Burroughs, Thomas Gallaudet, and William Russell (Cole, 1940:7). The handful of early women advocates for higher education for their sex, such as Emma Hart Willard, Catharine Beecher, Mary Lyon, and M. Carey Thomas, were forced to argue with great skill to achieve their initial goal: founding schools where young women could continue their education to prepare themselves scholastically and professionally for a productive and intellectually active life. That objective was made more difficult because the age enshrined females in the home and deemed it improper for women to speak in public.

There were few schools or prepared teachers at all educational levels. In colonial America, education had been a luxury. Dame schools provided boys and girls with the rudiments of literacy and arithmetic. Although the founders of the Republic had stressed the importance of an educated electorate, education generally remained a privilege for the wealthy. Many New England towns had coeducational primary schools by the time Massachusetts passed the first compulsory school law in 1852. By 1870, most northern and western states had followed suit, but in the South such laws were lacking well into the twentieth century (Stock, 1978:174).

Secondary education moved even more slowly. In 1827, Massachusetts decreed that every town of 500 families had to provide a high school; by 1840, there were sixteen. By 1857, eighty U.S. cities had high schools. The expansion created a demand for teachers, but rapid population growth left over 2 million children without educational opportunity in 1850 (Stock, 1978:186).

Women's opportunities were even more constrained. Girls often extended primary school education until they were sixteen or seventeen. Young women often served as "assistant teachers," taking over when their teacher married or moved on. The wealthy sent their daughters to academies that "finished" their education by providing "feminine accomplishments," such as music, drawing and painting, a bit of French or German, social dancing, and some ornamental needlework. Because these academies operated for profit, their quality depended mostly on the owner's personal integrity and accomplishments. Their curricula often catered to parental wishes or students' whims.

Emma Hart Willard's Troy Female Seminary (1821) was in the vanguard of dramatically improved educational opportunities for young women. It was quickly followed by Catharine Beecher's Hartford Female Seminary (1824), Zilpah Grant's Ipswich Seminary (1828), Mary Lyon's Mount Holyoke Seminary (1837), and others. These schools generally modeled their academic programs on New England's best male liberal arts institutions. ("Seminary" referred to any educational institution in which students were instructed in the several branches of learning with the objective of being prepared for future employment.) Female seminaries generally prepared their charges as teachers (Cole, 1940:9–10).

Pioneering women educators did not band together to seek a common cause. Although they knew and generally respected each other's accomplishments, they did not always agree on tactics or philosophy. They had a single goal that ultimately unified whatever they did: seeking ways to further higher educational opportunities for women.

The rhetoric of these advocates, however, was highly individualistic. Embodying the cultural norms of her times, Emma Hart Willard consistently appealed to influential men to establish her model school. Glorifying and glorying in True Womanhood, she chose rhetorical strategies to suit not only her audience but also her personal convictions about the role and functions of women in a republic. Assuming a crusader's role, Mary Lyon of Mount Holyoke persuaded ordinary New Englanders to finance a permanent seminary where young women could learn to serve God in whatever their calling, whether it be wife, mother, missionary, or teacher. Catharine Beecher's strident yet powerful logic hammered out a message that appealed to the pragmatic nature of her New England and

western audiences, yet always clothed the message in the most conservative of
True Womanhood's arguments. She elevated the "cult of domesticity" to "domestic science." M. Carey Thomas, higher education's radical feminist of her
day, capitalized on the achievements of the others to hone an image of the "Bryn
Mawr woman" as the prototype of a college woman for the twentieth century.

BACKGROUND

Emma Hart was born in 1787 in Berlin, Connecticut, the sixteenth of seventeen
children. She excelled at the town academy and at seventeen took over as
"schoolmistress" in nearby Kensington. Impressed with her talents and desire
for learning, her brothers helped her to continue her education in Hartford. Having
"a sense that it was important to know influential people, . . . she soon attached
herself, as a young person seeking guidance, to several of Hartford's leading
professional men. She was careful also to cultivate their wives" (Scott,
1978:683).

Having demonstrated her natural gift for teaching, in 1807 she was hired to
teach at the Middlebury Academy where she met her husband, Dr. John Willard,
a physician who nurtured her aspirations. Married in 1809, she bore her only
child, John, a year later. When Dr. Willard suffered financial reverses in 1812,
his resourceful wife opened a boarding school (Goodsell, 1931). She wrote:

When I began my boarding school in Middlebury, my leading motive was to relieve my
husband from financial difficulties. I had also the further motive of keeping a better school
. . . a year or two later, I formed the design of effecting an important change in education
by the introduction of a grade of schools for women higher than any heretofore known.
My neighborhood to Middlebury College made me bitterly feel the disparity in educational
facilities between the two sexes; and I hoped that if the matter was once set before the
men as legislators, they would be ready to correct the error. . . . It was merely on the
strength of argument I relied. I determined to inform myself, and increase my personal
influence and fame as a teacher, calculating that, in this way, I might be sought for in
other places, where influential men would carry my project before some Legislature for
the sake of obtaining a good school. (Lord, 1873:34–35)

Hart Willard improved her school, adding subjects to the curriculum as fast
as she could learn them: mathematics, history, geography, biological and physical
sciences, and philosophy. She lured influential men to the public examinations
that showcased her students' accomplishments. These brought her pupils and
fame. She explained: "I depend upon my examinations not only for the reputation
of my school, but for ultimately effecting change in the system of female education . . . of great importance not only to my own sex but to society in general"
(Lord, 1873:46).

THE PLAN, HER RHETORICAL MASTERWORK

Hart Willard dreamed of establishing a model female seminary. After observing female academies in her neighborhood, teaching in several, and directing one in Middlebury, she crafted her "Plan for Improving Female Education." Always the strategist, she sent a copy to New York Governor De Witt Clinton because she was convinced that it was the duty of the republic to support education for women. She was encouraged when he responded: "I shall be gratified to see this work in print, and still more pleased to see you at the head of the proposed institution, enlightening it by your talents, guiding it by your experience, and practically illustrating its merits and its blessings" (Lutz, 1929:63–64).

Dr. and Mrs. Willard moved to Albany for the 1819 legislative session where she read her Plan aloud to several groups of legislators (Goodsell, 1931:23). She remained seated throughout the address so as not to give the impression that she was delivering a speech. Lutz (1929) comments:

Although this [presentation] was very unconventional for a woman, she did not hesitate, so great was her enthusiasm for her *Plan*. She made a most favorable impression . . . for she was a woman to arouse admiration and respect. Well-dressed, handsome, with the bearing of a queen, intelligent but womanly, she impressed them not as the much-scorned female politician, but as a noble woman inspired by a great ideal. Yet, Willard, discussing her views on education with legislators, was probably the first woman lobbyist. (28)

She published 2,000 copies of her Plan, placing a copy on the desk of every New York legislator. Aware that "this is a world in which silent unpatronized merit is too often disregarded," Hart Willard sent copies to numerous influential men, including President James Monroe and various U.S. congressmen and judges (Lord, 1929:48). She would continue this practice throughout her life, using the printed word to present the strength of her arguments to those with the influence and power to enact them.

The Plan is a work of strategic artistry. Every element is tailored to appeal to her immediate audience, the distinguished male members of the New York State Legislature, but also to those middle- and upper-class citizens whose good opinion she desired and whose daughters she hoped would attend her school. She speaks to her audience as legislators, emphasizing that the Plan serves the national interest and demonstrating how "such institutions would tend to prolong or perpetuate our excellent government" (37). As Nina Baym comments, she reveals her

overriding commitment to republicanism and the extent to which an ideology of woman's place is articulated within the frame of that commitment [is] clear. Willard's thematics is consistently that of a filiopietistic patriotism uniting American men and women in a common republican heritage and differentiating them by the necessarily gendered tasks they must perform to serve the nation. . . . Men and women alike are required to subordinate themselves (subordination was one of Willard's favorite words) to the needs of their country; but they must do so in different ways. (1991:6)

She reinforces their traditional male self-images, appealing to their self-interest as fathers or brothers of the prospective beneficiaries of her Plan. Her long-range goal is the reformation of female education; her immediate objective is to secure public monies to endow a female seminary. She must refute the negative climate of popular opinion. Her traditional roles lend credence because she speaks as wife, mother, and teacher. Her arguments flow from the premise that what benefits a woman benefits the family, and thence the nation. Her tone is formal, her approach logical, and her voice authoritative yet republican.

It is from an intimate acquaintance with those parts of our country where education is said to flourish most that the writer has drawn her picture of the present state of female instruction, and she knows she is not alone in perceiving or deploring its faults. Her sentiments are shared by many an enlightened parent of a daughter who has received a boarding-school education. (33)

Lest her Plan be seen as aping male institutions, she assures them that her seminary will be "as different from those appropriated to the other sex as the female character and duties are from the male" (2). The proposed seminary will promote True Womanhood by educating young women to their role as mothers. She never alludes to education as a woman's right; women must be educated to perform well their natural duties.

Although she speaks in feminine style, the address depends primarily on methodical argument. She uses a problem-solution structure, which is sure to appeal to male legislators. First, she treats the "defects of the present mode of female education and their causes." Like a good lawyer, her brief leaves nothing to chance. She describes the woeful state of female institutions. She enumerates their financial shortfalls, pitiful equipment and library shortages, untrained teachers, lack of regularity and order, curricula emphasizing showy accomplishment rather than substance, and want of accountability, shortcomings likely to dismay businessmen and legislators. She hints that at times even "women of bad reputation . . . have been intrusted [sic] by our unsuspecting citizens with the instruction of their daughters" (10). Since these inadequacies attacked the very heart of nineteenth-century ideals, she aimed to appall her audience.

Next, the "principles by which education should be regulated" are clearly stated. Education should seek to perfect a young woman's "moral, intellectual and physical nature" and enable her "to perform with readiness those duties which [her] future life will most probably give [her] occasion to practice" (13). Here she contrasts the seriousness of male education with the frivolity of female education, which is turning girls into "pampered, wayward babies of society." She condemns the trend of educating "our sex to prepare them to please the other,'' noting that "our highest responsibility is to God and our highest interest is to please Him.'' Not the "taste of men" but the "will of God" should be "the only standard of perfection" (17). Rather than an attack on men, she makes a proper call to piety.

Finally, she sketches her vision for a female seminary, detailing the building, its equipment, a board of trustees, a suitable curriculum, and an ideal system of laws and regulations. She emphasizes that proposed curricular areas, Religious and Moral, Literary, Domestic, and Ornamental, will reinforce moral values. For example, "Natural Philosophy [science, mathematics] is calculated to brighten the moral taste, by bringing to view the majesty and beauty of order and design, and to enliven piety by enabling the mind more clearly to perceive, throughout the manifold works of God, that wisdom in which He made them all" (23). Domesticity is elevated to the systematic art of housewifery, "a system of principles . . . philosophically arranged and taught both in theory and practice" because "it is by promoting or destroying the comfort and prosperity of their own families that females serve or injure the community." Even ornamental subjects served piety. Music produced a "correspondent harmony of soul," and Art which "obliges us to the study of Nature in order to imitate her, enkindles adoration for [her] Author and a refined love for all His Works" (24–26).

Femininity clothes Hart Willard's masculine logic. Her serious and elevated tone, her lofty language, and her natural metaphors are highly consonant with the feminine image. She enacts "submission," relying on these worthy men to perform their duties. Her appeals stress nineteenth-century cultural values and demonstrate how the current straits of female education violate these standards. She appeals to male self-interest: "if the female character be raised, it must inevitably raise that of the other sex" (33).

The conclusion invokes republican civic virtue. She elucidates the benefits from establishing such a female seminary: (1) it will serve as a model for emulation and thus produce a ripple effect (an appeal to masculine pride and reform spirit); (2) it will benefit the whole of education, particularly the common schools, by providing a pool of educated women to act as teachers (an appeal to pragmatism and efficiency). Most important, "such institutions would tend to prolong or perpetuate our excellent government." She urges the education of women as a "preservative of national purity" (37).

She concludes in ringing rhetoric, heralding a nation that

having thrown off the shackles of authority and precedent, shrinks not from schemes of improvement because other nations have never attempted them; but which in its pride of independence would rather lead than follow in the march of human improvement—a nation wise and magnanimous to plan, enterprising to undertake and rich in resources to execute. Does not every American exult that this country is his own? And who knows how great and good a race of men may yet arise from the forming hand of mothers, enlightened by the bounty of that beloved country, to defend her liberties, to plan her future improvement, and to raise her to unparalleled glory? (46)

By reaffirming traditional American values, she urges auditors to cast away doubts stemming from lack of precedent. Invoking the nation's history of willingness to risk and dare, she challenges men to enable women to achieve their lofty goal: to raise sons worthy of liberty! James M. Taylor calls the Plan an "enlightened, skillful document, aiming in the spirit of true statesmanship at the best possible in existent conditions, pleading for a consistent and continuous course of education, and emphasizing ably the physical and intellectual, moral and spiritual conditions essential to it" (1914:5).

Unfortunately, the New York Legislature did not fund her request. However, wealthy Troy citizens, impressed by her Plan, underwrote her vision, and Troy Female Seminary opened its doors in 1821.

Hart Willard's rhetorical career was a lifelong extension and enactment of the principles outlined in this Plan. Discouraged by her failure to secure the public funding she desired, but encouraged by her success as educator and administrator, she continued to press for state support of schools for women. She wanted public funds to support the education of women not because they were poor and unfortunate, but because they were entitled to this education as citizens of the Republic. As Baym notes, "Willard envisages education for women as a discipline that will implicate them constructively (from her perspective) in the political and economic advancement of the nation-state" (1991:8).

To circumvent the social taboo against women speaking in public places, Hart Willard either remained seated and read or had prominent men read her "addresses" aloud for her at various gatherings. She usually had the "address" published as well, which not only guaranteed its preservation but also extended its audience and influence. Still considered a canny public relations move, it was a brilliant tactic in 1819. She used the profits from her textbook publications to further her primary cause, seeking improvement in the higher education available to women.

Although Troy Female Seminary was educationally and financially successful, Hart Willard never gave up pursuing public funding, on the principle that the state should support the education of the entire civic population. She consistently argued that since civic duties depended on character, and mothers formed character, therefore women should be educated by the state in order to become effective mothers. In 1823, she re-submitted her Plan to the New York Legislature, again unsuccessfully. Ten years later, she wrote again to the legislators appealing for funds for expansion. Although she had become a formidable voice for the education of women, well known throughout the East, she was never to secure the public funding for higher education that she felt was due to women as a political birthright.

Hart Willard also promoted the cause of female education internationally. In 1833, she published *The Advancement of Female Education, or A Series of Addresses in favor of establishing at Athens, Greece, a Female Seminary Especially Designed to Instruct Female Teachers*, a forty-six page booklet that sold for $1, the proceeds going to its establishment. In 1837, she exhorted the Latin

American liberator, Simón Bolívar: "Plant and endow institutions for female education, and you will have done more for your country than Washington did for his, and you will leave her on the way to greater glory" (Letter reprinted, *Lady's Book*, June 1937). In 1848, on the occasion of the French drafting of a new constitution, she wrote to the statesman Du Pont L'Eure on the "Political Position of Women." The letter, simultaneously sent to be printed in the *American Literary Magazine* (another of her favorite tactics), urged a "new principle in politics," whereby the women of France would meet to choose delegates to assemble in Paris to act for their sex, and according them "the advisory powers which in the family properly belong to the mother and mistress." She then advocated that women be made responsible for the care of schools for young children, of the poor, of public morals, and of female education beyond the primary schools. As in the Plan, Hart Willard emphasized man's naturally dominant role, but invoked civic virtues as the bedrock of her appeal for a voice for women in public governance. Once again, she invoked women's education as the means to make this voice effective.

Yet in 1848, she refused to support ELIZABETH CADY STANTON, a Troy graduate, in the campaign for political voice for U.S. women. Stephen Phelps notes that "she probably feared a backlash against women which would jeopardize their educational advancement, and in turn, the whole progress toward equality" (1979:19). In an open letter published just before the Seneca Falls Convention in 1848, Hart Willard wrote:

As a human being walks in safety with both his limbs, while with one only he hobbles and is in constant danger of falling; so has human government, forgetting that God has made two sexes, depended for its movement hitherto on one alone. The march of human improvement is scarce a proper term to express its past progress, since in order to march both limbs are required. (Quoted in Phelps, 1979:19)

It seems that she preferred to let others carry on the public fight which she apparently inwardly approved.

Whether or not Hart Willard was a closet feminist is still being argued. If only the Plan and her more commonly read textbooks and teaching manuals are considered, it appears not. But when some of her minor works, such as the Journals and Letters from France and Great Britain, her Memorials to individual legislators and other prominent men, and her private letters are added, a different picture emerges. In 1871, one year after her death, her former companion and secretary Celia Burleigh wrote an article for the *Woman's Journal* defending her former employer against attacks as an antifeminist:

During the whole of her long and useful life, Mrs. Willard was an extremist on the subject of woman's rights and duties. Her claim for the same educational advantages for women that were enjoyed by men was based upon her belief in the equality of the sexes, and those who were intimate with her cannot fail to remember how strenuously she insisted that government could never be rightly administered till women had a voice in making the laws.

Burleigh quoted from Hart Willard's letters to support her contention. At least two modern scholars, Alma Lutz and Anne Firor Scott, have examined Hart Willard from a feminist perspective, but more careful scrutiny of her works, particularly her letters, is needed to assess that claim.

In the turbulent years before and during the Civil War, Hart Willard worked determinedly to preserve peace and the unity of the republic she loved so dearly. In 1861, she wrote a "Peace Memorial" in the "Name of and by the Authority of American Women." It was signed by over 14,000 women and was presented to Congress on March 1, 1861. Again, she acted within the framework of her conviction that women must serve their country by persuading men to act justly on their behalf. However, her proposal for a commission of legal experts to act as mediators between the North and South to avert war fell on deaf ears.

Although she abhorred slavery, Hart Willard was not an abolitionist. In 1862, she advocated abolishing the slave market and the cruel separation of families, but she assumed that God had intended Africans to be servants. Talented Negroes should be freed and sent to Liberia if they wished to go. Northern families might take freed slaves into their homes where they would eventually be "fitted" to go to Liberia, which she thought would solve the "servant problem" of the northern housewife who, she believed, all too often worked herself to a premature death. Hart Willard's "motherly solution" to the slavery question received scant attention, but it prompted her nephew, John Willard, judge of the Supreme Court of the State of New York, to write her frankly that the time for such a plan was long past. To press it on the country at this moment, he said, would do more harm than good (Lutz, 1964:126).

In 1820, Hart Willard had drafted a memorial on Universal Peace in which she had proposed an international peacekeeping body. In 1864, she resurrected this idea in a final memorial on Universal Peace in which she suggested that the nations of the world "form a permanent tribunal to which by mutual consent, their disputes be referred, and Jerusalem was to be the seat of this tribunal." It reflected the thinking of Elihu Burritt, whose work on behalf of peace she admired:

One of my grounds of belief in the approach (whether near or far) of Universal Peace was the prophetic assertions of the Holy Writ, that there should come such a time, and that Jerusalem should be the chosen place. . . . The Jews stand waiting. Hasten to do the Lord's work, in preparing for them their promised abode. When the Gentile nations gather to Jerusalem to make it the seat of Universal Peace, then must they aid the Jews to return. (February 23, 1864, Emma Willard Archives, n.p.)

Thus, Hart Willard envisaged not only the United Nations almost a century before its realization, but also its links to the return of the Jews to Israel and the establishment of Jerusalem as an international city. Here, as on women's educational issues, she was ahead of her time, but her voice carried little weight in political circles. By the time her dream was realized, people had forgotten her prophetic words and recalled Emma Hart Willard only as an outstanding educator.

CONCLUSION

At her death in 1870, the *New York Times* called Emma Hart Willard the "most famous teacher in America." Perhaps her true genius in life as in her Plan was

to find a way to work within the framework of social expectations about women's proper behavior without allowing that framework to hamper seriously her very large plans or limit her ambition. The skill with which she did this is attested by the fact that while she achieved a public career stretching over fifty years, she was seldom criticized for stepping out of her place. . . . A close study of Willard's projects and methods shows that a determined woman dedicated to bringing about change could overcome these complexities and obstacles without alienating the men who controlled the money and power she needed, and how she could build a highly successful career by using for her own ends social stereotypes about woman's place . . . watching her, [her pupils] could learn something of the techniques for effective functioning in a male-dominated society. Few lessons could have been more useful to an ambitious nineteenth-century woman. (Quoted in Scott, 1978a:702–703)

Throughout her long life and in her voluminous writings, Hart Willard relied on the "strength of argument" to advocate her major cause: the improvement of society through the education of women. Her argument relied on the persona she created and enacted: a respectable, proper, pious homemaker and wife who was also intelligent and informed because she had been well educated. She never deviated from her singular strategy: to influence men in high places to do what would benefit her sex because it was part of their proper role as "the head of human society, and with him improvement should begin and it is his superior stability by which it must be sustained" (1848, Letter to L'Eure). Clothed in feminine propriety, she appealed to masculine superiority through an argument rooted in domesticated logic and pragmatic republicanism. One wonders why this woman who could argue like a lawyer but humbly asked men to read her speeches in public was never suspect. Did her deference to custom and her excellent reputation as an educator cloak her radical stance? Did men fail to realize the changes that her education would bring in young women to come? Was the erudite and articulate Hart Willard such a consummate actress that she convinced them that all future educated women would continue to defer, as she did, to "male superiority?"

Although arguing from the same premises of female equality and women's rights that created problems for her predecessor Mary Wollstonecraft in England

and for nearly all her contemporary woman's rights activists, Hart Willard's respectability and conservative rhetorical style won her almost universal admiration and acclaim. By carefully limiting her arguments to advancing the cause of higher education for women, she opened the doors for these newly educated women to lobby for the vote, for legal parity, and for professional equality.

When she was elected to the Hall of Fame for Great Americans at New York University in 1905, the citation read: "Emma Willard devoted her life to education. She was a woman of amazing vision for her times, and determination to work with courage for her conviction that education for women was essential to the development and well-being of the country." The medal that commemorates her selection shows her "drawing the symbolic curtain which had heretofore existed between the female student and 'higher' education."

SOURCES

Emma Hart Willard Correspondence, 1809–1866, Archives of the Emma Willard School, Troy, New York, contains original letters and copies or typed transcriptions of original letters with the location of original documents given. See annotated Finder's Guide prepared by Marion P. Munzler, 1986.

Willard, Emma (1829 circa). "Notes on Plan of Female Education." Holographic. Russell Sage College, Troy, New York.
"A Plan for Improving Female Education (1819)." *Woman and Higher Education.* Ed. Anna C. Brackett. New York: Harper Brothers, 1893.
Memorial of Emma Willard, Principal of Troy Female Seminary to the Honorable the Legislature of the State of New York. *Proceedings of the State Legislature of the State of New York,* January 25, 1823.
"A Letter to Bolivar." *The Lady's Book,* June 1837.
"Universal Terms—Disputes Concerning Them and Their Causes." *American Journal of Science & Arts* 23, no. 1 (1832):19–28.
Journal and Letters from France and Great Britain. New York: Tuttle, 1833.
Advancement of Female Education, or, A Series of Addresses, in Favor of Establishing at Athens, in Greece, a Female Seminary, Especially Designed to Instruct Female Teachers. Troy: Norman Tuttle, 1833.
Kensington or Berlin Third School Society; Berlin, First School Society, or Kensington; Kensington, or Berlin First School Society. *Connecticut Common School Journal* (June 2, 1840):241–244; (September 3, 1840):54–55; (November 15, 1840):29–31.
"The Relation of Females and Mothers especially to the Cause of Common School Improvement." *Connecticut Common School Journal* (March 15, 1842):64–66.
"Letter to the Editor." *The Trojan Sketchbook.* Troy, N.Y.: Young & Hart, 1846.
Answer to Marcius Willson's Reply, or Second Appeal to the Public. New York: A. S. Barnes, 1847.
"Letter to DuPont de L'Eure on the Political Position of Women." *American Literary Magazine* (April 1848).
Address on the time and teaching of little children. Read to the Rensselaer County

Teacher's Association. *New York Teacher* 2 (December 30, 1853):108–111; 136–141; 202–205.

"The School Mistress" (7 parts). *New York Teacher* 3 (February 1855):252; (March 1855):318–321; (April 1855):28–30; (May 1855):68–70; (June 1855):138–140; (July 1855):236–238; (September 1855):366–368.

"Mrs. Willard's Report on the Normal School." *Connecticut Common School Journal* (April 3, 1855):107–108.

To the Senate and Representatives of the U.S. of America in Congress Assembled. This Memorial Is Presented by Emma Willard in the Name of and by the Authority of American Women. Scroll and Printed Booklet, March 1, 1861.

Via Media: A Peaceful and Permanent Settlement of the Slavery Question. Washington, D.C.: Charles H. Anderson & Henry Polkinhorn, 1862.

"Universal Peace." *Our Country.* Ed. Mrs. Almira Hart Lincoln Phelps. 1864.

Hart Willard also wrote many textbooks that often appeared in multiple editions with somewhat slightly altered titles. These span her life from 1822 to 1865. Copies of at least one version of each is available in the New York Historical Society and the Emma Willard School in Troy, New York.

Biographical Sources

Anticaglia, Elizabeth. *Twelve American Women.* Chicago: Nelson Hall, 1975.

Brainerd, Ezra. *Mrs. Emma Willard's Life and Work in Middlebury.* 1895. Middlebury, Vt.: Middlebury College, 1918.

Burleigh, Celia. "Mrs. Emma Willard on the Woman Question." *TWJ* (April 1, 1871).

Fairbanks, A. W. *Emma Willard and Her Pupils or Fifty years of Troy Female Seminary 1822–1872.* New York: Mrs. Russell Sage, 1898.

Fowler, Henry. "Emma Willard." *Memoirs of Teachers and Educators.* Ed. Henry Barnard. 2nd ed. New York: F. C. Brownell, 1861, pp. 125–168.

Goodsell, Willystine. *Pioneers of Women's Education in the United States.* New York: McGraw-Hill, 1931.

Hale, Sarah Josepha. *Woman's Record: Sketches of Distinguished Women, The Creation to A.D. 1854 Arranged in Four Eras with Selections from Female Writers of Every Age.* New York: Harper & Brothers, 1855.

Lord, John. *The Life of Emma Willard.* New York: D. Appleton, 1873.

Lutz, Alma. *Emma Willard: Daughter of Democracy.* Boston: Houghton Mifflin, 1929.

Lutz, Alma. *Emma Willard: Pioneer Educator of American Women.* Boston: Beacon Press, 1964.

Lutz, Alma. "Woman's Hour: Present Generation Encouraged to Study Those Who Stood for Suffrage and Enlightenment." *Christian Science Monitor* (August 24, 1946):3.

Meyer, Margaret R. "Emma Willard and the New York State Teachers' Institutes of 1845." *Journal of Educational Research* 44 (1951):695–701.

Phelps, Almira Lincoln. *The Female Student, or, Lectures to Young Ladies on Female Education: For the Use of Mothers and Teachers.* Boston: Crockett & Brewster, 1833.

Phelps, Stephen. "The Indomitable Emma Willard." *Conservationist* (March-April 1979):17–19.

Rudolph, Frederick. "Willard, Emma Hart." *NAW* 3:610–613.

Woody, Thomas. *A History of Women's Education in the United States*, 2 vols. New York: Science Press, 1929.

Major Critical Sources

Baym, Nina. "Women and the Republic: Emma Willard's Rhetoric of History." *American Quarterly* 43 (1991):1–23.

Calhoun, Daniel H. "Eyes for the Jacksonian World: William C. Woodbridge and Emma Willard." *Journal of the Early Republic* 4 (1984):1–26.

Cross, Barbara M., ed. *The Educated Woman in America: Selected Writings of Catharine Beecher, Margaret Fuller, and M. Carey Thomas.* New York: Teachers College Press, 1965.

Fishburn, Eleanor, and Mildred Fenner. "Emma Willard and Her Plan for Improving Female Education." *National Educational Association Journal* 30, no. 6 (1941):177–178.

Fowler, Henry. "The Educational Services of Mrs. Emma Willard." *American Journal of Education* 6 (1859):125–128.

Nelson, Murray R. "Emma Willard: Pioneer in Social Studies Education." *Theory and Research in Social Education* 15, no. 4 (1987):245–256.

Rossiter, Margaret W. *Women Scientists in America: Struggles and Strategies to 1940.* Baltimore: Johns Hopkins University Press, 1982.

Scott, Anne Firor. "What, Then, Is the American: This New Woman?" *Journal of American History* 6, no. 2 (1978a):679–703.

———. "Emma Willard: Feminist." Paper presented at Emma Willard School, May 5, 1978b.

———. "The Ever-widening Circle: The Diffusion of Feminist Values from the Troy Female Seminary, 1822–1872." *History of Education Quarterly* 19 (1979):3–25.

———. *Soundings: An Interview by Wayne Pond with Dr. Anne Firor Scott about Emma Willard* (Cassette Recording). Research Triangle Park, N.C.: National Humanities Center, March 22, 1981.

———. *Making the Invisible Woman Visible.* Urbana: University of Illinois Press, 1984.

Historical and Social Background

Cole, Arthur C. *A Hundred Years of Mount Holyoke College.* New Haven: Yale University Press, 1940.

Green, Elizabeth Alden. *Mary Lyon and Mount Holyoke: Opening the Gates.* Hanover, N.H.: University Press of New England, 1979.

Harris, Barbara J. *Beyond Her Sphere: Women and the Professions in American History.* Westport, Conn.: Greenwood Press, 1978.

Heath, Kathryn G. "The Female Equation." *American Education* 10 (November 1974):20–33.

Kerber, Linda K. "The Republican Mother: Women and the Enlightenment—An American Perspective." *American Quarterly* 28 (Summer 1976):187–205.

———. *Women of the Republic: Intellect and Ideology in Revolutionary America.* Chapel Hill: University of North Carolina Press, 1980.

Melder, Keith. "Mask of Oppression: The Female Seminary Movement in the United States." *New York History* 55 (1974):261–279.

O'Neill, William L. *Feminism in America: A History*. 2nd ed. New Brunswick, N.J.: Transaction, 1989.

Scott, Donald M. "Women and Education." *History of Education Quarterly* 15 (1975):213–217.

Stock, Phyllis. *Better Than Rubies: A History of Women's Education*. New York: G. P. Putnam's Sons, 1978.

Taylor, James M. *Before Vassar Opened*. Boston: Houghton Mifflin, 1914.

Tenney, Tabitha. "Female Quixoticism." *Hidden Hands: An Anthology of American Women Writers, 1790–1870*. Eds. Lucy M. Freibert and Barbara A. White. New Brunswick, N.J.: Transaction, 1985, pp. 150–153.

Welter, Barbara. "The Cult of True Womanhood:1820–1860." *American Quarterly* 18, no. 2 (1966):151–174.

CLARINA HOWARD NICHOLS
(1810–1885), a modest voice for woman's rights

ADRIENNE E. CHRISTIANSEN

Clarina Howard Nichols was a prolific nineteenth-century writer and public speaker who devoted her adult life to improving the lives of women and their children. She was actively involved in the temperance and abolition movements, but it was through her efforts to win legal and economic gains for married women during the earliest years of the woman's rights movement that she distinguished herself. Her career as an activist spanned nearly forty years (1847–1885), and her thinking influenced legislators in many states as well as other woman's rights activists, such as SUSAN B. ANTHONY (Gambone, Spring 1973:16).

Howard Nichols had rare opportunities afforded her when she took over the work of her second husband, George Nichols, as the editor and publisher of the *Windham* [Vt.] *County Democrat*. She wrote a series of editorials that has been cited as ultimately persuading Vermont politicians to enact legislation liberalizing divorce laws and giving married women property rights, including the right to own, inherit, and bequeath property, and to insure their husbands' lives. Moreover, she was the first woman to address the Vermont Legislature and the only woman asked to speak at the Kansas Constitutional Convention.

Her work at the Kansas Constitutional Convention has been hailed as her most significant and enduring contribution to the cause of women. She singlehandedly ensured that several woman's rights provisions were incorporated into the state constitution, including property rights, equal guardianship of children, and the right to vote in school district elections. These provisions gave Kansas the distinction of entering the union in 1861 as the state with the most progressive woman's rights laws at the time (Madsen, 1975:11).

Clarina Howard Nichols is important in the history of woman's rights, not only because she succeeded in improving the lives of countless women through her legislative and constitutional achievements, but also because her speeches and writing are the handiwork of a highly skilled rhetor. Nonetheless, Joseph Gambone, the editor of her published papers, dubbed her the "forgotten feminist of Kansas." The paucity of scholarly attention is best accounted for by her decision in 1854, at the height of her career, to move from her home state of Vermont to Kansas as part of the New England Emigrant Aid Company in order to settle the territory and bring it into the Union as a free state. With her move came the increased demands of farming and a grueling pioneer existence. When her husband George Nichols died, she became sole support of their three children. These circumstances prevented her from continuing to speak at woman's rights and temperance conventions or participating in national organizations, thus diminishing her "presence" historically.

Although restricted geographically, Howard Nichols's activism did not cease; she embarked on lecture tours in the new territory, speaking to scattered, small audiences on the frontier. In addition, she began relying more extensively on her skills as a writer to reach audiences outside her immediate area. For example, she edited the Kansas *Quindaro Chindowan* and served as a contributor and correspondent for a variety of newspapers, including papers across Kansas, on the East Coast, and those focusing on woman's rights. She chafed under the physical restrictions she faced. She wrote to Anthony that she longed to "fight a *big* fight," saying, "I sometimes cry out at being hedged in by circumstances, from joining the triumphant march of womanhood. I seem almost to have dropped out by the way, unable to keep up. . . . But Oh, how I watch and pray! I do all I can with my pen (Letters to S. B. Anthony, January 1870, and February 15, 1870, quoted in Gambone 40 (Summer 1974):244, 250).

That Howard Nichols should be a "forgotten feminist" is lamentable because her capacities as a rhetor were significant. As one of the pioneers of the woman's rights movement who relished the "delightful collision of argument" ("Reminiscences," quoted in Bassett, *NAW* 2:626), she successfully contended with the double burden of justifying her right to speak as well as making a powerful case for woman's rights. An examination of her extant works demonstrates that she deftly used a variety of rhetorical strategies to overcome the prejudices and hostilities of her audiences and to justify her calls for legal and economic change.

In broad terms, she accomplished this by making herself appear to be traditional, even though much about her life and experiences was atypical. Her ability to portray herself as a traditional, feminine woman is especially significant because, in her rhetoric, she most often took on the contradictory and combative persona of a lawyer. The case she made for woman's rights was similarly noteworthy. She stressed that woman's rights would help women better fulfill their responsibilities as Christian wives and mothers, thus making the call for woman's rights seem like a modest rather than a radical proposal.

An additional reason Howard Nichols deserves critical attention is that her rhetoric exemplifies one of the argumentative schisms faced by woman's rights advocates—whether philosophically to ground their claims for political change in a natural rights perspective or in the perceived moral superiority of women. During the early years of her career, she tended to argue from woman's superiority, later embracing the natural rights perspective. Near the end of her life, she was trying, unsuccessfully, to combine these two philosophical positions. Her argumentative conflict was a microcosm of the broader "womanhood versus personhood" debate.

Howard Nichols's oral and written discourses suggest that she was a highly skilled, argumentative rhetor who could adapt her reasoning and evidence to fit the occasion and audiences to whom she spoke. However, to understand the importance of her rhetorical skill and her contributions to the cause of woman's rights, one must trace her development as a public advocate.

HOWARD NICHOLS AS A PUBLIC ADVOCATE

Her career as an advocate for temperance and woman's rights illustrates that public policy changes are often grounded in the experiences and tenacity of individuals. The legislative and social changes she sought evolved from her own life-changing, personal observations rather than from abstract reasoning. For example, she grew up in West Townshend, Vermont, where her father, Chapin Howard, was the town poormaster. During her formative years, she was allowed to study the poor laws at the same time she watched her father deal with those petitioning for pauper funds. (Poor laws were legal codes to arbitrate conflicts over indebtedness or to charge persons for nonpayment of debt.) In an editorial in 1856, she recalled her youthful outrage at the unjust laws that stripped women of property and inheritance rights, forcing many women to plead their cases unsuccessfully to her father. She wrote:

The conviction was forced upon my young heart that the electors and representatives of the State did not regard themselves as the representatives and protectors of women and children, and had no right to claim to be trusted as such. . . . I would shrink from myself as less than human, and an anomaly of womanhood, if I could have seen all this, and not resolve to *be*, that I might *do*. ("Letter to the Editor," *Herald of Freedom*, April 15, 1856, quoted in Gambone 39 [Summer 1973]:247)

Howard Nichols's experiences of knowing and observing the impact of the law on real women and children influenced her moral sensibilities. It also became the ground on which she developed her ideas about the need for women's property rights. Combining careful examination of the law with heartrending examples became a successful and trademark rhetorical strategy in her later public career.

Howard Nichols made her first public case for improving women's lives when she was quite young. At age eighteen, in her commencement address, she compared the value of a scientific education to that of an "ornamental" education for women. Her concern for women's education extended throughout her life. She founded a women's seminary at Herkimer, New York, while married to her first husband, Justin Carpenter. When she began editing the *Windham County Democrat*, she used the newspaper to encourage legislative changes that would allow women to vote in all school district elections. This effort garnered her an invitation to address the Vermont Legislature in 1852. Unfortunately, her speech at the state capitol did not result in immediate passage of such a law. Her concern for women's involvement in education followed her to Kansas, where she successfully lobbied for constitutional provisions that allowed women to vote in school district elections, and "as a result of her efforts, the University of Kansas, which opened in 1864, was the first state university in the United States or in the world to receive both men and women students on an equal basis" (Madsen 1975:15).

Just as her concern for women's economic security and education grew out of her own observations and experiences, so, too, did her views on divorce and temperance legislation. In these cases, however, she did not reveal publicly the personal motivation for her advocacy. Howard Nichols's first marriage to Justin Carpenter ended in divorce in 1843, apparently because of his intemperance. Obtaining a divorce was no easy matter; she had to petition the Vermont Legislature to enact a special law allowing her and a few other women to be divorced for "causes occurring out of the state" (Howard Nichols to Franklin G. Adams, March 25, 1884, quoted in Gambone 40 [Winter 1974]:557). This experience influenced her advocacy, as she explained in a letter in 1883 to Anthony: "My early marriage experience 'set me apart,' consecrated, called me to the work" (Gambone 40 [Winter 1974]:551). For example, in 1853, she addressed the New York Woman's State Temperance convention and became embroiled in a debate on divorce with Lucy Stone and ELIZABETH CADY STANTON. She argued that intemperance should not be made grounds for divorce because it would strip a woman of guardianship of children and control of property. Rather, she argued that intemperance should be grounds for obtaining a separation, thus protecting her few legal rights.

That Clarina Howard Nichols's public advocacy grew out of her own life experiences best explains why she focused her efforts and talents on removing women's legal and economic disabilities rather than working for woman suffrage. Early in her career she opposed the ballot for women, believing it improper. She publicly supported woman suffrage once she realized that the vote provided the best protection for the legal and economic gains that she and other woman's rights supporters had won. Just as she strategically adapted her own position on woman suffrage as a way to ensure that future legislators would not "undo" woman's rights, so, too, her rhetorical strategies were adapted as a way of overcoming the obstacles she faced.

Clarina Howard Nichols's rhetorical efforts are noteworthy because of the obstacles she faced as a speaker and because of the artistic and strategic ways she overcame them. Like many early woman's rights advocates, she had to contend with physical and attitudinal barriers. The physical obstacles she faced included finding care for her three children, having to pay for her own lecture tours, overcoming difficult traveling conditions, and facing threats of physical violence stemming from the tensions of the Civil War. Ellen Dubois writes that the early woman's rights speaking tours and legislative campaigns "were highly individualistic matters which put a premium on personal initiative and bravery" (1978:30). Some of these obstacles were mitigated by her husband George Nichols, who supported her in both word and deed.

After she moved with her children to the Kansas Territory and her husband died, she was forced to support her family through farming. She remarked in an 1883 letter to Anthony that in all her years of public speaking, she had given fewer than six lectures on woman's rights for which she had received any remuneration. To save money, she traveled across Kansas in a tiny mail carrier and stayed in filthy rooming houses.

Even these conditions paled in comparison to the obstacles created by the Civil War-related violence that broke out in Kansas. After Howard Nichols traveled to Vermont in 1855 to settle her husband's estate, she could not return to Kansas until 1857 because of dangerous conditions in the new territory. She responded by traveling across western New York, speaking in behalf of "bleeding Kansas," and by taking up her pen. She wrote a series of letters on woman's rights for the Lawrence, Kansas, *Herald of Freedom*. The last installment of the series was destroyed along with the newspaper's office when Lawrence was attacked in 1856 by Quantrill's pro-slavery raiders.

Her ability to overcome physical barriers is best illustrated by her reaction to the final move in her life. In 1871, at the age of sixty, Howard Nichols moved with her son to Pomo, California, believing that the change in climate would improve her health. Even if her health had allowed it, the financial costs and poor traveling conditions across the frontier insured that she would be unable to address subsequent national woman's rights and temperance conventions. Rather than decline invitations to speak at these gatherings, she wrote speeches that were read aloud at the conventions. In this way, she remained active in these movements.

The attitudinal barriers Howard Nichols faced were as taxing as the physical and material obstacles and required equally creative solutions. The attitudinal barriers were of two kinds—those arising out of the speaking situation itself (*MCSFH* 1:17–36) and those arising out of paternalistic attitudes toward women's intellectual, political, and moral capabilities. Women who spoke publicly violated social values consigning woman to the home (Welter, 1976). She knew that the penalties for addressing public audiences included ridicule, scorn, censure by friends and family, assaults from clergymen, and, in extreme cases, bodily injury. From the beginning, she confronted these ingrained attitudes. For example, one legislator publicly promised to present her with a suit of men's clothing if she were to address the Vermont Legislature on the issue of extending property rights to women. Fortunately, her address convinced him that this would be impolitic. This example, though colorful, was not atypical of the hostile reactions she faced. In her papers and speeches, she often commented on the pain she and other early activists felt at being stigmatized as "unsexed women," "Amazons," and "the self-willed women of the period" ("Letter to the Editors," *TWJ*, July 1877, quoted in Gambone 40 [Autumn 1974]425).

A related obstacle concerns the contradictory demands audiences placed on women speakers to be logical and feminine. A female rhetor was expected to reassure her audience that she was an emotional, demure, unthreatening woman. While assuaging the fears of her audience, she simultaneously had to make clear, forceful arguments in support of her position. The capacity to present onself as traditionally feminine while fulfilling logical requirements was a stubborn obstacle for Howard Nichols and her contemporaries, and it remains a rhetorical obstacle for today's female rhetors (Campbell and Jerry, 1988:123–133).

There were two other obstacles. Audiences believed that women did not need property rights because they were adequately cared for by fathers and husbands and that, even if rights were to be extended to them, women would be incapable of fulfilling their social, economic, and political obligations.

Howard Nichols used a variety of strategies in responding to the complex rhetorical situations in which she found herself. Her adaptation of argument, evidence, style, and persona illustrates her understanding of audience expectations (CHN:65–146; *MCSFH* 1:87–104). Nevertheless, two strategies that typify her oral and written discourses were designed to overcome recurring attitudinal obstacles: namely, beliefs about the impropriety of women as public advocates and their perceived limitations as women. In every case, she emphasized her own femininity and deftly linked the concept of woman's rights to the idea of woman's responsibilities in order to make her proposals appear to be modest reforms.

Highlighting the ways in which she was a traditional woman was a common theme in Howard Nichols's rhetoric. She conveyed this theme through a variety of verbal and nonverbal means, which included explicit claims about her femininity, her choice of metaphors and analogies, her selection of evidence, and her use of nonverbal "props."

An obvious way in which Howard Nichols attempted to reassure her audiences that she was a typical woman was by taking up the subject directly. Her most famous speech, "The Responsibilities of Woman," delivered at the 1851 Worcester, Massachusetts, National WRC, exemplifies this approach well. In this case, she told her audience that she believed that there was a proper sphere for women and that her "pride of womanhood lay within this nice sphere" (quoted in CHN:156). She added that she was a wife, mother, sister, and daughter and that she revered her husband, father, and brothers for their "manliness" (quoted in CHN:157). These statements and others like them served notice that she was not an "unsexed," mannish woman and that she shared audience assumptions about the proper relationships between men and women.

She did not always address the question of her femininity so directly. Instead, she would frequently use analogies and metaphors to emphasize her womanliness and assent to traditional ideas. Her 1853 address to the Whole World Temperance Convention stressed her belief that women were the "mother-fountain of humanity" and that in the cases of divorce or separation, children ought to be allowed to "drink the milk of human kindness that God has stored in the breast of woman" (quoted in CHN:173).

Howard Nichols's most common method of reassuring her audience that she was a typical, traditional, feminine woman was through her selection of supporting materials. These efforts are noteworthy because they aptly illustrate how skilled a rhetor she was while revealing the multiple ways that evidence can function persuasively. She would commonly use evidence that supported her logical arguments and simultaneously reinforced her own femininity. Only two types will be noted here: biblical allusions and lengthy, heartrending examples drawn from her own life experiences.

Howard Nichols used biblical allusions to help create audience identification and to allow audience participation in formulating her arguments. Biblical allusions effectively demonstrated that she shared the audience's religious beliefs and that she was pious, a key element in the Cult of True Womanhood (Welter, 1976). For example, in "The Responsibilities of Woman," she referred to her convention role as comparable to the gleaning of the biblical character of Ruth, and she compared the impossible task women faced as unpropertied wives and mothers to the difficulties faced by Jewish slaves in Egypt. She alluded to the fifth chapter of Exodus, in which Jewish slaves were forced to make bricks without being given straw. She said: "if we are not fitted to be capable wives and mothers—as contended by gentleman on the stand yesterday,—if we make poor brick, it is because our brother man has stolen our straw. Give us back our straw brother, and we will make you *good* brick" (quoted in CHN:163). Such allusions were persuasive because they acknowledged reverence for biblical authority and showed the speaker to be a good Christian woman. However, because biblical injunctions against women's speaking were often the main source of arguments *against* woman's rights activism, she risked reminding her audiences of these well-known arguments.

Howard Nichols used other kinds of evidence to buttress her arguments in creative, thoughtful ways while reassuring her audience that she was a traditional woman. Her use of heartrending personal examples and observations further substantiates her rhetorical skill. Traditionally, examples are relatively weak evidence because they are only one instance, but they have the ability to vivify difficult ideas and make them real for audiences. She used long, detailed personal examples in nearly every speech and written argument. Her decision to do so was an excellent one because it helped to balance the tightly reasoned, discursive style and lawyerly persona she often assumed in her rhetoric. The situations that women and children faced in her stories almost always arose from unjust laws, indicating that, rather than being atypical or unrepresentative, the circumstances described could happen to any woman. Thus, she was able to draw on the strength of the example and its ability to vivify while claiming its general applicability to women. One result was to stir the imagination, emotion, and indignation of her audience. In her speech to the 1853 Whole World Temperance Convention, she told a long story of a man on a stagecoach who was attempting to care for a small baby. The man had custody of the child in his legal right as its father but was woefully inept in caring for it. She was able alternately to make the audience laugh and grow incensed at her tale of the man's pathetic attempts to soothe the infant by feeding it sweet cakes. In another speech to the 1853 Woman's Rights Convention, she told a lengthy tale of a wealthy Vermont family. In the story, the father had taken one of the female children away from its mother and had hired a "vile Frenchman" to care for her. The girl was cruelly mistreated, and the mother undertook a protracted court battle to win custody of the girl. Unfortunately, the court awarded custody of the other child, a son, to the "unworthy father" (quoted in CHN:178). By drawing on the personal, emotional materials traditionally associated with women, she reinforced perceptions of her own femininity while offering powerful evidence in support of her demands.

Howard Nichols also portrayed herself as a traditional woman in nonverbal ways. One conspicuous tactic was to knit wherever she went, including during sessions of the Kansas Constitutional Convention. Historian T.D.S. Bassett claimed that she brandished her knitting as a kind of ideological flag, and Blanche Glassman Hersh concluded that she used her knitting as a "disarming image of domesticity" (1978:160). Various newspaper reports and biographical treatments have commented on the importance of her knitting, suggesting that her strategy was highly successful (Owen, 1939).

Howard Nichols faced another obstacle in pervasive attitudes that women did not need rights because they were protected adequately by their fathers or husbands and that extending rights to women would challenge traditional sex roles. She responded to this problem by making the extension of rights to women seem like a modest rather than a radical proposal. Rather than directly debate whether or not women should have legal and political rights, she redefined the issue as one of "responsibilities." Throughout her life, she argued that liberalized inheritance, property, guardianship, education, and divorce laws should be enacted so that women could better meet their God-given responsibilities as wives and mothers. This theme is best illustrated by "The Responsibilities of Woman." In 1851, she had only recently accepted suffrage as an appropriate goal for the woman's rights movement. Accordingly, she took pains to put distance between herself and explicit calls for "woman's rights." She differentiated woman's rights as an effort to obtain political privileges from an effort to correct *wrongs* against females. This distinction is apparent in her comment: "I shall say very little of woman's *rights*; but I would lay the axe at the root of the tree. I would impress upon you woman's *responsibilities*, and the means fitly to discharge them before heaven" (quoted in CHN:157).

"The Responsibilities of Woman" is Howard Nichols's most clearly developed statement of her views on woman's rights. Because the speech was so well received, it was reprinted as part of the Woman's Rights Tract Series. As one might anticipate, its argumentative approach was refined and adapted to different audiences throughout her life. For example, in her address to the Vermont Legislature, she claimed that women had family responsibilities that necessitated the ownership of property. She contrasted the experiences of men and women, arguing that men were recreant and incompetent, whereas women were morally upright, conscientious citizens who worked hard to fulfill their familial responsibilities. She claimed that women's past fulfillment of their responsibilities entitled them to their own property, as well as insuring that they could *better* fulfill their roles as wives and mothers. In her address to the Whole World Temperance Convention, she altered this argument in order to urge temperance activists to live up to what she saw as their Christian obligations. In her written speeches, she altered the argument to indict the Founding Fathers for not fulfilling the lofty ideals on which the government was based.

CONCLUSION

Although her call for granting rights to women was redefined as granting them the means to fulfill their responsibilities, Howard Nichols's basic ideas were much like those of her more radical contemporaries. Allowing women rights so that they might become better mothers and wives was a difficult argument for opponents to refute because it made her proposals seem modest and reasonable. It was a comforting argument for her listeners because it indicated that she was not interested in encouraging women to abdicate their socially appropriate roles. This argument was cautious and measured, even conservative, when compared to other calls for woman's rights based on the inherent personhood and citizenship of women.

An analysis of Clarina Howard Nichols's oral and written discourses demonstrates that she skillfully used a variety of strategies to put her audiences at ease and to overcome difficult rhetorical obstacles. Her emphasis on herself as a traditional woman, her selection of supporting materials, her nonverbal messages, and her argument about women's responsibilities were all developed as means of diverting the audience's attention away from her violations of social norms as a speaker and an activist. These strategies were also designed to make woman's rights seem like a reasonable, modest proposal. Finally, her life's work and her rhetorical skills indicate that Clarina Howard Nichols has earned a place as a memorable, rather than a "forgettable," champion of the rights of women.

SOURCES

The Clarina Howard Nichols Papers, Kansas State Historical Society, Topeka, have been edited and published by Joseph Gambone. A few letters and others documents, also edited and published by Gambone, are found in the Clarina I. Nichols Papers, Schlesinger Library, Radcliffe.

Gambone, Joseph G. "The Forgotten Feminist of Kansas: The Papers of Clarina I.H. Nichols, 1854–1885." *Kansas Historical Quarterly* 39 (Spring 1973):12–57; (Summer 1973):220–261; (Autumn 1973):392–444; (Winter 1973):515–563; 40 (Spring 1974):72–135; (Summer 1974):241–292; (Autumn 1974):410–459; (Winter 1974):504–562. (*FFK*)

Biographical Sources

Bassett, T.D. Seymour. "Nichols, Clarina Irene Howard." *NAW* 2:625–627.
Kunin, Madeleine M. "Clarina Howard Nichols: Green Mountain Suffragette." *Vermont Life* 28 (1978):14–17.
Nichols, Clarina I. Howard. "Reminiscences." *HWS* 1:171–200.

Critical Sources

Campbell, Karlyn Kohrs. *MCSFH* 1:87–93, 102–103.
Christiansen, Adrienne E. "Clarina Howard Nichols: A Rhetorical Criticism of Selected
    Speeches." M.A. thesis, University of Kansas, 1987. (*CHN*)

Historical and Rhetorical Background

Campbell, Karlyn Kohrs, and E. Claire Jerry. "Woman and Speaker: A Conflict in
    Roles." *Seeing Female: Social Roles and Personal Lives*. Ed. Sharon S. Brehm.
    Westport, Conn.: Greenwood Press, 1988, pp. 123–133.
Cowper, Mary O. "A History of Women's Suffrage in Kansas." M.A. thesis, Sociology,
    University of Kansas, 1914.
Dubois, Ellen Carol. *Feminism and Suffrage: The Emergence of an Independent Women's
    Movement in America, 1848–1869*. Ithaca, N.Y., and London: Cornell University
    Press, 1978.
Hersh, Blanche Glassman. *The Slavery of Sex: Feminist-Abolitionists in America*. Urbana:
    University of Illinois Press, 1978.
Madsen, Sandra, A. "The 1867 Campaign for Woman's Suffrage in Kansas: A Study
    in Rhetorical Situation." M.A. thesis, University of Kansas, 1975.
Owen, Jennie S. "Woman Knitted Her Way into First Constitution of the State of
    Kansas." *Topeka Journal* (March 2, 1939):9.
Pepe, Faith L. "Towards a History of Women in Vermont: An Essay." *Vermont History*
    45, no. 2 (Spring 1977):69–101.
Welter, Barbara. *Dimity Convictions: The American Woman in the 19th Century*. Athens:
    Ohio University Press, 1976.

Chronology of Major Speeches

Delivered Orally

"The Responsibilities of Woman." Woman's Rights Convention, Worcester, Mass.,
    October 15, 1851. *Series of Woman's Rights Tracts*. Rochester, N.Y.: Steam
    Press of Curtis, Butts, 1854. HOW; CHN:156–168; *MCSFH* 2:123–144.
Address, Second Woman's Temperance Convention, State of New York, Rochester,
    April 20, 1852. *Lily* (May 1852):38–39.
Address, Whole World Temperance Convention, New York City, September 3, 1853.
    New York Daily Times, September 3, 1853:1. 3–4. CHN:172–175.
Address, Woman's Rights Convention, New York City, September 6–7, 1853. CHN:176–
    178.
Address, Vermont State Legislature, December 3, 1853. Synopsis, CHN:169–171.

Delivered in Writing

Address, Women's National Loyal League Convention, New York City, May 14, 1863.
    CHN:180–181.
Address, NWSA Convention, Washington, D.C., January 16–17, 1873. CHN:182–184.

266

Women Public Speakers in the United States

Address, NWSA Convention, Philadelphia, July 19, 1876. *FFK* 40:418–421; CHN:185–187.

Address, NWSA Convention, New York City, May 25–26, 1877. *FFK* 40:421–423; CHN:188–189.

Address, NWSA Convention, St. Louis, Mo., May 7–9, 1979. *FFK* 40:429–433; CHN:191–194.

Address, NWSA Convention, Washington, D.C., January 21–22, 1880. *FFK* 40:439–441; CHN:195–196.

Address, Massachusetts WSA Convention, Worcester, Mass., October 20, 1880. *FFK* 40:445–446; CHN:198.

Address, NWSA Convention, Boston, Mass., May 26–27, 1881. *FFK* 40:515–517; CHN:199–200.

Address, NWSA Convention, Rochester, N.Y., March 4–7 1884. *FFK* 40:553–556; CHN:201–203.

HELEN JACKSON GOUGAR

(1843–1907), moral warrior for temperance and woman suffrage

Every social movement needs its organizers, its philosophers, its leaders, and, perhaps, even its martyrs. In addition, every social movement needs someone who will carry the battle to the enemy in the strongest possible terms. Helen Mar Jackson Gougar was such a person, a moral warrior for temperance and woman suffrage who was not afraid of confrontation and was willing to risk all, including her own good name, for her causes.

BACKGROUND

Helen Mar Jackson was born in Hillsdale County, Michigan, in 1843 and attended the local school until she was twelve; then she entered Hillsdale College where she studied for three years. In order to provide money for her younger sisters' education, she left college just before her sixteenth birthday to become an assistant school teacher in Lafayette, Indiana. Within three years, she was named the first woman school principal in Lafayette, a position she held until her marriage to John D. Gougar, a local attorney, in December 1863. Because her spouse suffered from weak eyesight, she regularly read his lawbooks to him, thereby gaining knowledge of the law that would later prove significant.

Jackson Gougar's rhetorical career began in the 1870s when Lafayette women began to organize around various causes such as treatment of the insane, disaster relief, temperance, and woman suffrage. After she gave her first public speech in 1877, her popularity quickly grew. Soon she was speaking on behalf of many groups, including the Social Science Association and the Sunday School Union, and in addition she made numerous appearances in behalf of temperance. She expanded her rhetorical efforts in November 1878 by becoming Lafayette's first woman newspaper columnist. For almost two years, she wrote "Bric-a-Brac," a column devoted to "Literature, Science, Art and Topics of the Day," for the *Lafayette Daily Courier*. In this column she dealt with such issues as charitable organization reform, labor agitation, home economy, and the relationship be-tween temperance and religion.

Jackson Gougar gradually increased her public speaking and her suffrage activity. On June 16, 1880, SUSAN B. ANTHONY appeared at a suffrage meeting in Lafayette at which Jackson Gougar was the opening speaker. This exposure to national suffrage leaders led to Jackson Gougar's appearances before national audiences. By 1881, she was a platform speaker at the AWSA annual convention, and in 1882, she was an Indiana delegate to the convention of the NWSA, appearing on their platform as well. That same year, Anthony chose her to be one of the "young and attractive" women to represent the NWSA before Congress. Jackson Gougar's most significant suffrage involvement was her role in the passage of the municipal suffrage bill she authored and lobbied for in Kansas in 1887. Her importance was noted by the *Wichita Eagle*: "Mrs. G. is, in many particulars, the most eloquent woman in America resembling in many respects Mrs. Elizabeth Cady Stanton, who is now too old to actively work on the platform" (Kriebel, 1985:107). Although the Indiana Equal Suffrage Association would remain officially affiliated with the AWSA until the NAWSA unification in 1890, Jackson Gougar (elected president of the Indiana society during this period) always preferred the NWSA's leaders and positions.

During this same period, Jackson Gougar expanded her publishing activity. Her full-fledged leap into reform publishing took place in August 1881, when she purchased the *Temperance Herald*, a local temperance newspaper. She outlined her purpose in the first issue of the paper, which she renamed *Our Herald* (*OH*): "It will be a fearless, outspoken advocate of all temperance principles. . . . Believing that 'Freedom and law know no sex,' as expressed in our motto, we shall also be outspoken in the interest of woman suffrage" (August 13, 1881:1). *Our Herald* was reasonably successful for a special interest newspaper; at its peak it achieved a circulation of 4,000. Jackson Gougar felt the work of the paper was extremely important, but she gave it up in 1885 in order to devote more time to speaking and traveling in behalf of her two causes.

In spite of her devotion to temperance and suffrage, her involvement with and similarity to national leaders lessened as her political activity and her confrontational tactics distanced her from the mainstream of these movements. Initially a Republican, Jackson Gougar became disillusioned with the major political parties and aligned herself with the Prohibition party from 1888 to 1896. Briefly attracted to the Populist party because its platform incorporated both of her causes, she finally focused her efforts on the formation of the National Prohibition party, a free-silver group that also favored woman suffrage. In 1896, she was this party's candidate for Indiana secretary of state. She led the National Prohibition party ticket but finished fourth out of a field of five, receiving only twenty-five out of over 10,000 votes cast in her own county. In 1900, she returned to the Democratic party, but the damage had already been done. The suffrage movement in general and Anthony in particular were opposed to suffragists dabbling in third-party politics. This "party hopping" contributed to her increasing estrangement from suffragists and temperance advocates. Even so, she would serve as president of the Indiana Equal Suffrage Association for twenty years (1887–1907).

Whatever her medium or outlet, Jackson Gougar labored for her two causes, temperance and woman suffrage, throughout her reform career. At times, depending on her audience and her specific purpose, she was more in one camp than the other. For example, on some occasions she was heard to argue that temperance was *the only* issue worth considering and on others that suffrage was *the paramount* issue of the age. However, such statements were not inconsistent because she saw an interrelationship between the two. As she explained in the opening issue of *Our Herald*: "Our present temperance legislation—as well as all the other legislation, does not express the will of the majority, because the women of the State are sent into prayer meeting on election day, instead of being called like thinking citizens, to the ballot-box as they have a right to be under the declaration that 'all men are created equal' " (August 13, 1881:1). She seemed to believe that if one of these two great battles were won, the other would, of moral necessity, follow. She simply could not separate them:

When I first became a temperance worker, I believed in praying away the evil. But I became convinced that the best way was to vote it away! After I really investigated the matter of woman suffrage, I became a fanatic on both subjects. And I am proud to say I am a fanatic. (Kriebel, 1985:53)

JACKSON GOUGAR'S RHETORICAL PHILOSOPHY AND STYLE

Jackson Gougar saw one unifying principle, one firm philosophical presumption, behind her two related causes: to do what is right because it is the right thing to do. "No question is ever permanently disposed of until it is settled in accordance with the laws of right" (*OH*, May 12, 1883:4), she affirmed. She held fast to one primary justification for all action—do what is moral and do not do what is immoral: "The whole theory of human Government must be according to that Divine plan which says: 'Thou shalt not'; and anything short of this will invariably demand the penalty of the State as well as the individual" ("High License").

Jackson Gougar believed that "goodness is greatness" and that there could be no compromises for political expediency. For example, she held that placing restrictions on the liquor traffic, rather than prohibiting it altogether, "gives it a new lease of [*sic*] life, and enables it to increase its dangerous power. Any crime, law protected, becomes constantly more powerful for evil" ("High License"). She was particularly strident in her belief that the problem with the mainstream parties was their lack of moral conviction. The Democrats had fallen in with the liquor lobby, and the Republicans refused to take a stand on the rightness of temperance or suffrage: "The American people prefer a brave knave to a moral coward. . . . The two great political parties of this Republic—Democratic and Republican—have assumed the relation of knave and coward before the eyes of the world. Both must die" ("New Political Party"). Having identified evil in the world, she felt there could be no choice but to respond: "To listen [to a vicious enemy] and keep silent is to sanction and encourage such an enemy. Such silence is the worst form of enmity" ("Bric-a-Brac," January 25, 1879, HGC).

This moral imperative to action did not mean that Jackson Gougar was uninterested in what would result from moral actions. She often cited the problems alcohol brought on the family and highlighted the positive influence women would have on government if they were allowed to vote. She maintained, however, that the reforms she sought should be enacted even if nothing good came of them *and* even if some undesirable acts were the result, as was possible. She did not believe that women would always seek the good, and she called on her coworkers to "cast off the garment of self-righteousness, and put on that of justice and self-examination" because women might not behave as the reformers would wish: "Give [woman] the same room and the same temptation, as the brother, and we feel safe in saying that she will be equal to the task of keeping even with him in the number and size of trespasses against the laws of right" ("Man's Rights"). What women did with the vote was beside the point, as she reminded Indiana legislators in 1881: "It is your duty to place the rights of citizenship upon the women of this State, and let them use it or not, as they see fit." Suffrage was a natural and inalienable right and, therefore, lawmakers (or judges) had a moral obligation to make it available to those disfranchised only by sex.

Jackson Gougar's belief in the morality and rightness of her views permitted her to hold that "God is always on the side of right." This belief had a clear impact on her rhetorical strategies and style. She was not particularly interested in adapting to her audiences, especially those who opposed her, but she was willing to create what Edwin Black called a "second persona" for any given audience (*Quarterly Journal of Speech* 56 [April 1970]:109–119). Her potential supporters were the "fair-minded readers" of her newspaper, the "Up-to-date Court" she faced in her voting trial, the courteous Indiana legislators who showed "gallantry" to suffrage speakers, and the "able men" who would finally pass the necessary reforms. She addressed them accordingly because she believed that "No honest man can stand the truth presented in this manner without being converted" ("Suffrage Work"). Conversely, she was also willing to identify those opponents in her audience as less than worthy. Once hissed at by a few in a crowd, she retorted: "I hear we have geese in the house" ("Reply to Anna Dickinson"). This separation of her audience into the "good" and the "bad" was consistent with her bipolar view of moral issues.

Her confidence that there were certain unassailable truths on her side contributed to Jackson Gougar's argumentative approach. She usually preferred not to introduce new evidence into the debate at hand, using direct clash instead, attacking her opponent's arguments and proving her own points by refuting her opponent's evidence. In her 1881 Address to the Indiana Assembly, refutation was her sole strategy: "I have been asked on this occasion to answer what is usually called some of the popular objections against enfranchising women." When she confronted the claim that women did not want to vote, she answered, "[N]ine-tenths of the women with brains above an oyster demand the ballot."

Jackson Gougar's moral convictions led to a use of language full of vivid analogies, both figurative and literal, as evidence. For example, she declared intemperance to be "the devil fish of our civilization" and intoxicating liquor to be the "devil's kindling wood." She compared temperance workers to Joshua "marching around the walls of this whisky Jericho." Her most common analogy was a comparison of her causes to slavery. Contrasting her positions to those of ANNA E. DICKINSON, she declared: "She entered into the defense of the abolition of slavery as I have in the defense of the abolition of the greater curse—the American saloon." Men were compared to the slaveholders themselves; "for us to expect that the masses of ignorant, prejudiced and dissolute men could be led to vote women free, simply for the sake of abstract justice, would be as unreasonable as to have expected the negro to have been made free by the votes of slaveholders" ("Civil and Political Rights"). This analogy led to a challenge when she attacked the party of Reconstruction: "I have always had a bone to pick with my Republican friends for doing this. You had no business to enfranchise any man who bore arms against this government until you enfranchise the loyal women of the North" ("Reply to Anna Dickinson"). Given a northern audience with many Civil War veterans, she recognized that this analogy would have persuasive impact.

In other words, Jackson Gougar's rhetorical strategy of first choice and the one that made her reputation was direct confrontation. One biographer put it this way: "Wit and sarcasm, like swords in jeweled scabbards, are ever in her sheath, and woe to the man against whom they leap forth" (*Biographical Record*, 639). She liked to attack, call names, poke fun at, and use the strongest language she could get away with. A savage humor was the rhetorical tool she often used in attacking her opponents' positions.

Her conclusions frequently were confirmed by personal refutation used to demolish a foe. For example, her article "Is Liquor Selling a Sin?" was chiefly a point-by-point attack on George Brown who had attempted to show that Christianity supported the liquor trade, a position that was anathema to Jackson Gougar. She offered no additional evidence but challenged his logic:

Does the writer believe that if Christ were on earth to-day He would engage in the wholesale liquor business or frequent saloons? . . . The very idea is shocking, doubtless, to him as well as to Prohibitionists and Methodists. Judging from His abundant teachings, and the fact that He came to bring peace and joy to all mankind, He would be a strict teetotaler and a Prohibition voter. (712)

She used the same technique on Dr. Henry Hartt who had tried to prove that Jesus must have used fermented wine at the Last Supper:

Inasmuch as the unfermented juice of the grape is the only exact counterpart of the human blood known to science, it is conclusive that it was the pure sweet juice of the grape used to symbolize His blood in the Holy Communion. . . . As his body was symbolized by unleavened or unfermented or uncorrupted bread, it is reasonable to conclude that His blood would be symbolized by uncorrupted juice of the grape. It is preposterous to hold that His blood would be symbolized by the poison of decay in the expressed juice ("Liquor Seller," 462–463).

No scientific evidence was adduced to support her claims; it was enough to show the weaknesses in Hartt's thinking.

Sometimes Jackson Gougar's confrontational style went beyond language and became excessive. She once struck a critic with her umbrella and offered $100 to anyone who would publicly whip him (*Washington Chronicle*, HGC). While such incidents might make her friends uncomfortable, they contributed to her image as a formidable and relentless adversary.

In addition, her commitment to her philosophical principle occasionally caused Jackson Gougar to attack those who were most closely allied with her. In 1892, she accused FRANCES E. WILLARD of poor judgment, of sacrificing her principles, and of lowering her standards in failing to demand total prohibition and in settling for limited municipal suffrage. In 1894, she called SUSAN B. ANTHONY a "moral coward" and a "failure as an organizer" for separating prohibition from the suffrage movement (Kriebel, 1985:148). Although the rifts that resulted were eventually healed, they demonstrate how far she was willing to go in defense of principle. Because character was defined by moral acts, one bad act, or one failure to act well, was sufficient cause to question the entirety of anyone's stance.

JACKSON GOUGAR'S RHETORICAL OUTLETS

Jackson Gougar used newspaper writing and publishing as her primary outlet for a relatively short period. She only wrote "Bric-a-Brac" for two years and edited *Our Herald* for four. Nonetheless, she used this medium to hone her rhetorical skills, which is quite evident in her writing. For instance, she first explored the effectiveness of humor in her editorials as when she poked fun at the scientific data presented by opponents of woman's rights. In an editorial in *Our Herald*, she contested the findings of a Dr. Hammond with respect to the significance of brain weight:

Broca . . . informs us that below 37 ounces a man becomes an idiot; but that a woman's brain must fall below 32 ounces before she becomes an idiot. . . . A woman with 32 ounces of brain can read her ballot. Above that she could judge the qualifications of candidates. Reaching 36 ounces, she might hold a minor office. But a man with 36 ounces of brain is such a helpless idiot that he cannot read his ballot, and his brain must weigh 37 ounces before he knows whether he is going to or from the ballot-box. Her brain is finer—that is the only explanation. (August 11, 1883:3)

Jackson Gougar's language in her writing reflected her intensity. When she responded to the Chicago Board of Education's ruling that marriage of a female teacher would result in an automatic "resignation," she showed her anger in a radical, if punning, attack: "We have had in this country the religious line, the color line, and now, after these have been swept away, come these ass-toot representatives of culture (?) and education with an attempt to create a sex line" ("Ass-Toot").

Jackson Gougar also used publishing to refine two of her most common rhetorical techniques: refutation and authority evidence. After first refuting the claims of unnamed opponents in the pamphlet "Some of the Idiots," she supplied her own list of highly authoritative sources:

[S]ome journals whose columns have never contained, and doubtless for a very good reason, a single argument against woman suffrage, are constantly proclaiming, in effect, that none but simpletons, fools, idiots, and "long-haired" men believe in the new reform. It may not be uninteresting to give to our readers the names and utterances of a few of these idiots.

She then quoted from John Stuart Mill, Ralph Waldo Emerson, Abraham Lincoln, William Seward, George William Curtis, Wendell Phillips, two university presidents, five senators, a bishop, and a governor and concluded, "With such royal idiots as we have named we are proud to stand."

The second rhetorical medium Jackson Gougar employed was lawsuits and the resultant court appearances. She could be compared to SUSAN B. ANTHONY in her unsuccessful bid to vote in the 1894 Indiana elections. Although she and Anthony both went to trial over their voting, Anthony was arrested and tried whereas Jackson sued the election board for $10,000 in damages for its failure to permit what she argued was a constitutionally permitted action. The suit was a friendly one, for her voting attempt had been arranged with the local election board in advance. Taking advantage of a change in Indiana law and of her informal legal "education," she was admitted to the Indiana bar on January 10, 1895, for the purpose of arguing her own case in Superior Court. Although she lost her case, including her appeal to the Indiana Supreme Court, she used this opportunity as one of the first women to speak before these courts to increase visibility for the cause. She issued her four-hour argument in pamphlet form and sold it as suffrage literature. Through these comparisons to Cady Stanton and Anthony, she, along with Frances Willard, was labeled one of the greatest of the second generation of women reformers.

Jackson Gougar was constantly involved in legal battles to defend the rights of women as well as her own reputation. Her lawsuit over voting was only one of many instances when she resorted to the courts. Her first suit was filed in 1881 against Western Union for delaying a telegram she had wanted to send in order to dispatch men's more "important looking" messages first. She was awarded $100 in damages but felt the more significant point was that "women's messages were as important as men's" (Kriebel, 1985:74–75). She also initiated several court cases in which she claimed to have been slandered or libeled. The most significant of these cases began after the political campaigns of 1882. She charged Lafayette, Indiana, police chief Henry Mandler with slander for spreading the rumor that she was having an affair with a local political figure, DeWitt Wallace. Mandler apparently had been influenced by political opponents of Wallace and Jackson Gougar who felt that these two, especially she, had been too active, and almost too successful, in campaigning for prohibition and woman suffrage. After a three-month trial filled with sensational testimony, she prevailed and was awarded $5,000 in damages, money she never received. This particular trial, although it generated much negative publicity, gave her national visibility.

Not all of her coworkers at the time appreciated her notoriety, but many recognized the significance of Jackson Gougar's victory. Immediately after the trial, Illinois suffragist Elizabeth Boynton Harbert wrote:

[This verdict] means that women who choose to enter public or political life are not to be lightly or wantonly assailed by those who disagree with them, or by those who cannot answer their arguments. It means that no one class of men, be they blackguards or reputable citizens, are to fix the standards of womanly character and to speak contemptuously of all who do not happen to be of their way of thinking. (*OH*, April 21, 1883:5)

Over time, more and more women came to acknowledge the importance of her legal efforts. In fact, these slander suits may have produced her most significant contribution to the movements she served. As Frances Willard observed: "In this battle she decided forever the right of women to take an active part in political warfare without being compelled to endure defamation" (Gougar, 1893:329).

Jackson Gougar knew how to marshal vast quantities of evidence. Her court argument on "The Constitutional Rights of the Women of Indiana" was reminiscent of Susan B. Anthony's defense of her vote (*MCSFH* 2:279–316) in its weight of legal and historical testimony. Like Anthony, she painstakingly analyzed the Declaration of Independence, Articles of Confederation, U.S. Constitution, and the Indiana Constitution to demonstrate their support for her claims. She offered thirteen definitions of citizenship and four of liberty and law. She called on English Common Law, the U.S. Supreme Court, and legal precedent from eight states. She even had testimony from one of the original drafters of the Indiana Constitution.

Jackson Gougar's aggressiveness was clear in her newspaper work and her courtroom appearances, but it was most striking in her public speaking. Her imposing style was matched by equally imposing delivery. She was famous for her strength and stamina on the platform. She typically spoke for two to three hours, demonstrating what the Rockford *Register* called "a rapidity of thought and expression that few men could display, and a physical endurance that would have floored hundreds of public speakers of the stronger sex" (HGC). She needed stamina because she averaged more than 200 speeches a year for more than twenty years (*TWJ*, June 15, 1907, HGC).

With very rare exceptions she spoke extemporaneously, without notes of any kind. This mode of delivery, cited by almost every Jackson Gougar biographer and observer, made a tremendous impact on her audiences. Frances Willard, for example, saw her as "earnest, easy, dignified and at times impassionedly eloquent, wholly without affectation or oratorical display. She speaks without manuscript or notes, rapidly and convincingly'' (329). Every aspect of her delivery seemed to contribute to her confrontational approach, as the Indianapolis *Patriot-Phalanx* observed: ''If she did not like a person or thing, she was very bitter. Her wit was bright and her sarcasm was keen'' (HGC). CLARA BEWICK COLBY concluded that she was more like ''the effective stump speaker'' than any of the other ladies of the NWSA (*Woman's Tribune*, April 1, 1884:1).

The most dramatic oral example of Jackson Gougar's point-by-point refutational style was her 1888 campaign speech in behalf of the Prohibition party. The party had hired Jackson Gougar to follow ANNA E. DICKINSON, who was stumping for the Republicans. By speaking after Dickinson, it was hoped that Jackson Gougar would neutralize or obliterate the Republican effect. The tone of her rebuttal was direct: ''I repudiate Miss Dickinson's language on that occasion as unjust, unwise, unchristian, unladylike and unpersuasive.'' She then proceeded to attack point by point, also refuting the Democratic and Republican platforms and the speeches and business practices of several Republican leaders.

In response to the tariff position of the 1888 Republican presidential candidate, James G. Blaine, she showed how humor could be used in refutation:

Blaine gives figures to show that a protective tariff has built up our great cities. He gives no credit to the incoming of a vast and intelligent population or the development of a new country; he lays it all to a high protective tariff; he shows how our commercial interests and our agricultural wealth have grown, and he lays all this to a high protective tariff, and now that he is back among the hills of New York, and he has seen the farmer of Indiana standing on his mule to pick the highest ear of corn, I expect him to say to New Yorkers that the corn crop in the West is owing to a high protective tariff (''Reply to Anna Dickinson'').

She knew how to use a humorous story to its best advantage and how to use humor to deal with interruptions, supportive or not, as illustrated in this example:

Voters are much like the little girl on a railroad train whom I met recently going from Crawfordsville to Indianapolis. The sweet-faced little body crawled up to one of the windows, and on looking out saw a picture of Mr. Harrison in a cottage window— [Applause]—I am glad to have so many Republican friends with us to night; it shows they have come to crowd the Democrats out. [Applause.] This little girl looked out upon that picture, and turning to the gentleman back of her she said, ''I just hate that picture— I'se a Democrat; my pa's a Democrat and I'se born a Democrat.'' [Great laughter.] That child has as intelligent a foundation for her political opinion as 99 out of every 100 of you voters have. (''Reply to Anna Dickinson'')

This excerpt is not unique; newspaper accounts of her speeches are replete with reports of audience laughter.

Jackson Gougar also used language to please her audiences. Rhetorical devices such as alliteration, rhythm, and rhyme made her confrontational statements easy to remember and a little gentler to the ear. For example, she encouraged workers to "Agitate! Educate! Legislate!" in "the parlor, the public place, the press, the pulpit." They needed to fight foes such as "the Republican party that has proven itself too cowardly and too craven to take up the great issue of home against saloon." She used these techniques to emphasize the urgency of her message: "There is absolutely no protection to life, liberty and happiness, but the bludgeon, the bullet or the ballot" ("Constitutional Rights").

Suffrage publisher Elizabeth Boynton Harbert reported an incident when Jackson Gougar's "bit of current slang," rather than pleasing the audience, resulted in a noticeably negative reaction:

I get so tired, she said, of answering the same old hackneyed, inane objections to woman's voting. If they would only ask me something new, but it is the same weary round. Why, the other night I had been speaking for about two hours and had answered every imaginable phase of the few moss covered questions which the opponents of our movement are forever putting forward, and thought I was about through with that day's troubles, when a man arose and said: "Well, if women have the ballot, won't the bad women vote?" I confess I was provoked, tired and worn as I was and I just answered him as the boys do in the streets. "OH RATS," I said. (HGC)

Boynton Harbert observed that when the "audience, mostly women, heard her says [sic] 'Rats,' it did rather give them a shiver. It was unexpected, but was used to point an illustration."

Finally, there was a darker side to Jackson Gougar's confrontational language. Deeply resentful of the attacks that had been leveled at her, she was not above a personal attack in response. She once compared Anna Dickinson to Rip Van Winkle, calling her "a failure," "a woman of the past" and lamenting her "demagogical discussion." She maligned Chaplain Lozier, a one-time debate opponent, revealing to an audience that he was "a man who has been tried twice before the Methodist conference for immoral conduct, and the second time came within two votes of being expelled and was only saved because he pleaded derangement of mind" ("Reply to Anna Dickinson"). She could turn humor to derision as when she mocked an anti-suffrage minister who had once addressed the Indiana Legislature:

The speech of Rev. Badger . . . is a literary curiosity, reminding one forcibly of the fanatical utterances of some puritanical politician of the time of Cromwell. Brother Badger quoted from Genesis to Revelation to show that the Lord was opposed to the resolution of Mr. Owen. It is a significant fact that old fogies are always, or pretend to be, on very intimate terms with the Lord. ("Civil and Political Rights")

For someone who always claimed to take the moral high ground, she knew how to fight in the oratorical trenches.

CONCLUSION

Making a final assessment of this prodigious rhetorical career is complicated because of the extremes to which Jackson Gougar and her critics went. On the one hand, she delivered more than 4,000 speeches during her career and was often paid between $50 and $100 per speech, impressive sums for her day. Coupled with the favorable critiques of her rhetorical prowess, these reports lead to the conclusion that she was, in at least some sense, a popular and successful rhetor.

On the other hand, Jackson Gougar inspired outspoken critics. One went so far as to spell her name "Hellen" saying "one l does not properly classify her" (HGC). In addition, her overpowering moral stance and singleminded determination to pursue her vision of the one true path made her an occasional organizational annoyance, if not an outright embarrassment. She never captured the imagination or the leadership of the movements which were, to her, dearer than life itself (*OH*, April 14, 1883:2). As a moral warrior, she crossed the line to become a fanatic zealot and alienated those with whom she was attempting to serve. Her failure to accomplish more as a reformer was probably caused as much by the internal conflicts she engendered in the movements as by any difficulties she had with liquor traffickers or recalcitrant legislators.

Jackson Gougar's confrontational rhetoric was, in many ways, a precursor of later feminist activism. At a time when few echoed her concerns, she called for "equal pay for equal work" and encouraged women to have more ambition. She was vicious in her sarcasm and abrasive in her attack. She willingly risked her character and her reputation in order to be politically active and to represent unpopular positions. Like so many first-and second-generation feminists, she did not live to see most of the reforms she advocated come into being. Nonetheless, she spoke, she wrote, she sued, she stood firm, believing to her death that "women are people" and that the right would prevail.

SOURCES

The Helen Gougar Collection (HGC), Alameda McCollough Library, Tippecanoe County Historical Association, Lafayette, Indiana, contains her notebook compilations of newspaper reports and transcripts of her speeches. These papers are important given her heavy use of extemporaneous delivery. The Indiana State Library, Indianapolis, has the only sizable holding of *Our Herald*; twenty-five issues (August 13, 1881, February 24–August 11, 1883) are on microfilm. The Library also owns the last five months of the paper (September 1884–January 1885) in original copy, but, at this writing, the issues are not available for study. The History of Women Collection (HOW) has two of Jackson Gougar's undated pamphlets; miscellaneous articles by her are in general circulation publications of the day such as the *Arena* and the *Voice*. Speech excerpts are found in *HWS* and in suffrage papers such as the *Woman's Tribune* and the *New Era*.

Selected Biographical Sources

Anthrop, Mary E. Unpublished mss. HGC

Biographical Record and Portrait Album of Tippecanoe County, Indiana. Chicago: Lewis, 1888, pp. 637–643.

Dunn, Jacob P. *Indiana and Indianans*. Chicago and New York: American Historical Society, 1919. Vol. 3:1311–1313.

"Gougar, Mrs. Helen M." *A Woman of the Century: Fourteen Hundred Biographical Sketches Accompanied by Portraits of Leading Women in All Walks of Life*. Eds. Frances E. Willard and Mary A. Livermore. 1893. Detroit: Gale Research, 1967, pp. 328–329.

Kriebel, Robert C. *Where the Saints Have Trod: The Life of Helen Gougar*. West Lafayette, Ind.: Purdue University Press, 1985.

Phillips, Clifton J. "Gougar, Helen Mar Jackson." *NAW* 2:69–71.

Chronology of Major Speeches and Articles

"Man's Rights, Bric-a-Brac." *Lafayette Daily Courier*, December 20, 1879. HGC

"Ass-Toot, Bric-a-Brac." *Lafayette Daily Courier*, February 7, 1880. HGC

"Temperance and Religion, Bric-a-Brac." *Lafayette Daily Courier*, April 10, 1880. HGC

"Welcoming Address, Woman Suffrage Convention." Lafayette, Indiana, June 16, 1880. HGC

Address at the Indiana State Assembly, February 15, 1881. *Brevier Legislative Reports* 19 (1881):193. See also Janice Marie LaFlamme. "The Strategy of Feminine Protest: A Rhetorical Study of the Campaign for Woman's Rights in Indiana, 1881." M.A. thesis, Indiana University, 1968, pp. 111–113.

"How Can the Civil and Political Rights of Indiana Women Be Enlarged Without Constitutional Amendment?" Indiana Woman Suffrage Society, Indianapolis, Indiana, no date (1881?). HGC

"The New Political Party." *Our Herald* (May 5, 1883):3.

"High License." *Our Herald* (July 28, 1883):4.

"Woman Suffrage Work: Plan for Local, State and National Woman Suffrage Societies." *Our Herald* (August 11, 1883):2.

"I Have All the Rights I Want." Pamphlet, n.d. (1883?). HOW

"Some of the Idiots." Pamphlet, n.d. (1883?). HOW

"Reply to Anna Dickinson." Delivered repeatedly October–November 1888. HGC

"Christ and the Liquor Seller." *Arena* (March 1893):461–470. HGC

"Is Liquor Selling a Sin?" *Arena* (October 1893):710–716. HGC.

"A Prohibitionist Points the Way Out." *Arena* (May 1894):831–836. HGC

"The Constitutional Rights of the Women of Indiana, An Argument in the Superior Court of Tippecanoe County, Ind., 10 January 1895." Lafayette: Morning Journal Printing, 1895. HGC; HOW

MATILDA JOSLYN GAGE
(1826–1898), suffragist and freethinker

To say that she was "outspoken," as the tactful did, is a little like describing a tornado as a grand gust of wind. "My Dear Mrs. [Harriet Hanson] Robinson, I think you are perfectly incomprehensible," Matilda Joslyn Gage began a letter to a coworker who had gotten cold feet in a decisive showdown (March 1890, Robinson Collection, HOW). "An appalling frankness of speech" is how the daughter of suffragist Lillie Devereux Blake described her. Katherine Devereux Blake went on to say, "She was absolutely honest in all her dealings, and I would take her word at any time as against anybody else's. I always loved and admired her greatly." Placing her alongside SUSAN B. ANTHONY, ELIZA- BETH CADY STANTON, and Isabella Beecher Hooker in her importance to the movement, she concluded, "I think that in some ways she was the greatest of those four women" (Blake, 1943:115).

CLARA BEWICK COLBY, editor of the *Woman's Tribune*, was another who recognized her importance: "Mrs. Gage has been conspicuous, and united with Mrs. Stanton since the early days; and the three names, Stanton, Anthony, and Gage, linked together in the authorship of The History of Woman Suffrage, will ever hold a grateful place in the hearts of posterity" (March 28, 1888).

But Joslyn Gage didn't simply fly off the handle. Her pen and tongue conveyed razor-sharp, focused fact. Olympia Brown observed that she was "always filled with matter, the results of careful research and thorough investigation" (1911:89), echoing Cady Stanton's amazement that she "always had a knack of rummaging through old libraries, bringing more startling facts to light than any woman I ever knew." Her "appalling frankness" and thorough research char- acterize her speeches. "To speak of atrocious crimes in mild language is treason to virtue," Edmund Burke said, and she was never, ever treasonous. The cost of unswerving truth-telling, of course, is generally the sort of isolation and historical neutralizing that she experienced.

"I think of her," a family friend reminisced with Joslyn Gage's daughter Julia, "as almost the one person in our community of intellectual vision, living as such persons must, somewhat isolated from her neighbors by no wish of her own but because of their inability to keep pace with her thought and sympathies."

Joslyn Gage entered the movement, as did Anthony, in 1852, four years after the first convention in Seneca Falls. Along with Cady Stanton, these women eventually became key figures in the radical wing of the woman's rights move- ment, sharing leadership positions in the NWSA. Anthony was the organizer; Cady Stanton and Joslyn Gage were the movement's theoreticians.

JOSLYN GAGE'S RHETORICAL CAREER

Joslyn Gage's career as a woman's rights advocate began when she was twenty-six, the youngest woman to mount the platform at the third national convention in 1852. Syracuse, only fifteen miles from her village of Fayetteville, was the site, and she attended with her oldest daughter in tow. Standing before the audience of 2,000, she read softly, perhaps from nervousness and a lack of knowledge of the projection necessary to fill a large hall. But if her voice was weak (and that would always be a problem), her theory was strong.

Drawing parallels between the position of women and feudalism, she celebrated the miracles, the many achievements made in art, science, and government "trammeled as women have been." Clearly the potential for greatness was there, "The question is, how can this mental and moral lethargy, which now binds the generality of women, be shaken off?" This "state of listlessness" was a "natural consequence" of women "educated to a state of entire dependence; taught before marriage, to expect a support from their fathers, and after, from their husbands, to suppress their convictions, if contrary to those of their fathers, brothers and husbands, and to allow others to act for them" (WRC 1852:3).

The solution Joslyn Gage posed was both personal and political. Women must be educated for self-respect and economic self-reliance, at the same time that institutions that perpetuated their oppression required changing. At this early date, perhaps because it weighed heaviest in her own life, she stressed the importance of economic independence, and the necessity to press for paid labor and the opening of more options to women than the marriage-or-prostitution choice they currently faced. Once they had the jobs, working conditions "must be revolutionized," because women working in northern industry were "driven by task-masters as merciless as those of the Southern cotton and rice plantations" (WRC 1852:4).

Joslyn Gage deftly showed the inseparability of the struggle of woman and the slave as they faced the same enemy:

Although our country makes great professions in regard to general liberty, yet the right to particular liberty, natural equality, and personal independence, of two great portions of this country, is treated, from custom, with the greatest contempt; and color in the one instance, and sex in the other, are brought as reasons why they should be so derided; and the mere mention of such natural rights is frowned upon, as tending to promote sedition and anarchy. (WRC 1852:5)

Knowing full well the ferocity of the backlash against justice and having grown up in an abolitionist household, she continued:

We need not expect the concessions demanded by women will be peaceably granted; there will be a long moral warfare, before the citadel yields; in the meantime, let us take possession of the outposts. The public must be aroused to a full sense of the justice of our claims. Beside the duty of educating our children, so as to make the path of right, easy to their feet, is that of discussion, newspaper articles, petitions. All great reforms are gradual. Fear not any attempt to frown down the revolution already commenced; nothing is more fertile aid of reform, than any attempt to check it; work on! (WRC 1852:8)

She concluded with a poem that exhorted the audience to work for woman suffrage:

Work sows the seed:
Even the rock may yield its flower:
No lot so hard, but human power,
Exerted to one end and aim;
May conquer fate, and capture fame!
  Press on!

Pause not in fear:
Preach no desponding, servile view—
Whate'er thou will'st thy Will may do.
Work on, and win!

Shall light from nature's depth arise,
And thou, whose mind can grasp the skies,
Sit down with fate, and idly rail?
No—ONWARD! Let the Truth prevail! (WRC 1852:8)

Interrupted several times by applause, her address, though not heard at the back of the hall, drew a great outburst of cheering and clapping at its conclusion. Audience appreciation increased when LUCRETIA COFFIN MOTT, the presiding officer, suggested that the text be published as one of their woman's rights tracts, ''which I always considered a great and appreciative compliment,'' Joslyn Gage recalled (Letter to Blake, May 2, 1890).

Shortly after the conclusion of this speech, SUSAN B. ANTHONY, a recent convert to woman's rights who was also attending her first convention as a temperance advocate, moved that no woman should be allowed to speak whose voice could not fill the house. PAULINA KELLOGG WRIGHT DAVIS, the next scheduled speaker, vindicated Joslyn Gage when she responded that she would not consent to this gag being placed on the convention, because

although she cared not to speak herself, yet many of her sisters had come here with full hearts, but with weak untrained voices. She would not consent that they should have their rights thus restricted, as such a course would only perpetuate the tyranny that woman came here to destroy. (*New York Tribune*, September 14, 1852)

Freedom of speech won the day as the resolution was defeated.

Within the next ten years, Joslyn Gage emerged as a major actor in the suffrage movement. She served as an officer and as a ''fluent and pleasant speaker'' at national, state, and local levels; she also published articles and short stories with a decidedly feminist cast.

In 1862, the women of Fayetteville called on her to present a flag from them to the local regiment of New York volunteers heading for the Civil War battlefields. The *Onondaga Standard* reported: "Monday last witnessed stirring times in this village. Crowds poured in from the country; the village was out en masse, everyone who could be present was here to witness this interesting ceremony" (September 3, 1862).

The moment that the villagers would long remember came when Joslyn Gage dramatically wrapped herself in the flag, "referring impressively to its symbolism of protection and freedom." The conflict between the North and the South, she declared, "is a war of principles. On the one hand, Liberty and the Union, and the poor man's rights forever, and on the other slavery and the aristocratic disunion of a few, over both the black man and the poor white man" ("Flag Presentation").

It was a far-reaching class and race analysis, at a time when radical abolitionists were outraged at Lincoln's footdragging over the issue of slavery. Although other women such as Amelia Jenks Bloomer and ELIZABETH CADY STANTON also made flag presentation speeches during the same period, Joslyn Gage's was unique in the demand she put on the government to fight the war, not to preserve the union (as Lincoln was insisting) but to end slavery:

There can be no permanent peace until the cause of the war is destroyed. And what caused the war? Slavery! and nothing else. That is the corner-stone and key-stone of the whole. The cries of down-trodden millions arising to the throne of God. Let each one of you feel the fate of the world to be upon your shoulders, and fight for yourselves, and us, and the future.

She went further, adding, "Let Liberty be your watch-word and your war-cry alike. Unless liberty is attained—the broadest, the deepest, the highest liberty for all,—not for one set alone, one clique alone, but for man and woman, black and white, Irish, Germans, Americans, and negroes, there can be no permanent peace" ("Flag Presentation").

Defined in these startlingly broad terms, there are those who would argue that the Civil War is still not over. There clearly was no permanent peace for women at the war's end when Congress passed the Fourteenth Amendment, which for the first time defined U.S. citizenship but limited it to males. Then Congress passed the Fifteenth Amendment, which limited suffrage to men for the first time in the country's history.

The Fourteenth Amendment was a double-edged sword: while it referred to citizens as "male" three times, it also defined the role of the federal government as protector of citizens whose rights were being violated by the states. The strategy of the radical NWSA (formed by those who broke from the conservative suffragists of the AWSA) was to hold the government accountable to its principles in a brilliant campaign of nonviolent civil disobedience.

The praxis was simple and clear. Women were not asking for the right to vote. That was theirs by virtue of being U.S. citizens. They were demanding that the federal government protect that right against the states, which had passed laws denying women suffrage. They would push the issue into public awareness by pointing out the contradition between the theory of political freedom and the practice of political slavery.

It was against the law for women to vote. By the hundreds, women all across the country broke the law and voted. They were arrested, like SUSAN B. ANTHONY, or they were denied, like Virginia Minor of St. Louis, and they sued the registrars who refused to let them vote. Minor, an NWSA officer, carried her case to the U.S. Supreme Court, whose decision was unanimous: "if the courts can consider any question settled, this is one," these nine white men agreed. In giving the Supreme Court's opinion, Chief Justice Morrison R. Waite declared that suffrage was not coexistent with citizenship, that states had the absolute right to grant or deny suffrage, and that the "Constitution of the United States does not confer the right of suffrage upon any one" (*Minor v. Happersett*, 1875).

Ably reviewing the case at a later NWSA convention, Joslyn Gage proved that the U.S. government had created eight different classes of voters, including franchised male slaves and Confederate leaders granted amnesty and reenfranchised by federal law. She predicted:

In the near future these trials of women under the XIV Amendment will be looked upon as the great State trials of the world; trials on which a republic, founded upon the acknowledged rights of all persons to self-government, through its courts decided against the right of one half of its citizens on the ground that sex was a barrier and a crime. (*HWS* 2:745)

Although Minor's case was the most important legally, it was Anthony's arrest and trial that drew the most attention. Whereas the other cases were brought against the government by women who wanted to vote, this was brought by the government against a woman for the "crime" of voting, which was against the law in New York, as it was in all states (Wyoming territory was the only exception).

Alone among the suffragists, Joslyn Gage understood it as a political trial, and joined Anthony in a campaign to educate potential jurors on the issue in a whirlwind tour of sixteen townships in the twenty-two days before the trial began. Her speech, "The United States on Trial, not Susan B. Anthony," ended with an impassioned appeal to potential jurors:

The eyes of all nations are upon us; their hopes of liberty are directed towards us; the United States is now on trial by the light of its own underlying principle. Its assertion of human right to self-government lies a hundred years back of it . . . it is at this trial that republican institutions will have their grand test, and as the decision is rendered for or against the political rights of citizenship, so will the people of the United States find themselves free or slaves, and so will the United States have tried itself, and paved its way for a speedy fall, or for a long and glorious continuance. (204)

She addressed the men of the audience personally, showing them their responsibility to history as potential jurors:

To you, men of Ontario county, has come an important hour. The fates have brought about that you, of all the men in this great land, have the responsibility of this trial. To you, freedom has come looking for fuller acknowledgment, for a wider area in which to work and grow. Your decision will not be for Susan B. Anthony alone; it will be for yourselves and for your children's children to the latest generations. . . . No more momentous hour has arisen in the interest of freedom, for the underlying principles of the republic, its warp and woof alike, is the exact and permanent political equality of every citizen of the nation, whether that citizen is native born or naturalized, white or black, man or woman. And may God help you. (205)

The judge, aware that virtually every potential juror in the county knew the significance of the case, placed himself above the law. Without consulting the jury or allowing them to indicate their opinion in any way, he found Anthony guilty of voting and fined her $100, plus the costs of the prosecution.

Until women were given their rights as citizens, they should not exercise their responsibilities. The next logical stage in the campaign was to launch a tax protest. "Oh, wise men," Joslyn Gage editorialized, "can you tell why he means she, when taxes are to be assessed, and does not mean she, when taxes are to be voted upon? The whole question of a woman's demand for a vote along with taxation is a simple question of justice," she wrote in the *Syracuse Journal* (May 7, 1871).

At a mass meeting called by the New York Woman Suffrage Association to organize a campaign of tax resistance on the centennial of the Boston Tea Party, Joslyn Gage reminded the audience that the original tax protesters had been the revolutionary mothers—not the fathers. These brave women had prepared the way for the famous Tea Party in Boston Harbor, which had precipitated the rebellion against English rule:

In 1770, six years before the Declaration of Independence, the women of New England made a public, combined protest against taxation without representation; and as tea was the article upon which Great Britain was then expending her strength, these women of the American Colonies united themselves into a league, and bound themselves, to use no more tea in their families until the tax upon it was repealed. This league was formed by the married women, but three days afterwards the young ladies held an anti-tax meeting. These young ladies publicly declared they did not take this step for themselves alone, but they protested against this taxation as a matter of principle, and with a view to benefit their posterity. These public protests against taxation were made more than five years before the commencement of the Revolutionary War. They, also, were the real origin of the famous Tea Party in Boston Harbor, which did not take place until three years after the public protest of the women. The women of today are the direct posterity of the women of the Revolution, and as our foremothers protested against "taxation without representation," so, do we, their descendants, protest against being taxed without being represented. ("Tea and Taxes," *Chicago Tribune* [1873], MJ Gage Scrapbook, Library of Congress)

The tax protest spread across the country; many women refused to pay their taxes and had their property seized and sold at public auction.

As the nation's centennial approached, the need for an organized, nationally focused protest in 1876 grew. Joslyn Gage alluded to the coming action when she testified before Congress in 1875 on behalf of the District of Columbia suffrage bill:

In asking you to secure the ballot to the women of the District we do not ask you to create a right. That is beyond your power. We ask you to protect in the exercise of a right. Some excellent women of this country have proposed to wear crepe upon their arms during the Centennial celebration, because half of the people are not free. The fitting celebration for the Congress of the United States, to crown itself and the country with glory, is to prove our national principles by securing to woman protection in the exercise of her right of self-government. Then, when the "Old Bell" peals out on July 4, 1876, it will in truth and in deed proclaim, "liberty unto the land and to all the inhabitants thereof." ("Memorial of Women Citizens of This Nation to the Senate and House of Representatives," 5)

But Congress failed to "crown itself with glory." Thus, Joslyn Gage's rhetoric was stronger the following year. She offered the following protest at the annual January NWSA meeting in Washington. It was adopted by the Convention, printed, and extensively circulated:

We, the undersigned women of the United States, asserting our faith in the principles of the Declaration of Independence and in the constitution [*sic*] of the United States, proclaiming it as the best form of government in the world, declare ourselves a part of the people of the nation unjustly deprived of the guaranteed and reserved rights belonging to citizens of the United States; because we have never given our consent to this government; because we have never delegated our rights to others; because this government is false to its underlying principles; because it has refused to one-half its citizens the only means of self-government—the ballot; because it has been deaf to our appeals, our petitions and our prayers.

Therefore, in the presence of the assembled nations of the world, we protest against this government of the United States as an oligarchy of sex, and not a true republic; and we protest against calling this a centennial celebration of the independence of the people of the United States. (*HWS* 3:4)

As NWSA president, Joslyn Gage had been threatened with arrest for refusing to pay the $5 license fee required for "itinerant showmen" and "traveling mountebanks" in the District of Columbia. She declared that she "wouldn't pay five cents," since the preamble of the Constitution granted free speech and the right of redress. "I shall remain in your District of Columbia jail," she promised, rather than pay the fee ("Woman Suffrage," *Washington Evening Star*, January 17, 1876, quoted in Wagner, 1987:60).

Joslyn Gage was not arrested then, nor was she several months later when she and four other NWSA officers presented a Woman's Declaration of Rights (penned by Joslyn Gage and Cady Stanton) at the official July 4 centennial celebration in Philadelphia after they had been denied permission to do so. Addressing their action "to the daughters of 1976," the women drew widespread newspaper coverage and gained more converts (*HWS* 3:42–44). At the mass celebration meeting following the Declaration's illegal presentation, Joslyn Gage pressed further by taking up the issues of marital rape and wife battering, declaring that women were denied the right of habeas corpus, "all married women being held outside its pale of protection against imprisonment by their husbands" (*Philadelphia Evening Post*, July 5, 1876).

Although suffrage was not achieved, the long-range impact of the civil disobedience campaign was summarized by Joslyn Gage:

There are defeats which mean more than victories in their remote results, and the decisions against woman in all these trials are of that character. Not a woman who before had striven for suffrage felt disheartened; their courage rose with every opposing argument or decision, while thousands and tens of thousands whose thoughts had not been turned to this battle for the rights of their sex, now felt the indignity heaped upon them through false interpretations of law by those in power, joined hands and worked with the heretofore despised reformer. (M. J. Gage ms., S.B. Anthony Scrapbook 6, Library of Congress, quoted in Wagner, 1978:24)

By the close of the centennial decade, Joslyn Gage had come to a decision. After thirty years of meeting, writing, petitioning, speaking, and protesting unsuccessfully for a suffrage right that was already theirs, it was clear that the source of woman's oppression was far deeper than a superficial and political one.

In 1878, Joslyn Gage spoke for the first time at a Free Thought convention and found kindred souls in that movement. "She looks anything but a reformer," the *New York Herald* commented, "and is more like a loving grandmother with a room full of grandchildren." The paper went on to describe her elegant attire: "black velvet, with passamenterie lace and silk trimming" and her nervousness as "she constantly played with a fan during her speech" ("The Watkins Convention," M. J. Gage Scrapbook).

While she may not have looked like a radical, she was, and this speech marked the shift of Joslyn Gage's attention from the political arena to the religious. It was the "political religion," Christianity, that she had come to see as the chief enemy of woman's rights. And the hatred of women was not peripheral to Christianity; it was its centerpiece. She challenged her audience:

Can one of you tell me what is the foundation doctrine of the Christian church to-day? Does one of you know what is the foundation principle of the three great divisions of the Christian Church—Catholic, Protestant, and Greek? The foundation is not upon Christ; not upon Paul; not upon the doctrine of immersion; it is not upon any of these, but the Christian Church is based upon the fact of woman servitude; upon the theory that woman brought sin and death into the world, and that therefore she was punished by being placed in a condition of inferiority to man—a condition of subjection, of subordination. This is the foundation to-day of the Christian Church. (Address, Watkins Convention, 212–213)

At this convention, a woman was arrested under the Comstock laws for selling a birth control manual. Joslyn Gage clarified and contextualized the arrest. She contended that the woman was arrested not for giving information on the prevention of pregnancy but, rather, for giving a woman the tools for self-power. The church was determined that woman should not have control of her body, or the fruits thereof, because, as she reminded the audience, "Do you know that every woman here who chances to be a married woman has the same danger of arrest if she dare to claim her child for her own?" (Address, Watkins Convention, 212). The church, through its agent, the state, decreed that woman was to produce children for man. She was not allowed to prevent birth, and once the children came, they were the "property" of the husband.

While increasingly focused on the church as the major enemy of woman's rights, Joslyn Gage did not retire from suffrage work. The following year (1879), she was part of an NWSA delegation that met with the president and read an address, which, according to newspaper reports, "evidently surprised President Hayes by its brevity and directness" ("Washington Society, Gossip from the Nation's Capital," *The Philadelphia Times*, January 19, 1879, quoted in Wagner, 1978:86). In 1880, she wrote and presented resolutions to the Republican, Democratic, and Greenback parties, and when BELVA BENNETT LOCKWOOD ran for president as the Equal Rights party candidate in 1884, she was one of two electors-at-large on the ticket. Still, Joslyn Gage increasingly believed that the vote was only a tool to remove the "fourfold bondage of women" at the hands of the State, the Church, the capitalist, and the home (*HWS* 3:vi).

Suffragists rented a boat and, banners flying, protested the unveiling of the Statue of Liberty in 1886, calling it a "gigantic lie, a travesty, a mockery" and "the greatest sarcasm of the nineteenth century" to present liberty as a woman, "while not one single woman throughout the length and breadth of the Land is as yet in possession of political Liberty." "Ah, women," Joslyn Gage pressed the audience on the boat, "I wish I could fill your hearts with a desire for liberty like that which boils in my heart" ("Women Express Their Preferences," *New York Tribune*, October 29, 1886, quoted in Wagner 1978:113).

That desire embraced, but far transcended, the mundane and increasingly meaningless political focus of the vote, as the era of the Robber Barons exposed suffrage as one more commodity to be purchased by the biggest pocketbook. As the scope of her analysis embraced more of woman's position, Joslyn Gage became more hopeful, as a speech at the 1887 NWSA convention showed:

The world is now full of subjects to compel great thoughts. Woman's experiences broaden, deepen, embolden her. She sees life as never before:—as never before she dares to be herself. The progress of life is a growth headword; as the spirit brain increases, morality increases and humanity becomes more free. True civilization is a recognition of the rights of others at every point of contact, and when this takes place the world will step out of the darkness of heathendom into a full light of a religious and political civilization grander than any of which it has yet dreamed. ("The Foundation of Sovereignty," TWJ, April 1887)

Her reputation as one of the suffrage movement's leaders was sealed. When women's rights advocates gathered internationally for the first time in March 1888, one paper noted, "There is not in all the body of women gathered on the platform of the International Council one whose life and acts are more bound up in its progress and influence than Matilda Joslyn Gage" (unidentified clipping, Gage scrapbook). The May *Cosmopolitan* described her as "tall and graceful in her bearing, attractive both in face and manner," adding, "her face is a sad one, but her speeches were all bright and gave evidence of deep thought. Her delivery is clear and distinct, and she speaks with considerable force" (1888:223).

One of the convention organizers, she spoke several times, but Joslyn Gage's most memorable address came during the Religious Symposium. At this meeting she chastised the International Council of Women for the "almost universal unanimity with which the delegates, both ministerial and lay, in invocation and speech, have ignored the feminine in the Divinity." Each session began with a prayer, and she had been hard-pressed to find a woman who would pray to the "Divine Motherhood of God." She was "profoundly surprised and astonished" by the continual references to a male God, because

All thoughtful persons, and foremost among them should be the women here represented, must be aware of the historical fact that the prevailing religious idea in regard to woman has been the base of all their restrictions and degradation. It underlies political, legal, educational, industrial, and social disabilities of whatever character and nature. The word "God," which simply means good, has everywhere been interpreted by the Christian Church, especially for the last hundreds of years, as well as by the later Jewish theocracy, as of but one gender—the masculine; and it has been the occasion for the priesthood of both dispensations to ignore the feminine principle everywhere. Inasmuch as history teaches us that the rack, the torture, the destruction of human will, the degradation of woman for the past eighteen hundred years, have been dependent upon masculine interpretation of the Bible, based upon belief in a purely masculine divinity, this Council has been to me a dangerous evidence of woman's ignorance upon this most important of questions. ("Woman in the Early Christian Church," 401)

This ignorance was recent because "In all ancient nations we find goddesses seated everywhere with gods, in many instances regarded as superior to them, and of greater influence in the affairs of the universe." Even in the early Christian church, "the equal feminine nature of the divine was accepted." Women clergy were needed, she asserted, "who shall dare break away from all the false traditions of the middle ages, fearless in preaching the truth as to the absolute and permanent equality of the feminine with the masculine, not alone in all material, but in all spiritual things" ("Woman in the Early Christian Church," 401).

Joslyn Gage's fears were well grounded, for the charismatic hit of the council was FRANCES E. WILLARD, conservative head of the WCTU. The Union was an "organized army of mother love" dedicated to placing God in the constitution and prayer in the public schools if they received suffrage. The effect of these women voting threatened to destroy religious freedom in America, she believed.

It was time to face the enemy head on, and so Joslyn Gage formed an antichurch organization, the Woman's National Liberal Union (WNLU). In her last major address, "The Dangers of the Hour," delivered as WNLU president at its founding convention, she identified "church aggression" as the "foremost danger of the day" and took her analysis further than she ever had.

She began with marriage and charged that the church lurked behind the legal oppression of women:

The authority of the church over marriage has always been especially prejudicial to woman; it is from teachings of the church, that in the family, power over the wife is given to the husband. It is the church and not the state, to which the teaching of woman's inferiority is due; it is the church which primally commanded the obedience of woman to man. It is the church which stamps with religious authority the political and domestic degradation of woman. It is the church which has placed itself in opposition to all efforts looking towards her enfranchisement and it has done this under professed divine authority, and wherever we find laws of the state bearing with greater hardship upon woman than upon man, we shall ever find them due to the teachings of the church. (4–5)

This was not a fluke or an accident, but a deliberate policy by the church to maintain its power:

The stronghold of the church has ever been the ignorance and degradation of women. Its control over woman in the two questions of marriage and education have given it keys of power more potent than those of Peter. With her uneducated, without civil or political rights, the church is sure of its authority; but once arouse woman to a disbelief in church teachings regarding her having brought sin into the world; once open to her all avenues of education, so that her teaching of the young in her charge will be of a broader, more scientific character than in the past and the doom of the church is sealed. (6)

Thought control was central to church power: "In order to maintain its authority over mankind it is necessary that the church should control human thought; freedom of the will has ever been its most dangerous foe" (6).

This doctrine of obedience stood in the way of democracy, Joslyn Gage contended:

The modern democratic-republican idea is the right of every individual to his own or her own judgment upon all matters. The centralized-clerical idea is that no person has a right to his or her own judgment upon either religious or political questions. In all that most deeply concerns the individual he or she is to bow to the church, embodied in the priesthood. (11)

With a population raised in fear of challenging the church's authority, "the chief danger of the present situation lies in the fact that the majority of the people do not see that there is a danger" (14).

Heralding the rise of democracy worldwide, U.S. citizens failed to realize that they didn't enjoy it in their own land.

Yes, it is daybreak everywhere; we see its radiance in Europe, in South America, in Africa. Peaceful revolutions are rapidly taking place on two hemispheres, yet just as a dark cloud shadows some parts of the earth even at break of day, heralding a coming storm, so while it is breaking day in many countries, yet over our own beloved land the fell shadow sweeps,—over it falls the pall of a coming storm. Amid so much liberty, people fail to see the gradual encroachments of organized power either in the church or in the state. (14–15)

Joslyn Gage predicted that individual liberty would only come in this country with bloodshed:

The struggle will be fierce and bitter . . . it will be a battle of the liberal element against the church and its dogmas of whatever name or nature. After a time liberty will triumph, and then and not until then shall we see a true Republic upon this soil. As the battle for political liberty began here so will that for full religious liberty end here. The conflict we were sure had gone by will again arise; the decisive battle has yet to be fought. It seems to me when that hour has passed there will be no more church forever, for science and the spirit of free thought will have destroyed its very foundations. (15)

When the speech concluded, it was clear that Joslyn Gage had threatened the status quo more deeply than any other suffragist. Her brilliant analysis of the withering away of the church mirrored Karl Marx's writings on the state. Just as Marx defined the state's function as the maintenance of power by one group over another, she asserted that the function of the church was to maintain male power over women. When woman took her freedom with her own hand, the church would disappear, no longer needed. Ideas this radical find small welcome in the United States. Her mail was intercepted by the government. She believed that she would be jailed under the repressive Comstock acts, as many of her freethinker friends had been.

When it became clear that the merger of the conservative AWSA with the radical NWSA in 1889 insured a middle-class, xenophobic direction for the movement, Joslyn Gage retired from the suffrage organization. But her voice was not silenced; it simply took another form. In probably her most prolific period of writing, she concentrated her attack on the church as the greatest enemy of woman. A contributor to Cady Stanton's *Woman's Bible*, she also published her major work, *Woman, Church and State*, which some recent feminist theorists believe to be the most important tract of the early woman's rights movement.

She paid a heavy price for her far-reaching, visionary analysis. She lost the friendship of her increasingly conservative coworkers in the woman's movement, who ultimately wrote her out of suffrage history. It was not unexpected. "We are battling for the good of those who shall come after us," she wrote in the final editorial of her newspaper; "they, not ourselves, shall enter into the harvest" (*National Citizen and Ballot Box*, October 1881).

SOURCES

Joslyn Gage's papers, gathered by her granddaughter, are available on microfilm from the Schlesinger Library. Her woman's rights scrapbooks, containing some published accounts of her speeches and newspaper clippings of her activities, as well as a sample of her published editorials and news stories, have been microfilmed by the Library of Congress, Rare Books Division, their repository. They represent a researcher's dream and a citation nightmare; most clippings are unidentified. In addition to the newspaper she edited, the *National Citizen and Ballot Box*, 1878–1881, Joslyn Gage wrote extensively for the *Revolution*. The *Woman's Tribune*, the *Sibyl*, the (Boston) *Index*, the (Portland) *New Northwest*, and the (San Francisco) *Golden Age* are also sources for her writings and speeches. Her hometown paper, the *Fayetteville Weekly Recorder*, documents her activities most extensively. The woman's rights clipping file at the Onondaga Historical Association in Syracuse, containing articles from the *Onondaga Standard*, the *New York Tribune*, and a scattering of other Syracuse papers, is a valuable source on her and on the movement. The New York Public Library's Free Thought Collection (housed in the annex), in addition to several of her writings, speeches, and obituaries, provides context for understanding the radical suffrage/Free Thought connection from the 1870s through the turn of the century. The New York City and State Woman Suffrage Collection, Rare Book and Manuscript Library at Columbia University and the Woman's Rights Collection, Rare Books Department, Olin Library, Cornell University, are important sources, as is *Lucifer the Light Bearer*, Moses Harmon's Kansas publication, which also shows her link to the early (pre-Sanger) birth control/body rights movement.

Other suffrage collections to consult are: Elizabeth Boynton Harbert at the Huntington Library, San Marino, California; Clara Bewick Colby at the Wisconsin Historical Society, Madison; Lillie Devereux Blake at the Missouri Historical Society, Columbia, and in the Sophia Smith Collection, Smith College; the Garrison family papers at Sophia Smith; the Robinson/Shattuck and Olympia Brown Papers at the Schlesinger; and the NAWSA collection, Library of Congress.

When Susan B. Anthony burned all of her papers after the completion of her commissioned biography, she destroyed her correspondence from Joslyn Gage. Elizabeth Cady Stanton and her children destroyed papers, doing away with almost all of Joslyn Gage's letters. While in the safekeeping of her daughter in Los Angeles, much of Joslyn Gage's correspondence disappeared during the 1920s. Hence, most of the letters between Joslyn Gage and her coeditors of the first three volumes of the *History of Woman Suffrage* are lost.

Selected Sources

Blake, Katherine Devereux, and Margaret Louise Wallace. *Champion of Women*. New York: Fleming H. Revell Co., 1943.
Brown, Olympia. *Acquaintances, Old and New, Among Reformers*. N.P.:1911.
Gage, Matilda Joslyn, to Lillie Devereux Blake, May 2, 1890, Blake Collection, Missouri Historical Society.
———. *Woman, Church and State*. Intro. Sally Roesch Wagner. 1893; rpt., Watertown, Mass.: Persephone Press, 1980.
Minor v. Happersett, 53 Mo., 58, and 21 Wallace, 162, 1875.
Squire, Belle. *The Woman Movement in America*. Chicago: A. C. McClurg & Co., 1911. (Virtually unrecognized by current historians, this book is a pithy summary of woman suffrage history that retains the passion and spark of the movement.)
Stanton, Elizabeth Cady, and the Revising Committee. *The Woman's Bible*. 2 vols. 1895, 1898. European Publishing ed. Seattle: Coalition Task Force on Women and Religion, 1974.
Wagner, Sally Roesch. *A Time of Protest: Suffragists Challenge the Republic, 1870–1887*. Carmichael, Calif.: Sky Carrier Press, 1988.
———. "That Word is Liberty: A Biography of Matilda Joslyn Gage." Ph. D. diss., University of California, Santa Cruz, 1978.
A Woman of the Century. Eds. Frances Willard and Mary Livermore. Buffalo, N.Y.: Charles Wells Moulton, 1893.

Speeches Cited

Speech of Mrs. M.E.J. Gage at the WRC held at Syracuse, N.Y., September 1852. Woman's Rights Tract No. 7. Syracuse: Master's Print, 1852. *New York Tribune*, September 14, 1852.
"Flag Presentation to the Third Onondaga Regiment." *Onondaga* (Syracuse) *Standard*, September 3, 1862.
"Voting Trial and Tax Protests." *HWS* 2:742–748; *HWS* 3:167–169, 415–416.
"Women Tax Payers; Centennial Letter No. 3." Schlesinger scrapbook.
"Tea and Taxes; Call for December 16, 1873, Mass Meeting." Library of Congress scrapbook.
"The United States on Trial; *not* Susan B. Anthony." *An Account of the Proceedings on the Trial of Susan B. Anthony, on the Charge of Illegal Voting, at the Presidential Election in November 1872*. 1874. New York: Arno Press, 1974, pp. 179–205.
"Memorial of Women Citizens of this Nation." To the Senate and House of Representatives of the United States in Congress Assembled. Arguments, Mrs. Matilda Joslyn Gage of New York. [1875], 3–5. Library of Congress scrapbook.
Centennial speech. (Boston) *New Age*, July 1, 1876.
Address of Mrs. Gage. The Watkins Convention [1878]. Free Thought Collection, New York Public Library.
1886 Statue of Liberty Speech. (Des Moines) *Woman's Standard*, December 1886; *HWS* 4:840; *New York Tribune*, March 25, 1886; *New York Times*, October 28, 1886.
"The Foundation of Sovereignty." *Woman's Tribune*, April 1887.

"Woman in the Early Christian Church." Religious Symposium of the International
    Council of Women, Washington, D.C., March 25, 1888. *Report of the Inter-
    national Council of Women.* Washington, D.C.: Rufus H. Darby, 1888, pp. 400–
    407.
"The Dangers of the Hour." Speech of Matilda Joslyn Gage at the Woman's National
    Liberal Convention, February 24, 1890. 15 pp. Gage Collection, Schlesinger
    Library; *MCSFH* 2:339–370.

FLORENCE KELLEY
(1859–1932), advocate for children, working women, and consumers

KAREN E. ALTMAN

Florence Kelley's achievements during the early decades of the twentieth century spanned industrial, political, and legal reform, but the unwavering focus of her life's work was labor reform for working women and children. Her rhetorical accomplishments included the ability to adapt to widely differing audiences and to analyze social problems, advocate specific solutions, and motivate others to action. Beginning with her bachelor's thesis in 1882 and continuing until her death in 1932, she built a corpus of translations, books, speeches, articles, editorials, organizational reports, social scientific surveys, congressional testimony, radio addresses, book reviews, correspondence, and an autobiography.

Widely recognized for her thirty-three year leadership of the National Consumers' League (NCL), Kelley contributed so much to changing social policy that, twenty years after her death, Supreme Court Justice Felix Frankfurter concluded that she was "a woman who had probably the largest single share in shaping the social history of the United States during the first thirty years of this century" (Goldmark, 1953:v).

Among the many reforms to which Kelley contributed as the voice of the NCL were the Louis Brandeis brief that undergirded *Muller v. Oregon* (1908), the first federal case upholding the constitutionality of protective labor legislation for women; enactment and enforcement of numerous minimum wage, maximum hour, and child labor laws; establishment of the U.S. Children's Bureau; passage of woman suffrage; and arguments, organizations, and networks that transformed much of nineteenth-century philanthropy into the profession of social work.

FORMATIVE EXPERIENCES

Florence Kelley was born and raised in Philadelphia. Her Irish Protestant father William Darrah Kelley was a lawyer and judge who worked with Abraham Lincoln to form the Republican party and capped his career with thirty years service in the U.S. House of Representatives. Her mother Caroline Bartram Bonsall grew up in the Quaker family of Isaac and Elizabeth Pugh, a household that included abolitionist Sarah Pugh. William and Caroline Kelley were the parents of eight children; only Florence and one brother reached adulthood.

Kelley's earliest challenges were illness and loneliness. Her mother was occupied with the sicknesses and deaths of many children; her father was often away for congressional work. She herself spent many years out of school due to illness.

During time spent at her maternal grandparents' home, Kelley absorbed Quaker values along with family commitments to anti-slavery and woman suffrage, especially from great-aunt Sarah Pugh and her friend, LUCRETIA COFFIN MOTT. References to these influences appeared years later. In 1905, in accepting the NAWSA vice-presidency, Kelley claimed: "I was born into this cause. My great-aunt, Sarah Pugh of Philadelphia, attended the meeting in London which led to the first suffrage convention in 1848. My father, William D. Kelley, spoke at the early Washington conventions for years" (*HWS* 5:145).

William Kelley took his young daughter on business trips during which she saw the conditions of factories, the working lives of laboring adults and children, and the neighborhood consequences of industrialization. He talked with her about the benefits and costs of industrial production, but the sight of boys tinier than herself hauling water amid the furnace blasts of steel plants remained etched in her memory. In 1931, at age seventy-one, she spoke to the National Child Labor Committee on a topic very old to her, "The Child and the Machine" (1931).

Kelley's training at Cornell University in languages, literature, rhetoric, and the new social sciences provided an educational base for her later work. The bachelor's degree featured four years of "Rhetoric, General Literature, and Oratory," including elementary rhetoric, composition, diction, elocution, advanced rhetoric, orations, essays, and general literature. She also studied Latin, Anglo-Saxon, French, and German (Mattson, 1956:46–48). As her political, moral, and social interests grew, she became a founding member and officer of the Social Science Club and, with some research on the law, wrote her thesis, "Some Changes in the Legal Status of the Child Since Blackstone" (Blumberg, 1966:24–27; *International Review*, August 1882; NCL Papers). Later, in 1894, she completed a law degree at Northwestern University, which honed skills in legal reasoning that structured much of her later writing and speaking.

In the mid-1880s, Kelley traveled in England investigating manufacturing systems and entered Zurich University, an institution that, unlike most others, accepted female students. There she met European socialists, learned socialist theory, and became involved in socialist politics. She also began a ten-year correspondence with Friedrich Engels, which "is the only example of a long-term exchange between an American and one of the two founders of the Marxist socialist movement" (Blumberg, 1964:103). She returned to the United States imbued with socialist theory and political commitments.

While in Europe, in 1884, Kelley married a Russian socialist physician, Lazare Wischnewetzky. During their six-year marriage, she used his name, but after their divorce, she returned to her birth name; their three children also took the name of Kelley. She was remarkably silent about her married life. The final paragraph of part three of her four-part autobiography said only:

I was, however, not to turn directly from my novitiate in American and European universities to a part in the intellectual life of my generation, nor the political, nor the economic life. Instead, having married a Russian physician, I returned to America in 1886 with him and my elder son, and the ensuing five years were devoted to domestic life. (April 1927, 35)

These sentences are significant for what they omit about the period 1886 to 1891, as seen by Kelley in 1927 when she wrote her life story partly to counter the conservative backlash against her four decades of advocating social change. During those "ensuing five years," she laid the philosophical and rhetorical foundations for her public career; she translated Engels's *The Condition of the Working Class in England in 1844* (1887), which remained the only English version published until 1958 (Sklar, 1985:661); she delivered and published her first significant speech, "The Need of Theoretical Preparation for Philanthropic Work" (1887), which challenged the assumptions underlying philanthropy and set a precedent whereby she would attack and be attacked in return throughout her career; and she crafted "An Address in Memory of Thomas Paine," which integrated socialist theory and practice into the American revolutionary tradition and specified the agenda and rhetorical frame for her life's work.

RHETORICAL BACKGROUND

Kelley's prolific rhetorical career was guided by her sense of purpose and socialist philosophy. She often summarized her guiding purpose in a word: education. Whether in personal letters to Engels or in public statements, she insisted that education was paramount in an industrial world. "Education is a lifelong process of fitting human beings for life in Society, for self-support, for sharing in the conduct of industry, for parenthood, for the fullest responsibility of citizenship, for all noble enjoyment," she declared in lectures to the Teachers' College of Columbia University, published as *Modern Industry in Relation to the Family, Health, Education and Morality* (80). Citizens needed to learn their constitutional rights; legislators, the conditions of laborers and immigrants; and manufacturers, the needs of working women and children.

Furthermore, in "The Working Child," an 1896 address to the National Conference on Charities and Corrections (later, the National Conference on Social Work), Kelley, then chief factory inspector in Illinois, argued for compulsory education despite resistance from manufacturers, department stores, and the telegraph company, all of which widely employed children:

Let us have every child in school every day of the school year, until he or she is sixteen years of age. Let us have manual training all the way up, and technical training the last two years. Let us prohibit employment of all children for wages until they are sixteen years of age, except at farming and gardening. Then, after ten years of rigid enforcement, let us see whether we have not taken an unexpectedly long step in the direction of solving several problems connected with delinquency, the tramp difficulty, and the incompetence of the employed. (2)

In other words, children needed to be schoolchildren, not working children.

Consumers, too, needed education. The "purchasing public" ought to know the health, wage-earning, manufacturing, and distribution conditions under which the products they bought were produced and sold. According to *Some Ethical Gains Through Legislation* (1905):

This great purchasing public, embracing the whole people, which ultimately decides everything, does so, on the whole, blindly, and in a manner injurious to itself, and particularly to that portion of itself which is engaged in production and distribution. (210)

Stressing education of "the whole people" was symptomatic of her guiding social philosophy: evolutionary socialism.

Having studied socialist philosophy in Europe, joined party politics, and translated Engels's book and Karl Marx's 1848 speech "Free Trade," Kelley was well versed in socialism by 1887. But she faced a huge rhetorical task as she began her public life: how to articulate a socialist theory and practice for the United States. Her first major speech, "The Need of Theoretical Preparation for Philanthropic Work," presented to an Association of Collegiate Alumnae meeting, used socialist principles, but they sounded like "foreign ideas" to American ears. As she addressed college-educated women whose main option for meaningful work outside the home was philanthropy, she challenged their assumptions and practices. She defined two kinds of philanthropy, bourgeois and working-class, and she methodically criticized "our bourgeois philanthropy, to which we college graduates are born and bred" as "merely palliative" and a "dogmatic apology for the social system as it is to-day." Instead, she advocated "critical investigation" and "theoretical preparation" for a "true" working-class philanthropy. The speech and its later publication generated much protest in the *Christian Union* (Blumberg, 1966:79–80).

Pivotal to her philosophy was a commitment to evolution of the whole, not revolution. The theories of Marx and Engels posited that the movement of human history involved feudalism giving way to capitalism, capitalism giving way to socialism, and socialism giving way to communism. This grand historical narrative of the human struggle to transform society from control by the powerful, propertied few to the classless, stateless, communal ownership of all wealth included evolutionary and revolutionary strands. Kelley held an evolutionary position that she called "the theory of the development of society, the theory which is to political economy what Darwinian theory is to the natural sciences" ("Need of Theoretical Preparation," 23). Her earliest success at integrating her socialism within the U.S. context occurred in her 1889 oration to Philadelphia's Friendship Liberal League, "An Address in Memory of Thomas Paine." She argued:

Paine's life embraced the period in European history of the dissolution of the old feudal order, the protest against royalty, aristocracy, nobility caste, against inequality and oppression of every kind. It was a time of decaying institutions. . . . The American Revolution came and the American republic arose. The French Revolution followed and feudalism fell, Paine doing a noble share toward bringing about both changes. (1)

This process of dissolution, decay, rise, and fall was, in her eyes, part of a gradual, step-by-step movement: "Hand in hand, step for step, in the progress of conquest and subjugation of the forces of nature, goes the work of centralization and accumulation" of capitalism, the current historical stage (3). After placing her socialist commitments into Paine's tradition, she specified the next tasks to be accomplished "until plutocracy is superseded by Social Democracy":

We must have factory inspection and truant officers. . . . We must have child-labor abolished, and childhood kept sacred to school life. Night work and overwork we must reduce to a minimum for everyone. The places of toil of men and women must be made wholesome; and the hours of labor shortened. (10)

With these words, Kelley publicly dedicated her life to accomplishing this agenda.

Her evolutionary philosophy also guided her arguments more than thirty years later in opposing a federal Equal Rights Amendment. She began an *American Review* article, "Should Women Be Treated Identically with Men by the Law?" this way:

It would be foolish to attempt to give, in 1923, a final or even a fairly complete reply to this question. What the answer may be in the year 2000, who can tell? The transition is so manifold in which we are living, and the space assigned to this discussion so limited, that we can only try to find a workable principle applicable to-day and in the near future. (276)

Hence, she analyzed each social issue and policy according to her overall philosophy rather than as an isolated problem to be resolved piecemeal.

MAJOR ADVOCACIES

Kelley's philosophy enabled her to make sophisticated analyses tailored to U.S. society. Her starting point was the class relationship of wage-laborers and capitalist-owners, from which she worked out multiple levels of analysis. Laborers differed by sex and age; hence, she analyzed working-class relations between laboring women and men and between laboring children and adults. Sex and age analyses resulted in her lifelong fight for legal protection of working women and children because, she argued, neither industrialists nor the newly forming labor unions specifically addressed the wage, health, safety, welfare, and family conditions of women and children. Numerous examples of these analyses are evident from the titles of her earliest writings, "Need Our Working Women Despair?" (1882) and "White Child Slavery" (1889), to much later arguments in the "Progress of Labor Legislation for Women" (1923) and "Challenge of the Working Children" (1930).

On the issue of child labor, Kelley advocated reforms and legislation on a state-by-state basis; only later did she support federal legislation. "The Working Child" began:

There are two ways of dealing with the problem of the working child. One is to prohibit outright the employment of children under sixteen years of age, as Switzerland is doing; the other is the method adopted by all manufacturing countries, including our own, and consists in legislating to keep in the market an abundant supply of child labor while restricting, to some extent, some of the most flagrant abuses which accompany it.

In endless arguments, she compared labor conditions and laws for children state by state. Phrases such as "in New York," "in South Carolina," and "in Pennsylvania" introduced data about the wages, hours, educational failures, and family needs of working children and the legal steps instituted to remedy problems by particular states. She rigorously assessed the costs against the potential benefits of national regulation, illustrated by her 1911 speech, "What Should We Sacrifice to Uniformity?" to the National Child Labor Committee. She predicted: "I think we shall have, by 1920, universally the prohibition of the employment of children under sixteen years of age at night and in dangerous occupations." But she tempered calls for immediate national uniformity with data about state laws, some of which were more favorable to children than others:

Everyone here would agree that it is better for employers to have a uniform pressure of competition and not have ten-year old children working in one state in competition with those of twelve and fourteen and fifteen years in other states; it is better for children to spend their youth in school and at play, and to have leisure in the South as well as in Montana. But we do not wish to arrive at uniformity by sacrificing what has been gained for the children. (27–28)

By 1922, however, she was a leading advocate of the proposed federal child labor amendment, which never succeeded, although its philosophy informed the 1938 Fair Labor Standards Act.

By contrast, on the issue of woman suffrage, Kelley always endorsed a federal amendment. In testimony in 1898, before the Senate committee on woman suffrage, she argued:

[T]he very fact that women now form about one-fifth of the employees in manufacture and commerce in this country has opened a vast field of industrial legislation directly affecting women as wage-earners. The courts in some of the States, notably in Illinois, are taking the position that women cannot be treated as a class apart and legislated for by themselves, as has been done in the factory laws of England and on the continent of Europe, but must abide by that universal freedom of contract which characterizes labor in the United States. This renders the situation of the working woman absolutely anomalous. On the one hand, she is cut off from the protection awarded to her sisters abroad; on the other, she has no such power to defend her interests at the polls, as is the heritage of her brothers at home. This position is untenable, and there can be no pause in the agitation for full political power and responsibility until these are granted to all the women of the nation. (*HWS* 4:313)

Her arguments for woman suffrage turned on the ballot's special potential to change industrial and social conditions for working women and children. At the 1905 NAWSA convention, she urged:

No one in this room to-night can feel free from such participation. The children make our shoes in the shoe factories; they knit our stockings, our knitted underwear in the knitting factories. They spin and weave our cotton underwear in the cotton mills. Children braid straw for our hats, they spin and weave the silk and velvet wherewith we trim our hats. They stamp buckles and metal ornaments of all kinds, as well as pins and hat-pins. Under the sweating system, tiny children make artificial flowers and neckwear for us to buy. They carry bundles of garments from the factories to the tenements, little beasts of burden, robbed of school life that they may work for us.

We do not wish this. We prefer to have our work done by men and women. But we are almost powerless. Not wholly powerless, however, are citizens who enjoy the right of petition. For myself, I shall use this power in every possible way until the right of the ballot is granted, and then I shall continue to use both. (*TWJ*, July 22, 1905:114–115)

Her NAWSA pamphlet on "What Women Might Do with the Ballot" also focused on "The Abolition of Child Labor" (1911).

With the passage of suffrage, however, Kelley strongly opposed a proposed Equal Rights Amendment because of class differences among women. Working women and professionals had differing needs and interests. She argued that the ERA, while beneficial to professional women, would erode the protections for women in industry that had taken decades of intense political and legal battles to secure. She was not willing to forego the hard-earned gains of the many exploited women and children for the greater benefit of professional women already privileged by class. Her 1923 *American Review* article "Should Women Be Treated Identically with Men by the Law?" left no doubt about how she saw the issue:

The query [should women be treated identically with men by the law?] is urgent because a group of extraordinarily active, articulate and well-financed new voters, under the name, The Woman's Party, adopted universal, identical, coercive equality of white women with white men before the law, as their sole and permanent goal. . . . Their dogma finds substantial backing in two quarters, among powerfully organized exploiting employers of women and children, and also, among many women in the professions and the highest salaried ranges of business who desire complete absence of interference by the law.

The answer to our question would, therefore, be Yes! if it were addressed to an audience of writers, teachers, lawyers, doctors, actresses, musicians, singers, dancers, sculptors, painters, highly paid confidential secretaries to business and professional men, and the small minority of women who hold lucrative, responsible positions in business. For these, however, no one wishes to legislate. Compared with the growing millions of women wage-earners, the professional women though articulate and, therefore, disproportionately influential, are exceptions. (276)

A year later in *Good Housekeeping*, she wrote that working women's

oldest, most widespread, and most insistent demands have been for seats, for more adequate wages, and short, firmly-regulated hours. . . . Whenever union men feel no need of laws, well and good. No one wishes to interfere with them any more than professional women are interfered with today by labor legislation. (165)

Her arguments for and against policies were structured according to social analysis of differences among laborers by sex and age and among women by class and race.

Kelley's success in changing industrial conditions and labor legislation began with her appointment as Illinois' chief factory inspector from 1893 to 1897. It continued as she became part of an 1890s consumer movement composed primarily of middle- and upper class, college-educated women. The early movement attempted to channel purchasing power into a force for changing workplace conditions, first in retailing and later in manufacturing, and for improving public health and welfare. The movement began in major industrial centers and became national in 1899 with the formation of the National Consumers' League (Nathan, 1986; Wolfe, 1975).

Kelley was asked to head the NCL, given her extensive background in social reform in Illinois as chief factory inspector, as a lawyer experienced in labor legislation and enforcement, and as a principal researcher and organizer of the *Hull House Maps and Papers* (1895), a social scientific survey of Chicago tenement and working conditions. As its leader, she addressed most of her messages in behalf of children, working women, laboring classes, and the citizenry as a whole. She spoke to local consumer groups as well as to international gatherings of consumer organizations. Her 1916 statement supporting Robert M. LaFollette's "seaman's bill," printed in the appendix of the fifty-third *Congressional Record*, demonstrates that she also spoke in the name of consumers:

The National Consumers' League, at its annual meeting in Buffalo in November 1913, indorsed [*sic*] the La Follette bill, and the writer appeared before the House committee on its behalf. So far as it is possible to learn no other person appeared at any stage of its legislative history to speak in the name of the passengers. (1198)

STRATEGIES AND STYLE

A particular practice fueled much of Kelley's discourse and is a key to her rhetoric: her epideictic impulse. Praise and blame filled her works. When she believed that credit was due, she praised, but frequently she attacked practices, policies, and organizations. Following the controversy aroused by ''The Need of Theoretical Preparation for Philanthropic Work,'' she carefully composed

"An Address in Memory of Thomas Paine." By using epideictic form, she was able to praise Paine and the American revolutionary tradition, blame the generations since Paine who had perverted the founders' democratic values, and enumerate the tasks on which she would work throughout her life. In a prophetic passage, she claimed:

Were Thomas Paine alive to-day, how his pen would flay the slavish, degenerate progeny of the founders of the republic! For he carried his critical thought and his rugged self-dependence in action into every department of life. In politics he was no mere critic, but the hero rich in persistent sacrifice of time, effort, fortune, and that liberty which he held so dear. (7)

For the next forty years, as her pen and tongue flayed opponents, she became the Thomas Paine of her generation.

Her impulse to praise and blame appeared in works not specifically epideictic in form or purpose. An example of praise occurred in "Use and Abuse of Factory Inspection":

Three different times has one inspector of the garment trades followed the path of duty into the sick room where a patient lay ill of malignant diphtheria, while garments in process of manufacture were exposed to the presence of germs of that dreaded disease. Each time that faithful officer contracted diphtheria, carried it home to his family, and twice lost a child of his own by death. This hero of the civic warfare against law-breaking is deputy Factory Inspector Griffin, garment trades inspector of the state of Massachusetts. (138)

Kelley was more likely to blame when engaged in refutation. Speaking in 1924 to the National Woman's party (NWP) about the NCL's objection to the ERA, she attacked them and the amendment:

We object to the new subordination of women for which the words, "Men and women shall have equal rights throughout the United States and all places subject to its jurisdiction," are used as a screen. When last year representatives of the Woman's Party appeared at Albany with the Associated Industries, to delay the passage of bills for a short working day and a minimum wage commission until wage-earning men shall demand for themselves identical measures, they thereby gave notice that what they seek is not the equal right of women to express their own will and conscience according to their own needs as they conceive those needs. That action proclaimed to both men and women that the intent of the Party, whatever its formula may be, is to delay and prevent labor laws for women. This is contrary to the established policy of Labor, both men and women, in the State of New York. And it is contrary to public policy and the general welfare. (2)

No policy or institution was beyond the reach of Kelley's lash, demonstrated by her critique of the Supreme Court. In a 1923 address to the National Con-

ference of Social Work, "Progress of Labor Legislation for Women," she
admonished:

The progress of labor legislation depends upon the personnel of the Supreme Court of
the United States and the social and economic opinions of the judges. The court incarnates
a world-old injustice. It has dealt with the whole people, but it has represented only half
of the people. We have seen two child-labor laws destroyed. No woman had any share
in that destruction, or opportunity to save it. We have seen the minimum-wage laws of
thirteen states endangered by the recent decision. No woman participated in that responsibility. Sooner or later women must be added to the court. The monopoly of the interpretation and administration of the law by men alone can never again be accepted without
criticism and protest. . . . Urgent, therefore, as is the modernizing of the Constitution, the
personnel of the court is the first essential. (115)

Praise and blame were made to serve varied purposes and ends, especially
criticism of past and present social conditions, creating and arousing opponents,
and motivational appeals.

As a keen rhetorical strategist, Kelley used all available means to influence
diverse audiences. In addition to speaking, she wrote extensively and, when
radio became available, she used the airwaves. She published books, articles,
essays, editorials, and reviews in scholarly journals, conference proceedings,
citizens' library collections, trade or union periodicals, popular and women's
magazines, newspapers, and pamphlets (Blumberg, 1966:29–31; Buechler,
1986:133–134; Hayden, 1982:170, 330 n.45). In "How Can We Best Utilize
the Press?," delivered to the 1905 NAWSA Convention, she described one
media strategy:

We all know to our sorrow that women cannot keep out of the papers but the question
is how to get our subject in them in a way to promote it. I can recommend the following
method: Write something in editorial style just about as you want it to appear and send
it to the editor with a deprecatory note to the effect that it is only raw material but perhaps
it could be whipped into an editorial by his able pen. The chances are that the first time
he is hard up for one he will use it—probably beheaded or with the end off or the middle
amputated to show that the editor is editing, but it will be published. (*HWS* 5:132)

Evidence that she was still using this strategy years later surfaced in a *Woman's
Home Companion* (January 1924) editorial opposing the ERA. The front-page
editorial was unsigned. However, in an endnote to "The Equal Rights Amendment" in the *Public Health Nurse* (April 1924), she identified herself as the
author.

Sometimes Kelley turned her writings into speeches; at other times, her writings prompted invitations to speak. At still others, she used the speaker's platform
to present messages that would be revised for publication (Mattson, 1956:215–
218). For example, she described *Some Ethical Gains Through Legislation* as
having "been presented in part to the students of several universities and col-

leges'' (vii); *Modern Industry and Its Relation to the Family, Health, Education, and Morality* began as lectures. She spoke often, sometimes three times a day, to audiences ranging from a few high school students to hundreds attending national conventions of suffragists, businesswomen (e.g., General Federation of Women's Clubs), politicians (e.g., National Republican Club), labor organizations (e.g., AFL), or consumer leagues. She addressed legislators, lawyers, activists, church groups, social workers, and the National Association for the Advancement of Colored People (NAACP).

Kelley consistently used a few basic strategies to adapt to audiences. Her speeches tended to be structured clearly in either a topical or problem-solution format. She often analyzed a problem straightforwardly to lead the audience to a solution and then called for some kind of action (Mattson, 1956). For example, her 1903 ''Use and Abuse of Factory Inspection'' is typical. It defined factory inspection, described its use, abuses, and means of improvement, and concluded with action needed to end abuses.

Another adaptive strategy was identification. Kelley favored the phrase ''speaking as a . . . '' to establish credibility and to identify with audiences. Speaking as a ''lawyer,'' ''grandmother,'' ''factory inspector,'' or ''General Secretary of the National Consumers' League'' enabled her to present herself in different roles. In 1925, she turned use of that phrase into the first third of an address to the National Republican Club. On this occasion, at the height of her work for the child labor amendment, she had become the target of backlash against socialism, unionism, and feminism and was the focus of attacks by manufacturers' associations, conservative politicians, and extreme right-wing women's groups. Under pressure to rally votes, she said:

I speak as General Secretary of the National Consumers' League, which has recently celebrated the twenty-fifth anniversary of its foundation. . . . I speak today, also, as one of the founders and an active member of two national organizations, both exclusively engaged in expediting ratification.

She went on to list twenty-three organizations affiliated with these coalitions, including the American Association of University Women, AFL, Federal Council of Churches, and the national WCTU. She continued her strategy for several more lines, but subverted audience expectations:

And one more word. A charge against the amendment is that it was drafted by three spinsters and a woman who, though married long ago, had never any children. . . . There is a humorous aspect to objecting to a bill drafter because of having no children. I have sons and grandsons (filial and delightful as any mother or grandmother could desire). But though I have had much to do in the past with bill drafting, I have not found the art of drafting among their gifts. And how could grandchildren be expected to help? Has anyone present ever heard of any Senator or Representative, or bill drafter such as many states now regularly employ, being chosen according to the number of his children?

Her strategies also included comparative or analogic reasoning and case studies or examples, which integrated argument and emotional appeal. For example, in her 1914 testimony in behalf of the Children's Bureau, printed in the fifty-first *Congressional Record* (6795–6796), she compared the protection of children working in fish canneries to the protection of scallops in the ocean. She marshalled facts, statistics, and legal precedents to support her positions and brought them to life in narratives of events that she had observed or others had reported to her. Many speeches contained illustrative stories. For instance, she told this story to illustrate preventable dangers in the workplace: In Chicago, at the Stockyards, in 1895, on an August day so hot that three employees died of sunstroke, young immigrant boys were serving as door-openers of the cooling rooms. A boy opening a door for little electric trains carrying sides of beef, was—as the door swung open—exposed to the scorching heat of the outside world. Then, as the train slowly passed him—the door swinging inward—he returned to his post inside the cooling room where icicles hung from the ceiling because that temperature was necessary for the meat. All day long, he oscillated between those extremes of temperature. Cynical, indeed, was the contrast between the provision for the well-being of the beef and the exposure of the immigrant boys to pneumonia or rheumatism! (*Modern Industry*, 57)

Kelley's style was typically direct. Although she had a large vocabulary and wide experience in translation, her speech was plain rather than ornate. She valued brevity over embellishment. She could turn a phrase, but the artistic quality of her discourse varied greatly. Compared to the carefully crafted "An Address in Memory of Thomas Paine" (1889), her later works appear more spontaneous and blunt. Across time or in a single speech, her tone could range from moral outrage and anger to deeply felt compassion to humor.

She used questions variously, frequently as transitions. As an illustration, in *Some Ethical Gains Through Legislation*, she said, "An unfailing test of the ethical standards of a community is the question, 'What citizens are being trained here?' " (4). Questions appear in the titles of her works, for example, "What Shall We Sacrifice to Uniformity?" and "Why Does Congress Let Babies Die?," or structure an entire text, for example, "Twenty Questions about the Federal Amendment Proposed by the National Woman's Party."

Kelley chose her words carefully and occasionally called attention to the importance of word choices or terms. In one annual factory inspector's report, she insisted on replacing "accidents" with "injuries," saying: "Injuries which recur thousands of times for want of adequate safeguards are not 'industrial accidents,' they are industrial injuries" (Mattson, 1956:375). In a 1924 *Woman's Home Companion* editorial on the ERA, she said: "The burning question concerning every proposed amendment to the Constitution is: What exactly do these words mean? In this case the ambiguous word is 'equal.' "

Like many career advocates, she was quick-witted. Responding to a congressman's query after a 1910 speech on woman suffrage, "Do you think that woman is physically and temperamentally fitted to give any return to the Government for any privilege she might have in the exercise of her right as a citizen? '' Kelley retorted:

Yes, I think we have always done it. We pay taxes, we teach the children to obey the laws, we fill their hearts with patriotism, but the principal thing is that we furnish the army at the risk of our own lives. Every time an army has been called for in the United States it has been the sons of American women on the whole who have carried the weapons and every son has been born at the risk of his mother's life. Her service is a very much greater contribution than the two or three years of the son's carrying a gun or perhaps dying of typhoid fever while in the service. (*HWS* 5:307–308)

CONCLUSION

No recordings of Kelley's speeches exist; only the memories of those who heard her remain. In a memorial tribute to the NAACP, her longtime friend Lillian D. Wald summed up her appeal: "[She] often appeared before legislatures to present her case, a ready crusader for just causes, and she knew her facts, which were strengthened by her driving power and her rich and lovely voice (*Congressional Record* 72 [1932]:13177). Josephine Goldmark, another longtime NCL colleague, testified that she

had preeminently the speaker's gift. At her best she was unrivaled. No other man or woman whom I have ever heard so blended knowledge of facts, wit, satire, burning indignation, prophetic denunciation—all poured out at white heat in a voice varying from flute-like tones to deep organ tones. (72)

However varied, hers was always a voice for those least able to speak for themselves.

SOURCES

A major source is the National Consumers' League Records (NCLR), Manuscript Division, Library of Congress, Washington, D.C. Other useful collections are the Nicholas Kelley Papers, New York Public Library; Jane Addams Collection, University of Illinois, Chicago, Library; Jack London Collection, Henry E. Huntington Library, San Marino, California.

Blumberg, Dorothy Rose. " 'Dear Mr. Engels': Unpublished Letters, 1884–1894, of Florence Kelley (-Wischnewetzky) to Friedrich Engels." *Labor History* 5 (1964):103–133.
Engels, Friedrich. *The Condition of the Working Class in England in 1844*. Trans. Florence Kelley Wischnewetzky. New York: J. W. Lovell, 1887; London: George Allen & Unwin, 1892.
Some Ethical Gains Through Legislation. New York: Macmillan, 1905. Ch.2, "The Child, the State and the Nation"; *OW*:98–101.
Modern Industry in Relation to the Family, Health, Education, Morality. New York: Longmans, Green, 1914.

"Notes of Sixty Years." 4 parts. *The Survey.* "My Philadelphia," October 1, 1926;
"When Co-Education was Young," February 1, 1927; "My Novitiate," April
1, 1927; "I Go to Work," June 1, 1927.
Notes of Sixty Years: The Autobiography of Florence Kelley. Ed. Kathryn Kish Sklar.
Chicago: Charles H. Kerr, 1986. Appendix: "The Need of Theoretical Preparation
for Philanthropic Work."

Biographical Sources

Blumberg, Dorothy Rose. *Florence Kelley: The Making of a Social Pioneer.* New York:
August M. Kelley, 1966.
Goldmark, Josephine. *Impatient Crusader.* Urbana: University of Illinois Press, 1953.
Sklar, Kathryn Kish. *Florence Kelley and Women's Political Culture: Doing the Nation's
Work, 1830–1930.* New Haven, Conn.: Yale University Press, forthcoming.
Wade, Louise C. "Kelley, Florence." *NAW* 2:316–319.

Critical Sources

Mattson, Ramona Tomlin. "A Critical Evaluation of Florence Kelley's Speaking on the
Child Labor Issue." Ph.D. diss., University of Iowa, 1956. Appendix: Address,
National Republican Club on the Child Labor Amendment, 1925; "Challenge of
the Working Children," 1930.

Historical Background

Buechler, Steven M. *The Transformation of the Woman Suffrage Movement: The Case
of Illinois, 1850–1920.* New Brunswick, N.J.: Rutgers University Press, 1986.
Cott, Nancy F. *The Grounding of Modern Feminism.* New Haven, Conn.: Yale University
Press, 1987.
Davis, Allen F. *American Heroine: The Life and Legend of Jane Addams.* New York:
Oxford University Press, 1973.
Ginger, Ray. *Altgeld's America.* New York: Funk & Wagnalls, 1958.
Hayden, Dolores. *The Grand Domestic Revolution.* Cambridge, Mass.: MIT Press, 1982.
Lemons, J. Stanley. *The Woman Citizen: Social Feminism in the 1920s.* Urbana: Uni-
versity of Illinois Press, 1973.
Nathan, Maud. *The Story of an Epoch-Making Movement.* 1926. Garland, 1986.
Sklar, Kathryn Kish. "Hull House in the 1890s: A Community of Women Reformers."
Signs 10 (1985):658–677.
Tax, Meredith. *The Rising of Women: Feminist Solidarity and Class Conflict, 1880–
1918.* New York: Monthly Review Press, 1980.
Wolfe, Allis Rosenberg. "Women, Consumerism, and the National Consumers' League
in the Progressive Era, 1900–1923." *Labor History* 16 (1975):378–392.

Chronology of Addresses and Writings

"Need Our Working Women Despair? " *International Review* (November 1882).
"The Need of Theoretical Preparation for Philanthropic Work." New York Association

of Collegiate Alumnae, May 14, 1887. Helen Hiscock Backus. *The Need and the Opportunity for College Trained Women in Philanthropic Work*. New York, 1887, pp. 15–26; Sklar, ed., *Notes*, Appendix, 91–104.

"An Address in Memory of Thomas Paine." Friendship Liberal League, Philadelphia, February 3, 1889. Florence Kelley Wischnewetzky, *Address in Memory of Thomas Paine*. Pittsburgh: Truth Publishing, (n.d.). London Collection.

"White Child Slavery." *Arena* 1 (1889):594–595.

"The Working Child." National Conference on Charities and Correction, Grand Rapids, Michigan, June 7, 1896. Addams Collection.

"Working Woman's Need of the Ballot." U.S. Senate committee hearing on woman suffrage, February 15, 1898. *HWS* 4:311–313.

"Use and Abuse of Factory Inspection." National Conference of Charities and Correction, Atlanta, May 1903. *Proceedings*. Ed. Isabel C. Barrows. Fred J. Heer Press, 1903, pp. 135–138.

"The Young Bread-winners' Need of Women's Enfranchisement." NAWSA Convention, Portland, Oregon, June 28–July 5, 1905. *TWJ*, July 22, 1905:114–115; WT:167.

"What Might Women Do with the Ballot? The Abolition of Child Labor." (NAWSA pamphlet.) New York: Co-Operative Press, [1911].

Four lectures, Teachers' College of Columbia University, 1913. Florence Kelley, *Modern Industry in Relation to the Family, Health, Education, and Morality*. New York: Longman, Green, 1914.

"Progress of Labor Legislation for Women." National Conference of Social Work, Washington, D.C., May 16–23, 1923. Reprint, NCLR

"Remarks to the Woman's Party on the Equal Rights Amendment." Woman's Party meeting, January 19, 1924. Typescript, NCLR

Address, National Republican Club, on the Child Labor Amendment. New York, January 31, 1925. Typescript, NCLR; Mattson, 442–447.

"What Should We Sacrifice to Uniformity? " Address to the National Child Labor Committee. *Uniform Child Labor Laws: Proceedings of the Seventh Annual Conference, Birmingham, Ala*. New York, 1911, pp. 24–30.

"Challenge of the Working Children." Address to the National Consumers League, Philadelphia, November 14–15, 1930. Mattson, 448–451.

"The Child and the Machine." National Child Labor Committee, June 16, 1931. Typescript, NCLR.

PAULINA KELLOGG WRIGHT DAVIS
(1813–1876), activist, organizer, publisher, lecturer

LYNNE DERBYSHIRE

Paulina S. Kellogg Wright Davis played an essential role in the development of the woman's rights movement as an organizer, lecturer, publisher, editor, financial supporter, and first historian of the movement. She is one of those to whom the first volume of *History of Woman Suffrage* is dedicated, along with Mary Wollstonecraft, LUCRETIA COFFIN MOTT, Margaret Fuller, SARAH and ANGELINA GRIMKÉ, and others. Her most significant contributions were organizing and chairing the earliest national woman's rights conventions, publishing the first newspaper dedicated exclusively to woman's rights, and lecturing on anatomy and physiology.

BACKGROUND

Paulina Kellogg Wright Davis's life exemplified the changing role of women in the first half of the nineteenth century, moving from private to public life through involvement in benevolent and reform organizations and activities. Born in what has been called the "burned over district" of New York State (a description stemming from the frequent religious revivals that fueled the fires of the spirit [Cross, 1950:1]), she participated in revival meetings and joined the Presbyterian Church in 1823. Shortly thereafter, according to ELIZABETH CADY STANTON, she was "roused to thought on woman's position by a [church] discussion as to whether women should be permitted to speak and pray in promiscuous assemblies" (*HWS* 1:284).

As a young adult in Utica, New York, she became a leader in reform as a founding member of the Female Anti-Slavery Society, the Female Moral Reform Society, and the Martha Washington Temperance Union. In 1835, she and her first husband, Francis Wright, a Utica, New York, merchant of wealth and position, organized the first anti-slavery convention held in Utica.

Kellogg Wright's first experience in speaking to mixed audiences occurred in the early 1840s when she presided over a joint convention of the Martha Washington Temperance Union and the Washingtonians. Afterward, Abby Kelley Foster described her as "bold as a lion for the truth," and she and her spouse Stephen S. Foster encouraged her to become an agent or lecturer (Kelley Foster to Foster, January 1843, K-FC). Although Kellogg Wright wrote of her desire to lecture on slavery, woman's rights, and physiology, she deferred such activity, citing responsibility for her husband who was ill (Kellogg Wright to Foster, February 27, 1843, K-FC). After her husband's death in January 1845, however, she studied anatomy and physiology; then, for four years, she traveled widely lecturing.

LECTURER

Kellogg Wright Davis's career as a lecturer on anatomy and physiology made a significant contribution to women. She helped to make lecturing a respectable and lucrative profession for women and to open the medical profession to women, and she supplied important information to women regarding their bodies and their health.

Little is known of her early education, but she apparently considered it inadequate. During her first marriage, she had studied anatomy and physiology on her own. Before she began lecturing, Kellogg Wright went to New York City to study and prepare. When barriers obstructed her formal education, she took resourceful action, persuading guards to lock her into libraries and classrooms overnight so that she could study and work with the skeletons and manikins. She also convinced professors to give her private lessons very early in the morning because she was prohibited from taking classes with male students at the regularly scheduled times (Finch, 1853:212).

Kellogg Wright Davis was not the first woman to lecture or even the first to lecture on anatomy and physiology, but she did so successfully. Some who lectured were considered disreputable; others created hostility wherever they went. Even though she was a close friend of the controversial Abby Kelley Foster and an admirer of Mary Neal Gove Nichols, she perceived their weaknesses as role models. She found that "Mrs. Jones [an anti-slavery lecturer] . . . left no prejudice behind her. It was easy to get a hall and an audience where she had been, almost impossible where the others [Kelley Foster and Gove Nichols] had pioneered." She believed it was "a field that could and must be redeemed for women" (Wright Davis to Caroline Healy Dall, September 24, 1855, CHDC).

Apparently, Kellogg Wright Davis did not arouse the antagonism others had engendered but instead helped to make lecturing more acceptable for women (Davis, 1871:31). She had prepared well; she had a thorough knowledge of her materials as well as life-sized color plates and the first *modelle du femme* in this country to illustrate what she said. Although she was generally well received, she told of women who dropped their veils, fled the room, or fainted when they saw the *modelle du femme*, a very lifelike reproduction of internal female anatomy.

Kellogg Wright Davis firmly believed in economic self-sufficiency and equal pay for equal work. According to LUCRETIA COFFIN MOTT, she was "the first woman to claim the right to equal pay with men for her lectures" (Davis, 1871:31). Although she was financially secure, she said that one of her goals in lecturing was to open more professions to women, including lecturing and medicine, in part for economic reasons. Many women who attended her classes later attended medical school and became physicians (Davis, 1871:32).

Kellogg Wright Davis's extant manuscripts on anatomy and physiology and the minutes of the Providence Physiological Society (PPS), which she helped found in 1850, reveal the extent of her knowledge of these subjects and her commitment to sharing her knowledge with others. The minutes mention that she frequently discussed and recommended new books or journal articles, and they note her proposal that the society subscribe to various medical journals. At one meeting she reviewed and recommended two articles from the *Boston Medical Journal*, one advocating the use of ether rather than chloroform for anesthesia (PPS: June 29, 1850). She also proposed creating a library, which she began by donating twenty-two volumes. The Providence group, which had formed after she gave a series of lectures in that city, sponsored an additional lecture series and frequently asked her to lecture as well.

The subjects of her lectures, which were attended by as many as 400 people, included "The Muscular System," "The Structure of the Eye," "The Nervous System," "Reproduction: The Origins of Life," "Pregnancy and the Changes It Causes," and "Diseases and Displacements of the Uterus." According to the PPS minutes, these topics were discussed very explicitly. "Mrs. Davis touched upon several points requiring moral courage with the prevailing ideal of delicacy," noted the secretary (May 22, 1851). She also spoke on dress reform, woman's rights and suffrage, and other social issues, indicating the extent to which she saw moral, social, and physical issues as interdependent. The Tenth Annual Report of the society praises her "sympathy for the moral, social and physical improvement of society" (PPS:3).

Her lectures were a combination of detailed technical information, philosophy, myth, history, religion, and reform. They reveal Kellogg Wright Davis's commitment to woman's rights principles as well as her belief in a pragmatic approach to reform. She considered issues of health and hygiene a responsibility as well as an opportunity for women. In response to an invitation by the *Water-Cure Journal* to advertise her lectures, she wrote:

Women are answerable, in a very large degree, for the imbecilities of disease, mental and bodily, and for the premature deaths prevailing throughout society—for the weakness, wretchedness, and shortness of life—and no one remedy will be radical till reformation of life and practice obtains among our sex, and there is no salvation for them but in knowledge (1 [1846]:29).

Once she had established the responsibilities of women, she offered them the means of fulfilling them: "Wives and mothers would superintend these departments much better by possessing a clear knowledge of them . . . we have a right to know everything that concerns our life and happiness." "Women themselves," she claimed, "to whom the offer of knowledge is made, will scarcely judge themselves incapable of learning, or unworthy of the responsibilities of knowledge" (*Water-Cure Journal* 1 [1846]:29). In her view, issues of anatomy and physiology were an integral part of social ideology (Morantz-Sanchez, 1985:43).

The lectures were usually presented as a series, with "Man Is a Microcosm" the first. In this lecture, Kellogg Wright Davis addressed the religious and social acceptability of her chosen work, lecturing on anatomy and physiology, and attendance by women at such a lecture. She assured the women of her audience that the laws of anatomy and physiology were the laws of God. Indeed, she argued that ignorance of these laws, "if it is not sin, is at least a culpable violation," making them virtually the religious duty of the audience to understand and hers to present them. "The necessity is laid upon me to preach this neglected portion of the bible," she stated (n.p.). In case any doubt remained as to the propriety of her endeavor, she further explained that she believed this to be a domestic reform, and that her dying husband's last injunction to her was that she "be faithful to suffering humanity . . . teaching that the natural laws are as binding as the moral because they originate from the same eternal source" ("Man Is a Microcosm"). In this way, she made her subject and herself acceptable to the audience.

Because the lectures generally were presented as a series, the later lectures did not repeat these defenses for lecturing or attending the lectures. References were made to woman's domestic role and the necessity of acquiring medical knowledge in order to fulfill that role adequately. The lectures follow the format of describing and explaining some part or system of the body, for example, the eye or the nervous system, followed by a discussion of the common problems associated with it and methods of treatment. She stressed the need for women to understand their bodies and take responsibility for their own health and that of their families. However, her reform efforts were not limited to instructing women about their bodies and their health.

WOMAN'S RIGHTS ACTIVIST

Kellogg Wright Davis was one of the earliest activists for woman's rights. She and ERNESTINE POTOWSKI ROSE were the first women to support the New York Married Woman's Property Bill, a measure designed to enable married women to retain inherited property in their own name. During the winter of 1836–1837, she collected thirty signatures on a petition in support of the proposed legislation, while Potowski Rose collected five signatures on a similar petition in another part of the state. However, she recognized that such efforts were not sufficient.

Without the efforts of Kellogg Wright Davis, the yearly national woman's rights conventions held throughout the 1850s might never have occurred. She was one of a group of women who met at the 1850 anti-slavery convention in Boston and decided to issue a call for a woman's rights convention. She is credited with organizing the first National Woman's Rights Convention held in Worcester in 1850 as well as taking primary responsibility for organizing the next two national conventions held at Worcester in 1851 and Syracuse in 1852. She presided over the two Worcester conventions and delivered addresses at all three.

Despite the demands placed on her by her second marriage in April 1849 to

Thomas Davis and the subsequent adoption of two daughters, Kellogg Wright Davis continued to help organize national conventions. She also helped organize and preside over state and regional conventions as a member and frequent chair of the Central Committee, the group responsible for organizing woman's rights activities, until the formation of a national organization after the Civil War. In addition, she participated in the founding of the American Equal Suffrage Association (1866), the New England Woman Suffrage Association, and, with Elizabeth Buffum Chace, was a founder and first president of the Rhode Island Woman Suffrage Association (RIWSA).

She continued to organize and preside at conventions and to promote lobbying and other activities as a member of the national organization. She organized and presided over the second decade celebration, which marked the twenty-year anniversary of the first National WRC at Worcester, Massachusetts. There she delivered the opening address on the history of the movement, which was later published along with the proceedings of the convention. Kellogg Wright Davis was one of the strong supporters of the Washington, D.C., conventions because they enabled the attendees to lobby the Congress, and she financially insured the presence of a full-time lobbyist and organizer in the capital for a time.

Following discussion of the need for a periodical devoted solely to woman's rights at the 1852 National WRC, she worked with Elizabeth Oakes Smith to form a joint stock company to start a paper. When that venture failed, she decided to publish and edit a paper herself (Paulina Wright Davis to Caroline Healy Dall, November 11 and December 18, 1852, CHDC). The *Una* debuted in February 1853, and was published and edited by Kellogg Wright Davis until the end of 1854. One goal of the paper was "to give a correct history of [the woman's rights movement's] progress, and be a faithful exponent of its principles." She hoped to be able to provide stenographic reporters at the conventions, and wrote that she would "endeavor to preserve a correct history, not only of this specific movement, but of the lives of those engaged in it" (*Una* 1, no. 1 [February 1853]:4). For the length of its existence, *Una* extensively covered national and regional conventions, and despite the demise of the paper, she accomplished her goal of maintaining a correct history of the movement. The history of the woman's rights movement that she presented to the 1870 convention became the basis for the first volume of the *History of Woman Suffrage*.

At the 1854 National WRC, Kellogg Wright Davis's proposal that the *Una* become the national organ of the woman's rights movement was discussed but ultimately rejected as inexpedient. Because of ill health and family obligations, she was unable to continue assuming sole responsibility for the paper. In December 1854, a new publisher moved the paper to Boston, and Caroline Healy Dall became co-editor; publication ceased a year later.

At the time the *Revolution*, published by SUSAN B. ANTHONY and edited by ELIZABETH CADY STANTON and Parker Pillsbury, began having serious financial problems, Kellogg Wright Davis became corresponding editor (1869–

1870) and provided financial assistance to ensure that women reformers would continue to have a voice. In 1870, with Kate Stanton of Rhode Island, she attempted publication of another reform paper, the *New World*, which apparently continued for about a year, but there is little information about it. In addition to her work on these papers, she wrote for the *Water-Cure Journal*, the *Liberty Bell*, the *Liberator*, the *New York Tribune*, the *Woman's Advocate*, and *Mc-Dowell's Journal*. She wrote articles, letters to the editor, and engaged in editorial exchanges with, for example, Horace Greeley in the *New York Tribune*.

The woman's rights discourse of Kellogg Wright Davis, like her anatomy and physiology lectures, demonstrated her belief in adapting appropriately to the audience. In her address to the first National WRC, she clearly confronted this perceived need: "A profound expediency, as true to principle as it is careful of success, is, above all things, rare and necessary" (WRC 1850:13). She demonstrated that "a good cause and good intentions alone" did not accomplish the goal, and therefore, she sought "to derive hints and suggestions as to the method and manner of successful advocacy" (WRC 1850:11). Accordingly, she suggested:

[T]he advocates of the right need none the less the wisest and kindest consideration for all the resistance we must encounter, and the most forbearing patience under the injustice and insolence to which we must expose ourselves. And we can help ourselves to much of the prudence and some of the knowledge we shall need, by treating the prejudices of the public as considerately as if they were principles, and the customs of society as if they once had some temporary necessity, and so meet them with the greater force for the claim to respect which we concede to them. (WRC 1850:12)

Kellogg Wright Davis demonstrated in her own speaking style the consideration and forbearance she recommended. She used materials such as history, mythology, and biblical references to support her positions, incorporating them into an argument designed to win assent rather than to provoke confrontation. There was little humor, irony, or sarcasm in her speeches; she saw no humor in what she usually referred to as "the work."

Her attitude of forbearance and consideration for public prejudices extended beyond discourse. In matters of dress, for example, she saw no need to seek confrontation. Regarding the "new costume" or "bloomers," she wrote to Caroline Healy Dall: "I wear it in the most quiet way and no one troubles me in the least. I shall not be confined to it nor yet laughed out of wearing it when I walk, work or ride" (September 1, 1851, CHDC). But when she wrote to ELIZABETH CADY STANTON on wearing the bloomer costume to lecture or to attend conventions, she observed, "If I put on this dress it would cripple my movements in relation to our work at this time and crucify me ere my hour had come" (Leach, 1980:245).

While willing to bow to expediency in terms of style, Kellogg Wright Davis was uncompromising in her adherence to principle. Her basic philosophy was one of equality in human rights, based on natural rights. In her address as chair of the first National Woman's Rights Convention, as in most of her discourse, she relied on natural rights philosophy as her basic premise. She argued: "Equality before the law, and the right of the governed to choose their governors, are established maxims of reformed political science" (WRC 1850:8). Refuting what she believed to be an implicit assumption regarding the inferior social and political position of women, she argued that natural rights did not depend on the ability physically to defend those rights: "The rights and liberties of one human being cannot be made the property of another, though they were redeemed for him or her by the life of that other; for rights cannot be forfeited by way of salvage, and they are in their nature unpurchasable and inalienable" (WRC 1850:10). In her addresses to both the first and second National Woman's Rights Conventions, she spoke not of woman's rights but of human rights. In 1850, she noted:

Nature does not teach that men and women are unequal, but only that they are unlike. . . . I ask only freedom for the natural unfolding of [woman's] powers, the conditions most favorable for her possibilities of growth, and then, I ask that she shall fill the place that she can attain to. (WRC 1850:9)

She clarified further in 1851: "I have said Human Rights, not Woman's Rights, for the relations, wants, duties, and rights of the sexes center upon the same great truth, and are logically, as they are practically, inseparable" (WRC 1851:7).

Her adherence to principle is exemplified by her split with the New England Woman Suffrage Association (NEWSA), forerunner of the AWSA, over the Fifteenth Amendment to the Constitution. NEWSA supported the amendment, which would grant suffrage to all male citizens. Kellogg Wright Davis's philosophy would not permit her to accept the idea that reformers should be content with half a loaf. In a letter to the *Revolution*, she wrote:

I have been trained in that school which taught children that they must do right for right's sake, without hope of reward or fear of punishment, leaving the consequences with the All Wise Ruler of events. Among the early Abolitionists this uncompromising spirit was manifest, and to me was the real gospel. (*HWS* 2:336–337)

She also resigned from the Rhode Island Woman Suffrage Association over their support of the Fifteenth Amendment.

Kellogg Wright Davis once again chose principle over expediency when she was confronted over a resolution she presented at the 1871 NWSA Convention: "Resolved: That the evils, sufferings and disabilities of the women, as well as of men, are social still more than they are political, and that a statement of woman's rights which ignores the right of self-ownership as the first of all rights is insufficient" (*Revolution*, 7, no 24 [June 15, 1871]:7).

She clarified this point, explaining that by advocating self-ownership she was referring to a married woman's right to reject compulsory sexual relations and compulsory maternity. Nonetheless, in the pages of the *New York Tribune*, editor Horace Greeley continued to challenge her either to repudiate this position or accept the label of "free-lover." She responded with a tactic characteristic of her discourse and redefined free love:

Passion, vanity, and convenience are bought and sold in the market, are forced into marriage and compelled into hated relations: but it is time that sensible people learned to use language correctly. Love is an emotion of the heart, founded upon respect, esteem, admiration, and devotion. To be free is to be exempt from the subjugation of the will of one or many, says Webster. I propose to stand upon this line and fight it out, rescuing the words from the base prostitution, and showing that only to the corrupt can corruption be made out of those resolutions. (*Revolution*, 7 no. 24 [June 15, 1871]:6)

Kellogg Wright Davis refused to bow to expediency and refute the free love charge. Rather, she chose, through calm, reasoned argument, to attempt to turn the exchange into an opportunity to clarify her position to those willing to hear it.

She often used logical reasoning, sometimes rather audaciously. For example, in a speech on that same subject in 1852 to the third National Woman's Rights Convention, she argued that the family is the central institution among humans, marriage is the bond of this institution, and the only institution given by God in the innocence of Eden. Therefore, she argued, "correction of [marriage's] abuses is the starting point of all other reforms." Furthermore, woman must be minister of the redemption of marriage, including social, moral, pecuniary, and political issues (WRC 1852:63). For her, the issue of equality in marriage brought together most of the important issues of the woman's rights movement and could not be forsaken.

Kellogg Wright Davis's frequent historical, mythological, and religious references demonstrate the extent to which she believed cultural perceptions of women to be based on the past. She often reinterpreted history, mythology, or religion in order to define or redefine the role of women. In her 1852 address on marriage, for example, she effectively reinterpreted the myth of Pandora to conclude: "It was her destiny to be the occasion of the fall; the instrument of doom; but her fortunes are linked to the resurrection and life, as well as the suffering and death, of the race." She then compared the myth of Pandora to the story of Eve and the serpent and the birth of Christ to Mary: "If she brought death into the world, she brought forth a Son who 'taketh away the sins of the world' " (WRC 1852:57, 58). She presented a compilation of the images of women on which the social perception is based and reinterpreted the compilation to show the wholeness of woman rather than the usual dichotomy. Rather than reject the traditional images, she appropriated them for her own purpose, and, in so doing, used images with which the audience already was familiar. She explained: "These myths, whether received as simple facts, or as poetic fiction, whose oracles always reveal the deepest signification of facts, alike indicate the eminent agency of woman in the fall and rising again of the human image of the divine upon earth'' (WRC 1852:58).

Rarely using anecdotes or personal experience, Kellogg Wright Davis's discourse was usually theoretical and carefully reasoned. As with the Pandora myth, she frequently redefined, reinterpreted, and reshaped concepts already held by her audience. She was usually more concerned with the ''social'' issues—marital disabilities, education, economic opportunities—than with suffrage. In the same speech discussed above, she elaborated the issue of marital disabilities with an uncharacteristic ''series of dissolving views'' meant to reshape the audience's view of the marital relationship. She described the child bride, ''the immolated child [who] saw not, in the ornamental bracelets, the vestige of the handcuff . . . had no clue to the riddle of the ring . . . as the sign of property.'' This was followed by the ''child wife withering away from life,'' the ''married coquette; at once seductive, heartless, and basely unprincipled'' (WRC 1852:60, 61). Marriage, she concluded, ''is only a name, a form without a soul, a bondage, legal and therefore honorable'' (WRC 1852:61). In this series of images she captured the tragedy not only of the unhappiness of the child wife, but also of the woman's loss of the complete human being she might have been. The ''series of dissolving views'' was introduced by a discussion of interrupted education leading to marriage. She claimed that if the child bride ''is ever developed as a woman, it will be through pain and suffering'' (WRC 1852:60). In a foreshadowing of Cady Stanton's ''Solitude of Self,'' she demanded: ''Give her strength, power and ability to stand alone, ere you demand of her duties from which an angel might shrink'' (WRC 1852:61).

CONCLUSION

Despite more than two decades of organizing, reporting on, chairing, attending, and financing conventions, Kellogg Wright Davis disliked conventions and doubted their efficacy in furthering the cause. She believed that writing, lecturing, and interpersonal contact were more useful in obtaining support for the movement. Personally, and on behalf of the central committee, she maintained a vast international correspondence with friends, acquaintances, and those she thought might be useful to the movement for the rights of women. She held parlor meetings everywhere she went and discussed the issues with everyone she met. Her home was always open to travelers, and she encouraged lecturers and agents to come to recuperate, frequently volunteering to help care for children. References to her frequently mention her charm, grace, and sincerity, in addition to her well-informed and able presentation of the issues. Letters in the *History of Woman Suffrage*, as well as those in her papers, testify to her interpersonal influence.

Kellogg Wright Davis was an early and constant advocate for the rights of women, arguing for property rights, educational and employment opportunities, equal pay, and marital equality. Through writing, lecturing, organizing, and interpersonal influence, she helped open the fields of medicine and lecturing to women, enhanced women's property rights, and chronicled as well as advanced the movement for the rights of women.

SOURCES

The Alma Lutz Collection, Vassar College Library, contains the Paulina Wright Davis Papers (PWDP), including holographic copies of seventeen speeches, an early draft and manuscript of *A History of the National Woman's Rights Movement*, and other manuscripts possibly intended for publication. There are also two travel diaries, possibly by a niece who accompanied her to Europe, and a notebook with autobiographical information about her early life.

The Isabella Beecher Hooker Collection (IBHC) at the Stowe-Day Library, Hartford, Connecticut, and the Caroline Healy Dall Collection (CHDC), Massachusetts Historical Society, each contain some three dozen letters written by or referring to Wright Davis.

The American Antiquarian Society (AAS), Worcester, Massachusetts, holds the Kelley-Foster Papers (KFP), with correspondence between Kellogg Wright Davis, Abby Kelley Foster, and Stephen S. Foster and between Kelley Foster and Foster discussing her (K-FC). The AAS also has a collection of nineteenth-century newspapers, including the *Una*, *Revolution*, *Liberator*, *Water-Cure Journal*, *TWJ*, *Woman's Advocate*, *Journal of Moral Reform*, and *McDowall's Journal*.

The papers, including full minutes, of the Providence Physiological Society (PPS) and the Rhode Island Woman Suffrage Association (RIWSA), organizations of which Kellogg Wright Davis was a founder and president, are held by the Rhode Island Historical Society.

Davis, Paulina Wright. *A History of the National Woman's Rights Movement, for Twenty Years, with the Proceedings of the Decade Meeting held at Apollo Hall, October 20, 1870*. New York: Journeymen Printers' Co-operative Association, 1871.

Historical Background

Anthony, Katherine Susan. *Susan B. Anthony: Her Personal History and Her Era*. Garden City, N.Y.: Doubleday, 1954.

Cross, Whitney R. *The Burned Over District: The Social and Intellectual History of Enthusiastic Religion in Western New York*. Ithaca, N.Y.: Cornell University Press, 1950.

Leach, William. *True Love and Perfect Union: The Feminist Reform of Sex and Society*. New York: Basic Books, 1980.

Lutz, Alma. *Created Equal: A Biography of Elizabeth Cady Stanton, 1815–1902*. New York: John Day, 1940.

Morantz-Sanchez, Regina Markell. *Sympathy and Science: Women Physicians in American Medicine*. New York: Oxford University Press, 1985.

Ryan, Mary P. *Cradle of the Middle Class: The Family in Oneida County, New York, 1790–1865*. Cambridge, England: Cambridge University Press, 1981.

Biographical Sources

"The Champions of Woman's Suffrage." *Harper's Bazaar* (June 12, 1869):379.

Elder, William. "Mrs. Wright's Lectures to Ladies on Anatomy, Physiology, and Health." *Water-Cure Journal* 2 (June 1, 1846):11–12.

Finch, Marianne. *An Englishwoman's Experience in America*. London: Richard Bentley, 1853.

Nathan, Amy. "Paulina Wright Davis." Senior honors thesis, Brown University, 1977.

"Paulina Wright Davis." *American Phrenological Journal* 18 (July 1853):11–13.

Stanton, Elizabeth Cady. "Mrs. Paulina Wright Davis." *Daughters of America or Women of the Century*. Ed. Phebe A. Coffin Hanaford. Augusta, Me.: True & Co., 1882.

———. "Reminiscences of Paulina Wright Davis." *HWS* 1:283–289.

Stone, Lucy. "In Memoriam." *TWJ* (September 2, 1876):285.

Wyman, Lillie B. Chace, and Arthur Wyman. *Elizabeth Buffum Chace, 1806–1899*. 2 vols. Boston: W. B. Clarke, 1914.

Critical Studies

Conrad, Susan Phinney. *Perish the Thought: Intellectual Women in Romantic America, 1830–1860*. New York: Oxford University Press, 1976.

O'Connor, Lillian. *Pioneer Women Orators: Rhetoric in the Ante-Bellum Reform Movement*. New York: Columbia University Press, 1954.

Phillips, Brenda D. "The Decade Of Origin: Resource Mobilization and Women's Rights in the 1850s." Ph.D. diss., Ohio State University, 1985. AAC 8510624

Steiner, Linda Clair. "The Women's Suffrage Press, 1850–1900: A Critical Analysis." Ph.D. diss., University of Illinois, Urbana-Champaign, 1979. AAC 8009181

Thompson, Eleanor Wolf. *Education For Ladies. 1830–1860: Ideas on Education in Magazines for Women*. New York: King's Cross, 1947.

Tonn, Mari Boor. "The *Una*, 1853–1855: The Premiere of the Woman's Rights Press." *A Voice of Their Own: The Woman Suffrage Press, 1840–1910*. Ed. Martha Solomon. Tuscaloosa: University of Alabama Press, 1991, pp. 48–70.

Chronology of Speeches

Address of the Chair, On Human Rights and Wrongs. October 23, 1850; National WRC Held at Worcester, October 23 and 24, 1850, *Proceedings*. New York: Boston: Prentiss & Sawyer, 1851, pp. 6–13. Holographic, PWDP.

Address of the Chair, Progress of the Movement, October 15, 1851; Report on the Education of Females, October 16, 1851; [second] National WRC, held at Worcester, October 15, 16, 1851. *Proceedings*. New York: Fowler & Wells, 1852, pp. 6–10; 77–89; *Una* (September 1853):360–362.

Address on Marriage, September 8, 1852; extracts, *Proceedings of the [third] Woman's Rights Convention held at Syracuse on September 8, 9, & 10, 1852*. Syracuse: J. E. Masters, 1852, pp. 56–63; *Liberator* 22 (October 1, 1852):76; *HWS* 1:533–535.

Remarks on the Bread Problem: Business and Professional Avocations, WRC, New York

City, Broadway Tabernacle, September 6 & 7, 1853. *Una* (September 1853):136–138.

History of the National Woman's Rights Movement for Twenty Years, WRC, Apollo Hall, New York City, October 20, 21, 1870. Davis, *A History*, pp. 6–31.

Holographic texts found in PWDP: "Mental Development"; "Nervous System"; "The Eye"; "Man Is a Microcosm"; "History of the Movement Since 1829"; Speech, Rhode Island Woman Suffrage Convention, 1869; "On the Renting of a Hall for Woman's Rights Meetings, 1870"; "Women's Rights"; "Despotism and Democracy."

CARRIE LANE CHAPMAN CATT
(1859–1947), leadership for woman suffrage and peace

DAVID S. BIRDSELL

Carrie Lane Chapman Catt's rhetorical career stretched from the late 1880s to shortly before her death in 1947. Though best known as president of NAWSA, first as SUSAN B. ANTHONY's successor, 1900–1904 and then from 1916 through ratification of the Nineteenth Amendment in 1920, she was also an early advocate of international woman suffrage efforts and, after 1920, a prominent peace activist. A second-generation suffragist, she inherited a powerful rhetorical tradition but a small power base. By 1904, only four states had full woman suffrage. A pragmatist, she devoted herself as chair of NAWSA's National Organization Committee and as president to political organization, first of the various state campaigns and then, from 1916 on, of the national amendment struggle (Fowler, 1986:105–154). Concern for organization also figured prominently in her peace work, for example, "What Shall We Do About War?" (December 8, 1936), but here she used rhetorical means that differed notably from her efforts as a suffragist.

Lane Catt was an indefatigable speaker. For a dissertation on her oratorical career, Ima Fuchs Clevenger collected full or partial texts of 723 speeches from 185 speaking tours (61). Many other speeches were given but not recorded (Peck, 1944; HWS 4:213). She also wrote extensively for the *Woman's Journal*, the *Woman Citizen*, and other publications. Sheer volume makes impractical a piece-by-piece review of her rhetoric. Instead, I present an overview of her rhetorical practice, followed by analysis of her suffrage speeches, emphasizing her arguments and style, with particular attention to matters that have received little stress in earlier studies. Finally, I analyze her peace rhetoric, emphasizing its sometimes radical departures from her earlier work.

OVERVIEW OF HER RHETORIC

Lane Catt understood speechmaking as an effective tool. She did not consider herself an expert speaker and rarely spoke to entertain (Clevenger, 1955:61–62). When asked to describe herself as a speaker, she told a story from an 1895 tour through the South that she made with Susan B. Anthony. After one speech, Lane Catt was bitterly disappointed with her performance.

When we went to the place at which we were staying, I asked Miss Anthony if she ever felt that she had made so bad a speech that she never wanted to make another for that was the way I felt. She replied: "Why, I always feel that way." In a few moments she came to me and said: "After I thought about it a little, I concluded that poor speeches were better than no speeches at all, so I have gone right on." That was really the philosophy of my speeches. I think I was better than nobody at all, but I never thought there was anything in my experience that could teach a Department in Public Speaking how to do it. (Catt to Clevenger, July 19, 1940, Clevenger, 1955:77; "Inheritance of the Woman Movement," April 14, 1938)

Nonetheless, she spent a great deal of time on the stump and was well received by audiences. Clearly, her poor opinion of her ability had little relationship to audience response and critical reaction (Clevenger, 1955: 74–76; Peck, 1944).

Lane Catt spoke to a wide variety of audiences in equally diverse situations. In late 1887, she earned a living as a professional lecturer speaking to genteel audiences in Iowa (Peck, 1944:46, 47; Van Voris, 1987:15). Three years later in South Dakota, during her first statewide suffrage campaign, she spoke in grain elevators and one-room prairie cottages, often after hours of uncomfortable travel (Peck, 1944:61–65). At the height of her prominence, she addressed members of Congress, European royalty, radio audiences, and international conventions. Though varied, these audiences rarely prompted major shifts in style or argument (Clevenger, 1955:100, 301). In an interview with Fuchs Clevenger, she explained that woman suffrage was a topic that demanded consistent treatment.

On campaign tours I felt that my audiences were rather similar in type; as a result I used the same subject matter on so many occasions that I tired of the extreme monotony. Often I wished that the purpose could vary more; that the material could be changed; and that the level could be raised; but I felt that I must work at all times with one motive, "To convert people to suffrage"; and that this one purpose did not permit a new presentation. (70)

Accordingly, the vast majority of her speeches were deliberate, straightforward, and logical, with little save the character of the immediate circumstances to distinguish those of any given period one from another.

Her hectic schedule encouraged an economical approach to crafting her speeches. Although her most important addresses were written, many more were extemporized from brief notes, which allowed her to use a single detailed presentation as material for several speeches (Clevenger, 1955:70). Many otherwise complete texts contain numerous references to stories whose details were provided orally (e.g., "The Bible and Woman Suffrage," 18, 23).

Although she often spoke extemporaneously, Lane Catt cared deeply about speaking and was keenly sensitive to the importance of making a good impression. As an Iowa State College student, she refused to accept rules that limited women to reading prepared essays while men could engage in debate and impromptu speaking; she insisted that women receive the same training as the men (Van Voris, 1987:8). She put her debate experience to good use in the suffrage cause. In 1903, she held a two-day debate with New York cleric Lyman Abbott. Confidently, she wrote to Anthony, "our two meetings were a fine climax and certainly the moral effect of Brother Lyman was quite overcome. He is as blind as a bat to the real situation, but I hope he will keep on, for he is a great help to us'' (n.d., quoted in Van Voris, 1987:58). In other words, speaking was important because of its practical value to the movement.

Furthermore, she saw popular reaction to women's speaking as an index of movement success. In "The Happenings of Eighty Years," delivered on her eightieth birthday in 1939, Lane Catt recalled:

Lucy Stone told me, when aged about seventy-five, that she, who came much later [than Abby Kelley], often had eggs thrown at her, but she added, "I never had any bad eggs as Abby Kelley had." So free speech for women moved forward through the prayerful opposition of earnest clergymen to the ferocity of wild mobs and through bad eggs to good eggs, and from good eggs to no eggs, and came out an established liberty. Let me say for myself that I have held office in a suffrage organization—local, state, national and international—without a break for fifty-four years and during that time I have visited and spoken in all the states, yet I have never seen a mob nor an egg thrown nor a meeting broken up. (20–21)

As a powerful tool for suffrage, a benchmark of progress, and a fundamental right, she valued her abilities as a public speaker.

SUFFRAGE RHETORIC

Examination of only complete speech texts in the Carrie Chapman Catt Papers, New York Public Library, reveals that her suffrage rhetoric was strongly logical. This quality was emphasized by contemporaries and later analysts alike (Clevenger, 1955:72, 301; *MCSFH* 1:164–171; Young and Immel in Clevenger, 1955:72–73). After a speech at the May Festival of the Massachusetts Suffrage Association in 1900, the *Boston Globe* wrote admiringly:

Hers is finished speech. There isn't much left to talk about when she gets through. There is never a slip of the tongue, no hesitancy, and her arguments are piled one on another like the charge of a judge to the jury. The effect is irresistible. . . . And her stage presence is perfect, with a splendid voice to crown it all. (Peck, 1944:114)

Her reasoned approach to speaking reflected her underlying beliefs. Lane Catt became a devotee of Herbert Spencer's Social Darwinism while she was still a student at Ames. She believed throughout her life that humankind was destined to evolve not just biologically, but socially and spiritually as well (Fowler, 1986:56–60; Peck, 1944:34; Van Voris, 1987:9, 30, 185). Her stress on the need for organization and fortitude, the susceptibility of government to reform, and the inevitability of victory are best understood as outgrowths of her evolutionist beliefs. Logical organization was apt because, in most respects, she understood herself to be a proponent of scientifically verifiable, logically entailed ideas.

Despite her use of logic, as the *Boston Globe* review suggests, Lane Catt was a powerful speaker who excited emotion. She made masterful and abundant use of narratives, some hardly more than vignettes, as examples of oppression and injustice. She devoted herself to inspiring listeners, even badgering or prodding them to action. As she said of sex prejudice, "neither logic nor common sense can dislodge it" (1902 President's Address, 13). Her speeches combined narrative, logic, and practical advice with an unshakable faith in human progress, allowing her to transcend ideological differences among her supporters and lead the successful national amendment campaign. She was aware of what she was doing, and time after time combined logic, narrative, and inspirational appeal to keep the movement from fragmenting.

She frequently opened speeches with a claim, which she then examined, drawing implications for suffrage in particular and woman's rights in general. For example, "The American Sovereign" (also "The Symbol of Liberty," Van Voris, 1987:19), with which she made her speaking debut at the 1890 NAWSA national convention, began much as a school exercise with a discussion of what different forms of government have held to be the common good, followed by the conclusion: "They have all declared that government will most nearly approach the perfect and ideal, which gives to all its citizens the strongest possible inducement to be virtuous, honest and law abiding" (59). The United States is judged to have fallen short because it denies the benefits of citizenship to its women. This deductive arrangement allows her to prove her claim against the government while calling for a good deal of supporting evidence, much of which stokes the fires of suffragist sentiment.

Lane Catt also used logic to narrow the range of opposing argument. "What Shall We Do About War?" (1936) used suffrage history to show how a public movement could defeat irrationality. She said that woman suffrage was inevitable from the beginning

[b]ecause our Republic was founded upon the voice of a majority of the people. Therefore, the only logical argument for excluding women was the claim that women were not people or, being people, they lacked the qualities which made other people capable as voters and these were, in fact, the two arguments upon which the case was founded at the first and finished at the last. With these two advantages, how long was it from the date when organized women started their campaign to the end? Exactly 72 years or 2 1/2 generations. (4)

By collecting all the anti-suffragist arguments under two implausible claims, she increased her inventional flexibility and put her opponents on the defensive. She also expressed her faith that logical necessity would, in time, be followed by practical victories.

The consistency of her logical case lent force to arguments that were not, in themselves, strictly rational. Lane Catt often demonized anti-suffragists as irrational, drunken, coopted, or even criminal. In a 1915 speech to a congressional committee, she said that the New York suffrage referendum had failed because "All the unscrupulous men of our State worked and voted against woman suffrage, and they were aided and abetted by the weak-minded and the illiterate, for both are permitted to vote in New York'' (5). Appearing before the House Judiciary Committee (February 16, 1904), she said that "the more ignorant a man is the more sure is he that a woman does not know enough to vote, and the more evil is he the more sure is he that a woman's character can not stand the strain of enfranchisement'' (19). These fierce denunciations of opposition votes resonated differently as parts of a logical case than they would as independent imputations. By denying the logic of anti-suffrage, she could indict opponents without appearing unreasonable; their incapacity as well as their intransigence was implied in the form of the argument.

She buttressed rational arguments with brief examples that supported and extended the force of her claims. The stories were evidence, instances of the oppression she alleged, proof of woman's capacity to achieve, proof of the chicanery by which a given referendum had been stolen. Moreover, they personalized injustices, inviting listeners to identify with suffering women.

Lane Catt was a woman of her time, and one of her favorite themes in the 1890s was the injustice of granting suffrage to Native Americans and immigrants while denying voting rights to women (Van Voris, 1987:16). This argument was questionable then as appealing to the worst impulses in her audiences, and today it would be seen as racist. Her stories of unqualified Sioux voters who shared neither language nor culture with white Americans emphasized her sense of the deep insult to U.S. womanhood. "Subject and Sovereign" details the differing populations of

two twin prairies, alike in fertility, in resources and climate. Both are occupied by a wronged and defrauded class. On the East side, the women just being freed from the thralldom the customs of centuries have imposed upon them. On the West side, the Indians just emerging from the darkness of Savagery. (12)

Clearly, the greater fraud was on the east side of the river because the Sioux were offered citizenship and the vote in return for their cooperation with white legal authorities.

The new provision was the promise of the government to give to each Sioux who would receipt [sic] these gifts as conditions, that sacred right and privilege we call the American ballot. It was the climax reached by 400 years of constant experiment—the last effort of a discouraged government, to win this people to peace and civilization. . . . Scarcely had the 300 who at first signed the treaty agreed to its provisions than the ghost dance came in fashion and the great majority of this newly enfranchised tribe joined in its fantasies. The U.S. troops were again called out at great expense in order that the honest settlers on the East Side of the River might be protected from the depridations [sic] of these insane and unreasoning voters on the West Side. This is the pedigree of the Sioux. It is not prejudice, no illiberal anti-Indian sentiment. It is the calm and unbiased testimony of authentic history. (6, 20)

While the Sioux had demonstrated their "unsuitability" for the ballot, women had proved their fitness many times over.

I dare say there is no territory in the U.S. where in proportion to the population there are so many women farmers as in that tract lying along the East side of the Missouri River. There are young maids and old maids, widows with and without children, but in accord with the homestead law, of course the [*sic*] were all unmarried women. . . . At one time I rode for many miles out into the country from the village of Pukivalla. We stopped at every farm and every farm was owned and cultivated by an American woman. I saw houses and barns and every nail in them had been driven by women. I saw a genteel cottage with an amazing red roof and porch and the stylish looking dressmaker who lived there assured me she painted it roof and all. (11, 10)

After contrasting the "savage" Indians and "civilized" women, she turned to anti-suffrage arguments: that women were incapable of fending for themselves and, hence, were undeserving of the vote; that women did not want the vote; that women were not intelligent enough to merit the vote. In each instance, she observed that, by every traditional measure, the women in the Dakotas were more qualified to vote than the Sioux who already did.

By turning her facts about the settlement of South Dakota into a story about the treatment of two groups, Lane Catt offered her listeners a concrete way to understand her principal points. The story plainly paralleled the arguments, but did not rely on them. In her account, the women are "civilized" and "domesticated"; they have nice homes and care about being "stylish." Their rugged competence is acknowledged quietly, without compromising their traditional womanhood. As women alone in a perilous environment, they were likely to arouse sympathy.

Lane Catt used the theme of women deserted later in the same speech. Pasted onto page 43 of the manuscript is a printed story of a "little waif" who is dying and asks the minister how Jesus will see him in the throng. The minister tells him to hold his hand up over his head, then tucks the boy in for the night. When the minister returns in the morning, the child is dead, his hand high above his head. She commented:

With a faith as absolute and as pitiful, millions of good women all over our land have been holding up their hands whenever any moral question has been before our people, but our political divinity has neither seen nor counted them. Every woman here tonight prays; if she doesn't pray in the orthodox way upon her knees, she prays anyway, for after all a prayer is only an earnest desire of the heart. So it is that every woman prays, and she prays for better conditions for temperance and purity and morality, for better and higher manhood and womanhood, but the political divinity who hears and answers prayers does not listen. (44)

In this passage, she reconciled the "factual" story of the Dakota women with a sentimental moral vignette and her sense that women need to stop quiet prayer and move into active campaigning for the vote. The stories illustrate, far more effectively than logical assertion, the difficulties of waiting.

An ardent advocate of organization from the time of her first state campaign,

she devoted herself even more intensively to organizational issues during her
second term as president of NAWSA (Fowler, 1986:137–154; Van Voris,
1987:115–165). She was convinced that a federal amendment was the only
reasonable strategy—''any other policy than this is weak, inefficient, illogical,
silly, insane, and ridiculous'' (''A National Survey,'' 5)—and that the amendment's success depended on NAWSA's ability to capitalize on the unique opportunities provided by World War I. Accordingly, her speeches after 1915 often
emphasized hard work and the necessity of immediate action. This was a delicate
period for Lane Catt and the NAWSA. Many suffragists, for example, LAURA
CLAY and Kate Gordon, felt that the federal amendment campaign compromised
their positions in the states and on states' rights in general (*IWSM*:163–218; Van
Voris, 1987:159–169). Furthermore, the war raised difficult issues. Many suffragists—including Lane Catt—sympathized with the pacifist movement. Some,
particularly during the early years of the war, actively opposed U.S. involvement.
On the other hand, protest risked creating the impression that suffragists were
unpatriotic and reinforced the longstanding anti-suffragist claim that women
should not vote because they could not and would not fight. She treated the war
as an opportunity for women, subordinating her own antiwar sentiment to the
needs of the movement and insisting on a patriotic profile for NAWSA. In
reaction, the Woman's Peace party stripped her of office, which she used as an
excuse to sever all relations with it (Van Voris, 1987:126–127, 138).

Lane Catt's overall rhetorical strategy was indicated in her major speech of
this period, ''The Crisis,'' delivered at the 1916 Atlantic City NAWSA convention in which she attempted to convey her sense of urgency, opportunity,
and mission. ''A crisis,'' she explained, ''is a culmination of events which calls
for new considerations and new decisions. A failure to answer the call may mean
an opportunity lost, a possible victory postponed'' (1). Postponement was un-
thinkable because circumstance and the movement's own successes had opened
a unique opportunity; ''the opposition to woman suffrage in our own country
has slowly disintegrated before the increasing strength of our movement'' (12).
Even so, much suffrage work remained to be done. Women could not afford to
wait for victory, because

[b]efore the vote is won, there must and will be a gigantic final conflict between the
forces of progress, righteousness and democracy and the forces of ignorance, evil and
reaction. That struggle may be postponed, but it cannot be evaded or avoided. There is
no question as to which side will be the victor. (17)

While reformulating the terms of conflict, her message also demanded effort.
''Behind us, in front of us, everywhere about us are suffragists,—millions of
them, but inactive and silent. They have been 'agitated and educated' and are
with us in belief,'' but they are quiescent (17).

The inspirational theme of ''The Crisis''—a major address that received much
public attention—was translated into pragmatic action in less prominent speeches

to the membership. The problem of the 1916–1920 amendment drive was pre-figured in 1915 when Lane Catt identified "apathy and indifference rather than opposition [as] the condition to be overcome" (Empire State Campaign Committee Report, 6). In a speech to the 1917 New York state suffrage convention, she applauded effort and condemned sloth. Consistent with the apocalyptic themes of "The Crisis," she cast work as a spiritual exercise: "You know nobody ever died and nobody ever broke down and nobody ever gave out or retired because of overwork. When people fall by the way it is a sign that the spirit is sick" (1). She spoke to different levels of the suffragist hierarchy. To Assembly leaders, she said:

Your captains are not perfect, because you are not perfect and God has never made anybody yet who was. So go to your captain, bear with her shortcomings if she has them, try to help her where she is weak, and remember that while she may not be doing perfect work, she is going to do better work, and with your aid she will do all that is needful. (3)

Lane Catt's inspirational message was complex. A leader who had long counseled patience, she recast the suffrage effort as an immediate battle rather than a long-term struggle. In a passage portending more recent theories of the stages of social movements, she insisted that "The object of the life of an organized movement is to secure its aim. Necessarily, it must obey the law of evolution and pass through the stages of agitation and education and finally through the stage of realization." By situating the struggle in its last phase and evoking battle metaphors for its conduct, she coopted contemporary war rhetoric and called for a new level of commitment and loyalty from NAWSA members in a final conflict between the forces of good and evil. Not content to let those abstract values stand on their own, she provided workers at every level with a program and an organizational philosophy. The combination of strategies not only inspired suffragists to work harder but also quelled dissension over goals and strategies. In these speeches, she spoke with an authority unusual for the president of NAWSA; she led the army of woman's millennium.

Of obvious interest for the light they shed on the life of a great suffrage leader and the most important of the suffrage organizations, Lane Catt's speeches are also of value for their contributions to the broader sweep of feminist thought. Of particular interest is her version of the expediency argument in favor of woman suffrage, one of the two principal justifications for suffrage (*IWSM*:43–75).

The expediency argument, broadly construed, holds that because men and women are different, both need to be represented in politics. As the sex more "naturally" interested in children and the home, more inclined toward mercy and forgiveness, women could have a salutary effect on national policy by voting *as women*. Their concerns were held by exponents of expediency to offer the prospect of improved child labor laws, a lessened risk of war, and better education policy, among others.

Aileen Kraditor discerns a gradual shift from early emphasis on natural rights to greater stress on expediency arguments (*IWSM*:43–75). She notes that these arguments tend to clash, particularly as vitiated versions of natural rights became increasingly common with the influx of large immigrant populations (52–53). Many woman suffragists held that voting restrictions might well be justified in the case of unlettered immigrants. Lane Catt relentlessly exploited the immigrant vote but in ways that modified the contradictions between these arguments.

In "The American Sovereign," Lane Catt characterized immigrants as a threat to good government, a dubious claim as noted earlier. "The gates of our Nationality are opened wide and through them into every port there comes marching an army thousands strong" (72). She saw this as a sickly army, coming from those areas "where poverty is greatest and intelligence is least" (74). She claimed not to object to the immigrant per se, for "America is generous. It may be she is amply able to build asylums for Europe's unfortunates, penetentiaries [*sic*] for her criminals, almshouses for her poor" (77). Her fear was the cooptation of government by bosses who would rule through purchased votes of these enfeebled new citizens. "The political boss," she said, "has come to be the great autocrat in America. By means of his well disciplined armies of hired and controlled voters, he holds unchallenged sway over the greatest of nations" (69). She herself underlined the term *expediency* in proposing her solution. "Cheap as the American ballot has become, women have asked in vain to share its privileges with men. They have asked it on grounds of reason, of common sense, of justice of chivalry. They now come asking it on the grounds of *expediency*" (85).

[I]t is only by the introduction into each political party of enough intelligence and patriotism to outvote this slum influence—an element whose vote and influence must be bid for in platforms and at the polls, exactly as today parties bid for this controlled vote— an element that shall have in its heart the purification of American politics and the perpetuity of the Republic. Where shall we find it? In American women. (85–86)

She then adduced figures from the U.S. Census to prove her point about the potential nativist power of the women's ballot.

Lane Catt was careful to mitigate the impression that she was against enfranchising the foreign born per se.

Do not misunderstand me. There are still good people among these immigrants. Men and women whom America gladly welcomes. She still has need of every honest brain and honest muscle; but the fact remains that every year we are receiving fewer good people and more of the slum element. (75)

She responded to the possibility that immigrants might be in the audience: "If there is any man, or woman of foreign birth here, who thinks I am making war upon foreigners, let him not mistake my meaning. A German vote, an Irish vote is as good as an American vote when they are honest votes'' (81). Though a weak defense of her position practically, the qualification of her nativism was important with respect to her expediency argument. U.S. institutions were not in danger from the foreign born, but because of ''the slum element,'' which posed a threat only when controlled by bosses. In other words, experience and behavior are the indices of virtue and of action. This was the same argument that she brought to the character of women.

She did not feature women as inherent bastions of virtue, but as people who experienced life differently from men. In a 1916 speech in Harrisburg, Pennsylvania, she told a story from a Massachusetts' suffrage campaign:

In Boston, I am told, that there is a perfumer, an Italian, a foreigner if you please, and he carried in his window all the way through the [suffrage] campaign a placard and on . . . it was announced that ''Men know all there is to be known about a great many subjects; women know all there is to be known about other subjects; men and women together know all there is to be known about all subjects.'' And, so it is true as the Italian tells us that no government is a government of the people if it does not put into the ballot box all the wisdom of all the people. (5)

The source of this wisdom invoked as evidence was an immigrant. The differences between men and women were not argued as inherent differences, but as differences in the things they know.

This sort of expediency argument does not run afoul of the natural rights argument quite so directly as do versions that argue that men and women are inherently different, nor does her nativism pose as clear a contradiction to the rationale for universal voting privileges. By rooting difference in perspective, not inherency, Lane Catt preserves a traditional ground for fundamental equality. Furthermore, by arguing that immigrants are not bad voters, but susceptible to influences that make them bad voters, she makes her principal distinction the character of the vote—''honest'' votes versus ''dishonest'' votes—rather than the character of the voter. Although this concern was not turned into a fully reasoned position early in her career, she developed a powerful argument for nonpartisan voter education and was a guiding influence in the League of Women Voters.

Her speeches show a variant of the expediency argument that broadens an understanding of what such argument might have meant. They also suggest a direct line of thought from her early, unabashed nativism to the internationalism and voter education she espoused later. They illustrate a version of inherency that was highly functional in terms of the rhetorical situation she faced during much of her career. By arguing that women were different by virtue of their experience, she could safely claim that they might know more about the home and about women's legal issues without having to concede to anti-suffragists that they were incapable of coming to terms with issues traditionally thought of as men's concerns.

Lane Catt played a vital role in the enfranchisement of U.S. women. However, an equally important figure in that process was Alice Paul, who headed what became the National Woman's party after her break with NAWSA over strategies to achieve the vote. Paul's clever use of agitation made Lane Catt's skillful organization of suffragists even more effective (*MCSFH* 1:171–177). Both, of course, built the final effort for passage and ratification of a federal amendment on the persuasive efforts of past woman's rights advocates.

ANTIWAR RHETORIC

After ratification of the woman suffrage amendment in 1920, Lane Catt devoted the bulk of her efforts to promoting world peace. She felt that humankind's "natural" evolution would eventually bring about peace, and she expected women's enfranchisement to quicken the pace. Still, she was unwilling to leave that process to chance, insisting that "evolvers" like herself needed to bring the cause to the world's attention ("Baccalaureate Address," 4). As with suffrage, much of her attention was devoted to organizing peace efforts. Yet there are important differences between the highly structured vision advanced during her years with NAWSA and the more individualistic action she championed in the campaign for peace. She was a principal organizer of the Conference on the Cause and Cure of War (CCCW), which sponsored sophisticated discussions of the reasons for war and practical programs to achieve its elimination (Katz, 1973:124; Van Voris 1987:198–210). However, she did not operate in it in the same way that she had in NAWSA or IWSA. Peace work was more loosely organized, the prospects for political effectiveness were less secure, and, most important, there were fewer peace advocates. In contrast to suffrage, she felt freer to insert her own thinking into her peace rhetoric rather than follow the precedents set by earlier advocates.

Though similar in many respects, her peace speeches were less argumentatively consistent than her suffrage addresses. The war metaphors that she had used to such effect in the suffrage campaign were curious in the context of peace activism. For thirty years a consistent critic of corruption, prejudice, and irrationality as the primary causes of hostility to woman suffrage, she now pointed to a number of different "single," or "genuine" causes of war. These sometimes disagreed with one another, on occasion, even to the point of contradiction. When she addressed gender and war—gender sometimes seemed to emerge as the most convincing "cause" of war—she was more inclined to rely on inherent differences between the sexes than she had during her suffrage career. She also allowed her emotions to figure prominently in several presentations.

Evolutionary change was a major theme of her antiwar rhetoric; the success of the suffrage movement had done much to reinforce her already substantial faith in human progress, especially when abetted by reformers. To echo her military metaphors: the forces of reason had battled the forces of reaction and emerged victorious. Peace became, simply, the next task. In her 1926 "Opening

Address'' to the second CCCW, she linked evolution to the less ominous notion of progress in assuring delegates of an improved humanity awaiting completion of their task.

What I want you to understand is: I believe there is a progress of the human race. If you are afraid of the word evolution you need not use it, but we will call it progress. Nobody can read history and not know it. Yet, within my lifetime (you can see how young I am), within my lifetime everybody believed that the human race had always been just what it is now, and that the only mission of change was when we should pass into the beyond, and that we lived for that. But since that day and in my lifetime [,] the proof has become so complete that all intelligent people know that there has been an upward trend of the human race since the beginning, whenever that was. We are more enlightened, more moral, have more comprehension, more tolerance. We have climbed upward and are still climbing. I don't think anybody has ever been able to point out why this is true or what the aim may be, but I, personally, do not believe this progress has come by chance. I believe it is a part of a great divine scheme of things. (4)

In joining evolution, progress, and religion, Lane Catt bid for broad legitimacy for peace and peace work. This was an important element in her campaign to provide solace to peace workers without excusing complacency. That the cause was supported by a relatively small band of advocates was not troublesome in her model. Since her early involvement in the suffrage movement, she had cast herself and her coworkers as part of an elite vanguard that represented the true direction of popular opinion.

She drew her expectation of public support into her evolutionary framework. "No citizen should expect War, Navy, or Department of State to build a new spirit for peace," she said at the third CCCW in 1927, "that must come from slow, determined, intelligent education and it must arise from the people" ("The Status of War v. Peace," 3). That such efforts could be relied on was proved for Lane Catt by the record of U.S. political action. In 1927, she told the Institute of Pacific Relations:

In fact, nearly, if not all the truly great things done by the United States have originated not with the government or the political party in power, but with a small group of citizens. When such movements have appealed to the people parties and administrations have eventually sponsored the idea and it has become established in law. ("Three Times Three," 2)

Her argument simultaneously advanced a general approach to change and reassured peace workers that their lonely labors ultimately would be rewarded. It also provided a solidly democratic rationale for the actions of an agitating elite that, in turn, blunted the attacks of the red-baiters who harried her and other peace activists in the 1920s (Fowler, 1986:35; Van Voris, 1987:189–191).

Her predictions of victory during this period took on a gently goading tone familiar from her suffrage speeches. In her 1926 CCCW address, she confessed to "a strange feeling which perhaps is silly and perhaps none of you would quite understand. I feel that there may be many of you who have not had the experience of being called names and of being misrepresented, and that perhaps it hurts your feelings" (2). Those so afflicted should not be disheartened, she said, because ridicule is simply a stage in the development of a social ideal. "Every new idea is attacked," she said at a dinner celebrating the sixth anniversary of the League of Nations; "It is ridiculed. When an idea is silly, it is laught [sic] out of sight. If it stands ridicule it proceeds to another stage. Have you not observed that if the stage of ridicule is passed the next stage is opposition and argument" (3). Her faith in evolution and her conviction that "evolvers" needed to work actively was a promise of victory and a prompting to further action. In peace work as in suffrage, she never ignored the need to rally her troops.

Evolution, however, was not a theme that guided all her antiwar rhetoric. As a result, her peace speeches, unlike her suffrage speeches, were not always argumentatively consistent one with another. For example, Lane Catt generally identified war as a product of the "war system," a broad class of institutions and attitudes ranging from government agencies to the presumed need to prepare a "defense" against an "aggressor" (Clevenger, 1955:264; Katz, 1973:51–60; Van Voris, 1987:184–210). Under this line of reasoning, she argued flexibly about economic causes, the danger of stockpiling armaments, and the will of political elites. But it was somewhat confusing when she also claimed that "few wars have been based upon actual causes. Wars have always had excuses, but the real cause was the desire for war itself" ("What Shall We Do About War?," 9).

In part, the shifting rationales reflected her choice of aspects of the "war system" argument early in her antiwar work, and in part, the development of her ideas over time. They also reflect her response to events. Lane Catt became increasingly frustrated with the pace of the peace movement, eventually offering arguments that seemed to conflict with her work in the CCCW. That organization was explicitly devoted to advanced and enlightened analyses of war. These analyses were expected to produce practicable programs, but such efforts were to have been an outgrowth of the conferences, not their substance. In 1936, she reviewed the theories of "college-bred men, polite and sincere" who offered economic, political, and other reasons for war and said:

With these theories, I sincerely disagree. I regard them as very large and fat red herrings. In reply, I say that wars will go on for thousands of years if public opinion does not demand their abolition and that when a nation wishes to go to war, it will pick out an excuse for so doing and announce it as a cause. ("What Shall We Do About War?," 18–19)

In 1934, she said that "from no meeting does one go away with a sense that peace is nearer or war less threatening" ("World Alliance for International Friendship," 3).

These differing rationales might have meshed comfortably as so many different arguments in an advocate's repertoire had they not been phrased in such absolute language and been productive of different programs of action. No "single cause" can long be convincing if its defender also asserts that there is no such thing as a cause at all. The scholarly explorations of the CCCW seem irrelevant at best in light of the "red herring" remarks. Gradually, she modified her educator's role and resorted to the language of religious conversion. On June 4, 1936, she told the International Farm Women that the people of the world can stop war "when they demand it. They and they alone can stop war. 'How?' do you say. By the conversion of the people and that can be done simply" (7). She elaborated the conversion motif in "What Shall We Do About War?"

What, then, shall we do about war? I invite each one of you to become an anti-war Committee of One. You will be its Chairman, it Treasurer, and its constitution. The aim of your Committee is to build up public opinion for the complete abolition of war. There are at least one hundred reasons why war should be abolished. Select one, study it well. Make yourself a perfect master of that one reason. Then go forth to preach and persuade whoever and wherever you can. One man or woman, healthy in body and mind, equipped with correct information of one reason why war should be abolished, ought to be able to convert a whole county in a year. (9)

Though addressed to the public, the pacifism in these speeches suggests a more private commitment of the soul than the constitutional amendments Lane Catt championed during the suffrage period. Peace advocates, circulating in their "Committees of One," would be public apostles of private conviction. Together, their enlightened converts would constitute a new body politic. For a pragmatist, the emphasis here created an oddity in that, though relying for practical purposes on the behavior of states, it began and had its greatest force in the beliefs of individuals. It may be going too far to say that she had abandoned the pragmatic and organizational aim she had so stressed in her suffrage work. Certainly, there was little chance of any practical success: she had far too few followers; the obstacles she faced in building first a national and then an international antiwar movement were greater than any she had confronted in her suffrage rhetoric; World War I provided opportunities for suffrage action, but World War II, with the demonic figure of Hitler, dwarfed other social ills.

Perhaps the sharpest divergence between her suffragist and peace rhetoric appeared in arguments about differences between men and women, which became more clearly inherent in her peace rhetoric. In "A Call to Action" in 1921, she specified women's role in combatting male belligerence:

I say to you women, you know that war is in the blood of men; they can't help it. They have been fighting ever since the days of the cave-men. There is a sort of honor about it. But it seems to me that God is giving a call to the women of the world to come forward and stay the hands of men and say: "No, you shall no longer kill your fellow man." (3)

Four years later, speaking to the Ethical Culture Society ("Men, Women and War"), she drew her recommendations for action from her reconstruction of human history: "[I]n the very beginning women invented work and man invented war. Women invented those processes which were constructive of the foundation upon which civilization was to be based, and men invented the destructive activities" (69). Her contemporaries were to "retaliate now and destroy the immemorial occupation of men, which was war" (70).

Lane Catt often asked for the support of both men and women, but stressed women's natural advantages in the cause of peace. Indeed, her solid and repeated identification of men with the attitudes that lead to war made "men" almost synonymous with the "will to war" that she had identified as a principal cause of war in her speeches.

Hitler's rise to power in the thirties outraged and frustrated her because the brutality of his regime and the threat it posed made a credible peace seem so much less likely. Accordingly, her speeches during this period grew increasingly angry. In 1938, she made a number of speeches recommending a global campaign to acquaint the people of the world with the virtues of U.S. democracy. In "The Outlook Today," she recommended a full-scale effort on behalf of liberty:

Germany has a Nazi primer; Russia a Red primer. We should have an American primer. It must tell the story of the struggle on this continent, not for power but for liberty. It must not be spoiled by dullness. It must be inspired by the great spirit of freedom. It must be radiant with the rosiest of hopes, joyous with the most confident faith in mankind, and most certain of Divine guidance toward peace. Somewhere in this country there are men and women who can write such a Red-White-and-Blue primer. (9)

This speech ended, as did at least one other during 1938, with the chant: "Heil Democracy! Heil Democracy! Sieg Heil!" (10) which, though chilling to modern ears, may have been an effort to evoke the popular enthusiasm that she identified as the real strength of the Nazis (Speech at the Cause and Cure Dinner).

This coda can also be read as a deeply ironic response to talk of war among the Allied powers, a reading supported by a passage in another 1938 speech. Though clearly disgusted by the Nazis and hopeful that U.S. institutions could provide a sufficiently strong moral counter to war, Lane Catt refused to lay blame for the coming conflict entirely on Germany's shoulders:

In a new book on THE DEFENCE OF DEMOCRACY an alleged *German proverb* is quoted (page 13): "Be my brother; or I will bash your head in." The Germans may have written the proverb, but they certainly did not invent it for long centuries before any German appeared upon this earth the bashing method of making brothers was well under way. Bash, bash, bash; guns, guns, guns, blood, blood, blood, bash bash, bash; this is about all there ever has been to world history. (Speech at the Cause and Cure Dinner, 5)

She also vented her frustration in a grotesque scenario of the state of human evolution as it related to the coming war:

Let us paint a wee picture and call it THE EVOLUTION OF MAN. Beneath the picture, it is written: THIS WAS THE KING OF MEN IN THE YEAR OF OUR LORD 1939. HE HAD THE LARGEST BRAIN EVER DISCOVERED, THE MOST EDUCATION POSSIBLE FOR ANY MAN TO RECEIVE; LOOK, HIS BREAST IS COVERED WITH THE RECORD OF SUPER-DEGREES FROM UNIVERSITIES. HE WEARS THE KEY. Solomon, in all his glory, knew little compared with this, wisest of all men, the climax of a million years of human evolution. Look again; this man wears a gas mask. He is followed by a woman and a baby, a dog and a cat, and all four wear gas masks. He shepherds them into a dark hole and scuttles in after them in the hope that he may escape the effects of the war neither he nor any other man knows how to stop. Shall we acknowledge that picture as the final climax or do something about it? (10–11)

Here she contrasted the evolutionary ideal with the stage of evolution actually achieved, and the vivid contrast expressed her own frustration with the stubborn persistence of war.

CONCLUSION

These brief excerpts cannot fully represent Lane Catt's antiwar rhetoric. In assessing this material, readers should keep in mind that, although she held office in a number of peace organizations and was a prominent speaker on pacifism, her public role was less constrained by executive responsibility than it had been during her career with NAWSA. In addition, she entered the peace movement after spearheading a successful suffrage campaign against enormous odds. She was a formidable political leader, accustomed to results and inclined to speak her mind. It may not have been politic to do so, but she did not hesitate to voice her rage at human stupidity and her seething contempt for male belligerence.

SOURCES

Early in her career, Lane Catt was determined not to become an object of worship among supporters and destroyed many of her own papers. She never organized what remained. Accordingly, records left by colleagues and intimates are unusually important sources of information. However, the New York Public Library's Carrie Chapman Catt Papers, 1887–1947, contain speech manuscripts and typescripts collected and edited by Mary Gray Peck, many annotated by Lane Catt, as well as letters, articles, pamphlets, and meeting reports. Some are dated approximately, some erroneously, and some not at all. Dating is problematic because Lane Catt sometimes gave many different versions of the same speech. Peck's datings generally reflect the first time a speech was delivered, and she sometimes labeled much later versions of a speech with the earlier date.

That is the only major collection that biographer Ralph Fowler did not draw on extensively. I have relied on his discussion of sources (xiv–xv) to describe the following: The Library of Congress houses the Carrie Chapman Catt Collection and the papers of the National American Woman Suffrage Association and of Alice Stone Blackwell, who edited and published much of her work. Smith College's Sophia Smith Library and Radcliffe's Schlesinger Library hold correspondence, speeches, and speech fragments.

The *New York Times* published many of her speeches following her election as NAWSA president in 1900. Coverage was less regular during the hiatus from 1904 to 1915, when she was active in international suffrage work and remained in charge of the International Woman Suffrage Alliance. Many speeches were also published in *TWJ*, later the *Woman Citizen*. Others were circulated as NAWSA pamphlets.

Biographical Sources

Fowler, Robert Booth. *Carrie Catt: Feminist Politician*. Boston: Northeastern University Press, 1986.
Peck, Mary Gray. *Carrie Chapman Catt: A Biography*. New York: H. W. Wilson, 1944.
Van Voris, Jacqueline. *Carrie Chapman Catt: A Public Life*. New York: Feminist Press at the CUNY, 1987.

Dissertations

Clevenger, Ima Fuchs. "Invention and Arrangement in the Public Address of Carrie Chapman Catt." Ph.D. diss., University of Oklahoma, 1955. AAC 0014000
Katz, David Howard. "Carrie Chapman Catt and the Struggle for Peace." Ph.D. diss., Syracuse University, 1973. AAC 7408358
Walker, Lola Carolyn. "The Speeches and Speaking of Carrie Chapman Catt." Ph.D. diss., Northwestern University, 1950. AAC0277275

Chronology of Speeches (Box and file numbers refer to the Carrie Chapman Catt Papers, 1887–1947, New York Public Library)

"The American Sovereign." 1888/1892. Box 4, File 3.
"Subject and Sovereign." 1888/1892. Box 4, File 12. Catt refers to census figures not available before 1890 and to the Wyoming referendum as having occurred "23 years ago." Perhaps it was given in 1888 and revised in 1892.
"The Bible and Woman Suffrage." 1890/1891. Box 4, File 4.
President's Address. 1902. Box 4, File 6.
Statement, Mrs. Carrie Chapman Catt, Judiciary Committee, U.S. House of Representatives, February 16, 1904. Box 4, File 7.
"Empire State Campaign Committee Report." 1914. Box 4, File 8.
Speech Before the Congressional Committee. 1915. Box 4, File 9.
Speech, Harrisburg, Pennsylvania. March 7, 1916. Box 4, File 10.
"The Crisis." 1916. Box 4, File 10.
"A National Survey." 1916. Box 4, File 10.
"A Call to Action." April 13, 1921. Box 5, File 4.
Baccalaureate Address. *University of Wyoming Bulletin* 18 (December 1921). Box 5, File 4.
"The Problem Stated." 1924. Box 5, File 5.
"Men, Women and War." *The Standard* (April 1925). Box 5, File 5.
"Report of the Sixth Anniversary League of Nations Dinner." January 11, 1926. Box 5, File 6.
Opening Address. December 6, 1926. Box 5, File 6.

"The Status of War v. Peace." 1927. Box 5, File 6.
"Three Times Three." July 18, 1927. Box 5, File 6.
"World Alliance for International Friendship." November 14, 1934. Box 5, File 10.
"International Farm Women." June 4, 1936. Box 6, File 2.
"What Shall We Do About War?" November 11, 1936. Box 6, File 3.
"What Shall We Do About War?" December 8, 1936. Box 6, File 3.
Speech at the Cause and Cure Dinner. 1938. Box 6, File 4.
"The Inheritance of the Woman Movement." April 14 1938. Box 6, File 4.
"The Outlook Today." October 19, 1938. Box 6, File 4.
"The Happenings of Eighty Years." January 9, 1939. Box 6, File 5.
"Who Can Answer?" December 8, 1939. Box 6, File 5.

The author wishes to thank the staff of the New York Public Library's Manuscript Division for their assistance on this project.

MARIA W. MILLER STEWART

(1803–1879), first African-American woman to lecture in public

LAURA R. SELLS

When scholars of rhetoric and history map women's emergence on the public platform, they mark abolitionism as a seedbed of women's public speaking. In general, early women abolitionists, especially the famous Grimké sisters, represent a vanguard that opened the public sphere to women speakers (Hersh, 1979; Melder, 1977).

When Maria W. Miller Stewart addressed Boston's African-American abolitionist community between 1831 and 1833, six years prior to the Grimkés' acclaimed success, she became an important forerunner for many key abolitionists and woman's rights activists. She is considered "the first Black feminist-abolitionist in America" (Andrews, 1986:22). She prefigures the major African-American activists of the nineteenth century, including Frederick Douglass, SOJOURNER TRUTH, Frances Harper, and Henry Highland Garnet. In an introduction to an edited collection of Miller Stewart's work, historian Marilyn Richardson writes: "In both the formulation and the articulation of the ideas central to the emerging struggle for Black freedom and human rights, Stewart was a clear forerunner to generations of the best known and most influential champions of Black activism" (1987:xiv; also Flexner, 1974:44; Giddings, 1985:46–55; Lerner, 1971:4). As the first U.S.-born woman and the first Black woman known to address mixed-sex and mixed-race audiences on political issues, she is a significant figure in the U.S. rhetorical tradition and in the history of women's oratory.

Miller Stewart was concerned primarily with reviving the waning spirit of militant activism among African-Americans in Boston (Giddings, 1985:52). She encouraged her listeners to improve their oppressed condition by participating in abolition and moral reform movements. Although the exact composition of her audience is unknown, her discourse indicates she directed her message to the men and women of her own community. Her immediate audience was probably entirely African-American, predominantly laborers, and probably involved in "the politically dynamic" atmosphere of the Black abolitionist movement (Lintin, 1989:3–5; Richardson, 1987:xvi).

Two events in Miller Stewart's life led her to the public sphere. After only three years of marriage, her husband died, leaving her an inheritance that was stolen from her by white lawyers. Soon thereafter, her political and intellectual mentor, David Walker, also died. Walker had been Boston's most militant Black abolitionist and was the author of the incendiary pamphlet "Appeal to the Colored Citizens of the World." In her grief over these deaths, she experienced a conversion to evangelical Christianity, which proved central to her political ideology and her rhetorical style. She wrote that her fears of assuming a public role were tempered by her faith in God:

I felt that I had a great work to perform; and was in haste to make a profession of my faith in Christ. . . . Soon after . . . [t]he Spirit of God came before me, and I spake before many. When going home, reflecting on what I had said, I felt ashamed, and knew not where I should hide myself. A something said within my breast, "Press forward, I will be with thee." And my heart made this reply, Lord, if thou wilt be with me, then I will speak for thee as long as I live. (FA:74)

She saw herself as a Christian prophet authorized by God to enter the public sphere (1835; Flexner, *NAW* 3; Richardson, 1987:8–9).

Miller Stewart's brief oratorical career in Boston was quite remarkable given the perceived lack of support from her community and given the overwhelming constraints she faced as an African-American woman speaker. By overstepping the boundaries drawn for their activities, women who entered the political arena invited severe controversy and hostility. The antagonism that her outspokenness evoked was evident in her final speech:

I am about to leave you, perhaps never more to return. For I find it is no use for me as an individual to try to make myself useful among my color in this city. . . . Had experience more plainly shown me that it was the nature of man to crush his fellow, I should not have thought it so hard. (FA:78)

Rather than brave the hostility she aroused, she chose to withdraw from the platform and leave Boston in 1834 after delivering only four public lectures.

Miller Stewart's speeches reached other audiences, however. Full texts of three of them appeared in the *Liberator*, the primary abolitionist publication, but of its 2,300 subscribers, three-quarters were African-American. This suggests that her larger audience was also primarily African-American (Linton, 1989:3).

In addition to four public speeches, Miller Stewart's rhetorical activities included political and spiritual writings. During a time when writing in the public sphere exceeded the limits of acceptable behavior for women, illustrated by ANGELINA GRIMKÉ's experience, she composed two pamphlets, which were published by William Lloyd Garrison. Sections of the first, "Religion and the Pure Principles Of Morality" (1831), also appeared in the *Liberator*. Like most of her discourse, this pamphlet combines the religious fervor, spiritual narrative, and political argument common in nineteenth-century Black political discourse (Moses, 1982:161). Her second pamphlet, "Meditations from the Pen of Mrs. Maria W. Stewart" (1832), is a collection of meditations and prayers written in the tradition of African-American women's spiritual autobiographies (Houchins, 1988:xxxix). In 1835, her pamphlets and speeches were collected and published as the "Productions of Mrs. Maria W. Stewart." In 1879, she republished "Productions" with an autobiographical sketch and several letters. The collection was advertised along with "the major anti-slavery and human rights writings of the abolitionist movement" (Richardson, 1987:27).

While her oratorical career lasted less than three years, Miller Stewart's rhetorical and political activities spanned five decades. The little that we know about her life comes mostly from her personal narratives and her spiritual meditations. She participated in numerous women's organizations that were crucial to the abolitionist movement and to the improvement of conditions for African-Americans. After leaving Boston in 1834, she joined an African-American women's literary society; she attended the Woman's Anti-Slavery Convention of 1837; and in 1850, she organized fundraisers for Frederick Douglass's *North Star*. Her strong belief in education as a means to improve the condition of free Blacks was reflected in her decision to become a school teacher, and eventually she established a school for African-American children in Washington, D.C. (Richardson, 1987:xvi, 25, 27).

MILLER STEWART AS BLACK "TRUE WOMAN" AND PUBLIC ADVOCATE

The dominant ideology governing women's roles during the nineteenth century prohibited them from activity in the public sphere. This ideology, which required women to uphold the four gender-based "virtues" of piety, purity, domesticity, and submissiveness, is commonly called the cult of True Womanhood (Welter, 1966:158–159). African-American women's experiences of True Womanhood differed from those of advantaged whites. For most women, embodying True Womanhood was difficult; for Black women, it was impossible. Economic factors drove free Black women out of the domestic sphere into the workforce. Moreover, Black women faced the additional obstacle of proving their humanity as well as their femininity. Many free African-Americans believed that approximating white gender roles would ensure upward mobility, self-respect, and racial progress. Thus, embodying True Womanhood became a racial responsibility (Higginbotham, 1989:59; Horton, 1986).

Yet as free African-Americans appropriated the dominant culture's values, they altered True Womanhood to fit their own social and material conditions. They accepted women's movement into the public sphere when limited to employment, education, and participation in political or religious organizations. Thus, the free Black community adhered to a slightly wider conception of women's public role by fostering activism along with the virtues of True Womanhood (Foster, 1985; Horton, 1986; Sealander, 1982).

To Miller Stewart, True Womanhood constituted a philosophical principle that she advocated in her discourse. Although her primary rhetorical purpose was to exhort her audience to political and social activism, she believed that change would come only when African-Americans assumed a public character that would explode negative stereotypes. She urged political action, such as petitioning Congress and engaging in rhetorical campaigns: "O ye sons of Africa, when will your voices be heard in our legislative hall, in defiance of your enemies, contending for equal rights and liberty?" (MH:66). Yet she repeatedly argued that Black people could win social justice only through virtuous behavior: "Our condition as a people has been low for hundreds of years, and it will continue to be so, unless by piety and virtue, we strive to gain what we have lost'' (MH:65–66). The gender conventions of Black True Womanhood constituted the virtuous public character she wanted her women auditors to uphold. She believed that true Black women inspired Black men to assert their human rights. The pamphlet establishes this central tenet of her philosophy:

Did the daughters of our land possess a delicacy of manners . . . did their pure minds hold vice in abhorrence, . . . would not their influence become great and powerful? [W]ould not our brethren fall in love with their virtues? Their souls would become fired with a holy zeal for freedom's cause. They would become ambitious to distinguish themselves. (RP:7)

Yet her acceptance of True Womanhood's tenets was not uncritical. Her rhetoric pointed to the hypocrisy of a system that forced Black women into the public sphere in order to maintain their households and to fulfill their domestic obligations and then questioned their purity because they moved outside the domestic realm. In a passage anticipating SOJOURNER TRUTH's ''Aren't I a Woman'' speech, she referred to the racist and classist biases of True Womanhood:

O, ye fairer sisters, whose hands are never soiled. . . . Had it been our lot to have been nursed in the lap of affluence and ease . . . should we have naturally supposed that we were never made to toil? And why are not our forms as delicate, and our constitutions as slender, as yours? (FH:54–55)

Moreover, True Womanhood was a barrier to her own success as a speaker. She was acutely aware of the obstacles created by even the broadest definition of true womanhood in her community. She knew that, as a woman speaker, she was subject to ''calumny and reproach'' (RP:6). Paradoxically, she publicly advocated a value system that forbade her own public advocacy (Sells, 1991:47).

As a central feature of Miller Stewart's rhetoric, the gender ideology of True Womanhood, particularly as it relates to her conception of virtuous public character and social activism, is best understood within the context of her strong religious beliefs. As Richardson explains:

From the start, her religious vision and her sociopolitical agenda were intrinsically bound together, one defined by the other. . . . Religion and social justice are so closely allied in her analysis that, to her mind, one could not be properly served without a clear commitment to the other. (1987:9)

The relation between her religious beliefs and the way she defined public activism was crucial to her political goals. She prescribed for her audience an activism infused with her religious world view:

That day we, as a people . . . become distinguished for our ease, elegance and grace, combined with the other virtues, that day the Lord will raise us up, and enough to aid and befriend us, and we shall begin to flourish. (RP:17–18)

Miller Stewart based her discourse on the spiritual principles of nineteenth-century African-American intellectual and religious thought. By seeing African-Americans as a separate people or nation, much like the Old Testament Hebrews, she espoused a Christian Black nationalist ideology (Moses, 1990:161). She expressed this religious philosophy in the militant "Zionist" rhetoric of what Wilson Moses calls the "Black jeremiad."

Moses describes the Black jeremiad as an adaptation of the traditional jeremiad, exemplified by the Puritan sermon, dominant in antebellum America. The Puritan jeremiad explains the sufferings of God's chosen people as a result of sinfulness and predicts greater tribulations to come (Moses, 1982:30–31). In the Black jeremiad, however, African-Americans issued "constant warnings" of God's judgment for the sin of slavery: "Their use of the jeremiad revealed a conception of themselves as a chosen people, but it also showed a clever ability to play on the belief that America as a whole was a chosen nation with a covenantal duty to deal justly with blacks" (Moses, 1982:30–31). Moses argues that Miller Stewart's oratory typifies the tone of this rhetorical form (1982:31; 1990:161; Lintin, 1989:13–16). The following passage from Miller Stewart's "Masonic Hall" speech illustrates this claim:

It appears to me that America has become like the great city of Babylon. . . . She has made the Africans drunk with the wine of her fornication; she has put them completely beneath her feet, and she means to keep them there. . . . The oppression of injured Africa has come up before the majesty of Heaven . . . it will be a tremendous day to the people of this land; for strong is the hand of the Lord God Almighty. (71)

Miller Stewart's political philosophy of civil religion was undergirded by the tenets of True Womanhood and Christian Black nationalist ideology. To encourage her audience's participation in her political agenda, she relied on several rhetorical strategies. Her philosophical beliefs often proved to be the seat of many of these strategies. Her discourse also reflects techniques common to the feminine style of other nineteenth-century woman's rights advocates (*MCSFH* 1:12–15). Because it is a "less confrontational violation of taboos against public speaking by women," feminine style is often an adaptive strategy to the obstacles of gender (*MCSFH* 1:13). Her frequent reliance on feminine style stands in direct contrast to her use of the militant Black jeremiad.

Through her personal narratives, a move typical in feminine style, Miller Stewart justified her public role and articulated an alternative role for the Black women in her audience. Her spiritual narratives demonstrated women's ability to act in the public sphere. The theological support of separate spheres represented a particularly difficult obstacle for women orators. Consequently, the religious nature of her response to her gender role constraints is not surprising. By appropriating God's word and using the high style of biblical language, she authorized her public voice and strengthened her rhetorical purpose (Andrews, 1986; *MCSFH* 1:34).

An important component of feminine style is consciousness-raising, which empowers the audience by showing them that they possess the ability to be agents of change (*MCSFH* 1:13–14). Miller Stewart used consciousness-raising as a primary strategy to overcome her audience's powerlessness in the face of their overwhelming oppression. Her final speech illustrates her use of argument from precedent as a consciousness-raising tactic to empower African-American women.

One instance of consciousness-raising occurred in the "Farewell Address" when Miller Stewart argued from biblical and historical precedent urging women's activity outside the home. She raised a procession of famous women figures who acted outside traditional gender roles. This procession constitutes the longest section of her speech. Her list of biblical figures portrayed women's activism as ordained by God. This section also anticipates the arguments of later women rhetoricians, especially those of ANGELINA and SARAH GRIMKÉ. She entreated:

What if I am a woman; is not the God of ancient times the God of these modern days? Did he not raise up Deborah, to be a mother, and a judge in Israel? Did not queen Esther save the lives of the Jews? And Mary Magdalene first declare the resurrection of Christ from the dead? (FA:75)

The "Masonic Hall" address represents another instance of Miller Stewart's approach to empowering her audience through consciousness-raising. She sought to create an empowered identity for her audience by establishing a shared cultural history that symbolized pride and power (Lintin, 1989:9). In describing the audience's common African heritage, she assumed the role of a teacher, a stance often associated with feminine style (Campbell, 1986:440).

History informs us that we sprung [sic] from one of the most learned nations of the whole earth; from the seat, if not the parent, of science. Yes, poor despised Africa was once the resort of sages and legislators of other nations, was esteemed the school for learning, and the most illustrious men in Greece flocked thither for instruction. (MH:65)

Although Miller Stewart relied on personal narrative, consciousness-raising, and other strategies of feminine style, she also used direct confrontation to instigate her audience to action. Her address delivered at the African Masonic Hall reflects her extensive use of conflict as a rhetorical tactic. In this speech she publicly chastised the men in her audience for their political inactivity. With this confrontational strategy she justified her own presence in the public sphere by arguing from expedience. In the wake of David Walker's death and the ensuing political lethargy of African-American men, she issued this challenge: "But where is the man that has distinguished himself in these modern days by acting wholly in defence [*sic*] of African rights and liberty? There was one, although he sleeps, his memory lives" (MH:64). By deploring the lack of men of distinction, she justified her entry into masculine territory. In other words, she challenged men in the audience to emulate David Walker. Because this challenge went unanswered, she justified her appearance on the public platform.

In her "Masonic Hall" speech, Miller Stewart repeatedly accused Black men of having no ambition. Although she firmly believed that free Blacks had the responsibility to improve their circumstances, she also knew that their condition resulted directly from the weight of white oppression. She argued that fear of strong opposition prevented "distinguished men" from making themselves "more influential" (MH:70).

At the literal level, Miller Stewart insulted Black men for their inactivity: "Had those men among us who had an opportunity turned their attention as assiduously to mental and moral improvement as they have to gambling and dancing, I might have remained quietly at home and they stood contending in my place" (MH:67). At the figurative level, however, the intent of her remarks changed significantly. She sought to empower Black men rather than to humiliate them. She did not intend her insults to offend her male listeners, but to motivate them toward action. This strategic insulting or baiting is an instance of the rhetorical form called "signifyin(g)." In this type of signifyin(g), "the first person to give in to anger loses." Henry Louis Gates, Jr., defines signifyin(g) as the Black trope of repetition and revision, of reversal and indirection (1988:68; see also Kochman, 1981).

Implicit in Miller Stewart's "signifyin(g) on" the Black men in her audience is an argument by indirection for male activism. The insults that she hurled at her audience often were *repetitions* of the insults made by white society: "Have the sons of Africa no souls? feel they no ambitious desires? . . . [S]hall the insipid appellation of 'clever negroes,' or 'good creatures,' any longer content them?" (MH:64). Signifyin(g) is repetition with revision. In repeating these insults, she illustrated her own contempt ("insipid appellation") for the epithets whites hurled at Blacks. Furthermore, by repeating such insults, she also attempted to insinuate herself between her Black male listeners and the larger white society where the insults actually originated. Like a trickster attempting to "stir up a fight between neighbors" by carrying tales (Gates, 1988:54), she repeated white sentiments regarding Blacks to incite her audience's anger—not toward her, but toward white society.

For any nineteenth-century woman speaker, the task of carving out a public character was formidable; for an African-American like Miller Stewart, it was Amazonian. In order to establish a public image consistent with her own definitions of femininity, she frequently assumed a passive rhetorical stance. In contrast to her strategies to incite anger in her audience, her public statements are also rife with modest apologies for overstepping her bounds. In this stance, which diminished her self-assertion, she embodied the virtue of submissiveness, a primary tenet of True Womanhood. The following passage is representative of her humility in taking to the platform: "I am but as a drop in the bucket— as one particle of the small dust of the earth. God will surely raise up those among us who will plead the cause of virtue and the pure principles of morality more eloquently than I am able to do so" (MH:70–71).

The act of public expression directly challenged women's prescribed roles. Miller Stewart's public expression, however, came from divine inspiration. Even though she boldly violated the norms of feminine behavior, she characterized this violation as a submissive and Christian act. She repeatedly reinforced her identity as a prophet touched by God. For instance:

Methinks I heard a spiritual interrogation—"Who shall go forward, and take off the reproach that is cast upon the people of color? Shall it be a woman?" And my heart made this reply—"If it is thy will, be it even so, Lord Jesus!" (FH:51)

She located the virtues of submissiveness and piety within her Christian morality. By following God's call, she adhered to a higher authority. She recast her acts of interpreting God's will and becoming God's prophet—decidedly masculine behaviors for her time—as Christian piety and feminine submission.

The final strategy Miller Stewart used to handle the obstacles she faced was to withdraw from the public platform altogether. As a prophet, not only did she prophesy the collapse of the United States in her resounding jeremiads, but she also predicted the death of her own public character by equating death with silence in juxtaposed images. Beginning with the introduction to her pamphlet, where she associated herself with the martyred image of David Walker, she repeatedly foreshadowed her withdrawal from the platform:

Many will suffer for pleading the cause of oppressed Africa, and I shall glory in being one of her martyrs; for I am firmly persuaded, that the God in whom I trust . . . is able to protect me . . . and if there is no other way for me to escape, he is able to take me to himself, as he did the most noble, fearless, and undaunted David Walker. (RP:5)

Aware of the constraints that gender placed on her character as a speaker, Miller Stewart constructed a paradoxical persona that was militant and modest. She sought to maintain her femininity by crafting a public character consonant with the piety and deference of a true woman. Yet her piety and deference to God, as she constructed it, required militant activism. As a result, she assumed a persona antithetical to the true woman persona she sought to embody (Sells, 1991:88).

CONCLUSION

The contradictions in Miller Stewart's rhetoric make sense in light of her unique historical position, the philosophy she espoused, and the considerable constraints of her situation. While her rhetoric is similar to that of many nine-teenth-century Black male rhetoricians (Moses, 1961:161), it is noteworthy be-cause of the strategies she used to overcome the contradictions of a woman engaged in public speaking and writing. Her rhetoric demonstrates the ways in which Black women activists shared with their white counterparts the difficulties of True Womanhood. Yet her discourse also illustrates the important differences in the meaning of True Womanhood for Black women. While she did not singlehandedly break the barrier of separate spheres for women, she was part of a vanguard of women speakers who challenged prescribed gender roles. She helped inaugurate a new role for U.S. women—that of speaker. And she pi-oneered that role with the deference of a true woman and with a militancy quite unlike the feminine style of many women speakers who followed her:

For he hath clothed my face with steel, and lined my forehead with brass. He hath put his testimony within me, and engraven his seal upon my forehead. And with these weapons I have indeed set the fiends of earth and hell at defiance. (FA:75)

SOURCES

Original texts of Miller Stewart's works are found in:

Religion and the Pure Principles of Morality, The Sure Foundation on Which We Must Build. Productions from the Pen Of Mrs. Maria W. Steward [sic], Widow of the Late James W. Steward, of Boston. Boston: Garrison & Knapp, 1831. Boston Public Library; Howard University Library; SUNY, Brockport.
Meditations from the Pen of Mrs. Maria W. Stewart. Boston: Garrison & Knapp, 1832. Boston Public Library; Boston Athenaeum.
Productions of Mrs. Maria W. Stewart, Presented to the First African Baptist Church & Society, of the City of Boston. Boston: Published By Friends of Freedom and Virtue, 1835. Howard University Library; New York Historical Society Library; New York Public Library Schomburg Collection; Western Reserve Historical Society, Cleveland.
Meditations from the Pen of Mrs. Maria W. Stewart. Washington, D.C.: n.p., 1879. Indiana University, Bloomington; Library of Congress.

Selections from these works are reprinted in:

Bormann, Ernest G. *Forerunners of Black Power: The Rhetoric of Abolition.* Englewood Cliffs, N.J.: Prentice-Hall, 1971. (*FBP*)
Spiritual Narratives. Ed. Henry Louis Gates, Jr. Intro. Sue E. Houchins. Schomburg Library of Nineteenth-Century Black Women Writers. New York: Oxford University Press, 1988. (*SN*)
Black Women in Nineteenth-Century American Life: Their Words, Their Thoughts, Their Feelings. Ed. and intro. Bert J. Loewenberg and Ruth Bogin. University Park, Pa.: Pennsylvania State University Press, 1976. (*BW*)
Early Negro Writing: 1760–1837. Ed. Dorothy Porter. Boston: Beacon Press, 1971. (*ENW*)
Maria W. Stewart, America's First Black Woman Political Writer: Essays and Speeches.

Ed. and intro. Marilyn Richardson. Bloomington: Indiana University Press, 1987.
(*MWS*)

Biographical Sources

Flexner, Eleanor. "Stewart, Maria W. Miller." *NAW* 3:377–378.
Giddings, Paula. *When and Where I Enter: The Impact of Black Women on Race and Sex in America*. New York: Bantam Books, 1985.
We Are Your Sisters: Black Women in the Nineteenth Century. Ed. Dorothy Sterling. New York: W. W. Norton, 1984.

Critical Sources

Campbell, Karlyn Kohrs. "Style and Content in the Rhetoric of Early Afro-American Feminists." *Quarterly Journal of Speech* 72 (1986):434–455.
Lintin, Dan. "Maria Miller Stewart, an Afro-American Woman, Speaks in the 1830s: A Study in Consciousness Raising and Religious Personas." Unpublished paper, University of Minnesota, 1989.
———. " 'Shall It Be a Woman?': Rhetorical Analysis of Maria W. Miller Stewart." M.A. thesis, University of Minnesota, 1989.
Sells, Laura R. "The Rhetoric of Paradox in the Discourse of Maria W. Stewart." M.A. thesis, University of South Florida, 1991.
Thompson, Julie M. "Managing the Public/Private Dichotomy: Maria W. Stewart and the Problem of Rhetorical Status." M.A. thesis, Indiana University, 1991.

Background Sources

Andrews, William L. *Sisters of the Spirit: Three Black Women's Autobiographies of the Nineteenth Century*. Bloomington: Indiana University Press, 1986.
Flexner, Eleanor. *Century of Struggle: The Woman's Rights Movement in the United States*. 1959. New York: Atheneum, 1974.
Foster, Frances Smith. "Adding Color and Contour to Early American Self-Portraits: Autobiograpical Writings of Afro-American Women." *Conjuring: Black Women, Fiction, and Literary Tradition*. Eds. Marjorie Pryse and Hortense J. Spillers. Bloomington: Indiana University Press, 1985, pp. 25–38.
Gates, Henry Louis, Jr. *The Signifying Monkey: A Theory of African-American Literary Criticism*. New York: Oxford University Press, 1988.
Hersh, Blanche Glassman. "Am I Not a Woman and a Sister?: Abolitionist Beginnings of Nineteenth-Century Feminism." *Antislavery Reconsidered: New Perspectives on the Abolitionists*. Eds. Lewis Perry and Michael Fellman. Baton Rouge: Louisiana State University Press, 1979, pp. 252–283.
Higginbotham, Evelyn Brooks. "Beyond the Sound of Silence: Afro-American Women in History." *Gender and History* 1 (1989):50–67.
Horton, James Oliver. "Freedom's Yoke: Gender Conventions Among Antebellum Free Blacks." *Feminist Studies* 12 (1986):51–56.
Kochman, Thomas. *Black and White Styles in Conflict*. Chicago: University of Chicago Press, 1981.

Maria W. Miller Stewart   349

Lerner, Gerda. *The Grimké Sisters from South Carolina: Pioneers for Woman's Rights and Abolition.* New York: Schocken, 1971.

Melder, Keith E. *Beginnings of Sisterhood: The American Woman's Rights Movement, 1800–1850.* New York: Schocken, 1977.

Moses, Wilson Jeremiah. *Black Messiahs and Uncle Toms: Social and Literary Manipulations of a Religious Myth.* University Park, Pa.: Pennsylvania State University Press, 1982.

————. *The Wings of Ethiopia: Studies in African-American Life and Letters.* Ames: Iowa State University Press, 1990.

Quarles, Benjamin. *Black Abolitionists.* London: Oxford University Press, 1969.

Maria W. Stewart, America's First Black Woman Political Writer: Essays and Speeches. Ed. Marilyn Richardson. Bloomington: Indiana University Press, 1987.

Sealander, Judith. "Antebellum Black Press Images of Women." *Western Journal of Black Studies* 6, no. 3 (1982):159–165.

Welter, Barbara. "The Cult of True Womanhood: 1820–1860." *American Quarterly* 18 (1966):151–175.

Chronology of Major Works (Citations in the entry are from the *Productions* of Mrs. Maria W. Stewart [1835].)

"Religion and the Pure Principles of Morality" (RP). 1831. *MWS*:28–42; *ENW*:460–471; *BW*:183–200; *SN*

"An Address, Delivered Before the Afric-American Female Intelligence Society" (AA). *Liberator*, April 28, 1832:66–67; *MWS*:50–55; *SN*

"Lecture Delivered at the Franklin Hall" (FH), Boston, September 21, 1832. *Liberator*, November 17, 1832:183; *MWS*:44–49; *ENW*:136–140; *MCSFH* 2:1–10; *SN*

"Meditations from the Pen of Mrs. Maria W. Stewart." 1832. *SN*; Preface; Sufferings During the War; Letters and Commendations, *MWS*:87–109.

"An Address, Delivered at the African Masonic Hall" (MH), Boston, February 27, 1833. *Liberator*, April 27:68 and May 4, 1833:72; *MWS*:56–64; *ENW*:129–135; *FBP*:177–181; *SN*

"Mrs. Stewart's Farewell Address to Her Friends in the City of Boston" (FA), September 21, 1833. *MWS*:65–74; *SN*

"Productions of Mrs. Maria W. Stewart, Presented to the First African Baptist Church & Society, of the City of Boston." 1835. *SN*

ERNESTINE POTOWSKI ROSE
(1810–1892), unfolding the rhetoric of identity

CHARLES CONRAD

In the middle of the nineteenth century, Ernestine Potowski Rose was known to thousands of Americans. In an era of social and cultural ferment, when movements for intellectual freedom and political emancipation dominated the cultural milieu of the United States and Europe, virtually every cultural assumption was being challenged, even prevailing conceptions of God. In the United States, she was linked with many of these movements—woman's rights, abolitionism, socialism, free public education, elimination of child labor, and alternative religious beliefs. Potowski Rose was only the second foreign woman to lecture publicly in the United States (her friend Frances Wright had been the first). Her exceptional oratorical skills gained her the title "Queen of the Platform" and led woman's rights activists to view her as the most effective speaker of the movement's early years:

Those who sat with her on the platform in bygone days, well remember her matchless powers as a speaker; and how safe we all felt while she had the floor, that neither in manner, sentiment, argument, nor repartee, would she in any way compromise the dignity of the occasion. . . . She had a rich musical voice, with just enough of a foreign accent and idiom to add to the charm of her oratory. As a speaker she was pointed, logical, and impassioned. She not only dealt in abstract principles clearly, but in their application touched the deepest emotions of the human soul. (*HWS* 1:100)

Although the editors of the first volume of *History of Woman Suffrage* list the rhetoric of Ernestine Rose and Frances Wright as one of the three factors most responsible for the early movement, her name is not among the nineteen pioneers to whom the work is dedicated. Although her work on behalf of woman's rights ranged from going door-to-door through New York with a petition for women's property rights to election as president of the National Woman's Rights Association, some movement histories do not mention her, and few provide a systematic commentary on her rhetoric or her role in the movement. And although her humanistic views served as the cornerstone of woman's rights ideology and influenced the ideas of such future leaders as ELIZABETH CADY STANTON and SUSAN B. ANTHONY, it is her successors who usually are credited as the key movement philosophers and rhetors.

When her name is mentioned, she typically is treated as an enigma, both by modern-day scholars and by the women who knew her best. Anthony's diary records a conversation during an 1854 speaking trip to Washington, D.C., that reveals both her frustrations with this enigmatic figure and Potowski Rose's feelings about her place in the movement:

[After she criticized Lucy Stone and Wendell Phillips for their willingness to compromise movement ideals] I said, Mrs. Rose there is not *one* in the Reform ranks, whom you think true, not one but whom panders to the popular feeling. She answered I can't help it, I take them by the words of their own mouths. I trust all until their words or acts declare them false to truth and right and continued she, no one can tell the hours of anguish I have suffered, as one after another I have seen those I had trusted betray falsity of motive as I have been compelled to place one after another on the list of panderers to public favor. Said I, do you know Mrs. Rose, that I can but feel that you place me too on that list. Said she, I will tell you when I see you untrue. A silence ensued. . . . I observed tears in her eyes. Said I, Mrs. Rose, have I been wicked and hurt your feelings? She answered, no, but I expect never to be understood while I live. Her anguish was extreme. I too wept, . . . even though I felt I could not comprehend her . . . Mrs. Rose is not appreciated, nor cannot be by this age. She is too much in advance of the extreme ultraists [liberal reformers] even, to be understood by them. Almost every reformer feels that the odium of his [*sic*] own ultraisms is as much as he is able to bear and therefore shrinks from being identified with one in whose view their ultraism is sheer conservatism. (Quoted in Dubois, 1981:75–76)

The extreme liberalism of her beliefs, her unwillingness to compromise or conciliate, and her refusal to accept anything less than total commitment from other reformers created a barrier that persisted throughout her career. This chapter explores the enigma that was Ernestine Potowski Rose and attempts to explain her background and beliefs, illuminate her rhetoric, and evaluate her relationship to the movement for woman's rights/woman suffrage.

BACKGROUND

Ernestine L. Siismondi Potowski was born in a Jewish ghetto in Piotrkow, Poland, on January 13, 1810 (Suhl, 1959). Family tradition hints that early in life she rebelled against the constraints imposed on a female child in an orthodox Jewish household. She insisted that Torah was not the exclusive province of males and began to study it in Hebrew. She read critically, once arguing that the illnesses her father suffered from regular fasting were evidence of God's cruelty. By age fourteen, her neighbors and the members of her father's congregation viewed her as a heretic.

At age sixteen, her rebellious nature became a matter of public record. Her mother died, leaving her a substantial inheritance. As was typical in orthodox families, her father arranged her betrothal to a man much older than she without her knowledge or consent, and her inheritance became her dowry. She decided to challenge her father's arrangement in court, an action possible only because of the size of her inheritance. She represented herself before the Regional Tribunal of the Polish Court and left with a court decree that made her the sole owner of the property she had inherited. When she returned home, she presented her property to her father, and he presented her with a seventeen-year-old stepmother.

Within a year she decided that there was no place for her in her father's house or in the community of devout believers who saw her as a heretic. Her commitment to her heritage and to her nation was unquestioned—later, she described herself as "a daughter of poor crushed Poland, and the downtrodden and persecuted people called the Jews" (Suhl, 1959:21), but her curiosity about the outside world and her obsession with freedom and equality were even stronger. She traveled alone to Berlin and found a Jewish community immersed in theological schism. Polish Jews were not welcome in Germany, but she arranged an audience with the Prussian king who granted her special permission to stay. Needing a source of income, she invented a kind of paper that, when burned, functioned as a room deodorizer. Within two years she had become fluent in German and immigrated to Holland, perhaps as the result of a shipwreck on the way to London. In 1830, she traveled to Paris and found herself in the midst of the revolutions against autocratic rule sweeping across Europe. Late that year, she attempted to return to Poland to support a tragic revolt against the Czar, but Austrian authorities prevented her. She then went to London where she was to make the most important contacts of her life.

England was torn with social strife. Labor unions and reform societies advocated a wide range of changes—restrictions on child labor, higher wages and improved working conditions, universal suffrage—as farm workers destroyed buildings and machinery. The most visible social reformer was Robert Owen, then more than sixty years of age, who believed that human beings are the product of their environments; that we are who we are because of forces and circumstances largely outside our control. Potowski Rose summarized her version of this belief in a speech to the 1845 Infidel Convention:

What makes man [sic] act wrong? Is it his desire to do it? We have been and are yet told that the heart of man is wicked and in accordance with this, such arrangements have been made in society as to fulfill the prophecy and make him bad indeed. It is the greatest libel that has ever been put upon nature. Every human being has a tendency to do good, but the fundamental error, that man forms his own opinions, feelings and acts, has made him bad. He was considered as a being independent of every man around him; hence followed the isolated condition of society. These two fundamental errors are the cause of all evil; they make every man an enemy to his neighbor. (Suhl, 1959:279)

In 1900, Owen put his theories into practice when he purchased New Lanark, a typical cotton mill town of the day. The workers lived in extreme poverty, children of five and six years worked fourteen- or fifteen-hour days in the mills or mines, few workers could read or write, and drunkenness and wife/child abuse were common. Owen changed the workers' environment by improving working conditions, building new homes, creating a public education system, and substantially reducing alcohol consumption. New Lanark was a success, and after working for legislation restricting child labor, he attempted to replicate the experiment in Harmony, Indiana, and a number of smaller U.S. communities. These efforts failed, and Owen returned to England in 1829. For six years he cooperated with the labor movement, but in 1835, he rejected the concept of class militancy at the core of labor organizing and founded the Association of All Classes of All Nations, an organization Potowski Rose later said was "for the protection of human rights which embraced all colors, and nations, and sects" (Suhl, 1959:32). During this period, Potowski Rose met Owen and accepted the key principles of Owenist socialism.

Alienated from established religions much earlier, she found in its "Religion of a New Moral World" a body of belief she could accept:

The religion of the New Moral World consists of the unceasing practice of promoting the happiness of every man, woman and child. . . . [T]here will be therefore no worship . . . no anger on account of religious differences—no persecutions. . . . [A]ll that will be required by man for the Glory of God, will be to make himself and all other living things, as happy as possible. . . . [A]nd the worship of God will consist in the practice of useful industry; in the acquisition of knowledge; in uniformly speaking the truth; and in the expression of joyous feelings which a life in accordance with nature and truth will be sure to produce. (Suhl, 1959:33)

Her involvement with Owen had provided her with a radical religious faith and her first opportunity to speak in public. Sometime between 1932 and 1936, it also gave her a lifelong partner, William Ella Rose.

In May 1836, the new couple immigrated to the United States. New York City was the fastest growing city in the world, and the United States was in the midst of political and religious change. Jacksonian Democracy had fostered universal suffrage for white males, and the opening of the frontier and the early Industrial Revolution were responsible for rapid economic growth. Ralph Waldo Emerson, Henry Thoreau, Theodore Parker, and the other members of a group called the Symposium were developing Transcendentalism, which held that human beings were nature's highest achievement, were divine in themselves, and had unlimited potential for personal growth and self-development. They were humanists in the fullest sense of the term and opponents of virtually any kind of conformity of thought or action.

Soon after arriving, Potowski Rose met Frances ("Fanny") Wright, another Owenite who was one of the most visible and controversial figures of the era. Both believed in a new society based on the principles of human equality and community property, were branded as infidels for their nontraditional religious beliefs, and developed a passion for public rhetoric. "Agitate! Agitate!" Potowski Rose once said, "ought to be the motto of every reformer. Agitation is the opposite of stagnation—the one is life, the other death" (Suhl, 1959:65). But during 1836, her rhetoric was private, not public. Her exhausting door-to-door campaign to obtain signatures for the New York Married Woman's Property Bill netted only five signatures and confronted her with women's apathy, an attitude she would encounter throughout her career. She admitted that women who said, "we have rights enough," were "indeed discouraging, for the most hopeless condition is that when a patient loses all sensation of pain and suffering'' (Suhl, 1959:55). But she sent the five signatures to Albany and continued her work until its passage in 1848.

In the summer of 1837, the Society for Moral Philanthropists, headed by Benjamin Offen and described by the press as a society of infidels whose goal was to undermine religion, offered Potowski Rose her first U.S. public platform. In a thirteen-week debate, she answered objections by anyone who wished to contest her radical ideas. The debates drew large audiences and evoked repeated accusations that she was an infidel. This label was abhorrent to most Americans, but she found it attractive because to her it signified reformer. In December of that year, she was among 5,000 in the audience at a debate on public school reform held at New York City's Broadway Tabernacle. L. E. Barnard described the events that followed:

Mrs. Rose, sitting in the gallery, called the reverend gentleman [the Reverend Robert Breckenridge] to order for violating the sense of the audience, in entirely overlooking the important object which had called the people together [a discussion of public school reform], and indulging in a violent clerical harangue against a class whom he stigmatized as infidels. This bold innovation of a woman upon the hitherto unquestioned prerogatives of the clergy, at once caused a tremendous excitement. Loud cries of ''Throw her down!'' ''Drag her out!'' ''She's an infidel!'' resounded in all parts of the building. She, however, held her ground, calm and collected while the tumult lasted, and after quiet was restored, continued her remarks in a most dignified manner, making a deep impression upon all present. Certain religious papers declared it a forewarning of some terrible calamity, that a woman should call a minister to account, and that, too, in a church. (*HWS* 1:97)

By Christmas of 1837, she was launched on a career as a public speaker with a reputation as an eloquent but radical infidel. Moreover, her views of the world and of human beings had solidified.

IDEOLOGY IN POTOWSKI ROSE'S RHETORIC

Potowski Rose's ideology can be defined by five concepts, three of which concern human nature: (1) all humans have inalienable rights stemming directly from their membership in the species; (2) all humans are capable of self-awareness and self-control; and (3) all humans have the same potential for self-development (*MCSFH* 1; Conrad, 1981). Social conditions often rob persons or groups of their rights to life, liberty, and the pursuit of happiness; cultural assumptions often cause individuals to lose sight of their essential value and competencies; and differential opportunities frequently make it appear that some persons or groups have inherently different capacities and limitations. However, these limitations arise out of the constraining effects of social structures and cultural assumptions, not from human nature. The final two components of her ideology involved (4) the processes through which social change can be realized and (5) the role of religious beliefs and institutions in society.

A Humanistic Ontology

For Potowski Rose, woman's rights "are as old as humanity itself" (AERA 1867; *HWS* 2:209; *MCSFH* 1:133–144). Although not derived from any legal document, inherent human rights are expressed most effectively in the U.S. Declaration of Independence:

Resolved, That by Human Rights, we mean Natural Rights, in contradistinction from conventional usages, &c. Upon that ground we claim our rights, and upon that ground our rights have already been conceded by the Declaration of Independence, in that first great and immutable truth which is proclaimed in that instrument, "that all men [sic] are created equal," and that therefore all are entitled to "certain inalienable rights, among which are life, liberty and the pursuit of happiness." Our claims are based upon that great and immutable truth, the rights of all humanity. (WRC 1853:33)

These inalienable rights are the same, regardless of sex or race:

Humanity recognizes no sex—virtue recognizes no sex—mind recognizes no sex—life and death, pleasure and pain, happiness and misery recognize no sex. Like man, woman comes involuntarily into existence; like him she possesses physical and mental and moral powers, on the proper cultivation of which depends her happiness; like him she is subject to all the vicissitudes of life; like him she has to pay the penalty for disobeying nature's laws, and far greater penalties has she to suffer from ignorance of her far more complicated nature than he; like him she enjoys or suffers with her country. Yet she is not recognized as his equal! (WRC 1851:37; also WRC 1853:35)

Because human beings are inherently alike, she supported

emancipation of all kinds—white and black, man and woman. Humanity's children are, in my estimation all one and the same family, inheriting the same earth; therefore there should be no slaves of any kind among them. . . . But permit me to say that the slaves of the South are not the only people that are in bondage. All women are excluded from the enjoyment of that liberty which your Declaration of Independence asserts to be the inalienable right of all. The same right to life, liberty, and the pursuit of happiness, that pertains to man, pertains to woman also. For what is life without liberty? Which of you here before me would not willingly risk his or her life, if in danger of being made a slave? Emancipation from every kind of bondage is my principle. I go for the recognition of human rights, without distinction of sect, party, sex, or color. (Address on the Anniversary of West Indian Emancipation, quoted in Schappes, 1949:351, 354–355)

For Potowski Rose, the issue was not which humans possessed certain rights, or what was the basis of those rights—they belonged equally to all as humans. The issue was what attributes defined the human experience.

The characteristic that most clearly defines humans as unique creatures is our awareness of who we are and our ability to exercise individual control over our identity. Slavery was the most dehumanizing of socially prescribed situations because it denied individuals the exercise of this uniquely human feature:

Not to be your own, bodily, mentally, or morally—that is to be a slave. Ay, even if slaveholders treated their slaves with the utmost kindness and charity . . . it is none the less slavery; for what does slavery mean? To work hard, to fare ill, to suffer hardship, that is not slavery; for many of us white men and women have to work hard, have to fare ill, have to suffer hardship, and yet we are not slaves. Slavery is not to belong to yourself—to be robbed of yourself. There is nothing that I so much abhor as that single thing—to be robbed of one's self. (Address on the Anniversary of West Indian Emancipation, quoted in Schappes, 1949:350)

Although not slaves in the same sense as southern Blacks, women were also denied their personhood:

Moreover we claim not only the right of woman to make herself independent in the accumulation of wealth, and in keeping it after it is accumulated, but above all these, we claim the right to her own person. For here lies the cornerstone of all the injustices done woman, the wrong idea from which all other wrongs proceed. She is not acknowledged as mistress of herself. From her cradle to her grave she is another's. We do indeed need and demand the other rights of which I have spoken, but let us first obtain *ourselves.* Give us ourselves, and all that belongs to us will follow. We claim that no lawmaker, man or husband, shall control woman except as man allows himself to be controlled. (WRC 1853:41)

The depersonalization of women was most pressing within marriage:

At marriage she loses her entire identity, and her being is said to have become merged in her husband. Has nature thus merged it? Has she ceased to exist and feel pleasure and pain? When she violates the laws of her being, does her husband pay the penalty? When she breaks moral laws, does he suffer the punishment? When he supplies his wants, is it enough to satisfy her nature? And when at his nightly orgies, in the grog shop and the oyster cellar, or at the gaming-table, he squanders the means she helped by her cooperation and economy to accumulate, and she awakens to penury and destitution, will it supply the wants of her children to tell them, that owing to the superiority of man she had no redress by law; and that as her being was merged in his, so also ought theirs to be? What an inconsistency, that from the moment she enters that compact, in which she assumes the high responsibility of wife and mother, she ceases legally to exist, and becomes a purely submissive being. . . . When *he* marries again [after a wife's death], he still retains his identity and power to act; but *she* becomes merged once more into a mere nonentity. (WRC 1851:37, 40; *MCSFH* 1:71–86)

For Potowski Rose the situation women faced was the quintessential example of how social systems denied persons the right to control their own identities. But in the negative attitudes of women toward increasing their rights, she found an especially offensive illustration of the ways that cultural assumptions led women to lose their sense of selfhood. Taught that "she was created for his [man's] benefit only, women have learned not to assert a discrete identity":

[U]ntil this falsehood is eradicated from her mind, until she feels that the necessities, services, and obligations of the sexes are mutual, that she is as independent of him as he is of her, that she is formed for the same aims and ends in life that he is—until, in fact, she has all rights equal with man, there will be no other object in her education, except to get married, and what will best promote that desirable end will be cultivated in her. Do you not yet understand what has made woman what she is? Then see what the sickly taste and perverted judgment of man now admires in woman. Not physical and mental vigor, but a pale, delicate face . . . and above all, that nervous sensibility which sees a ghost in every passing shadow, that beautiful diffidence which dares not take a step without the protecting arm of a man to support her tender frame. . . . Oh! the crying injustice towards woman. She is crushed at every step, and then insulted for being what a most pernicious education and corrupt public sentiment have made her. But there is no confidence in her powers, nor principles. (WRC 1851:44–45)

All humans are born with an awareness of self and a need to control their own identities. Both law and custom robbed women of the capacity for self-awareness necessary to live life as fully functioning humans.

The third element of her humanism was her belief that all humans had an equal potential for self-development. Unfortunately, social systems (unfair laws, barriers to equal education, unequal access to capital, and so on) combined with cultural assumptions to prevent many people from realizing their potential. In an insight that seems quite modern (Gusfield, 1975), Potowski Rose recognized that the core beliefs of members of a culture provide the basis on which unequal social structures arise, while the legal, political, and economic structure of a society simultaneously support discriminatory cultural beliefs:

[A]s long as woman shall be oppressed by unequal laws, so long will she be degraded by man. We have hardly an adequate idea of how all-powerful law is in forming public opinion, in giving tone and character to the mass of society. . . . Hence also the reason why we call on the nation to remove the legal shackles from woman, and it will have a beneficial effect on that still greater tyrant she has to contend with, Public Opinion. (WRC 1851:39)

This duality of cultural ideas and social structures defines the situations that humans face. For nineteenth-century women, cultural beliefs and social structures allowed only partial development of their human capacities—nurturance, emotionality, domesticity, and piety—while men were allowed only partial development as well—aggressiveness, initiative, and rationality. Changing the structures and beliefs that made artificial distinctions between the sexes would allow all to develop the full range of human capacities. Thus, for her, one of the potential effects of the changes advocated by woman's rights advocates would be to change humans, which, in turn, would generate new ideas and social structures that would support the fullest possible development of all.

This view differentiates Potowski Rose's ideology from that of most other nineteenth-century women activists. Throughout the history of the movement, there was a tension between justifications based on humanist ideology and justifications based on what came to be called expediency, that is, "claims based on the benefits to be derived from change" (*MCSFH* 1:64). K. K. Campbell notes that

such arguments ordinarily contradict those based on natural rights because they presume that woman's nature is distinctive and that her influence will improve whatever sphere she enters. These two kinds of argument were both prevalent throughout the early women's movement, and the contradictions between them bedeviled movement ideology. (*MCSFH* 1:64–65)

During the latter half of the century, arguments from expediency became dominant in the movement, with important implications for its direction and rhetoric (Conrad, 1981b; *IWSM*). But in her belief system, humanism and expediency were not incongruent.

If given the opportunities that should be granted to all, women would fully develop their inherently human capacities:

Open to her all the avenues of emolument, distinction, and greatness; give her an object for which to cultivate her powers, and a fair chance to do so, and there will be no need to speculate as to her proper sphere. She will find her own sphere in accordance with her capacities, powers, and tastes; and yet she will be woman still. Her rights will not change, but [rather] strengthen, develop and elevate her [human] nature. Away, then, with that folly and absurdity, that a possession of her rights would be detrimental to her character; that if she is recognized as the equal of man, she would cease to be woman. Have his rights as citizens of a republic, the elective franchise with all its advantages, so changed man's nature, that he has ceased to be a man? Oh, no! But woman could not bear such a degree of power; what has benefited him, would injure her; what has strengthened him, would weaken her; what has prompted him to the performance of his duties, would make her neglect hers! (WRC 1851:41, 43–44)

Conversely, if cultural beliefs and social structures accepted the inherent humanness of so-called feminine characteristics instead of defining them as inferior, men would be able to develop more fully:

[T]he subjection of woman has caused, to some extent, the subjection of man; for no one can be truly free, so long as he enslaves another. So long as man has deprived woman of her natural rights, he has never known how fully and best to use and prize his own. When woman has her rights, when both have equal rights, the race will advance far beyond the present stage of human greatness, human development, and human ability. (WRC 1853:39; WRC 1851:38,42)

For Potowski Rose, eliminating artificial sex-related beliefs and social structures would improve society, not because women are inherently morally superior to men as the usual expediency argument asserted, but because their removal would rid society of the barriers constraining the development of both sexes. Thus, she could talk simultaneously about the positive social effects of changes sought by the movement and deny that her position was based on considerations of expediency (as typically defined):

There is one argument which in my estimation is the argument of arguments, why woman should have her rights; *not on account of expediency*, not on account of policy, though these too show the reasons why she should have her rights; but we claim—I for one claim, and I presume all our friends claim—our rights on the broad ground of human rights; and I for one again will say, I promise not how we shall use them. I will no more promise how we shall use our rights than man has promised before he obtained them how he would use them. We all know that rights are often abused; and above all things have human rights in this country been abused, from the very fact that they have been withheld from half of the community. (WRC 1853:33)

The notion that women were somehow morally superior to men, just like the belief that men were somehow intellectually superior to women, was wholly inconsistent with Potowski Rose's ideology. To her all *persons* had the same attributes, and if placed in the same social and cultural circumstances would exhibit the same variety of actions and attitudes regardless of their sex or ethnic background. To assert that women and men were essentially different in any respect violated the humanitarian ideology that was the basis of all her beliefs.

The Role of Rhetoric in Social Change

Like many of the social reformers of her era, Potowski Rose had what modern readers would see as a naive faith in the essential goodness of human beings. Opposition to woman's rights resulted from ignorance; once that was eradicated, society would change. In a speech to the 1851 WRC, she argued:

It is from ignorance, not malice, that man acts toward woman as he does. In ignorance of her nature, and the interest and happiness of both sexes, he conceived ideas, laid down rules, and enacted laws concerning her destiny and rights. The same ignorance, strengthened by age, sanctified by superstition, ingrafted into his being by habit, makes him carry these convictions out to the detriment of his own as well as her happiness. . . . Those men who have their eyes already open to these facts, earnestly desire the restoration of woman's rights, as the means of enabling her to take her proper position in the scale of humanity. If all men could see the truth, all would desire to aid this reform, as they desire their own happiness; for the interest and happiness of the sexes cannot be divided. . . . I cast no more blame or reproach on man, however, than on woman, for she, from habit based on the same errors, is as much opposed to her interest and happiness as he is. (46)

Two years later she elaborated these ideas:

We do not fight men—we fight bad principles. We war against the laws which have made men bad and tyranical. Some will say, "But these laws are made by men." True, but they were made in ignorance of right and wrong, made in ignorance of the eternal principles of justice and truth. They were sanctioned by superstition, and engrafted on society by long usage. (*HWS* 1:144–145)

Ignorance would be overcome through public discourse. "Both [men and women] are the victims of error and ignorance," she said; "Hence the necessity for active, earnest endeavors to enlighten their minds; hence the necessity for this, and many more Conventions, to protest against the wrong and claim our rights" (WRC 1851:46). Her goal was to press women's issues in public until opponents were forced to respond in open debate:

On these grounds [human rights; no taxation without representation] we ask man to meet us, and meet us in the spirit of inquiry, in the spirit of candor and honesty, as rational human beings ought to meet each other, face to face, and adduce arguments, if they can, to convince us that we are not included in that great Declaration of Independence; that although it is a right principle that taxation and representation are inseparable, yet woman ought to be taxed, and ought not be represented; and that although it is an acknowledged principle that all just power of government is derived from the consent of the governed, yet woman should be governed without her consent. Let them meet us fairly and openly; let them meet us like rational men, men who appreciate their own freedom, and we will hear them. If they can convince us that we are wrong, we will give up our claims; but if we can convince them that we are right in claiming our rights, as they are in claiming theirs, then we expect them in a spirit of candor and honesty to acknowledge it. (WRC 1853:34)

Because she believed in inherent human goodness and rationality, she assumed that cultural assumptions and social structures could be modified through public deliberation. Inequities were based on ignorance, which could readily be overcome through symbolic action.

Religion in the Ideology of Potowski Rose

Although recognized as a key figure in the early years of the woman's rights movement, Potowski Rose was also active in many other reform efforts, one of which was a loosely organized group of intellectuals who sought changes in the religious beliefs that dominated Western cultures. Cady Stanton, Anthony, and MATILDA JOSLYN GAGE recognized this dual interest and the links that she saw between the two movements:

All through these eventful years Mrs. Rose has fought a double battle; not only for the political rights of her sex as women, but for their religious rights as individual souls; to do their own thinking and believing. How much of the freedom they now enjoy, the women of America owe to this noble Polish woman, can not be estimated, for moral influences are too subtle for measurement. (*HWS* 1:100)

In this, too, she was atypical because reform movements of this time tended to be grounded in traditional religious beliefs. From the outset, woman's rights advocates found clerics to be their strongest opponents and traditional theology their greatest barrier (IWSM). Usually, movement activists responded by arguing that, properly interpreted, Christian teachings supported the humanist assumptions of the movement, but she took a different position.

By the time she was a teenager, Potowski Rose had abandoned her belief in God as defined in the Judeo-Christian tradition. By the time she came to the United States, she had accepted the Owenite view that religious faith should be faith in human beings, and religious action should be devoted to making people's lives as fulfilling as possible, not to obtaining some rewards in an afterlife:

Ignorance is the evil—knowledge will be the remedy. Knowledge not of what sort of beings we shall be hereafter, or what is beyond the skies, but a knowledge pertaining to *terra firma*, and we may have here all the power, goodness and love that we have been taught to God himself. (1845 Infidel Convention, quoted in Suhl, 1959:279)

If "God" existed, she or he existed in the spirit of all living humans, not in a realm apart from human action. Society should be based, not on a conception of God, but on a conception of humanity. Thus, discussions of the proper interpretation of religious texts were, at best, irrelevant to woman's rights and, at worst, counterproductive.

At the 1852 WRC, Potowski Rose challenged the Reverend ANTOINETTE BROWN's interpretation of scripture, saying, "[W]e require no written authority from Moses or Paul, because those laws and our claim are prior even to these two great men" (Harper, 1969, 1:7). At the 1856 convention she continued her argument:

[O]ur [authority] is older than all books, and whatever of good there is in any written revelations, must necessarily agree with ours, or it is not true, for ours only is the true revelation, based in nature and in life. That revelation is no less than the living, breathing, thinking, feeling, acting revelation manifested in the nature of woman. In her manifold powers, capacities, needs, hopes, aspirations, lies her title-deed, and whether that revelation was written by nature or nature's God, matters not, for here it is. No one can disprove it. No one can bring an older, broader, higher, and more sacred basis for human rights. Do you tell me that the Bible is against our rights? Then again I reply that our claims do not rest on the opinions of any one, not even on those of Paul and Peter, for they [woman's rights] are older than they. Books and opinions, no matter from whom they came, if they are in opposition to human rights, are nothing but dead letters. I have shown you that we derive our claims from humanity, from revelation, from nature, and from your Declaration of Independence; all proclaim our right to life, liberty, and the pursuit of happiness; and having life, which fact I presume you do not question, then we demand all of the rights and privileges society is capable of bestowing, to make life useful, virtuous, honorable, and happy. (*HWS* 1:662)

To discuss woman's rights in terms of biblical texts or theological concepts served only to legitimize clerics and their attacks on the movement. Potowski Rose's attacks on the clergy were as direct as any aspect of her rhetoric. In 1853, she identified them as a key source of the cultural assumptions that the movement had to overcome:

[N]ot only do the law-makers give woman her ideas of morality, but our pulpit preachers. I beg pardon—no, I do not either—for Antoinette L. Brown is not a priest. Our priests have given us public sentiment called morals, and they have always made or recognized in daily life, distinctions between man and woman. Man, from the time of Adam to the present, has had utmost license, while woman must not commit the slightest degree of "impropriety," as it is termed. (*HWS* 1:133)

Given their consistent opposition to women's interests, she had difficulty understanding why so many women focused so much of their lives around churches. She attacked this inconsistency explicitly:

And when your minister asks you for money for missionary purposes, tell him there are higher, and holier, and nobler missions to be performed at home. When he asks for colleges to educate ministers, tell him you must educate woman, that she may do away with the necessity of ministers, so that they may be able to go to some useful employment. If he asks you to give to the churches (which means to himself) then ask him what he has done for the salvation of woman. When he speaks to you of leading a virtuous life, ask him whether he understands the causes that have prevented so many of your sisters from being virtuous, and have driven them to degradation, sin, and wretchedness. When he speaks to you of a hereafter, tell him to help educate woman, to enable her to live a life of intelligence, independence, virtue, and happiness here, as the best preparatory step for any other life. And if he has not told you from the pulpit of all these things; if he does not know them; it is high time you inform him, and teach him his duty here in this life. (WRC 1856; *HWS* 1:662–663)

In a society dominated by religious belief, Potowski Rose's heresies created a constant rhetorical problem for the movement. She was known to audiences as much for her religious heresies as for her humanistic ideology (Harper, 1969, 1:203), which fostered the perception that the woman's rights movement was even more radical than it was. Her beliefs also created tangible problems. For example, in 1854, Cady Stanton and she journeyed to Washington for a series of lectures. The chaplain of Congress would not allow them to speak in the Capitol because of Potowski Rose's religious beliefs, even though he admitted that barring them violated their First Amendment rights to freedom of speech and religion. A crisis also occurred in the early years when some movement supporters argued that she should not be allowed to speak at WRCs. Alma Lutz (1940:115) notes that Cady Stanton, after hearing her speech during the "Divorce Debate" at the 1860 WRC, "admired Ernestine Rose more than ever, remembering the warning which Wendell Phillips and George William Curtis had given

Susan [Anthony] that such a woman—an atheist they called her—would harm their cause.'' Similarly, when Anthony defended Cady Stanton's heretical *Woman's Bible* at the 1896 NAWSA convention, she recalled the turmoil caused by Potowski Rose's religious beliefs:

The one distinct feature of our association has been the right of individual opinion for every member. We have been beset at each step with the cry that somebody was injuring the cause by the expression of sentiments which differed from those held by the majority. The religious persecution of the ages has been carried on under what was claimed to be the command of God. I distrust those people who know so well what God wants them to do, because I notice it always coincides with their own desires. All the way along the history of our movement there has been this same contest on account of religious theories. Forty years ago one of our noblest men [Phillips] said to me, ''You would be better never [to] hold another convention than allow Ernestine L. Rose on your platform;'' because that eloquent woman, who ever stood for justice and freedom, did not believe in the plenary inspiration of the Bible. Did we banish Mrs. Rose? No, indeed! (Quoted in Dubois, 1981:243; on the debate see *HWS* 4:263; Behnke, 1969; Welter, 1985)

Potowski Rose believed that all humans possessed the same nature and capacities and that individuals and groups differed from one another solely because of their experiences and the opportunities provided them by society. When social conditions robbed persons of their inalienable right to develop to the fullest, it was the duty of all citizens to act to redress such imbalances in power or opportunity. Because bad laws and intolerable social conditions were the result of ignorance, not evil intent, education—to be achieved through open, public argument and advocacy—was the solution to those social ills. These assumptions served as the basis of her rhetoric throughout her career and were the core beliefs underlying the rhetoric of the early years of the woman's rights movement.

Why, then, has a woman who was among the first to speak in public for woman's rights, who was instrumental in the passage of the first Married Woman's Property Act (New York), and was president of the Woman's Rights Association and co-founder of the National Woman's Rights Association, in the words of her biographer, been ''virtually forgotten?'' The answer may be relatively simple: she was not in the country during the years when movement histories were being written, and so she was unable to provide movement historians with documents necessary to preserve a record of her place and role. She left the United States in June 1869, three weeks after the bitter convention that resulted in the formation of the competing American and National Woman Suffrage Associations. She returned only once, in 1873, to liquidate her property and to speak briefly to the National Woman's Rights Convention, where she announced her retirement from the public platform (Suhl, 1959:242–261). For AWSA leaders—Lucy Stone, Wendell Phillips, Henry Blackwell, and JULIA WARD HOWE—the final contact with her was as part of an alliance with Anthony and Cady Stanton. Thus, they had little incentive to preserve her memory. Although her name was included in the Executive Council of the National

Association until 1885, her contribution to the movement virtually disappeared from its discourse within a year. A brief history of the movement that appeared in a summer 1870 issue of the *Revolution* omitted Potowski Rose entirely (Suhl, 1950:253). Her ill health also complicated the situation.

Potowski Rose responded to Anthony's request to contribute her memoirs to the *History of Woman's Suffrage* in this way:

Believe me it would give me great pleasure to comply with your request, to tell you all about myself and my past labors; but I suffer so much from neuralgia in my head and general debility, that I could not undertake the task, especially as I have nothing to refer to. I have never spoken from notes; and as I did not intend to publish anything about myself. . . . I made no memorandum of places, dates, or names; and thirty or forty years ago the press was not sufficiently educated in the rights of woman, even to notice, much less to report speeches as it does now; and therefore I have not anything to assist me or you. All I can tell you is, that I used my humble powers to the uttermost, and raised my voice in behalf of Human Rights in general, and the elevation and Rights of Woman in particular, nearly all my life. . . . I look back to that time, when a stranger and alone, I went from place to place, in high-ways and by-ways, did the work and paid my bills with great pleasure and satisfaction; for the cause gained ground, and in spite of my heresies I had always good audiences, attentive listeners, and was well received wherever I went. (Letter, January 9, 1877, *HWS* 1:98–99; Suhl, 1959:263)

By the time the histories of the early movement were being written, a new generation of women had appeared. Few of them remembered her or knew of her struggles. Oral histories become incomplete and unreliable as eyewitnesses die. Because she spoke impromptu, no records exist except for speeches transcribed at the WRCs and other settings.

But there may be more subtle reasons for these omissions that reveal the ways in which the movement changed between 1848 and 1890 (Conrad, 1981a; IWSM). One change involved its focus. In calling for acceptance of the humanness of women, woman's rights rhetors called for a number of socioeconomic changes, only one of which was suffrage (Conrad, 1981a). Put differently, early advocates did not act "for the poor claim, that a woman shall put a piece of paper into a box in the month of November; that she shall have a right to crowd up to your ballot and name one or the other of the candidates" (Wendell Phillips, WRC 1850:31). But by the end of the Civil War, suffrage had become the focus of the movement (Cady Stanton, WRC 1866:5). By 1870, male suffragists would look at past movement rhetoric and would accurately note that

in the early days of the discussions about woman's position . . . was a period of great agitation in regard to all social problems. . . . In the resolutions of these [1850–1852] conventions, the claim for suffrage is buried under such a load of words that you can hardly find it, while they ascend very far into dim air in their vague demands. . . . This rather vague and high-flown element in the movement was fortunately met and controlled by an element of clear common sense (T. W. Higginson, *TWJ*, October 15, 1870:321).

The woman's rights movement had become the woman suffrage movement.

During the same era, the justification offered for movement demands also changed. Whereas woman's rights rhetoric grounded its demands in the humanness and individual identities of women, suffragist rhetoric concentrated on what giving women the ballot would do for society at large. In 1866, Cady Stanton proclaimed:

Instead of demanding the rights of our self-hood, we would make the broader claim for that education and position that shall best fit us to do our duty to the race. Instead of the satisfaction we now feel when all is well in the home, we would let our sympathies go forth into the outer world; we would peer into garrets and cellars of this great metropolis [New York City], into the dens of vice and folly, into the jails, prisons and asylums; for a wise selfishness would teach us there are duties there." (WRC:6; emphasis added)

This expediency argument asserted that woman's ballot would have three effects on society. First, if women became politically active, their sphere of interest would broaden. Second, the ballot would broaden opportunities for employment, bringing "bread and wages" to women. Third, it would unleash an army of women to "abate drunkenness, gambling, licentiousness; to watch and warn the young, the weak, the ignorant; to counsel and comfort the criminal and the unfortunate; to look after the order and cleanliness of our tenement houses, streets and prisons" (Stanton, 1866 WRC:7). A rhetoric based on selfhood had been replaced by a suffragist rhetoric of national improvement.

In addition, suffragist rhetors had become more concerned with and responsive to antimovement rhetoric. The radical, assertive, often uncompromising rhetoric of the 1850s was replaced by a more pragmatic rhetoric of response. Antoinette Brown Blackwell's argument that if the Bible was interpreted properly, readers would realize that Christian principles demanded acceptance of the essential equality of human beings became the "official" response to clerical opposition. Fears that suffrage would undermine the family were assuaged with the argument that woman's moral superiority, coupled with the enhanced power of the ballot, would lead to improvements in the institutions of marriage and family. Discussions of issues that might distract from the call for suffrage were purged (Conrad, 1981b).

In sum, woman suffrage rhetoric could not accommodate an Ernestine Potowski Rose. Her broadly defined humanism and concern for a plethora of social issues would have added unacceptable distractions; her atheism would have complicated the process of actively seeking support from reformist clergy; her version of the expediency argument contradicted the new movement ideology; and her confrontational, uncompromising style would only have undermined efforts to appear moderate and acceptable to outsiders.

Finally, she was a foreigner in an era in which nativism was rampant, both inside and outside of the movement (Higham, 1988). Throughout her career her lineage had been a point of contention. For example, an 1854 Albany *Register* article responded to her testimony to the New York Legislature by saying, ''it is a melancholy reflection that, among our American women, who have been educated to better things, there should be found any who are willing to follow the lead of such foreign propagandists as the ringleted, gloved exotic, Ernestine Rose'' (Cady Stanton, 1898, 1971:191). Her response to the *Register* presented her as one of a long series of foreigners contributing to U.S. freedom:

I chose to make this country my home in preference to any other, because if you carried out the theories you profess, it would indeed be the noblest country on earth. And as my countrymen so nobly aided in the physical struggle for freedom and independence, I felt, and still feel it equally my duty to use my humble abilities to the uttermost in my power to aid in the great moral struggle for human rights and human freedom. (Suhl, 1959:157)

On other occasions, she responded:

[T]hough I am not myself an American by birth, and have never had the pleasure of attending such an anniversary [of the Plymouth Rock landing], yet my heart is always with those who do, for they hail a day of freedom. But there are other anniversaries kept in this country, one of which I presume you all love to celebrate; and that is the anniversary of the Declaration of Independence. That great and glorious day did not create, but gave to the world a great truth—that all men are born free and equal, and are therefore entitled to life, liberty and the pursuit of happiness. My heart always rejoices in that day, and I shall never forget the emotions I felt when I first witnessed its celebration in this country. It seemed to me as if the sun shone brighter, the birds sang sweeter, the grass grew greener. Everything in nature seemed transformed from deformity to beauty. (Address on the Anniversary of West Indian Emancipation, quoted in Schappes, 1949:348)

Thus, she responded to nativist rhetoric on two levels: explicitly, that humanism transcends national boundaries; and implicitly, that her love for this country paralleled the love expressed by Americans on patriotic occasions.

But when nativist attacks came from inside the movement, responding was more difficult. As early as 1854, Potowski Rose complained privately to Anthony about the nativism of Lucy Stone and Wendell Phillips, AWSA founders, who opposed granting foreign immigrants the rights of citizenship (Dubois, 1981:74–75). Ironically, she herself contributed to the growing racism and nativism of the movement. During an emotional debate at the 1869 convention, Potowski Rose, Cady Stanton, and Anthony each said things that violated the humanist ideology of the movement:

Potowski Rose: ''Congress has enacted resolutions for the suffrage of men and brothers. They don't speak of women and sisters. . . . We might commence by calling the Chinaman a man and a brother, or the Hottentot, or the Calmuck [Canuck], or the Indian, the idiot or the criminal, but where shall we stop? They will bring all these in before us, and then they will bring in the babies—the *male* babies.''

Cady Stanton: ''It isn't merely giving suffrage to the black men, but giving it to ignorant men of every color landing on our shores.''

Anthony: "[I]f you will not give the whole loaf of suffrage to the entire people, give it to the most intelligent first." (Suhl, 1959:238)

During the 1870s and 1880s, nativist sentiment increasingly permeated suffragist rhetoric. The moral superiority of white women, suffragists argued, would offset the treachery of Chinese immigrants, counteract the drunkenness of the Irish, and civilize Eastern and Southern Europeans. Granting white women the vote would be a counterweight to immigrant votes. As anti-suffragist rhetors often argued, white women would vote as their husbands did or white women's votes would offset African-American votes. This second argument was less pronounced after the turn of the century, perhaps because the advent of Jim Crow laws had effectively eliminated Black male suffrage (Woodward, 1974). Of course, nativism is wholly inconsistent with an ideology of humanism, but by the latter decades of the nineteenth century, suffragist rhetoric was grounded more in issues of expediency than questions of inherent human rights. Potowski Rose's ideology had always contradicted arguments from expediency; her persona as a foreigner living in a foreign land alienated her from the movement she helped create. Thus, movement historians would have very little incentive to seek out, record, or publicize the rhetoric of a woman whose ideology was so inconsistent with the views of the woman suffrage movement.

CONCLUSION

One of the realities faced by members of movements for societal change is that they must adapt if they are either to survive or succeed (Simons, 1970). Another reality is that movements will be attractive to potential members only if they offer a sufficiently broad ideology to be relevant to the experiences, needs, and desires of their audiences. If the espoused ideology changes, so does the potential appeal of its rhetoric. Demands for adaptation that audiences and opposing rhetors impose on movement rhetors inevitably create tensions between ideological purity and practical demands for effective political action. Rhetors may respond to these tensions in two ways. They may strive to maintain internal unity by retaining a pure ideology, which may not only lead to a cohesive and homogeneous movement, but may also increase the alienation between movement and society (Shils, 1968). Alternatively, they may sacrifice ideological purity in an attempt to obtain enhanced opportunities to effect desired sociopolitical changes, resulting in an ideology altered to make it more palatable to outsiders. The cost of reducing ideological purity is an increased potential for internal schism. As an ideology becomes more pragmatic, it becomes less visionary. When visions are modified or abandoned, the grounds for unification of the movement are lost. As the early women's movement progressed, the originating ideology of the essential humanness of women was transformed into the essentially different ideology of national improvement that characterized the later movement.

Regardless of how movement rhetors manage the dilemma of ideological purity and strategic adaptation, some members will be purged, either overtly or covertly, as their contributions and beliefs simply disappear from movement rhetoric. After the Civil War, Potowski Rose's belief in the essential humanness of all persons became irrelevant, then problematic, for suffragists. Her persona was even more difficult to integrate into a rhetoric of moderation and expediency. As movements progress they change in fundamental ways. The lessons of that transformative process may be Potowski Rose's most important legacy to contemporary feminists.

SOURCES

Behnke, Donna. *Religious Issues in Nineteenth Century Feminism*. Troy, N.Y.: Whitston, 1969.
Conrad, Charles. "Agon and Rhetorical Form: The Essence of the 'Old Feminist' Movement." *Central States Speech Journal* 32 (1981a):45–53.
———. "The Transformation of the 'Old Feminist' Movement." *Quarterly Journal of Speech* 67 (August 1981b):284–297.
DuBois, Ellen Carol. Ed. *Elizabeth Cady Stanton, Susan B. Anthony: Correspondence, Writings, Speeches*. New York: Schocken Books, 1981.
Elizabeth Cady Stanton As Revealed in Her Letters, Diary and Reminiscences. 2 vols. Ed. Theodore Stanton and Harriot Stanton Blatch. New York: Arno, 1969.
Gusfield, Joseph R. *Community: A Critical Response*. New York: Harper & Row, 1975.
Harper, Ida Husted. *The Life and Work of Susan B. Anthony*. 3 vols. 1898. New York: Arno, 1969.
Higham, John. *Strangers in the Land: Patterns of American Nativism, 1860–1925*. 3rd ed. New Brunswick, N.J.: Rutgers University Press, 1988.
Lutz, Alma. *Created Equal: A Biography of Elizabeth Cady Stanton*. New York: John Day, 1940.
Schappes, Morris U. "Ernestine L. Rose: Her Address on the Anniversary of West Indian Emancipation [4 August 1853]." *Journal of Negro History* 34 (July 1949):344–355.
Shils, Edward. "The Concept and Function of Ideology." *The International Encyclopedia of the Social Sciences*. Ed. David Sills. New York: Crowell, Collier & Macmillan. Vol. 7 (1968):66–76.
Simons, Herbert W. "Requirements, Problems, and Strategies: A Theory of Persuasion for Social Movements." *Quarterly Journal of Speech* 56 (February 1970):1–11.
Stanton, Elizabeth Cady. *Eighty Years and More: Reminiscences*. 1898. New York: Schocken, 1971.
Suhl, Yuri. *Ernestine L. Rose and the Battle for Human Rights*. New York: Reynal, 1959.
Welter, Barbara. "Introduction: Something Remains to be Done." *The Original Feminist Attack on the Bible (The Woman's Bible)*. Ed. Elizabeth Cady Stanton. New York: Arno and the New York Times, 1985, pp. v–xxxvi.
Woodward, C. Vann. *The Strange Career of Jim Crow*. 3rd rev. ed. New York: Oxford University Press, 1974.

KATE RICHARDS O'HARE CUNNINGHAM
(1876–1948), socialist, antiwar activist, prison reformer

DEBRA K. JAPP

Kate Richards O'Hare has been called the United States' "premier barnstorming orator." She was active in the Socialist party in the first two decades of the twentieth century and was a well-known and popular lecturer and writer for the socialist cause. She championed the causes of women workers, tenant farmers, and those whose voices were not heard. She was convinced that under socialism, a more just, democratic, and Christian society would result. According to Neil Basen, a noted authority on her life, by 1910, she had "carved a national reputation as a scintillating spellbinder second only to [Eugene] Debs in popularity on the socialist platform" (1980:174). She "covered more territory and delivered more lectures on the Socialist hustings than almost any other member of the party" (Basen, 1980:168). With the onset of World War I, she joined other socialists in protesting U.S. involvement. Her antiwar rhetoric eventually led to her arrest and conviction of sedition under the Espionage Act of 1917. After her release from prison, she fervently pursued prison reform.

But despite her successful career as a socialist speaker, antiwar activist, and prison reformer, Kate Richards O'Hare Cunningham has been virtually ignored by both historians and rhetorical scholars. There are several possible reasons. First, she was a member of a nontraditional U.S. political party. Second, as a woman, she has taken a backseat to her male counterparts in the Socialist party— Eugene Debs, Morris Hillquit, Victor Berger. Finally, when she divorced her first husband, Frank P. O'Hare, he destroyed most of her correspondence; a significant part of her work is still available, however. Historians are beginning to recognize the important role Kate Richards O'Hare Cunningham played in the socialist movement of the early twentieth century.

BACKGROUND

Christened Carrie Katherine, Richards was born on a farm in Ottawa County, Kansas, in 1876. She was one of five children and the second of three daughters born to Andrew and Lucy Richards, "well-to-do" landowners. According to Richards' reports, her early years were idyllic. Later, in her speeches and writings, she romanticized her early years on the ranch:

Those were wonderful days and I shall never cease to be thankful that I knew them. Days that laid the foundation of my whole life, gave me health and strength and love of freedom, taught me to depend on myself, to love nature, to honor rugged strength of mind and body and to know no shams in life. Everything is very real, very much alive and in close touch with nature on the broad sweep of the prairie amid the longhorns. ("How I Became a Socialist Agitator," 4)

At age ten, however, her life took a dramatic shift. Her father lost the family farm in the drought of 1887 and moved the family to Kansas City. The first winter in the city was difficult, and, according to Richards, her family lived "the life of a wage-worker's family in the poverty-cursed section of town" (*Socialist Woman* 2 [October 1908]:4). This early experience sensitized her to the plight of the poor and destitute. She would devote the rest of her life to relieving the suffering of society's less fortunate.

Early in her life Richards showed a tendency to flaunt social convention. After completing her high school education, she attended a normal school in Nebraska, where it is reported she took a class from William Jennings Bryan (*Progressive Woman* 4 [August 1910]:2). After a brief stint teaching, which she discovered paid her barely enough to live, she accepted a position as a bookkeeper in the machine shop where her father was now a partner. Unsuited to a sedentary life of books and ledgers, she became a machinist's apprentice and, despite its male-only membership practice, joined the International Association of Machinists.

Like other young women of her era, Richards was deeply religious and actively campaigned for social reform in her community. At one time she hoped to become a missionary for the Disciples of Christ. Working in the WCTU and the Florence Crittenton Mission, which maintained a home in Kansas City for "fallen women," exposed her to the social problems resulting from poverty. Gradually, however, she became disenchanted with the role the church and clergy played in improving the conditions of the poor and downtrodden. In one of her early writings, she explains her gradual disillusionment with organized religion:

I began to realize that . . . prayers would never fill an empty stomach. . . . I also learned that intemperance and vice did not cause poverty, but that poverty was the mother of the whole hateful brood we had been trying to exterminate and the increase of her offspring was endless. Dimly I began to realize that if we would win we must study poverty . . . to try to understand why there should be so much want in such a world of plenty. ("How I Became a Socialist Agitator," 4)

When she discovered that two of the largest brothels in Kansas City were on church-owned land, her estrangement from the church was complete. By the turn of the century, she had permanently severed her ties with organized religion.

Richards' search for a solution to poverty and vice led her to the lectures of well-known reformers and agitators, including one by the already legendary MARY HARRIS "MOTHER" JONES. Harris Jones introduced her to Julius Wayland, publisher of the socialist newspaper *Appeal to Reason*. Discussions with Wayland, along with study of such reform tracts as Edward Bellamy's *Looking Backward*, convinced her that socialism held the answers to society's ills. After a brief period with the Socialist Labor party, in 1901, she joined the newly formed Socialist party of America.

Richards met her first husband, Francis Patrick O'Hare, in 1901 while attending a training school for Socialist party workers in Girard, Kansas. They were married on New Year's Day, 1902. Their honeymoon was spent agitating for the Socialist party. Until the birth of their first child in November, 1903, they traveled the midwestern and eastern states, working to gain converts to the socialist cause.

In 1904, the O'Hares moved to Chandler, Oklahoma Territory. By 1908, they had added three more children to their family. Motherhood did not slow her down, however. While in Oklahoma, she continued to stump for the Socialist party, and she wrote a column for a small socialist newspaper. According to Basen, she "helped to build in the Sooner State the strongest American grass-roots Socialist organization" (1980:174). In 1909, she began to travel the country extensively on socialist lyceum speaking tours organized by her husband.

Despite her heavy lecture schedule and her time-consuming roles as wife and mother of four children, Richards O'Hare found the time to run for election to the U.S. House of Representatives on the Socialist ticket and to hold several prominent positions in the Socialist party. In 1912, she and her husband accepted positions on the editorial board of the *National Rip-Saw*, a socialist monthly for which she also wrote a column. During her six-year tenure with the *Rip-Saw*, the circulation of the paper increased to 150,000 subscribers, becoming the second largest socialist newspaper in the United States, after the *Appeal to Reason* (Basen, 1980:175).

In 1913, she defeated incumbent Morris Hillquit in an election for the party's international secretary. Much to the consternation of some male party members who thought a woman would look "ridiculous," in her position of international secretary, she represented the United States in a meeting of the International Socialist Bureau in London later that same year (Basen, 1980:190). Richards O'Hare was so successful, and her oratorical skills were so powerful, that Jean Jaurès, a leading French socialist, invited her to France to help organize and convert the French peasants to the socialist movement.

In 1916, she was a candidate for the vice-presidency of the Socialist party but was defeated by George Kirkpatrick of New Jersey. Later that same year, Richards O'Hare became the first woman to run for election to the U.S. Senate, when she stood for election on the Socialist ticket in Missouri. And in 1917, when the U.S. government officially entered World War I, she served as chair of the Socialist party's Committee on War and Militarism during the party's Emergency Convention in St. Louis. In this position she helped to develop the party's majority report, which censured U.S. involvement in the "European conflict."

While numerous socialists, among them the O'Hares, Eugene Debs, and Morris Hillquit, opposed U.S. intervention, an equal number of prominent socialists supported the war effort, including John Spargo, May Wood Simons, and her husband A. M. Simons. As in every other cause she supported, Richards O'Hare wholeheartedly devoted herself to ending U.S. participation in the war effort once again by taking to the lecture circuit. By December 1917, she had delivered her lecture "Socialism and the World War" over 130 times to audiences all over the United States. Ultimately, it would result in her arrest and incarceration.

On July 17, 1917, Richards O'Hare delivered that speech before approximately 125 people in Bowman, North Dakota. Although she later denied that she deviated from her standard text on that evening, she was quoted as saying "that the women of the United States were nothing more or less than brood sows, to raise children to get into the army and be made into fertilizer" (Foner and Miller, 1982:19). For her alleged, irreverent remarks, she was arrested and charged with "intent to interfere with the enlistment and recruiting of the United States."

Richards O'Hare was found guilty of sedition under the Espionage Act of 1917 and sentenced to five years confinement on December 17, 1917. She entered the Missouri State Penitentiary in mid-April 1919, after exhausting every avenue of appeal, and there joined another famous radical, EMMA GOLDMAN, who had also been incarcerated for her antiwar rhetoric.

While in prison, Richards O'Hare worked to improve the conditions of the female prisoners and collected data for a scientific study on prisons. Much of this research was lost when her manuscript was confiscated by prison officials prior to her release. However, a partial record of her prison experience exists in the weekly letters she wrote to her family. In an effort to sustain public sympathy, her husband mimeographed and circulated her letters. In 1919, the *Appeal to Reason* press published sixteen of these letters under the title *Kate Richards O'Hare's Prison Letters*. In 1920, after her release, she published *Crime and Criminals*, a pamphlet about her prison experiences. *In Prison*, a more sustained examination of crime and the U.S. penal system, was published in 1923.

President Woodrow Wilson commuted her sentence on May 29, 1920. Upon release, Richards O'Hare began to concentrate her energies on gaining the freedom of other "federals" and "politicals" incarcerated for their antiwar rhetoric. In 1922, she and her husband helped to organize the Children's Crusade, a cross-country tour by thirty-five women and children, the families of those antiwar advocates still in prison.

The O'Hares were divorced in June 1928; in November, she married California attorney and engineer, Charles C. Cunningham. In the years prior to her death, she devoted her time and energy to prison reform. She led a successful campaign to ban contract work by prisoners. In 1938, Culbert L. Olson, governor of California, appointed her assistant director of the Department of Penology. In this position she helped to overhaul the administration of the California penal system. She died on January 10, 1948, of a coronary thrombosis.

A SOCIALIST ORATOR AND EDUCATOR

At 5'10'' and "imperially slim," Richards O'Hare was an imposing figure on the platform. Her socialist lecture tours took her to the large cities of the

East and West coasts and the small towns of the Midwest and Southwest. She was an immensely popular speaker—able to draw large audiences for the socialist cause. However, as a native daughter of the Midwest, she shared a special rapport with her rural audiences. She was a favorite of the thousands of poor dirt farmers, migratory sharecroppers, and railroad workers who attended the socialist encampments during the hot summers in the Midwest and the Southwest. Here she preached the gospel of socialism to crowds that sometimes exceeded 5,000. In her autobiography, *The Rebel Girl*, Elizabeth Gurley Flynn (see entry in Volume 2) provided perhaps one of the most vivid pictures of her at the summer encampments:

Kate was their star attraction, sometimes speaking three and four times a day. She spoke with such fervor that she would be wringing wet with perspiration at the end of each performance. She loved to dress in white and her laundry bills caused the committee to remark she should buy stock in a laundry. So she started to wash and iron all her garments herself. This was before the days of nylon, and women wore a lot more clothes— petticoats, corset covers, etc. She had a clothesline up in her room and an ironingboard which fitted into her suitcase, and she worked at her chores as she talked to me. She was a splendid orator and a militant Socialist. She made a big hit with the IWW men in my audience. They sang for her all the Joe Hill songs that had any reference to women, like: "One little girl, fair as a pearl, Worked everyday in a laundry." (1973:212)

Unlike many radicals, Richards O'Hare did not advocate the overthrow of the current system, but argued instead that cherished American values would sooner be realized in a socialist society. Thus, she incorporated Christianity and democracy as the fundamental building blocks of her rhetoric. Big business and organized religion consistently served as villains in her speeches. According to her, socialism would restore true Christianity and democracy to U.S. society. Although at least one historian has attributed her successes to the organizing abilities of her husband, Frank O'Hare, few can deny the dynamism of her fiery words (Ginger, 1949:325).

Several of Richards O'Hare's rhetorical strategies help to explain her popularity. First, she worked to adapt her message to audiences. Second, she frequently referred to her gender, and, in her capacity as a woman, wife, and mother, tried to speak for all U.S. women. Finally, she developed a narrative style that provided her audience with an intimate portrait of U.S. working classes.

Richards O'Hare's speeches were carefully planned and written out in advance, developed "just as I write a book, or as a musician prepares a composition in music, or as a mechanic draws a blueprint for a machine" (Transcript of Testimony, *U.S.A. v. Kate Richards O'Hare*, 49). And although the content of the lectures she delivered to audiences all over the United States was primarily the same, she admitted to making stylistic changes, depending on the audience she was addressing. In her trial for sedition, she said:

I always adjust the vocabulary of a lecture to the intellectual requirements of my audience. If I am speaking to a college group, a group of college students, I use the academic language common in college. If I am speaking to a southern audience I use the words common to the south. If I am speaking to a farmer audience I use the words and terms most commonly used by farmers in order to bring the thing directly to their mind; so while I use the same outline exactly in its sense and meaning, I vary my vocabulary always to the intellectual needs of the audience. (Transcript of Testimony, *U.S.A. v. Kate Richards O'Hare*, 50)

Thus, she was always aware of her audience, and, like any effective speaker, she adapted her content and the style to them.

A second strategy Richards O'Hare used to her benefit was her gender. Although some considered her speaking in public unwomanly, she and her followers made much of her role as mother and wife. She used an argument common among women agitators—that the conditions of the country compelled her to act. In fact, several times in her speeches and in her writings she stated that she had accepted the public platform reluctantly, and that, like any woman, she preferred to be with her children and to tend the home for her family. When she announced her candidacy to represent the second congressional district of Kansas in 1910, she was reported to have said:

I long for domestic life, home and children with every fiber of my being. . . . Nothing is of less interest to me than practical politics and public speaking has lost its novelty. I always start on a trip with a feeling of depression. But there is the call of Socialism. The home is becoming archaic. Socialism is needed to restore the home. I agree to run for congress to advertise Socialism. If the voters will become Socialists I will agree to become a candidate for nothing different than what the average woman's life should be. But now I am running for congress. (*Progressive Woman* 4 [August 1910]:2)

Socialist literature supported Richards O'Hare's image as a devoted wife and mother by frequently picturing her surrounded by her children. One newspaper article reassured its readers that "There is nothing in her of the pathological feminist or the acrimonious radical. Rather she is normally feminine, and quite conscious of her charm and the leverage it gives her in a man-run world" (Bronco, 1926:5–6).

Richards O'Hare frequently referred to her children in her speeches, and she was not above mentioning her family to gain sympathy when necessary. On her farewell tour in the early months of 1919 as she made her way to Fargo, North Dakota, to surrender to federal officials, she told her audiences:

When I go to prison, I leave four children outside: a boy of fifteen, a girl of twelve, and twins, boys ten years of age. And to my children, I know no one can take a mother's place, but they too come of good fighting stock, and they will face the loss of their mother with courage worthy of their ancestry. When they are old enough to understand, they will rather have a mother inside prison walls true to her ideals and principles than outside, a craven coward who dared not protest when our rights were wrested from us and when grievous wrongs were thrust upon us. ("Americanism and Bolshevism," 45)

Richards O'Hare spoke to her audiences as a woman, wife and mother, and in this role she spoke for those who had no political voice. In her famous antiwar speech, "Socialism and the World War," she depicted the war from the perspective of working-class wives and mothers whose husbands and children were being forced to fight in the war:

Dead and decaying on these battlefields are the pick and flower of modern civilization. ... When I picture the bearded face of a man, swollen and bloated in the July heat, it is not only the man I see, but the women he left behind. Oh! I see his wife the victim of invading soldiers, his children starved and maimed and mutilated and I wonder what hope the future holds for that man's wife and children? When I see the downy face of a boy upturned in death on the battlefield, I see not only the young life wasted, but I see back of that boy the mother who gave him life. ... I know that when the boy died there on the battlefield, the hope of the mother's life ended as well. I can sense the agony and hopelessness and despair of the mother whose boy lies dead on the battlefield, for I am a mother and I have sons. (16)

A third strategy Richards O'Hare used was to incorporate narratives of true, or apparently true, stories in her writings and lectures. These narratives took the form of personal accounts of individuals who had suffered at the hands of the capitalists. For example, when she wrote about how war was destroying families, she did not just talk about the problems in generic terms, but instead introduced her audience to her immigrant cook, Mary, whose brother was soon to be conscripted into the army in Europe: "Each night and morning when we read the paper Mary's eyes, dumbly beseeching, asked for news, and as I tried to tell her all that I could find and listened to her broken stories of what war meant to her father land, it ceased to be an academic question and was a living, vital thing" ("Peace," *Progressive Woman* 4 [February 1913]:4).

In another essay, she took her readers into the home of a poor farm family. She described how poverty had squeezed the joy from the mother, who in a moment of complete desperation, blamed her children for the family's troubles. After the death of one of her sons, the mother was inconsolable. Richards O'Hare wrote of this funeral:

About me were the faces of three-score men, women and children, toil-scarred and awed into breathless silence. The little bell tolled a harsh, uneven strain, a lumber wagon rumbled up to the door, there was a scuffling of heavy feet, and four young men stumbled up the aisle bearing between them a tiny, home-made coffin. Behind it walked the farmer, his face drawn with a dumb look of agony, the little son frightened and pale, and the mother dressed in the cheap, rusty mourning with which the poor must show the world their sorrow. ("As a Man Thinketh," *Socialist Woman* 1 [March 1908]:7)

Through her vivid descriptions, she brought to life the fears and trials of the poor and forgotten citizens of the United States.

Richards O'Hare's stories often provided her audience with a view of the "enemy." In one article, "The Employer's Story," she wrote about a conversation with a manufacturer who employed a large number of children in his factory. When she condemned his child labor practices, she said that the factory owner responded:

I am so sick of it all, so tired of watching that crowd of children glide in through the gates at morning like felons, and out like ghosts at night, so heartsick with hearing poverty pinched mothers lie their children's childhood away for the scanty wage we pay, so disgusted with lobbying legislatures, bribing officials and juggling laws, I want to escape it if I can. (*Socialist Woman* 2 [February 1909]:10)

Whether this story is true is unimportant. By portraying the factory owner sympathetically, she encouraged her audience to see that the victims of the capitalist system extended beyond poor women and children. Many business owners were victims as well, forced by capitalism to exploit their fellow human beings to make a living for their own families. Her inclusion of these personal biographies and narratives provided her audience with insight into the complexity of such social problems as insufficient wages, child labor, and prostitution.

RICHARDS O'HARE'S PHILOSOPHY OF
WOMAN'S RIGHTS

From the beginning of her career, Richards O'Hare focused much of her rhetoric on the impact of capitalism on the lives of poor women. Many of her writings, such as *The Sorrows of Cupid* (1912), examined social problems such as prostitution, alcoholism, and divorce, and their impact on U.S. society and its women. Capitalism was, of course, the primary cause of the subjugation and degradation of women. Socialism was the solution.

An active supporter of woman suffrage, she maintained the traditional socialist view that the woman question must submit to the larger question of the rights of the working class. Richards O'Hare argued that the ballot would help women reform society and purify the home. She believed that U.S. women had earned the right to the ballot and that the vote was necessary for women to protect their families and their homes. In the article, "Shall Women Vote," she answered the charge that women should be protected from the dirt of politics—that they were "too good" to vote:

If we are good enough to bear the children we are not "too good" to use our ballots for their protection. If we are good enough to produce the wealth of the world we are not "too good" to use our ballots to get possession and enjoyment of what we have created. If we are good enough to bear the burdens of civilization upon our shoulders we are not "too good" to demand the right to share in the blessings of the civilization we have made possible. (*SWAS*:102)

Although the Socialist party recognized the equality of its women members and supported suffrage for women in theory, the practices of party members were not consistent with their stated beliefs. Richards O'Hare was often the target of the chauvinism of the male party members. In a prominent socialist newspaper, she wrote: "Scratch a scientific male socialist and you will find an ordinary he-man. And that he-man will resent as bitterly and fight as unscrupulously the invasion of women into his domain as possible" ("The Eternal Feminine," *New York Call*, June 6, 1915, quoted in Basen, 1980:191).

Regardless of her treatment by the men of her party, Richards O'Hare did not change her philosophy on woman's rights until much later in her life. According to Sally Miller (1984), although Richards O'Hare's social, economic, and political views remained relatively constant throughout her incarceration, prison experience changed her understanding of woman's rights. Her prison letters reflected a new awareness of and sensitivity to women's total lack of social and political power. In one letter she wrote:

You know I have never been a particularly rampant feminist; I have always felt that the "woman question" was only a part of the great "social problem," but my two months here have changed my views materially, and I know now, as never before, that "women bear the heaviest burdens and walk the roughest road" and that this is true in all walks of life, and becomes more damnably true as you descend the social scale, until it reaches the very extreme here in prison. (*Prison Letters* [June 8, 1919]:31)

Ironically, it was only with her victimization as a political prisoner that she began to understand fully the lives of the women for whom she had fought so hard.

CONCLUSION

Despite her reputation as a radical, Richards O'Hare Cunningham was an ardent reformist. She actively campaigned for a shorter workday, protective legislation for women, abolition of child labor, and, after her confinement in the Missouri State Penitentiary, prison reform. Through her rhetoric, she recreated the struggles of the working classes—the farmer, the factory worker, the miner, the housewife. In her speeches and writings, she preached the gospel of socialism, but not necessarily the conventional socialism of the party's hardliners. When necessary, she was not above altering socialist policy to fit her audience, much to the dismay of some party members (Basen, 1980:177). Her sincerity was evident to all who came to listen to her, and helped to make her a popular and powerful force within the socialist movement in the United States.

Far from the traditionally sympathetic audiences in the large cities of the eastern United States and Europe, Kate Richards O'Hare Cunningham managed to forge a loyal following in the Great Plains. She sought to expose the deplorable conditions in which many Americans lived by painting rich, compelling pictures of the poor and downtrodden in her speeches and her writings. Her personal, intimate portraits of people used and discarded by the capitalist system forced her audiences to recognize the impact capitalism had on human beings. Her fiery words and vivid depictions of destitute Americans convinced thousands of midwestern men and women that the solution to poverty and inequality could be found in the principles of the socialist cooperative commonwealth.

SOURCES

Because Frank O'Hare destroyed much of her correspondence, no complete collection of Richards O'Hare's work exists. The Frank P. O'Hare Papers, Missouri Historical Society, Columbia, contain copies of her prison letters, some information about her speaking schedule, letters they wrote to each other, and some of her essays. Mimeographed copies of her prison letters are available at the Schlesinger Library, Radcliffe, the University of Missouri Library, and the University of Oregon Library. The Anne Henrietta Martin papers, California Historical Society, include some correspondence. Some of her essays were printed in the *National Rip-Saw*, a St. Louis-based socialist newspaper, renamed *Social Revolution* in 1917.

Kate Richards O'Hare: Selected Writings and Speeches. Eds. Philip S. Foner and Sally M. Miller. Baton Rouge: Louisiana State University Press, 1982. (*SWAS*)
Richards, Kate. *The Sorrows of Cupid*. St. Louis: National Rip-Saw, 1912. HOW
Kate O'Hare's Prison Letters. Girard, Kan.: Appeal to Reason, 1919. HOW
In Prison. 1923. Intro. Jack M. Holl. Seattle: University of Washington Press, 1976.

Biographical Sources

No complete biography exists; several historical essays treat specific aspects of her life. However, these sources are not always consistent on details. Where there is disagreement, I have relied on Basen, which appears to be the most complete.

Basen, Neil. "Kate Richards O'Hare: The 'First Lady' of American Socialism, 1901–1917." *Labor History* 21 (Spring 1980):165–199.
Bronco, Harold. "The Family Album: Kate Richards O'Hare." *World Tomorrow* 9 (February 1926):55–56.
Cobb, William H. "Commonwealth College Comes to Arkansas, 1923–1925." *Arkansas Historical Quarterly* 23 (Summer 1964):99–122. Covers her association with the college.
Flynn, Elizabeth Gurley. *The Rebel Girl: An Autobiography, My First Life (1906–1926)*. New rev. ed. New York: International Publishers, 1973.
Foner, Philip S., and Sally M. Miller. Introduction. *Kate Richard O'Hare: Selected Writings and Speeches*. Eds. Foner and Miller. Baton Rouge: Louisiana State University Press, 1982, pp. 1–31. Summarizes her career in socialism.
Ginger, Ray. *The Bending Cross*. New Brunswick, N.J.: Rutgers University Press, 1949. A biography of Eugene V. Debs.

Holl, Jack M. Introduction. *In Prison*. By Kate Richards. 1923. Seattle: University of
    Washington Press, 1976. Deals with her prison experience and reform efforts.
Shannon, David A. "Cunningham, Kate Richards O'Hare." *NAW* 1:417–420.

Critical/Descriptive Sources

Most critical studies are by historians; two exceptions are:

Brommel, Bernard. "Kate Richards O'Hare: A Midwestern Pacifist's Fight for Free
    Speech." *North Dakota Quarterly* 44 (Winter 1976):5–19. Details her arrest and
    trial in Bismarck, N.D.
Japp, Debra K. "Socialist-Feminist Rhetoric: The Case of Kate Richards O'Hare."
    Unpublished paper. St. Cloud State University, 1987. Analyzes "Socialism and
    the World War" speech.

Other critical works include:

Miller, Sally M. "Kate Richards O'Hare: Progression Toward Feminism." *Kansas History* 7 (1984):263–279.
Roediger, David. "Americanism and Fordism: American Style: Kate Richards O'Hare's
    'Has Henry Ford Made Good?' " *Labor History* 29 (Spring 1988):241–252. Reprints some writings on Henry Ford's factory methods and describes their impact
    on her.
Zeuch, W. E. "The Truth about the O'Hare Case" (pamphlet). St. Louis: Frank P.
    O'Hare, 1918. Describes political infighting in Bowman that may have led to her
    arrest.

Chronology of Major Speeches and Writings (Actual
speech texts are difficult to obtain. Several were printed in
pamphlet form.)

"How I Became a Socialist Agitator." *Socialist Woman* 2 (October 1908):4–5. *SWAS*:35–
    41.
"Socialism and the World War, Bowman, N.D. 17 July 1917." Pamphlet. St. Louis:
    Frank P. O'Hare, 1919. Senator Porter McCumber, N.D., read two letters condemning it in the U.S. Senate, July 23, 1917. *Congressional Record*, 65th Cong.,
    1st Sess., 55, no. 5:5390–5391.
Address to the Court (after sentencing), December 14, 1917. Proceedings on the sentencing of Mrs. Kate Richards O'Hare, by Hon. Martin J. Wade. Transcript of
    Testimony, *U.S.A. v. Kate Richards O'Hare*, on deposit at the Federal Records
    Center, Kansas City, Mo. (in the District Court of the United States for the District
    of North Dakota; case #2737); Zeuch.
Farewell address, delivered in twenty-four cities in the first four months of 1919, prior
    to her incarceration. Parts were incorporated into her pamphlet "Americanism
    and Bolshevism."

DEBORAH SAMPSON GANNETT

(1760–1827), Revolutionary War veteran and early lecturer

JANE ELMES-CRAHALL

Deborah Sampson Gannett was the first woman to masquerade as a man and serve in the nation's armed forces, and she may have been the first U.S. woman to appear on public platforms speaking to audiences of men and women. Thus, during her life, she violated some of the most fundamental taboos that imprisoned the women of her time.

Sampson holds a unique place in U.S. military history as the only female veteran of the Continental Army, having served with distinction as a soldier from 1781 to 1783 under the name of Robert Shurtleff (Different sources have variant spellings; see Stickley, 1972, on military records.) in the 4th Massachusetts Regiment. She fought in the battles of White Plains, Tarrytown, and Yorktown and was wounded twice, most seriously near Tarrytown. Apparently, by remaining aloof and making "light of her injuries," her true sex remained undiscovered for over two years (Stickley, 1972:233). In awarding Sampson Gannett's widower a pension in 1838, the U.S. Congressional Committee on Revolutionary Pensions concluded that "the whole of history of the American Revolution . . . furnishes no other similar example of female heroism, fidelity, and courage" (Rep. #159:2, 25th Cong., Serial 333, NA). In 1802, nearly twenty years after her honorable discharge, she lectured publicly at least twenty times on her experience as a soldier in the Revolutionary War, perhaps "initiating women's rhetorical history in the United States" (*MCSFH* 1:17).

HISTORICAL BACKGROUND

Deborah Sampson's father died when she was five, and like many poor children, she was bound out as a servant from age nine to age eighteen. She was strong and athletic; she taught herself to read and write (Ellet, 1969:125; Friedenberg, 1976:2); she was interested in the political debates she heard in the home of her foster father, Deacon Cephrus Thomas, who was an ardent patriot. After age eighteen, she supported herself, first as a teacher in the Middleborough school and then by taking in sewing, chiefly making suits of clothes for young men joining the Continental Army.

In April 1781, wearing a suit of clothes she had made and using the name Robert Shurtleff, she traveled to Uxbridge and successfully enlisted in Captain George Webb's Company, 4th Massachusetts Regiment. Private Shurtleff was known to be a "good soldier," although quiet and of a "smock face." Signed statements from commanding officers attested that Shurtleff was brave and athletic and was "noted in the forefront of every action" (MSA; NA). After surviving two wounds, in 1783, she was assigned as an orderly to General John

Patterson's staff in Philadelphia, where she became ill with a fever and was taken unconscious to an Army hospital. Dr. Barnabas Binney "discreetly kept the secret of the girl soldier until her discharge could be quietly arranged" (Stickley, 1972:233).

Following her military discharge in November 1783, Sampson returned to Stoughton, where she faced concerned relatives. One descendant wrote: "My step Grandmother told me [they] were not at all proud of her escapade" but were relieved that she "retained her virtue" during her two and one-half year enlistment (L. Tolman letter, December 4, 1903, HSS).

In April 1784, she married a young farmer, Benjamin Gannett, and moved to Sharon. Life for the Gannetts and their three children was not easy. Evidence from correspondence by and about Sampson Gannett and official documents filed to support various pension applications suggest a long struggle with poor health and poverty. Twenty years later, Paul Revere, who owned copper works near the Gannetts' home, took it upon himself to inquire about her "situation, and character, since she quitted the Male habit, and Soldiers uniform; for the more decent apparel of her own Sex" (Letter to W. Eustis, February 20, 1804, MHS). Revere's letter provides details about her condition:

She is now much out of health; She has several Children; her husband is a good sort of man, 'tho of Small force in business; They have a few acres of poor land which they cultivate, but they are really poor. She told me, she had no doubt that her ill health is in consequence of her being exposed when She did a Soldiers duty; and that while in the Army, she was wounded.

Sampson Gannett made application for a pension from the Commonwealth of Massachusetts because she and her family needed the money to survive, but she faced formidable barriers in seeking official compensation for her service in the army. The credibility of her claim was challenged partly because her discharge papers had been lost and partly because as a woman she was held to the higher standard of virtuous conduct expected of women. The implicit question was, how could a woman preserve her softer virtues while fighting in the army as a man?

In 1792, John Hancock would argue on her behalf that "it further appears that the said Deborah exhibited an extraordinary instance of female heroism by discharging the duties of a faithful gallant soldier, and at the same time preserving the virtue of Chastity of her Sex unsuspected and unblemished, and was discharged from the service with a fair and honorable character" (Letter to D. Cobb, January 19, 1792, MSA). That year the state of Massachusetts awarded her the amount of £34 with interest from 1783. Following Paul Revere's letter, in 1805, "she was placed on the pension list of the United States at the rate of four dollars per month," and after her death, her widower was awarded "$466.66, the equivalent of a full pension of eighty dollars per annum" (NAW 3:228).

RHETORICAL BACKGROUND

In many ways, Deborah Sampson Gannett is an unsettling figure; she is a Revolutionary-era woman whose actions are difficult to interpret. As a "notable woman in history," her experiences were "exceptional, even deviant" for women of her time (Lerner, 1979:146). Her actions take on broader historical and rhetorical significance if viewed as evidence of "the tensions created in the culture between the prescribed patriarchal assumptions and women's efforts to attain autonomy and emancipation" (Lerner, 1979:158–159). In her analysis of women in the colonies, Linda Kerber writes: "Americans inherited their political vocabulary from Aristotle" and the major works of the Enlightenment, "which criticized and helped to change attitudes toward the state, [but] offered no guidance to women analyzing their relationship to liberty and civic virtue" (1980:27). She also notes that the Revolutionary War "raised again the old question of whether a woman could be a patriot—that is, an essentially political person—and it also raised the question of what form female patriotism might take" (9).

To George Washington, female patriotism was "the love of country . . . blended with those softer virtues" (Letter to Anne Francis [1781], quoted in Kerber, 1980:106). But less affluent women could not survive on their softer virtues. The war meant that they had to support their families in the absence of husbands or go to war with their spouses, cooking, nursing, and doing laundry for the troops. Like their more privileged sisters who organized sewing societies and boycotts, "They did not change their domestic identity (though they put it to a broader service), and they did not seriously challenge the traditional definition of the woman's domestic domain" (Kerber, 1980:73–74).

Within such a social context, Deborah Sampson "declared a political allegiance" (Evans, 1989:52) and made a decision to risk her life in the war for independence. By enacting the values of self-reliance, bravery, and willfulness, she demonstrated that an individual woman could successfully function in the polis, first as a citizen-soldier and patriot, later as an orator.

The timing of Sampson Gannett's 1792 petition for a pension coincided with the short-lived popularity of several magazines targeting men and women readers. In March 1792, her wartime adventures were featured in a Philadelphia magazine, the *American Museum* (6 [March 1792]:110). In light of publicity from that article, and with public assurances from patriots like John Hancock that her sexual virtue was "unblemished," she was evolving into a romantic heroine of the Revolution. Many accounts of her life as a soldier incorporated two enduring myths about female fighters—the fierce Amazons and the saintly Joan of Arc. One biographer wrote, "It cannot be denied that this romantic girl exhibited something of the same spirit as the lowly herdsmaid" (Ellet, 1969:123). Like Joan, Sampson the soldier was a "troubling sexual figure" (Campbell, 1989:105), and early biographies included romantic tales of her exploits (Ellet, 1969; Mann, 1972).

Herman Mann's fanciful 1797 biography generated additional public curiosity about the female soldier, and it was he who first approached Sampson Gannett, probably sometime in 1801, about the possibility of a lecture tour. In 1802, seeking to support her family and perhaps to refute charges that she had made up the entire affair, she took another unprecedented step as the first U.S. woman to undertake a lecture tour.

By the time she delivered her lecture, two changes in the nature of rhetorical practice were taking place: "The oration itself began to change its form and would appear as the lecture," and the theater "became an accepted part of the cultural pattern" (Robb, 1954:179). The age of elocution was dawning, with an emphasis on formal, literary style, declamation, and dramatic performance. Public lectures were seen as a form of entertainment that also had the potential to instruct. In Boston, for example, she shared the bill with other acts, including scenes from Shakespeare's *Henry IV* and a mime performance of "Harlequin's Frolic" (Tappan, *Diary* notes, 34–37).

The publisher's introduction to the address claimed that she *"procured the following, which she remarkably soon committed, verbatim, to memory except an addition since of about three pages."* There is much disagreement regarding the extent of Herman Mann's role in the creation of the lecture. What is most plausible is that Sampson Gannett needed Mann's help to prepare a text appropriate for a paid lecture tour, but the speech itself made no false claims and even incorporated facts that were not generally known. In effect, she told her story to Mann who cast it in a form suited to the oratorical conventions of the day. The address was in "high style," incorporating ornamental, literary language, including poetry. Nevertheless, it was she who appeared in public and addressed mixed audiences.

Hers was a lecture for which audiences of men and women paid twenty-five cents admission, with children admitted for half price. Because it was designed to generate revenue for her family, Sampson Gannett concerned herself with business details throughout the fifteen-month tour. Her diary indicates that she managed her own business affairs—bookings, advanced publicity, and accounting. For example, she paid $1.34 for "printing bills—3 hundred and 1 hundred tickets" for her Albany, New York, appearances (*Diary*, 29). After arranging to have her publicity bill printed in Providence, Rhode Island, "they were set up in the most publick places in town" (*Diary* [May 3, 1802], 10). Her diary contains detailed accounting and promotional efforts for many of the lectures. It is unlikely that any other woman had attempted to travel alone from town to town, delivering public lectures, while managing her own business affairs.

The tour, which took her to at least twenty towns in Massachusetts, Rhode Island, and New York, was an economic success; Sampson Gannett cleared at least $100, perhaps slightly more. The purchasing power of $100 in 1802 equals over $3,000 earned today. Moreover, at a time when a woman school teacher typically earned one dollar or less a week plus room and board and a seamstress typically earned twenty-five to forty cents a day, her profits were equivalent to the earnings it might otherwise have taken her a year or more to accrue (Friedenberg, 1976:13–14). The popularity of the lecture tour is also suggested by the efforts of William Dunlap, one of the nation's most engaging theatrical managers, to secure her appearance at his Park Theatre in New York City, which was in financial difficulty. His desire to have her appear at the Park apparently reflected his knowledge of the large crowds her appearances were attracting (O'Dell, 1970,2:176, quoted in Friedenberg, 1976:27n.46).

THE RHETORIC

The introduction to the printed text of her address listed three goals Sampson Gannett hoped to achieve during the tour: (1) to "enhance the pecuniary interest of her family"; (2) to "open the eyes of the incredulous, and . . . wipe off any aspersions, which the whispers of satire, caprice, or malevolence may have been wantonly thrown upon her"; and (3) to "re-visit some of the principal places, which were the theatre of her personating the soldier."

Her need for income was evident, and, with a pension application awaiting congressional action, she had to be sensitive to public opinion. For Sampson Gannett, the lecture tour was an attempt to solidify her credibility as a soldier while simultaneously trying to present herself as feminine within the context of Republican Motherhood. Thus, she faced a thorny rhetorical dilemma. On one hand, she had to convince audiences that she had the wherewithal to serve and fight in the army. On the other hand, if that proof was made too forcefully, they would reject her as a woman.

Demonstrating her skill as a soldier, and thereby establishing her credibility, proved to be a challenging task. As her story spread in romanticized accounts in the popular press, many people apparently doubted that a woman could actually have fought in the war. She proved the truth of her military service in several ways: (1) by using facts about the war not known to the general public; (2) by demonstrating her skill with "Old Betsy" in the Manual of Arms; (3) by staying in the homes of her former commanding officers while on tour, including Captain George Webb and General John Patterson; and (4) by presenting a compelling rationale for joining the army in terms her audience could accept.

On May 5, 1802, in Providence, she observed the following about her audience.

When I entred [sic] the Hall, I must say I was much pleased at the appearence [sic] of the audience. It appeared from almost every countenence [sic] that they were full of unblieff [sic]—I mean in Reguard [sic] to my being the person that served in the Revolutionary Army. Some of them which I happened to overhear Swore that I was a lad of not more than Eighteen years of age. (Diary, 11)

In her address, Sampson Gannett acknowledged that her "achievements, which some have believed, but which many still doubt . . . once seemed to me as impossible." She offered "a tale of truth" (17), "a narration of facts" (19) about her soldiering experience. She described her role in "the progress of this horrid delusion of war," as she beheld "the parched soil of *White-Plains* drink insatiate the blood of her most peaceful and industrious proprietors. . . . I was there! The recollection makes me shudder!—A dislocated limb draws fresh anguish from my heart!" She was referring to a wound she received near Tarrytown. About Yorktown she recalled, "Three successive weeks, after a long and rapid march, found me amidst this storm.—But, happy for AMERICA . . . when, on the delivery of Cornwallis's sword to the illustrious, the immortal *WASHINGTON*, or rather by his order, to the brave LINCOLN." If audience members were skeptical about her involvement at Yorktown, this passage put their doubts to rest. Few people other than the soldiers involved would have known how long it took the 4th Massachusetts Regiment to march from West Point, and perhaps few remembered that it was not to Washington, but to General Benjamin Lincoln that Cornwallis surrendered his sword at Yorktown (Friedenberg, 1976:9).

Careful to mention the specific commanding officers and locations, Sampson Gannett also spoke of an "attempt to reinforce the brave SCHUYLER, then on the borders of Canada" and of the "death-like doors of the hospital in Philadelphia, whose avenues were crouded [*sic*] with the sick, the dying and the dead; though myself made one of the unhappy croud [*sic*]!"

Sampson Gannett's credibility as a soldier was further assured by her exhibition of the "Manual of Arms." For this part of the performance, she appeared on stage dressed in her full military uniform, with the regulation Army musket. One witness to the exhibition wrote that she went through the routine "briskly and with perfection and she brought the musket butt smartly down to the floor with a Thud" (Holbrook, 1947:60). It was the type of performance that could only be done with the benefit of training, and considering that she was forty-two and in poor health at the time, it was probably physically taxing. As program notices indicate, the exhibition was usually followed by the audience singing, "God save the sixteen states." Thus, her exhibition enhanced the entertainment aspect of the performance, proved her skill as a soldier, and involved the audience in linking her soldiering to a public show of patriotism.

To further ensure belief in her truthfulness, Friedenberg notes, Sampson Gannett "deliberately spoke in many communities where her former colleagues in arms had settled" (1976:10). Indeed, her lecture tour took her to Holden, the home of Captain George Webb, and, more important, she reestablished contact with former General John Patterson, now a judge in Lisle, New York. She stayed in his home from November 11 to December 11, 1802. In her diary, she writes of a warm reception and feelings of melancholy.

I arrived at Judge Patersons [*sic*] at Lisle. This Respectable family treated me with Every mark of Distinction and friendship, and likewise all the people did the same. I realy [*sic*] want for Words to Express my Gratitude. They often met together in the Neghbourhood [*sic*] and had the most Social meetings. They seemed to unite in hearty Congratulations with my old friend Judge Patterson on our happy meeting. Thus I spent my time as agreeably as one can Imagin [*sic*] Considering my Circumstances. But oh, how often my mind harrowed up by recollection! (22)

Her close association with such well-known citizens eased her entry into the communities where she spoke and reinforced her claims about her previous role in the army. In the case of Judge Patterson, her visit was fortunate for another reason; he served in Congress from 1803 to 1805, during the time when her pension was approved.

With her credibility established, Sampson Gannett could deal with the matter of character. She used several rhetorical strategies to show herself to be a virtuous woman. First, in a mildly apologetic voice, she argued that a sense of patriotic duty led her, as a youth, to demonstrate civic virtue as a soldier. Then, she subordinated her heroics to the feminine virtues of motherhood that she had embraced since the war. In what was certainly an unusual strategy, she spoke directly to women in the speech, asking them to accept her sincerity in praising the virtues of Republican Motherhood. A female lecturer, speaking directly to women in the mixed audience, in praise of Republican Motherhood must have been a rare event indeed, "a presumption," to use her own words. Could she convince her audiences that, as a female patriot *in extremis*, she was a virtuous woman worthy of public recognition of her heroics?

In her lecture, Sampson Gannett posed what was no doubt the central question in the minds of the New Englanders who came to hear her speak:

What particular inducement could she have thus to elope from the soft sphere of her own sex, to perform a deed of valor by way of sacrilege on unhallowed ground—voluntarily to face the storms of both elements and war, in the character of him, who is more fitly made to brave and endure all danger? (27–28)

Her answer voiced her desire for emancipation from popular notions of what an eighteenth-century woman patriot could do for her country.

Wrought upon at length, you may say, by an enthusiasm and phrenzy, that could brook no control—I burst the tyrant bands, which *held my sex in awe*, and clandestinely, or by stealth, grasped an opportunity, which custom and the world seemed to deny, as a natural priviledge [*sic*]. (21)

She was not a reformer who sought to use public address to attain rights for herself or others. Instead, she enacted women's emancipation; her very presence on stage raised questions about the way women were defined as political beings in the Republic. Within the address, she never renounced her motives, her conduct, or her pride in her accomplishments. She did not use the address to recant the political allegiance she swore to defend the nation. However, she did not appeal for other women to follow her example. Such a plea would have implied that every citizen, male and female, has a duty to participate in the armed defense of the nation. This argument still generates heated debate, even among feminists. Nor did she call for granting women a greater role within the polity by extending citizenship to them.

In the address, Sampson Gannett said, "I am indeed willing to acknowledge what I have done, an error and presumption. I will call it an *error* and *presumption*, because I swerved from the accustomed flowery paths of female *delicacy*" (28–29). However, she confessed, "I recollect it with a kind of satisfaction . . . recollecting the *good intentions* of a *bad deed*" (18). She recalled hearing discussions of the British assaults on Lexington and Concord when young, and said, "Know then, that my juvenile mind early became inquisitive to understand . . . why [man] should march out tranquilly, or in a paroxism [*sic*] of rage against his fellow-man, to butcher, and be butchered?" (19). Going to war, she argued, was not "a demoralization of human nature"; she spoke of "the rouzing [*sic*] of every latent spark of humanity," and called the debate over the war "a theme of universal speculation and concern to man" (26).

Sampson Gannett avoided the polarizing language of men as life takers and women as life givers; she recognized that men fought for just causes, and the war for independence was such a just cause. Thus, she invested men with noble motives for going to war, thereby subtly implying that her own motives for enlisting were similar. She explained her growing patriotic fervor: "Confirmed by this time in the justness of a defensive war. . . . I only seemed to want the *license* to become one of the severest *avengers* of the wrong" (21).

As her "mind ripened with [her] strength," she was moved to act by "scenes of havoc, rapacity and devistation [*sic*], as one looks on a drowning man . . . without being able to extend the rescuing hand" (21). Thus, deeply stirred by "an enthusiasm and phrenzy, that could brook no control" (21) she prepared for battle, "with an inflexible resolution to persevere through the last scene; when we might be permitted and acknowledged to enjoy what we had so nobly declared we would possess, or lose with our lives—FREEDOM and INDE-PENDENCE!" (22).

She fought not out of curiosity, but because the nation's armed forces were sorely pressed. She left the world of womanhood and faced danger and death. This was, perhaps, the first time a U.S. woman addressed the belief, firmly grounded in Western political thought and cultural myths, that "martial fervor [is] at odds . . . with maternalism in women" (Elshtain, 1987:4). Shifting into the language of Republican Motherhood, she conceded that her actions "are a breach in the decorum of my sex" (19), "deemed unnatural in my sex" (20), and "thought to have been unnatural, unwise, and indelicate" (31). She used such literary devices as poems, vivid imagery, and extended analogies to link her martial acts to feminine virtue, thus raising questions about how society views the patriotic efforts of women.

Sampson Gannett repeatedly used the analogy of turbulence, which causes objects in nature to stray from their accustomed path, orbit, or course, to explain her experience. She compared herself to a mariner who survived a deadly storm:

she had "performed an important part assigned for another—like a bewildered star traversing out of its accustomed orbit" (30).

She risked offending the guardians of virtue by claiming unfair treatment for her actions when she pointed out: "Had all this been achieved by the rougher hand, more properly assigned to wield the sword in duty and danger in a defensive war, . . . these thorns might have been converted into wreaths of immortal glory and fame" (29). Had she pressed the point, she would have been arguing that her actions should be judged by the same standards as those used to judge the records of men. Instead, she subordinated her heroics to those of her male peers: "I therefore yield every claim of honor and distinction to the hero and patriot, who met the foe in his own name" (29). After all, it was her personage, Robert Shurtleff, who fought in the army, and he ceased to exist when she returned home—to the woman's sphere.

Sampson Gannett also used poetry to argue that her breach of conduct was justifiable:

> And dost thou ask what fairy hand inspired
> A *Nymph* to be with martial glory fired?
> Or, what from art, or yet from nature's laws,
> Has join'd a *Female* to her country's cause?
> Why on great Mars's theatre she drew
> Her *female* pourtrait [*sic*], though in soldier's hue?

She concluded:

> Else must he tell, who would this truth attain,
> Why one is formed for pleasure—one for pain:
> Or, boldly, why our MAKER made us such—
> Why *here* he gives too *little—there* too *much!* (28)

In one of the more confrontational passages, she challenged other women to compare the merits of her soldiering to their own patriotic conduct during the war:

I would appeal to the soft bosom of my own sex to draw a parallel between the perils and sexual inconveniences of a girl in her teens, and not only in the armour, but in the capacity, at any rate, obliged to perform the duties in the field—and those who go to the camp without a masquerade, and consequently subject only to what toils and sacrifices they please: Or, will a conclusion be more natural from those who sometimes take occasion to complain by their own domestic fire-sides; but who, indeed, are at the same time in affluence, cherished in the arms of their companions, and sheltered from the storms of war by the rougher sex in arms. (23)

Having so challenged women, Sampson Gannett drew a stark picture of what she risked by enlisting. She compared her experience to the despair of losing a child, an analogy clearly selected to have an impact on women in the audience: "Such is my experience—not that I ever mourned the loss of a child, but that I considered myself as lost!'' (26). A woman willing to sacrifice her life for the Republic might be seen as extreme, but not corrupt. Her offense was having an excess of civic virtue in exercising what she saw as her patriotic duty.

In the concluding paragraphs, Sampson Gannett moved to strengthen the bond between herself and women in the audience by pledging "high respect and veneration for my own SEX'' (30). To women she said, "you surely will not be wholly indifferent to my sincere declaration of friendship for that sex, for which this checkered flight of my life may have rendered me the least ornamental example'' (30). She praised Republican Mothers:

The rank you hold in the scale of beings is, in many respects, superior to that of man. *Nurses* of his growth, and invariable models of his habits, he becomes a suppliant at your shrine, emulous to please, assiduous to cherish and support, to live and to die for you! *Blossoms* from your very birth, you become his admiration, his joy, his eden companions in this world. (31–32)

Thus, even she, who fought during the Revolutionary War, did not argue against the view that men and women lived in separate spheres. In the concluding paragraph of the address, she wholly embraced Republican Motherhood:

On the whole, as we readily acquiesce in the acknowledgment, that the *field* and the *cabinet* are the proper spheres assigned to our MASTERS and our LORDS; may *we*, also, deserve the dignified title and encomium of MISTRESS and LADY, in our *kitchens* and in our *parlours*. And as an overruling providence may succeed our wishes—let us rear an offspring in every respect worthy to fill the most illustrious stations of their predecessors. (32)

Considering her status as a pioneering woman, it is likely that any hint of impropriety or insincerity in her claim to maternal virtue would have become the basis for ridiculing her public appearances. In her letters and diary, the sacrifices she made for her family's welfare during the tour were clear. Numerous diary entries indicated her sadness at being separated from her family. When she became ill in Boston and had to return home, she wrote the following on May 28, 1802:

Returned home in much anxiety of mind, which is natural to Sore Disappointments. I tarried with my family the most of the month of June, much agitated in mind—anxious to persevere in my Journey—tho' a heart filled with pain when I Realized parting with my three Dear Children and other friends. I may say four Dear children—my Dear Little Susanna Shepperd, which I took at five days old at her mother's Death. (*Diary*, 13)

Thus, her praise of Republican Motherhood in the lecture can be understood as a heartfelt expression of her own beliefs, supported by concern for her children and her willingness to go to extraordinary ends to ensure their welfare.

Sampson Gannett reminded her female listeners of the interdependence of family members and of the woman's role within the family: "How important then is it, that these *blossoms* bring forth such *fruit*, as will best secure your own delights and felicity, and those of him, whose every enjoyment, and even his very existence, is so peculiarly interwoven with your own!"

CONCLUSION

Deborah Sampson Gannett contributed to the history of women: as "a first woman" to fight in the army; as one whose work adds to the diversity of female voices of the Revolutionary era; and as "a first woman" to speak in public to articulate an alternative point of view about women and war.

Sampson Gannett was not a fighter for expanded civil and property rights. She was a poor woman, an indentured servant, for whom improved property and inheritance laws and the vote offered little. As an individual, she did not plead for, but *enacted*, emancipation for early nineteenth-century women.

In an age in which women did not speak in public, her lecture attracted large audiences of men and women, successfully generated money she needed to support her family, and probably played a role in the congressional approval of her pension. Her soldiering experience challenged the assumption that women *could* not fight in combat, but she did not refute the argument that women *should* not fight in combat. Her soldiering experience implied that both men and women can be part of an armed civil militia, but it did not result in reform efforts to extend citizenship to women. That same experience showed that a woman could function on equal terms with men when gender biases were removed (or temporarily "equalized" by means of a disguise or personage), but it did not diminish the double standard used to judge the worth of women's experiences.

As a pioneer, the impact of her experiences in 1802 was limited because there was no organized effort to advance arguments provoked by her example. However, as recently as July 1991, when the U.S. Senate debated the role of women in combat, her performance figured in the argument. "Whether women can go into combat with the armies of the United States has, in a sense, already been answered . . . Deborah Sampson . . . served . . . in the waning days of the Revolution" (MacNeil, 1991:E3). And, it should be added, she explained and justified what she had done in public lectures.

SOURCES

The Deborah Sampson Gannett Collection, Public Library, Sharon, Massachusetts, holds original texts, second-generation hand copies, photocopies of her "Address" and "Diary, 1802," files of unbound, uncatalogued correspondence about her, various secondary publications, and letters written by her descendants. Some official documents in the collection are dated inaccurately. For example, her original discharge and enlistment papers were destroyed; the copies made when she was applying for pensions give 1782 rather than 1781 as the date of her enlistment, which the National Archives determined was a copying error.

In celebration of the centennial of her tour, the Historical Society of Sharon (HSS) reprinted her original lecture, including Mann's introduction, which is cited throughout: "An ADDRSS [sic], Delivered with Applause, at the Federal-Street Theatre, Boston, four successive nights of the different plays, beginning March 22, 1802; By Mrs. DEBORAH SAMPSON GANNET [sic], The American Heroine, Who Served with reputation (undiscovered as a Female) in the late American Army. (1802). Dedham, Mass.: Published and Sold by H. Mann, for Mrs. Gannet." Intro. Eugene Tappan. Sharon, Mass.: Sharon Historical Society, 1905. See also the corrected version minus Mann's introduction: "An Address Delivered in 1802 in Various Towns in Massachusetts, Rhode Island and New York, BY Mrs. Deborah Sampson Gannett, A Soldier of the American Revolution." Intro. Eugene Tappan. Boston: H. M. Hight Press, 1905.

Diary of 1802, with introductory and end notes by Eugene Tappan (July 11, 1901). Sharon, Mass.: Sharon Historical Society. Unpublished, handwritten copy [by Eugene Tappan]; original HSS.

The Gannett Collection, Massachusetts Historical Society (MHS), contains her 1791 pension application to the Massachusetts Legislature; a letter from her to Paul Revere, February 22, 1806 [Unbound papers, 1802–1813, Revere Family Papers, Roll 2, p. 230]; and a letter from Paul Revere to W. Eustis, Esq., February 20, 1804 [Misc. Bound Papers of Paul Revere, 1801–1808], supporting her congressional pension application.

The Deborah Sampson Gannett (also listed under Robert Shirtliff [sic]) Collection, National Archives (NA), Washington, D.C., is housed in the Military Records Division, pension File S32722; Microfilm Publication Papers of the Continental Congress, M–247, M–332. Other Revolutionary War pension applications from women to Congress are found in film M–804.

The Deborah Sampson Gannett Collection, Massachusetts State Archives (MSA), contains copies of her pension applications, a number of detailed sworn statements by Private Shirtleff's commanding officers taken during 1791–1792; and a letter from John Hancock to D. Cobb, speaker of the Massachusetts Legislature, January 19, 1792, approving her 1791 pension request. See also Acts and Laws of the Commonwealth of Massachusetts (January 30, 1792), Ch. 23, and Massachusetts Soldiers and Sailors of the Revolutionary War, Vol. 14 (1906):185.

Secondary sources

Campbell, Karlyn Kohrs. "*La Pucelle D'Orleans* Becomes An American Girl: Anna Dickinson's 'Jeanne D'Arc.' " *Texts in Context*. Eds. Michael Leff and Fred Kauffeld. Davis, Calif.: Hermagoras Press, 1989, pp. 91–111.

Cometti, Elizabeth. "Sampson, Deborah." *NAW* 3:227–228.

Deborah Sampson the Girl Soldier. Ed. E. S. Ellis. New York: Beadle & Adams, 1863.

Ellet, Elizabeth F., ed. *The Women of the American Revolution*, 1848. New York: Haskell House, 1969. Vol. 2:123–134.

Elshtain, Jean Bethke. *Women and War*. New York: Basic Books, 1987.

Evans, Sara. *Born for Liberty: A History of Women in America*. New York: Free Press, 1989.

Friedenberg, Robert. "I Burst the Tyrant Bands Which Held My Sex: Deborah Sampson Gannett, America's First Feminist Speaker." Paper presented at the National

Endowment for the Humanities Symposium on Women in American History, 1976.

Harkness, David J. *Northeastern Heroines of the American Revolution*. Knoxville, Tenn., 1974, pp. 8–9.

Holbrook, Stewart H. *Lost Men of the American Revolution*. New York: Macmillan, 1947, pp. 55–62.

Kerber, Linda. *Women of the Republic: Intellect and Ideology in Revolutionary America*. Chapel Hill: University of North Carolina Press, 1980.

Lerner, Gerda. *The Majority Finds Its Past: Placing Women in History*. New York: Oxford University Press, 1979.

Life of Deborah Sampson: The Female Soldier. Ed. John A. Vinton. Boston: Wiggins & Lunt, 1866.

MacNeil, Donald G. "Private Robert Shurtleff, Well-Camouflaged Fighter." *New York Times*, July 21, 1991, p. E–3.

Mann, Herman. *The Female Review or Memoirs of an American Young Lady*. 1797. New York: Arno, 1972.

Memoirs of the Sampson Family in America. Ed. John A. Vinton. Boston: Wiggins & Lunt, 1864.

Norton, Mary Beth. *Liberty's Daughters: The Revolutionary Experience of American Women, 1750–1800*. New York: Little, Brown, 1980.

O'Dell, George C.D. *Annals of the New York Stage*. 15 vols. 1927–1949. New York: AMS Press, 1970.

Robb, Mary Margaret. "The Elocutionary Movement and Its Chief Figures." *History of Speech Education in America*. Ed. Karl Wallace. New York: Appleton-Century-Crofts, 1954, pp. 178–201.

Stickley, Julia Ward. "The Records of Deborah Sampson Gannett, Woman Soldier of the Revolution." *Prologue: The Journal of the National Archives* (Winter 1972):233–241.

Wright, Eugene A. *The Tales of Old Plympton*. Plympton, Mass.:1977. Vol. 1:71–73.

Wright, Richardson L. *Forgotten Ladies: Nine Portraits from the American Family Album*. Philadelphia: J. B. Lippincott, 1928.

ABIGAIL SCOTT DUNIWAY

(1834–1915), praise and blame for woman's rights "Where Rolls the Oregon"

RANDALL A. LAKE

An Illinois native who migrated with her family to Oregon in 1852 at the age of seventeen, Abigail Scott Duniway devoted more than four decades of her life to the cause of equal rights for women. With less than a year of formal education and responsibility for an invalid farmer husband and six children, "Jennie" nonetheless became a school teacher, milliner, businesswoman, journalist, author, and vigorous proponent of equal rights. She was well informed on and broadly interested in public issues, trends, and reforms of the day, including spiritualism, abolitionism, temperance, bimetallism, immigration, and party politics, and was particularly concerned about women's economic plight. She fought for a woman's right to own property in her own name and to secure that property from her husband and his creditors. She railed against unequal wages on the job and unpaid labor at home, urging that marriage be organized as a business (Address, Progressive Party, 1914:8). Above all, she toiled ceaselessly for that one right on which, she believed, all improvements in woman's lot depended: the right to vote.

To this end, Scott Duniway traveled thousands of miles, spoke on thousands of occasions, and wrote thousands of pages. She cut her teeth on the lecture circuit during SUSAN B. ANTHONY's thousand-mile speaking tour of Oregon and Washington in 1871, for which Scott Duniway served as business manager and delivered speeches of introduction. Thereafter, she stumped the territory herself, organizing local suffrage associations and canvassing for her woman's rights newspaper, *The New Northwest* (*NNW*). Her energies were spent primarily in her "chosen bailiwick," the Pacific Northwest. She divided the first twelve and one-half years of her efforts equally between Oregon and Washington, estimating that she delivered seventy speeches in each place every year for a total of 1,750 from 1871 to 1884. She was also the chief advocate for woman's rights in Idaho for nearly twenty years; her work there, she estimated, involved 140 public lectures and 12,000 miles of travel from 1876 to 1895. In 1886, she reported walking five miles every day except Sunday to collect subscriptions for the *NNW*, writing 100 pages, and delivering three to four public lectures per week (Larson, 1976: 4; Myres, 1982:36n.42; ASD to Mrs. M. C. Athey, January 6, 1897, in ASD II; Address, NWSA, 1884). In addition, she lectured throughout northern California and in states across the country, including Illinois, Iowa, Wyoming, Utah, Michigan, Minnesota, Ohio, and Washington, D.C., on her way to and from national suffrage conventions. Finally, she participated actively in related reform organizations, including temperance alliances and women's clubs.

RHETORICAL CAREER

Scott Duniway was a distinguished rhetor for two fundamental reasons. First, as the activities described suggest, her rhetorical corpus is remarkably large and diverse. There is Scott Duniway the orator, articulate and self-assured, described as a "forceful, logical platform orator, with a touch of sarcasm and a dash of humor that make her arguments effective. As an impromptu speaker she has few equals" (*TWJ*, October 28, 1905:1).

There is also Scott Duniway the journalist. In addition to *The New Northwest*, which she, with substantial help from her family, edited for sixteen years (1871–1887), she also became involved in two other enterprises: editing and contributing to the *Pacific Empire* (1895–1897) and the *Coming Century*, which apparently was issued only once (December 2, 1891). She faithfully attended sessions of the Oregon Legislature to report its doings, to lobby, and, on occasion, to speak. When on the stump, she would send editorial correspondence, a combination of travelogue and biting commentary, for publication. And she wrote countless letters to the editors of other newspapers throughout the region. Harvey Scott, editor of the powerful *Oregonian* for almost forty years, did not share his sister's views of suffrage, among other public issues, and the two engaged in heated discussions in the columns of their newspapers for many years.

Finally, there is Scott Duniway the *littérateur*. She published a bit of "poesy" in the *Illinois Journal* at age sixteen and continued to write verse all her life. In 1875, she published a collection entitled *My Musings*, and the epic poem *David and Anna Matson* a year later. Her poetic impulse often found secondary outlets in lyrics for suffrage songs and in vivid metaphors, colorful imagery, and actual verse in her public speeches. Over the course of forty-six years, she published twenty-two didactic novels, most in serialized form in her newspapers, featuring heroines whose lives taught lessons bearing on the Woman Question. She believed that allegorical fiction was her most effective medium ("How I Became a Literary Woman," *Western Lady*, 1904, DCD).

Second, Scott Duniway is notable as a Western, pioneer woman activist. Studies of the nineteenth-century woman's rights movement have concentrated on Easterners and suffrage campaigns in the more settled states. But conditions in the West were different, and many Western suffragists believed their rhetorical situation to be somewhat different from that of their Eastern sisters. Many believed that the spirit of freedom, independence, perseverance, and self-reliance fostered by the pioneer experience rendered frontier men especially amenable to certain appeals and particularly averse to others (Myres, 1982:232; Larson, 1972a:14). Hence, rhetors like Scott Duniway looked for their models to the discourse, ideals, and values of the American Revolution, when the nation was new. Her rationale for equal rights consisted largely of arguments from principle rather than expediency. Her addresses were often epideictic in character and, only indirectly, deliberative. She protested vociferously, frequently, and often undiplomatically against "interference" in regional efforts by "imported" workers and strategies from "the National," which she often blamed for campaign failures in Oregon and elsewhere. Finally, as her territory became increasingly settled and its frontier origins more distant, she strove to maintain the salience of her message by recreating the pioneer experience in historical narrative. Hence, her rhetoric is noteworthy for both its similarities to and its differences from the discourse of other, better known advocates and the insight gained thereby into the diversity of, and tensions within, the nineteenth-century equal rights movement.

In some respects, Scott Duniway's analysis of her rhetorical situation was typical. Like others, she noted the unique barriers to women's advocacy posed by the "unwomanly" character of the public podium. At the same time, she was aware of the sense in which women's *only* power was rhetorical. Women could not enfranchise themselves, she noted; they could obtain their rights only by the hand of men. It followed indisputably, she believed, that women should take care not to antagonize men or give them cause to fear women's enfranchisement, and should appeal only to men's noblest instincts. In "How to Win the Ballot," she analyzed women's rhetorical situation and prescribed her approach:

The first fact to be considered, when working to win the ballot, is that there is but one way by which we may hope to obtain it, and that is by and through the affirmative votes of men. . . . we must show them that we are inspired by the same patriotic motives that induce them to prize it. . . . [and] impress upon all men the fact that we are not intending to interfere, in any way, with their rights; and all we ask is to be allowed to decide, for ourselves, also as to what our rights should be.

To this end, Scott Duniway's arguments for women's rights stressed "the great principles" of liberty and justice laid out in the U.S. Constitution and Declaration of Independence. She echoed the natural rights doctrines of men from the Founders to Lincoln. She repeated the common but controversial suffragist argument that the Fourteenth and Fifteenth amendments had extended the franchise to women. And she invoked the catch-phrases of the nation's birth. "Government by consent of the governed," she contended, remained a mockery as long as women, who clearly were numbered among the governed, could neither grant nor withhold their consent via the ballot. Similarly, "taxation without representation," she cried, "is tyranny." (Indeed, the 1910 Oregon campaign exploited this theme, as the initiative under consideration would have extended suffrage only to taxpaying women of the state.) Her 1877 address to the Illinois Legislature on "Constitutional Liberty and the 'Aristocracy of Sex' " is a classic statement of these principles.

These themes were commonplace in woman's rights rhetoric of the day, but few pursued them as singlemindedly as Scott Duniway, who strenuously resisted many expediency-based rationales. In her address to the twenty-sixth annual convention of the Oregon State Equal Suffrage Association (OSESA), she declared:

We have from our first existence as an association demanded our right to vote because it belongs to us by every sacred right vouch-safed to every citizen of the United States through the [D]eclaration of Independence and the Federal Constitution. We make no pledges as to what we will do or will not do with the ballot when we get it. Women differ as widely over side issues as do men.

Railing against the "one-idead," she steadfastly maintained that suffrage ought not favor any particular "ism." Her presidential address to the thirty-ninth anniversary convention of the OSESA declared:

Our platform is strictly non-partisan and nonsectarian. It welcomes to its standard every Jew and Catholic, Protestant and Mormon, Christian Scientist, Spiritualist, Theosophist and Pagan who will support our plea against taxation without representation. It appeals for support at the polls to every Democrat, Republican, Prohibitionist, Socialist, Anti-Prohibitionist, Anarchist and Union Labor partisan.

Scott Duniway reserved the greatest measure of her ire for the White Ribboners of the WCTU. Although a lifelong temperance advocate herself, she appears to have abandoned advocacy of prohibition by 1881 (Larson, 1976:54). In principle, she came to believe, women could not seek individual natural rights for them-selves and simultaneously seek to deprive men of theirs. Prohibition *qua* pro-hibition, whether of the liquor traffic or of women's right to vote, was wrong. In a letter to the *Oregonian* (October 13, 1887), she wrote:

The two ideas of prohibition and liberty are in exact juxtaposition to each other. It is just as impossible to reconcile the two ideas and make them win together as it was impossible for this government to maintain itself any longer under the old discordant regime of freedom and slavery.

True temperance, she maintained, was a matter of personal moral responsibility. In 1914, addressing a Progressive party luncheon in Portland, she argued:

"Oh" somebody says, "doesn't God prohibit everything that is evil? Aren't the Ten Commandments full of prohibition?" Yes, the Ten Commandments say, "Thou shalt not steal," but the Ten [C]ommandments do not hide away in the bowels of the earth everything that man can steal. On the contrary, the Ten Commandments place in your way and mine temptation and say to us, "Resist it or take the consequences." ... We can never have temperance in its truest sense until we have raised men and women who are willing to abide by the rule of self-protection.

Only by successfully surmounting temptation could this morality be perfected, a process that the law would short-circuit. Her thirty-ninth anniversary address to OSESA continued:

Don't imagine that you can ever make laws to govern men. All you can do through the law of liberty, is to so elevate the standard of morality, through expanding opportunities for yourselves, that men will strive instinctively to meet, from within their own consciousnesses, the highest laws that are innate within even the lowliest and most depraved man or woman, and only await the soul of development under the laws of liberty and responsibility.

Moreover, she believed, prohibition would doom suffrage by arousing the organized opposition not only of the liquor industry but also of secondary trades including farmers, coopers, and barrel-makers. In "Ballots and Bullets," perhaps her most famous address on the topic, she warned: "Whenever our demand for our right to vote is based upon an alleged purpose to take away from men any degree of what they deem their liberties, or own right of choice we simply throw boomerangs that recoil upon our own heads."

Scott Duniway vigorously defended these views at every opportunity. Her 1914 autobiography, *Path-Breaking*, is largely an *apologia* for this position. As a result, she endured repeated and often vicious charges that she had sold out to liquor interests, and she faced efforts, both overt and covert, to subvert her leadership.

Scott Duniway advanced arguments from principle in response to her understanding of women's rhetorical situation. She believed that men would find it more difficult to oppose woman's rights that were claimed according to the same principles by which they claimed their own. In addition, because principles are abstract, transcendent, and universalizing, they possess a moral authority that expediency lacks, and they can be less contentious than concrete policy proposals. That prohibition aroused division rather than harmony in fact illustrates the relative danger of tying principles to concrete actions, whether to promote or oppose them.

Scott Duniway was keenly aware of the importance of political expediency and employed such appeals when she judged that they would not antagonize men. Frequently, she sought to allay fears that suffrage would undermine the home. To standard charges that suffragists were man-haters and home-wreckers, she responded in several ways. Although the interests of men and women differed, she insisted, they were always complementary. She often compared unequal relations between the sexes to dislocated shears that could not function effectively; suffrage would make these relations more, not less, harmonious. In "Woman in Oregon History," commemorating the fortieth anniversary of Oregon statehood, she averred: "The interests of the sexes can never be identically the same; but they are always mutual, always interdependent, and every effort to separate them results, primarily, in discontent and ultimately in failure." She stressed that most women were not man-haters but, in fact, liked men a good deal better than they liked each other. She berated the "sour-souled, vinegar-visaged" exceptions to this rule, who should "steal away and die" ("Home and Mother"; "How to Win the Ballot"). She commonly used the experiences in states that had approved woman suffrage to disprove the "theoretical" claims of doomsayers. She often turned anti-suffrage arguments on their heads. For example, in reply to the charge that equal rights would cause women to abandon home and family, she conceded women's maternal instinct and domestic inclination, arguing that these were so powerful that equal rights could not overwhelm them. She proudly held up her own successful children as further refutation of the claim that suffragists would destroy motherhood.

While most of these arguments were not original, they illustrate three important points. First, Scott Duniway sought to reassure often hostile audiences by arguing from generally accepted principles of liberty and premises about woman's sphere. Second, she was familiar with the repertoire of pro and con arguments on equal rights. Third, she had a keen, analytical mind and was a skillful arguer. Her "Opposition" and "Equal Rights for All" speeches are notable examples of her refutational skills (and "Opposition" also illustrates her use of humor). In these ways, she demonstrated her talents in deliberative address.

More important, Scott Duniway quite literally courted favor by engaging in epideictic. Aristotle's *Rhetoric* observes that epideictic and deliberative addresses are related, since to praise or blame is, in some respects, akin to urging a course of action: "the suggestions which would be made in the latter case become encomiums when differently expressed" (1367b36–1368a1). Her rhetoric splendidly illustrates the way in which flattery and censure can be made to serve deliberative ends by indirection.

Scott Duniway lavished praise on the men of the Pacific Northwest, particularly the deeds of pioneer men in clearing and settling the land, their independent spirit and love of liberty, and their sense of fairness. Similarly, she praised the region's women, particularly their strength and courage in enduring pioneer hardships at least as great as those faced by men, their endless domestic toil, and their accomplishments in business and the professions (e.g., "Eminent Women I Have Met" and "Woman in Journalism"). In "A Pioneer Incident," she claimed:

The men and women who first take up their line of march across untracked continents, who settle upon the outposts of civilization and raise the standard of Liberty for all the people to higher planes are the very best and most enterprising citizens of any land.

Her address at the Lewis and Clark Exposition appealed to "the broad-brained, big-hearted men of this mighty State, in the midst of whose splendid achievements we are so proudly standing . . . to arise in the majesty of your patriotism and chivalry and swing wide the doors to our joint inheritance."

Praise of women's exploits in particular "demonstrated" that they had earned equal rights. "Success in Sight" contains Scott Duniway's most explicit expression of this theme:

Nowhere else upon this planet are the inalienable rights of women as much appreciated as on the newly settled borders of the United States. Men have had opportunities in our remote counties to see the worth of the civilized woman who came with them or among them to new settlements after the Indian woman's day. And they have seen her, not as the parasitic woman who inherits wealth, or the equally selfish woman who lives in idleness upon her husband's toil, but as their helpmate, companion, counselor and fellow homemaker.

Whether celebrating men or women, flesh-and-blood people or somewhat mythic frontier personae, such praise invited audiences to live up to these models of humanity, to become them.

Scott Duniway's own persona also augmented the epideictic mode. Her speeches often were partly autobiographical, recounting her experiences as a mother of six, a pioneer settler of Oregon, and a pioneer in the equal rights movement. They typically dwelt on the unceasing toil and drudgery that were the lot of a frontier wife and emphasized her decades-long, back-breaking, sometimes solitary, and often ill-appreciated labors, at great personal sacrifice, for the cause. As she grew older, she often attributed her infirmities to overwork and expressed hope that she would live to see her life's work consummated. Such passages can appear self-aggrandizing and as plays on cheap emotionalism, including maternal respect and guilt over disobedience. But they should be considered in their larger epideictic context. In praising herself, she also praises the women of the Pacific Northwest whose virtues and experiences she shares and comes synecdochically to represent. They all are "path-breakers" in this dual sense, pioneers of the Pacific Northwest and for equal rights, and her life comes to stand for Everywoman's. If her life demonstrates that she has earned equal rights, she enacts her larger epideictic "claim" that women deserve the ballot.

Like argument from principle, epideictic furthers Scott Duniway's rhetorical purpose. Praise ingratiates and does not threaten. Unlike deliberative address, as Aristotle first noted, epideictic's focus on the present reduces a rhetor's need to envision a future of uncertain appeal to audiences (*Rhetoric*, 1358b14–21). Moreover, just as appeals to principle avoid discussion of the expediency of policies, the epideictic emphasizes character, not courses of action. Characterizing temperance as a moral rather than legal matter and praising the rugged individualism of the pioneer were mutually reinforcing; both emphasized personal responsibility without specifying what responsible action must entail. Hence, rather than challenging audience beliefs about right and wrong actions, Scott Duniway invited audiences to become certain kinds of people, those who live according to certain accepted principles, presupposing that people of right character will do the right thing.

The danger of epideictic, however, is that while praise assuages, blame estranges. Herein lies the great irony of Scott Duniway's strategic choice given her understanding of women's rhetorical situation. Generous with flattery in high style, she was also liberal with censure couched in low style. Sharp-witted and sharp-tongued, she could excoriate an opponent as quickly as laud an ally. Reportedly, her extemporaneous stump speeches were laced with prickly humor.

Her more formal addresses were comparatively circumspect. In them, she invariably praised the support for suffrage shown by "all the best classes" of men, but scornfully condemned the opposition of the "vicious" classes, particularly immigrants. At the tenth Oregon Pioneer Association reunion, she appealed to the patriotic and chivalrous instincts of the "best classes" for protection from the "vicious":

We are not afraid of the votes of wise men, moral men, intelligent, liberty-loving, progressive men; but we know, alas! that every ignorant, vicious, drunken, law-breaking or tyrannical man has a vote which counts at the polls as surely as the vote of a thinker, statesman and philanthropist. Women cannot reach the prejudiced, ignorant and vicious voting elements to educate and enlighten them. Such men consider themselves *superior* to those Oregon pioneers—these wives and mothers of orderly and law-abiding citizens— and we must look to the leading men of the State, like those around me, for protection from the proscriptive ballots of the lawless, ignorant and wicked hordes who presume to dictate our destiny.

Here, in a typical move, the appeals to chivalry and to suffrage as reward for pioneering combine with concerns over immigration to argue that woman suffrage would strengthen the "home element" against the less virtuous classes (Myres, 1982:232). She was fond of condemning the injustice that placed the "wives and mothers" of "self-respecting men" in the same political category as "idiots, insane persons, criminals, Chinamen not native-born, and Indians not taxed" ("Campaign Leaflet," 1, no.7 [November 1900]:6 in DCD). In this way, flattery and guilt are reinforced by fear.

As noted, Scott Duniway was equally impatient with wealthy, privileged women who, because they hired others to perform their labor for them, felt no need for equal rights, and with the "one-idead" and "man-haters" among suffragists. But her disagreements with others were not only philosophical and substantive. She frequently came into heated conflict with regional and national suffrage leaders over political tactics as well. She cautioned against what she called "hurrah campaigns," run by workers "imported" from the eastern states, which, with public rallies and demonstrations, brought much attention to the cause. Such publicity, she believed, was counterproductive, arousing also the organized opposition. These campaigns, she contended, invariably failed. She favored instead the "still hunt" method that sought, through letter-writing and personal lobbying, to win the quiet support of key officials, respected organizations, and leading men of the state.

In her most conciliatory moments, Scott Duniway's approach to those with whom she disagreed was to admonish and correct, not to assail and humiliate. In "Ballots and Bullets," she concluded: "If in anything I have said tonight I have given any one of my sincere co-workers a moment's pain, I can only say I am sorry, but I must not withhold the facts." Defending her views on prohibition in *NNW* (June 17, 1886), she wrote:

We do not say these things in a spirit of faultfinding or dictation. It pains us inexpressibly to thus proclaim the truth and arouse your hostility. But it is the truth, and we hereby tell it in love and kindliness, not seeking or expecting personal reward, but braving even your own condemnation if haply we can humbly help to make you free indeed.

But Scott Duniway's capacity for vituperation is also evident in her newspaper columns and letters, which often engaged in the name-calling, witty sarcasm and bitter invective characteristic of the "Oregon-style journalism" of her day. She lambasted Supreme Court Justice Ward Hunt, who rejected the Fourteenth Amendment defense in SUSAN B. ANTHONY's 1873 trial for illegal voting, as "an angular brained, one idead old fossil, who would excel as a first class donkey" (*NNW*, July 18, 1873). When Horace Greeley refused to endorse suffrage, she called him "an infinitessimal political pigmy of reality" (*NNW*, June 7, 1872) and "a coarse, bigoted, narrow-minded old dotard" (*NNW*, September 13, 1872). And she exchanged fire with opposition editors, nicknaming one Prohibition paper the "Temperance Turkey Buzzard" and denouncing its editor as "a noisy simpleton" (*NNW*, July 17, 1874). In the vilification arena, she clearly could hold her own.

This habit of personalizing disagreement unquestionably generated intense hostility, transforming potential allies into bitter adversaries. She alienated many regional and national suffrage leaders. In 1895, CARRIE LANE CHAPMAN CATT confided to Emma Smith DeVoe of Illinois, "I now believe that Mrs. Duniway is a jealous-minded and dangerous woman." Scott Duniway was ordered to remove herself from the campaign in Idaho; NAWSA sent Smith DeVoe and Laura M. Johns of Kansas to spearhead the effort, and Lane Catt herself spent a month campaigning and strategizing in 1896. Afterward, Scott Duniway felt denied proper credit for her role in the victory. But even her mentor Anthony admitted to CLARA BEWICK COLBY that her head was "so full of crochets that it is impossible for her to co-operate with anybody." Thereafter, Scott Duniway confined her work chiefly to Oregon. She directed the "still hunt" campaign of 1900, which failed by fewer than 2,000 votes. But her resentment of eastern "interference" boiled over in the aftermath of the NAWSA-directed campaign of 1905–1906, which failed by over 10,000 votes. She termed the effort "disastrous" and interpreted the results as exonerating her methods and repudiating those of the National's leadership. She earned the enmity of ANNA HOWARD SHAW (whose name she sometimes spelled "Pshaw") in particular, accusing the NAWSA president of malfeasance in office. Shortly after this setback, she beat back a prohibitionist attempt involving Bewick Colby, publisher of the *Woman's Tribune*, to seize control of OSESA. Her subsequent appeal to NAWSA for seed money with which to launch a new effort was, unsurprisingly, rebuffed. The National, she was told, had concluded that "the only thing that could be done for Oregon was to leave her severely alone" (Kate Gordon to ASD, June 7, 1907 in "Suffrage Correspondence 1907–1909," DCD; see also

Catt to DeVoe March 7, 1895; Anthony to Bewick Colby, May 19, 1899, quoted in Larson, 1976:56).

Scott Duniway often was not gracious even when she could have been. Years after the 1906 defeat, when suffrage had come to the Pacific Northwest, she used the occasion of Shaw's refusal to pay income taxes to reopen old wounds:

It has been my experience that it has been better to obey the laws until we get the chance to amend them. If we had pursued the tactics of Dr. Shaw in the Northwest, we should never have had equal suffrage in Washington, Idaho or Oregon. I consider our victory here in Oregon, after the 42 years of my work, a repudiation of Anna Shaw's method. ("Income Tax Fought by Suffragist Chief," in Duniway Family Clippings, DCD)

In 1914, when a member of the WCTU, in polite disagreement, returned the copy of the polemical *Path-Breaking* that Scott Duniway had sent her, the latter shot back:

You are not the only woman who owes her enfranchisement to my humble efforts who has proved ungrateful. But you and—you know who—are the only ones who have capped the climax by refusing to accept my little History that will live and flourish long after you are both forgotten. *And thou too, Brutus*? (Elizabeth Eggert to ASD, October 1, 1914, and ASD to Eggert, October 2, 1914, in "Suffrage Correspondence 1914," DCD)

Clearly, Scott Duniway was opinionated, often strident, even vain. Yet, by defining repellent characters, her vilification of opponents magnified the contrast between noble and ignoble personae, rendering more stark and compelling the choice between characters with which she confronted audiences. Because blame is but the counterpart of praise, her outbursts, though impolitic, were understandable.

However, Scott Duniway reserved her most lyrical and effusive praise, expressed in verse and prose, for the "paradise" that was the Pacific Northwest. At virtually every opportunity, she lauded its magnificent scenery, abundant natural resources, temperate climate, space for settlement, and prospects for commerce.

At first blush, these encomia to nature seem little more than somewhat provincial boosterism. But they played a vital role in Scott Duniway's larger epideictic efforts by literally grounding the cause of equal rights in a place. Moreover, because the place itself was unique, this cause became its special destiny. In "Woman in Oregon History," she contended: "All great uprisings of the race, looking to the establishment of a larger liberty for all the people, have first been generated in new countries, where plastic conditions adapt themselves to larger growth." She often argued that the West in general, and the Pacific Northwest in particular, was the most fertile of grounds, in which the cause of equal rights could and would take deepest and firmest root. In addressing the Oregon Pioneer Association in 1882, she sounded the theme she was to echo before the 1899 NAWSA Convention:

There are lessons of liberty in the rock-ribbed mountains that pierce our blue horizon with their snow-crowned heads and laugh to scorn the warring elements of the earth and air; lessons of freedom in the broad prairies that roll away into illimitable distances; in the gigantic forests that rear their hydra heads to the very zenith and touch the horizon with extended arms; lessons of truth, equality and justice in the very air we breathe, and lessons of irresistible progress in the mighty waters that surge with irresistible power through the overshadowing bluffs where rolls the Oregon. It is not strange that noble men living in such a country should have early learned to preach and practice the grand gospel of equal rights. (Address, Oregon Pioneer Association)

In Burkean terms, this strategy features the scene, which then, according to the logic of the pentadic ratios, calls forth suitable acts and agents (1969:3–15). In Scott Duniway's case, the land is free, just, and irresistible and calls forth a pioneer people imbued with the spirit of liberty; here is the scene-agent ratio at work. It remains for this people to consummate the acts consistent with this scene, that is, to free women by granting them suffrage. Yet by the logic of the scene-act ratio, because the scene is free and just, the acts it contains will partake of these qualities. Furthermore, the scene itself is described as irresistible. Hence, the victory of suffrage is inevitable; the region demands and of necessity will result in a civilization founded on principles of equality between the sexes.

Variations on this central theme of irresistible progress are common in Scott Duniway's rhetoric. A firm believer in human improvement, she often marveled at advances in science and technology that were transforming labor both in and outside the home, and commented frequently on the evolving state of spiritual awareness. The advance of woman's rights was for her a natural, ineluctable part of human sociopolitical development. "The world is moving," she was fond of saying, "and women are moving with it." She unfailingly heralded the inevitable triumph of her cause, even in the face of defeat after defeat. She began her 1884 address to the Senate select committee on woman suffrage with a rhetorical question: "Gentlemen of the committee: Do you think it is possible that an agitation like this can go on and on forever without a victory?" Twelve years later, she still prophesied that "equal suffrage is marching toward victory just as surely as the light which leaves the sun and travels toward the earth will reach the human eye" ("Among the Suffragists," *PE*, April 23, 1896:1).

This scenic emphasis accomplishes four important rhetorical objectives. First, it mitigates the temporal and pragmatic limitations of epideictic appeals grounded in arguments from principle. No longer restricted to abstractions adhered to in the present, Scott Duniway can envision the future of a place, predicting the amelioration of drunkenness, divorce, political corruption, prostitution, crime, war, labor unrest, and myriad other social ills.

Second, a scenic emphasis reinforces the contrast between noble and vicious characters, between which audiences are asked to choose, with a complementary and equally loaded choice between alternative futures of progress and regress. Indeed, because inevitable progress is a feature of the scene, there really is no choice at all; audiences of the Pacific Northwest must become what the land requires.

Third, the momentum generated by the scene can evoke optimism in those who favor its direction and pessimism in those it threatens to leave behind. In many of Scott Duniway's addresses, notably in "Upward Steps in a Third of a Century," ever-increasing support for the cause of woman's rights is part of the broader advance of human progress. Thus, her discourse offers hope to woman's rights advocates while it resigns opponents to defeat.

Fourth, by locating the future in the inexorable unfolding scene itself, she deflects responsibility from woman's rights advocates, insulating the movement from the criticism of those who would oppose and obstruct this future. Even her own rhetorical insensitivity can be excused at least partially; in her plain speaking, she often averred, she intended no "personal" offense, but sought only to speak the "truth." In so doing, she simply gives voice to the scene. What the land has set in motion is something for which no woman can be blamed and no man can stop; it is destiny.

These deliberative and epideictic strategies span Scott Duniway's entire public career. As time passed and Oregon became more settled, and the original pioneer experience more remote, she strove to maintain the salience of her message by recreating this experience in historical narrative. Often, she would be a prominent character herself; at other times, she would recount the exploits of others. In either case, she sought to keep alive not simply the memory of an era, but that era itself. In addition to those already quoted, illustrative addresses include "The Pacific Northwest" (1893); her speech to the Oregon Federation of Women's Clubs (1906); "The Woman Suffrage Movement and Two Kinds of Prohibition" (1914); and her otherwise unidentified October 1915 speech.

CONCLUSION

In sum, Abigail Scott Duniway was a controversial advocate whose rhetoric, adapted to frontier conditions, could inspire as well as infuriate. Her combativeness and insistence on running campaigns in her own way arguably slowed the progress of the equal rights movement in the Pacific Northwest by alienating potential allies both within and outside the movement. Yet, her prodigious pen and outspoken voice, her indefatigable determination, and, ultimately, her stature as a public woman were unmatched in the region. The triumph of woman suffrage in the Pacific Northwest was in large measure her personal triumph as well. Admittedly, she played a larger role in Washington Territory's brief experiment with suffrage in 1883 than in subsequent campaigns and, as noted above, she was removed from the decisive drive in Idaho (Larson, 1976:55–56, 62). Nonetheless, her early efforts laid the groundwork for extensions of suffrage in Idaho in 1896 and Washington in 1910. When, after five unsuccessful campaigns that had begun in 1884, the voters of Oregon finally extended the franchise in 1912, the labors of the acknowledged "mother of woman suffrage in the Pacific Northwest'' were rewarded. Scott Duniway penned and countersigned the gubernatorial proclamation that made suffrage a reality.

SOURCES

Those who wish to study Scott Duniway's rhetoric will want to consult two major primary sources. The holdings of the Oregon Historical Society Library, Portland, include scrapbooks with clippings and other material related to woman suffrage, the *Pacific Empire* (*PE*) in text, the *New Northwest* (*NNW*) on microfilm (5 reels), other regional newspapers that printed her work, notably the *Oregon Farmer*, the *Oregon City Argus*, and the (Portland) *Oregonian* (*OR*), all on microfilm, the records of the Duniway Publishing Company and the Oregon State Equal Suffrage Association, and some correspondence, notably in the Eva Emery Dye Papers (two boxes). Scott Duniway's personal papers are in the possession of her grandson, David C. Duniway (DCD) of Salem, Oregon. Included here are manuscripts of speeches, poetry, and novels, two scrapbooks (ASD I & II) primarily of news clippings and editorial columns (as a journalist, Scott Duniway subscribed to a clipping service), suffrage campaign materials, the overland diary she kept on the trip from Illinois, business records, and correspondence with family and others. Because she also wrote occasionally for the *Revolution*, *TWJ*, and the *Woman's Tribune*, scholars may wish to consult the History of Women collection microfilmed by the Schlesinger Library at Radcliffe. Finally, the Archives of the Oregon State Library (OSL) contain some miscellaneous materials.

Duniway, Abigail Scott. *Path Breaking: An Autobiographical History of the Equal Suffrage Movement in Pacific Coast States*. 2nd ed. 1914. New York: Schocken, 1971. (*PB*)
Edwards, G. Thomas. *Sowing Good Seeds: The Northwest Suffrage Campaigns of Susan B. Anthony*. Portland: Oregon Historical Society, 1990.
HWS 4:Ch. 54; *HWS* 5:Ch. 60; *HWS* 6:Ch. 56.

Selected Critical References

Bandow, Gayle R. '' 'In Pursuit of a Purpose': Abigail Scott Duniway and the New Northwest.'' M.A. thesis, University of Oregon, 1973.
Bennion, Sherilyn Cox. "The New Northwest and Woman's Exponent: Early Voices for Suffrage." *Journalism Quarterly* 54 (1977):286–292.
Burke, Kenneth. *A Grammar of Motives*. 1945. Berkeley, Calif.: University of California Press, 1969.
Kessler, Lauren. "A Siege of the Citadels: Search for a Public Forum for the Ideas of Oregon Woman Suffrage." *Oregon Historical Quarterly* 84 (1983):117–149.
Mansfield, Dorothy M. "Abigail S. Duniway: Suffragette [*sic*] with Not-so-common Sense." *Western Speech* 35 (1971):24–29.
McKern, Roberta O. "The Woman Suffrage Movement in Oregon and the Oregon Press." M.A. thesis, University of Oregon, 1975.
Montague, Martha Frances. "The Woman Suffrage Movement in Oregon." M.A. thesis, University of Oregon, 1930.
Ward, Jean M. "The Emergence of a Mentor-Protege Relationship: The 1871 Pacific Northwest Lecture Tour of Susan B. Anthony and Abigail Scott Duniway."

Proceedings of the 1982 Northwest Women's Heritage Conference Sponsored by the University of Washington and the Ford Foundation. Seattle: University of Washington, 1984, pp. 120–145.

———. "Women's Responses to Systems of Male Authority: Communication Strategies in the Novels of Abigail Scott Duniway." 2 vols. Ph.D. diss., University of Oregon, 1989.

Selected Biographical and Historical Works

"Abigail Scott Duniway: Oregon's Foremost Suffragette" [*sic*]. *The Table Rock Sentinel* 5 (1985):3–17.

Capell, Letitia Lee. "A Biography of Abigail Scott Duniway." M.A. thesis, University of Oregon, 1934.

Chittenden, Elizabeth F. " 'By No Means Excluding Women': Abigail Scott Duniway, Western Pioneer in the Struggle for Equal Voting Rights." *The Northwest Mosaic: Minority Conflicts in Pacific Northwest History.* Eds. James A. Halseth and Bruce A. Glasrud. Boulder, Colo.: Pruett, 1977, pp. 191–198.

Clark, Robert Carlton. *History of the Willamette Valley, Oregon.* Chicago: S. J. Clarke, 1927. Vol. 1:702–724.

Duniway, David Cushing. "Abigail Scott Duniway, Path Breaker." *With Her Own Wings: Historical Sketches, Reminiscences, and Anecdotes of Pioneer Women.* Ed. Helen Krebs Smith. Comp. Portland Federation of Women's Organizations. Portland, Oreg.: Beattie, 1948, pp. 202–205.

Holbrook, Stewart H. "No Doll Was Abigail." *Dreamers of the American Dream.* Garden City, N.Y.: Doubleday, 1957, Ch. 6:205–212.

Johnson, L. C. "Duniway, Abigail Jane Scott." *NAW* 1:531–533.

Larson, T.A. "Dolls, Vassals, and Drudges: Pioneer Women in the West." *Western Historical Quarterly* 3 (January 1972a):5–16.

———. "The Woman's Rights Movement in Idaho." *Idaho Yesterdays* 16 (Spring 1972b):2–15, 18–19.

———. "The Woman Suffrage Movement in Washington." *Pacific Northwest Quarterly* 67 (1976):49–62.

Morrison, Dorothy Nafus. "Ladies Were Not Expected: Abigail Scott Duniway and Women's Rights." New York: Atheneum, 1977; rpt. Western Imprints, Oregon Historical Society Press, 1985.

Moynihan, Ruth Barnes. "Abigail Scott Duniway of Oregon: Woman and Suffragist of the American Frontier." 2 vols. Ph.D. diss., Yale University, 1979. Ed. and rev. *Rebel for Rights: Abigail Scott Duniway.* New Haven, Conn.: Yale University Press, 1983.

———. "Of Women's Rights and Freedom: Abigail Scott Duniway." *Women in Pacific Northwest History: An Anthology.* Ed. Karen J. Blair. Seattle: University of Washington Press, 1988, pp. 9–24.

Myres, Sandra L. *Westering Women and the Frontier Experience, 1800–1915.* Albuquerque, N.M.: University of New Mexico Press, 1982.

Richey, Elinor. "The Unsinkable Abigail." *American Heritage* 26 (1975):72–89.

———. "Abigail Scott Duniway: Up from Hard Scrabble." *Eminent Women of the West.* Berkeley, Calif.: Howell-North, 1975, pp. 73–96.

Roberts, Leslie McKay. "Suffragist of the New West: Abigail Scott Duniway and the

Development of the Oregon Woman Suffrage Movement.'' B.A. thesis, Reed College, 1969.

Ross, Nancy Wilson. "The Prophet." *Westward the Women*. New York: Random House, 1944, Ch. 8:137–154.

Smith, Helen Krebs. *The Presumptuous Dreamers: A Sociological History of the Life and Times of Abigail Scott Duniway (1834–1915)*. 2 vols. Lake Oswego, Oreg.: Smith, Smith & Smith, 1974.

Chronology of Major Speeches (Codes are listed above.)

"Opposition." Washington Territory Woman Suffrage Association, November 11, 1873. *NNW* (November 28, 1873):1.

"Constitutional Liberty and the 'Aristocracy of Sex.' " Illinois State Legislature, Springfield, Ill., January 19, 1877. DCD, ms. in folder.

Address, Tenth Annual Reunion, Oregon Pioneer Association, Salem, Oreg., June 16, 1882. OSL; *Transactions of the Tenth Annual Reunion of the Oregon Pioneer Association for 1882*. Salem: E. M. Waite, 1883, pp. 36–39.

Address, Eleventh Annual Convention OSESA, Portland, Oreg., February 14, 1883. DCD, ASD II:44.

Address, suffrage rally, Astoria, Oreg., August 1883. *NNW* (August 16, 1883):1.

Address, NWSA Convention, Washington, D.C., March 1884. DCD, excerpt in ASD II:18.

Address, U.S. Senate Select Committee on Woman Suffrage, Washington, D.C., March 7, 1884. *NNW* (April 24, 1884):6.

"Ballots and Bullets." NWSA Convention, Washington, D.C., February 1889. *PB*, 188–200; *OR* (September 9, 1906):33.

"Equal Rights for All." Idaho Constitutional Convention, Boise, Idaho, July 16, 1889. *PE* (June 9, 1898):3–8; excerpted in *PB*, 133–141.

"Woman Suffrage and the Republican Party." To various equal suffrage societies prior to the reelection of Grover Cleveland in 1893. DCD, typescript in ASD II.

"The Pacific Northwest." World's Congress of Women, Columbian Exposition, Chicago, June 1, 1893. DCD, ms. in folder; typescript in ASD II.

Address, Twenty-fifth Annual OSESA Convention, Portland, Oreg., December 5, 1896. *PE* (December 10, 1896):3–6.

Address, Twenty-sixth Annual OSESA Convention, 1897. DCD, typescript in ASD I.

"Woman in Oregon History." Oregon Legislative Assembly, Salem, Oreg., in commemoration of the fortieth anniversary of statehood, February 14, 1899. OSL; *Fortieth Anniversary of the Statehood of Oregon*. Salem: W. H. Leeds, 1899, pp. 55–60; *OR* (February 15, 1899):12; *PB*, 144–153; DCD, clipping in folder.

"How to Win the Ballot." NAWSA Convention, Grand Rapids, Mich., May 2, 1899. *PB*, 156–168.

"Success in Sight." NAWSA Convention, Washington, D.C., February 14, 1900. *PB*, 169–178. Also dated February 12, in *Portland Evening Telegram*, February 13, 1900; DCD, clipping in folder.

"Eminent Women I Have Met." State Federation of Women's Clubs, Pendleton, Oreg., June 1, 1900. *OR* (June 2, 1900):5; DCD, portions of typescript in ASD I and II.

"Presidents Past and Future." Presidential inaugural address, Portland Women's Club,
        Portland, Oreg., October 11, 1902. DCD, typescript in folder.
Address at "Abigail Scott Duniway Day," Lewis and Clark Exposition, Portland, Oreg.,
        October 6, 1905. DCD, clipping (excerpts) in ASD I; rpt. *Woman's Tribune*
        (October 28, 1905):1, 72; copies in ASD I:46–47, and folder.
Address, Business Women's League, San Francisco, November 1905. DCD, clipping
        (excerpts) in ASD I.
"A Pioneer Incident." Oregon Historical Society fourth annual meeting, Portland, Oreg.,
        December 20, 1905. DCD, reconstructed from memory in letter from ASD to Dr.
        Annice Jeffreys, December 21, 1905.
Address, State Federation of Women's Clubs, 1906 (?). DCD, ms. in folder.
"Upward Steps in a Third of a Century." NAWSA Convention, Baltimore, Md., February
        1906. *OR* (February 11, 1906):30; clippings in DCD, ASD I:18–19, ASD II:15;
        OSL, Scrapbook 88, 181–182.
Presidential address, OSESA Convention, Portland, Oreg., November 1906. *OR*, No-
        vember 22, 1906; DCD, ASD I.
"Early Pioneer Nursing." Quarterly meeting, Oregon State Nurses' Association, Port-
        land, Oreg., July 10, 1907. *OR* (July 11, 1907); DCD, ASD I.
"The Powers of Thought." Society of Bible Spiritualists, Portland, Oreg., October 6,
        1907. Excerpts *OR* (October 7, 1907); DCD, ASD I:27.
Address to a company of soldiers, Willamette Valley Chautauqua Assembly, July 1908.
        DCD, typescript in ASD II.
Presidential address, thirty-seventh anniversary OSESA meeting, Portland, Oreg., No-
        vember 1908. DCD, ASD II:10–11.
"The Tax-Paying Woman's Suffrage Amendment." People's Forum, Portland, Oreg.
        OR: May 17, 1909.
Presidential Address at thirty-ninth anniversary OSESA meeting, Portland, Oreg., No-
        vember 20, 1909. *OR* (December 5, 1909): Sec. "Woman's and Books," 4;
        DCD, ASD II:12.
Address, luncheon meeting, Progressive party, Portland, Oreg., February 25, 1914. DCD,
        typescript in ASD I.
"Home and Mother." Federation of Labor, Portland, Oreg., Labor Day, 1914. DCD,
        ms. in folder (reconstructed in letter to the editor, September 22, 1914).
"The Woman Suffrage Movement and Two Kinds of Prohibition." Library Hall, Portland,
        Oreg., October 5, 1914. DCD, typescript in folder (stenographic report by D. A.
        Norton, October 6, 1914).
Address on the history of the Oregon Territory, October 1915. DCD, ms. in folder.

The following undated addresses are also extant:

Address on domestic servants and housekeeping. DCD, ASD I (typescript).
"Woman in Journalism." DCD, ASD II (ms.).
Address, State Federation of Women's Clubs, Hood River, Oreg. DCD, ASD II
        (typescript).
Address, Charter Commission, Portland, Oreg. DCD, ASD II (ms.).

ANNA HOWARD SHAW
(1847–1919), a case study in rhetorical enactment

WILMER A. LINKUGEL

"I was born on a cold, dreary morning in February," wrote the Reverend Dr. Anna Howard Shaw, "and it is said that my protests against existing conditions began immediately and that they have continued without cessation ever since" (*SP*, Box 19, Folder 436). For forty years Shaw protested existing social conditions and proclaimed equal rights for women in every American state and in most European countries. She spoke to the English, the Swedes, and the Germans; she addressed leading American colleges and universities; she presided at packed meetings in Carnegie Hall and Cooper Union; and she pleaded with numerous congressional committees and state legislatures. She delivered several hundred speeches a year, and often spoke as many as eight times a day, often for temperance but mostly for woman suffrage.

BACKGROUND

This remarkable woman was born in England on Valentine's Day, 1847, but when she was four, her father, Thomas Shaw, moved the family to the United States, settling first in New Bedford, Massachusetts, but moving within the year to Lawrence where they lived for almost seven years. In 1859, Thomas Shaw's restlessness prompted him to move the family to Michigan, where he left them to build a home in the wilderness while he returned to the East to earn money for their support. Life in the Michigan wilderness left little time for formal education, and so Shaw received much of her elementary education at home. It was not until she was twenty-four years old that she entered Big Rapids High School. While there, she became interested in the school's speech activities and demonstrated considerable skill as a reader, debater, and orator. After two years, because of her age, in 1873, she decided not to finish high school but to enter Albion College, where she once more was drawn to the public speaking platform. The school's literary societies attracted her, and she joined an all-woman society because a representative of the mixed society pompously told her, "Women need to be associated with men, because they don't know how to manage meetings" (*SP*:69). Her oratorical reputation grew so quickly on campus that by the end of the year the men nominated her to be the orator for a quinquennial reunion of all the societies.

What attracted Shaw the most, however, was the pulpit. As a young girl, her desire to preach was already so great that often she stood on a stump in the solitude of the Michigan wilderness and delivered youthful eloquence to the mute trees. Liberal-minded Methodist ministers in the area occasionally invited her to deliver the Sunday sermon in their churches. Thus, after two years of college, she felt a strong urge to pursue a ministerial career. Showing some of her father's impulsiveness, she made a hard decision to leave financial and family security in Michigan to matriculate at Boston University Seminary to work toward a theological degree. Since the ministry was not a generally accepted profession for women, her move to Boston produced temporary alienation from her family, leaving her with few resources. Thus, as a seminarian she not only encountered a heavy dose of prejudice from teachers and peers, but also nearly starved while weathering the Boston winter in an unheated attic. Serendipity came to her rescue, however, when a Mrs. Barrett, the superintendent of the Women's Foreign Missionary Society, told her that an unnamed friend would pay her three dollars and a half a week if she would promise to rest, study, and take care of her health (*SP*:89).

On completion of her work at the seminary, Shaw accepted a parish pastorate at East Dennis on Cape Cod. Her work as a pastor was both eventful and controversial. Early in her ministry she repeatedly encountered challenges, and she dealt with each dispute resolutely. Although pastoral duties absorbed her, she still felt her preparation for life unfulfilled. So it was that she commuted to Boston for three years to study medicine at the Boston University Medical School, taking her M.D. in 1886. Now equipped to treat both soul and body, she resigned her pastorate, not to practice medicine, but to preach woman's rights. She was appointed National Lecturer by the AWSA in 1888, and two years later the newly merged NAWSA continued her in that post. From that time forward until the adoption of the Nineteenth Amendment, she was an advocate of woman suffrage. From 1904 until 1915, she served as president of NAWSA.

SHAW'S RHETORIC: ENACTING THE "NEW WOMAN"

That Shaw was highly regarded as an orator, even the greatest woman orator of her day, can easily be demonstrated from reading journalistic reports and peer assessments of her speaking. Newspapers, large and small, praised her oratory profusely. "A magnificent speaker," "brilliant, clever, and humorous," "The foremost orator of her generation," "Queen of the platform" were typical journalistic plaudits. On the day after her death, the Philadelphia *North American* proclaimed that "Dr. Shaw was without equal as an orator among women. She is generally conceded as the greatest woman speaker who ever lived. Some believe her to have been without peer in either sex among orators of her day" (July 3, 1919). CARRIE LANE CHAPMAN CATT, herself a capable speaker, said that she "stood unchallenged as the greatest orator among women the world has ever known" (Catt and Shuler, 1926:268). Even opponents acknowledged her talents. Fearing rhetorical embarrassment, for example, the Anti-Suffrage Association eventually prohibited their members from debating her. The evidence is overwhelming: Shaw was regarded as an unusually capable advocate of woman suffrage. Why?

The response that she was so effective simply because she was such a good public speaker seems simplistic. A better answer may lie in the rhetorical concept of *enactment*. In *Form and Genre: Shaping Rhetorical Action*, Karlyn Kohrs Campbell and Kathleen Jamieson describe enactment as occurring when "the speaker incarnates the argument, *is* proof of the truth of what is said" (1978:9). Campbell elsewhere adds, "Enactment is powerful evidence because members of the audience see and hear the evidence for themselves, directly. The proof is particularly vivid—it is alive in front of them!" (1982:273). Support for this thought also comes from the Reverend Samuel Longfellow, brother of the famous poet, who, in 1860, at the outset of his address at the Tenth Annual National Woman's Rights Convention, said:

It might seem, that on a platform like this, when a woman speaks, her presence is not merely a plea and an argument, but also a proof. When a woman speaks, and speaks well, speaks so as to interest and move and persuade men, there is no need of any argment back of that to prove that she has the liberty and the right, and that it is a part of her sphere to do it. She has done it; and that of itself is the whole argument—both premise and conclusion in one. (*HWS* 1:711)

To understand how Shaw enacted the citizen-voter or the "new woman," we must understand that woman's fate in the nineteenth century was largely determined by stereotyping and role prescription. It was generally believed that the primary attributes of men were "courage and boldness"; the male was to leave the domestic scene to encounter the "turmoil and bustle of an active selfish world"; he had to "meet with a lion's heart the dangers which threaten him." Woman, by contrast, was to be shielded by man from the "rude shocks of the world" and "because of her inferior strength and sedentary habits confine her[self] within the domestic circle." In 1935, Thomas R. Dew, a writer on the subject, announced: "Woman we behold dependent and weak" (quoted in Kraditor, 1968:45–47). Women were also seen as being nervous and prone to fainting. The "clinging vine" metaphor prescribed that a woman was to be the "helpmate" of her man, to stand behind him in all things, and to look to him for her strength and protection (Pastoral Letter of the Massachusetts Congregationalist Clergy, 1837, quoted in Kraditor, 1968:51–52). She was to yield to him in matters outside the hearth. The male of the species was thought to be stronger not only in body but also in mind. Men were logical; women were emotional. Men sought answers through a search for evidence and reasoned from that evidence to logical conclusions; women found answers intuitively. And women certainly should not vote, except in school elections because schools involved children, a subject on which women as mothers were thought to be natural experts. To make the female even more drab, she was thought to be relatively humorless. A nineteenth-century woman was to be a "true" woman—and a true woman was to possess the four cardinal female virtues of piety, purity, submissiveness, and domesticity (Welter, 1976). Given the stereotype, it is easy to understand why anyone would conclude that women should stay in the home and let the superior male meet the dangerous vicissitudes of life.

Thus, a woman rhetor in the nineteenth century had the task of creating a "new woman" in the minds of people: a woman who was capable of doing things, including public speaking; a woman who could think logically and deal with political questions of the day; a woman who was not too emotional to vote meaningfully; a woman who could stand on her own without having man protect her from the "slings and arrows" of the hard, cruel world; and perhaps even, a woman who had a sense of humor. In addition, the woman rhetor needed to convince men that this "new woman" was not an aberration, that she was not "manlike" but "humanlike." Shaw was ideally suited to enact this "new woman." She often spoke about such a new woman, especially in relationship to the "new man," as she did in her lecture of that title. The purpose of this chapter is to search out *the manner in which Shaw and her rhetoric enacted the new woman*—a woman equally qualified with males as a citizen-voter.

Shaw capably demonstrated her physical endurance through rugged campaigning in the hinterlands of South Dakota, Wyoming, and Kansas. Travel in these western states was primitive. Trains went to the leading cities, but not always passenger trains; on more than one occasion, Shaw traveled in the splendid comfort of a cattle car. She was snowbound in a train near Faribault, Minnesota, with no one but herself and a group of cattlemen on board; her sleigh was chased by wolves one night in the Kansas winter, and only the lights of a small town that suddenly appeared saved her life; she pumped a railroad handcar from Newton to Hutchinson in Kansas in order to keep a speaking appointment. Shaw herself relates in her autobiography:

To drive fifty or sixty miles in a day to meet a lecture engagement was a frequent experience. I have been driven across the prairies in June when they were like a mammoth flower-bed, and in January when they seemed one huge snow-covered grave—my grave, I thought, at times. Once during a thirty-mile drive, when the thermometer was twenty degrees below zero, I suddenly realized that my face was freezing. I opened my satchel, took out the tissue-paper that protected my best gown, and put the paper over my face as a veil, tucking it inside my bonnet. When I reached my destination the tissue was a perfect mask, frozen stiff, and I had to be lifted from the sleigh. I was due on the lecture platform in half an hour, so I drank a huge bowl of boiling ginger tea and appeared on time. (*SP*:163)

Shaw earned the respect of her audiences in these out-of-the-way places just by showing up—no one given to fainting would have been able to be there. Courage was also involved. Any woman who would venture into the Minnesota or South Dakota winter on a sled or on a cattle train in order to reach her speaking destination did not lack for courage and boldness. She had to meet with a "lion's heart" the dangers that threatened her. Evidence shows that auditors admired Shaw's courage and pluck. On one occasion, she gained the respect of hearty cattlemen, lumbermen and townspeople alike, when she courageously stood on the stage of the speaking hall which was on fire and told the audience to march out singing while she beat time to "Jesus, Lover of My Soul" (*SP*:170–171).

Shaw also enacted the "new woman" through her speaking ability. With few exceptions, she delivered her speeches in a lively, extemporaneous manner, a style of speaking that allowed her to adapt to difficult situations. Sometimes she discarded her prepared speech on the spur of the moment and spoke extemporaneously; at other times she totally reshaped her speech to fit the needs of the occasion. Audiences were aware of the directness of Shaw's speech. She was not a shy, clinging vine reading from a manuscript with a weak voice; rather, her voice was resonant and carried exceptionally well. With considerable ease, Shaw projected her voice into "the back rows in the topmost galleries of such places as the Hippodrome in New York City and Albert Hall in London. Outdoors she could be heard at extreme edges of immense crowds" (AHSP, Box 19, Folder 441; Harper unpublished biography, 49). A German man, on hearing that Shaw was going to speak, snorted, "That old woman! She cannot make herself heard." However, when she started to speak, he was so stunned by her voice that he listened attentively, and exclaimed, "Mein Gott, she could be heard *anywhere*" (*SP*:333). The *Washington Post* asserted, "Her voice, while it is sweet, and musical, is strong and carries a tone of conviction" (*HWS* 4:361). Another reporter declared that Shaw's rich contralto voice cast such a spell that it "was not to be evaded. Even in conversation, her voice had the indefinable quality which makes the orator" (AHSP, Box 20).

Shaw approached each speech with energy and enthusiasm, in direct contrast to the retiring nineteenth-century female stereotype. Her auditors admired her quenchless, superabundant vitality, and some hostile listeners gave her a fair hearing because of it. Once at Coatesville, Pennsylvania, she addressed a group of women and a few sympathetic men on temperance. As she was leaving the hall, a prominent citizen stopped her and told her he wished she were a man. He explained that the town was to have a big outdoor meeting that night, but the orator had failed them. He said there were thousands of men in the streets waiting for a speech, "and the saloons are sending them free drinks to get them drunk and carry the town tomorrow." Whereupon Shaw, despite the man's protests as to the rowdiness of the crowd, forced her way to the speaker's stand, mounted the platform, and proceeded to so enthrall the crowd that they were led by an African-American man in punctuating the key ideas of her speech with "Hallelujah to the Lamb!" (*SP*:175).

Rhetorically, Shaw enacted the "new woman" in three ways: (1) She was thoroughly logical; (2) she was incisive in dealing with opposing arguments; and (3) she spoke with considerable humor.

Early in her lecture career Shaw argued the woman suffrage question from expediency. One of her most famous addresses, "The Fate of Republics," was grounded in the thought that the life of a republic was seriously eroded by a lack of female participation in political action. However, after the turn of the century, her fundamental stance shifted almost entirely to republican principles as the bases of her arguments. She began most speeches by establishing the grounds on which the woman suffrage question should *not* be resolved. The consequences of woman suffrage, or issues of expediency, had the potential for strong emotional overtones, but she told New Jersey legislators at a hearing that "whether all women vote once they receive the ballot or no women vote, whether all women vote right or all women vote wrong, whether women will love their husbands after they vote or forsake them, whether they will neglect their children" or be loving and attentive mothers—were irrelevant to the fundamental issue (January 25, 1915, AHSP, Box 22, Folder 539). What was relevant, Shaw told her listeners, was that the issue be decided on the principles of "a republican form of government." She then inquired into the nature of a democracy, and, for an answer, she turned to the writings and sayings of the Founders. With delight, she quoted such able advocates of democracy and the rights of man as James Otis, Benjamin Franklin, and Samuel Adams: "No taxation without representation"; "The voice of the people is the voice of God"; "Under God, the people rule." From these axioms of the Founders, she concluded that the essence of a republican form of government was that laws were made by representatives of the people. If, then, women were people, logically, they should be represented in the lawmaking and governing processes with men. Thus, she had established not only basic premises about a republican form of government but also her position as a student of government who identified herself with the Founders.

Next, Shaw indicated that women were indeed people because they were generally acknowledged to have souls. For the humor it embodied, she often inquired into this question; for an answer she referred to a seventeenth-century church council that, by a very small majority, decided that women had souls. Mirthfully, she remarked at San Jose in 1895; "How thankful we should be for that decision, for unless it had been reached there is no telling what we would have been decided to be by this time" (*San Jose Daily Mirror*, October 16, 1895). Then, with a degree of mock surprise, she pointed out that a Massachusetts court had even declared women to be "persons" in the eyes of the law in an 1883 opinion (*Opinion of Justices*, 136 Mass. [1883], 578, 580). If women were people—and even persons in the eyes of the law—they should have the same political privileges as men, and to deny them these privileges abridged the fundamental principles of a republican form of government.

Shaw thus arrived at her conclusion through an argument from genus. By inquiring into the nature of democracy, she revealed it was a form of government that guaranteed certain "unalienable rights" to its people; by legal definition, she established that women were persons, thus making them people; by logical inference, she concluded that the rights of the whole must be predicated to all its parts. As long as a woman, because of her sex, was denied the right of the ballot, no true democracy could exist.

Shaw continued her logical train of thought by applying the fundamental principles of a republican form of government to existing conditions, only to discover that the status quo did not fit the definition of a democracy. Laws were being made in the nation by half the human family. Women had no voice in the government, yet they were expected to obey all its laws and pay taxes to support it. This was not democracy, but tyranny—as the Revolutionary Founders had so loudly proclaimed. In a democracy, voting qualifications must be uniform. The only restrictions that the nature of democracy decreed was that voters be rational beings susceptible of ideas and capable of reasoning from them. All humans could meet age or residency qualifications; however, sex, she said, was not a qualification, but an insuperable barrier. To place this barrier before women grouped them with criminals, idiots, children, and the insane—who were all excluded on grounds of irresponsibility. She staunchly adhered to these principles. She rejected racist inclinations prominent in her day and called for equal rights for all. She also rejected the "educated vote" that ELIZABETH CADY STANTON advocated late in life, insisting that the fundamental principles of a democracy must apply to all.

In addition to responsibility, the citizen-voter should be able to compare and contrast competing points of view. Shaw demonstrated this ability in most of her suffrage addresses by analyzing and refuting anti-suffrage contentions. She relied on three refutative techniques: exposing inconsistencies, reducing opponents' arguments to absurdity, and attacking the evidence of the opposition.

Exposing inconsistencies was Shaw's deadliest tactic. She announced that the beauty of the anti-suffragists' arguments was that they came in pairs: They would spend five minutes developing an argument and then proceed to present a second argument that was so contradictory that it thoroughly refuted the first one. Once, when asked to answer an anti-suffrage debater, she replied, "What's the use? Divide up their literature and let them destroy themselves." With eyes twinkling, she pointed out that one minute the anti-suffragists contended that it was no use for women to vote because they would vote like their husbands—even if they had no husbands; in the next breath the same speakers said that great discord, broken homes, and divorce would be the consequences of equal suffrage. A similar inconsistency was that women did not really want the ballot, and if it were given to them, they would not use it. Subsequently, these anti-suffragists argued that women would neglect their homes and families because of the great amount of time spent in voting—as though voting would take several hours of each day of the year (Linkugel, 1960).

Shaw often skillfully reduced an opponent's arguments to absurdity. A good example was her response to the argument that women should not be given the ballot because that would add large numbers of ignorant voters to the electorate. To begin with, she asserted, the nation would also be adding a large number of intelligent voters—as a matter of fact, the proportion of literate women was considerably higher than that of men, and in this regard the female characterized the "citizen-voter" better than the male. She thought it strange that an objection to woman suffrage should be made on the grounds of female ignorance, because such painstaking effort was made to protect male illiteracy.

In order to avoid corruption, the Australian ballot was imported into the United States, but a voter needed to be able to read to vote the ballot. Because a large number of men could not read, a rooster was used to identify the candidates of one party and an eagle to identify those of the other party. Since even illiterate men could tell the difference between a rooster and an eagle, ignorant males were able to vote. Shaw suggested that ignorant women also could tell the difference between a rooster and an eagle; if not, the eagle could be replaced by a hen, which they certainly would be able to differentiate (*MCSFH* 2:441).

She frequently attacked the evidence of the opposition. Anti-suffragists often cited figures in support of their stand, but, according to Shaw, all they proved was that liars could figure. For example, in dry states the anti-suffragists offered statistics to show that women would legalize liquor if given the vote; but in wet states they presented figures to show that women would vote the state dry.

Sometimes Shaw dealt directly with the issue of the emotionality of women versus the rationality of men. "By some objectors women are supposed to be unfit to vote because they are hysterical and emotional," she told her audience in a 1913 speech on "The Emotional Sex," "and, of course, men would not like to have emotion enter into a political campaign." She acknowledged that, on a few occasions at their annual conventions, women had stood up and waved white handkerchiefs and had even sung "Blest Be the Tie That Binds." However, she countered that that seemed considerably less hysterical to her than the men at the last Democratic national convention held in Baltimore, where she had gone "to observe the calm repose of the male politicians." She said that she saw some men carry a picture of one candidate that was so big that they had to walk sideways as they carried it down the aisle, and

they were followed by hundreds of other men screaming and yelling, shouting and singing the "Houn' Dawg;" then, there was a lull, another set of men would start forward under another man's picture, not to be outdone by the "Houn' Dawg" melody, whooping and howling still louder. I saw men jump upon the seats and throw their hats in the air and shout: "What's the matter with Champ Clark?" Then, when those hats came down, other men would kick them back into the air shouting at the top of their voices: "He's all right!" Then I heard others howling for "Underwood, Underwood, first, last, and all the time!" No hysteria about it—just patriotic loyalty, splendid manly devotion to principle.

Shaw then allowed that she had never seen a "woman leap up on a chair and take her bonnet and toss it up in the air and shout: 'What's the matter with somebody.' I never saw a woman knock another woman's bonnet off her head as she screamed: 'She's all right!' " She concluded that whenever she heard how emotional and excitable women were, she could not help but see in her mind's eye "the fine repose and dignity of this Baltimore and other political conventions I have attended" (*HWS* 5:370).

If Thomas Dew's (1835) stereotypical woman lacked a sense of humor, the "new woman" as enacted by Shaw certainly did not. For example, she had a talent for clever repartee in heckling situations. At Wichita, in 1912, an anti-suffragist informed her that suffrage was unnecessary because her husband voted for her. She retorted that she didn't believe it because no man could vote for another and for himself. Turning to another anti-suffragist who contended that she controlled her husband's vote, Shaw said she doubted that too, because no woman who had a fool for a husband would publicly announce it (*Wichita Eagle*, October 24, 1912). The crowd was delighted. She sometimes used a question box technique, and her responses usually provided a good deal of levity for the audience. For example:

If women had the ballot, would she not sell her vote for a new bonnet? Perhaps she might. Who knows? A new bonnet is a fine thing, and most women hanker after it. But a good bonnet costs more than a glass of whiskey, and that, they say, is the marketplace of male votes nowadays.

Why does the Scripture say that there shall be no marriages in heaven? Ah, my dear friends (and she drew a long sigh), some one has answered that by saying, because there will be no men there.

The crowd loved it. The loudest guffaws often came from the men in the audience. Anecdotes, odd conceits, wit, gentle sarcasm, irony, and amusing comparisons abounded in her suffrage campaign speeches. Early in her career, she was prone to sarcasm but later she sweetened her satire and modified it with a gracious smile. In her eulogy, CARRIE LANE CHAPMAN CATT said that ''as the cause gained, [Shaw] put aside ridicule and sarcasms and assumed a gentler and sunnier humor'' (*New York Times*, November 23, 1915). Instead of scolding men for their shortcomings, Shaw poked fun at them in a way that made them laugh with her. Even the man who quivered under her blows usually smiled, applauded, and admired her. Her touches of humor tended to keep even the crustiest listeners on pleasant terms with her. As a rule, newspapers reporting her speeches noted the crispness of her logic, but then proceeded to call special attention to her sense of humor. The *Nebraska State Journal* (October 6, 1906) asserted: "Greater entertainment is seldom enjoyed than that delivered from the address of the Reverend Anna Howard Shaw." Her infectious humor was an important good-will device in her suffrage speeches, and as such was one of her most important avenues to persuasion.

Clearly, then, Shaw enacted the qualities of the citizen-voter in contrast to the stereotypical qualities ascribed to women throughout most of the nineteenth century. Her logic, incisive analysis, emotional control, sense of humor, and speaking ability—in both voice and action—were dimensions of her rhetoric that were not lost on her audiences. Even men staunchly opposed to woman suffrage often acknowledged the logic of her arguments. One Senate Judiciary Committee chair, after listening to her speak, remarked: "Your arguments are logical. Your cause is just. The trouble is that women don't want suffrage. My wife doesn't want it." Unfortunately for that senator, his wife was in the audience, and she stood up to say that not only did she want the vote, but also that she had wanted it for twenty years. Shaw slyly observed, "I am afraid his wife had a bad quarter of an hour when they met a little later in the privacy of their home'' (*SP*:255–256). Another committee chair admitted, ''There is no man living who can answer the argument of those women, but I'd rather see my wife dead in her coffin than voting, and I'd die myself before I'd vote to submit that amendment!'' (Catt and Shuler, 1926:268). Small wonder that the Paola, Kansas, *Miami Republican* spoke of the ''woman preacher, with the clear, keen, unanswerable logic'' (May 25, 1894). After listening to her at a committee hearing, a reporter remarked: ''If this woman has not sufficient intelligence to vote, how many men have sufficient mental capacity?'' (AHSP, Box 20). A reporter from the Topeka, Kansas, *Daily Capital* wrote: ''If anything could convince a disbeliever in woman suffrage it would be the sight of a woman with such a remarkable intellect'' (May 11, 1894).

Although logical appeal was often bluntly rebuffed, as illustrated previously, men such as President Woodrow Wilson in the midst of a great war ''to make the world safe for democracy'' eventually found it awkward to uphold democratic principles while continuing to ignore woman's right to suffrage; the equal suffrage amendment was adopted in 1919 and ratified a year later as the Nineteenth Amendment. Shaw died on July 2, 1919. She lived to see the amendment passed, but she never voted in a national election.

CONCLUSION

During the forty years that Shaw spoke for suffrage, membership in the national association increased from 17,000 to more than 200,000. Many factors doubtless contributed to this rise. Nevertheless, she spoke more often for woman suffrage than anyone else, which was not lost on CARRIE LANE CHAPMAN CATT when she eulogized her:

There are no words with which to measure the part which Dr. Shaw played in this monumental victory. She was of the suffrage struggle its greatest orator, its wit, its humor, its deathless spirit. She staked her whole life on the cause, she conquered it, and death cannot rob her nor us of the victory that was so largely her work. (*New York Times*, November 23, 1915)

In her own day, the *Seattle Post-Intelligencer* called Shaw ''*a living demonstration* of the ability of her sex and the justice of her cause'' (AHSP, Box 23, Folder 566, italics added). The *Springfield Republican* pointedly stated that Shaw ''illustrated *in her own person* the truth which she preached'' (AHSP, Box 23, Folder 566, 22; italics added). The Reverend Dr. Anna Howard Shaw clearly was a speaker who incarnated her argument; she *was* the proof of what she claimed. In her rhetoric and in her life she was the ''new woman.''

SOURCES

The Anna Howard Shaw Papers (AHSP), Dillon Collection, Schlesinger Library, Radcliffe College, Cambridge, Massachusetts, are the major primary source and contain correspondence, newspaper clippings, speeches, diaries and appointment books, and other miscellaneous manuscripts.

Biographical sources

Harper, Ida Husted. Anna Howard Shaw. Unpublished ms. AHSP, Box 19, Folder 436; Michigan Historical Collection, University of Michigan Library, Ann Arbor.

Linkugel, Wil A., and Martha Solomon. *Anna Howard Shaw: Suffrage Orator and Social Reformer*. Westport, Conn.: Greenwood, 1991.

Shaw, Anna Howard. *The Story of a Pioneer*. New York: Harper & Brothers, 1915. (*SP*)

Theses and Dissertations

Eggleston, Jean Marie. "A Study of the Development of Dr. Anna Howard Shaw— Reformer and Orator." M.A. thesis, Northwestern University, 1934.

Giel, Dorothy. "Anna Howard Shaw: A Leadership Study." M.A. thesis, Central Michigan University, Mount Pleasant, 1987. MA 1330128

Linkugel, Wilmer Albert. "The Speeches of Anna Howard Shaw: Collected and Edited with Introduction and Notes." 2 vols. Ph.D. diss., University of Wisconsin, 1960. AAC6005761

Critical Essays

Jordan, Elizabeth. "Anna Howard Shaw: An Intimate Study." *Chicago Tribune*, July 27, 1919.

Linkugel, Wil A. "The Speech Style of Anna Howard Shaw." *Central States Speech Journal* 13, no.3 (Spring 1961):171–179.

————. "The Woman Suffrage Argument of Anna Howard Shaw." *Quarterly Journal of Speech* 49 (April 1963):165–174.

————, and Kim Giffin. "The Distinguished War Service of Dr. Anna Howard Shaw." *Pennsylvania History* 28, no.4 (October 1961):372–385.

McGovern, James R. "Anna Howard Shaw: New Approaches to Feminism." *Journal of Social History* 3 (Winter 1969–1970):135–153. Uses psychology to attack woman's rights advocates.

Other References

And Blessed Is She: Sermons by Women. Eds. David Farmer and Edwina Hunter. San Francisco: Harper & Row, 1990. Shaw's "The Path Is Plain," September 30, 1877, pp. 22–30.

Campbell, Karlyn Kohrs. *The Rhetorical Act*. Belmont, Calif.: Wadsworth, 1982.

Campbell, Karlyn Kohrs, and Kathleen Jamieson. *Form and Genre: Shaping Rhetorical Action*. Falls Church, Va.: Speech Communication Association, 1978.

Catt, Carrie Chapman, and Nettie Rogers Shuler. *Woman Suffrage and Politics: The Inner Story of the Suffrage Movement*. New York: Charles Scribner's Sons, 1926.

Dew, Thomas R. "Dissertation on the Characteristic Differences Between the Sexes, and on the Position and Influence of Women in Society." *Southern Literary Messenger*

1 (May 1835):493–512. Rpt. *Up from the Pedestal: Selected Writings on the History of American Feminism*. Ed. Aileen S. Kraditor. Chicago: Quadrangle, 1968, pp. 45–47.

Kraditor, Aileen S. Ed. *Up from the Pedestal: Selected Writings on the History of American Feminism*. Chicago: Quadrangle, 1968.

Welter, Barbara. *Dimity Convictions: The American Women in the Nineteenth Century*. Athens: Ohio University Press, 1976.

A chronology of Shaw's extant speeches is found in the Linkugel dissertation. Texts in Linkugel and Solomon are:

"The Heavenly Vision," March 25, 1888, pp. 115–126; also OW:158–162.

"The New Man," delivered frequently during the late 1890s, pp. 127–130.

"God's Women," February 22–25, 1891, National Council of Women, Washington, D.C., pp. 131–138.

"The Fate of Republics," Congress of Women, World's Columbian Exposition, Chicago, Ill., 1893, pp. 139–146; excerpt *WSBH*:201–209.

"The Fundamental Principle of a Republic," June 21, 1915, pp. 147–164; also *MCSFH* 2:433–460.

"The Other Half of Humanity," undated, pp. 165–184.

"Select Your Principle of Life," undated, pp. 185–191.

"What the War Meant to Women" (speech and pamphlet), undated, pp. 193–204.

SOJOURNER TRUTH

(1797?–1883), legendary anti-slavery and woman's rights agitator

SUZANNE PULLON FITCH

Sojourner Truth was an advocate for anti-slavery and woman's rights. As a freed Black woman, she epitomized both causes and from this position gained much of her influence as spokesperson for both reforms. As a slave, Truth was denied any opportunity for an education, and even after gaining her freedom, she never learned to read or write. Thus, extant texts of her speeches were transcribed by others as she spoke; probably none is accurate. Because they were transcribed, most of the content is fragmentary at best, and often the only records are reports of what she said that quote a phrase or two to show her ability to make a point.

A further problem in quoted fragments of her speeches concerns the language that she used. Because her first language was Dutch, and she did not learn English until she was nine or so, it is difficult to judge her language and accent. She may have spoken with a Germanic accent, but she may also have acquired some southern Black dialect from fellow slaves. However, there is little or no proof of this background in reports of her speaking. Truth did not approve of those who transcribed her speeches in a thick dialect. In her only remaining scrapbook, a fragment of an article in the *Kalamazoo Telegraph* that she kept states:

Sojourner also prides herself on a fairly correct English, which is in all senses a foreign tongue to her, she having spent her early years among people speaking "Low Dutch." People who report her often exaggerate her expressions, putting into her mouth the most marked southern dialect, which Sojourner feels is rather taking an unfair advantage of her. (1)

Given such strong indications of her unusual language background, the most extreme "negroisms" attributed to her have been removed in this chapter.

Despite the fragmentary nature of her extant rhetoric, what we know of Sojourner Truth's speeches provides enough evidence to show that she was an orator of great personal power whose words "came with direct and terrible force, moving friend and foe alike" (Stone, 1976:252) at times, or softly and gently as she talked about prejudice to Sunday School children. Her use of the simple language of the uneducated, which she could weave into striking narrative and metaphors, her nearly six-foot frame that revealed the strength developed working as a farmhand and house maid, and her powerful low voice telling of her denied rights as a woman and an African-American made her one of the most forceful instruments of reform. She was more than a symbol for the two causes. Described as this "weird, wonderful creature, who was at once a marvel and a mystery" (Gage, 1863:4), she set her own goals for both causes when she said, "So I am for keeping the thing going while things are stirring; because if we wait till it is still, it will take a great while to get it going again'' (May 9, 1867). She was also quoted as saying, ''I go in for agitatin','' and responded to one heckler who said he didn't mind her talk anymore than the bite of a flea, ''Perhaps not, but, the Lord willin', I'll keep you scratchin' '' (Carter, 1887:479). Using humor, sarcasm, and homely logic, coupled with a unique persona, she did just that.

Most of what is known about her comes from the *Narrative of Sojourner Truth: A Bondswoman of Olden Times* (hereafter *Narrative*), written for her from her own story by Olive Gilbert. Frances Titus later added the ''Book of Life'' section, which consists of newspaper clippings, autographs of famous people she met, and other artifacts, some kept in three small scrapbooks.

The *Narrative* is an autobiography with two qualifications. First, Gilbert often added her own material, especially when discussing the woes of slavery. Second, there is an omission of several years of her life when she was owned by John J. Dumont, the master whom Truth considered kind. She kept in touch and even visited Dumont after freedom was granted her. However, she did not always get along well with Mrs. Dumont. Gilbert wrote:

From this source [Mrs. Dumont] arose a long series of trials in the life of our heroine, which we must pass over in silence; some from motives of delicacy, and others, because the relation of them might inflict undeserved pain on some now living, whom Isabel [Truth's slave name] remembers only with esteem and love; therefore, the reader will not be surprised if our narrative appear somewhat tame at this point, and may rest assured that it is not for want of facts, as most thrilling incidents of this portion of her life are from various motives suppressed. (*Narrative*, 30)

The *Narrative* explained that to tell her slave tale of this period might hurt those still living, that it was not for the ''public ear,'' and that she feared many would not credit her because ''it would seem to others, especially the uninitiated, so unaccountable, so unreasonable, and what is usually called unnatural, . . . they would not easily believe it'' (82).

The omission of details appears even stranger because slave narratives were written to attract public attention to the brutality of slavery, as illustrated by the autobiographies of Frederick Douglass and Harriet Jacobs. Thus, to omit details that would show the evils of slavery seems paradoxical. But, in *Many Thousand Gone* (1963), Charles Nichols lists Truth as one of the cooperative and loyal slaves and comments: ''The narratives of such loyal slaves are less bitter in tone and even when describing the outrages of the system preserve a restraint that is surprising'' (76). Perhaps the omission was strategic; she was a northern slave whose duties resembled those of the farmhands and hired girls of that day. By her own admission as noted below, she had only one severe master. If the criteria for a harsh slave existence are set by the narratives of Douglass and Jacobs, Truth did not live such a life.

However incomplete and dubious it may be at times, the *Narrative* is the only source of some of Truth's history. Equally important, it is her own view of that history, and from it comes the story of her early life. She was born Isabella Baumfree in Ulster County, New York, probably in 1797. She led a fairly stable life living with her parents and a brother until her second master died when she was about nine years old. Her parents were freed at this time, but she was sold to Mr. John Nealy, whom she considered a cruel master, and she reported her one severe beating when owned by Nealy. She was later sold to John J. Dumont with whom she stayed until the year she was promised her freedom. Under the New York emancipation law of 1817, slaves who were born before the 1799 emancipation act were to be given freedom on July 4, 1827 (Dumond, 1961:50). Dumont had promised her that he would give her "free papers" a year earlier, but as the time approached, he refused, claiming that she had not put in a full year in 1826 because of a problem with her hand. She left Dumont, and a friend paid for the rest of her last year so that she would not have to return (*Narrative*, 39–43); she was finally freed in 1828.

Although a large proportion of Sojourner Truth's adult slave life is missing from her *Narrative*, the story of her religious experiences dominates almost a quarter of the book. The selection of what was excluded and what was included in the book had to have been, at least in part, her choice. She chose to emphasize religion and her religious conversion both in her *Narrative* and whenever she told her life's story, as illustrated by Harriet Beecher Stowe's article about her in the *Atlantic Monthly* (1863).

Truth's first religious experience took place while she was still a slave. Before this experience, she believed she had to shout for God to hear her, so she created a wall and arch from woven branches for privacy on an island near her home and prayed loudly to God in her self-made wilderness. Gilbert wrote: "She demanded, with little expenditure of reverence or fear, a supply of her most pressing wants, and at times her demands approached very near commands. She felt as if God was under obligation to her, much more than she was to him" (61).

According to one version of her story, in this first experience, Truth was waiting for a ride to her old home to visit friends when "God revealed himself to her, with all the suddenness of a flash of lightning, showing her, 'in the twinkling of an eye, that he was all over'—that he pervaded the universe—'and that there was no place where God was not' " (*Narrative*, 65). She continued her story, saying that she "began to wish for some one to speak to God for her" (66) because, until this time, she had considered God someone like herself. There then appeared a space between Truth and God, and a bright form filled that space. Thinking at first it was someone she knew, she soon realized it was not the friend she thought it was. This became her vision of Jesus, to whom she said, "I know you, and I don't know you" (67). She retold the story of this vision to Harriet Beecher Stowe, who asked her if she had not heard about Jesus. She replied, "No, honey I hadn't heard no preaching'—been to no meetin'. Nobody hadn't told me. I'd kind o' heard of Jesus, but thought he was like

General Lafayette, or some o' them'' (*Narrative*, 159). She also claimed she did not know that others knew of this Christ (*Narrative*, 68).

The second important religious experience came after she was free. While living in New York, she became associated with Robert Matthews or Matthias, as he preferred to be called, and Elijah Pierson. Matthias considered himself the Father, God upon earth, and Pierson considered his mission to be like that of John the Baptist (*Narrative*, 92). Truth followed these men and their teachings, even fasting as Pierson had done, in order to see the light, but she soon discovered that only her body became light (97). Other matters arose that soon made her realize that these men were pretenders, and in 1843, she left them and New York (100). She referred to this experience as her second Sodom.

Truth saw all the issues she supported—anti-slavery, woman's rights, temperance, and even a place for the freed slave to live as part of her religious calling. Nichols refers to her as one of the "God-intoxicated" ex-slaves (2). Her insistence on recounting her religious visions and experiences coupled with the story of her slave life, albeit not one of the more dreadful histories, lent her tale a legendary quality. Indeed, the story she told repeatedly of her life was a legend she helped build for herself. After leaving New York in 1843, Truth took the name "Sojourner" and began her travels to preach her interpretation of Jesus. Later, she added the surname "Truth" because she wanted a "name with a handle on it" (Carter, 1887:478; Wyman, 1901:62). "Lecturin' ,'' as she called it, took her to religious camp meetings where she developed an ability to handle the zealots and hecklers who often disrupted the services.

She was next heard of in 1850 when she began her work with the anti-slavery movement. Sallie Holley reported on her work with the Ohio agents in the summer of 1851: "Every few days Sojourner Truth joins us and aids in our meetings. She travels in a buggy by herself. An anti-slavery friend loaned her a pony and buggy for the entire summer" (Chadwick, 1969:80). In May 1851, Truth gave her famous "Aren't I a Woman?" speech in Akron, Ohio, thus beginning her association with the woman's rights movement.

Truth's third cause was to help the freed slaves. Her efforts to gain support to move the slaves from the cities in order to wean them away from a life of handouts and into a life of independence with land of their own were tireless. She petitioned Congress, spoke in any town or city that would have her, raising money and securing support for her cause, and even visited the West to encourage ex-slaves to move to what she considered a better life. She lived to see her people freed, but she was defeated in her battle to create a real home for them. She died at her home in Battle Creek, Michigan, in 1883, also without having attained her goal of the right to vote.

Throughout her career as an advocate, Truth remained independent. Although associated with the abolitionist and woman's rights movements, she was never a part of their leadership. Historian Carleton Mabee comments that, unlike Frederick Douglass, she was never a part of the inner councils (73). He attributes that to her illiteracy, but organizational records show that she did not attend their meetings with any consistency. She can best be described as an itinerant reformer who chose her own time and place to speak. Her contributions to the movements she espoused were as an agitator, as she described herself, and as a folk heroine, a figure she created through her speaking.

SOJOURNER TRUTH'S RHETORICAL PRESENCE

Truth's speeches reflected the reforms she supported. Her abolitionist speaking carried over into her later effort to aid freed slaves. Abolitionist speeches consisted of telling the story of her own life as a slave and, later, recounting the problems of crime and destitution among freed Blacks. These speeches were given in both major cities and small towns. Although no texts exist, reports of them appear in newspaper accounts, but not in great detail. After delivering this type of speech, she often took the opportunity to sell her *Narrative* and her "shadow," as she called her photograph. With the profits from these two items, she supported herself.

She also advocated the rights of women. Woman's rights and slave rights were often intermingled in her speeches because she saw both causes as essentially the denial of natural rights. In the Akron, Ohio, speech of 1851, Truth forcefully brought the two elements together when she told of her work as a slave and then asked, "and aren't I a woman?" In a calmer manner, she exploited her ethical appeal as a freed Black when she began one of her speeches at the American Equal Rights Association convention by saying, "I come from another field—the country of the slave" (May 9, 1867). She used this same appeal twice more, once in 1853 when she told the audience, "I know that it feels a kind o' hissin' and ticklin' to see a colored woman get up and tell you 'bout Woman's Rights, too" (*HWS* 1:567), and, again, when she said: "There is a great stir about colored men getting their rights, but not a word about the colored women; and if colored men get their rights, and not colored women get theirs, there will be a bad time about it. . . . I suppose I am about the only colored woman that goes about to speak for the rights of the colored woman" (May 9, 1867; quoted in *MCSFH* 2:252–253). She also combined issues of slavery and woman's rights to attack men. In a report of her Akron, Ohio, speech in the *Anti-Slavery Bugle*, she supposedly ended her speech by saying, "But man is in a tight place, the poor slave is on him, woman is coming on him, and he is surely between a hawk and a buzzard" (1851).

Some speeches were based on her religious beliefs. One interesting example, in which Truth combined her legendary ability to converse directly with God and her struggle for rights, was reported by a friend, James A. Dugdale. Using the analogy of wheat infected by the weevil (which she called a "weasel") and the Constitution, she told this tale:

Children, I talk to God and God talks to me. I go out and talk to God in the fields and the woods. This morning I was walking out, and I got over the fence. I saw the wheat a holding up its head, looking very big. I go up and take hold of it. You believe it, there was no wheat there? I say, "God what is the matter with the wheat?" and He says to me, "Sojourner, there is a little weasel in it." Now I hear talkin' about the Constitution and the rights of man. I come up and take hold of this Constitution. It looks mighty big, and, I feel for my rights, but there ain't any there. Then I say, "God, what ails this Constitution?" He says to me, "Sojourner, there is a little weasel in it." (3)

Although religion played an important part in many of her speeches, speeches on strictly religious matters dealt with what she considered to be acts against the will of God. Her speech against the Wycoff Hanging Bill of Michigan in 1881 is an example. In it, she argued from the premise that hanging was not Jesus's law: "In the olden times it was 'an eye for an eye and a tooth for a tooth,' but the Savior taught us better things than these, and commanded us to love one another." Later, she linked her claim to another of her causes, temperance, by saying, "I should like to see you make a law that would hang whisky out the United States, for I believe that it is at the bottom of a great many crimes."

In all her speeches, she used an aggressive blend of wit and sarcasm and unassailable logic. Her friend Samuel Rogers said of her:

The severe sarcasm conveyed in the tone of her voice was marvelous. She was quick also at repartee. On one occasion at Battle Creek, Mich. [sic], during the war, a well known and noisy citizen had bantered her with questions until, getting impatient, she exclaimed, "who be you any how?" The answer given was, "The only son of my mother." With uplifted hands, in a moment came these thrilling words: "Thank God there are no more." (n.p.)

However, her most famous retort, "Frederick, is God dead?" was her way of challenging the great Frederick Douglass's belief that only bloodshed could end slavery (Douglass, 1982:275).

In Angola, Indiana, in 1861, she and her friend Horatio Roby were arrested— she because she was Black, and he because he violated an 1851 state law that forbade mulattoes or Blacks from entering the state. Josephine Griffing, a fellow anti-slavery advocate and companion, was outraged and wrote to the *Liberator* that it was a treasonous act to arrest these two (98). The local *Steuben Republican* expressed embarrassment over the incident and turned it into a plea for the right of free speech (May 18, 1861:3). Truth, however, made light of the incident, telling with a good deal of zeal and humor how the ladies dressed her up in patriotic uniform and advised her to carry a weapon, which she refused to do. They wanted to get her to the courthouse where she was to speak without being molested on the way by a mob of pro-slavery advocates. Later, she described her trial this way:

[T]wo half-drunken lawyers, who looked like the scrapings of the Democratic party, made their appearance, eyed us for a few moments, then left. Presently we saw them enter a tavern across the way, and this ended the trial. We now went to the house of a friend and had a grand picnic. (*Narrative*, 143)

In her speech to the 1851 Akron, Ohio, Woman's Rights Convention, Truth took the argument that "women can't have as much rights as man, 'cause Christ wasn't a woman," and answered, "Where did your Christ come from? Where did your Christ come from? From God and a woman. Man had nothing to do with him."

In 1876, she said someone told her women were not fit to rule because they had seven devils in them, and responded:

"Seven devils is of no account"—(laughter)—said I, "just behold, the man had a legion." (Loud laughter.) They never thought about that. A man had a legion—(laughter)—and the devils didn't know where to go. That was the trouble. (Laughter and applause.) They asked if they might get among the swine; they thought it was about as good a place as where they came from. (Laughter.) Why didn't the devils ask to go among the sheep? (Laughter.) But no. But (laughter)—and certainly a man has a little touch of that selfishness that don't want to give the women their right. I have been twitted many times about this, and I thought how queer it is that men don't think of that. (May 10, 1867:3)

And it was with a bit of irony that Truth accused men of "having our [women's] right so long, that you think, like a slaveholder, that you own us," after appealing to get equal pay for equal work for women (May 9, 1867:3).

As for logic, in a dignified little speech in 1863 to Sunday School children in Battle Creek, Michigan, she used a chain argument built on a rhetorical question.

Children who made your skin white? Was it not God? Who made mine black? Was it not the same God? Am I to blame, therefore, because my skin is black? Does it not cast a reproach on our Maker to despise a part of his children, because he has been pleased to give them a black skin?

She used a cooking metaphor to refute the argument that women did not have the intellect to handle certain rights (Foss, 1987:386), responding: "If my cup won't hold but a pint and yours holds a quart, wouldn't you be mean not to let me have my little half-measure full?" (Truth, 1851). She equated the size and use of a church with the lack of decent housing for her people. In a report on one of her lectures, she was described as having said that churches were "big, lumbering things, covering up costly space and doing good to no one," while "citizens . . . were living in low dens and sky-lighted garrets" (Truth, 1853). Her argument for freed slaves was that these people needed land in order to become self-supporting at this time, not civil rights (Titus, n.p.). Lucy Stone quoted her as saying:

Tain't rations that this people needs. As long as there is those that get a salary for giving out rations, rations will be begged for them; and as long as these poor things can get food and clothes for nothin', they won't work. They have always seen the white folks do just so, and they do just like them. If the government would only take 'em out west and give 'em land, and just start 'em, it would be better for them, and, in the end, a great deal cheaper for the government. (252)

Of course, her sarcasm and logic met with varied reactions. A pro-slavery newspaper in New Jersey wrote a scathing report of one of her appearances before a church group, which began: "Sojourner Truth—who fifty years ago was considered a crazy woman; who was wont to address street meetings and Garrison abolition conventicles," and continued to described her speech as "not on religion, but at random, on copperhead Jersey, hypocrites, freemen, woman's rights, etc." It concluded: "She is a crazy, ignorant, repelling negress, and her guardians would do a Christian act to restrict her entirely to private life" (*Narrative*, 204). The *New York Tribune* remarked on her loose organization positively when it reported: "Her matter and manner were simply indescribable, often straying far away from the starting point; but each digression was fraught with telling logic, rough humor, or effective sarcasm" (*Narrative*, 242).

But by far the most powerful element of Sojourner Truth's rhetoric was her use of herself as a symbol, an image, a living example of the claims she made. She enhanced her imposing physical presence by adopting the Quaker costume, although she was not a member of that sect, and topping her six-foot frame with a turban. Frances Barker Gage described her first appearance at a woman's rights convention:

The leaders of the movement . . . were many of them almost thrown into panics on the first day of the meeting, by seeing a tall, gaunt black woman in a gray dress and white turban, surmounted by an uncouth sun-bonnet, march deliberately into the church, walk with the air of a queen up the aisle, and take her seat upon the pulpit steps. (1863:4)

Samuel Rogers confirmed the report of her self-assured presence when he described Truth this way: "With all the masculine traits of character, developed by the rough life in early years, and the apparent consciousness of superiority, there was still in her nature much of the true woman" (1883:n.p.).

No contemporary contributed more to creating the legendary image of Sojourner Truth than Harriet Beecher Stowe, who called her the "Libyan Sibyl." This title was picked up by her supporters, giving her an air of mystery. It stayed with her throughout her life, sometimes slightly altered, as in Parker Pillsbury's reference to her as "the Ethiopian Sybil" (1883/1970:487).

Caroline Putnam described the format for the anti-slavery meetings in Ohio. Commenting on Truth's role, she said:

Following Mr. Pillsbury, would arise, towering, the striking form and features of Sojourner Truth, in her turban, and with wit and pathos she would wring our hearts, and wreathe our faces with smiles, and even convulse us with laughter, at her story of her old slave life in New York, before the act of emancipation in the Empire State in 1828. (Chadwick, 1899:63)

Lucy Stone related an incident in which abolitionist Stephen S. Foster was describing the horrors of slavery when a member of the audience accused him of making statements that were too sweeping. Stone continued:

When he ceased, Sojourner sprang to her feet, and, in a speech of not more than five minutes, she drew a picture which every one present both saw and felt, of what slavery is to its victims, and of the guilt of those who inflict it and of those who uphold it; and, with the tone of one of the old prophets, turning to Mr. Foster, she said: "Sweep away, Stephen, sweep away." (1876:252)

Sojourner Truth seemed unconcerned about her inability to read or write. She not only claimed to be a better judge of people and God than those who could, but also chided the literate for their weaknesses. She referred to the clergy as "[b]ig Greek-crammed mouthing men, who, for many a long century had been befogging the world, and getting its affairs into the most terrible snarl and confusion, and then when women came to their assistance, cried 'shame on women!' " (1853). When lecturing to college students, "[n]oticing several of them taking notes while she was speaking, she stopped and looking scornfully around, advised to them 'put their notes in their heads' " (Carter, 1887:479). In fact, she often used her illiteracy to further her causes. ELIZABETH CADY STANTON quoted her as saying:

You know, children, I don't read such small stuff as letters, I read men and nations. I can see through a millstone, though I can't see through a spelling-book. What a narrow idea a reading qualification is for a voter! I know and do what is right better than many big men who read. (HWS2:926)

Carleton Mabee put it best: "Remarkably, she seemed to be able to use her illiteracy to lift herself up into a high pulpit from which she then could more effectively scold an audience" (1988:71).

And there were times when she used her own persona and her own experiences to the end of high drama. Pro-slavery groups and college students felt the force of her sarcasm. In Silver Lake, Indiana, Truth was accused of being a man because of her height and low voice. A Dr. W. T. Strain suggested she disrobe for some of the ladies present to prove her femaleness. Truth replied that "her breasts had suckled many a white babe, to the exclusion of her own off-spring." She went on to say that "some of those white babies had grown to man's estate, that, although they had suckled her colored breasts, they were, in her estimation, far more manly than they [her persecutors] appeared to be." As she disrobed in front of all present, two young men ran towards the platform. To intensify her

searing demonstration, ''she quietly asked them if they too, 'wished to suck' ''
(Hayward, 1858:n.p.).

On another occasion, she focused her ridicule on the prejudices of her audience.
Frances Titus reported the following incident which took place at Kalamazoo
College during the Civil War.

When she rose to speak there was quite a commotion among the students. Some broke
into hilarious laughter, some thumped on the seats, others hissed. Sojourner stood upon
the platform proud and grand, her tall, unbent form had a slightly swaying, graceful
motion, as she fixed her keen eyes on the audience. At length she addressed them with,
''Well, children, when you go to heaven and God asks you what made you hate the
colored people, have you got your answer ready.'' After a pause she continued in a deep
voice like rolling thunder: ''When I go before the throne of God and God says, 'Sojourner,
what made you hate the white people?' I have got my answer ready.'' She undid the
collar of her dress and bared her arms, to the shoulders, showing them covered with a
perfect network of scars made by the slave master's lash. The effect was overwhelming.
The confusion ceased. Hisses and scoffs were succeeded by a baptism of tears. (n.p.)

Almost everyone who wrote about Truth attempted to describe her. Graves,
her grandson's playmate, wrote:

I knew Sojourner Truth and remember her very well. She was tall, thin and angular, with
a deep voice and as I remember her always with a turban. Although illerate [sic], she
possessed a keen mind and ready wit. She was a most impressive speaker, especially
when dwelling on the wrongs and aspirations of her race. I can see her now addressing
an attentive audience and extending a long bony forefinger to emphasize her points. (n.p.)

The ''long bony forefinger'' described by Graves and the reference to her
''uplifted hands'' by Rogers mentioned earlier were bywords repeatedly used to
describe her delivery. Caroline Putnam also noted her ''towering'' and ''striking
form . . . in her turban.'' Besides her physical appearance, those who knew her
and wrote about her often mentioned her quick wit and intellect, despite her lack
of education and illiteracy.

CONCLUSION

Sojourner Truth understood that a public advocate needed to fashion an un-
forgettable image. She also understood Americans' appreciation of public advocates who were ''full of shrewd wit and homespun resourcefulness'' (Lerner,
1957:802). She used wit and sarcasm to ''scatter her enemies with dismay and
confusion, winning more than victory in every battle'' (*Narrative*, 137). She
fought for her causes with every weapon she had, and she remains one of the
classic folk heroines of U.S. history.

SOURCES

Primary sources are the Bernice Lowe Collection, Bentley Historical Library, Ann Arbor, Michigan, the Amy Post Collection, Rush Rhees Library, University of Rochester, Rochester, New York, and the Sojourner Truth, Bernice Lowe, and Dorothy and Michael Martich collections, Willard Library, Battle Creek, Michigan. Some correspondence with Amy Post was published in *We Are Your Sisters*. Ed. Dorothy Sterling. New York: W. W. Norton, 1984.

Narrative of Sojourner Truth: A Bondswoman of Olden Times. With Olive Gilbert. 1878. Ed. Frances W. Titus. New York: Arno, 1968.

Critical Sources

Campbell, Karlyn Kohrs. *MCSFH* 1:19–22.

———. "Style and Content in the Rhetoric of Early Afro-American Feminists." *Quarterly Journal of Speech* 72 (1986):434–445.

Carter, Harriet. "Sojourner Truth." *Chautauquan* 7 (May 1887):477–480.

Dugdale, James A. "Sojourner Truth." *National Anti-Slavery Standard* 24 (July 4, 1863):3.

Foss, Karen A. "Sojourner Truth." *American Orators Before 1900: Critical Studies and Sources*. Ed. Bernard K. Duffy and Halford R. Ryan. Westport, Conn.: Greenwood, 1987, pp. 383–390.

Gage, Frances D. "Sojourner Truth." *National Anti-Slavery Standard* 23 (May 2, 1863).

Galvin, Corrine Brown. "Sojourner Truth, the Libyan Sibyl." *New York Folklore Quarterly* (Spring 1950):5–21.

Graves, Henry B. "Memoirs, December 30, 1939: Sojourner Truth." Martich Collection.

Griffing, Josephine S. "Treason in Disguise." *Liberator*, June 21, 1861.

Hayward, William. "Pro-Slavery in Indiana." *Northern Indianian* [Warsaw, Ind.], October 8, 1858; *Liberator*, October 15, 1858.

Kalamazoo *Telegraph*. "Sojourner Truth." July 8, 1879:1.

Lebedun, Jean. "Harriet Beecher Stowe's Interest in Sojourner Truth, Black Feminist." *American Literature* 46 (1974):359–363.

Lowe, Berenice. "A Woman of Courage, Causes." *Battle Creek Enquirer and News*, March 30, 1975.

———. "History Is Legend *and* Truth." (History Society of Battle Creek) 17 (1975): n.p.

———. "The Family of Sojourner Truth." *Michigan Heritage* 3 (1962):181–185.

———. "Truth About Sojourner Truth: Her Michigan Days." *New York Folklore Quarterly*. Rpt. *Battle Creek Enquirer and News*, July 21, 1956.

Mabee, Carleton. "Sojourner Truth, Bold Prophet: Why Did She Never Learn to Read?" *New York History* (January 1988):55–77.

Montgomery, Janey Weinhold. *A Comparative Analysis of the Rhetoric of Two Negro Women Orators–Sojourner Truth and Frances E. Watkins Harper*. Fort Hays Studies-New Series Literature Series no. 6. Hays, Kans.: Fort Hays Kansas State College, December 1968.

Nichols, Charles H. *Many Thousand Gone: The Ex-Slaves' Account of Their Bondage and Freedom*. Leiden: E. J. Brill, 1963.

Rogers, Samuel J. "Sojourner Truth: An Orthodox View of her Character." [Battle Creek, Mich.] *Journal*, December 12, 1883.

Shafer, Elizabeth. "Sojourner Truth: A 'Self-Made Woman.' " *American History Illustrated* 8 (1974):34–39.

Stone, Lucy. "Sojourner Truth." *TWJ* 5 (August 1876):252.

Stowe, Harriet Beecher. "Sojourner Truth, the Libyan Sibyl." *Atlantic Monthly* 11 (April 1863):473–481.

Steuben Republican [Angola, Ind.]. May 18, 1861:3.

Titus, Frances W. "Sojourner Truth: Some Notable Incidents of an Active and Useful Career in Behalf of Philanthropy." Truth Collection.

Wagner, Gerard A. "Sojourner Truth: God's Appointed Apostle of Reform." *Southern Speech Journal* 28 (1962):123–130.

Wyman, Lillie B. Chace. "Sojourner Truth." *New England Magazine* 24 (March 1901):59–66.

Biographical Sources

Chadwick, John White. *A Life for Liberty: Anti-Slavery and Other Letters of Sallie Holley*. 1899. New York: Negro University Press, 1969.

Fauset, Arthur Huff. *Sojourner Truth: God's Faithful Pilgrim*. Chapel Hill: University of North Carolina Press, 1938.

Pauli, Hertha. *Her Name was Sojourner Truth*. 1962. New York: Avon, 1976.

Redding, Saunders. "Truth, Sojourner." *NAW* 3:479–481.

Vale, Gilbert. *Fanaticism: Its Source and Influence, Illustrated by the Simple Narrative of Isabella, in the Case of Matthias*. New York, 1835.

Background Sources

Douglass, Frederick. *Life and Times of Frederick Douglass*. 1882. New York: Collier, 1962.

Dumond, Dwight L. *Antislavery: The Crusade for Freedom in America*. 1961. New York: W. W. Norton, 1966.

Jacobs, Harriet. *Incidents in the Life of a Slave Girl*. 1861. New York: Oxford University Press, 1988.

Lerner, Max. *America as a Civilization*. Vol. 2. New York: Simon & Schuster, 1957.

Pillsbury, Parker. *Acts of the Anti-Slavery Apostles*. 1883. New York: Books for Libraries, 1970.

Chronology of Speeches

Address, Akron, Ohio, Woman's Rights Convention, May 29, 1851. *Anti-Slavery Bugle*, June 21, 1851; as reported by Frances Gage: *National Anti-Slavery Standard*, May 2, 1863:4; *HWS* 1:115; *Narrative*, 131–135; *MCSFH* 2:99–102.

Address, New York Woman's Rights Convention, September 7(?), 1853. *HWS* 1:567.

Address, Michigan Friends of Human Progress Annual Convention, Battle Creek, October 4, 1856. Rpt. Lowe, "A Woman of Courage, Causes," *Battle Creek Enquirer and News*, March 30, 1975. Willard Library.

Address, State Sabbath School Convention, Battle Creek, June 3, 1863. *National Anti-Slavery Standard*, July 11, 1863. Black Abolition Papers 979; Willard Library.

Addresses (3) to First Annual Meeting, AERA Convention, New York, May 9, 1867: *National Anti-Slavery Standard*, June 1, 1867:3; *HWS* 2:193; *MCSFH* 2:251–254; May 10, 1867: *National Anti-Slavery Standard*, June 1, 1867:3; *HWS* 2:222; *MCSFH* 2:254–257; Speech #2, May 10, 1867: *HWS* 2:224.

Address, Commemoration of the Eighth Anniversary of Negro Freedom in the United States, Boston, January 1, 1871. *Narrative*, 213–216.

Address Opposing Wycoff Hanging Bill, East Lansing, Mich., June 3, 1881?. [Battle Creek] *Michigan Nightly Moon*, June 8, 1881. Lowe Collection.

Reports of Speeches

Address to First Congregational Church, New York, September 6, 1853. *New York Daily Tribune*, September 7, 1853.

Lecture, New York?, 1853. *National Anti-Slavery Standard*, December 10, 1853 (reprinted from the *New York Tribune*).

Address at Anti-Slavery Celebration, Farmington, N.Y., July 4, 1854. *Liberator*, July 14, 1854; Black Abolition Papers.

"Weasel" Speech. *National Anti-Slavery Standard*, July 4, 1863:3; *Narrative*, 146.

JULIA WARD HOWE

(1819–1910), patriotic crusader for woman's rights and peace

SUSAN SCHULTZ HUXMAN

"Mine eyes have seen the glory of the coming of the Lord."

With that stirring line of her famous poem, "Battle Hymn of the Republic," Julia Ward Howe launched a whirlwind career as poet, philosopher, journalist, and public speaker for a host of causes, including woman's rights and peace. Riding a wave of popularity as the nation's spirit personified, she joined the cause for woman suffrage in 1868, arguing that the United States would achieve its true glory only when women received the political and educational advantages they deserved. For forty years she waxed eloquent on the righteousness of woman suffrage.

Despite her profound influence on the women's movement and her legacy as an "American institution," her rhetorical skills have been overlooked, despite large amounts of primary materials. One reason may be that her life and work reveal a paradoxical figure. First, relatively late in life, she entered a movement she had earlier rejected, which exposed the contrast between her public and private lives. Second, she did not fit the standard suffragist mold; she juggled many causes, used poetry and philosophic essays more than the platform, and assumed the role of patriotic mother, not committed activist.

This critical portrait juxtaposes Ward Howe's legendary status as "Great American Mother," "Queen Victoria," and "a national institution" against her career as a patriotic crusader for woman's rights and other causes. In the following pages, a biographical sketch precedes analysis of the substance and style of her rhetoric and assessment of her role as a suffragist.

EARLY YEARS

Born in New York City, Julia Ward lived a privileged, but secluded, childhood with two brothers and two sisters. She was described by her mother as the most incorrigible, impulsive, but vivacious, of the Ward brood. At an early age, the energies of this precocious, red-haired child were diverted to studies. Samuel Ward, a wealthy banker, spent lavishly on the private education of his children. Languages, literature, art, music, philosophy, and the Bible comprised their core curriculum. She spoke fluent French before she could read or write, was an accomplished singer before she was twelve, and published her first poems in the New York *American* at age fourteen. However, when she was six, her mother died bearing the Wards' eighth child. That loss deprived her of maternal affection and domestic instruction, and irreparably tainted her impression of childbirth. Her father responded to his wife's death by grieving long and fervently in private, severely curtailing the children's social activities, and imposing on them the strict, Calvinist religion of his wife. His youngest daughter took refuge in books and imaginary companions, but later reminisced: "I seemed to myself like a young damsel of olden time, shut up within an enchanted castle. And I must say that my dear father, with all his noble generosity sometimes appeared to me as my jailer" (*Reminiscences*, 49).

Entering young adulthood ill equipped for a life of marital and domestic bliss, she was married to Samuel Gridley Howe in 1843. "Chev," as she called him, for "The Chevalier," a title conferred on him for his spirited crusade for Greek independence, had already established himself as a pioneer for his work with the blind at the Perkins Institute in Boston. At age forty, he was some twenty years older than she.

Age was just the beginning of the differences between them. Dr. Howe was a domineering man with a volatile disposition who, for all his reform efforts, staunchly believed that a woman's place was in the home. He thwarted his wife's writing at every turn, criticized her housekeeping and cooking, drained her inheritance, moved her constantly and abruptly, controlled all household decision making, denied her affection, and, after engaging in an adulterous relationship, threatened her repeatedly with divorce (Grant, 1982).

The unhappy marriage did not change with the addition of children. Ward Howe bore six children in sixteen years, and between caring for babies and nursing her spouse through his repeated bouts of migraines and malaria, she grew wearied and hopelessly depressed, bordering on madness (Grant, 1982). Her journal registered her deep despair at their strained relationship. Of his endless nagging, she wrote: "I have never known my husband to approve of any act of mine which I myself valued" (April 23, 1865, Howe Papers, HL). Of his usurpation of her household duties, she confided: "The longer I live the more I do feel my utter, childlike helplessness about all practical affairs" (May 15, 1847, Howe Papers, HL). Of the constancy of childrearing, she lamented: "Must I sew and trot babies, and sing songs, and tell Mother Goose stories and be expected to know how to write?" and, finally, of marriage, she declared: "Marriage, like death, is a debt we owe to nature" (June 1846, Howe Papers, HL).

The oppressive marital conditions under which Ward Howe languished for thirty-three years were eased slightly in three ways. First, as the wife of a renowned reformer, she became more knowledgeable and sophisticated. She traveled extensively all over the world; was exposed to many of her husband's pet causes, including abolitionism, prison reform, the plight of Armenian and Turkish peoples, education of the handicapped, annexation of Santa Domingo, and Greek independence; and conversed with many notable reformers, including Wendell Phillips, John Brown, Ralph Waldo Emerson, Theodore Parker, Thomas Mann, James Freeman Clarke, William Lloyd Garrison, and Charles Sumner.

Second, Dr. Howe's lengthy absences gave her time to rediscover her first love: books. Writing and reading poetry and philosophy was an "emotional sanctuary'' from the realities of a failed marriage, a surrogate companion to replace her husband's inattention, and an outlet to vent angers, sorrows, and desires. Her journal recorded the release she found in writing: ''My husband has scarcely half an hour in twenty-four to give me. So, as I think much, in my way, and nobody takes the least interest in what I think, I am forced to take an imaginary public, and to tell it the secrets of my poor ridiculous brain'' (Howe Scrapbook, n.d., p. 31, Howe Papers, HL). The hours she stole from her children to write in wasp-infested attics produced her first volume of poetry, *Passion Flowers* (1854), which she felt compelled to publish anonymously to avoid her husband's wrath. Two plays, two travelogues, and another collection of poems were published over the next fourteen years, but received little critical praise. During this time she also began speaking on ethics and philosophy to her husband's cadre of reformers in the ''Boston Radical Club,'' much to his chagrin.

Third, in 1848, Ward Howe underwent a religious conversion at the hands of Theodore Parker, Boston's celebrated Transcendentalist minister. Casting aside the Calvinist's vengeful God and depraved view of humankind for the more joyful and optimistic view of a loving God, the fundamental goodness of humankind, and the exaltation of the individual conscience over societal strictures, she clung to the soothing words of liberal Christianity in order to sustain her self and preserve her sanity (Clifford, 1978). Her crowning moment as an accomplished writer came shortly after her conversion with the publication in 1861 of ''The Battle Hymn of the Republic.'' From that moment on, she was no longer merely the wife of Dr. Howe. She became an overnight sensation as a first-rate poet and true-blue patriot. From the depths of depression to the heights of literary stardom, she stood ready to change the direction of her life.

SUFFRAGE YEARS

With the death of her husband in 1876, Ward Howe, now fifty-seven, moved full-swing into a new, productive role as a woman suffragist. But her late entry into the movement cannot be attributed solely to her late husband's objections. In the early 1850s, she harbored stereotypes of women activists as unhappy, eccentric sirens, and associated Frances Wright and her ''odious'' ideas with the very essence of the Woman Question. Four decades later, in a speech on equal rights to NAWSA, she said:

I can well recall the years in which I felt myself averse to the participation of women in political life. The feminine type appeared to me so precious, so indispensable to humanity, that I dreaded any enlargement of its function, lest something of its charm and real power should therein be lost. (*JWH and the Woman Suffrage Movement*, 222–229)

She had no reason to look kindly on her sex in those early years. From the time of her mother's death, she had no close female friends. In her *Reminiscences*, she recalled: ''During the first two thirds of my life I looked to the masculine ideal of character as the only true one'' (372). Later, when asked about the true value of the woman suffrage movement, she would always hasten to reply: "the better acquaintance with my own sex'' (372). For these reasons, she shunned the cause until 1868.

Like many women who converted to the cause after the Civil War and passage of the Fourteenth and Fifteenth amendments giving freed African-American males the vote, Ward Howe was stung by the exclusion of her sex from full citizenship. In an essay "Woman and the Suffrage," later a suffrage tract, she denounced the amendments in words with biting racist and classist overtones:

[T]here seemed a special incongruity in putting this great mass of ignorant men into a position of political superiority to all women. The newly enfranchised men were generally illiterate and of rather low morality. Should they, simply on account of sex, be invested with a power and dignity withheld from women, who at that time were unquestionably better fitted to intervene in matters of government than men could be who for many generations past had been bought and sold like cattle, men who would have the whole gamut of civilization to learn by heart before they could have any availing knowledge of what a vote should really mean? (3)

Ward Howe found an audience for her views in an 1868 meeting called in Boston for the express purpose of founding a New England Woman Suffrage Club. There, for the first time, she saw Lucy Stone, a woman whom she had earlier pegged as a strident suffragist but who now appeared "sweet-faced and silver-voiced" and whose arguments were "simple, strong, and convincing." When asked to speak at the meeting, Ward Howe could only utter feebly: "I am with you" (*Reminiscences*, 375).

True to her word, Ward Howe remained with the movement until her death. Leadership in woman suffrage and a host of other causes came naturally to her over the next forty years. Tirelessly, she founded, presided over, or held membership in nearly twenty clubs and associations. Her fond memories of her first two Boston club associations: the "Brain Club" in 1864, a club formed for women for the sole purpose of "just carrying on," and the "Radical Club" in 1867, a club formed mostly for men to discuss religion and philosophy, were catalysts for her promotion of other social networks for women's self-improvement.

In 1868, Ward Howe joined the New England Woman's Club (NEWC), which became her primary affiliation. From 1871 to 1910, she was its president and seldom missed a meeting. Committed to becoming "an organized social centre for united thought and action," the NEWC boasted 118 female and 17 male members at the outset in its promotion of "domestic feminism" (Blair, 1980). Other club commitments followed, including co-founding AWSA with Lucy Stone in 1869, and founding and presiding over the International Women's Peace Association, the Saturday Morning Club for teenage women in 1871, and the Association for the Advancement of Women in 1873 (forerunner of the General

Federation of Women's Clubs of 1892). She also served as vice-president of the merged NAWSA in 1891 and was a loyal member of the Boston Author's Club, the Women's Rest Tour, Friends of Armenia, Friends of Russian Freedom, Il Circolo Italiano, Daughters of the American Revolution, Society of Colonial Dames, and the Industrial Council of Women, among others. Little wonder that she was pronounced ''The Mother of Clubs.''

When not attending club meetings, Ward Howe was churning out articles on women's issues for several national publications, but mostly for the *Woman's Journal*, the weekly mouthpiece of the AWSA and later NAWSA. Lucy Stone, the newspaper's editor-in-chief, asked her to become one of four associate editors in 1870. She gladly accepted and was the only one to remain in that capacity until Stone's death in 1893.

Ward Howe also found a national platform for her ideas by editing *A Reply to Dr. E. H. Clarke's 'Sex in Education'* (1874), a work of refutational brilliance, and by writing *Margaret Fuller* (1883), a book about her first woman's rights role model, and two collections of essays on woman's rights, *Modern Society* (1881) and *Is Polite Society Polite?* (1895). Though not as gifted a speaker as her friend Lucy Stone, she lectured all across the country, often accompanied by Illinois suffragist and fellow journalist, Mary Rice Livermore. Two speeches, ''Woman and the Suffrage'' and ''Mrs. Howe on Equal Rights,'' became suffrage tracts.

While her Calvinist upbringing taught her the value of a hard day's work, Ward Howe lived by a simple rule in her widowhood: ''The ideal aim of life is to learn, to teach, to serve, and to enjoy!'' (Maud Howe, 1911:74). True to the last of these ideals, she initiated Mother's Day on June 2, 1878, in connection with her crusade for world peace. As she conceived it, the United States needed a national holiday to honor mothers who had lost sons in the Civil War and other wars and to dedicate the nation anew to the task of bringing world peace.

To honor Ward Howe's tremendous efforts on behalf of a variety of social reforms, but, particularly, for woman's rights, Tufts, Smith, and Brown universities bestowed honorary degrees on her. She also became the first woman to be elected to the American Academy of Arts and Letters (1908).

RHETORICAL SUBSTANCE AND STYLE

After the ''Battle Hymn'' brought Ward Howe the literary celebrity she so desperately sought, she patterned subsequent volumes of poetry after its recognizably commemorative form. Her verses rang with patriotic fervor for all kinds of occasions. Her philosophic predilections were expressed in scholarly essays. Membership in the Boston Radical Club and the Brain Club gave her an opportunity to discuss a range of metaphysical topics in the long, unwieldy, digressive style of the parlor lecture setting. But despite her prodigious output as poet and thinker, she was not prepared for the difficulty of becoming an accomplished rhetor.

By 1870, Ward Howe recognized the limitations of poetic and philosophic genres. Of the limits of poetry as a medium of reform, she wrote: "I had much to say to my day and generation which could not and should not be communicated in rhyme, or even in rhythm" (*Reminiscences*, 305). Of the limits of philosophy as a medium of popular discourse, she noted with dismay: "I made no real progress, but went round and round in a sort of circle of metaphysical and mystical reasoning which rather separated me from the minds of others" (Sermon, n.d., JWH Collection, Box 9, HL). Neither permitted the creation of a simple, compelling justification for woman suffrage. But moving from writing commemorative and timeless words to speaking agitative and timely ones produced no small degree of difficulty. She struggled with how to communicate with a live audience, how to modulate her voice, and how to follow parliamentary procedures at conventions. She was indebted to Lucy Stone and Mary Rice Livermore for their exemplary instruction on effective public speaking.

As a budding woman's rights rhetor, Ward Howe had special difficulty in communicating her conversion to woman's rights principles. The substantive and stylistic moves she made are connected to her conversion to liberal Christianity with its social millennialist overtones.

Transcendentalism swept New England in the early 1800s, with its emphasis on the innate goodness of humans, the presence of God in all nature, and insistence on the authority of individual conscience. Ward Howe felt at home in two unorthodox denominations that embraced all but the agnostic overtones of this philosophy: the Unitarian Church and the Church of the Disciples. Under the tutelage of Theodore Parker and James Freeman Clarke, she embraced what came to be called "practical Christianity," whose watchword was that a Christian conscience mandates social activism; love of God necessitates a love of justice (Clifford, 1978).

Into this theology Ward Howe integrated a nationalistic millennialism of fervent proportions. She believed in the return of Christ to earth, but not before humankind had been perfected. Adapting the rhetoric of the evolutionists to the moral sphere, she often repeated: "We know that civilization is a progress of light and intelligence and that this progress cannot at the world's present age be forcibly interrupted or thrown back" (*TWJ*, January 7, 1882:4). Drawing on the residual theme of the "Battle Hymn," she proclaimed that the United States would become the beacon of light in the advance of civilization and herald Christ's coming. "We should all thank God for America," she reminded *Journal* readers, because "it is, and is to be a surpassing gift to the human race" (May 31, 1879:172).

Based on this amalgam of religious presuppositions, Ward Howe attempted to justify the righteousness of the woman suffrage cause in several ways. She asserted the divine origin of the reformer's impulse in hastening society's perfection, the exaltation of individual conscience over societal strictures, the androgyny of personhood, and the civic responsibility of men and women to help the United States take the lead in preparing Christ's kingdom on earth.

Specifically, Ward Howe championed eight key issues over her forty years of woman's rights advocacy: the primacy of self-reliance including repudiation of wives living for husbands, the glorification and enlargement of motherhood, the value of club participation in cultivating self-esteem and civic awareness in women, dress reform, the education of women especially in regard to personal and household hygiene and the world of finance, property rights, divorce rights, and women in the ministry. Restoring motherhood to its honored place became her most identifiable issue—an inexplicable choice given her own miserable home life. Strangely enough, the woman who had every motive for repudiating the stranglehold of family responsiblities on women ended up championing them.

Argumentatively, Ward Howe exploited the pragmatic value or expediency rather than the philosophic value or natural rights position of the cause in promoting these issues via the ballot. In "Woman and the Suffrage," she advanced no less than twelve reasons that woman deserved to be enfranchised:

1. "it gives women a position of increased dignity and worth";
2. "it leads to improvements of laws";
3. "it allows women to bring their influence to bear on legislation more quickly";
4. "it leads to the defeat of bad candidates";
5. "it broadens women's minds";
6. "it makes elections and political meetings more orderly";
7. "it makes it easier to secure liberal appropriations for educational and humanitarian purposes";
8. "it opens to women important positions now closed to them because they are not electors";
9. "it increases the number of women chosen to such offices as are already open to them";
10. "it raises the average of political honesty among the voters";
11. "it tends to modify a too exclusively commercial view of public affairs"; and
12. "it binds the family more closely together."

Ward Howe's expedient reasons for granting suffrage relied heavily on her belief in women's superior moral sensibilities, which contradicted her belief in the androgyny of personhood. Nonetheless, by associating herself with expediency arguments, she was leading the surge of suffragists who, by the late 1870s, had all but abandoned natural rights in favor of social and personal betterment arguments (*IWSM*).

Ward Howe also became adept at refuting the objections to suffrage that originated out of theology. These objections used scripture to justify woman's subordination, sociological views that supported "separate spheres" for men and women in order to preserve the social order, and biological assumptions that claimed women are defined and limited by their anatomy (*IWSM*).

To the first and most powerful of these prevailing convictions, she formed her most frequent defense. Arguing for the equal status of all believers, regardless of sex, she quoted the "misunderstood" Apostle Paul many times over: "In Christ Jesus there is neither male nor female, neither bond nor free" [Gal. 3:28]. She would often add: "Christianity could only work upon this basis, and all that founds itself upon the inherent superiority of one class of human beings to another, is not Christianity" (*TWJ*, June 5, 1875:180). To those who pointed to St. Paul's saying: "I suffer not a woman to teach," she retorted: "Yes, but remember that, in another place, he says that a woman may prophesy wearing a veil" (*Reminiscences*, 357). Taking this passage to heart, she always spoke in public wearing a white lace cap.

She rejected the concept of a separate sphere for woman as an artificial construction of the "barbarous past," not the "enlightened day of a new civilization" (*WSM*:123). Removing restrictions on women would advance civilization, she reasoned. Speaking extemporaneously in 1884 to the Massachusetts Legislature, she argued for women's custody rights, explaining: "In a low state of civilization the father might abandon the children and mother. The law was devised to prevent this. . . . [But] those laws, which protected women from the older barbarism, now defraud them of the newer civilization" (*WSM*:200).

Of all the justifications for the subjugation of woman, Ward Howe found "biology is destiny" the most preposterous. The celebrated physician Edward Clarke gave scientific credence to the biological rationale in his *Sex in Education* (1873). He argued that U.S. women were not designed to be stimulated intellectually because their education caused physical dysfunctioning and mental impairment. In a grand display of parody, she debunked the doctor's sloppy research in *Sex and Education: A Reply* (1874), for which she wrote the lead rebuttal. Recalling earlier medical theories that had proved false and now seemed silly, she placed them alongside Clarke's "polemics":

Before this pet theory of the incompatibility of health with intellectual activity, for women only, was discovered, men of science speculated concerning the deficient busts of American women. The dry, stimulating climate was supposed, in a great measure to account for it. . . . As you go south, you find fuller forms, but not always combined with emptier heads. (25)

Obviously enjoying this exercise in belittlement, she continued: "The effect of the climate of this portion of the country upon the masculine physique is equally noticeable, and has long been a subject of remark. Men here are for the most part wiry, sinewy, nervous, and brainy" (25). She refused to treat Clarke's version of the biological rationale as worthy of serious debate.

From her positions as a book and newspaper editor, club officer, and lay preacher, Ward Howe championed a host of woman's rights issues. She hotly contested the prevailing justifications for woman's subjugation by exploiting the democratic presuppositions of transcendentalism and the religious patriotism of millennialism. In so doing, she could present everything from dress reform to divorce reform under a veneer of righteousness and respectability. Concomitantly, she projected a likable persona that encouraged the public to associate the controversial issue of woman suffrage with her, the "Mother of America."

Although other woman's rights leaders suffered from adverse publicity as "sharp-tongued, godless sirens or frustrated old maids," Ward Howe basked in the public perception of her as a cultured, maternal voice of reform. When NWSA was casting about for its first leader, they offered the job to her despite her lack of experience. The rationale, according to historian Mary Hetherington Grant, was that she gave the organization a "sheen of propriety" with her large family, high social status, extensive travels, and celebrated philanthropist husband (1979:383). In other words, she had the credentials to be regarded as a member of the intellectual and social elite.

Ward Howe also enhanced this image rhetorically. Four recurring stylistic flourishes preserved her genteel role in the movement: (1) Battle imagery drawn from the Bible dramatized the cause; (2) buoyant optimism preserved the vision; (3) diplomacy toward the opposition deflected confrontation; and (4) heartfelt advancement of timeless ideals reinforced her motherly persona. Each helped her in overcoming many of the rhetorical obstacles endemic to the movement.

Drawing liberally from scripture to bathe the cause in a kind of religious righteousness, Ward Howe appealed to God-fearing women who desperately needed guidance on how to counter the cry of "heresy" and "atheism" from the Antis (Huxman, 1991:91). Military metaphors, some drawn from the Old Testament, added a heroic element and cast an aura of invincibility over their efforts. Her speeches, essays, and journal entries are replete with such language as: "We are a Grand Army of the Republic of Women." We are engaging in "a new maneuver," "a fresh phalanx in the good fight of faith." We have donned "the crystal armour of our chief." Favorite expressions were: "The weapon of Christian warfare is the ballot," and "The armor of Paul will become us, the shield and breast plate of strong and shining virtue" (*TWJ*, January 8, 1870:4; January 2, 1875:4; February 1, 1873:36; March 1, 1873:68; "Woman and the Suffrage," 5).

Complementing the strategy of polarizing the forces of good and evil, Ward Howe was the optimistic "Herald of Glad Tidings." She used her voice and pen to proclaim the glorious days of a not-too-distant suffrage victory. By transforming despair into hope, she rekindled enthusiasm in a movement that witnessed meager victories and primed members for seemingly endless mobilization efforts (Huxman, 1991:91). As a cheerleader for the cause, she was relentless in commanding women to "be up and doing" and to act as if "there was no such word as fail" (*TWJ*, January 4, 1873:4). Her buoyant optimism was contagious because she detailed instances of progress, movement, and success with gusto. She spoke repeatedly of "marching onward with firm and majestic tread," "the unfolding of Divine Providence," "the dawn of a new day," and "the progress of light and intelligence." By cataloguing successes, as she did in a

1901 speech entitled "Duty of Women" ("We have women in the pulpit, at the bar, in the countinghouse, in the medical colleges, we have women of established position in art, literature, business, and science—women walking beside their brothers with every tread"), and sounding the bugle of victory in 1905 in "Let There Be Light" ("Friends, behold the dawn! The brighter day is already here. Prepare to set your thoughts and deeds in order fit for the splendor of its high noon"), she depicted a panoramic view of human history marching ever onward to embrace progressive causes.

Even when the movement reeled from setbacks, as in the late 1870s when female "remonstrants" or "anti-suffragists" formed an official organization, Ward Howe had a constructive answer. She elected not to enter a debate that pitted woman against woman but treated female "antis" with deference and deflected confrontation from sources to ideals. Ironically, the first female organization of "antis" was founded in Boston by an old friend, Lizzie Homan. Moreover, a leading advocate against suffrage in England, Mrs. Humphrey Ward, was also a longtime friend. Not surprisingly, then, as her daughter Maud Howe recollected: "Whenever any great question of public interest, not connected with Woman Suffrage, came up, the 'Antis' were continually coming to ask her help." Howe rationalized her mother's association with remonstrants in this way: "She was no respecter of persons; the cause was the thing" (1911:30). Ward Howe was able to continue her campaign for woman's rights without alienating her more traditional friends by debating principles, not persons. In 1875, she admonished readers of the *Woman's Journal*: "[We should] war not against individuals, but against institutions and tendencies" (June 5, 1875:180). In her exceedingly popular lecture, later published as *Modern Society*, she pleaded with audiences not to cast the "battle" as "one sex against the other, but by the very gospel of fairness and justice against the intrenched might of selfish, passion, inertia, and prejudice" (84). Diplomacy did not preclude harsh indictments of opposition arguments, only a moratorium on name-calling.

Ward Howe could be razor-sharp in debating Massachusetts legislators or the antis on the various exigencies of the day, but, ultimately, she seemed more comfortable as an armchair philosopher. The traditional feminine virtues of nurturing, love, and Christian stewardship found an outlet in her exposition of timeless principles. Each week her "grandmotherly advice" on right living appeared in the *Woman's Journal*. Nuggets of wisdom from her column, "Some Rules for Everday Life," became her trademark: "Let no one apply criticism to others until he has thoroughly applied it to himself" (August 23, 1873:268); "Wisdom itself is practically weak until it has allied itself to sympathy" (August 23, 1873:268); "To have intended to do the right thing is a success" (March 22, 1873:92); "The fruitful exchange of thought is one of the greatest agencies in human progress" (January 11, 1873:12). Her warm words of wisdom garnered a larger, unsuspecting, mainstream audience, and indirectly encouraged suffragists not to become one dimensional and consumed by a single issue.

CONCLUSION

Julia Ward Howe was a luminary in the woman suffrage movement. She added to its credibility, despite being a figure of some contradiction. For suffragists everywhere, she was a cheerleader for the cause, rekindling optimism in the rank and file, and forecasting victory at every turn.

For conservative women, she was a role model for how a "society lady" could turn reformer gracefully. In a biography of their mother, Laura Richards and Maud Howe Elliott recalled that a male friend once said: "Her great importance to this cause is that she forms a bridge between the world of society and the world of reform" (1925:197).

By age seventy, she had become almost a permanent fixture at any grand commemorative occasion in Boston and Washington, where encore performances of "The Battle Hymn of the Republic" were common occurrences. Presidents from Lincoln to Taft praised her civic-mindedness. The public's perception of her as a "true-blue patriot" enhanced her efforts to attract a large forum for causes like woman's rights and world peace. While the pessimistic rhetoric of some reformers was too disturbing for most people's taste, her social millennialism was hard to resist. As her daughter Florence Howe Hall observed, "her rare culture and wide acquaintance with the best and most distinguished men and women of her day invest[ed] her words with authority" (Intro., *WSM*:5).

Yet for suffrage leaders, Ward Howe must have been a puzzlement and, to an extent, a disappointment. First, her inability to embrace a consistent woman's rights ideology made her less effective at articulating the philosophic core of the movement and, ultimately, made her less recognizable as a persuasive figure within the movement's rank and file. In keeping with the tenets of Transcendentalism, she advanced the androgyny of the sexes, yet she also repeatedly argued that women were specially endowed as moral creatures. She celebrated civic pride and military prowess, as part of beliefs in social millennialism, yet embraced pacifism in her affiliation with the peace movement. The woman who sang the Union's praises in "The Battle Hymn" also exhorted readers of the *Journal* to "Disarm! disarm!," warning that "The sword of murder is not the balance of justice" (September 24, 1870:297). She refused to associate with "radicals" of the movement, yet she idolized Margaret Fuller, a radical in her time.

Second, Ward Howe's long list of club memberships may have won her a diverse following, but it compromised her loyalty to woman suffrage. Her lack of focus disturbed some suffragists. In 1888, when the two rival associations were contemplating unification, SUSAN B. ANTHONY suggested that Ward Howe not be considered for offices in the new organization because she had not developed her reputation solely as a suffragist.

Third, conspicuously absent from Ward Howe's rhetoric was any real disaffection with the status quo—a key movement characteristic. She did not chronicle the injustices done to women; she did not revel in castigating a scapegoat; she did not linger long at itemizing grievances. She was more at home with proclaiming "redemption" than calling for "purification." She was, simply, more a club leader than a movement leader.

Finally, for scholars, Ward Howe continues to be an anomaly. Her divergent private and public lives may invite some to question the authenticity of a woman who survived a miserable marriage only to parade it as "the nation's most sacred institution"; who found motherhood a distraction from writing, yet founded a national holiday honoring mothers; who suffered repeated bouts of depression, yet became the voice of eternal optimism. To be sure, her troubles antedated her leadership in the movement, but the inconsistencies remain a mystery. However, her rhetorical status as "patriotic crusader for woman's rights" capably filled the movement's need to mainstream its message, and her legendary status as "Great American Mother" gave the movement a veneer of propriety that it so desperately desired.

SOURCES

Primary sources are the Julia Ward Howe Collections, Houghton Library (HL), Harvard, and Schlesinger Library, Radcliffe; Library of Congress; Sophia Smith Collection, Smith College Library, Northampton, Massachusetts.

Howe, Julia Ward. *Julia Ward Howe and the Woman Suffrage Movement: A Selection from Her Speeches and Essays*. Intro. Florence Howe Hall. Boston: D. Estes, 1913. (*WSM*)
A Reply to Dr. E. H. Clarke's 'Sex in Education.' Ed. and intro. Julia Ward Howe. Boston: Roberts Brothers, 1874.
Howe, Julia Ward. *Is Polite Society Polite? and Other Essays*. Boston: Lamson, Wolffe, 1895.
———. *Modern Society*. Boston: Roberts Brothers, 1881.
———. *The Woman's Journal*. Selected Entries. 1870–1893. (*TWJ*)

Collected Poetry, Plays, and Autobiographies

———. *Passion Flowers*. Boston: Ticknor & Fields, 1854.
———. *Words for the Hour*. Boston: Ticknor & Fields, 1856.
———. *The World's Own*. Boston: Ticknor & Fields, 1857.
———. *A Trip to Cuba*. Boston: Ticknor & Fields, 1860.
———. *Reminiscences, 1819–99*. Boston: Houghton Mifflin, 1900.
———. *Later Lyrics*. Boston: J. E. Tilton, 1866.
———. *From the Oak to the Olive. A Plain Record of a Pleasant Journey*. Boston: Lee & Shepard, 1868.

Selected Biographical Sources

Clifford, Deborah Pickman. *Mine Eyes Have Seen the Glory: A Biography of Julia Ward Howe*. Boston: Little, Brown, 1978. See reviews by Karen J. Blair, *Journal of American History* 66 (March 1980):952–953; Judy Barrett Litoff, *American His-*

torical Review 85 (February 1980):215; Robert J. Niess, *American Literature* 57 (January 1980):584–587; Anne Firor Scott, *Wisconsin Magazine of History* 63 (August 1979):53–55; Willard Thorp, *Pennsylvania Magazine of History and Biography* 103 (October 1979):544–545.

Howe, Maud. *The Eleventh Hour in the Life of Julia Ward Howe.* Boston: Little, Brown, 1911.

Richards, Laura E., and Maud Howe Elliott. *Julia Ward Howe, 1819–1910.* Boston: Houghton Mifflin, 1925.

Stern, Madeleine B. "Julia Ward Howe." *Dictionary of Literary Biography.* Gale, 1978. 1:114–115.

Tharp, Louise Hall. *Three Saints and a Sinner: Julia Ward Howe, Louisa, Annie and Sam Ward.* Boston: Little, Brown, 1956.

Selected Critical Studies

Grant, Mary H. "Domestic Experience and Feminist Theory: The Case of Julia Ward Howe." *Woman's Being, Woman's Place: Female Identity and Vocation in American History.* Ed. Mary Kelley. Boston: G. K. Hall, 1979.

———. "Julia Ward Howe." *American Women Writers.* Ed. Linda Mainiero. Ungar, 1980. Vol. 2:340–342.

———. "Private Woman, Public Person: An Account of the Life of Julia Ward Howe from 1819–1868." Ph.D. diss., George Washington University, 1982.

Huxman, Susan Schultz. "The *Woman's Journal* 1870–1890: The Torchbearer for Suffrage." *A Voice of Their Own: The Woman Suffrage Press, 1840–1910.* Ed. Martha M. Solomon. University of Alabama Press, 1991, pp. 87–109.

Chronology of Major Speeches

"Woman and the Suffrage." n.d. HOW rpt. *Outlook,* April 3, 1909.

"The Patience of Faith" (opening address); "How to Extend the Sympathies of Women." Twelfth annual congress, Association for the Advancement of Women, Baltimore, Md., n.d. *WSM*:230–234, 235–241.

Speech at a Suffrage Hearing before the Massachusetts Legislature. n.d. *WSM*:189–197.

Speech at Legislative Hearing. Massachusetts Legislature, March 7, n.d. *WSM*:202–205.

"The Woman's Peace Festival." International Women's Peace Movement, June 5, 1875. *TWJ* (June 5, 1875):180.

"Look After Your Legislature." Massachusetts State Legislature, February 1880. *TWJ* (February 21, 1880):60.

Address of Mrs. Howe's. New England WSA, June 1881. *TWJ* (June 11, 1881):169.

"The Moral Initiative As Belonging to Women." Second Council of Women, May 16, 1893. *WSM*:113–135.

Speech at the Annual Meeting of an Equal Suffrage Association. New England WSA, 1895. *WSM*:212–216.

"Why Are Women the Natural Guardians of Social Morals?" Association for the Advancement of Women, 1896. *WSM*:93–112.

"Let There Be Light." n.p. 1905. *WSM*:217–221.

"Mrs. Howe on Equal Rights." Speech read at the 38th annual NAWSA Convention, Baltimore, Md., February 12, 1906. *WSM*:222–229.

"Boston, A Little Island of Darkness." Address, Suffrage Hearing, State House, Boston, February 4, 1908. *WSM*:206–211.

Secondary Sources

Blair, Karen J. *The Clubwoman as Feminist: True Womanhood Redefined, 1868–1914*. New York: Holmes & Meier, 1980.
Clarke, Edward H. *Sex in Education: A Fair Chance for the Girls*. Boston: James R. Osgood, 1873.
Conrad, Susan Phinney. *Perish the Thought: Intellectual Women in Romantic America 1830–1860*. New York: Oxford University Press, 1976.
Cott, Nancy F. *The Bonds of Womanhood: "Woman's Sphere" in New England, 1780–1835*. New Haven, Conn.: Yale University Press, 1977.
———. "Young Women in the Second Great Awakening In New England." *Feminist Studies* 3 (Fall 1975):15–29.
Douglas, Ann. *The Feminization of American Culture*. New York: Alfred A. Knopf, 1977.
Griffin, Clifford S. *Their Brothers' Keepers. Moral Stewardship in the United States, 1800–1865*. New Brunswick, N.J.: Rutgers University Press, 1960.
Higginson, Thomas Wentworth. *Common Sense About Women*. Boston: Lee & Shepard, 1882.
Hutchison, William R. *The Transcendentalist Ministers*. New Haven, Conn.: Yale University Press, 1959.
Mitgang, Herbert. "Her Song Goes Marching On." *New York Times Magazine* (January 28, 1962):14, 38.
Smith-Rosenberg, Carroll. "The Female World of Love and Ritual: Relations Between Women in Nineteenth-Century America." *Signs* 1 (1975):1–29.

CATHARINE WAUGH MCCULLOCH

(1862–1945), drama, humor, and legal argument in support of woman suffrage, peace, temperance, and social justice

CHARLES M. KAUFFMAN

From 1890 through the ratification of the suffrage amendment, Catharine Waugh McCulloch was one of the principal legal advisers to the suffrage movement. She was legislative superintendent of the Illinois Equal Suffrage Association (IESA), 1890–1912, and the author of bills that gave Illinois women joint guardianship of children and raised the legal age of consent for women. She was the author and principal advocate of the "brilliant idea" to give Illinois women partial suffrage by revising Illinois statutes rather than by constitutional amendment (Brown, 1946:83); suffrage historians called the 1913 Illinois victory "the turning point in the enfranchisement of twenty-five millions of women" (Brown, 1946:94). She was elected justice of the peace in 1907, the first U.S. woman elected to judicial office. She worked for many causes: temperance, pacifism, and the legal rights of women and children. She served as a presidential elector for Woodrow Wilson in 1916. She was married in 1890 to Frank Hathorn McCulloch, and they raised four children in a large house two blocks from the Northwestern University campus in Evanston. After ratification of the Nineteenth Amendment, she continued to work for the causes to which she had dedicated her life: peace, temperance, and social justice. A sought-after speaker, she was famous for her biting wit and careful argument. Although she is not well known today, in her lifetime her words inspired thousands, while her work bettered conditions for families throughout the United States.

BACKGROUND

Catharine Gouger Waugh was born in New York, but the family soon moved to a farm in northern Illinois. Her father Abraham Waugh had wanted to become a lawyer but lacked the money to realize his ambition. Although he spent his life as a farmer, he never lost his interest in the law. When court was in session, he spent whatever time he could observing trials and serving as a juror. He argued in his own behalf and for local merchants in several lawsuits to collect debts (*NAW* 2). At home, he encouraged a love of argument and interest in controversy. In a family history written for her children, she remembered, "So when he said to his argufying daughter, 'That's my little lawyer' he was apparently hoping to have me realize his own ambitions" (SL E29, 165). Her father debated the question of woman suffrage in Grange meetings during the 1870s, and both her parents came from families opposed to alcohol (SL E32, 792; E29, 119). It seems to have been a matter of faith that "anti" sentiments were a product of big city vices (SL E32, 792). Early in her life she saw a close connection between temperance and suffrage, and to these causes she devoted herself.

Waugh began her higher education at the Rockford Seminary. While there, she joined the Oratorical Society and was selected to represent the school in intercollegiate competition (SL E29, 165). Evidently, she thought such training quite valuable. When in 1884, members of the sophomore class objected to participation in oratory, she, by then a graduate, wrote a five-page letter in response to the *Rockford Seminary Magazine* (SL E29, 313–316). It reveals the depth of her belief in the value of oratorical training and is an early demonstration of her style, which joined forensic argument with a derisive wit. After castigating the sophomores for their lack of loyalty and generosity, she wrote: "Upon the 'mature deliberation' of girls of eighteen, their blinded eyes 'see no benefits.' So I will not dwell on school loyalty, generosity or consistency, but will show some of the many instances in which these duties will bring personal mental profit and honor" (SL E29, 316). Her case for oratory rests on pragmatic arguments. If women are to take advantage of the new opportunities open to them, "the brain must formulate grand plans and arguments, and these must the mouth utter." Without training in oratory, even the greatest thoughts will fail to convert the recalcitrant. "Perhaps an old fogy of eighteen will say, 'We women never intend to speak in public on a stage, and so what good will this drill do us?' Poor, benighted intellects, poor blinded eyes! If you ever expect to have any ideas in your heads you will be anxious enough to share them with others" (SL E29, 316). She advised the "timid weaklings" who desire nothing more than to "officiate as 'angels of the fireside,' or 'queen of home' " that they will find drill in oratory useful in training their children and for participation in prayer meetings (SL E29, 316).

By the time she was graduated from Rockford Seminary, Waugh had become an effective orator and was fully committed to the cause of woman suffrage. At first glance her commencement address to the class of 1882, "Cogito Ergo Sum," seems to be a forgettable encomium to the virtues of knowledge. Instead, the speech subtly predicted a radical reorganization of society in which the rule of the stronger would give way to the rule of intellect:

The careful development of man's physical nature, which makes him a leader just as one animal leads the herd, did not tend to show that there was any thing superior to brute force; it completely overlooked those higher elements which give an insight into the world's thought, and link him with divinity. But now that the power of thought has arisen and begun to sway the world with our calculating nineteenth century ideas, we ask what chance this new course has of practical success and of outliving its rival. (SL E29, 310)

The power of knowledge was irresistible. Therefore, she called on her classmates to develop their minds: "Knowledge is a power, and he who has it has far wider fields of usefulness than his untaught fellows; for not only will others be intellectually elevated, but by skilled effort, using always the best ways and means, material prosperity will also be enhanced'' (SL E29, 310). For her, the value of knowledge depended on the use to which it was put. "The student should be no ethereal creature among the clouds,'' she said. Woman's lot would improve only through the cultivation of her intellect:

Equal power for manual labor, for living and suffering proved nothing, only when woman came forward as a thinker and author, an intellectual force was she recognized as more than a mere cypher; and now, in general literature, once man's domain, she is taking a leading place throughout Europe and our own land. She has been allowed to step from the nursery and kitchen to attempt this solution of social problems, by the power of her own mind, and may it soon be by the power of her own vote. (SL E29, 312)

This is the only reference to suffrage in the speech; there are no references to specific social reforms. Yet, the implications of her ideas are clear enough. Because women think, they must be treated as thinking beings, with all the rights, privileges, and responsibilities that thought entails. In the process, as they become full members of their communities, women will contribute to the general betterment of humankind. Male-dominated governments based on the rule of the stronger will give way to egalitarian governments based on intellectual ability. "The former boundaries of society, the power of wealth, beauty and high birth, are giving place to this new force which makes its division on the ground of culture and effective working power,'' she said (SL E29, 312). These sentiments informed her public argument throughout her life.

After her graduation from Rockford Seminary, Waugh read law in the offices of a Rockford attorney, but the experience proved unsatisfactory. In 1885, she enrolled in the two-year curriculum of the Union College of Law, later to become the Northwestern University Law School. One of two women in her class, she completed her studies in 1886 and was admitted to the Illinois bar, but she was unsuccessful in her search for a position with a Chicago law firm. Returning to Rockford, she established a legal practice and became active in the local chapter of the WCTU and the Rockford Equal Suffrage Association.

While in Rockford, she also completed work on an advanced degree at Rockford Seminary. In 1888, her thesis, "Woman's Wages,'' was accepted for the degrees of bachelor and master of arts. The thesis took issue with the reasons advanced by one of her faculty advisers justifying a lower wage for women and was developed in three parts. In part one, "Excuses for Inequality in Wages,'' Waugh wrote, "women received from one-third to one-half less wages than did men for the same amount of work, and any one who has eyes to see can observe this unjust discrimination between men and women wage-workers, but fail to behold any just reason therefor'' (5). Part two described the "real reasons" for the wage disparity. Women were disadvantaged because many professions were closed to them and by a lack of adequate education and training. Part three advanced solutions: legislation to make women eligible for all professions, better educational opportunities, reforms in the treatment of female delinquents, and so on (44). Reform would never come, she concluded, until women had the right to vote. She frequently used this argument over the next twenty years. Legislators represented the interests of their constituents. Legislative reforms directed to the interests of women would not, and could not, be expected to receive a full and fair hearing until women became constituents and legislators. "So when women ask for justice concerning wages can any simpler, more decisive method be devised than that of giving women the ballot?" (49).

This is an early instance of what Aileen Kraditor calls the "expediency" argument for suffrage (Buechler, 1986:193; *IWSM*:52ff.). There is no question that Waugh supported the ballot for the tangible benefits it would confer. But the vote offered something more: it was the fundamental ritual of democracy. Without it, women could not fully participate in their communities; without it, women could not give free rein to their intellects; without it, women could not be fully human, as she argued in "Cogito Ergo Sum." Thus, the vote was both an end in itself and a means to secure social reform. Although the expediency argument was always in the foreground, it was grounded in recognition of the ballot as a fundamental human right.

As president of the Rockford Equal Suffrage Association, Waugh refined her skills as a public advocate. Two events from her tenure are noteworthy. She invited HELEN JACKSON GOUGAR to speak at a District Suffrage convention. In her speech, Jackson Gougar took issue with local clergy who were anti-suffrage. She invited any minister opposed to woman suffrage to the platform for an impromptu debate. None came forward. After she left town, six local ministers granted interviews with a local newspaper and came out against suffrage.

Waugh challenged them to debate Jackson Gougar the following week at the Opera House, offered to pay all expenses, and invited the public to attend free of charge. Newspaper accounts played up the debate and aroused considerable interest in it. She remembered:

We had some noble old Republican to introduce the speakers. When no clergyman came to anyone [*sic*] of the six chairs on the platform provided for the six clergyman, I put on a large placard, "He who fights and runs away, will live to fight another day." This was enjoyed. Then Helen spoke, using the newspaper interviews for the speeches of the six. . . . It was great and the next day there was more publicity routing the enemy. (SL E29, 188)

This may be the first recorded instance of an "empty chair" debate in U.S. politics.

The second noteworthy event from the Rockford years is a debate in which Waugh participated. Fred Smith, an attorney from a nearby town, challenged her to debate the suffrage question. Posters advertised the encounter: "SHALL WOMEN VOTE. Come to Cole's Opera House, Thursday Evening, December 20, at 8 o'clock to see who is left on the field, Mr. Fred Smith or the Lady

Lawyer of Rockford. Admission 15 cents'' (SL E34, 278). A newspaper article
headlined ''Walloped Her Challenger'' described the outcome:

Now Mr. Smith can say, ''I have met the enemy and I am theirs,'' for when the debate
was concluded, the house voted for Miss Waugh's side by a tremendous majority. In
fact, she convinced all . . . with the solitary exception of Mr. Smith, who still maintains
that he has a case, but somehow can't make the people see it. (SL E34, 276)

Her victory was a source of local pride. A newspaper announced: ''A Rockford
Girl Victorious in Debating'' and described the outcome graphically: ''Thursday
night he [Fred Smith] was the cheapest young man in the state. You could have
bought him for a sou and a hole as big as your fist would have contained him.
Attorney Catherine [sic] G. Waugh was the cause of Mr. Smith's chagrin.'' The
article concluded by way of explanation, ''Well, after all a Rockford girl beats
a man from any other section of the globe'' (SL E34, 277). By 1890, she had
become an effective organizer and advocate for the cause of suffrage. When she
married Frank McCulloch in 1890 and moved to Chicago to establish the law
firm, McCulloch & McCulloch, she brought the skills that were to make her
one of the most influential women of her era.

PUBLIC ADVOCACY

Waugh McCulloch was an extremely gifted speaker; she was in constant
demand to fill speaking engagements not only in Illinois but also across the
United States (HWS 6:145–165). Her legal education made her the ideal figure
to speak before groups of men empowered to alter the conditions of women:
legislatures, business and church groups, and so forth. Wherever she went, she
brought much the same message: women were threatened by laws and customs
that jeopardized their well-being. Laws written by men and the decisions of a
male judiciary threatened women's economic status, their rights of guardianship,
their physical well-being and safety, their ability to gain employment at a fair
wage, and their ability to work for redress of these grievances. While the substance of her message remained much the same, the method of her appeal differed
considerably depending on her audience.

Waugh McCulloch advocated suffrage to solve the legal inequities suffered
by women and the social problems that accompanied disfranchisement. Government was a product of the interests it represented; without representation,
women could expect nothing better than benevolent protection, and the reality
was often much worse. With the vote would come the ability to participate in
government and influence the direction of the legislature and the judiciary. With
the vote, a woman controlled her destiny. Much the same reasoning was behind
her argument favoring teaching young women the art of boxing, a position that
attracted considerable attention in the press (SL E32, 885ff). Her concerns encompassed two broad but related issues: the legal and economic status of women.

Waugh McCulloch dedicated much of her career as a lawyer to improving the legal status of women and children. She felt that the laws governing women in most states were the product of an earlier era in the evolution of civilization when despots ruled the state and men were both protectors and providers in the home. Furthermore, most laws were framed for rural, rather than urban, societies. Questions that were formerly decided by farm families were, in cities, left to "men-aldermen elected by men voters" even though their decisions affected "women's homes and the surroundings of their children" (SL E33, 106). The evolution of civilization and the transformation of the United States from a rural to an urban society demanded changes in the law. She wrote:

[T]he conditions which gave rise to these laws no longer prevail. Mothers are today responsible, cultivated, discreet, experienced, and, under the changed conditions of society, are entirely capable of sharing with fathers in the guardianship and control of their children. (*Mr. Lex*, 6)

The best summary of her argument is found in her fictional *Mr. Lex or The Legal Status of Mother and Child*, published in 1899. A copy was sent to the wife of every member of the Illinois Legislature and to many newspapers. *Mr. Lex* began as a speech; Waugh McCulloch recalled that " 'Mr. Lex' was my address at many a club meeting" (SL E32, 739). Despite its fictional form, it was accompanied by a four-page table of citations documenting the legal authorities from which the incidents in the novel were derived.

Mr. Lex was a grocer, a conceited grocer because he had a legal education and was admitted to the bar. Married to Mrs. Lex, he had tried for ten years to build a practice, but "Either his nervous, irritable manner, or lack of thoroughness, or one or two great blunders, or lack of tact, or all combined, had conspired to bring him few clients" (11). Mrs. Lex had an inheritance from her father, which she used to support the growing family. After ten years of a failed law practice, all that remained of Mrs. Lex's inheritance was a grocery store that Mr. Lex finally consented to run. But he never forgot that he was a lawyer, and he conducted all of his personal and social relations in strict accord with the law.

Mrs. Lex offered to help reduce household expenses by using her knowledge and expertise to purchase food and clothing for the family, but Mr. Lex refused to give her any money whatsoever. He controlled all the family assets, and his was the right to choose clothing for the children and the food the family would eat (14–15). When Mrs. Lex bought a winter coat on credit for her daughter, Mr. Lex refused to pay the bill and took the case to court, arguing that the garment "was not for the welfare of the family," and that he had given "no authority to make this purchase" (16–17). The judge decided in favor of Mr. Lex, and when the merchant threatened Mrs. Lex with arrest "for obtaining the cloak under false pretenses," she stripped the coat off her daughter's back and returned it to the merchant. "Mrs. Lex did not try to buy any more clothes, and her husband did not let her forget that his choice must prevail" (18).

Subsequently, Mr. Lex asserted his authority to "devise unusual and humiliating punishments for the children" (18), to force the children to attend the church of his choice (19), to decide the course of medical treatment for the children, which cost the youngest daughter her life (19–20). Mr. Lex asserted his authority to determine where the dead child would be buried, and he ruined the health of the eldest son by requiring him to do hard labor in the store. Their daughter Mary, who helped in the store, was seduced by "an evil man" at the age of fourteen (26). When Mrs. Lex sought the arrest of the man, she was informed that "girls over fourteen are considered old enough to consent" (27). When Mr. Lex discovered their daughter's condition, he "turned [her] out on the street" (31). With her daughter destitute, Mrs. Lex attempted a civil suit to recover damages done her by the "evil man," only to discover that she lacked standing to sue: "The father has the exclusive right of action" (33).

Thereafter, Mrs. Lex discovered that creditors had the right to attach her savings to pay her husband's personal debts (41); that her husband had sole authority to consent to her daughter's marriage (47); that after sixteen weeks of schooling, her children could be withdrawn from school to work in the store (49); that her husband could have her infant child removed to a baby farm (51); and that she could be arrested for abducting her child when she tried to prevent its removal (53). She found she could not divorce Mr. Lex because she had no legal ground (67). Only when her husband was declared legally insane did Mrs. Lex find relief.

During her troubles, generous men helped Mrs. Lex, including an attorney who took her case without charge. She received the sympathy of judges and magistrates who, though compelled to rule against her, saw the essential justice of her cause. The lesson was that, despite the good intentions of even the majority of men, a single man could, by the power of the law, deprive a woman of everything important in life. Reflecting on her experience, Mrs. Lex decides that she must share her misfortune. In a scolding like that given the sophomores who rejected oratory, Waugh McCulloch's Mrs. Lex concludes that women must offer up their voices:

[T]he time is coming when women of education and wealth and leisure and social prestige will take up the cause of women, other women, all women. Just now some of them are more interested in "society," clubs, Hindoo [sic] philosophy, whist, or the heathen or drunkards, criminals or incompetents. They are busy studying, entertaining, reforming, curing. They are only sleeping on women's needs. They will wake up soon. (80)

Although *Mr. Lex* was reviewed negatively in scholarly outlets (Freund, 1900; W.H.A., 1899), it had an impact (*HWS* 4:602–604).

Waugh McCulloch became legislative superintendent of the IESA in 1890 and pushed for changes in guardianship law at every legislative session. Years later, she recalled: "My bill passed in 1901" (SL E32, 739). Four years later, her bill raising the age of consent from fourteen to sixteen also became law in Illinois. Despite these reforms, injustices remained in Illinois and elsewhere. Their elimination awaited the advent of full suffrage. In an address to the Michigan Legislature, she concluded: "When complete woman suffrage is established in the constitution, the minor injustices, the inconsistencies, the many absurdities now in Michigan law will be replaced with laws more fair and equal and righteous" (SL E33, 107).

Waugh McCulloch's second great concern was the economic status of women. In *Mr. Lex*, she wrote: "Women must have some financial resources before they can ever stand equal to their husbands in the control of their children. If women continued financially dependent, they would still be inferior" (74). Her concern with the economic status of women, first voiced in her M.A. thesis, continued long after ratification of the Nineteenth Amendment. But whereas her thesis dealt with women in the workforce, her later concerns were directed to women working in the home. Despite legal reforms giving women control over their earnings, most women still labored in the home, receiving no wages for their efforts, and remaining economically dependent on their husbands: "In no state is a wife entitled to any pay for her service for the family. The mythical 'one dollar a week pin money' has no foundation in law" (SL E33, 188).

Waugh McCulloch argued that women's contribution to the maintenance of the home was "essential to the continuance of the Republic" (SL E33, 191). Recognition in "poems" and "Mother's Day Addresses" was insufficient: "Sentiment is good but there is no money in it" (SL E33, 191). Legal reforms making the "marriage relationship an attractive business undertaking, and just to both partners" were required (SL E33, 190). Citing cases from trial records in which women had worked their entire lives only to be deprived of the wealth accumulated in marriage, she advocated the establishment of community property arrangements whereby "every wife should have full economic control of a half of the family income and a half ownership in family wages" (SL E33, 191). The advantages of this arrangement to women were obvious. To men, she argued that community property might cause young men to "hesitate to marry an idle woman, a parasite, a vampire, or a spendthrift. If such women were never wed, the world would not be cumbered by their lazy spendthrift progeny, a great indirect benefit" (SL E33, 191).

Together, economic and legal reform would help to emancipate women and eliminate the provision of rights and privileges based solely on sex. Reform was an inevitable byproduct of the franchise. When women's interests were represented, better legislation would follow. Waugh McCulloch concluded: "When laws are drafted by men only, who have only a man's viewpoint, they are liable to work out unjustly. Women and men together can prepare a safer, more just family-property law than can be found on the statute book of any state" (SL E33, 192).

With the ratification of the Nineteenth Amendment, Waugh McCulloch's public advocacy merely shifted its focus. She was active in the League of Women Voters, preparing pamphlets and speaking the need for legal reform of property laws (McCulloch and McCulloch, *A Manual*). She continued her work in support of prohibition (e.g., "A Word to Wise Drys," 1928) and in the years after World War I advocated pacifism ("The Crooked Made Straight" 1917: SL E32, 272). She and her husband turned their attention to the problems of social reform throughout the world. Traveling widely, they used their travels to "watch developments in other countries whose problems are similar to ours and fit ourselves to evaluate economic and social ends and to discover the proper means to achieve the best" (McCulloch and McCulloch, *Social Welfare Legislation*, 2).

The most striking attribute of Waugh McCulloch's rhetoric is the range of its formal expression. She presented her message in poems, fables, plays, novels, prayers, speeches, debates, articles, pamphlets, and books. The variety of rhetorical forms enabled her to speak comfortably and effectively to many different audiences. For more than twenty years, she spent her winters buttonholing state legislators in Springfield, Illinois. After the invention of the automobile, she spent vacations with her family touring Wisconsin and Illinois speaking to groups of strangers in small towns from the back of the family car. She was equally comfortable giving testimony to the U.S. Congress, discussing scripture in church, or citing legal precedents in court. Although her basic message never changed, the arguments were adapted to her immediate audience. A comparison of her rhetoric before legislators, men's groups, and women's groups illustrates her strategies.

Two themes unified all her presentations. First, the principle of consistency, a basic tenet of rational deliberation, required the acceptance of woman suffrage. Second, suffrage, once obtained, would enable women to help themselves and their society.

To legislators, Waugh McCulloch was the realistic lawyer. Human beings act out of self-interest. In some respects, the interests of men and women are the same, and in other respects, their interests differ. Men, possessing power, are naturally reluctant to share it. Therefore, it is understandable that male juries and legislatures had not acted to protect the rights and liberties of women. In testimony to the House of Representatives, she said, "One class cannot, will not legislate better for all than all for all. So men alone cannot legislate better for women and men than can men and women together for men and women both" ("Protective Value of the Ballot," *TWJ*, February 24, 1900). Of the courts, she said, "Men jurors generally fix inadequate penalties for wrongs done women and girls. They can never be expected to go ahead of the law, and the law shows little delicate discrimination between wrongs against women and animals" (SL E33, 105). This argument presaged what has come to be known as feminist jurisprudence (MacKinnon, 1987). Thus, her task was to demonstrate to legislators that it was in their interest to enfranchise women.

Her strategy was to treat male legislators as part of the legal and legislative community, bound by training, law, and custom to respect the conventions of evidence and argument. Specifically, she expected legislators to honor the principle of consistency as they examined the case for suffrage. The principle of consistency is the foundation of U.S. jurisprudence, embodied in the doctrines of *stare decisis* and precedent. If it can be shown that statutes and court decisions are incompatible with constitutional presumptions and the social realities of the twentieth century, then legislators have either to forfeit their status as reasoning beings or to change the laws. Waugh McCulloch always demonstrated a lawyer's faith in the power of argument to change minds. In the middle of a legislative fight, she once claimed: "If there are men making these unusual conditions, I want to know their names, and I am positive that by argument I can persuade them to withdraw such conditions" (SL E32, 741).

Waugh McCulloch's position was thoughtfully argued; her arguments were carefully documented. She examined both sides of a controversy and was meticulous with her facts and documentation. Her argument demonstrated that the laws disadvantaging women were inconsistent with current legislative enactments; they were outmoded vestiges of a less civilized era (SL E33, 98–107). If discriminatory laws were not revised to remove these inconsistencies, the only inference to be drawn was that legislators themselves were irrational and unworthy. Her speech to the Michigan Legislature is a good example of this strategy. Noting that the old Michigan Constitution had been written before women came to positions of prominence and when the state had no great cities, Waugh McCulloch, citing Michigan court decisions, demonstrated the need for legislative change. Her analysis of tax law illustrates the point:

Women's right to representation in government because of their payment of taxes is only recognized by Michigan in the matter of school elections. If this principle should be carried out concerning the schoolhouse . . . why should not women taxpayers also vote for or against a town house, a city hall, a county courthouse, or a state capital building[?]" (SL E33, 106)

The law on a wife's services was similarly inconsistent, as were the laws governing contracts (SL E33, 101–102). Property laws deprived women of their earnings and confused their legal status by grouping women and children (a category error that suggests that someone wasn't thinking) (SL E33, 103). Similarly, laws on death and divorce, on competency as a witness, on the guardianship of children, on taxation, and on jury service all demonstrated inconsistency and, therefore, the need for revision. Waugh McCulloch's appeal is the appeal of a well-crafted argument, an appeal rooted in the forms and language of law and legislation. The appeal recognizes the distinctiveness and the power of the human rational faculty and attempts to engage it and so to affirm it. At the same time, she enacted her argument; her rhetoric demonstrated the power of woman's intellect. Confronted with her arguments, rational men must give their assent. Other men may, perhaps, invent irrational reasons to oppose suffrage. But in a curious reversal, to do so was to enact the irrationality they feared in women.

Waugh McCulloch often spoke to male audiences in less formal surroundings. Civic and church groups were a powerful influence on public opinion in the early twentieth century, and she sought them out. In these settings, as in public debate, she often personalized the suffrage question by locating opposition in a single individual. Using her wit to skewer her opponent, she built identification with herself and the cause of suffrage. A typical example is "A Chicago Fable" (SL E32, 917–919).

A representative of the Chicago Chamber of Commerce entertains a Scotsman, a Dane, a Norwegian, an Icelander, a Finn, a Welshman, a South African, an Australian, a Canadian, a New Zealander, a Kansan, a Tasmanian, and residents of Wyoming, Colorado, Utah, and Idaho. As the delegation travels the city, much impressed, one asks, "Do you have privileged classes who do all the voting?" "No," the Chicago Man answers, "all citizens vote here without regard to rank." "That's the way it is with us," said the New Zealander. "Men and women vote on all matters." The rest of the fable describes Chicago Man's attempts to explain why women are not citizens and why they cannot vote. Each visitor, to be polite, offers a different possible justification: the Australian hypothesizes that the women of Chicago must have been criminals deported from some other land; the Scot suggests that Chicago women are lazy. To each explanation the Chicago Man offers an indignant rebuttal until he can stand no more: "Please stop," he says. "Even if I am your host, I can no longer endure the slurs which you are all casting at our Chicago women. I must tell you point blank that no women on earth are superior to ours" (SL E32, 919). "Why then," said the Finn, "do you politically disgrace your women by classing them with men guilty of election frauds and with unpardoned criminals? Why do you not enfranchise them as our countries have done?" Bewildered and dazed, the Chicago Man could only answer, "I don't know" (SL E32, 919).

The consistency principle was again at work. Just as Chicago Man could not justify his treatment of women, Waugh McCulloch's audiences either had to invent novel reasons to withhold suffrage or to change their views. Furthermore, there was an appeal to parochial pride. Without the vote, Chicago women were "less worthy" than other women, a position that Chicago Man was loath to accept. Civic boosterism, if nothing else, should be sufficient reason to advance the status of women: "there is no good reason why our women should be treated with less justice or honor than are the women of these other states and countries" (SL E32, 919).

Before church groups, Waugh McCulloch was more restrained but used the same strategies. To a group of Congregational men, she gave a speech entitled "Colonial Mothers" in which she argued that the denomination's history showed a commitment to the full participation of women in community affairs: "No real Congregational Church with any remnant of the Pilgrim spirit ever puts up bars against a woman holding any position" (SL E32, 146). To reject the appeal was to become unworthy of one's heritage. "The spirit of the men who in 1636

based their new laws on the consent of the governed is needed in Illinois'' (SL
E32, 147).

When Waugh McCulloch spoke to groups of women, she often gave her wit
greater freedom, especially as she dealt with anti-suffrage arguments. Speeches
such as ''Shall Men Vote'' (SL, Box 3, Folder 44) and ''Jury Service for Women
in Illinois'' (SL, Box 3, Folder 37) took prominent anti-suffrage arguments and
applied them to male behavior, proving that men were unworthy of the ballot
or jury service (''they are too emotional. I have observed it at football
games . . . ''). Nor did she spare women with whom she disagreed. Yet, before
women's groups, she did attempt to temper wit with understanding by using the
power of dramatization to bring the plight of women immediately before her
audiences. Her play, *Bridget's Sisters*, attempts to bridge ethnic and class barriers
by demonstrating the need for all women to work together to overcome their
common problems.

''Bridget'' and her drunkard husband ''Patrick'' are Irish immigrants (Waugh
McCulloch's ancestors were Irish) who represent recent immigrants whom many
thought unworthy of the vote. Margaret Deland, for example, wrote in the
Atlantic Monthly, ''We have suffered many things at the hands of Patrick; the
New Woman would add Bridget also. And—graver danger—to the vote of that
fierce, silly, amiable creature, the uneducated Negro, she would add (if logical)
the vote of his sillier, baser female'' (299). *Bridget's Sisters* depicts women of
middle- and upper-class backgrounds and interests coming together to support
their cleaning woman, Bridget, when a saloon-keeper attempts to take her wages
in payment for Patrick's liquor bill. Waugh McCulloch intended the play to
demonstrate that the interests of all women run deeper than ethnic and class
divisions. Her characters, Mrs. Takerights, Mrs. Pious, Mrs. Adoremen, Mrs.
Equity, and Mrs. Bitter, discover that they have much in common with Bridget
and with one another. They pledge to work together, following the example of
''Miss Anthony and Lucy Stone,'' to ''get the ballot for Illinois women'' (179).

CONCLUSION

Waugh McCulloch used dramatization to make the plight of women come to
life. *Mr. Lex* used ''the form of fiction . . . in order to place more vividly before
the reader the injustice which results from laws which make fathers sole guardians
and custodians of their children'' (5). ''A Selfish Prayer Turned Altruistic'' used
a mother's prayer to illustrate the perils facing children: ''Oh, Father of all,
follow my children into the ill lighted, poorly ventilated, over crowded school
room; save their eyes from being injured . . . direct some streams of fresh air to
the needy lungs of my children'' (*Survey* 14, March 1914:752). Detailing the
horrors that confronted children, ills from disease to sexual slavery, she concluded with a plea for the ballot: ''Yes, Lord, I hear thy voice. Thou wouldst
save us all through us thy servants. Thou wouldst use our ballots to make safe

conditions for all thy little ones. If the ballot is what we now need, give us the complete ballot." By setting forth the condition of women in dramatic form, she showed women from every background that their collective experience of injustice bound them to a common cause.

SOURCES

There are no dissertations, articles, or books about Waugh McCulloch. Standard histories of the suffrage movement mention her only briefly (*HWS* 4 and 6; *IWSM*; Flexner, 256). The primary source of information is the Catharine Waugh McCulloch papers, History of Women Collection, Schlesinger Library (SL), Radcliffe College, available on six reels of microfilm, E29-E34; documents are numbered consecutively. Citations in the text follow the Schlesinger Library system.

Secondary Sources

Beldon, Gertrude May. "A History of the Woman Suffrage Movement in Illinois." M.A. thesis, University of Chicago, 1913.

Boyer, Paul. "McCulloch, Catharine Gouger Waugh." *NAW* 2:459–460.

Brown, Gertrude Foster. "The Opposition Breaks." *Victory and How Women Won It.* New York: H. W. Wilson, 1946, pp 83–94.

Buechler, Steven M. *The Transformation of the Woman Suffrage Movement: The Case Study of Illinois, 1850–1920.* New Brunswick, N.J.: Rutgers University Press, 1986.

Deland, Margaret Wade (Campbell). "Change in the Feminine Ideal." *Atlantic Monthly* 105 (March 1910): 289–302.

Freund, Ernst. "Review of *Mr. Lex.*" *American Journal of Sociology* 5 (July 1899-May 1900):277.

MacKinnon, Catharine. *Feminism Unmodified: Discourses on Life and Law.* Cambridge, Mass.: Harvard University Press, 1987.

Trout, Grace Wilbur. "Sidelights on Illinois Suffrage History." *Journal of the Illinois State Historical Society* 12, no. 2 (July 1920):145–179.

W.H.A. "Review of *Mr. Lex.*" *Journal of Political Economy* 7 (December 1898-September 1899).

Wheeler, Adade Mitchell. "Conflict in the Illinois Woman Suffrage Movement of 1913." *Journal of the Illinois State Historical Society* 76, no. 2 (Summer 1983):95–114.

Chronology of Major Works

The following speeches are in the McCulloch Papers; most are on SL 32 and 33.
"Cogito Ergo Sum," June 1882.
"School Suffrage for Illinois Women," ca. 1891.
"Colonial Mothers," ca. 1905.
"A Chicago Fable," ca. 1907.
"Some Wrongs of Michigan Women, 1850–1908." Address, Michigan Constitutional Convention, January 8, 1908.
"Guardianship of Children." *Chicago Legal News,* January 13, 1912.

"A Selfish Prayer Turned Altruistic," January 1914. *Survey* 14 (March 1914):752.
"Patriotism and Feminism," ca. 1916.
"The Crooked Made Straight," ca. 1917–1918.
"The Economic Status of a Wife Working in the Home," January 1924.
"Excerpts, Address, Woman's Guild of Evanston," September 1937.

Congressional Testimony

"The Protective Value of the Ballot." House Judiciary Committee, February 13, 1900;
    rpt. *The Woman's Journal*, February 24, 1900.
Statement of Mrs. Catharine Waugh McCulloch. Hearings, Senate Committee on Woman
    Suffrage, April 19, 1910, pp. 6–9.

Books and Plays

Woman's Wages. Rockford, Ill.: Daily Gazette Book and Job Office, 1888.
Mr. Lex or The Legal Status of Mother and Child. Chicago: Fleming H. Revell, 1899.
Bridget's Sisters or The Legal Status of Illinois Women in 1868. Chicago: IESA, 1911;
    rpt. *On to Victory: Propaganda Plays of the Woman Suffrage Movement*. Ed.
    Bettina Friedl. Boston: Northeastern University Press, 1987, pp. 163–188.
A Manual of the Law of Will Contests in Illinois. Chicago: Callaghan & Co., 1929. With
    Frank H. McCulloch.
Social Welfare Legislation and Governmental Participation in Business. Evanston, Ill.:
    n.p., 1936. With Frank H. McCulloch.

IDA B. WELLS BARNETT
(1862–1931), agitator for African-American rights

MARY M. BOONE HUTTON

Ida B. Wells Barnett dedicated herself to eradicating lynch law. In that effort, she interpreted and expressed the suffering and oppression inflicted on African-Americans through the press and on the platform in the United States and Great Britain. She believed that "the people must know before they can act," and she was strongly convinced that "there is no educator to compare with the press" (*Southern Horrors*, 23). A contemporary called her "a special envoy and ambassador extraordinary, sent to earth in behalf of great movements of democracy, interracial concord and cooperation" (Gaines Box 1, March, 1931). Her great hatred of injustice, her militant spirit, and her experiences in the South, along with her talents as a writer and speaker, combined to make her ideally suited to be an advocate for African-Americans.

BACKGROUND

Ida Bell Wells was born on July 16, 1862, in Holly Springs, Mississippi (*Crusade*, 15). Her parents died in a yellow fever epidemic in 1878, and at age sixteen, the oldest of three sisters and two brothers, she assumed the responsibilities of head-of-household. She obtained a position teaching in a rural Holly Springs school, but after one term, she moved to Memphis, where she first taught in rural Shelby County while studying to obtain city certification (*Crusade*, 18; Fortune's account [1893:35] differs). While teaching in Memphis, she worked to improve her academic skills, taking private lessons, including lessons in elocution and dramatics. As a member of the local lyceum she was elected to edit the *Evening Star*, and when she read aloud the items she had written, attendance increased. Among those attending was the Reverend R. N. Countee, publisher of the *Living Way*, who invited her to write for his paper, which she did for two years (*Crusade*, 22–23).

Although she had no journalistic training, Wells quickly observed that most of her readers had little formal schooling and needed reading material that addressed their problems simply and helpfully. "I wrote in a plain, common-sense way on the things which concerned our people," she said in her autobiography. "Knowing that their education was limited, I never used a word of two syllables where one would serve the purpose" (*Crusade*, 24). Her articles were reprinted in and commented on by African-American newspapers around the country. She became widely known by the pen name "Iola," which she used during her early journalistic career.

Wells believed that if African-Americans were to change the conditions under which they lived, they had to rise and free themselves. Decisions handed down by the Supreme Court during the last quarter of the nineteenth century had weakened the protection afforded African-Americans by the Fourteenth and Fifteenth amendments and underscored the need for self-help. In 1876, the Court limited the federal government's right to enforce suffrage in cases involving race and color. In 1878, the Court declared unconstitutional a Louisiana law forbidding segregated facilities in interstate travel on the grounds that it placed an undue burden on privately owned interstate commerce. Then, in 1883, the Court ruled that the 1875 Civil Rights Act, which provided for equal accommodations for all citizens in public places regardless of color, was unconstitutional.

Consistent with her belief in self-help, Wells sued the Chesapeake, Ohio and Southwestern Railroad for its discriminatory practices. In December 1884, the Circuit Court returned a judgment in her favor, awarding her $500 in damages, but on appeal, the Tennessee Supreme Court reversed the decision, ordering her to pay the costs (*Crusade*, 18–20). Her account of this suit in the newspaper *Living Way* introduced her to the press as a skilled writer; by 1891, she had written for many leading African-American newspapers (*Crusade*, 32–33).

Wells's first regular salaried position as a journalist was on the staff of *American Baptists*. On one occasion, she published an "earnest plea" to support T. Thomas Fortune in his efforts to establish the Afro-American League, an organization founded to protect African-Americans' life, citizenship, and property. Promoting African-American self-help, she chided her readers: "All who give the matter earnest thought realize that something should be done and that something by ourselves." She continued:

Because it is the first move of a practical nature toward self-protection, of which colored men have been the originators, it is deserving of the deepest consideration at the hands of the people. We have reached a state in the world's history where we can no longer be passive onlookers, but must join in the fray for our recognition, or be stigmatized forever as a race of cowards. (*New York Freeman*, July 9, 1887:1; quoted in Louisville *American Baptists*)

In 1889, Wells was invited to write for the *Memphis Free Speech and Headlight*, an African-American weekly. Explaining her acceptance, she wrote:

I was one among those who believed the condition of the masses gave large excuse for the humiliations and proscriptions under which we labored; that when wealth, education and character became more general among us,—the cause being removed—the effect would cease, and justice be accorded to all alike. I shared the general belief that good newspapers entering regularly the homes of our people in every state could do more to bring about this result than any agency. Preaching the doctrine of self-help, thrift and economy every week, they would be the teachers to those who had been deprived of school advantages, yet were making history every day.... And so, ... I became editor and part owner of the *Memphis Free Speech* ("Lynch Law in All Its Phases," 334).

In editorials, Wells criticized the white Memphis school board for its "one-sided" administration, claiming that funds were not evenly distributed between

African-American and white schools. As a result, she was fired from her teaching position, which she had held for seven years. She now devoted all her efforts to the paper, attempting, in her words, "to make a race newspaper pay—a thing which older and wiser heads said could not be done" ("Lynch Law in All Its Phases," 334). Acting as advertising agent and solicitor as well as editor, she traveled through Mississippi, Arkansas, and Tennessee canvassing for subscriptions. Within nine months, circulation had increased from 1,500 to 3,500; at the end of a year, she had achieved her goal: the *Free Speech* was paying its way.

Wells's world was shattered when, on March 9, 1892, three of her Memphis friends—Thomas Moss, Calvin McDowell, and Henry Stewart—were lynched. Prior to these murders, she admitted that she, too, had believed that the unreasoning anger of whites over the terrible crime of rape had led to the lynchings of African-Americans, that perhaps those lynched had deserved their fate (*Crusade*, 64). But her friends had not even been accused of rape. They were peaceful, law-abiding citizens, "three of the best specimens of young since-the-war Afro-American manhood," she observed (*Southern Horrors*, 18). In an interview, she explained that these men were

energetic businessmen, who had accumulated a little money which they invested in a grocery business. The white monopolists did not like their rivalry; there was an altercation, my friends defended themselves, were thrown in gaol, and bail was refused. The whites thought they were getting too independent, so they were taken out of gaol and lynched. (*London Methodist Times*, May 24, 1894:330)

She concluded that lynching was really "[a]n excuse to get rid of Negroes who were acquiring wealth and property and thus keep the race terrorized and 'keep the nigger down' " (*Crusade*, 64).

Impelled by these murders, Wells began to investigate reported lynchings and discovered that, of those recorded during the next three-month period, every case of alleged rape "became such only when it became public" (*Crusade*, 64–65). In other words, whenever an illicit relationship between a white woman and an African-American man came to light, the cry of "rape" went up, the man was lynched, and all was well with the white woman's reputation.

These findings prompted Wells to respond to a *Memphis Commercial* editorial, "More Rapes, More Lynchings" (May 17, 1892), which charged that five out of eight African-Americans lynched within a week had raped white women. She contested this claim in an explosive editorial (*Free Speech*, May 21) in which she wrote:

Nobody in this section believes the old threadbare lie that negro men rape white women. If Southern white men are not careful, they will overreach themselves and public sentiment will have a reaction. A conclusion will be reached which will be very damaging to the moral reputation of their women. ("Lynch Law in All Its Phases," 339)

In response, the Memphis *Commercial Appeal* called on chivalrous white men to avenge the insult to the honor of white women, stating that the editorialist should be burned at the stake (*Crusade*, 66). The white community destroyed the newspaper office and threatened the owners of the *Free Speech*, effectively exiling them from Memphis and suppressing their paper. Wells, who was in New York City, received letters and telegrams from friends warning her that she would be killed if she returned ("Lynch Law in All Its Phases," 340).

If Memphis whites hoped to silence Wells by these actions, they failed. Reflecting on these events, she wrote that losing her paper, having a price put on her life, and being exiled from her home for hinting at the truth made her feel that she owed it to herself and to her fellow African-Americans to tell the whole truth now that she could do so freely (*Crusade*, 69). She believed that in order to justify lynching, southern whites were branding African-American men as rapists. To her it was a cruel irony that white men, who had sired mulattoes by raping African-American women, were lynching African-American men for illicit relationships with willing white women. That death in its most terrible form should be meted out to African-Americans who consorted with a white woman was horrible enough, but that all African-Americans "should be branded as despoilers of white womanhood and childhood," she contended, "was bound to rob us of all the friends we had and silence any protests that they might make for us." Accordingly, she judged, "it seemed a stern duty to give the facts I had collected to the world" (*Crusade*, 71).

Wells accepted a position with the *New York Age* and continued her fight against lynching through its columns. The opportunity to expose the lies behind the lynchings of African-Americans was made possible, in large measure, through the help of T. Thomas Fortune and Jerome B. Peterson, the owners and editors of the *New York Age*. They printed 10,000 copies of the June 25, 1892, issue and circulated them throughout the nation; in Memphis alone, 1,000 copies were sold (*Crusade*, 63, 71). On the front page was a seven-column article titled "Exiled," giving the names, dates, and places of many of the lynchings for alleged rape. In Wells's estimation, these statistics proved conclusively that the charges in her *Free Speech* editorial had been based "on facts of illicit association between black men and white women" (*Crusade*, 69; "Lynch Law in All Its Phases," 341; "Preface," *Southern Horrors*).

Responding to that article, Victoria Earle Matthews of New York City and Maritcha Lyons of Brooklyn decided that women should do something to support Wells's work and to protest the treatment she had received. Their efforts led to a testimonial held in Lyric Hall, New York City, on October 5, 1892. Wells was presented with a gold brooch and $500, which she later used to publish her first pamphlet, *Southern Horrors* ("Preface"). On this occasion she first delivered what she called her first "honest-to-goodness address" (*Crusade*, 79).

According to Wells, that event was also the real beginning of the club movement among African-American women and the genesis of her public speaking career. The sponsoring women organized the Women's Loyal Union, which was the first strictly African-American women's club in New York City. The exposure Wells received brought invitations, primarily from African-American churches and organizations, to speak in cities and towns in Pennsylvania, Delaware, Washington, D.C., and Massachusetts (*Crusade*, 81).

On February 1, 1893, Henry Smith, an African-American, was burned alive in Paris, Texas, an act of mob violence that "exceeded all others in its horrible details" ("Lynch Law in All Its Phases," 9). When news of this atrocity reached England, Catherine Impey, an Englishwoman who had heard Wells speak during a visit to the United States, wrote inviting her to tell the truth about lynch law in Great Britain. Wells had been unsuccessful in reaching white Americans: "Only in one city—Boston—had I been given even a meager hearing, and the [white] press was dumb" (*Crusade*, 86). She seized this opportunity to spread her message, and from April to June, she lectured in England and Scotland. Of her reception, she wrote: "My audiences have been often large, and always enthusiastic. Everywhere I have met with cordial and friendly sympathy" ("Lynch Law in the United States," 9). Moreover, the Society for the Recognition of the Brotherhood of Man (SRBM) was founded, and its members passed resolutions of condemnation and protest, many of which were published in the Society's journal *Fraternity* and in other newspapers (*Crusade*, 128).

During her second British tour, from March through July 1894, Wells delivered 102 speeches and wrote of her experiences for the white *Chicago InterOcean*. Consequently, her speeches told the grim story to British audiences, while her newspaper articles recounted her British successes for Americans. She also carried back with her a document signed by well-known English clergy appealing to the ministers and congregations of U.S. churches to accord her the same opportunity to speak from their pulpits as had been accorded her in England (Aked, 1894:545). After hearing her speak in Hope Street Unitarian Church in Liverpool, its pastor, the Reverend R. A. Armstrong, wrote a letter to the *Christian Register* of Boston, the leading Unitarian organ in the United States, in which he pleaded with his New England brothers and sisters to "bestir" themselves to save the good name of their nation (Armstrong, 1894:5). The letter helped her gain a hearing from white Americans and provoked considerable response.

Back in New York in July, she announced that if funds could be raised, she would "give the year to carrying the message across the country" (*Crusade*, 218). To this end, an Anti-lynching Association was formed, and while Wells waited for funds, invitations to lecture came from African-American groups. When the funds raised proved insufficient, she accepted the invitations, charging a fee. Beginning in New York, her lecture tour took her to Philadelphia, Chicago, St. Louis, Kansas City, and San Francisco.

Wells continued her agitation against lynching until she was "physically and morally bankrupt." Concluding that she had done her duty, she wrote: "So, when at last I came back to Chicago, in June 1895, it was to accept the offer

of a home of my own which had been made to me before my last trip to England''
(*Crusade*, 238). On June 27, 1895, she was married to Ferdinand L. Barnett.

After the birth of their first child, she retired from public life, but in the spring
of 1898, an African-American postmaster was lynched in Anderson, South Carolina. Fired by the hope that the federal government would intervene to punish
those responsible on the grounds that the outrage had been perpetrated on a
federal officer, African-Americans in Chicago passed resolutions denouncing the
act and prevailed on Wells Barnett to take them (along with a nursing baby) to
Washington, D.C., to press for government action. She agreed; accompanied
by Senator William E. Mason and seven members of Congress from Chicago
districts, she called on President McKinley (*Crusade*, 252–253). She said:

Nowhere in the civilized world save the United States of America do men, possessing
all civil and political power, go out in bands of 50 to 5,000 to hunt down, shoot, hang
or burn to death a single individual, unarmed and absolutely powerless. Statistics show
that nearly 10,000 American citizens have been lynched in the past 20 years. To our
appeals for justice, the stereotyped reply has been that the government could not interfere
in a state matter. . . . We refuse to believe this country, so powerful to defend its citizens
abroad, is unable to protect its citizens at home. Italy and China have been indemnified
by this government for the lynching of their citizens. We ask that the government do as
much for its own. (*Cleveland Gazette*, April 9, 1898:2)

Despite her eloquent plea and five weeks spent in daily trips to the Capitol in
an effort to secure passage of a bill to indemnify the postmaster's widow and
children, she retreated in defeat. Congress had just declared war on Spain; Senator
William E. Lorimer advised her that further efforts at that time would be useless.

Steadfast in her conviction that the conscience of the nation would not remain
forever silent in the face of continued lynchings, Wells Barnett continued to
make the facts known. In 1889, she issued *Lynch Law in Georgia*, reporting six
weeks of mob violence that had resulted in the horrible deaths of more than a
dozen African-Americans in that state. In 1900, she published *Mob Rule in New
Orleans*, a detailed account of a week of rioting ushered in by unprovoked
assaults on two African-Americans by white police officers. The pamphlet also
included a history of humans burned alive in the United States and a table of
lynchings as presented by the *Chicago Tribune* for the period 1882 through 1899.
In 1901, the National Afro-American Council, for which she chaired the Anti-
Lynching Bureau, published another of her protests entitled ''Lynching and the
Excuse for It.''

Seven years later, she again found herself actively caught up in the anti-
lynching movement when a race riot broke out in Springfield, Illinois. At the
end of a three-day reign of terror, three law-abiding African-American men in
no way involved with the riot were lynched. In response, the Negro Fellowship
League, forerunner of the National Urban League, was organized with Wells
Barnett as its president.

In 1909, a race riot erupted in Cairo, Illinois, after the body of a white woman was found in an alley. A penniless African-American known as "Frog" James was locked up in the police station, and the sheriff, Frank Davis, was called. James was taken from the sheriff's custody by a mob and killed. African-Americans maintained that the sheriff had been negligent, and Davis was suspended. Wells Barnett was asked to represent Illinois African-Americans and was sent to Cairo to obtain facts with which to confront the sheriff, who planned to petition the governor for reinstatement. She drew up resolutions to deny the sheriff's petition, which were adopted by the African-Americans of Cairo. In presenting these resolutions to the governor, she related the facts of the lynching and those gleaned from interviews with the African-Americans of Cairo and from reading the files of every newspaper in that city published during the riot. In this way, it was hoped to find some account of the steps the sheriff had taken to protect his prisoner. She concluded:

Governor [Charles S. Deneen], the state of Illinois has had too many terrible lynchings within her borders within the last few years. If this man is sent back[,] it will be an encouragement to those who resort to mob violence and [who] will do so at any time, well knowing they will not be called to account for so doing. (*Crusade*, 317)

After hearing the facts and the arguments of both sides, the governor decreed that the sheriff could not be reinstated because he had not provided proper protection for the prisoner within his keeping and that lynch law could have no place in Illinois. From that time until 1929, when she wrote her autobiography, there were no lynchings in Illinois (*Crusade*, 319).

A year after the violence in Cairo, Wells Barnett published "How Enfranchisement Stops Lynching" in which she discussed the impact of the vote on eradicating lynch law. Unless the ballot was sacred, she argued, human life could not be sacred because if the strong could take the ballot of the weak whenever it suited their purposes, they would also take their lives. Without the vote, African-Americans could not protest against discriminatory legislation by electing other lawmakers, and the more complete the disfranchisement, the more frequent and horrible the killings. As proof that African-Americans, by unified effort and sagacious use of the ballot, could help to end lynch law, she recounted how African-Americans in Illinois had united to work against lynching and, in 1904, elected one of their number, Edward D. Green, to the state legislature. Green introduced and secured passage of the Mob Violence Act, the legal instrument used in denying reinstatement to Sheriff Davis.

As a member of the National Equal Rights League, Wells Barnett investigated the race riot that erupted in East Saint Louis, Illinois, in July 1917, during which 150 African-Americans were killed. She appealed to the same organization to protest the riot in Elaine, Arkansas, in 1919, when African-Americans refused to sell their cotton below market price. During that riot, more than twenty-five African-Americans were killed. Many others were herded into prison in Helena,

Arkansas, where a mob beat and tortured them in an effort to make them confess that they were part of a conspiracy to kill whites. After the mockery of a trial, twelve were sentenced to death. Wells Barnett urged: "We can at least protest against it and let the world know that there is one organization of Negroes which refuses to be silent under such an outrage" (*Crusade*, 398).

A committee was formed that Wells Barnett chaired to send protest letters. Through the columns of the *Chicago Defender*, she appealed to African-Americans to use their influence and money to aid the twelve men sentenced to be electrocuted; people from all over the country responded. Returning to the South for the first time in thirty years, Wells Barnett concealed herself among a group of the prisoners' wives and mothers to visit the men at the penitentiary to gather facts about the riot. She assisted legal efforts by publishing and circulating these facts (*The Arkansas Race Riot*, 4–5; *Crusade*, 401, 404). All were freed.

Wells Barnett's anti-lynching agitation was not in vain. Between 1892 and 1895, when she was most active, the number of lynchings decreased from the all-time high of 241 in 1892 to 200 in 1893, 190 in 1894, 171 in 1895, and 107 in 1899 (*Mob Rule*, 46–47). Even the southern press reported unusual public sentiment against lynching, manifested in several states by passage of special legislation to suppress mob violence. The press further maintained that public sentiment against lynching was having the positive effect of making law enforcement officers more vigilant and determined in the protection of their prisoners (*New York Times*, December 8, 1895:32).

Wells Barnett continued to work to end lynching until her death in 1931. At that time, W.E.B. Du Bois wrote: "The passing of Ida Wells-Barnett calls for more than the ordinary obituary. [She] was the pioneer of the anti-lynching crusade in the United States. . . . She roused the white South to vigorous and bitter defense, and she began the awakening of the conscience of the nation" (*Crisis*, 40 [June 1931]:207; quoted in Thompson, 1990:126). In 1930, the struggle against lynching was taken up by white women, who formed the Association of Southern Women to Prevent Lynching led by Jessie Daniel Ames (see entry in Volume 2).

WELLS BARNETT'S RHETORICAL CAREER

As champion of the anti-lynching movement, Wells Barnett proved to be a skillful persuader. In attempting to convince audiences, she needed to make a strong case to refute prevailing views that justified lynching as a violent response to the alleged rapes of white women. She also had to present a plausible alternative explanation. Moreover, given post-Reconstruction appeals to states' rights, she needed to preempt arguments for noninterference. Finally, she faced a severe credibility problem. As an African-American woman, she had to draw her evidence from unimpeachable sources, which meant that she used data collected by prestigious white sources and the statements of whites, particularly southern whites, to support her conclusions.

Wells Barnett's most basic argument was straightforward refutation, based on statistics gathered by the *Chicago Tribune* and other white sources. She showed that fewer than one third of the African-Americans who were lynched were even charged with assaults on white women. This gave the lie to the claim that it was primarily for the crime of rape that African-Americans were lynched.

Her alternative explanation was more complex. She argued that lynching was a means of social control. This argument was supported by her analysis of the cry of rape as justification, by examples such as that of her three friends lynched for economic reasons, and by the editorial statements that appeared in white southern newspapers, illustrated by the long quotations in *Southern Horrors* (16–18). These were buttressed by four additional arguments.

Historically, she asserted that lynch law could be explained "by the well-known opposition growing out of slavery to the progress of the race" (*Southern Horrors*, 13). As an institution, she contended, slavery had shaped a contemptuous attitude in southern whites that caused them to view African-Americans as subhumans. Accordingly, they were committed to using any method, however extreme, to perpetuate their subjugation (*Southern Horrors*, 20).

A second argument was that the false view of lynching as prompted by rape was rendered plausible because southern whites suppressed the truth. Through threats and physical attacks on anyone who attempted to reveal the details of mob action, they prevented accurate reports from being made public, as dramatically illustrated by her own experience. For concealing and misrepresenting the facts of lynching, she indicted the pulpit and the white press as accomplices of and "apologists for lynchers" ([London] *Inquirer*, May 5, 1894:274–275).

A third argument was an attack on states' rights. Wells Barnett argued that U.S. political and legal institutions failed to extend their protective powers to African-Americans. Instead, these were administered entirely in behalf of southern whites and often in connivance with the lynchers. In her words, "the southern people . . . have demanded the right to administer their own justice, and they have obtained it" (*New York Sun*, July 30, 1894:2). Pointing to recent Supreme Court decisions, she said: "The Repeal of the Civil Rights Law removed their last barrier and the black man's last bulwark and refuge. The rule of the mob is absolute" ("Lynch Law in All Its Phases," 345). She responded to southern pleas for noninterference by casting her anti-lynching campaign as a moral crusade that transcended state and national boundaries and by calling on Christians everywhere to act against this great moral wrong. She insisted that the solution to lynching was strong public sentiment against it, sentiment that she attempted to arouse ("Lynch Law in All Its Phases," 346).

Finally, she empowered her African-American audiences by urging them to seek out the facts and disseminate them in person and through their newspapers, to bring economic pressure in the form of boycotts or mass emigration to deter future mob action, and to defend themselves, with arms if necessary, when attacked by mobs (*Southern Horrors*, 22–24).

Her arguments were developed deductively and were asserted emphatically, but she used evidence, particularly examples, to allow audiences to weigh the evidence and draw their own conclusions. Examples were also the primary source of emotional appeals—the details prompted sympathy for the victims and horror at the atrocities. However, she scrupulously avoided horrific particulars, dramatic language, and overtly emotional entreaties. Instead, she sought to convert through facts, argument, and appeals to widely held legal and moral principles. In some cases, numerous examples functioned almost statistically by piling instance upon instance. In *Southern Horrors*, for instance, seventeen relatively detailed cases were presented in support of her claim that "White men lynch the offending Afro-American, not because he is a despoiler of virtue, but because he succumbs to the smiles of white women" (7–12).

Her style was direct, even blunt. Early in her career, T. Thomas Fortune described her rhetorical methods in terms that remained accurate throughout her life: "She has plenty of nerve; she is smart as a steel trap, and she has no sympathy with humbug" (*New York Age*, August 11, 1888; quoted in Thompson, 1990:127). Somewhat later, he commented: "Her style is one of great strength and directness" (Fortune, 1893:39; quoted in Thompson 1990:84).

Whether quantitative, illustrative, or authoritative, she drew her evidence, in her words, from "the news gathered by white correspondents, compiled by white press bureaus and disseminated among white people" (*A Red Record*, 71). Her refutation of the charge that lynching was a response to rape relied on statistics amassed by northern white newspapers, but she also supported her charges with examples reported in southern white newspapers. For instance, to illustrate the connivance of the custodians of law and order in lynching, Wells Barnett quoted the description of a lynching in the *Memphis Commercial* (July 23, 1893): "The entire performance, from the assault on the jail to the burning of the dead Negro [*sic*] was witnessed by a score or so of policemen and as many deputy sheriffs, but not a hand was lifted to stop the proceedings after the door yielded" (*The Reason Why*, 32).

CONCLUSION

Wells Barnett should be remembered for spearheading the anti-lynching campaign and for her courage in debunking the claim that rapes of white women by African-American men were the cause of lynching. Emphasizing the barriers she faced, her daughter, Alfreda M. Barnett Duster, wrote:

Ida B. Wells was a black woman born into slavery who began openly carrying her torch against lynching in the very South bent upon the degradation of the blacks. . . . The most remarkable thing about [her] is . . . that she fought . . . with the single-mindedness of a crusader, long before men or women of any race entered the arena. (*Crusade*, xxxi–xxxii)

However great her dedication and fearlessness, she should be acclaimed equally for her rhetorical skills. In the words of historian John Hope Franklin, "For more than forty years Ida B. Wells was one of the most fearless and one of the most respected women in the United States. She was also one of the most articulate" (*Crusade*, ix). She constructed messages that could withstand scrutiny and skepticism. She developed arguments that, collectively, made a strong case for viewing lynching as a form of social control. Most important, she selected and deployed her evidence so that it could not be impeached, and she used the words of southern whites so effectively that, as she said, "out of their mouths shall the murderers be condemned" (*A Red Record*, 15).

SOURCES

Much of Wells Barnett's rhetoric appeared as articles in newspapers and other periodicals. Of the three newspapers that she edited and/or owned, only the June 22, 1911, issue of the *Fellowship Herald*, Chicago, which she edited, is extant (DuSable Museum, Chicago). Copies of *Free Speech*, like twenty-five other African-American newspapers published in Memphis, were not preserved. No copies of the Chicago *Conservator* for the period when she edited and owned it, June 1895–ca. January 1897, are extant. Her articles were widely quoted by the Black press; some are preserved in northern newspapers. No copy of her explosive essay "Exiled," *New York Age*, June 25, 1892, which was the basis for her *Southern Horrors* and *United States Atrocities* pamphlets, still exists. The most comprehensive record of her early anti-lynching campaign rhetoric is located in the British Library Newspaper Library. The best U.S. sources of information are her autobiography, Mildred Thompson's exploratory study, and the Ida B. Wells Papers, University of Chicago Library.

Other source materials are available in the Lynching Files (the most comprehensive in the United States) and the Margaret Murray Washington Papers, Tuskegee Institute, Tuskegee, Alabama; Joel E. Spingarn Papers and nineteenth-century African-American newspapers, Moorland-Spingarn Center, Howard University, Washington, D.C.; Commission on Interracial Cooperation Papers, Committee on Civil Rights Papers, and Association of Southern Women for the Prevention of Lynching Papers, Trevor Arnett Library, Atlanta, Georgia; Ida B. Wells-Barnett Clippings File and the Irene McCoy Gaines Papers, Chicago Historical Society; Tuskegee Institute Clippings File (lynching), nineteenth-century African-American newspapers and periodicals, Chicago Public Library; Jane Addams Papers, University of Illinois, Chicago; William Monroe Trotter Papers, Boston University Library; *The Woman's Era* [newspaper], Boston Public Library; Mary White Ovington Papers, Wayne University Archives of Labor History and Urban Affairs, Detroit, Michigan; Southern Historical Collection's Jessie Daniel Ames Papers and Southern Tenant Farmer's Union Collection, University of North Carolina Library, Chapel Hill; local newspapers, Public Library and Information Center, Memphis, Tennessee; Ida B. Wells File, including *United States Atrocities* [microfilm], Lynching Files, National Negro Congress Papers, and W.E.B. DuBois Papers, New York City Public Library; *Fraternity* [SRBM journal] and assorted British newspapers, especially *The*

Manchester Guardian, The Liverpool Review, and *The Methodist Times, The Christian World*, and *The Inquirer*, London, May-June 1893 and March-July 1894, British Library Newspaper Library, London; *Anti-Caste* [forerunner of *Fraternity*], March 1888–1895, Religious Society of Friends Library, London, England.

Biographical Sources

Flexner, Eleanor. "Wells-Barnett, Ida Bell." *NAW* 3:565–567.

Fortune, T. Thomas. "Ida B. Wells, A.M." *Women of Distinction*. Ed. Lawson A. Scruggs. Raleigh, N.C.: L. A. Scruggs, 1893, pp. 33–39.

Giddings, Paula. *When and Where I Enter: The Impact of Black Women on Race and Sex in America*. New York: William Morrow, 1984.

Hughes, Langston. "Ida B. Wells: Crusader 1869 [*sic*]–1931." *Famous Negro Heroes of America*. New York: Dodd Mead, 1958, pp. 155–162.

Sterling, Dorothy. *Black Foremothers: Three Lives*. New York: Feminist Press, 1979, pp. 61–117.

Thompson, Mildred I. "Ida B. Wells–Barnett: An Exploratory Study of an American Black Woman, 1893–1930." Ph.D. diss., George Washington University, 1970. Ed. and rev. *Ida B. Wells–Barnett: An Exploratory Study of an American Black Woman, 1893–1930*. Black Women in U.S. History Series. Ed. Darlene Clark Hines. Brooklyn, N.Y.: Carlson, 1990. Contains eleven essays by Wells-Barnett. (*IBWB*)

Wells, Ida B. *Crusade for Justice*. Ed. Alfreda M. Duster. Chicago: University of Chicago Press, 1970.

Critical Sources

Campbell, Karlyn Kohrs. "The Heavy Burdens of Afro-American Women: Sex, Race, and Class." *MCSFH* 1:145–156.

———. "Style and Content in the Rhetoric of Early Afro-American Feminists." *Quarterly Journal of Speech* 72 (1986):434–445.

Hutton, Mary Magdalene Boone. "The Rhetoric of Ida B. Wells: The Genesis of the Anti-Lynch Movement." Ph.D. diss., Indiana University, 1975.

———. "The Rhetorical Strategies of Ida B. Wells in the Anti-Lynch Movement." *In Search of Justice: The Indiana Tradition in Speech Communication*. Eds. Richard J. Jensen and John C. Hammerback. Amsterdam, Holland: Rodopi B.V. Press, 1987, pp. 89–116.

Lerner, Gerda. *Black Women in White America: A Documentary History*. New York: Vintage, 1973. (*BWWA*)

Lynching and Rape: An Exchange of Views by Jane Addams and Ida B. Wells. Ed. and intro. Bettina Aptheker. Occasional paper no. 25. New York, San Jose, Calif.: American Institute for Marxist Studies, 1977.

Selected Works of Ida B. Wells-Barnett. Comp. and intro. Trudier Harris. Schomburg Library. Ed. Henry Louise Gates, Jr. New York: Oxford University Press, 1991.

Historical Background

Aked, Charles F. "One Woman's Work—The Mission of Miss Ida Wells." *London Christian World* 38 (July 19, 1894):545.

"An American Problem: An Interview with Miss Wells." *London Methodist Times* 10 (May 24, 1894):330.

Armstrong, Richard Acland, "Lynching in the United States." *Liverpool Mercury*, April 3, 1894, p. 5.

Cutler, James Elbert. *Lynch Law: An Investigation into the History of Lynching in the United States*. New York: Longmans Green, 1905.

Diggs, Charles C., Sr. "Ida B. Wells Barnett: Militant Foe of Lynching." *A Brochure Concerning Little Known History of the Negro*. Detroit: Metropolitan Mutual Insurance, n.d., 12 pp.

"Ida B. Wells Heard Here—She Urges the Negroes of America to Organize." *New York Sun* (July 30, 1894):2.

Logan, Rayford W., and Irving S. Cohen. *The American Negro: Old World Background and New World Experience*. Boston: Houghton Mifflin, 1916.

"Lynch Law in the United States." *The Manchester Guardian* (May 9, 1893):9.

"A Nineteenth Century Pilgrim in Liverpool—The Gospel of the Second Emancipation of the Colored Race—Miss Ida B. Wells and Her Mission." *Liverpool Review* (March 24, 1894):12.

Penn, Irving Garland. *The Afro-American Press and Its Editors*. 1891. New York: Arno and the New York Times, 1969.

Pickens, William. *Lynching and Debt Slavery*. New York: American Civil Liberties Union, 1921.

Salem, Dorothy. *To Better Our World: Black Women in Organized Reform, 1890–1920*. Black Women in United States History Series. Ed. Darlene Clark Hine. Brooklyn, N.Y.: Carlson, 1990.

Chronology of Works

Southern Horrors. Lynch Law in All Its Phases. 1892. Rpt. *On Lynchings*. New York: Arno and the New York Times, 1969, 24 pp.; *MCSFH* 2:385–420; *Selected Works*, 4–25.

United States Atrocities. London: Newspaper and Publishing Co., 1892. 28 pp. [Rpt. of *Southern Horrors* with a three-page introduction and ten-page summary added].

"Lynch Law in All Its Phases." Tremont Temple, Boston Monday Lectureship (February 13, 1893). *Our Day* 11 (April 1893):333–347; *IBWB*:171–187.

The Reason Why the Colored American Is Not in the World's Columbian Exposition. With Frederick Douglass, I. Garland Penn, and Ferdinand L. Barnett. Chicago: Ida B. Wells, 1893. Rpt. Ch. 4, "Lynch Law," *IBWB*:195–207.

A Red Record, 1895. Rpt. *On Lynchings*. Pref. August Meier. New York: Arno and the New York Times, 1969, 101 pp.; *Selected Works*, pp. 138–252; *BWWA* [excerpt]:196–205.

Lynch Law in Georgia. Chicago: Pamphlet circulated by Chicago Colored Citizens, 1899, 18 pp.

"Lynch Law in America." *Arena* 23 (January 1900):15–24; *IBWB*: 235–243.

"The Negro's Cause in Equity." *The Independent* 52 (April 26, 1900):1010–1011; *IBWB*:245–248.

Mob Rule in New Orleans: Robert Charles and His Fight to the Death. 1900. *On Lynchings*. New York: Arno and the New York Times, 1969, 48 pp.; *Selected Works*, 253–322.

"Lynching and the Excuse for It." *The Independent* 53 (May 16, 1901):1133–1136. Rpt. *Lynching and Rape: An Exchange*, 29–34; *IBWB*:249–254.

"Booker T. Washington and His Critics." *The World Today* 6 (April 1904):518–521; *IBWB*:255–60.

"Lynching, Our National Crime." *Proceedings of the National Negro Conference, New York, May 31–June 1, 1909*, pp. 174–179. Rpt. New York: Arno and the New York Times, 1969; *Major Speeches by Negroes in the United States, 1797–1971*. Ed. Philip S. Foner. New York: Simon & Schuster, 1972, pp. 687–691; *IBWB*:261–265.

"How Enfranchisement Stops Lynching." National Negro Conference, 1910, NAACP Papers, Reel 8, 00034–00053.

"How Enfranchisement Stops Lynchings." *Original Rights Magazine* 1 (June 1910):42–53; *IBWB*:267–76.

"Our Country's Lynching Record." *Survey* 29 (February 1, 1913):573–574; *IBWB*:277–280.

The Arkansas Race Riot. Chicago: Mrs. Ida B. Wells-Barnett, May 15, 1920.

FRANCES E. WILLARD
(1839–1898), reinventor of "True Womanhood"

BONNIE J. DOW

President of the Woman's Christian Temperance Union (WCTU) from 1879 until her death in 1898, Frances E. Willard was an indefatigable rhetorician and organizer. Her unique brand of woman's rights rhetoric and her work on behalf of a wide range of innovative reforms make her one of the most creative and strategic of nineteenth-century woman orators. In her rhetoric, Willard relied on the rationale of womanhood (emphasizing woman's allegedly superior moral character and the social and political benefits resulting from increased rights for women) rather than natural rights to support her arguments for reform. This strategy set her apart from such prominent woman's rights orators as ELIZABETH CADY STANTON and SUSAN B. ANTHONY and allowed her to attract significant support from men as well as women.

Through the persuasive power of her discourse, Willard built the WCTU into the largest and most diverse all-female reform organization of its time, and she personally led the conservative members of the WCTU to endorse woman suffrage in 1881 (Bordin, 1986:110–111). Her religious upbringing, her education and work experiences, and her strategic understanding of the opportunities offered by women's temperance reform were instrumental in the development of the complex matrix of religious, social, and gender-related beliefs that constituted her rhetorical appeal.

Frances Willard was born into an educated and religious family on September 28, 1839, in Churchville, New York. Both of her parents briefly attended Oberlin College, then the only coeducational institution in the country, and they were devout Methodists. At eighteen, Willard and her sister were sent to Evanston, Illinois, to study at the newly formed North Western Female College. Although its curriculum was not equal to men's college-level study, it provided a fairly good education. Willard graduated in 1859 with a Laureate of Science (Bordin, 1986:24). While a student there, she expressed admiration for Margaret Fuller, an early woman's rights advocate and author of *Woman in the Nineteenth Century* (1845).

Willard's growing resolve to reject a traditional female role was intimated in her decision to pursue a teaching career upon graduation from North Western. Against her father's wishes, she left home in 1860, and until 1874, she taught at eleven schools in six different cities. In 1871, she became president of the newly formed Ladies College of Northwestern University in Evanston, Illinois, a position she held until 1874 (Willard, 1889:133–134). Her commitment to an independent life was also reflected in her rejection of opportunities to marry, including one serious engagement in 1861 (Bordin, 1986:36). However, her diaries and correspondence indicate that close friendships with women provided primary emotional support throughout her life (Bordin, 1986:44–47).

When Willard decided to leave teaching, she searched for a career that would allow her to continue her interest in women's issues. Her choice to identify herself with women's temperance activities rather than with woman's rights reflects the strategic thinking she would demonstrate as the leader of the WCTU. The woman suffrage movement had a negative public image for many. Conversely, temperance was a nascent woman's movement that could achieve advances for women while presenting itself in the guise of moral reform, a more respectable pursuit.

Still in its early development in 1874, the woman's temperance movement offered her the opportunity to establish herself as a leader. During 1873–1874, Willard's last year at Northwestern University, grass-roots activity for temperance began in the Midwest in a series of "Women's Crusades" aimed at eliminating the sale and use of alcoholic beverages. Responding to the lectures of a traveling evangelist, groups of women marched on saloons and drugstores where liquor was sold, persuading their owners to close their doors or to cease the sale of alcohol. While moved by religious appeals, the women involved in the crusades and later temperance activity were also motivated by an acute awareness of the damage inflicted on women and children by drunken, profligate husbands and by the unhealthy connection between saloons and prostitution. The spread of a nationwide chain of crusades, involving an estimated 56,711 women, culminated in the formation of the WCTU in November 1874 (Bordin, 1981:Ch. 2).

Unlike most women who would meet to form the WCTU, Willard never participated fully in a crusade, and her experience with saloons and the alcohol problem was limited. For her, involvement in temperance was a conscious and pragmatic career choice rather than a decision growing out of moral commitment and religious revivalism as was the case for most early WCTU members (Bordin, 1986:69–73). She accepted the presidency of the Chicago WCTU in the fall of 1874. Later that year, she was elected secretary of the Illinois WCTU, and then corresponding secretary of the national WCTU.

Willard's reform activities would dominate the rest of her life. She became president of the WCTU in 1879. As president she traveled widely, speaking and organizing on behalf of the Union. Through these efforts, she helped change it from a one-issue organization into a group supporting many social reforms, including woman suffrage, labor reform, prison reform, and changes in prostitution and rape laws (Bordin, 1981:Ch. 6). Until 1892, her base was in Evanston, where she shared a home with her mother. After her mother's death that year, she spent most of her time in England, at the home of Lady Henry Somerset, British WCTU president, with whom she became friends after their meeting in 1891.

Between 1892 and 1898, Willard continued in her duties as president of the Union, returning to the United States for conventions and other WCTU activities, but she was much less visible. During these years, her health began to fail because of recurring attacks of anemia. Early in 1898, this condition was complicated by a severe cold; she died in New York City on February 17, 1898, at the age of fifty-nine. Until the day she died, her life was devoted to reform work under the auspices of the WCTU. Her influence as leader of the Union is attested by the steady decline in the organization's power following her death. After 1898, the Union reverted to emphasis on a single issue, temperance, the position that it had held before her leadership (Bordin, 1981:151–155).

WILLARD AS ORGANIZATIONAL LEADER

Frances Willard's organizational genius and rhetorical acumen were the primary reasons for the growth of the WCTU under her leadership. By the time she became president of the national WCTU in 1879, she was well prepared for a career in the public arena. She was an experienced educator and administrator, and she had honed her skills as a public rhetor in various forums. As president of the Ladies College of Northwestern University, she spoke in public numerous times, often delivering a lecture on "The New Chivalry." This lecture consisted primarily of her observations on the situation of women in Europe but included an argument for women's education with mild woman's rights overtones:

No picture dawns upon me so refulgent as this Home that yet shall be the gift of this Better Age to the New America, in which a *three-fold tie* shall bind the husband to his wife, the father to his daughter, the mother to her son. Religion and affection—as heretofore in all true homes—shall form two of the strands in this magic three-fold tie; the third *this* age is weaving, and it is *intellectual sympathy*, than which no purer or more enduring bond survived the curse of Eden.

Willard clearly perceived the importance of rhetorical skill to reform activities. In her autobiography, she named ANNA E. DICKINSON, a famous lecturer and reform speaker, as her primary role model for female public speakers. She wrote that "beyond all men and women to whom I have yet listened, Anna Dickinson has been to me an inspiration" (*Glimpses*, 1889:570). For part of 1877, she developed her public speaking skills lecturing to huge crowds in the East as a member of the staff of prominent Methodist evangelist Dwight E. Moody. She was also prepared for her role as WCTU president in 1878 when she briefly took over the editorship of the *Chicago Evening Post*, a small general newspaper formerly edited by her brother Oliver, following his death in March 1878 (Bordin, 1986:94–95).

Willard's rhetorical skill in her public appearances, and in the numerous articles, pamphlets, and letters that she composed, indicate that her early experiences served her well. Her first major WCTU organizing tour in the South in 1881 received highly favorable reviews. In most towns she was supported by the local Protestant churches, and her speeches were introduced by clergymen and politicians. The enthusiasm that she generated as an orator continued for the rest of her career. By 1883, she had spoken in more than 1,000 communities at least once, in most cities with populations over 5,000, and in all cities of more than 10,000 (Bordin, 1981:73).

Beyond adding to her own visibility and popularity, the organizational vision and rhetorical skills Willard demonstrated during these tours attracted new members and support for the Union's causes. By 1884, women had organized WCTU chapters in every state and territory. Local unions were visible everywhere except in rural areas (Bordin, 1981:89–94). The popularity of the all-female WCTU is evident in a comparison with other women's organizations of the time. By 1892, the WCTU had over 200,000 members, including auxiliaries. In contrast, in the same year, the General Federation of Women's Clubs claimed 20,000 members; in 1893, NAWSA had 13,000 dues-paying members (Bordin, 1981:3).

At Willard's request, in 1884 a WCTU "missionary" was sent to organize unions in foreign countries. As part of this campaign to reach out to other nations, she wrote the "Polyglot Petition," a document calling for laws against alcohol and opium. WCTU missionaries eventually gathered nearly a million signatures from women around the world, and she presented the petition to President Grover Cleveland in 1895 (Bordin, 1986:191–192, 221). In 1891, the first World WCTU convention, including women from Unions around the world, met in Boston (Bordin, 1986:192).

Under Willard's direction, publishing became another major strength of the Union. By 1890, the *Union Signal*, the official WCTU journal, was the most popular women's paper in the world, with a circulation of almost 100,000 (Bordin, 1981:90). Although she had little to do with its management, she became its editor in 1892. In the early 1880s, she also engineered the founding of the Woman's Temperance Publishing Association (WTPA) to publish the tracts, pamphlets, and books of the Union as well as the *Union Signal*. The WTPA published several of her books as well as printing her essays, popular speeches, and annual addresses in pamphlet and leaflet form. She was a prolific writer; although her books were more valuable as propaganda than as literature, they were widely read in the nineteenth century. The first 50,000 copies of her autobiography sold within a few months (Bordin, 1986:116–118).

As president of the WCTU, Willard was the catalyst for adoption of the "Do Everything" policy, a broad program of reform. When she joined the WCTU, it was an organization devoted solely to achieving temperance through the personal moral suasion of its members. By 1890, her initiatives had led to thirty-nine departments within the national Union, classified into three major areas: temperance, labor, and woman (Dillon, 1944:92). She described the sweeping policies of the Union as a natural extension of woman's nature and of temperance:

The "Do Everything Policy" was not of our choosing, but is an evolution, as inevitable as any traced by the naturalist or described by the historian. Woman's genius for details, and her patient steadfastness in following the enemies of those she loves "through every lane of life," have led her to antagonize the alcohol habit, and the liquor traffic, just where they are, wherever that may be. If she does this, since they are everywhere, her policy will be "Do Everything." (Quoted in Gordon, 1898:113)

As the WCTU grew, so did its range of interests. By 1892, nontemperance issues dominated twenty-five out of thirty-nine departments (Bordin, 1981:98). The issues included prison reform, manual training for girls, kindergartens, organized labor, working women, health and hygiene, peace and arbitration, woman suffrage, and social purity, a term referring to reforms such as an increased age of consent for women, a single standard of chastity for men and women, stricter prostitution and rape laws, and sex education for children.

As Willard's power and influence grew, so did her interest in radical politics, including organized labor and gospel socialism. In 1886, she began to work for WCTU endorsement of the Knights of Labor, a union and reform organization with eclectic membership that advocated the elimination of conflict between capital and labor through class cooperation (Epstein, 1981:137–138). Her attraction to the cooperative philosophy of the Knights of Labor presaged the socialist sympathies that she exhibited in the late 1880s and 1890s. The socialist vision of Edward Bellamy's utopian novel *Looking Backward*, which she read in 1887 or 1888, deeply affected her (Bordin, 1986:146). In her 1888 and 1889 annual addresses, she promoted Christian or gospel socialism:

We must change the system. We must found business upon Social Law. Combination must take the place of competition; we must have a system in which business shall be carried on, not for private profits, but for the public good. We must apply our Christianity to the Social Order . . . realizing at last the ideal of Christian Socialism, the Fatherhood of God, the Brotherhood of Man, the spirit of Jesus Christ. (*Annual Address*, 1889)

Although the values of gospel socialism appealed to many WCTU members, Willard's endorsement generated some uneasiness. In the 1880s and 1890s, socialism came to be associated with anarchy and violence, and many WCTU members were uncomfortable with her leftist sympathies. There is evidence that, by the time of her death in 1898, the large amount of time she spent overseas as well as her increasingly radical beliefs, were undermining her influence within the WCTU (Bordin, 1981:154–155; Epstein, 1981:143–144).

WILLARD AS RHETORICAL STRATEGIST

Willard's genius as a rhetorical strategist is apparent in her ability to obtain support for various controversial causes from the women who joined the WCTU and the men who supported the organization financially and ideologically. Temperance supporters were an essentially conservative group characterized by a Protestant religious outlook and a belief in the supremacy of middle-class values, including the pure, pious, domestic, and submissive ideals of True Womanhood (Epstein, 1981).

In the 1880s, the WCTU's major growth period, temperance supporters were unlikely to affiliate with the "mainstream" woman suffrage movement; instead, they were part of a moral reformism based in values of sobriety, sexual morality, and Protestant religious ethics (Gusfield, 1963). The WCTU received significant support from Protestant churches, and many of its members were wives of clergymen (Bordin, 1981: 173). WCTU supporters saw themselves as missionaries less intent on reforming those of their own class than on extending middle-class standards for behavior to the lower classes as a move toward an improved, Christianized society (Gusfield, 1963).

Willard's appeal for her conservative audiences was her framing of all reforms within the boundaries of True Womanhood. Her entire public philosophy radiated from the argument that reforms were necessary to protect the home, woman's traditional sphere: "The Woman's Christian Temperance Unions have taken up this sacred cause of protection for the home, and we shall never cease our efforts until women shall have all the help that law can furnish them throughout America" ("Social Purity"). In her rhetoric, "home protection" was an overarching strategy, and the home was a crucial factor in every political issue:

The three questions that alone engross our people are the Temperance, the Labor and the Woman Questions, and these three agree in one. Only by convincing labor that a high tariff meant material protection for the home, was the last Presidential battle won; only by convincing wage-workers and women that the outlawing of the saloon means protection for those who dwell within the home, will Prohibition ever gain the day; only by convincing wage-workers and temperance voters that through equal suffrage women will help to protect both the external and the internal interests of the home, will the Woman Question ever be wrought out in government. ("Social Purity")

Willard's linkage of reform to the traditional beliefs of her audience provided powerful motivation for women's activism. When "home," the sphere of women, became the context that encompassed all reforms, women's public action to protect it was legitimated. Moreover, by drawing on beliefs about women's moral superiority implied in the ideal of True Womanhood, she was able to argue that society, the larger "home," would benefit from women's influence.

Willard's rhetorical strategies were based in a philosophy that held that the motivation of all reform action lay in women's maternal concern for the purity and sanctity of the home and in men's chivalric duty to protect their idealized vision of True Womanhood. Based on examples of her rhetoric on woman suffrage, social purity, and the Prohibition party, three of the most controversial issues that she consistently espoused during the 1880s, three primary rhetorical strategies emerge: (1) her use of euphemisms to avoid controversy in her social purity rhetoric; (2) her use of redefinition in her arguments for woman suffrage as "home protection"; and (3) her use of metaphors to present prohibition and social purity reform as holy crusades.

While all of Willard's rhetoric exhibits a highly sentimental, "feminine" style that relied on poetry, religious and biblical allusions, romantic metaphors, and euphemisms, her use of euphemisms to discuss controversial issues is particularly vivid in her social purity rhetoric. In 1885, she became superintendent of the WCTU's controversial Department of Social Purity, a branch of the larger social purity movement in the United States and Britain. The department was concerned with age of consent laws, prostitution, sex education, and a single standard of chastity for men and women.

To avoid offending the Victorian modesty of her audience, Willard substituted vague concepts for specific terms. For example, stricter statutory rape laws were a major cause for the WCTU, and in her social purity discourse, rape became "stealing away a woman's honor," and rapists were "the outragers of women" ("Social Purity"). She referred to the age of consent as "the age of protection," and the laws the WCTU desired were "legislation for the protection of woman's honor" ("Social Purity," 39; "Social Purity: The Latest and Greatest Crusade," 7). Through the use of such phrases, she was able to cast the controversial issue in the language of fairy tales and epics. She described a woman's virginity as her "honor," drawing on notions of chivalric protection for women and the value of virginity inherent in True Womanhood.

Evidence suggests that this strategy was successful for Willard and the WCTU. In 1886, the year after the WCTU became involved in social purity reform, the age of consent in twenty states was ten years of age. In one state the age was as low as seven. By 1894, twenty states had raised the legal age of consent to sixteen; only four states still maintained laws placing consent at ten years. WCTU petitions were a major force behind these developments (Bordin, 1981:110).

Related to Willard's use of euphemisms was her dominant strategy of redefinition, particularly her redefinition of reform as "home protection." Although she eventually used the term "home protection" to refer to any WCTU cause, she originally coined the term as a strategy to promote woman suffrage. In 1881, she persuaded the WCTU membership to declare its support for woman suffrage as a means of achieving a federal prohibition amendment. However, she differentiated the WCTU's purpose from that of other suffragists who relied on a natural rights philosophy that was at odds with True Womanhood. Her discourse emphasized that women entered the public sphere and agitated for the vote because they desired to protect their traditional sphere: "Every day brings fresh accessions of women, translated out of the passive and into the active voice on this great question of the protection of their homes." Because women were "the necessary and tender guardians of the home, of tempted manhood and untaught little children," they needed the vote to protect these interests ("Home Protection Address").

Willard's definition of woman suffrage as home protection made it an other-centered reform consonant with woman's nature. She stressed woman's special moral power that is "effectively exercised by giving her a voice in the decision by which the rum-shop door shall be opened or closed beside her home." The vote was women's "power to protect, along life's treacherous highways, those whom they have so loved" ("Temperance and Home Protection"). Thus, the vote became a natural extension of woman's protective instinct used to safeguard her traditional interests. In this context, suffrage was an issue of "not rights, but duties; not [woman's] need alone, but that of her children and her country; not the 'woman' but the 'human' question" ("Home Protection Address"). Thus, the vote did not threaten to change women, as many anti-suffragists feared. Rather, Willard claimed that women would change the vote into a weapon for "home protection" against intemperance. Woman suffrage was merely a means to the end of moral reform, not an end in itself.

WCTU members who did not support the woman suffrage movement accepted "home protection" as a cause. Until the 1890s, at least twice as many WCTU members claimed involvement in missionary work as claimed connections with the suffrage movement outside the Union (Bordin, 1981: 174–175). However, Willard's letters and diaries suggest that her personal commitment to woman's equality was stronger than her rhetoric demonstrated (Bordin, 1986:100–101; 1981:57–58). Although the WCTU declared for full suffrage (not just the temperance ballot) for women in 1883, her rhetoric in the 1880s continued to justify the ballot as a means of "home protection." By 1892, her power secure, she was openly using natural rights arguments for suffrage and advocating full female participation in the political process. In her 1892 Annual Address to the WCTU, she stated: "We claim suffrage as an indefeasible human right," a clear change from her earlier rationale.

A third important strategy in Willard's rhetoric was her use of quixotic war and crusade metaphors, accompanied by allusions to chivalry. Her depiction of WCTU reforms as holy crusades blessed by God accomplished dual purposes. First, appeals to the need for women's pious and moral influence offered a way to overcome resistance to women's participation in reform. Second, the need for men's participation in a chivalrous effort devoted to protection of the home was attractive to male audiences.

In the war metaphors that dominated her woman suffrage rhetoric, women, because of their piety and caretaking instincts, were the natural enemy of alcohol: "By the changeless instincts of her nature and through the most sacred relationships of which that nature has been rendered capable, God has indicated woman, who is the born conservator of home, to be the Nemesis of home's arch enemy, King Alcohol" ("Temperance and Home Protection"). For Willard, women comprised "a great army, gentle of mien and mild of utterance" on "the splendid battlefield of this [the temperance] reform," and their ballots would be weapons in the "quick, decisive battle of election day" ("Temperance and Home Protection"). The exercise of woman's moral influence through woman suffrage, she claimed, would save society: "I solemnly call upon my countrymen to release those other hands, familiar with the pages of the Book of God, busied with sacred duties of the home and gracious deeds of charity, that they may drop in those whiter ballots, which, as God lives, alone can save the state" ("Home Protection Address").

Her strategy of metaphorically presenting temperance reform as a holy war against the liquor industry permeated her rhetoric on behalf of the Prohibition party as well as her discourse on temperance and woman suffrage. Most WCTU members were opposed to the outright politicization of the Union, but Willard, attracted by the Prohibition party's support for woman suffrage, eventually obtained endorsement of the party in 1882 through the strategic maneuvering that characterized her leadership. The WCTU's affiliation with the Prohibition party presented additional rhetorical problems to those she faced in her discourse on temperance and suffrage. Association with a political party took women even farther into the male-dominated realm of politics. Support of a specific political party demonstrated an active interest in the machinations of political life, which was clearly outside woman's sphere. In addition, many temperance supporters questioned the wisdom of third-party affiliation in general (Bordin, 1986:214–215).

To overcome these obstacles, Willard effectively extended her war metaphor to embrace the Prohibition party as the "army" necessary for successful battle. According to her, "parties are like armies, recruited man by man, to defend a cause concerning which all of them think alike; drilled, disciplined, and having brave, trusty and veteran leadership." The "cause" that the party defended was the "beleaguered home," which would be saved through prohibition ("Latest Evolutions of the Temperance Reform"). She compared the Prohibition party to Martin Luther's rebellion against Catholicism, to the Pilgrims, "a hunted minority [that] sought freedom to worship God," and to the Methodists who left the Anglican Church. She concluded that "minorities are the Protestants of each new age, with their earnest *'Here I stand. I can do no other; God help me, Amen'* " ("Latest Evolutions of the Temperance Reform").

In Willard's rhetoric, the noble males of the Prohibition party, motivated by their reverence for suffering mothers, would do battle with liquor on behalf of women:

If any beings on this earth have the right to come to the manhood of this nation and ask protection for themselves and for their children and for their homes, it is the mothers, and the vested interests they represent are those the voting population intends in the last analysis to take care of, and will take care of, in place of the brewers' vat and the distillers' bottles. The mother's home, her heart, her son, are dear to the manhood of America. ("Principle Before Politics")

Willard emphasized the importance of the Prohibition party when she totally discounted the possibilities for reform under the Republican or Democratic parties. She portrayed them as enemies of traditional homes and Christian religion:

The politicians of the saloon are bidding for [the child in the marketplace], and they turn the crank of the party machine with such tireless industry that measures dear to the heart of the home are voted down, the Ten Commandments and the Sermon on the Mount are voted down and the aims and wishes of the liquor traffic are voted up to success. ("Principle Before Politics")

Again, religious associations were used to portray prohibition supporters as being on the side of God.

The appeals to chivalry implied in Willard's Prohibition party rhetoric were also central to her social purity rhetoric. In the social purity rhetoric, the war was depicted as a Christian crusade; she appealed to beliefs in the sanctity of woman's purity and men's natural desire to protect it. She made the chivalric link explicit when she said: "Noble knights of the new chivalry are rallying to their [women's] help and encouraging them by word and deed and bank-note as they hasten to the rescue of the fallen" ("Social Purity: The Latest and Greatest Crusade").

The function of the "knights" was to aid women as they pursued social purity reform. With the support of chivalrous men, the "movement goes forward. It has been a great battle of heart and brain, and in it every woman has been counted a man's daughter, and every man as a woman's son" ("A White Life for Two," 1891). In Willard's utopian vision, the pure home that came from men's dedication to purity led to domestic bliss and fulfillment of God's wishes: "The manhood of the nation at large will reach the heights that purity insists upon; then shall come the blessed, sacred, pure, home life, the fair sweet future that Christ wants to see in our republic" ("The White Cross and Social Purity"). This brief outline of her depiction of the crusade indicates her dominant themes: The enemy is vice; the warriors are chivalrous men, guided by the maternal power of women; the reward is fulfillment of God's vision for America.

Particularly important in her social purity rhetoric, as in all of her discourse, was Willard's unfailingly charitable attitude toward men. Instead of blaming them for destructive attitudes and actions toward women, she depicted men as victims of outdated laws, social customs, and lack of education, which combined to make them victims of temptation:

Thus under the conditions of a civilization crude and material, grew up that well-worn maxim of the common-law, "Husband and wife are one, and that one is the husband." But such supreme power as this brought to the man supreme temptation. By the laws of mind he legislated first for himself and afterward for the physically weaker one within "his" home. ("Social Purity")

She stressed that men as well as women would benefit from reform, because a "pure" man would be more attractive to a woman and would be more likely to achieve domestic happiness: "[T]here is no man who[m] women honor so deeply as the man of chaste life, the man who breasts temptation's swelling waves, like some strong swimmer in his agony, and makes the port of perfect self-control" ("Social Purity").

CONCLUSION

Under the leadership of Frances Willard, the WCTU became not only a temperance organization, but also a reform society with a broad agenda. By the mid–1880s, many of the Union's goals were openly supportive of woman's rights positions. Clearly, it was she who led the Union down this political, and in contemporary terms, feminist path. Through her strategic use of arguments based on the central tenets of home protection and true womanhood, she redefined the controversial issues she espoused into reforms necessary to protect and enrich the traditional role of women as caretakers, nurturers, and guardians of piety and morality. Any rights that women gained, she implied, would benefit cultural ideals of womanhood, rather than undermine them.

In the 1880s and 1890s, the WCTU was a tremendously visible and popular organization promoting a variety of reforms to benefit women. However, Willard is less well remembered than other advocates for woman's rights and woman suffrage, which can be traced to two factors. First, the WCTU's reversion to its narrow concern with temperance following her death meant that her charisma and iconoclastic vision were allowed to die with her, and the WCTU contributed little to the final, decisive campaign for woman suffrage waged between 1900 and 1920. Second, although the natural rights philosophy used by other woman's rights activists has maintained its resonance over time, Willard's brand of "feminine feminism" (Bordin, 1986:39) seems outdated and contrary to most contemporary feminist goals. Her rhetorical strategies achieved important short-term victories but have not stood the test of time.

Yet Willard was undoubtedly committed to an enlarged sphere for women, in both personal belief and public practice. Her rhetoric had the effect of bringing thousands of women into public reform work. The breadth of the WCTU's organization at the local, state, national, and international levels provided extensive networks for disseminating arguments in support of greater rights for women (Bordin, 1981:157). Her success with the "home protection" rationale clearly increased the public acceptance of woman suffrage that resulted in the passage of the Nineteenth Amendment in 1920. After her death, many of the women she attracted to the WCTU continued to work for woman suffrage outside it. Moreover, her rhetorical success influenced other women reformers. Her basic argument for the superior moral influence of women and the resultant societal benefits to be derived from women's enfranchisement was a strategy used successfully by other activists in the final stages of the woman suffrage movement. The importance of understanding Frances Willard's brand of activist, reform rhetoric ultimately rests in her vivid enactment of a unique and an important strain in the complex, multidimensional character of nineteenth-century rhetorical action in support of advancement for women.

SOURCES

The Frances E. Willard Memorial Library (FEWML), Evanston, Illinois, houses her papers, including correspondence, scrapbooks, speeches, essays, and books. The library also has extensive secondary materials on the temperance movement and her life. Much of the library's primary material is on the microfilm edition of the Temperance and Prohibition Papers (TPP) compiled by the Michigan Historical Society, the WCTU, and the Ohio Historical Society. See *Guide to the Microfilm Edition of the Temperance and Prohibition Papers*. Eds. Randall C. Jimerson, Francis X. Blouin, and Charles A. Isetts. Ann Arbor: University of Michigan, 1977.

The History of Women (HOW) Collection, available on microfilm, also contains a few of her speeches and pamphlets, as well as many of her books, including her autobiography.

Speech Sources

Gordon, Anna. *The Beautiful Life of Frances Willard: A Memorial Volume*. Chicago: WTPA, 1898. (*BLFW*)
Willard, Frances E. *Glimpses of Fifty Years: The Autobiography of an American Woman*. Intro. Hannah Whitehall Smith. Chicago: WTPA, 1889. HOW, Reel 495, No. 3747. (*GFY*)
———. *Woman and Temperance: Or, the Work and Workers of the Woman's Christian Temperance Union*. 1883. New York: Arno Press, 1972. HOW, Reel 495, No. 3749; excerpt *WT*:92–93.

Selected Critical Studies

Campbell, K. Kohrs. "Femininity and Feminism: To Be or Not to Be a Woman." *Communication Quarterly* 31 (Spring 1983):101–108.
———. "Social Feminism: Frances Willard, 'Feminine Feminist.' " *MCSFH* 1:121–132.
Caroli, Betty Boyd. "Women Speak Out for Reform." *The Rhetoric of Protest and Reform, 1878–1898*. Ed. Paul Boase. Athens: Ohio University Press, 1980, pp. 212–231.
Dow, Bonnie J. "The Reformist Rhetoric of Frances E. Willard: The Romantic Appeal of Mother, God, and Home." M.A. thesis, University of Kansas, 1987.
———. "The Womanhood Rationale in the Woman Suffrage Rhetoric of Frances E. Willard." *Southern Communication Journal* 56 (Summer 1991):298–307.
Gifford, Carolyn DeSwarte. "Home Protection: The WCTU's Conversion to Woman Suffrage." *Gender, Ideology, and Action: Historical Perspectives on Women's Public Lives*. Ed. Janet Sharistanian. Westport, Conn.: Greenwood, 1986, pp. 95–120.
Oliver, Robert T. "Denouncing Demon Drink: Frances E. Willard and John B. Gough." *History of Public Speaking in America*. Boston: Allyn & Bacon, 1965, pp. 450–459.

Selected Biographies and Historical Works

Bordin, Ruth. *Woman and Temperance: The Quest for Power and Liberty, 1873–1900*. Philadelphia: Temple University Press, 1981.
———. *Frances Willard: A Biography*. Chapel Hill: University of North Carolina Press, 1986.
Dillon, Mary Earhart. "Willard, Frances Elizabeth Caroline." *NAW* 3:613–619.

————. *Frances Willard: From Prayers to Politics*. Chicago: University of Chicago Press, 1944.

Epstein, Barbara Leslie. *The Politics of Domesticity: Women, Evangelism, and Temperance in Nineteenth Century America*. Middletown, Conn.: Wesleyan University Press, 1981.

Gusfield, Joseph R. *Symbolic Crusade: Status Politics and The American Temperance Movement*. Urbana: University of Illinois Press, 1963.

Chronology of Willard's Major Published Works (Some works, for example, biographies of her mother and sister, are not included.)

How to Win: A Book for Girls. New York: Funk & Wagnalls, 1888. HOW, Reel 495, No. 3748.

Woman in the Pulpit. Chicago: WTPA, 1889. HOW, Reel 496, No. 3750.

A Woman of the Century; Fourteen Hundred Seventy Biographical Sketches Accompanied by Portraits of Leading American Women in All Walks of Life. Ed. with Mary A. Livermore. Buffalo, N.Y.: Charles Wells Moulton, 1893. HOW, Reel 620, No. 4940.

Do Everything: A Handbook for the World's White Ribboners. Chicago: WTPA, 1895[?]. HOW, Reel 619, No. 4937.

Occupations for Women. A Book of Practical Suggestions, for the Maternal Advancement, the Mental and Physical Development, and the Moral and Spiritual Uplift of Women. With Helen M. Winslow and Sallie Joy White. New York: Success, 1897. HOW, Reel 620, No. 4939.

Chronology of Willard's Major Speeches (Speeches often were reprinted as WCTU pamphlets, in local newspapers, in magazines, or in the minutes of an organization she addressed. Some are listed twice because she often gave the same speech with slight variations many times over a period of years.)

"The New Chivalry, or, The School-Mistress Abroad" [on woman's rights]. *GFY*:576–589; TPP Series 3, Roll 26, File 112.

"Everybody's War" [first temperance speech, 1874]. Holograph FEWML; TPP Series 3, Roll 26, File 112.

"Temperance and Home Protection" [first home protection address], 1876 WCTU Convention. *WT*:452–459; *BLFW*:116–125; *TWJ* (October 14, 1876):1; *OW*:221–226.

"Home Protection Address." *Home Protection Manual: Containing An Argument for the Temperance Ballot for Woman, How to Obtain It, as a Means of Home Protection*. New York: The "Independent" Office, 1879. FEWML; TPP Series 3, Roll 29, File 125.

"Latest Evolutions of the Temperance Reform." *Demorest's Monthly Magazine* 22 (March 1886):361–362. FEWML

"Social Purity: The Latest and Greatest Crusade." *Voice Extra* [National Prohibition party publication] 1 (June 1886) [New York: Funk & Wagnalls]. FEWML; TPP, Roll 35, scrapbook 26.

"The White Cross and Social Purity." *Chautauqua Assembly Herald* (August 6, 1886):2. FEWML

"The Coming Brotherhood." 1888. FEWML; *The Rhetoric of Christian Socialism*. Ed. Paul Boase. New York: Random House, 1969, pp. 78–87.

Speeches, International Council of Women. *Report of the International Council of Women, Assembled by the National Woman Suffrage Association, Washington, D.C., March 25–April 1, 1888*. Washington, D.C.: Rufus H. Darby, 1888, pp. 222–224 [on organization]; pp. 286–289 [on social purity]; pp. 319–332 [on women and politics]; pp. 422–424 [on religion]. Minutes, *Woman's Tribune*, March 29–April 1, 1888.

"Principle Before Politics: Miss Willard's Stirring Plea at Springfield, Massachusetts." October 7, 1889. *Our Message Supplement* [WCTU Publication], 1–4; FEWML

"Social Purity." *Papers Read Before the Association for the Advancement of Women, 16th Women's Congress, November, 1888*. Fall River, Mass.: J. H. Franklin, 1889.

"The White Cross Movement in Education." *National Education Association Journal of Proceedings and Addresses. Session of the Year 1890, held at Saint Paul, Minnesota*. Topeka: Kansas Publishing House, Clifford C. Baker, 1890, pp. 159–178; *The Minnesota White Ribboner* [Mpls.] 1, no. 2 (July 15, 1890):1–6; FEWML; TPP Roll 31, scrapbook 12.

"A White Life for Two" [WCTU Pamphlet]. Chicago: WTPA, 1890. FEWML; *MCSFH* 2:317–338; *WSBH*:146–154.

Presidential Address, National Council of Women. *Transactions of the National Council of Women of the United States, Assembled in Washington, D.C., February 22–25, 1891*. Ed. Rachel Foster Avery. Philadelphia: J. B. Lippincott, 1891. FEWML; HOW, Reel 619, No. 4934.

"A White Life for Two." Delivered August 1, 1891. *Chautauqua Assembly Herald*, August 2, 1891. FEWML; TPP Roll 35, scrapbook 12.

"A White Life for Two." *Lexington Church Record* (December 7, 1895):1. FEWML; TPP Roll 35, scrapbook 12.

"First Address, Presentation of the Polyglot Petition." 1895. FEWML; excerpted in *BLFW*:150–157.

Presidential Addresses to National Meetings of the WCTU, 1879–1898, are in the Annual Meeting Minutes of the National WCTU published by the WTPA. FEWML; TPP Rolls 1–5.

INDEX

ABOUT THE CONTRIBUTORS _____

KAREN E. ALTMAN is a professor in the Department of Communication Arts and Sciences, University of Southern California, Los Angeles.

KATHLEEN L. BARRY is a professor in the Department of Human Development and Family Studies, Pennsylvania State University, University Park.

TRUDY BAYER is a professor in the Department of Communication at Thiel College, Greenville, Pennsylvania.

SANDRA J. BERKOWITZ is a doctoral student in the Department of Speech-Communication, University of Minnesota, Minneapolis.

DAVID S. BIRDSELL is a professor in the Department of Speech Communication, Baruch College, City University of New York.

THOMAS R. BURKHOLDER is a professor in the Department of Speech Communication, Southwest Texas State University, San Marcos.

KARLYN KOHRS CAMPBELL is a professor in the Department of Speech-Communication, University of Minnesota, Minneapolis.

ADRIENNE E. CHRISTIANSEN is a professor in the Department of Speech Communication, Macalester College, St. Paul, Minnesota.

SUZANNE E. CONDRAY is a professor in the Department of Communication, Denison University, Granville, Ohio.

CHARLES CONRAD is a professor in the Department of Speech Communication & Theatre Arts, Texas A & M University, College Station, Texas.

SISTER SHARON DEI teaches Communications at the Media Centre, Kaduna, Nigeria, and at St. Augustine Major Seminary, Jos, Plateau State, Nigeria.

LYNNE DERBYSHIRE is a lecturer in the Department of Speech Communication, University of Rhode Island, Kingston.

BONNIE J. DOW is a professor in the Department of Communication, North Dakota State University, Fargo.

JANE ELMES-CRAHALL is a professor in the Department of Communication, Wilkes University, Wilkes-Barre, Pennsylvania.

SUZANNE PULLON FITCH is a professor in the Department of Speech Communication, Southwest Texas State University, San Marcos.

FRAN HASSENCAHL is a professor in the Department of Speech Communication and Theatre Arts, Old Dominion University, Norfolk, Virginia.

MARY M. BOONE HUTTON is a professor of Speech Communication in the Department of English, Foreign Languages, Philosophy, Speech and Theatre, Alabama State University, Montgomery.

SUSAN SCHULTZ HUXMAN is a professor in the Elliott School of Communication, Wichita State University, Wichita, Kansas.

DEBRA K. JAPP is a professor in the Department of Speech Communication, St. Cloud State University, St. Cloud, Minnesota.

PHYLLIS M. JAPP is a professor, Department of Speech Communication, University of Nebraska, Lincoln.

E. CLAIRE JERRY is an adjunct professor, Department of Communications, Illinois College, Jacksonville.

CHARLES M. KAUFFMAN is a professor in the Department of Speech Communication, California State University, Northridge.

RANDALL A. LAKE is a professor in the Department of Communication Arts and Sciences, University of Southern California, Los Angeles.

WARREN L. LASHLEY is a professor in the Department of Communication, University of Cincinnati.

WILMER A. LINKUGEL is a professor in the Department of Communication Studies, University of Kansas, Lawrence.

JOHN M. MURPHY is a professor in the Department of Communication, North Dakota State University, Fargo.

LESTER C. OLSON is a professor in the Department of Communication, University of Pittsburgh.

CATHERINE HELEN PALCZEWSKI is a professor in the Communication Department, St. John's University, Collegeville, Minnesota.

PAULA TOMPKINS PRIBBLE is a professor in the Speech Communication Department, St. Cloud State University, St. Cloud, Minnesota.

MARY M. ROBERTS is a professor emeritus, Department of Communication, Kansas State University, Pittsburg.

LAURA R. SELLS is a doctoral student in the Department of Communication, University of South Florida, Tampa.

MARTHA SOLOMON is a professor in the Department of Speech Communication at the University of Maryland, College Park.

BARBARA S. SPIES is a doctoral student in the Department of Speech Communication, Pennsylvania State University Park.

MARI BOOR TONN is a professor in the department of Communication, University of New Hampshire, Durham.

KRISTIN S. VONNEGUT is a professor in the Communication Department of St. John's University, Collegeville, Minnesota.

SALLY ROESCH WAGNER is a research affiliate of the Women's Resources and Research Center, University of California, Davis.